TRUTH
OR
CONSEQUENCES

The Quiz Program That Became
a National Phenomenon

MARTIN GRAMS, JR.

BearManor
Media

Orlando, Florida

Truth or Consequences: The Quiz Program That Became a National Phenomenon
© 2020 Martin Grams, Jr. All rights reserved.

No portion of this publication may be reproduced, stored, and/or copied electronically (except for academic use as a source), nor transmitted in any form or by any means without the prior written permission of the publisher and/or author.

Published in the USA by
BearManor Media
1317 Edgewater Dr. #110
Orlando, FL 32804
www.BearManorMedia.com

Softcover Edition
ISBN-10: 1-62933-528-2
ISBN-13: 978-1-62933-528-5

Printed in the United States of America

Table of Contents

Foreword by Bob Barker	vii
Introduction	ix
1. Ralph Edwards and the Origin of Truth or Consequences	1
2. The Early Years, 1940 – 1945	15
3. The War Bond Tours	43
4. The Mr. Wickel Gag	63
5. Babe Ruth and Children Charities	71
6. Jack Dempsey and the Mr. Hush Contest	85
7. The Mrs. Hush Contests: Clara Bow and Martha Graham	91
8. Hubert Smith and a Christmas to Remember	131
9. This is Your Life, Lawrence Tranter	143
10. Jack Benny and The Walking Man Contest	159
11. Truth or Consequences, New Mexico	187
12. The Longest Golf Game in History	221
13. The Truth or Consequences Fiesta	239
14. Additional Consequences	249
15. The Television Program	297
16. The Jack Bailey and Bob Barker Years	305
The Episode Guide	321
Index	649

Bob Barker hosting the television version of *Truth or Consequences*.

Foreword by Bob Barker

After a series of auditions, on December 21, 1956, at five minutes past 12 noon, Ralph Edwards called me and told me I had been chosen to emcee Truth or Consequences on NBC. After that telephone call, as long as Ralph lived, we met for lunch on December 21 and, at five minutes past 12 noon, we drank a toast to our long and enduring friendship.

Ralph Edwards was not only brilliantly intelligent, he was a man of endless talents. He was a splendid host on radio and then on television. He was a masterful producer, an excellent writer and a top-notch salesman. Also, he was a true gentleman of the old school.

I consider myself blessed to have had Ralph as my friend, and to have had the opportunity to work for him. As I write this, a picture of Ralph hangs on the wall above me. On it Ralph wrote, "For Bob from Ralph, for bringing us together two decades ago, for Dorothy Jo and Barbara, and for our continuing brotherhood, I thank thee God." In closing, I should like to say "Amen."

INTRODUCTION

Popularly known today as a radio and television quiz program designed to humiliate their contestants through practical jokes, *Truth or Consequences* raised the bar for audience participation, inspiring imitation. Of recent, aficionados of game shows have faced a major disenchantment with the decline of quiz programs. The decay stems from an era when soap operas and quiz programs, facing obsolescence, step aside for reality-themed programs, which can be produced on the cheap. While preservation in a digital age ensures the longevity of past quiz programs, an official accounting of *Truth or Consequences* verifies a disturbing statistic: thousands of radio and television broadcasts no longer exist in recorded form. A sad statement when you consider how much was accomplished during the heyday when quiz programs reigned supreme.

On the evening of January 10, 1948, screen actress Lizabeth Scott made a surprise guest appearance on the radio quiz program, *Truth or Consequences*, to assist host Ralph Edwards in a unique publicity stunt. It seems a student at Fairfax High School in Los Angeles was suffering a dilemma after his "girl" rudely called off the original date. Edwards learned the boy had no girl to go with, he contracted Producer Hal Wallis, whose movie *I Walk Alone* was about to be released theatrically nationwide, co-starring Lizabeth Scott, to arrange for the actress to accompany the boy to the ball. Surely the publicity and mention of the up-coming movie would compensate Wallis – and Scott – for their time. Sure enough, days later, the actress accompanied him to the dance.

Flash forward to December 2014 when I came across a dozen candid photographs from that memorable evening – the actress laughing on stage with the young contestant, her initial meeting with Edwards to iron out the details of the stunt, her visit to the contestant's house, the trip in the limo, and her dancing and mingling with other men at the ball. Five weeks later I arranged for duplicates to be made of the photographs and slid them into an envelope – along with a letter to the actress in the hopes she would recall some behind-the-scenes story or two regarding that particular evening. The photos were sure to jog her memory. With her reputation for responding to fan letters, I addressed the envelope to Lizabeth Scott, a resident of Los Angeles. It was the day after I mailed the envelope that my wife reported the news trending on Facebook… Lizabeth Scott passed away at the age of 92. They say when someone passes away, a library burns. It became apparent that the history and legacy of *Truth or Consequences* was suffering the ill effects of Father Time.

Edwards attained success with charitable contributions that remains unequaled in the history of broadcasting entertainment; raising millions of dollars for various health agencies and wartime projects, including a half-billion dollars in "E" Bonds sold through the *Truth or Consequences* broadcasts. The quiz program played before a live studio audience, willing to purchase a war bond in exchange for admission to the program. The practical jokes pulled on the contestants, referred to as "consequences" on the program, were entertainment for the masses, not just the audience sitting in the theater.

For Thanksgiving, *Truth or Consequences* gave a contestant a Turkey dinner; that is to say, he was sent to Turkey – the country – for dinner. A contestant was once made to play a piano upside down, hanging from the ceiling, while strapped to a number of contraptions. Edwards conducted a race between one man on a pogo stick and a man in an airplane, made another fellow live for three weeks on a traffic island, and sent a sea lion to France to swim the English Channel.

After performing a Cinderella act, giving away lavish prizes for a worthy beauty temporarily down on her luck, Ralph Edwards quickly discovered how producers of other radio quiz programs latched onto the idea, giving away ridiculous prizes for ridiculously easy questions. This was where the now-famous Hush Contests originated – voices of famous people giving riddles and clues to their identity, which gave contestants a chance to win a jackpot of prizes that grew with each passing week. The Hush Contests originated from Edwards' disdain for the quiz programs giving away so much for so little.

"The Hush Contest was called, originally, not 'jackpot' but 'crackpot,' satirizing the situation by giving away fantastic prizes for identifying the mystery subject," Edwards later recalled. "The first Mr. Hush was Jack Dempsey. People flew in from all over America, wearing crazy hats and carrying signs to gain my attention when I was selecting contestants from the audience. When I saw all the greedy hands go up in the audience to get a crack at the 'crackpot,' I realized we had an enormous agent for good if we opened other mystery contests to our radio listeners benefiting the March of Dimes, the Heart Association, etc." In the following contest, "Mrs. Hush" (a.k.a. silent screen actress Clara Bow), Edwards suggested to the listeners that they include a donation to the health agency aligned with the contest, along with a brief essay for supporting that particular charity.

"The results were phenomenal," Edwards continued. "Not only did millions of dollars come in for these health agencies, but with Jack Benny as the Walking Man, it raised us to the number one rated show in America, and with the million and one-half dollars contributed, started the American Heart Association as a full-fledged health agency." To say that The Walking Man contest was a national phenomenon would be an understatement. As you will soon discover when you read this book, *Truth or Consequences* was more than a radio quiz program.

The American Cancer Society tremendously benefited by a series of stunts and acts on the *Truth or Consequences* radio show, based on the inspirational appeal of brave young people, such as little Bobby Riggio, a paralyzed boy for whom dimes were contributed by the radio audience to the March of Dimes. Through the magic of radio, the program was able to go into homes and hospitals, as they did in New Jersey where a little boy named Buster Roos talked with Roy Rogers, Frank Sinatra, and met Babe Ruth, to influence the American public to contribute hundreds of thousands of dollars to the Cancer Crusade.

In 1948, the now-famous Jimmy Fund of Boston was created through a *Truth or Consequences* act, talking from Hollywood to Boston with a young leukemia victim named "Jimmy," who loved baseball. The entire Boston Braves championship baseball team visited the boy in the hospital, took him out to the ball game; and the end result was that through the funds received from that broadcast, plus the tremendous work of the New England Variety Club, the Jimmy Fund has been responsible for building not just the original Sidney Farber Cancer Clinic, but now two cancer research centers.

The resilience, the power, the total platform *Truth or Consequences* offered for almost every kind of emotion in entertainment, proved to be its staying power. *Truth or Consequences* served as a public service message for rehabilitating war veterans following the Second World War, proving miracles could come true and setting the stage for another of Edwards' success stories: *This is Your Life*. "I couldn't get over the wide range of entertainment we covered," Edwards later recalled, "from the unbelievable pranks we put our contestants through, to the heart-strings we pulled within the homes all over America."

The largest of stunts, however, was in 1950 when the producers of *Truth or Consequences* induced the city of Hot Springs, New Mexico, to officially change its name to Truth or Consequences, New Mexico, in recognition of the show's tenth anniversary. Known for its medicinal climate and hot springs, the town expanded from a natural health resort to a major tourist attraction. Following the success (and minor opposition from some of the locals) of putting Truth or Consequences on the Rand McNally maps, the quiz program went one step further by helping put Hollywood on the map – literally.

It was inevitable that numerous efforts would be made to cash in on variations of the quiz parlor game formula. As it happened with all success stories in primetime network broadcasting, imitation spawned competition, and *Truth or Consequences*, having made a successful transition to television, was relegated to the status of a daytime quiz program. Spanning decades amid a healthy and lengthy run on both radio and television, the quiz program has since been demoted to academic entries in both electronic and print encyclopedias. Long forgotten are the stories of war veterans who owe their rehabilitation and new purpose in life as a result of those broadcasts. Long forgotten stands Al Baker and his challenge to hit a golf ball from Los Angeles, California, to Truth or Consequences, New Mexico, an improvised golf course stretching 823 miles… completed in six weeks. Trivia Pursuit fanatics are quick to point out Jack Benny was The Walking Man. How many remember the name of the woman who won the contest, the prizes she won, or the details regarding contest applicants? These are the stories that are documented within the pages of this book with as much detail as possible to ensure preservation of the legacy of Ralph Edward, and *Truth or Consequences*.

Today's aficionados are often preoccupied with the television counterpart of their favorite quiz programs, thinking no more of the radio version than a brief facet of broadcasting history. Rather than squander valuable time theorizing why no one has yet written a book about *Truth or Consequences*, I took it upon myself to rectify that oversight. With primary focus on the major contests and charities, the majority of this book will extensively cover the radio years from 1940 to 1955. Assuming someone also has intentions of writing a book on the quiz program – or in the future decides to do so – it is a fair assumption that their coverage will focus primarily on the television component. Therefore, I have left the door open for the next devotee.

A book such as this could not be possible without the benevolent endeavors of these good folks who donated time, recordings, archival materials, permissions, photographs, and other materials that were needed for this project. In alphabetical order: Melanie Aultman, Bob Barker, David Blumberg (for contributing many of the photos in this book), Brian Boswell, Ryan Ellett, Karen Fishman, Steve Forster, John Gassman, Larry Gassman, Irene Theodore Heinstein, Walden Hughes, Gary Lowe, Mary Ann Lowe, Bill McMahon, Ralph Edwards Passmore, David Simon, Rene Thompson and Steve Thompson. Special thanks to the library staff of UCLA, the staff at the Library of Congress, The Jimmy Fund in Boston, Massachusetts, and Ralph Edwards Productions. Special recognition goes out to Chuck Harter, who spent many days helping me research materials at UCLA, and Terry Salomonson of Audio Classics who sent me numerous photographs that are reprinted in this book.

Regarding a legal issue, the concern of whether or not to list the names of game show contestants and/or their place of residence in this book, which was provided over the air at the time of broadcast, was debated for a short time. Over the years, thousands of people have been seeking the broadcast date, as well as the "consequence," for which their family relative later recollected. Most seek this information for genealogy purposes. During the early eighties, Ralph Edwards himself had a secretary who spent considerable time providing this information at the request of ex-contestants and/or their relatives; a professional courtesy to the public. That public service, however, has long since expired. It is a known fact (and verified within the pages of this book) that each and every contestant signed a disclosure before appearing on the broadcasts – both for legal and insurance purposes. Upon the signing of those disclosures, contestants waived any privacy concerns they had beforehand.

As you will find throughout this book, whenever known, names of quiz show contestants are listed under their respective episode entry. Such information can be found through archives across the country, open to the public, as well as newspaper archives on both microfilm and digital copy. Small-town newspapers across the country, after discovering local residents appeared on a national broadcast, regarded them as momentary celebrities and treated them as such in their columns. Like a county census, contestants on *Truth or Consequences* are a matter of public record. Like a good archeologist, one just needs to know where to look. For this reason, the names of all contestants listed in this book were not withheld because they can be found through such venues that have already been made public.

Six years of research took me across the country to compile the material contained within the pages of this book, including a trip to Truth or Consequences, New Mexico. I was able to assist a number of families with information they were seeking, about their relatives, who were contestants on the program. Some of the stories contained within the pages of this book might rival those of Robert Ripley and Bill Stern, but I can assure you they are true… proof that during the late 1940s and early 1950s, the quiz program truly was a national phenomenon and it is my hope that in some way I have preserved the legacy of Ralph Edwards.

Martin Grams, Jr.
July 2018

Chapter 1
Ralph Edwards and the Origin of *Truth or Consequences*

Ralph Edwards first saw the light of day in the front (and only) bedroom of a farmhouse in Merino, Colorado, at 13 minutes after nine on June 13, 1913 (a Friday, of course). It was here that he learned the importance of neighborliness. "In a Colorado Plains blizzard, you may have only one contact," Edwards later recalled. "The farmer a mile away who would hitch up and come to help. If it were a crop planting need, several helped out." The nationwide contests Edwards would later devise and apply on *Truth or Consequences*, especially for America's health agencies, raising millions of dollars, were a throwback to that American spirit of combined aid for those in need.

Work began at an early age, soon after he moved with his family to Oakland, California when he was 12, peddling the *Oakland Tribune* on a paper route, working at a neighborhood drug store, and clerking at the Tenth Street Produce Market.

His first "break" came as the result of a skit he wrote and in which he appeared in the annual Oakland High School "spectacular" broadcast on the local radio station, KROW. His appearance was in conjunction with the recent announcement that he was made class president. Edwards was 15 at the time and the cast included Jack Farnell, who would later work for the Leo Burnett Advertising Agency in

Chicago. The station manager heard Edwards doing the skit, liked what he heard, and hired the youth to read the news at a salary of $5.00 a week. Edwards also got the job of writing, announcing, and acting in a 15-minute serial every weekday, at $1.00 per script. He was a senior at high school at the time, circa 1930. The most mail he received was from three people who assured him it was "Marine Corps" and not Marine "Corpse," as he pronounced it. Since then, Ralph Edwards was meticulous in his pronunciation.

During the six-month period between December 1930 and June 1931, when Edwards graduated from high school, and June enrollment at the University of California in Berkeley, he was introduced to Alfred Penn, director of a group called "Penn Players," who performed once a week on KROW. Edwards did several parts for free. He spieled commercials for such accounts as the Star Outfitting Company and Silvers, both clothing stores. That same year, he found himself writing and selling radio commercials for a small (one man) advertising agency. Among his assignments was *Alvin and Betty*, the story of a married couple and their trials and humorous tribulations. On this program, he conducted his first contest (a forerunner to the later Mr. and Mrs. Hush contests) in which radio listeners wrote in to name a pet goat in the script. Edwards also played the role of the goat in the program. The judge of this contest was silent screen actress Colleen Moore. She was playing in *Church Mouse* at the Fulton Theatre in Oakland at the time. Edwards went backstage with Carl Botino, his employer, and asked her to be the judge. (The winning name, by the way, was Anthracite since it was a black goat.)

Ralph Edwards

Between 1931 and 1932, Edwards was re-writing the news, following up leads and writing his own stories, and broadcasting them as news programs as well as performing together, turning records, and doing sound effects in a nightly program known as *March of Events*, similar to the popular radio program, *The March of Time*. In rewriting the stories from the morning papers, Edwards would get up before 5:00 a.m., be at the corner when the papers arrived, and rush home to pound out his own dramatized version of the news. His Little Theatre pals from U.C. Berkeley would meet him at the radio station – KTAB, 14th and Franklin Streets, Oakland. This was Frank Wright's Penthouse Studios, where they would act out the news. Then he would hop into his Model T and whiz up Telegraph Avenue to his "8 o'clock" at Cal. All this while he was still working at Pedley's Drug Store and going to Merritt Business School.

On top of this, he took on a job of writing and announcing a two-hour evening radio program sponsored by Morgan's Stomach Tablets and featuring the music of Dude Martin and his Nevada Night Herders. He also did other programs ranging from reading the funny papers to classic music. He continued to spiel commercials for such accounts as the Star Outfitting Company and Silvers. Tom Morgan was the owner of the Pickwick Stages Bus Line in that area, and a health pill called "Morgan's Stomach Tablets." It was Morgan who hired Edwards to fill in two hours of programming on KTAB. This was a rare opportunity for the creative urges of the young sophomore at Cal. Lunch time would find Edwards writing his nighttime scripts at Stephens Union Lounge on campus. After class, he would write another script, perform some of his broadcasting assignments for Frank Wright, go home, eat the big meal his mother cooked, study, and rush down to KTAB to prepare his assignment with all involved.

The principal purveyors of Morgan's Stomach Tablets was Dude Martin and his Nevada Night Herders. Ralph Edwards would announce the program, sell a few pills, and get on with the next assignment: *Bats in the Belfry*, the forerunner of *Truth or Consequences*. Shows ranged from reading the funny papers on *Uncle Ralph*, and enacted the lines of great composers, playing recordings of their master works, on *Children of Orpheus*.

Joe Walters, later a CBS staff announcer, got into radio as a result of Edwards by having him substitute when Edwards went to Cal games to lead yells as assistant varsity yell leader. Phil Lasky, the manager, finally called Edwards and said, "Don't you think you ought to at least introduce me to the young fellow you seem to have hired?" (Later, when Edwards left for New York, Walters gave him $100 to use if he ever needed it. Returning the favor, Walters was later to announce on *Truth or Consequence).

Working on this small station, he had about every possible kind of radio experience from engineering, acting and writing, to selling and production. Throughout this time he kept up with his studies and graduated as an English major and with a B.A. in Letters and Science. Approximately 1933-1935, KTAB was bought by Wesley Dumm, and hired Phil Lasky as manager. The station call letters were quickly changed to KSFO, with the main offices in San Francisco's Russ Building, and Oakland offices in the old Penthouse Studios of Frank Wright. Edwards was hired as an announcer in charge of all Oakland programs with occasional assignments in San Francisco. Ralph was assigned Bob Dumm, the owner's son. He used to borrow Bob's tuxedo for the Junior Prom and Senior Ball at Cal.

Ralph Edwards

Until graduation from U.C. in June 1935 with his B.A. in Letters and Science, an English major, Ralph kept a schedule in which only the stout survive. Aside from his cheerleading activities, he was the lead in most of the campus Little Theatre productions, and in the classic productions of Professor Charles Von Neumayer and Sarah Huntsman Sturgess. Edwards was Louis Dubedat in Shaw's *Doctor's Dilemma*, Dr. Carroll in Sidney Howard's *Yellow Jack*, the Death-takes-a-holiday character in Giraudoux's *Intermezzo*, and the wild Darrell Blake in Lewis Johnston's *The Moon in the Yellow River*.

Ralph Edwards

Edwards also played in Shakespeare's *Macbeth*, *A Midsummer Night's Dream* and *King Lear* and the title role of Orestes in the Greek tragedy *The Choepheri*, at the U.C. Greek Theatre. The month he entered the university he appeared at the Fulton Theatre, Oakland, for a brief run of *Late Springtime*, directed by Norman Field. During his university years, he gave up his Sunday School teaching assignment, but he usually managed to accompany his mother to church every Sunday.

The rest of 1935 was eaten up by graduation and full assignment in the San Francisco studios of KSFO, writing, acting, announcing, and producing. In February 1936, Pat (Sylvester) Weaver called Ralph one Saturday afternoon and asked if he would audition for an announcer's job at KFRC, the CBS outlet in San Francisco, of which Weaver was program manager. Freeman Sergeant, Ralph's acting buddy at Cal, had recommended him. When Ralph took the audition, Weaver had gone on to greater glory in New York. Jack Van Nostrand was production chief. He hired Ralph and it was there on the announcer's "board" at KFRC that Ralph listened to announcers such as Paul Douglas, David Ross, Frank Gallop, Andre Baruch, Ken Roberts and Bert Parks from New York, and decided if they could do it, so could he.

At KFRC at the time was Murray Bolen, the piano playing partner of the team Murray and Harris. Ralph Edwards announced their act. Tom Brenneman, who constantly told Edwards what a great job he was always doing. Elbert Lachelle, organist, who figured with Edwards in a funny "filler" of the program, *Hawaii Calls*. Charlie Concannon, the engineer for *Hawaii Calls* where Edwards uttered his first words to a network – and, in his mind, blew it. Grant Pollock, a fellow announcer, who urged Edwards to go to New York and get on Broadway on network radio. Sam Taylor (later a successful Broadway playwright), who wrote a postcard to Edwards from New York remembering Edwards' acting at U.C., and said, "If you can get back here, I can get you a walk-on on Broadway."

Ralph Edwards had been stage struck since putting on his own plays in the family's barn as a boy back in Colorado. He borrowed $200 from a bank. Mrs. Fisher, the apartment manager across the street, and Chris Madsen, ex-roomer at the Edwards home, signed as co-signers on the loan. Wilma Blurton, a girlfriend at the time, assumed half the loan; Ralph paid $30 for transportation to Philadelphia. Ralsten Lewis, a junior salesman at KFRC, who successfully sought a position at Lewis & Gilman, a Philadelphia ad agency, split driving duties with Edwards as the two ventured east. Edwards' mother, to whom he was devoted, gave him parting advice, which he always remembered: "Son, go to church." (The stories of Edwards' mother and her influence on his life were an important part of the "humanity" approach in all of Ralph's radio programs.)

Upon reaching New York on July 16, 1936, Edwards found that the show in which he had hoped to appear had folded, but he stayed on, having to borrow $50 from a friend to make ends meet. After three months of struggling, Ralph Edwards saw Pat Weaver in person at the Young & Rubicam Advertising Agency in New York, where Weaver was Director of Programs. Weaver hired Ralph as "the voice" in a Sal Hepatica-Ipana commercial read by Harry Von Zell on the *Stoopnagle and Budd* radio program, a summer replacement for Fred Allen on NBC. For this, Edwards received $35 and made it possible for him to exist until the middle of October, when he was down to his last 15 cents, which he spent on a salmon sandwich and a cup of hot chocolate in the Greeley Square Automat Cafeteria. He then went back to his hotel, the Stratford, 34th and Broadway.* He wired Joe Walters for $25, and charged the wire to his room. Joe wired back $50. Ralph's family could have "scrounged" up the money but things were tough enough for everyone as it was and he did not want to worry them. The $50 kept him in New York until he was called by Ernie Bush at CBS to come back for a final audition as an announcer.

Ralph had auditioned at every radio network in New York. He tore out the "recording" section of the Yellow Pages in the phone book and had run them all down. Two of those contacts bore fruit later: Allan Ward got Edwards a job for the *George Jessel Show* for DeSoto, and *The Phil Arden Orchestra*, among others.

The date was October 24, 1936. Ralph Edwards and one other fellow were auditioning for the post Del Charbert had vacated as CBS staff announcer. Ralph was called first; the other man was still waiting. Doug Coulter hired Edwards. He later recalled the terse interview with the rugged Mr. Coulter and his final words: "I like your work." Then, picking up the phone to Harry Burgess, Coulter said, "Hello, Harry. I'm sending down a new announcer." A handshake confirmed the big struggle was over. This may have been inspiration for Edwards later exploring the unsung as well as the celebrated on such programs as *Truth or Consequences* and *This is Your Life*.

Edwards met Harry Burgess with one hand hiding the "elbow in his right sleeve," signed the contract and then immediately did two things. One, he wired the good news to his mother. Two, hit a University of California alumnus he had met in New York for enough money for a new suit. It was "iron black" and wore forever.

Supposedly the job was originally sought by 69 competitors – at least that was the number he was told from third party sources at CBS. What was certain, Edwards later recalled, "There were two us at the final call back. I got called first; the other fella became a judge in upstate New York." His starting salary was $45,

---

* Numerous newspapers and magazines reported Edwards slept in the most "reasonable" places, including the balcony of a church, and slept in a movie house, but it appears that was mere publicity exaggerations, proving that newspaper accounts should not always be taken as the gospel.

good money in November of 1936. The first checks went to pay back his half of the bank loan in Oakland. The latter suggested he move to a room on Riverside Drive; inexpensive, but not a hotel. He shared the apartment with fellow announcer Andre Baruch and Mel Allen.

Within six weeks, Edwards won his first commercial audition after having become a CBS staff announcer. He tried out for the *Horace Heidt* show, which he would serve for two years. His fresh approach to on-the-air selling, by inserting "conversational punctuation" into advertising copy as if he was addressing each feminine listener individually, landed him assignments on other radio programs. Six daily soap operas, four nighttime programs, and occasionally substituting on *Your Hit Parade* for his friend Andre Baruch, whom he roomed with.* Reportedly he was working on as many as 40 shows a week, announcing for Big Band remotes and delivering the news. Edwards was announcing for *Pick and Pat, Against the Storm, Vic and Sade, The O'Neils, The Road of Life, Pepper Young's Family, Major Bowes' Original Amateur Hour, 99 Men and a Girl, The Silver Theatre, Honolulu Bound, Life Can Be Beautiful,* and Tony Wons, Ben Bernie, Phil Baker, Emily Post, and Edward MacHugh's radio program, *The Gospel Singer*. Within two years, his earnings rose from $45 a week to $1,100 a week.

It was in 1937 that Ralph Edwards met a very attractive girl from New York named Barbara Sheldon. Ralston Lewis insisted on taking Edwards to Scarsdale on a blind date and there Edwards met the woman who would ultimately become his wife. She was a popular girl and every time he called, she was busy with previous engagements. One day he sent her tickets for her grandfather to see the Ben Bernie radio show. She brought him into the city to see the show and following the broadcast, he took her family to dinner. He eventually won her over and in July of 1937, took a vacation to the West Coast to introduce his fiancé to his parents.

In February of 1938, in between announcing chores on radio programs in New York City, Edwards had a tooth pulled and returned to the studio in time to deliver Crisco commercials for *The Right to Happiness*. The deadening after-effect

---

* In July 1937, Ralph Edwards discovered there was another announcer of the same name, blind, formerly on the staff of KIRO, Seattle, who moved to San Francisco to become an announcer for the same territory Edwards vacated. The blind announcer prepares his own announcements in Braille and read them over the air.

Ralph Edwards (bottom right) with CBS staff announcers including Ken Roberts (above Edwards) and his good friend Andre Baruch (middle bottom).

of the anesthetic gave his jaw a tough tussle for a while, but he completed his chore to the amazement of the radio cast. When executives at Procter & Gamble learned that Edwards pulled off the task without any noticeable difficulty, they complimented him for "an especially good job."

On August 19, 1939, Edwards married Barbara Sheldon. They resided in West Redding, Connecticut. They were joined in time by two daughters, Christine and Lauren, and a son, Gary. He commuted back and forth to New York City while she remained home to raise the children.

From his very first audition as an announcer in 1936 to his last in 1940, Edwards lost only one audition: for Pall Mall Cigarettes. "Maybe it's because I never smoked," Edwards later joked. He would run from one studio to another during the day with Bill Meeder, organist, holding the studio door for each other–depending on whether the announcer or the organist started the show. With all of these program, Edwards recalled "I was beginning to see box tops in front of my eyes." He wanted one nighttime show so he might divest himself of his day-to-day footrace and sales spiels.

It was in 1939 that while Edwards was an announcer for multiple programs sponsored by Procter & Gamble that he heard the soap manufacturer was looking for a new half-hour radio program. John McMillin of the Compton Advertising Agency, encouraged Edwards to think of a show for Procter & Gamble. He tried the spelling game "Ghosts," but it didn't work. His next idea would be an audience participation game.

"I dreamed of a show of my very own," Ralph Edwards later recalled. "After mulling over lots of ideas, I thought of the old parlor game we used to play back on the farm called 'Heavy, Heavy Hangs Over Thy Head'." Edwards recalled that he was the youngest of a family of three boys on the Colorado farm where he grew up. The winter nights were long in Logan County, and the nearest town, Merino, was a good buggy drive away, so it was natural that the Edwards kids should play games like *Truth or Consequences* very often. In the late eighties, Edwards recalled the idea for *Truth or Consequences* dated back to the old post-office parlor game in which the penalty often was a kiss. "People like to laugh at the ridiculous or absurd dilemmas other folks get into and like to see how they act to get out of their fix," recalled Edwards. "So I devised the unique radio show in which the victims must do the ludicrous, absurd and side-splitting things. Surveys have credited the show with being the most popular of any in which the audience participates."

He discussed the idea of a show with his wife, and invited a few friends over to try it out. The next day he took the idea to the agency. Their interest serious, the executives wanted to hear an audition. So in front of the audience for the *Horn and Hardart Children's Hour*, Edwards made a pilot for *Truth or Consequences*. (Horn and Hardart was an Automat in New York City, the same establishment Edwards spent his remaining 15 cents before a jump in his career.) Jack Farnell, a friend from Oakland, who was then in New York, went to the public library to research questions. Barbara, her parents and Ralph began thinking up consequences. Andre Baruch, with whom he had shared an apartment in his bachelor days, and his wife Bea Wain, made celebrity appearances on the program. Mr. Goldblatt was his first contestant. He was supposed to be a sound effect man imitating an automobile horn – but actually he wouldn't open his mouth. "His consequence was to be a sound effects man, ending with a scream," Edwards recalled. "No matter how I prodded him, Mr. Goldblatt just wouldn't scream. I was frustrated. My show was dying before it got started. So I walked up behind Mr. Goldblatt, extended my thumb. As hard as I could I poked Mr. Goldblatt in his derriere. Mr. Goldblatt screamed and I sold the show." Edwards later joked that he had "the golden thumb of radio."

The recording was played back for William Ramsey, then head of Proctor & Gamble's radio division, who asked: "How on Earth do you get them to do those things, Ralph?" Those on the inside often referred to Edward's "golden thumb."

With the assistance of John McMillin, Edwards sold the program and quickly enlisted Herb Rosenthal, who was then at CBS' Artist Bureau to handle the details. The sponsor carried the option for renewal of an additional 13 weeks, after the initial test run. Uncertain of the results, Procter & Gamble devoted funds for prime time instead of daytime to promote Ivory soap flakes, which debuted over WBAC in New York, and four CBS stations in New England including WDRC, Hartford; WPRO, Providence; and WROC, Worcester. If the series was deemed successful, the program would be extended to the whole CBS network, coast-to-coast.

The cast of the *Horn and Hardart Children's Hour*.

Truth or Consequences was referred to by executives at Procter & Gamble as "an experimental show," scripted, directed and emceed by Ralph Edwards, announcer on several other P&G programs. The traditional parlor game had various names, depending of what part of the country people played the game, some referred to it as "Fine or Superfine." But a radio contest in which contestants had to pay a forfeit for giving incorrect answers to a variety of amusing questions, *Truth or Consequences* was risky business. At that time, *Information, Please* was considered the only audience participation show on the air, but contestants were not subjected to parlor tricks. CBS sold the show through the Compton Advertising Agency, supervised by Gilbert Ralston. Bill Meeder supplied the organ accompaniment. The bulk of Compton's lineup of programs were daytime serials.

In the same month Edwards celebrated his third year as an announcer for *Major Bowes*, *Truth or Consequences* asked the initial contestants who fizzled on questions to talk and spell through the impediment of an all-day sucker, imitate a one-man band with such implements as dishpans, garbage cans and coffeepots, and conduct good-humored interviews with strangers in the audience.

"Saturday night house parties should enjoy this one after everybody has flung off two or three highballs," *Variety* commented in their review of the premiere broadcast. "There's hardly a limit to which this twist to pinning the tail on the donkey could be put… Silly and entertaining and, considering the season and the limited hookup of four stations, quite inexpensive. Edwards proves a choice fit for the assignment. He's fleet of tongue, a suave party man and adept at keeping things moving snappily."

Ken Roberts was the announcer for the first few broadcasts, replaced in late April by Mel Allen, who was in Florida when the series premiered. Roberts was hired with the understanding that the position was temporary. Allen's job was also to convince contestants to help with the sponsor plugs. About that time Ralph Edwards opened an office at CBS in New York City, to handle the ambitious task of continuing his announcing duties on other radio programs, as well as moderate a program of his own, which required fresh stunts every week.

Variety reviewed the series in their May 1 issue, citing the program "shapes up as that ideal of radio commercials, a cheap novelty show, with the customers making their own fun for relatively modest $5, $10, $15 and $20 fees. The double sawbuck is the grand prize, determined by the applause-meter, for the one getting the most exuberant audience reaction. As the old parlor tag indicates, the $15 prizes go for 'truth,' i.e. guessing a query right, and $5 for the 'consequence,' which calls for some novelty penalty, to be fulfilled by the victim."

By late May, Procter & Gamble agreed to renew the contract for an additional 13 weeks. But the stress of creating a weekly radio program during what little free time he had between announcing assignments was starting to play a toll. About the time he received notice of the renewal, Edwards was struck ill and spent his down time consulting with his wife, Barbara. While he didn't let his illness keep him from doing the show on the evening of May 26, he had to make an important career decision. With approval of the producers and sponsors at Compton, Edwards took a vacation from announcing the five network shows for a period of six weeks over the summer. His only return to the radio microphone was for his *Truth or Consequences* radio program, which ran until July 27. Shortly before vacation, Edwards had discussions with executives at P&G, making a corporate decision regarding the quiz program. The soap manufacturer wanted to take the program coast-to-coast during prime time but CBS was unable to find a suitable time slot for the company. As a result, *Truth or Consequences* would return in late August under a 46-week contract, on a different network, NBC. This did not fare well for CBS, having a staff announcer hosting his own program on a rival network. P&G agreed to raise the weekly cost of the radio program to offer larger prizes and Edwards' salary would be raised – justifying his resignation from CBS as a staff announcer. The series would now be featured on Saturday evenings over NBC, at 8:30 p.m., Eastern. It was on NBC that *Truth or Consequences* would become synonymous during the remainder of the radio era.

Ralph Edwards and crew as guests performing *Truth or Consequences* for the April 15, 1942, broadcast of *Stage Door Canteen*.

Ralph Edwards and crew as guests performing *Truth or Consequences* for the April 15, 1942, broadcast of *Stage Door Canteen*.

Chapter 2
The Early Years, 1940 - 1945

"If you miss the question, you'll look good in custard..."
-- Ralph Edwards to a contestant

Week after week, starting in 1940, Ralph Edwards and his crew had fun dishing out the consequences, purposely devising questions that were fair, but difficult to answer. Contestants selected from the audience were asked a question and promised money and prizes if they knew the answer. In most cases, the contestants failed to answer correctly and were then subjected to numerous humiliations... completion and participation rewarded them with both cash prizes and samples of the sponsor's product. At first, the acts were simple parlor stunts. The radio audience required little explanation of the elaboration of the stunts: One contestant had to make up a poem about specific objects and subjects. Another had to imitate the sounds of animals. One contestant had to describe a boxing match. A short contestant had to ride an electric horse. It was not until 1946 that Edwards struck gold with "carry-over" stunts that boosted ratings, involved numerous Hollywood celebrities, and discovered a winning formula that would truly make *Truth or Consequences* a national phenomenon.

His first stunt on the premiere broadcast (March 23, 1940), involved a sailor who had to address the nationwide audience with a mouth full of cherry lollipops. That stunt was simple, but they never were all that easy and as the months passed, the consequences became challenging; the questions became almost completely unanswerable.

"What letter is omitted from the dial telephones?" (Q)

"What are the words on a mailbox? (Pull Down)

"If it is January in Buenos Aires, what month is it in British Columbia?" (January)

"Where do you find diamonds in the U.S.?" (a jewelry store)

"What number is spelled with ten different letters? (Eighty-Four)

"What is bought by the yard, worn by the foot?" (carpet)

The structure of the consequences was both strategic and essential. An average of five new stunts had to be devised every week. Every facet of the stunt had to be ironed out to the minute detail. Threat of physical harm had to be ruled out. The consequence had to go over well with the studio and radio audience. Setting up the stunts through third parties, consulting legals, and verifying insurance policies was only a fraction of the enterprise. Some stunts (referred to as "consequences" on the program) pulled off on stage did not go over as well as planned and used only once; others were repeated a number of times over the years, with variation or improvements.

Contestants find themselves covered in mud.

Ralph Edwards once explained that as emcee (the host), he could not be derisive in any way or make fun of a contestant or hold them up to ridicule. He never used the contestant to get their barbs across because that would have made the show take on a whole new attitude. Before any stunt, interaction with the audience was necessary, by allowing the contestant to answer a couple questions about themselves. The contestant was considered the patsy – never the victim. The contestant was never to feel victimized. Edwards always complimented the contestants before and after each stunt, i.e. "You've been wonderful" and "I'm going to remember what you said." Having learned the hard way in an early broadcast, children were never asked yes or no questions. Else, they would simply answer "yes" or "no." With jovial freshness and sharp wit, Edwards made contestants feel at home on stage, accepting of their challenges.

The warm-up with the audience before the show was essential to the success of the broadcast. This helped get the audience going and kept them in high spirits. It was during the warm-up that Edwards selected the contestants. He always set up a joke or two prior to each broadcast opened with the sound of laughter originating from the audience before the announcer came to the microphone.

Producer Al Paschall kissing a woman in the audience during the pre-show warm-up, circa 1946.

While the contestants were exposed to unexpected surprises, they themselves provided some unexpected laughs. In one broadcast, a contestant admitted his profession was delivering frozen fish. When asked if he liked his job, he responded how "it smells." Mrs. Lebarr, a female contestant, was once asked if she was ready to start the consequence and over the air she admitted, "I want to get out of here." A Brooklyn taxi driver was once asked who made a better passenger – a man or a woman? "A young girl," was his response. Edwards immediately moved on to the game before the contestant, eager to explain why, could finish answering the question. To face her consequence, an old woman had to play a wind instrument and, after a couple brief failures at playing the overture, admitted over the air that she had to take her teeth out to perform the task.

A high school girl from the Bronx found herself talking to Tyrone Power, on long-distance from the stage, in front of several hundred people. As soon as she discovered the gag was real, and who she was really talking to, she took hold of her senses, got her breath and quipped, "Gee, what's Annabella got that I haven't got?"

When a contestant was sent to Columbus Circle, at a corner of Central Park in New York, where impromptu orators hold forth, he was instructed to stand up on a soap box and make a speech on "Why America Should Have a Be-Kind-to-Flies Week." The contestant proved to be unexpectedly eloquent. Then the hecklers stepped in and punched up the program with their own unrehearsed comments: "You don't hear the flies complaining, do you?" and "So what's the matter? They're not kicking!"

A man who had to pretend he was a seal was surprised when a real seal wandered out onto the stage while he had to complete the consequence: singing "Let Me Call You Sweetheart," while the seal barked an accompaniment. When he completed his assignment, the man observed over the air, "Well, I've had some dates I've liked less."

One contestant was dressed up in an 1890 swimming suit and made to walk the plank over a big tank of water. When Ralph Edwards told him he was a good sport for playing the game, the contestant brought Edwards into the game. "I had just made a contestant walk the plank, pirate-style," Edwards recalled. "I leaned over the tank to interview him as he came out and he gave me a tug. Into the water I went, microphone, watch, wallet, tuxedo and all." The plunge into the water could be heard over the air and when Edwards climbed out of the tank, he reached for a dry microphone and remarked, "This is certainly a heck of a way to make a living."

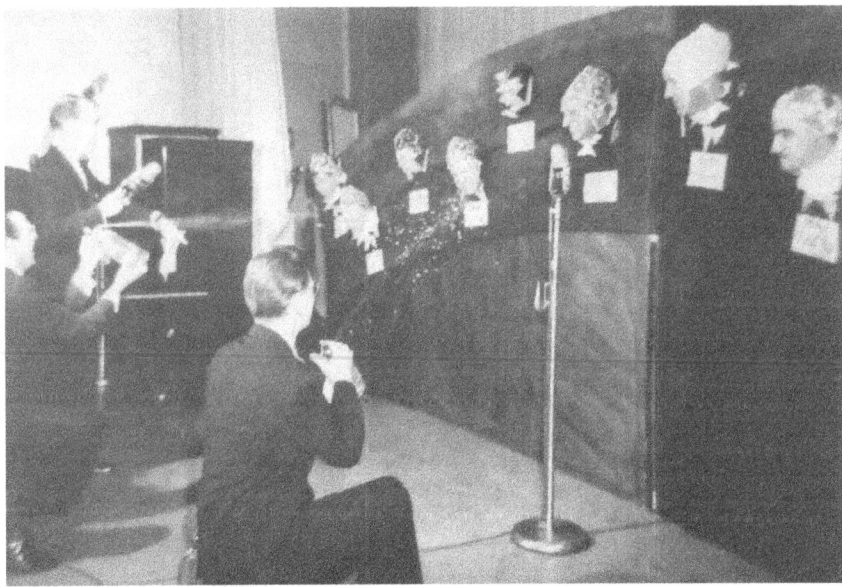

The Stunts

Radio quiz programs often applied terminology employed behind the microphone. By definition, a "frame" was identified by Ralph Edwards and Jerry Payne (head writer of *Truth or Consequences*) as the most used of the basic ideas. In the "I'm Joe" stunt featured on the broadcast of November 28, 1942, a contestant found himself framed for a caper he never committed. "Flowers were sent to a woman each day for a week," Edwards recalled. "They contained a message, 'You are beautiful, love you, Joe,' 'I hope to meet you some day, Joe,' 'To my secret love, Joe,' and so on.

No one knew we were doing this. We brought a contestant up on stage. For his consequence, he had to go to a home at a particular address, ring the buzzer and say, 'I am Joe.'"

There were group frames, where a group of people were selected from the audience and placed into a combination act. They could be told to play the Copacabana (or some well-known club), etc. "They really go up and practice," Edwards recalled. "We have a singer and film the reaction at Las Vegas or the Copacabana and come back to the show and play it. You could build it up one week and play it the next week but that can cause a problem because possibly the Las Vegas people would have seen it or heard about it on the radio. You may have to just do it and bring it back."

"Once a lady who couldn't sing at all was sent over to The Plaza to sing with Eddy Duchin," Edwards recalled. "Eddy Duchin introduced her as the new vocalist. She was not passable in any way, shape nor form and confounded the very elegant group at The Plaza."

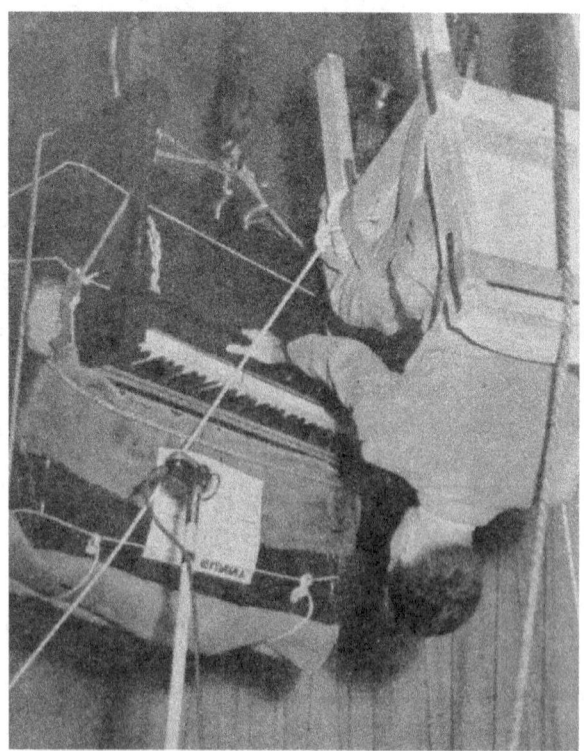

A contestant is strapped into a chair and hanging upside down
from the ceiling to play "Keep Your Sunny Side Up" on the piano.
(Broadcast of September 4, 1943.)

"The mind reader" was another frame. A man helped frame his wife and we introduced another contestant as a mind reader. We once used Billy Barty for this stunt. The woman contestant was going to have her mind ready by 'Lady Gasava' who was another contestant with earphones hidden under a turban. She was plugged into a man under the table, fed backstage to a speaker at which was the woman's husband. Any question was asked, the husband provided the correct answer. The woman was completely confounded that the turbaned woman knew everything about her. Finally, the man came out from behind, holding the mike, getting closer and closer until she realized he was the one 'spilling the beans.'"

"The Lady Ralph was a great frame where a man contestant was brought up to the stage," Jeremy Fox explained. "He was sent out to the street to find someone and tell that person he was Ralph Edwards and came on back and gave them a question and if they told the truth they could avoid the consequence – which was to dance the samba. He was sent out under the leadership of an aide and went on the street. In the meantime, Ralph Edwards dressed up like a lady, wearing a wig. The aide went on the street and got the contestant (we had arranged for the street to be closed so he could find no one. An aide brought him back and we sent out another aide to find someone. Aide comes back with Ralph as a lady and is introduced to the man as Mrs. So and So, and the consequence started. The man had to pretend he was Ralph and took the real Ralph (whom he didn't realize was the real Edwards) on stage and they started to dance and the result was a lot of fun. He was a small fellow, purposely picked so Ralph could swing him around, etc. He whirled him around and landed on top of him and then the real Ralph asked him, "Who are you?" The man replied that he was Ralph Edwards. The real Ralph said, "No, you're not, because I am! It played far better than it could be told."

"Another wonderful frame was the little old lady from the audience who would do a pole vault, pitted against a real athlete," Fox continued. "We said we would give her a head start. Get on your mark, get ready, set, go! The old lady ran like the dickens until she got to the back of the auditorium where there was a little ten-foot divider behind which was a real champion vaulter of the same size."

On the more elaborate frames, they were planned often a week of more ahead. The contestant's spouse or close relative was consulted ahead of time for approval. Some research was done two weeks or more in advance (i.e., train an elephant, teach a woman to juggle, go to Berlitz to learn a language, etc.). Contestants had to sign a disclaimer, printed in advance on an index card, with no exceptions. By the early fifties, the disclaimer had expanded to a full sheet of paper.

Announcer Art Balinger

A "carry-over" was a stunt that was featured on more than one consecutive broadcast and the contestant came back week after week to deliver a progress report. Rarely used in the early years, the "carry-over" became more commonplace as the years progressed.

Some stunts were the impediment type of act, such as relaying a message in a marching band. Marine Band members had to relay a message to each other, such as "be sure to peel the potatoes" and then watch how funny the message came out in the end. Another was having a sexpot type playing opposite a survey man, and having a contestant trying to get a survey accomplished over the phone. He has to get answers and the woman kept making very suggestive type of comments. Another simple impediment was having someone whistle while chewing on a cracker.

Child acts were rarely done due to the lack of children in the audience and the producers' attempt to avoid anything remotely similar to radio's *The Quiz Kids*. In one episode, Humpty Dumpty talked to a little boy and then fell off the wall. Humpty broke into many pieces and asked the child to put him back together again. The youth actually started putting him back together.

"Once we had three little boys sitting in a remote studio," Edwards remarked. "A *Truth or Consequences* person dressed like Superman came out of a phone booth and flew. The children thought they were seeing their hero. We brought them back later and asked if they had seen anything unusual happen. Not one of them mentioned Superman!" In another episode, a child was asked how much his mother paid for his clothes. His mom got to keep however much the child said she paid for each item.

The youngster was asked to sing "Pistol Packin' Mama" to win tickets to the rodeo at Madison Square Garden. The boy was surprised when Roy Rogers stepped out on the stage to sing a duet with him. Broadcast of October 23, 1943.

Ralph Edwards recalled the moment when they played the Blindfold Guess Where game, where they told someone who they sent out somewhere in New York, to guess where they were. If they succeeded, they got a very large prize. "The person was sent out and we gave them an appropriate entourage – under the guidance of a strong, nice guy so the blindfolded person would feel at ease. We took him around the actual playing of the show – all over the city where the contestant could hear the sound effects of boats, cars, and so on. They ended up on the old stage for *Hellzapoppin'* – a show they could stop at any point. The guy was brought on stage and sat in the middle of the stage. Ahead of time, the audience was told to keep quiet. They tuned me in back at the studio and I said, 'Can you guess where you are?' because of the boat sounds he heard, his guess was down at the dock. Then the audience told him, 'No, you aren't!'" After he discovered he was on stage in front of an audience, his response was completely natural and spontaneous: "I feel like a damn fool." The audience roared with laughter.

Among the straight acts was one called Mouse in the Box. "We got more laughs than almost anything we've ever done," Edwards explained. "Four boxes on a table, four ladies. Last lady to play is one who will give the biggest reaction. An assistant comes on stage and while the women close their eyes, a white rat on a cushion is supposed to be put into one of the boxes. The lady doesn't know what box it is. The audience knows that really it was taken away. Ladies think the rat is still there. To win prizes, each lady has to reach in their box and discover nothing there. Nothing is in the first three ladies boxes and the timid lady knows the rat has to be in her box. I milked it for all I could get."

Edwards later recalled how it was easier to get a celebrity to participate on the phone than at the studio. There was the frustration over the phone gag when a wife called her husband (who was really off stage) at the office. She pretended to be downtown and there was a fur coat on sale at a terrific price. He said, naturally, 'no way.' She was told that is she could convince the husband into letting her buy the coat, she could get the prize for free. Finally, he reveals his presence and she received the prize. Pre-dating *The Dating Game*, one stand-up act involved a husband and wife who stood back to back and picked subjects at random. The husband was told to write how many girls he kissed before he was married. The wife writes her answer and then they compared answers. The audience played for the reaction. Other questions along the same principal were "How many hours does the husband help the wife at home?" or "How many times did you kiss your wife before you were married?"

One man was asked to whistle "Yankee Doodle Dandy" while sucking a lollipop. Some women were blindfolded and had to sniff men lined up, to determine their husbands. Contestants were asked to chew a cracker and whistle at the same time; eat an apple on a string while reciting an epic poem; go through the motions of driving an imaginary dog team, shouting "Mush! Mush!" while the contestant was fed a spoonful of mush at every cry; and two boys once had to sing "Down by the Old Mill Stream" while feeding each other blackberry pie blindfolded."

On one particular broadcast, a woman was asked to step to the microphone and sing, "Oh, Tell Me, Pretty Maiden, Are There Any More at Home Like You?" while reviewing a bathing parade without giggling or laughing. Then, four men from the audience passed across the stage wearing historic bathing suits. The last

one was the woman's husband, carrying a sign, "Miss Lettuce Leaf of 1840." Only after the stunt was completed was it revealed that newsreel cameras had been grinding away throughout and pictures of the event would be shown in all the Embassy newsreel theaters.

One woman was blindfolded and asked to give a lecture on "The Right Way to Dance," illustrating her talk with an unknown partner. She provided the most appropriate remarks: "You're so clumsy! Why don't you keep off my feet?" And when the blindfold was removed, she was introduced to her partner – Arthur Murray, the best-known dancing instructor in America.

A young male contestant was told he would receive a thousand dollars if he could call the correct heads or tails when a penny was flipped. The penny was tossed into the air, landing in the Hudson River, encased in cement. In the intervening week, the young man practiced deep-sea diving in a diving helmet; and on the *Truth or Consequences* broadcast, down he went to the bottom of the Hudson River to broadcast the results.

The staff of *Truth or Consequences*, circa 1942.

Animal Acts

Animals were always welcome props on the quiz program. In Hartford, Connecticut, two old ladies had to wash an elephant before the show was over. A contestant was asked if she wouldn't mind taking a couple of kids to dinner and her reply was "delighted"… until she found out they were the four-legged kids. In Minneapolis, a male contestant lay on the floor imitating a seal barking. On stage came a big female seal – barking.

The audience had seen a cow before, but not on the stage of the Orpheum Theatre in Minneapolis, where a little farm lady was to accompany the Minneapolis Symphony Orchestra, under the direction of Dimitri Mitropoulos, on a "Bovina." The little lady was the featured accompanist. The "Bovina" she was to play turned out to be the sound made when the little farm lady milked the cow, squirting the milk into a galvanized bucket in tempo with a section of the "Blue Danube Waltz." The cow, incidentally, upstaged them all by adlibbing all over the stage on her way out.

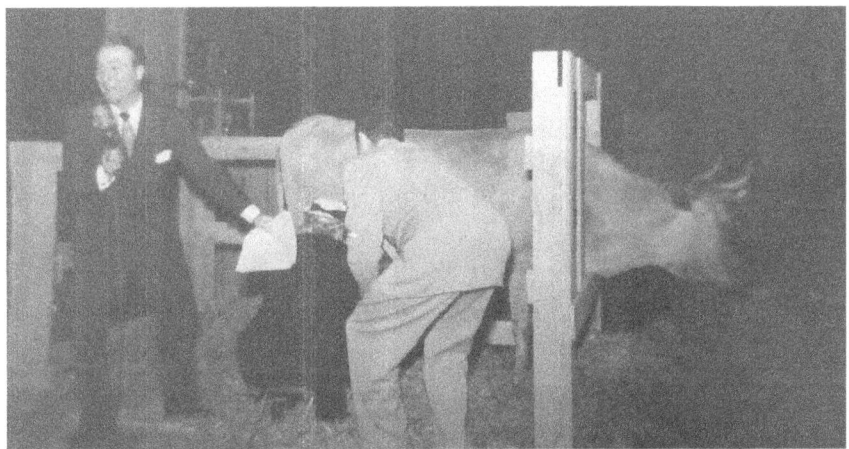
Contestant has to milk a cow on stage.

When a contestant was required to cry loudly for a cigarette, she asked for a Camel. Imagine her surprise when she got one - and had to mount it.

A live elephant was used in a circus stunt. Broadcast of March 31, 1945.

On the evening of November 6, 1948, Herbert Scherr, age 43, had to push an elephant past the New York headquarters of President Truman to pay off an election bet. The bet was made with Howard Heisley of Elkhorn, Wisconsin, on *Truth or Consequences* when it was broadcast from the Auditorium. Scherr flew to New York City, the day before the broadcast, expecting that he would have to push a peanut with his nose. At the last moment, he learned that the peanut was in an elephant!

In Baltimore, newspaper reporters and cameraman covered the big news story of "Man Bites Dog." One male contestant, hearing the ferocious barks and snarls inside the dog cage, braced himself, ready as the cage door swung open, and he did bite – a hot dog.

Two women had a race milking two nanny goats. The Bronx-born assistant in charge of nanny goats screwed up. On the air they discovered he brought billy goats and Edwards took the consequences.

Edwards recalled having to register a horse at a hotel. "We have an impersonator, a feedbag over the horse – done at the Essex in New York. The contestant had to take it up and say, 'How do you do, Mr. George and I am registering.' George says, 'I want a suite because I don't like to sleep with you.' Try to get a junior fellow for the desk clerk – chatter can go back and forth about what he wants for breakfast (little hay, little barley). See how long the banter can go on before the guy blows his mind-contestant and Mr. George finally walk out saying they don't want to stay in the place."

On the evening of December 27, 1947, a contestant's husband gave permission to the producers of the quiz program for a two-way mike set-up between the home and the radio studio, to broadcast his wife's reaction when she came home to find a camel in her Hollywood home on Bronson Avenue. Broadcast of December 27, 1947.

"I remember at one of the theaters there was a seal act," recalled Lillie Buchstane, the woman who handed over the prizes from the booth on stage. "I was in the Treasurer's Booth placed in front of the curtain. Al and Phil Davis knew how frightened I was of anything that crawled or walked on four legs. So they started poking me with a broom. The curtain was between us. I thought it was the seal and kept moving the Treasurer's Booth further on the stage. T'was the night that I almost ruined the show!"

At the Roxy in New York, one of the most talked-about stunts involved a real bear. A man and woman stood on stage before the radio audience. The man, wearing a complete bearskin with bear head that made it impossible for him to see, embraced his supposed wife, who he imagined also would be wearing a bearskin. But the "wife" proved to be a live bear – and was that husband surprised when he got a real bear hug!

"We brought four ladies to the studio," Edwards recalled. "They knew nothing about *Truth or Consequences*. They were seated on a couch. We had a tiger (who was actually declawed) and we had dragged a sack of hamburger along a 100-foot trail. It made the tiger turn to the couch and across in front of it and back and away. We turned the tiger loose with the ladies just sitting there on the couch, talking. The tiger appears, no one else is around the area – he walks along, following the trail of the hamburger. That was called the 'Tiger, Friendly Tiger Act.'"

The Cinderella Stunt

A pretty young, out-of-work secretary was made Cinderella on *Truth or Consequences* in March of 1941. She was given a Saks Fifth Avenue gown, an I.J. Fox fur coat, an I. Miller pair of shoes to wear, and a Charles of the Ritz hair-do; and as a modern Cinderella, was sent off with a young lieutenant of the National Guard to the Big Ball at the Armory on Park Avenue in New York. As she was leaving with her Prince Charming to get in her carriage limousine, Edwards said, "Unlike the real Cinderella, the clothes you are wearing will not turn to rags at the end of the evening. They are yours to keep." Further, the quiz show had a job waiting for the young lady with a law firm starting the following Monday. This act, by the way, much to Edwards' unhappiness, started what became many "give-away" shows. Although Edwards mentioned the well-known names of stores, the quiz program paid for the wardrobe and everything else came out of Edwards' pocket.

"We were putting the show on in New York at the time and it occurred to me what fun we could have lending a helping hand to some of the struggling young people trying to make the 'big time' in New York. That was the start of the Cinderella idea," Edwards later recalled. "We took a girl who was trying to hit Broadway, invited her to attend the show, and after the usual nonsense, gave her the glamor treatment, outfitting her from top to toe, sending her on a round of the right places, etc. The photographers moved in on the stunt and the girl got the 'chance of a lifetime' break."

"I personally got a bang out of doing that stunt," he continued, "and that same idea went on in various phases throughout the years. On the Town Hall plane it gave a struggling musician a chance to enjoy a fake premiere and maybe cash in on his talents. During the war years it was used to reunite families of GIs. Of course, prizes or gifts were involved, but surely no one could question their distribution or their intention."

How a Parlor Game Works

"A visit to a broadcast of *Truth or Consequences* is about as soothing to the nerves as taking a bath in a tub full of snakes," wrote columnist Terrence O'Flaherty of the San Francisco *Chronicle*. "There is never a quiet moment either on stage or off and there are times when a more conservative segment of the audience might wish they were in the middle arena of a nice quiet three-ring circus. Ten minutes before show time, the stage of Studio B at NBC's entertainment emporium was cluttered with a great variety of objects: barrels, sailors, Indians, a crate of eggs and several assistant producers with curly hair. In one corner, a man in argyle socks and a bow tie was seated at a small electric organ playing "Merrily We Roll Along." Here was confusion – but on a paying basis – as one look at the sponsor's sales curves will show. Harlow Wilcox, the announcer, made the usual preliminary introduction to the audience while standing in front of the curtain. As he finished a stranger walked up on the stage, pulled a gun and shot him 'dead.' He fell back through the opening of the curtains into the arms of two assistants who had been waiting there presumably for that."

"One important thing to remember about the *Truth or Consequences* show is that it is crawling with assistants and they're busy all of the time," O'Flaherty continued. "They're in the audience. They're registering people (all participants willing to be contestants are registered). Some are helping old folks to the microphone. Others are gently removing people from the microphone. And others are catching announcers who have been shot, as noted. Everything looks completely unrehearsed, but persons close to the station management say that each assistant has an itinerary to follow. On each program Edwards had what he calls a 'human' touch. This provides a nice relief from the ham-bone aspects of the rest of the show. But it requires a deft bit of handling on his part to keep the heartwarming element in this one act from growing cold – or, worse yet, from becoming slapstick."

In the Los Angeles home of contestant John Dalton, his wife is engaged in conversation with a friend. The conversation is picked up by a hidden microphone and every time Mrs. Dalton said something unpleasant about husbands, John was dumped in a water tank. Broadcast of November 22, 1947.

Remote Broadcasts

Many times Ralph Edwards claimed that *Truth or Consequences* was the first radio program to do an out of the studio remote. In May 1940, a contestant was sent to Alaska to sell an ice box to an Eskimo and he was tuned in live from there and sang "Baby It's Cold Outside." Broadcasting from remote was relatively new until news coverage of the war brought the latest from overseas into American living rooms. But remote broadcasts for a quiz program involved costs that the sponsor had to approve in advance. Justification became more prominent when competition made remote broadcasts essential.

Broadcasting the program from a different location than the NBC Studios required legwork from numerous parties. Clearances, permissions, permits and budgets all had to be approved in advance. In late September 1940, Edwards secured permission from the sponsor, Proctor & Gamble, to broadcast the quiz show from the stage of the Municipal Auditorium at the annual Food Show in Omaha, Nebraska. It was rare for a radio quiz program to originate remote, rather than the confines of the studio, but Edwards convinced executives at the advertising agency the importance of media manipulation and self-promotion. The local newspapers would pick up on the program, creating numerous references to the quiz show over a period of a week, and thus gain additional listeners. The agency's two concerns were budget and the risk of technical disaster.

The broadcast went off without a hitch, however, and in early November, Procter & Gamble considered originating *Truth or Consequences* from various cities – provided extensive coverage in local newspapers ensured the growth of radio listenership. This, according to one inter-office memo, "would be policy departure for the account." Approval was granted by mid-November, and Ralph Edwards was given permission to broadcast *Truth or Consequences* from the stage of The Palace in Cleveland, Ohio, as part of the stage show for the week beginning Friday, November 29. The radio broadcast on Saturday night, November 30, also included Mel Allen making the trip from New York City for the single day. (Gloria Jean and the Merry Macs were also on the vaudeville bill.)

Circa Christmas 1940, Ralph Edwards dropped his announcing jobs on *Life Can Be Beautiful* and *Against the Storm* to devote full time to his own radio program. With approval from the sponsor to broadcast the program via remote, his new schedule would not have afforded him the occasion to continue announcing for other programs. He continued for a brief spell on the Horn & Hardart series on Sundays, but he would eventually drop that assignment as well. "If *Truth or Consequences* failed to succeed," Edwards later recalled, "I had my announcing career to fall back on."

During the week of December 25, Edwards played to a packed house in Detroit. The Fox seated 5,000 fans and was successful for Procter & Gamble. "You can't mistake the sponsor, with a 10-foot banner unfurled taking over the final portion," wrote one reviewer. On stage a contestant did a fan dance impersonation of Sally Rand, a housewife rattled away as a one-woman orchestra among kitchen utensils, a guy imitated a woman getting ready to take a bath, two performers (boy and girl) chewed on string toward a centered marshmallow, and another contestant stuck his head into a bird cage and sang "I'm Only A Bird In A Gilded Cage," while being fed crackers. The most valuable prize on the menu was $5 cash and Ivory soap.

Beulah, the Buzzer

Radio made a lady of Beulah the Buzzer. When contestants failed to answer a question and must pay for the consequence, the dulcet voice of Beulah was heard.

Described in a press release as "the Edgar Bergen of a sound effects dummy," Beulah was a nondescript gadget with a half-shot reed before she was discovered, growing old and dusty in a music shop, by Jack Farnell, assistant to Ralph Edwards. Beulah was repaired, dressed up and given a fine new reed and was insured for $5,000.

> As verified by an extant recording, when Mel Allen and Ralph Edwards attempted to sing the first musical commercial for Ivory Soap, they couldn't help but chuckle over the air. The sponsor was not pleased with the results and for years Allen denied the story.

Sound man Ted Slade using Beulah the Buzzer.

If a press release dated February 24, 1941, can be believed, supposedly the only one of her kind in existence and part of Farnell's job was to safeguard her between Saturdays. "Before locating Beulah, Farnell combed every sound effects studio in the city," the release stated. "Because there was no telling what it would sound like over the air, he had to buy every possible instrument. He spent over $100, to no avail. Finally, Farnell walked into a music shop and the clerk dug among a bunch of sound effects instruments marked "Duck Calls." Farnell said he did not want a duck call but the store owner assured him it was not altogether a duck call. It was half duck call and half cow's moo. "I bought the gadget just for a lark," Farnell recalled. "It turned out to be just what we were looking for." Something of a razzing nature crossed with a tone of finality, the sound effect heard on the radio program suggested the contestant was in for it.

"Guest actors in *Truth or Consequences* put on better shows than professional actors," said Edwards in a press release. "Visitors are here to have fun, and not to give a performance. They play my game just as if they were playing it at home in the front parlor. They disregard the 'mike' and the audience and have a good time by concentrating on the consequences they had been asked to do. Of course, many of the amateurs are nervous, and so polished performances are rare. But, in this game, nervousness is just part of the fun!"

Edwards was known for having a superb memory, remembering whether someone had been on the program before. He once called up a group of "regulars" when he was selecting contestants and took them backstage to talk to them. "He said they made it difficult for him since they knew and anticipated all the jokes in the warm-up," recalled Fred Carney. "He said he didn't mind their coming to the broadcast but in a warm and friendly way he requested they sit in the back and not try to be contestants."

The only contestant who is "planted" was the man or woman who was to be surprised by the presence of a wife, a husband, a mother or some neighbor or relatives who were in on the stunt and got the contestant there by hook or by crook.

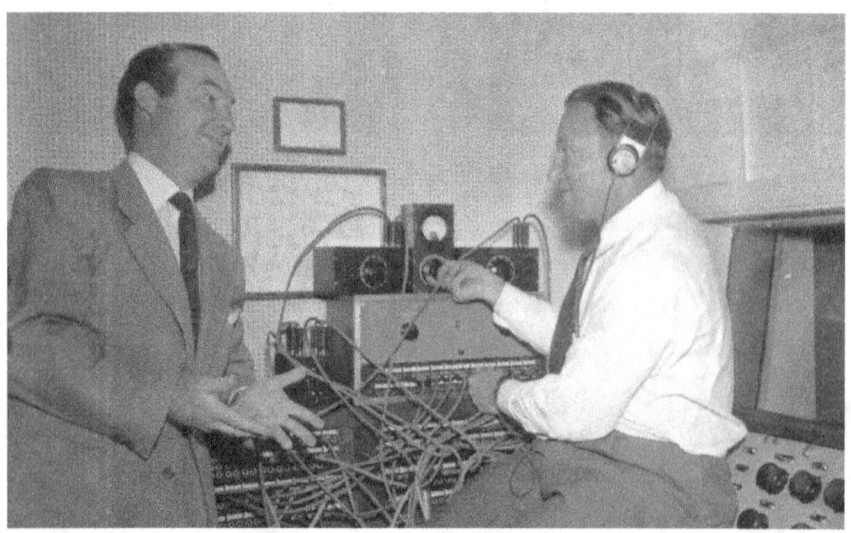

Ralph Edwards and engineer Johnny Pawlek.

Engineer Johnny Pawlek (reprinted from *Engineer's Journal*).

When stunts required the use of police escorts, a member of the force who was off duty was hired and paid by Edwards. If the man did not own a motorcycle, he rented one. Policemen were not only hired for the need of speed, but also if there might be any danger to curious bystanders.

Fred Carney, once had 20 donkeys on stage "to accompany" a contestant in "Donkey Serenade."

If the facts in a press release can be believed, when a pig was needed for an act on the show involving a greased pig, Edwards found the ham in Cleveland, at a local stockyard. "He poked at the porkers with a long stick," the press release stated. "The men in the stockyards gaped at the dude's familiarity with their rugged charges and gaped still more when he specified the kind of hay needed for bedding down the pig, and the kind of food that the animal actor would appreciate. And whether pigs, seals or Eskimos are needed, Ralph Edwards, the 27-year-old producer of what has become, in a short time, the top-flight act in radio and on the stage, knows what he wants."

Fred Carney replaced Jack Farnell, the man who was responsible for finding all sorts of props for the radio program. Farnell was responsible for finding an Eskimo mother and child, a Chinese laundryman and ironing board, talking dogs, a barking seal, a greased pig, a 1921 Chevrolet, feminine lingerie, an elephant and a bag of peanuts. Farnell later recalled that he had no trouble getting the elephant, but he spent considerable time finding a bag of peanuts.

Over time, Edwards convinced the sponsor to raise the weekly budget, allowing for expansion in the form of Government defense and larger prizes. With the U.S. entry into World War II, Edwards knew the program had to wave a patriotic flag of support by encouraging radio listeners to contribute to the cause. Contestants were promised $15 in "cash" (always in the form of a check) if they answered their question correctly, $5 if they paid the consequence. The audience voted on the best consequence act of the evening, shown by the applause meter, rewarding the lucky recipient a $25 Defense Bond. Each contestant, whether appearing on the program or not, receives five large cakes of Ivory Soap. The radio audience may not have had the luxury of winning the prize money, but they could count their blessings that Ivory Soap was available from their local retailer.

Contestant Vernon Keene had to take the sixth-grade exam and failed. His consequence was to be sent to the corner of Hollywood and Vine and sit on the stool, wearing a dunce cap and shout publicly "I am a Dunce." Ralph Edwards spoke with the 41-year-old contestant to inform him that he still received the Kit Camper Trailer even though he failed the exam.

The radio audience was also asked to send in both "questions" and "consequences." For each question used, the sender received $5. For each consequence used, $10. This audience participation was already a success with *Information, Please*, which premiered in 1938, ensuring the radio audience would tune in and participate – with the hopes of hearing their submissions used. Another clever ploy of increasing listenership.

On the evening of January 10, 1942, Ralph Edwards was unexpectedly thrown for a loss during the repeat (West Coast) broadcast. Confidently tossing an ultra-complicated question at a studio-audience contestant, Edwards received the correct answer after only a split-second pause. While the broadcaster and his production aides were doing comic salaams and expressed amazed admiration, the contestant, a resident of Chicago, opened his mouth too soon and volunteered the explanation that he heard the same question used on the repeat broadcast of the previous week's show and thus knew the answer. He then offered to take the "consequences," but Edwards settled the matter by giving him another question. The contestant missed that one. And going forward, Edwards and his crew never used the same question twice.

In late April, Edwards was momentarily outsmarted by a member of his studio audience again when he called for the audience member to compete in an announcers' contest, against Milton Cross, Ben Grauer, and David Ross. After the three spielers had read just a few lines each, for comedy, the chap from the studio audience was handed the script. He looked blank and faltered, "I can't read. I don't know how to read or write." Edwards and his aides were flabbergasted for a few moments, but then the stranger admitted he was only kidding.

"Commentary on the kind of people who attend the show is that they're usually disappointed if they correctly answer the question and thus don't have to do the required stunt," one columnist reported in *Variety* (September 16, 1942 issue). "The show is still a field day for exhibitionists, a glorified parlor game for people who enjoy making spectacles of themselves in public. It frankly has no appeal to the intellect, aiming at the same instinct that makes people laugh when someone slips on a banana peel."

After 26 weeks on the air, Procter & Gamble dropped *Junior Miss*, starring Shirley Temple, when the contract expired in August of 1942. The program started with a satisfactory rating, but steadily dropped as the weeks passed. There was trouble with the production, the director having been changed even before the final broadcast and the scripting setup having been revised weeks into the program. Despite the decline in the rating and production difficulties, however, a major factor in the cancellation, according to inter-office memos at Procter & Gamble, was said to be the inability of the company to maintain its output of Dreft soap, the product on the West Coast, and Ivory Soap, the product hocked on the East Coast. Executives at P&G decided that it was too costly to sponsor four programs, especially with the steady rise in popularity polls and ratings for *Truth or Consequences* and made a budgetary decision in the favor of the quiz program, a contributing factor to the decline of Shirley Temple's career in weekly radio. If there were any remaining doubt of radio's power to build a draw, Ralph Edwards would extinguish any doubts with the 1943 War Bond tour for *Truth or Consequences*. Little did he know at the time how large a contribution he would make for the war cause.

Ralph Edwards playing around.

Contestant prepares to get dunked in a tank of water.

A contestant was unaware that more than one seltzer bottle was involved in the stunt, believing it was a squirt-less bottle until he sprayed himself. Broadcast of November 8, 1947.

Chapter 3
The War Bond Tours

World War II had an immediate impact on *Truth or Consequences* as it did for hundreds of radio programs throughout the rest of the country. Public service announcements were one way of pitching the sale of War Bonds but Edwards went beyond the call of duty – and at his own personal expense – to assist the U.S. Government. Edwards and his troupe crisscrossed the country in an exhausting series of War Bond tours, with the purchase of War Bonds ensuring admission to the radio program, and larger purchases ensuring prime seating location. During the Second World War, Ralph Edwards and his crew racked up more than 100,000 miles and sold more than half a billion dollars in "E" bonds… an impressive feat that could not be rivaled by any other celebrity in Hollywood.

"Yeah, you could really get spoiled by all the attention the troops gave you, but occasionally something would snap you back to Earth," Edwards later recalled. "I remember finding a seat at a table beside a Colonel for a quick bite to eat before our stage show there in the Marine mess hall in Quantico, Virginia. The Colonel talked to me all through dinner, and when I was finished and headed for backstage, the Colonel said, 'Oh, aren't you sticking around for the show?' Ah, the anonymity of radio."

Before the historic War Bond tours, Edwards was inducing patriotism on the quiz program through a variety of "consequences." In recognition of the new 20th Century Fox movie, *My Gal Sal*, a barber shop quartette performed for Rita Hayworth, who was listening to their rendition of "My Gal Sal." The quartette consisted of one contestant in the studio, a Coast Guardsman in New York; Pfc. George Michael O'Keafe, a Marine in Washington, D.C.; Seaman First Class Verne Anderson, a sailor from the Great Lakes Naval Training Base in Chicago; and Private Ernest N. Joy, a soldier in Hollywood. The vocal quartet was broadcast by means of a four-way pickup between New York, Washington, Chicago and Hollywood and aired on the evening of May 9, 1942.

When the guardsman failed to name the "First Lady of the Nile," his answer was that he didn't know because the Coast Guard doesn't go out that far. As his consequence, four servicemen harmonized "My Gal Sal," the theme song from the current 20th Century Fox picture of that name. Because of the value of the network plug involved, the studio paid the line charges for the hookup, amounting to $1,417.

On the evening of June 6, 1942, the program provided a novel approach by originating from the front parlor of the home of Daniel A. Doyle, in West Townsend, Massachusetts, with Edwards and his staff of 14 people, surprise guests and a mess of props. Mrs. Doyle was a contestant on the program a week before. When she missed her question and she was from a small town, Edwards asked about her neighbors, the size of her front parlor, and eventually finagled an invitation from her to come up and meet the folks. Her neighbors and friends became contestants.

During the broadcast, radio listeners were provided a surprise stroke during a conversational passage with the mother of the household. Inquiry about the whereabouts of her son disclosed that he was an ensign on duty, supposedly at that moment, in Norfolk. Edwards told her that the reward for her cooperation in the broadcast was to be found behind the parlor draperies. She drew them back and there stood her son, the ensign. Edwards had arranged for the furlough sub-rosa with the Norfolk commandant. "Two things that can be counted on in Ralph Edwards' *Truth or Consequences* series are enterprise and emphasis on human interest values," reviewed *Variety*, following the broadcast.

 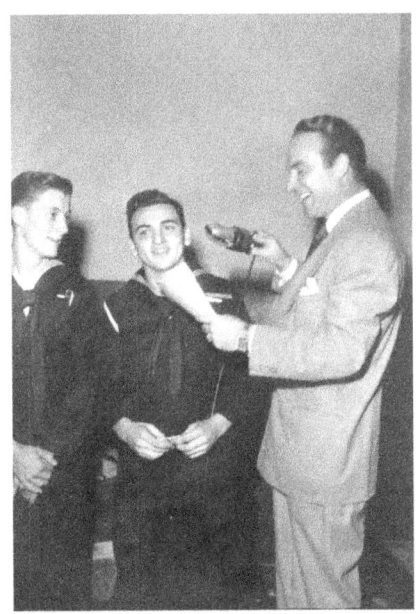

One week later, Harry Fox, who licensed mechanical rights for publishers, jabbed a temporary thorn in the side of Ralph Edwards, when he asked for fees of $50 to $100 for the use of parodied lyrics in connection with Government messages on *Truth or Consequences*. In answer to the protests of the Compton Agency, which handled the program for Procter & Gamble, Fox stated that the publishers involved would gladly waive collection of a fee if the program did not also contain copy plugging the sponsor's product. Government business aside, Fox contended that the parodies were strictly commercial and such use required a fee. There had been several previous instances of costly stunts on *Truth or Consequences*, and they were always paid for by Ralph Edwards, out of the package price for the program. Edwards had to write a check written out payable to Fox not from the package price, but out of his own pocket.

It wasn't until the broadcast of October 24, 1942, that Ralph Edwards discovered just how persuasive *Truth or Consequences* was regarding War Bonds. On the West Coast broadcast of that evening, Mrs. Jeanette Brenner, a female riveter in a war plant for the American Women's Volunteer Services, also billed as a housewife in New York City, missed her question and as her consequence had to deliver a 30-minute speech on the importance of purchasing War Bonds. Many people were put on the spot to do the same throughout the war years, but Mrs. Brenner, with two boys in service, broke down during her improvised speech and cried over the air.

The radio audience had been told that if they purchase at least $10,000 worth of bonds, she would be awarded the prize any mother, with a young man in service, would want. The response from listeners from the 22 radio stations (the repeat broadcast rode west of Denver), totaled more than the producers expected. Her winnings for the job amounted to $107,460 worth of War Bonds and a phone call to Hawaii to a son in service and a trip to Camp Shelby, Mississippi, to visit another in training, in addition to a complete outfit to wear. By December 16, it was reported that a total of $407,000 in sales had been made as a result of her plea. She was also sent to Fort Logan, Colorado, to see her soldier son – possibly relocated to a new camp since the initial radio broadcast.

Two types of admission tickets to attend *Truth or Consequences* as a result of the purchase of a war bond.

On the evening of November 28, 1942, *Truth or Consequences* originated from CBC's Playhouse in Toronto, Ontario, in a good-neighbor stunt in support of our allies. A columnist for *Variety* listened in to the broadcast and noted that Canadians "react in almost the same manner as do Americans to the hair-brained stunts, the hokum and all the other things which go to make up this unusual half-hour paced by Ralph Edwards over NBC. The Canadians also appeared just as good sports and just as ready to take the 'consequences' as do the people on this side of the border."

When government copper was scarce, Edwards dreamed up a consequence for a housewife who had a son in the Marines. The broadcast of January 23, 1943 featured Mrs. Dennis J. Mullane, a Staten Island mother of 17-year-old Harold Mullane, serving in the U.S. Marines, who failed to answer her question. As a consequence, she agreed to help the government's drive to put copper pennies into circulation. Listeners were asked to send in their pennies to Mrs. Mullane, to exchange for War Bonds for her son so he would have some financial security to come home to after the war. The result – more than 300,000 pennies, or $3,000 in cold copper cash.

The following week, Mrs. Mullane returned to the program to thank the listeners for their overwhelming contributions in pennies. Her son, Pvt. Harold Mullane, was also brought to the program, rushed over from the Marine's Camp Lejeune at New River, North Carolina, to join his mother on the program. To prove they actually did receive the pennies, which broke all expectations, under special guard, attendants brought in casks of pennies and coins and poured them into containers in front of the microphone. Radio listeners actually heard the sound of 300,157 pennies being dropped. Private Mullane then said he would like to turn over every fiftieth penny to buy sports equipment for the Marines on Parris Island. With the rest he was going to buy War Bonds and after the war complete his education.

Additional pennies were sent through the mail as a result of the second broadcast and the official count was 204,000 letters and a fiscal total of $3,361.42 in cash.* The Government wanted the copper and Edwards arranged for the pennies to be shipped to the mint. Even the postage stamps were removed from the postcards and envelopes, so the dye could be recovered. This cost Edwards

* The February 3, 1943, issue of *Variety* reported the total was approximately $3,560 in pennies, silver and folding money. Up to February 2, they received 236,000 pieces of mail. NBC made a survey of postmarks on the letters received, to breakdown the response into individual station areas.

$1,507 out of his pocket carry out the "practical joke." He underwrote the cost of some 197 temporary clerks to open the letters, rent for office space to do the work, approximately $50 for letters which arrived with insufficient postage, and the expenses of bringing the soldier involved to New York from North Carolina for the January 30, 1943 broadcast, entertaining him and his family while they were in the Big Apple. Numerous newspapers gave the story attention, along with wire services and newsreels.

When the recent stunts resulted in an avalanche of outpouring and support, Edwards agreed to take the show on the road – in the interest of the U.S. Treasury, the War Manpower Commission, and provide entertainment in service camps across the nation. The quiz show could easily be adapted for vaudeville, which made it possible to use the vaudeville medium to pay the expense of his staff

A contestant named Mrs. Siering was asked to spend 30 seconds telling the American people why they would like to buy War Bonds. After her spontaneous plea, she took her position in the Comet Ship at the end of the giant rainbow to head toward the treasure at the other end. The goal was to reach the treasure in 20 to 25 minutes. If she raised $50,000, she would receive an all-expenses paid trip to see her son who was stationed at an undisclosed camp. (Among the pledges that came in was $5,000 from comedian Danny Kaye, who was listening to the broadcast that evening!)

throughout the tour. With Procter & Gamble assuming the line charges, including the expenses of engineer, announcer and agency man, a plan was put into place. The U.S. Government asked Edwards to reach a goal of $20,000,000 in the sale of War Bonds in the three months of engagements in fourteen key cities.

With cooperation from local communities, sales of War Bonds for the *Truth or Consequences* appearance was put in the hands of local groups such as a savings and loan, or the advertising clubs. The cities' eyes were opened to the power of radio with the rapidity of sales for the show. In many instances the theaters were sold out two or three days after the sale had been announced. In Topeka, Kansas, a city of 73,000, over 9,000 people made immediate response to the bond sales announcement, and they came early Saturday afternoon, with lunch baskets, and sat on the grass outside the auditorium waiting for the doors to open. "Business at the dinner hour performance opening day was turn away, almost unheard of at that time of day. Attendance has remained spectacular since then," reported *Variety*. In Denver, 1,500 extra seats had been promised for bond purchases before the local committee noticed the over-sale, so quickly did the show sell out. To avoid ill will, a Friday night version of *Truth or Consequences* helped ring up another $1,000,000. After five weeks, the total sale of War Bonds exceeded the $20,000,000 goal.

On Wednesday, prior to the broadcast from Taft Auditorium in Cincinnati, Ohio (April 3, 1943), Edwards had breakfast at the Netherland Plaza with a group of officials who were in competition with the radio program. Hilary H. Evers, chairman of the Hamilton County Savings and Loan War Bond Committee, explained to Edwards that his organization, responsible for the sale of the War Bonds and arranging for tickets to the show, sold more than $6,000,000 in War Bonds by the time Edwards arrived in Cincinnati, with only 600 seats left. Tickets to the radio program could be obtained only through the purchase of War Bonds. Advanced publicity announced a live pig (not greased) and soldiers from Ft. Thomas as part of the evening's entertainment. Local listeners were not able to listen to the East Coast broadcast but were able to hear a transcription on Sunday night.

During the breakfast at the Netherland Plaza, Edwards failed – by a dime – to guess how many bonds his show already sold. The consequence was that he had to eat the flowers that decorated the table, for vegetables were becoming high-priced. He pitched into the red carnations and golden jonquils with gusto after duly salting them.

Weeks following, the citizens of Portland, Oregon, pulled off a monumental feat that would never be accomplished again during any of Ralph Edwards' fundraisers: the sale of $109,000,000 worth of bonds.

First Tour (Spring 1943)

March 13 – Providence, Rhode Island	$504,000.00
March 20 – Buffalo, New York	$811,725.00
March 27 – Toledo, Ohio	$1,025,455.00
April 3 – Cincinnati, Ohio	$7,498,475.00
April 10 – Indianapolis, Indiana	$10,619,425.00
April 17 – Topeka, Kansas	$3,408,864.04
April 24 – Denver, Colorado	$6,118,129.25
May 1 – Spokane, Washington	$7,518,830.00
May 8 – Seattle, Washington	$32,112,625.00
May 15 – Portland, Oregon	$109,925,319.50
May 22 – Salt Lake City, Utah	$1,579,650.00
May 29 – San Francisco, California	$4,101,000.00
June 5 – Glendale, California	$2,058,088.00
June 12 – Oakland, California	<u>$1,210,000.00</u>
Total	$188,481,082.79

Regarding May 15: 8,000 people attended, 7,800 bought $107,515,000.

After a total of 107 performances, Edwards and his staff succeeded in raising more than nine times the amount requested by the Treasury. To add to this accomplishment, during the War Bond tour, Edwards also inaugurated local manpower recruiting shows in various defense industry cities, besides making numerous camp show appearances. The manpower programs, called "Know Your Neighbor," were started in Indianapolis, Wichita, and Denver. In each case, Edwards went on a local radio station and broadcast the conversation as he phoned women picked at random from the phone book, asking them about taking jobs to relieve men for Army service or heavy industry. In each city, a local broadcaster took over the series after Edwards moved on to the next city. Reportedly, Edwards did both the manpower and camp show stints at his own expense.

In the fall of 1943, while Ralph Edwards was setting up a second War Bond tour for early 1944, he spent a couple weeks negotiating for the vaudeville stage in

New York City, where the weekly radio broadcasts originated. By late September, the Capitol booked the *Truth or Consequences* radio show, which Roxy passed up when $7,500 weekly was asked. The Roxy paid $4,000 weekly for *Truth or Consequences* the year prior, but Edwards had sales figures from the recent War Bond tour to verify the popularity of the radio program, justifying the additional expense. Edwards also wanted the extra funds to afford the second tour, planned for launch in January. The Capitol had no regrets with their investment. During the first week at the Capitol, a screening of Columbia's *Sahara*, along with stage entertainment by Lawrence Welk and Ralph Edwards, grossed the theater $78,000 in receipts; more than $90,000 for the second week and $55,000 during the third and final week.

> From the October 20, 1943 issue of *Variety*
>
> The slated guest shot of the *Can You Top This?* trio on *Truth or Consequences* was nixed at the last moment by Palmolive-Peet, the sponsor. Palmolive did not want to create competition for its *Inner Sanctum* show that aired on CBS, the same time as *Truth or Consequences*.

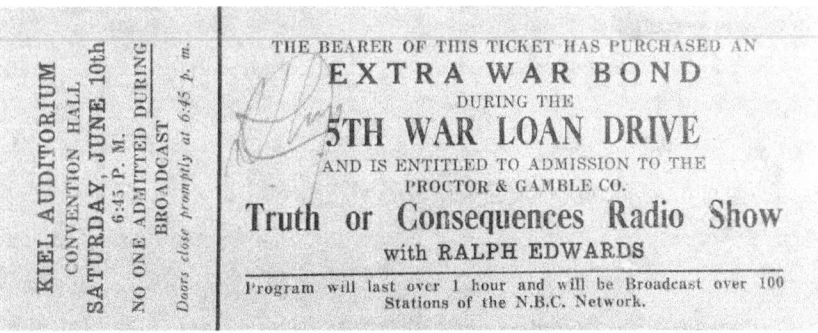

For the purchase of a War Bond, a radio listener would receive an admission ticket like this one.

The Paper Drive

During World War II, Americans were called upon repeatedly to salvage raw materials for the war effort, often during brief, highly publicized "drives." Stories about the salvage drives are a staple in both popular and scholarly histories of the home front, and in film documentaries, because the drives appear to demonstrate the potential importance of non-economic motives such as patriotism and community spirit. To aid in the government's paper drive, on the evening of November 6, 1943, Ralph Edwards offered to put on a show in whatever school of the nation would collect the most paper; the results provided almost a fifth of the total goal of the entire drive.

The contest started November 8 and closed November 15. It was not until the broadcast of November 27 that the results were tallied and the winner was proclaimed. A total of 4,420 high and grade schools, representing every state in the U.S., sent in entries. The contest was conducted on a per pupil basis. Regardless of size or location, the winning school would be visited by *Truth or Consequences*. The total amount of paper collected by all school students who entered the contest was 42,761,829 pounds. Mr. Norman Greenway, member of the Executive Committee of the Paper Consuming Industries of America, and one of the contest judges, announced the winner. The Moore School, District 81, Linn Co., Missouri, a rural school with only 12 students, collected a total of 274,000 pounds of paper, an average of over 22,000 pounds per pupil. The winning school of each state received a special Scroll Award from the War Production Board. Edwards was assisted in this drive by the Office of War Information and the War Production Board. As for the winners, the quiz program originated in Moore School in Missouri, on the evening of December 11, and the students were the contestants.

Having originated a radio broadcast from a high school auditorium, and the living room parlor of a Massachusetts home, broadcasting from a one-room schoolhouse initially seemed less complicated. When Edwards and his crew boarded a train to Brookfield, they encountered a complication. Early one morning the train porter assumed that they had arrived at Brookfield and heaved the props trucks off the train. Just as Edwards and his troupe were about to follow their precious trunks, the train started again and as Edwards watched his irreplaceable props settle into the Missouri mud, the train gained speed and the porter explained that he was new on that run and "that must not have been Brookfield after all." The crew had to drive back 32 miles to retrieve the trunks.

The little white schoolhouse was located in a rural section of Missouri, near Brookfield, in Linn County. Sitting in a field of snow, with the bright Missouri moon shining down, the one-room schoolhouse had a big stove right in the middle of the room. There were only 12 pupils in Moore School, and Mrs. Zoe Harwood, the teacher, gave a roll call of her 12 pupils. The children responsible for the collection of 274,000 pounds of waste paper told the radio audience that paper came by hay wagon and Model T. As contestants for the evening, the students performed for an audience of 50 people – fathers and mothers and people who helped with the waste paper drive such as George Breen, the salvage director, and John Ed Fuhrman, county Superintendent of Schools.

The fan mail for *Truth or Consequences* grew over the years, so did the contributions for the purchase of war bonds.

The Second and Third War Bond Tour

Phoenix, Arizona, was the kickoff for the second War Bond tour; five weeks and five major cities that provided a modest total of $5,474,990, compared to prior achievements. In the fall of 1943, Ralph Edwards performed for an audience totaling 9,600 in Springfield, Illinois, grossing $4,250,975 in the sale of War Bonds in five days. Four-fifths of what he raised in five weeks.

In the same manner as the previous War Bond tour, the NBC program aired from theaters where the admission would be the cash purchase of E series bonds. Edwards was paying all expenses of the tour, using the proceeds he made for his daily performances at the Capitol in New York, with the sponsor paying the line charge. Accompanying him were Carl Jampel, public relations; Herb Moss, director; Ted Bell, representing the Compton Agency; Al Paschall, stage manager; Lamont Johnson, announcer; and Lily Engle, secretary to Edwards.

The biggest sale was in Memphis, Tennessee, raising more than half the funds of the entire five-week tour. But the stage performances almost never happened. Local newspapers let the Musicians' union have it with both barrels after reporting alleged attempts to halt the *Truth or Consequences* radio broadcast for War Bonds on the evening of January 29, from the stage at Ellis Auditorium. The Memphis and Shelby County War Finance Committee asserted that R.L. (Spike) Lesem, business agent for the Memphis Federation of Musicians, ordered them to halt the program, which was originated from WMC, a station belonging to the Memphis Commercial Appeal and currently on the union's "unfair list" because it had been recording hillbilly music for re-broadcast. The Press-Scimitar reported that Lesem, unable to convince the War Finance Committee, then told Col. C. A. McElravy, the Auditorium's managing director, that the *Truth or Consequences* program could not go on from his stage, implying that stagehands and other union men would be jerked.

The broadcast went on as planned, without interference, and sold almost $3,000,000 worth of War Bonds to Memphis residents as admission to the radio show. This was not the first occurrence against Edwards during his patriotic tour across the nation. Months prior in the first War Bond tour, Edwards and his crew ran into an age old feud between newspapers and radio. Apparently not even the urgency of war had eased the strain in some cases. Newspapers felt threatened by radio, which provided up-to-the-minute news at an advantage to the competition. Newspapers, in turn, hesitated printing articles publicizing any radio broadcasts without advertising revenue. The newspapers in the majority of the cities cooperated with the advance notices of Edwards' appearances for the War Bond tour, but in Toledo there was almost complete disregard of a radio program's appearance. Even though radio had the power to serve Uncle Sam, there was occasional opposition from the locals.

Second Tour (Fall 1943)

Springfield, Illinois (9,600 people)	$4,250,975.00
(Contributions from Industry)	<u>$23,734,750.00</u>
Total	$27,984,825.00

Third Tour (January and February 1944)

January 15 – Phoenix, Arizona	$915,475.00
January 22 – Dallas, Texas (8,600 people)	$1,828,500.00

January 29 – Memphis, Tennessee (12,800 people)	$2,891,225.00
February 5 – Atlanta, Georgia	$1,163,575.00
February 12 – Richmond, Virginia (15,000 people)	$576,215.00
Total	$5,474,990.00

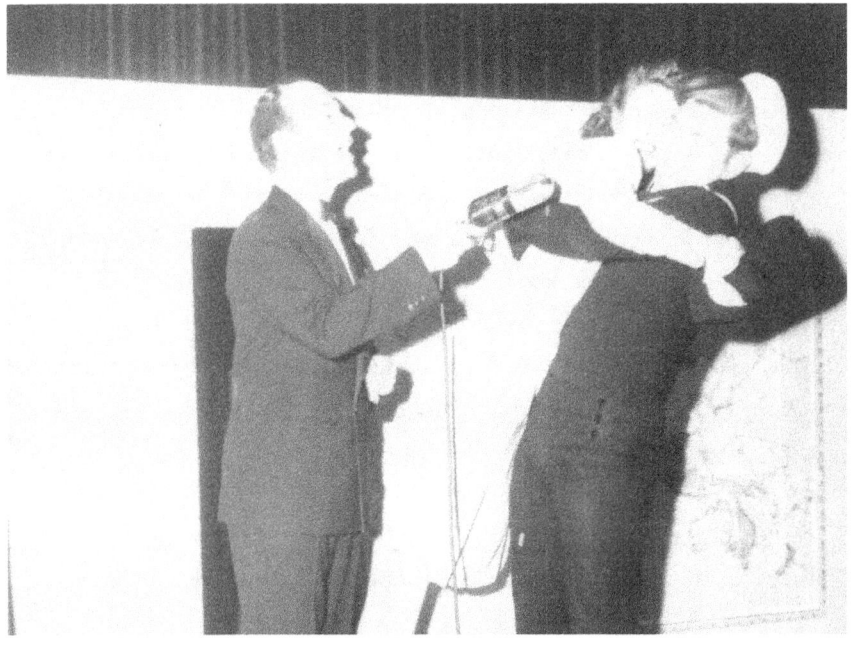

On a number of radio broadcasts a female contestant would speak her to soldier boy by phone in a booth, unaware that the loved one on the phone is standing just offstage.

The Draft

The War Bond tour was originally slated for five weeks, even though a few historians theorized in the past that Ralph Edwards was forced to cut his tour short when he received official notice that he was being called in to active duty. Before the end of the month, radio announcer Harry Von Zell auditioned for director Herb Moss, who did not feel Von Zell had what it took to "deliver the goods" in place of Edwards, who passed his physical. As imminent induction of Edwards intensified, the search for a successor continued with one rejection after another from Moss. By the end of the month, Edwards informed Moss that the numerous auditions were unnecessary, and it was Edwards who personally appointed Von Zell as the new emcee. According to Army notifications, Edwards was to be inducted in early May. With time against him, Edwards wanted to break in Von Zell, introducing him to the radio audience with the broadcast of April 8. The terms of the contract called for Von Zell to perform the task for five months of the year, allowing him to continue with his other contracted assignments.

Meanwhile, backstage in the office of the Draft Board, discussions from influential officials were attempting to void Edwards from military service, based on his performance regarding the sale of War Bonds, which was considered a vital component to winning the war. Edwards was more valuable to the U.S. Government encouraging the sale of War Bonds than fighting in the trenches. Edwards was over the age of 26 and an effort to have him "permanently deferred" by the military was under consideration. Pending clarification from the Army, Edwards went about the necessary planning stages of breaking in Von Zell for the spotlight. Numerous letters and telegrams were exchanged regarding the status of Edwards' induction, keeping all concerned in the dark for weeks until the middle of May, when confirmation was finally approved. The uncertainty on the part of the Army as to whether they wanted Ralph Edwards ultimately cost the *Truth or Consequences* host $14,000. That's the figure for which he settled with Harry Von Zell when the latter was released from contract under which he was to have succeeded Edwards on the show. The arrangement was entirely amicable and Von Zell was kept under option for the spot should selective service procedure shift again and call Edwards into service.

"When Ralph Edwards had to register for the Draft, the staff tried to make it a bit more 'pleasant' for him," recalled staff member Lillie Buchstane. "We all rented different military outfits and came to his apartment on Park Avenue at 3:00 a.m. Barbara had arranged with the doorman to allow us to enter the building at that hour. She left the door unlocked so that we could sneak into your living room. We sat in the darkened room without a word being spoken. Ralph finally came to the dining room and saw these familiar shadows and almost fainted! We all came back to my apartment for a send-off breakfast. When we suggested that we would accompany him to the Draft Board, he was horrified and nixed that pronto!"

After straightening out the draft issue, Edwards made preparation for another War Bond tour, raising almost $20,000,000 in five weeks.

Fourth Tour (June to July 1944)

Philadelphia, Pennsylvania	$2,504,475.00
St. Louis, Missouri	$5,700,130.00
Cleveland, Ohio	$2,058,312.00

Boston, Massachusetts	$1,829,375.00
Raleigh, North Carolina	$2,085,000.00
One Night Stands*	$5,164,465.00
Total	$19,341,757.00

*One Night Stands included Charleston, Illinois; Columbus, Ohio; Charlotte, North Carolina, Washington, D.C. and Baltimore, Maryland.

In March, Edwards and his crew moved to California and took up origination at NBC in Hollywood starting with the broadcast of March 17. They were originally to remain on the West Coast as long as Edwards was needed for the RKO picture, *Radio Stars on Parade*. By June of 1945, Edwards signed a contract with RKO to appear in two movies per calendar year. Beginning the day Edwards signed the contract with the movie studio, it was official: *Truth or Consequences* would officially originate from the West Coast. Saying good-bye to New York City, the Edwards family purchased a home and settled in "The Golden State."

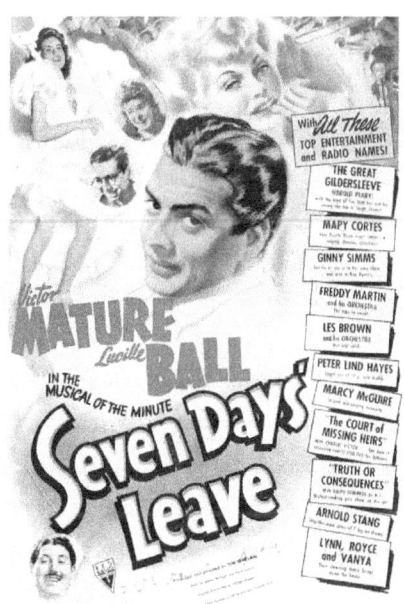

Ralph Edwards played supporting roles in half a dozen motion-pictures, including *Seven Days to Leave* (1942), *The Bamboo Blonde* (1946) and *Beat the Band* (1947). Edwards worked with singer/actress Frances Langford in three movies. To promote *Radio Stars on Parade*, Langford was a guest on the March 31, 1945 broadcast of *Truth or Consequences*.

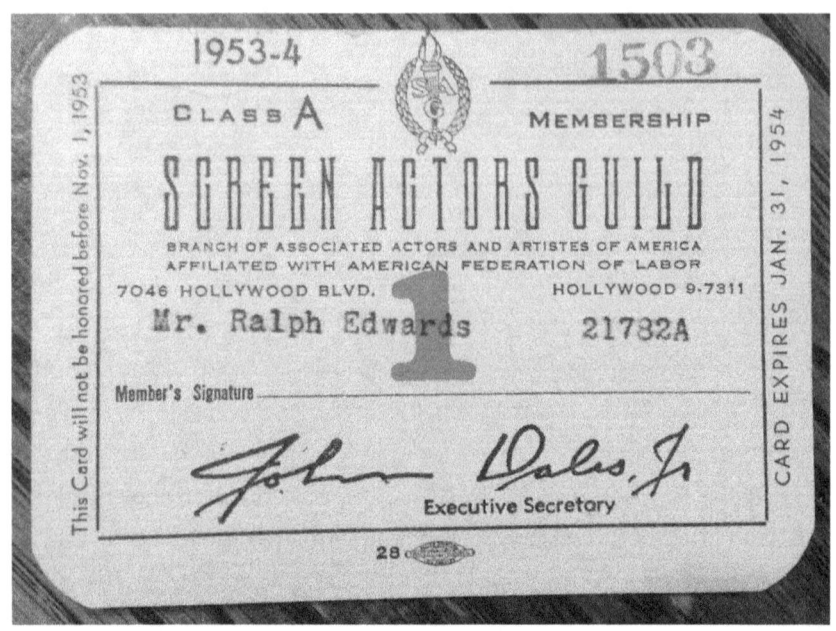

Ralph Edwards' Screen Actors Guild Card necessary to appear in front of the cameras when filming movies such as *Radio Stars on Parade*.

The move to California required a number of staff changes. Herb Moss, the director for the past few years, needed to return to New York to complete his assignments, making room for new director. Murray Bolen, West Coast radio head of the Compton Agency, took over production, relieving Floyd Holm, who returned to New York.

On January 17, 1945, a salute to the Entertainment Corps of War-Time America was held at the Bellevue-Stratford Hotel in Philadelphia, Pennsylvania, known as the 40th Annual Dinner of the Poor Richard Club. Following the dinner, Bob Hope received a gold medal for his dedication to entertaining servicemen overseas. Frances Langford, Vera Vague, Jerry Colonna, and Tony Romano, regulars on Hope's radio program, received citation awards. With Ed Wynn as master of ceremonies, Ralph Edwards was introduced on stage, followed by his receiving of a citation award. "Over $400,000,000 worth of Series 'E' U.S. War Bonds have been sold by Mr. Edwards and his *Truth or Consequences* radio program – through 45 War Bond meetings, 90 special bond broadcasts, and 169 bond shows, from Nome, Alaska, to the Panama Canal," it was explained by Ed Wynn. "For this extraordinary service, Poor Richard is pleased to award Mr. Edwards a special Citation of Merit." The ceremonies were broadcast over network radio.

Participating in the Fifth War Loan Drive, Edwards went back on the road in late 1944 to raise another $5 million. In 1945, he went on his sixth and final War Bond tour, selling "E" Bonds. Combined with Bond pulls on various radio broadcasts, the total of all sales accredited to Ralph Edwards amounted to over $500,000,000. Reviewing a cross-section of the fan mail received, Edwards and his staff were able to determine the general attitude of the public towards the program. What they learned was the program became a welcome relief to the unhappy news of world affairs. Combined with the total sum of Edwards' pooling power, it is no wonder that *Truth or Consequences* was the first and only radio program to receive the Eisenhower Award.

Fifth Tour (November and December 1944)

November 15 – Albany, New York	$500,075.00
November 20 – Pittsburgh, Pennsylvania	$290,000.00
November 22 – Youngstown, Ohio	$277,000.00
November 29 – Philadelphia, Pennsylvania	$1,280,000.00
December 2 – Chicago, Illinois	$50,000.00
New Haven, Connecticut	$700,325.00
Hartford, Connecticut	$800,600.00
Elizabeth-Newark, New Jersey	$1,200,000.00
Ridgefield, Conn.-Pound Ridge, N.Y.	$75,000.00
Total	$5,173,000.00

The Sixth Tour (October to December 1945)

October 29	Wichita, Kansas
October 30	Kansas City, Kansas
October 31	Tulsa, Oklahoma
November 3	Omaha, Nebraska
November 5	Denver, Colorado
November 6	Salt Lake City, Utah
November 7	Reno, Nevada
November 10	Hollywood, California
November 17	Hollywood, California
November 19	Milwaukee, Wisconsin
November 20	Detroit, Michigan
November 21	Indianapolis, Indiana

November 24   Chicago, Illinois
November 26   Oklahoma City, Oklahoma
November 27   Dallas, Texas
December 1   Hollywood, California
December 3   Spokane, Washington
December 4   Seattle, Washington
December 5   Portland, Oregon

Lucille Ball participated in a *Truth or Consequences* stunt on the May 9, 1945 radio broadcast of *Mail Call*.

Other Bond Pulls
MARY
(*Truth or Consequences* appeal) $5,117,962.00

MRS. SIERING
(*Truth or Consequences* appeal) $501,000.00

MRS. STEWART
(*Truth or Consequences* appeal) $1,300,000.00

COS COB
(Personal appearance) $119,000.00

PENNIES
(*Truth or Consequences* stunt to return
pennies to U.S. mint for defense.) $3,300.00

JASPER
(Personal appearance, Alabama) $158,000.00

THEATRES
(Strand & Waterbury –
Personal appearance, Connecticut) $209,000.00

POLO GROUNDS
(Personal appeal) $800,000.00

McCREERY'S
(Advertised personal appearance) $1,500,000

Total $9,708,262.00

Chapter 4
The Mr. Wickel Gag

The earliest stunt to cost Ralph Edwards' expenditures beyond initial projection began in November 1944, costing about $3,000, but Edwards told the press he figured it was well worth it from the publicity angle. Gag involved "burying" $1,000 in silver dollars in an empty lot in Holyoke, Mass., the grand supposed to have gone to one Rudolph J. Wickel, of Vernon, NJ, a contestant on the Nov. 4 program. Little did he know that the stunt would backfire when radio listeners rushed out to dig up buried loot, meant for the radio contestant, after learning of the location over the radio.

Edwards had a running gag for some time asking each studio audience if Mr. Wickel was in the house. He picked the name out of a hat. For weeks, radio listeners were writing in to ask clarification of the question that was asked every week on the program, for which no explanation was provided. Mr. Wickel's wife, Lillian, encouraged her husband to telephone NBC to find out what it was about. After all, they shared the same name. The only thing an NBC staff member could explain was that it was some sort of gag. Curiosity getting the better of him, he applied for tickets for the family to attend the program on the evening of November 4, 1944, which was all that was necessary, as it turned out, to claim the $1,000. While on stage in New York, Edwards asked, "If there is a Mr. Wickel in the house, let him come on stage." There was, and Mr. Wickel honored the request. Edwards explained "Old Peckinaw Wickel" had willed 1,000 silver dollars to Rudolph Wickel.

Mr. Wickel was told that the money was waiting for him at the corner of Prospect and Walnut Streets, where the prize was deposited by the conductors of the program. Moments before Wickel boarded the train that evening, and long before he reached Massachusetts, Holyoke residents turned out by the hundreds, (1,500 residents according to the *Los Angeles Times*) many of them in pajamas and nightgowns, armed with everything from spoons, trowels, shovels, frying pans, and a bulldozer to dig for the grand. It was an angle Edwards had not counted on, even though care had been exercised in stashing the scratch deep under a bench. When the contestant arrived in Holyoke, the city's mayor was waiting with bad news. People had heard the story over the radio and had been out digging.

Al Simon, known as the idea man for the quiz show.

Among the first on the scene was native son, Joseph E. Roy, 23, a carpenter and his 11-year-old brother-in-law, Henry Martell. They struck pay dirt with shovels and found the money in silver dollars; under law, buried treasure belongs to the finders. Wickel received $1,000 consolation money on the broadcast of November 11. Holyoke authorities had given their okay to the stunt in advance and on Monday, November 6, it was announced that the corner lot was to be made into a park named after Wickel. Edwards then did a non-broadcast show in the town on November 13 to raise proceeds to pay the cost of converting the lot into a park.

The consolation prize, however, had another catch. Only one bank would cash the check. It was up to Mr. Wickel to find the right one. The contestant was also provided a list of 14,000 banks in the United States. When he finally found the correct bank, he discovered his $1,000 was in Confederate money. The next week, Mr. Wickel was given a safe containing half of a $1,000 bill. Edwards promised to mail the missing half to Wickel between pages 12 and 13 of a book. Without the contestant's knowledge, radio listeners were invited to send books over to Camp Shanks, New York, to give Mr. Wickel a challenge. The more books that arrived, the bigger the challenge. And Edwards promised to have the other half of the $1,000 bill in a book, also mailed to Camp Shanks. Mr. Wickel soon discovered the gag as he opened books at page 13 for an entire week, eventually finding the missing half in a copy in *Blood, Sweat and Tears*.

Comedian Jerry Colonna prepares for a stunt with donkey.

Following the conclusion of the contest, librarians volunteered their time peeking between pages 12 and 13 of each book, aware that Mr. Wickel had already retrieved the other half of the prize. They discovered radio listeners placed one dollar bills, Chinese money, assorted coins, a rubber dollar, Christmas cards, an empty envelope with the notation "Ha-ha; not here," girls' names and telephone numbers, and several rather suspect offers from volunteers who wanted to help Mr. Wickel open the books and search for the prize. The gag ultimately provided more than 17,000 books which were shipped overseas for fighting men. Everyone was happy. Wickel got his $1,000, servicemen received books for reading, and there was a planned park in the memory of the Wickel stunt in Holyoke, Mass. Many of the radio listeners, however, were not happy listening in on the stunt.

"Your 'carry on' of the Mr. Wickel and the $1,000 episode is getting tiresome to listeners and no doubt is to Mr. Wickel. It was a rotten trick (although it may have been funny to you) to have people all over the country send books to the man's house. I'd refuse to accept these when they came whether they were for servicemen or not. You're just making a clown out of the man and if it was me I'd tell you to take your other half of the $1,000 bill and go to hell. It was a grand boner on your part in the first place telling everybody in Holyoke where the original $1,000 was hid. Your program ceased to be funny to a lot of people since Saturday night."
—John J. Jack, Sharon Hill, Pennsylvania

"The program of *Truth or Consequences* of Saturday, December 2, 1944, has clearly demonstrated to me the unfunny, and, I might add, the extreme childishness, to which a once fine program has descended."
—Emrys D. Nuneville, Drexel Hill, Pennsylvania

"Will the other half of the $1,000 bill be found between the 12th and 13th pages of the Bible when it is found?"

—F.J.F., Huntington, New York

Closing chapter in the saga: In September 1947, a "Wickel Park" had not yet been established and Henry J. Toepfert, Mayor of the city of Holyoke, Massachusetts, discussed with producer Al Paschall the real estate situation in making such a park possible. As a result, the money from the Wickel Fund was turned over for playground equipment for the new Memorial Village. The Memorial Village consisted of sixty-two beautiful four and five-room homes, built exclusively for Veterans and their families. With Rudy Wickel's approval, the funds were donated for the playground equipment, thus consummating the act.

In October of 1945, Ralph Edwards was warming up the audience preparatory to going on the air with his quiz show the other night. Suddenly, he remembered he was to meet writer Sidney Singer before the broadcast. Hastily, Edwards instructed his secretary, Lorayne Pyle, to scout the studio and hallway, to bring Mr. Singer to the control booth. Unacquainted with the object of her search, Lorayne accosted a lone gentleman pacing in the corridor, asked if he were Singer. She was rewarded with a look of blank wonderment and she repeated, "Are you Mr. Sidney Singer?"

"No, young lady," smiled the gentleman. "I'm not the Singer you want. I'm just a singer. My name is Thomas – John Charles."

Laughs aside, Ralph Edwards and his crew were not content merely to entertain. The wartime fundraising success had proved to him the medium's ability to generate money for many worthy causes. Three young boys in particular involved baseball and the foundation of a charity that continues today.

Notice the empty chair in the front row reserved for Mr. Wickel for every radio broadcast following the conclusion of the stunt.

Radio actress Joan Alexander and actor Jim Backus performs his "Hubert Updike" in a radio sketch required for a stunt.

The Mr. Wickel Gag

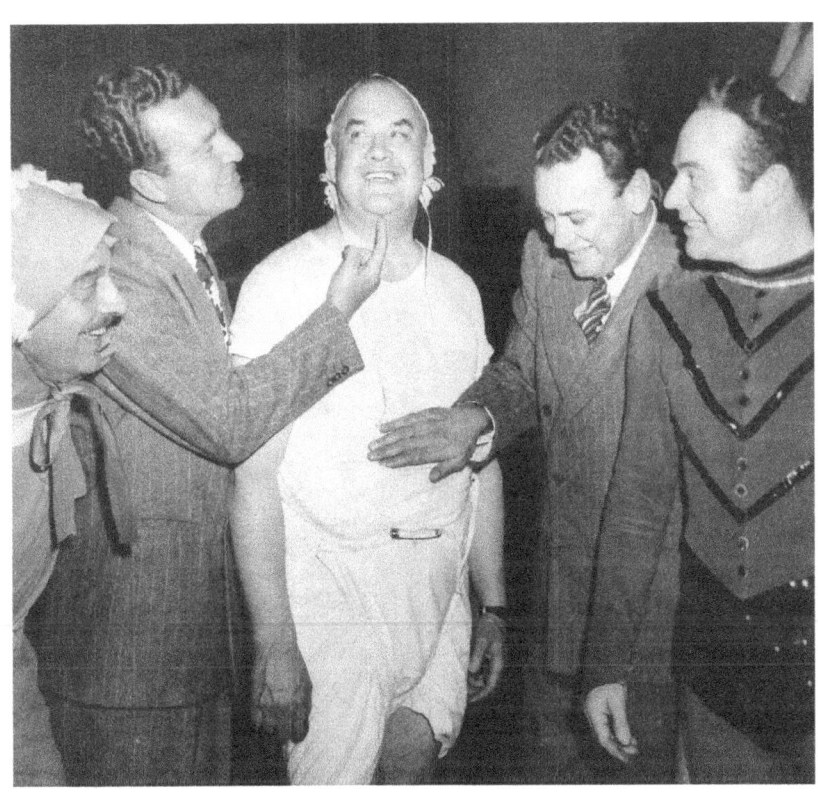

(Left to Right) Hanley Stafford, Phil Harris, Don Wilson, and Ralph Edwards during the Sixth Anniversary party for *Truth or Consequences*.

Chapter 5
Babe Ruth and Children Charities

On the evening of January 20, 1945, the first March of Dimes act for polio concerned a little boy, Bobby Riggio, a ten-year-old infantile paralysis victim, of 561 Seventeenth Street, Brooklyn. Edwards told Bobby, who lived in Washington, D.C., that the program would give him a $1,000 War Bond for his education if the listeners would send $10,000 in dimes. To pluck the heart-strings of radio listeners, Bobby sang a song on the program, his personal rendition of "Over the Rainbow." Bobby's song had such an impact that the NBC switchboard was immediately swamped by people willing to donate and in the days that followed, thousands of dimes poured in to the network. So many in fact that NBC sent the bags of dimes over to the producers of the radio program after the banks closed for the day. Afraid to leave the money unattended, a staff member, Carl Frederick, slept on the bags all night until the bank opened the next day.

A week following the broadcast, on the evening of January 27, the program briefly switched to Washington, D.C., so announcer Don Fisher could present the youth with the $1,000 War Bond and an autographed football. Earlier that afternoon, young Bobby accompanied a representative in a visit to the White House on crutches to present to Mrs. Roosevelt $50,000 representing a week's donations. By the time of the broadcast, a total of $79,642 worth of dimes had been accounted for, with more still unaccounted. By the time the contributions concluded, $137,000 worth of dimes had been counted.

Babe Ruth and Buster Roos

On the evening of April 13, 1946, *Truth or Consequences* attempted to provide short-lived joy to a young victim of cancer. Switching to Parkertown, New Jersey, via two-way set-up, a small town of about 500 inhabitants and home to "Buster" Leonard Roos, Ralph Edwards spoke with an eight-year-old boy who at Christmas time was given only three weeks to live and proving the doctors wrong; even with his right leg amputated at the hip and his only lung infected with cancer. The child suffered from club-shaped fingers and toes; a swollen stomach and ankles. Buster, who rarely smiled since he was stricken in December of 1944, was assisted by an NBC engineer who also set up the equipment and microphone by Busters' bedside, so that the child did not have to exert himself needlessly. During the broadcast, Buster told Ralph Edwards about some of the things he would like to have: movies of Mickey Mouse because he could not go to the neighborhood theaters; he wanted to hear Frank Sinatra sing; an entire freezer of ice cream; hear "Uncle Don"; see a big baseball game and meet Babe Ruth in person; a collie dog and a pony and a cart; and he wanted to see Roy Rogers and his horse, Trigger.

After the interview, Ralph Edwards asked Buster to turn off the speaker to his radio for a minute because the next part was a secret. Assured by the engineer that Buster could not hear the next portion of the program, Edwards told listeners the truth about Buster's condition and then made an appeal for help so that other children may not suffer the way little Buster has. Back in the Roos home, the speaker was turned up again and Buster was told that all of the things for which he asked would be his: even a ball team from New York Big Leagues will visit his home and practice a warm up outside his window; Roy Rogers will telephone Buster tonight and everything will come true for little Buster in the few weeks he may yet live… And Buster was officially proclaimed Honorary Treasurer of the American Cancer Society Drive for Funds. All of the radio listeners are asked to send contributions directly to: "Buster, Parkertown, New Jersey." If the amount of contributions reached $10,000 by next week's broadcast, Buster's mother would receive an additional $1,000 in cash to help with medical bills.

Within a week, Buster Roos received a visit by Babe Ruth himself, two clowns (Charles Bell and Frankie Saluto) from the Ringling Brothers and Barnum & Bailey Circus in Madison Square Garden in New York, Buster's ride in a cart pulled by a Shetland pony, and seeing the better part of the town's 400 residents on the lawn of his one-story wooden home. Even the truckload of toys, valued at $500, was delivered as Edwards promised. Babe Ruth showed the youngster the stance and grip he used in hitting home runs, but the boy was too weak to hold the bat. "I'm mighty glad to see you," Buster told the mighty Bambino with a broad smile. It was fulfillment of a long-cherished ambition when he shook hands with Ruth, the pair chatted about baseball, and posed for photographs for the local newspaper.

The clowns did somersaults while a trick dog jumped through a hoop. Buster watched – and occasionally showed a tired smile. He never knew he was going to die and the news was never broke to the youth. He also didn't understand why so much money was placed in his lap. He didn't utter a word, possibly because his breath was short. Even his mother, Mrs. Pearl Roos, couldn't get anything from him. All he remembered was that he was kicked by a playmate in December 1944, and as a result his disease discovered; his leg amputated in an effort to stop the spread of the disease. A few weeks after the amputation he returned to school on crutches – but he collapsed. Cancer had spread to his lungs. At the time of the radio broadcast, he was down to one lung.

Despite his condition, Buster was an immediate celebrity – a poster boy for a good cause – and posed for newsreel pictures with money that poured in as a result of the national broadcast. "This youngster should have been dead months ago," said Dr. L.R. Carmona, who had been treating the youth. "His pulse rate has been way above normal for the last six weeks. There just isn't any hope for him. There's no telling how long he'll linger; it may be anywhere from three weeks to a year. This boy is one of many children who gives the lie to a common belief that cancer is only an older person's disease. He won't benefit by the money rolling in, but other people will." One week following Buster's radio debut, on the broadcast of April 20, an announcement was made that little Buster Roos had all of his wishes come true about the various things he wanted. Mrs. Roos also received the gift of $1,000 in cash, to help with the medical bills, because the donations sent to him for use by the National Cancer Society surpassed the $10,000 mark in one week's time. By the time the public outpouring concluded, a total of $72,000 had been raised for the cause.

Four weeks after his wish fulfillment, on Sunday, May 19, Leonard Roos died. Buster had amazed physicians with his tenacity in surviving one amputation and the removal of a lung… accepting a fate that was never disclosed to him. When asked during the media sensation what he liked best – Babe Ruth, Uncle Don, the clowns, the toys or Roy Rogers giving him a ten-gallon hat – the youth said it was the postcards that brought sunshine into his life when things looked darkest.

Little "Buster" Leonard Roos

Buster and his friend on *Truth or Consequences*.

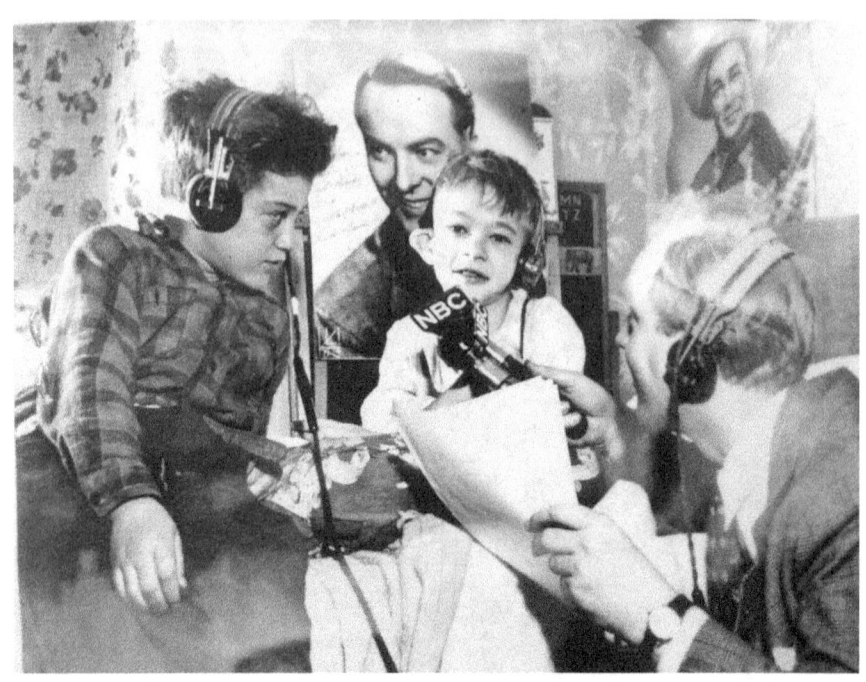

Buster and his friend on *Truth or Consequences*.

Media frenzy outside the house of "Buster" Leonard Roos.

Letters from radio listeners as a result of the Buster Roos contest.

The Jimmy Fund

The Jimmy Fund solely supports Boston's Dana-Farber Cancer Institute, raising funds for adult and pediatric cancer care and research to improve the chances of survival for cancer patients around the world. Since its founding in 1948, the Jimmy Fund has raised millions of dollars through thousands of community fundraising events. The story of the Jimmy Fund is one of grassroots involvement — of thousands of people organizing bake sales, lemonade stands, runs, walks, golf tournaments, dances, and softball games to raise money for cancer research and care. *Truth or Consequences* was not involved with establishing the charity, but it dramatized the need for research funds. William S. Koster and his Variety Club colleagues had been quietly laying the groundwork in the early forties for this unique venture.

The Variety Club sponsored a blood bank at the local Children's Hospital, and pledged $50,000, at the rate of $10,000 a year. One afternoon towards the end of 1945, they took a visitor from the national office to the hospital. "As we walked through a ward, a theater owner asked a doctor what was wrong with these children," Koster recalled. "The physician told us that, in a period of 50 to 75 days, the children would die from leukemia and other cancers. That was shocking to hear. When asked what could be done, the doctor said that the only hope was research, which was very expensive. We returned to the club and asked ourselves whether we could help. We decided to hold a raffle, from which we raised $47,000. We presented a check to the doctor – Sidney Farber – and asked him whether he could use this money for research. Dr. Farber suggested that we start our own foundation, which we did in 1946. We called it the Variety Club Children's Cancer Research Foundation."

The name was quickly shortened to the Children's Cancer Research Foundation, Inc. At Dr. Farber's suggestion, it became popularly known as the Jimmy Fund. "He said that if we wanted a common name, why not Jimmy, who is everybody's child," Koster remembered.

Dr. Farber had a small basement office at the Children's Hospital, where he was the first full-time pathologist. He was also the first S. Burt Wolbach Professor of Pathology at Harvard Medical School. One of the first, too, to recognize that a new, focused approach was needed to study and treat childhood cancer. He conducted research which, in 1947, resulted in the development of aminopterin, the folic acid (a member of the vitamin-B complex) antagonist. This chemical produced remissions in children with acute leukemia and demonstrated the effectiveness of a new treatment method, chemotherapy.

The subsequent publicity concerning this major medical discovery called attention to the large sums of money that would be necessary for continuing research. The Variety Club decided to seek a national forum… and the solution came in the form of *Truth or Consequences*. In early 1948, Richard Robie, known as the Rent-A-Car King, was also the Chairman of the Boston Children's Hospital Fund Drive, phoned Dan Sullivan, his advertising man, regarding the great Dr. Sidney Farber of the Children's Hospital, who needed funds for children's cancer research, the Variety Club's fund for that project.

"Uncle Dan called Billy, who talked with Lou Perini, owner of the old Boston Braves, and I was approached to do a *Truth or Consequences* stunt to start the ball rolling," Edwards later recalled. "George Swartz, a great gentleman and indefatigable volunteer worker for scores of worthy projects in and around Boston, called me in Hollywood one night. I knew George when he enlisted Jack Benny, Phil Harris, and myself for a volunteer tour for the March of Dimes (polio drive) to New York, Philadelphia and Boston.* George said, 'Ralph, do you remember that *Truth or Consequences* act where you had Babe Ruth visit a little leukemia patient in New Jersey and you raised several thousand dollars for the American Cancer Society?' I recalled how the Babe had taken an autographed baseball and bat down to the child and we heard him talk baseball with the young boy. When Babe Ruth had left him, we told the radio audience that if they sent in a certain number of dollars for the Cancer Society, we would get the boy a nice gift. I've forgotten what the gift was, but several thousand dollars came in."

* Swartz was in charge of the President's birthday parties for the Infantile Paralysis fund. Swartz knew Jack Benny, and Benny agreed to bring his whole company, saying he would not even charge travel expenses. Edwards was invited and he said he would, asking for equal billing with Jack Benny. When the two were in Boston, Swartz was responsible for their meeting and the two struck up a friendship. Another member of that group of friends was Eddie Cantor.

"Well, George Swartz, the unsung hero of this whole thing, said that he could deliver me the Boston Braves and a young leukemia patient who was a real baseball fan and had been particularly interested that year because the Braves were going to play in the World Series," Edwards continued. "I agreed to do a similar surprise visit, as we had done a few years earlier in New Jersey. It was agreed we would keep the boy's name anonymous and the name 'Jimmy' was suggested… Dr. Farber, as a matter of fact, called on my wife and me in our home in Beverly Hills soon after the event to express his appreciation."

Swartz himself would call Edwards and plead with him. First Edwards said that he just could not do it. Then, as Swartz again called him, he told of the other philanthropies that would have prior rights. And George would come back with, "There are no prior rights over sick children. This is not just a Boston thing. This is something that reaches every youngster all over the world. There are children from all over the United States at the Children's Hospital. The work being done with them may mean healthy kids a generation from now, kids who won't have to go through fear and pain." Edwards finally said that if he could get clearances from those people who previously had asked him, he would devote some time on his radio show. For a few minutes there was a temporary halt to the lunatic-fringe entertainment of the quiz show, devoting time for the young boy and a good cause.

On the evening of May 22, Ralph Edwards used part of his radio program to address the listening audience: "Tonight, we take you to a little fellow named Jimmy. We're not going to give you his last name because he's just like thousands of other young fellows and girls in private homes and hospitals all over the country. Jimmy is suffering from cancer, but he doesn't know he has it. He's a swell little guy and although he can't figure out why he isn't with the other kids, he does love his baseball and follows every move of his favorite team, the Boston Braves. By the magic of radio, we're going to span the breadth of the United States and take you right up to the bedside of Jimmy… Up to now, Jimmy has not heard us. Now we tune in a speaker in the hospital."

Edwards, from Hollywood, then had a conversation with the young boy. "We had our remote lines hooked up to the hospital bed when I tuned in Jimmy and introduced him to our nationwide *Truth or Consequences* audience," Edwards later recalled. "After chatting with him a bit, and letting the listeners know just what a baseball buff he was, I asked him if he would like to meet the Boston Braves team – Sain, Spahn, Billy Southworth, the manager and all the rest of those champions – and in they all walked. After having several of them talk to Jimmy, I told him they were going to sing a song for him, and these nice guys bellowed forth with 'Take Me Out to the Ball Game,' which led me into what we knew would happen, but Jimmy didn't. We said he was truly going out to the ball game, and he did. They had a special place for him with special care."

When Edwards asked Jimmy who his favorite player was, the boy replied Phil Masi, the catcher for the Boston Braves. Edwards asked the youth whether he had ever met Masi. Jimmy said no. That was when Masi walked into the room and corrected the lad. "Oh, sure you have, Jimmy. My name is Phil Masi." Following Masi were the others in the Braves' starting lineup, along with Sain and Manager Billy Southworth, who announced that the next day's doubleheader against the Chicago Cubs would be called "Jimmy Day." As Southworth explained over the air, "We're dedicating that first game to you, Jimmy." The youngster was then given a regulation Braves' uniform, an outfielder's glove autographed by the team, and a season pass for him and a friend. Finally, he led the team in singing "Take Me Out to the Ballgame."

When the pick-up from Boston concluded, Edwards, back in Hollywood, then made a public plea for the boy. "Then, after bidding Jimmy and the players goodbye, I told our radio audience that little Jimmy can watch the baseball championship games, *Truth or Consequences* will give Jimmy a television set if you folks listening will donate at least $20,000 to the Children's Cancer Research Foundation.' Thousands of dollars came in and the Jimmy Fund was born."

The real "Jimmy," a.k.a. Einar Gustafson, age 12.

"Now this isn't a contest where you'll win anything," Edwards reminded the audience. "This is our chance to help helpless little boys and girls such as Jimmy win a greater prize – the prize of life." Soon after the program went off the air, a Cambridge company donated a television set. Motorists who heard the program on their car radios stopped by the Children's Hospital and left off small contributions. On May 29, one week after Edwards made his appeal, 22,000 letters were received and contributions grossed $16,813.33. One week later, on the June 5 broadcast, Edwards reported contributions reaching $32,854.50. Some 18,000 letters were received by the end of the month, all addressed to Jimmy.

As for the doubleheader between the Braves and the Cubs, sportscaster Jim Britt re-told the story heard first on *Truth or Consequences*, heard throughout New England. Fittingly, the Braves, with Jimmy cheering them on, swept the doubleheader. The doctor in charge of the Children's Hospital gave permission for Jimmy to go to the game. Jimmy sat in a box at Braves Field under the supervision of a nurse and cheered the Braves to an 8-5 victory over the Chicago Cubs in the opening game of a double-header. He cheered so well the Braves won the second game, too, 12-4.

"That's when the Jimmy Fund took off," recalled William S. Koster. Large sums of money were raised – in pennies, nickels, dimes, quarters and dollar bills. Collections were taken in theaters. Policemen, firemen, taxi drivers and people from all occupations and income levels contributed to the Jimmy Fund. Britt recalled a time when a group of young girls waited for him outside radio station WHDH. "One of the girls was holding a large, black bag," Britt recalled. "She reached in and took out nine dollars and some change. 'Nobody died today,' she said, explaining that things had been quiet that day in her father's funeral parlor in Boston's North End, where she and her friends had presented a play."

When Jim Britt and Warren Spahn of the Braves made a visit to Plymouth High School, they disregarded the norm. Instead of giving a gift to the school, which was traditional, the senior class made a contribution to the Jimmy Fund. Students from the Perkins School for the Blind in Watertown held a five-mile walkathon for the Jimmy Fund. A stained dollar bill was donated, along with a short note written in a woman's shaky hand. The donor wrote that her son was killed on Guadalcanal. She wanted the Jimmy Fund to have the dollar bill, which had been returned with his personal effects. By the end of the summer, $282,000 had been raised to further research of cancer in children.

In 1949, Jimmy Fund movie theater collections begin, with volunteers asking for contributions before a feature film is shown while passing a collection canister. Movie trailers precede the passing of the canisters and have featured movie stars of the time including Spencer Tracy, Joan Crawford, and Bing Crosby.

A brand new four story building constructed in 1952. Dr. Sidney Farber wearing white lab coat in center.

In 1954, Dr. Sidney Farber discovered that the antibiotic actinomycin, when combined with surgery and radiotherapy, produced tumor regressions in patients with Wilms' tumor, a common – and deadly – growth. Dr. Farber also introduced the "total care concept," which was geared to the whole patient. There were always, for example, psychological and sociological factors affecting a patient and his family. "We never say nothing more can be done," he once said. "We say, 'Why don't we try?'" Dr. Farber died on March 30, 1973, while working in the building that had been a haven for young cancer victims from around the world.

On Friday, September 4, 1981, Ralph Edwards received the Yawkey Memorial Award, on behalf of The Jimmy Fund.

On November 13, 1996, a 50th anniversary celebration of the Dana-Farber Cancer Institute included a recognition to The Jimmy Fund. In the format of *This is Your Life*, a host of national recognition and credibility was involved with the entertainment. The honorary chairman was Ted Williams, who was on the radio broadcast that helped launch the *Truth or Consequences* pledge drive.

Organist Buddy Cole

Organist Buddy Cole

Chapter 6
Jack Dempsey and the Mr. Hush Contest

On the evening of May 10, 1941, *Truth or Consequences* did a Cinderella "consequence" in which a girl was given a whole layout of clothes – gown, mink coat, slippers, etc. This stunt has been credited by many as the act that led to the "give-away" shows of the 1940s. Ralph Edwards detested this indiscriminate giving away of gifts made on other shows merely for answering a single question. He devised, therefore, the "Mr. Hush" contest in December of 1945, which was meant to serve as a satire on the big giveaways and to build a backfire against them. On the evening of December 29, he introduced to his radio audience a mystery voice referred to as "Mr. Hush," and said that the first contestant to identify the individual would win a Bendix Washer, a dozen pairs of Nylons, and a new Mercury Sedan Coupe, and each week, three more unbelievable prizes would be added to the pot. It would take five weeks for a contestant to guess correctly. As promised, the pot continued to build week after week, providing the winner of that contest a total of $13,500. Each week the veiled mystery man, known only as "Mr. Hush," provided clues to his identity in doggerel.

> "Hickory, Dickory, Dock,
> The hands went round the clock.
> The clock struck ten,
> Lights out, goodnight."

To take part in this "Crack-Pot Consequence," all of the contestants of the evening sat around a long table. In front of every person was a different kind of sound effect, such as a whistle, a bird-call, a fight gong, a chime, and others. Then, the voice of "Mr. Hush" was broadcast and the contestant who thought they recognized the voice and named the owner was allowed to make a "noise" with his or her sound effect. The first person to recognize the voice wrote the name of the mystery man on a slip of paper and handed it in. Ralph Edwards read the answers publicly, but week after week, no one guessed correctly.

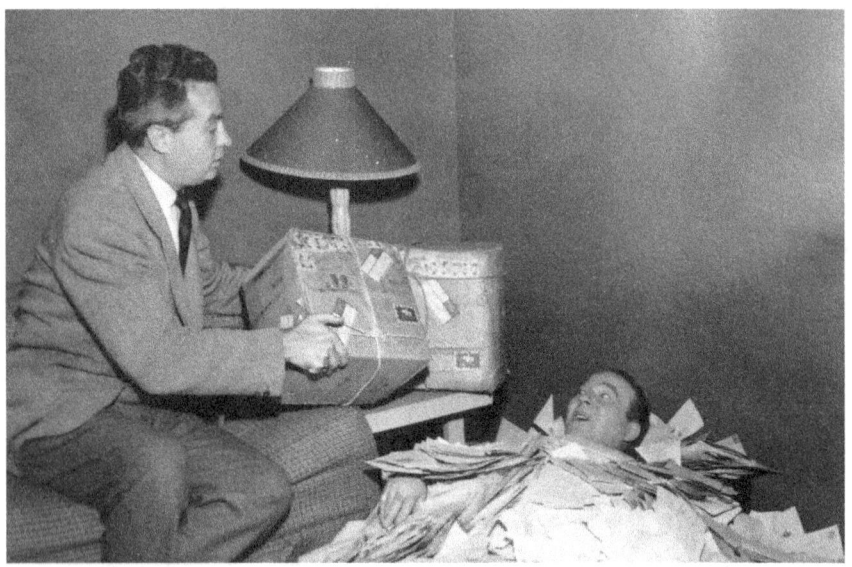

Ed Bailey and Ralph Edwards with the outpouring of mail.

After five weeks, on the evening of January 26, the voice of "Mr. Hush" was identified by contestant Ensign Richard Bartholomew of Fayetteville, Arkansas, who recognized the voice as that of Jack Dempsey. After the identification was made, Dempsey came on the air via two-way pick-up from New York to congratulate the winner. Ensign Bartholomew's prize, an accumulation of five weeks' give-away prizes included a $1,000 diamond ring designed by J.R. Wood, a $1,000 I.J. Fox silver fur coat, a $1,000 diamond-and-ruby Bulova wrist watch, a 1946 Mercury car, an RCA-Victor radio phonograph console with 100 Red Seal Popular records, a Bendix washing machine, a two-year supply of Hollyvogue Nylon stockings, a Knabe piano, a Tappan gas range, a Crosley Shelvador refrigerator, round-trip ticket to New York by plane with a weekend at the Waldorf Astoria hotel, two weeks paid vacation for two at Banff Springs Hotel in the Canadian Rockies, an Electrolux vacuum cleaner with all attachments, maid service for one year, and two complete men's head-to-toe outfits including two Hart Schaffner & Marx suits and overcoats. The entire winning was estimated at approximately $13,500.

On that windy cold Saturday night, the Bartholomews were at home relaxing, unaware that their life was about to change. Father was in bed with a severe attack of asthma, also suffering with a blinding headache. Mother was seated by the radio, reading a magazine and listening to the program at the same time, not doing a very good job of either. The program was *Truth or Consequences*. Edwards came to the mike to introduce an ensign. Mother pricked up her ears but it was only a boy from San Antonio. There was a rigmarole of questions and incorrect answers and Mother desultorily turned a page of the magazine. "Gosh, I wish Dick would get on a quiz program some time," Mother thought to herself. "I'll bet he'd get the right answer." The second contestant came to the microphone and introduced himself as Dick Bartholomew, from 604 Whitham Street in Fayetteville, Arkansas. Mother screams, Father jumps up from the bed, and both listen with bated breath.

"What was the original use of the pendulum?" Edwards asked. "To determine gravity," was the incorrect answer. Now young Bartholomew must pay the consequences. He is to take two people to the Earl Carroll's Vanities, with all expenses paid. One of them is a person from the Old Ladies' Home and the other is from Earl Carroll's Vanities. "I'll take the old lady," chose the Arkansas gentlemen. Enter stage left a beautiful woman who worked as the secretary at the Old Ladies' Home. The other woman was a bit older, the dietitian at the Vanities.

In the meantime, the phone at the Bartholomews' has been ringing constantly, calls coming from friend and foe alike even as far away as Siloam Springs. That was when Edwards offered Ensign Dick Bartholomew the same as all other contestants. "Now we come to the crackpot," Edwards proclaimed. "We have the voice of a well-known person reciting a jingle. You have 30 seconds to guess the identity. Ring the bell when you think you have the correct name." Bartholomew guessed Jack Dempsey. After a few seconds of stunned silence, Edwards shouted, "Jack Dempsey it is!"

Mother fainted. Father's asthma was gone. The phone did not stop ringing for two hours. Calls from all over the nation were jamming the switchboard. Ralph Edwards was also on the wire, giving the phone to Dick who is as excited as anyone ever was. He was provided the opportunity to tell his mother and father the news, unaware at first that they heard the program over the radio. The phone calls at the Bartholomew home began again at 8:00 a.m. Sunday morning. Bartholomew gave the Silver Fox coat and the expensive ring to his mother, who expressed an interest in the two prizes.

Allan H. Keith in Greenville, Illinois, wrote a letter to his local radio station, who forwarded his query to Ralph Edwards. "My friend argues that the list of prizes offered the winner was a fake and that he did not win all of the things as stated on the program. I contend that he did, and I would surely appreciate some proof from your station or from the sponsor of *Truth or Consequences* that this was a bona fide award as stated on the program." The producers of the radio quiz show would not normally respond to such a query, uncertain if the author of the letter was merely feeling them out or partially unstable for even writing such a letter, but the General Manager of KSD in St. Louis, James Martin of NBC, and Murray Bolen of Compton Advertising suggested Edwards address the query if for no other reason than to propose a newspaper article or news feature verifying such prizes were legit. Edwards wrote a brief response to Allan H. Keith, consisting of two sentences: "Please assure your friend that Ensign Bartholomew really did receive all those prizes. We, naturally, could not make a claim over the air that we could not substantiate."

Edwards originally wanted Albert Einstein, who wasn't interested, so he settled for his second choice: Jack Dempsey. The origin of Mr. Hush's voice was at no time announced on the air and his voice was heard as if originating from a small room near the studio, where the rest of the broadcast was being given. Because the champion was on the road at the time of the contest, his voice originated from a different remote each week – unknown to the radio audience. His voice originated from a dressing room at the Hollywood Bowl on December 29; his private home in Hollywood, January 5; from The Forum in Wichita, Kansas, January 12; the Lennox Hotel in St. Louis, Missouri, January 19; and New York City January 26.

At the time of the contest, Jack Dempsey resided at 5254 Los Feliz in Hollywood, California. Weeks following the contest, on May 9, Ralph Edwards sent a personal thank-you letter to Dempsey. "The days keep flying by and I'm constantly reminded of the fact that your good turn for us is still going unpaid.

Please contact me or my secretary, Miss Pyle, or my press gal, Miss Curry at Crestview 5-3153, when you get a few minutes and tell me at your earliest convenient date to get together for your thoughts on a settlement with a good cup of coffee or a highball at the same time. I can never thank you enough for the way you entered into the stunt. There isn't a day goes by that we are not pleasantly reminded of Mr. Hush." Dempsey responded with a suitable payment for his services: a couple of savings bonds – one in the name of daughters Joan Hannah and the other Barbara J. Dempsey. Having verbally agreed to pay Dempsey $250 for each week of services, the five weeks totaled $1,250. Edwards rounded the fee up a little and had each girl receive a $500 Bond, three $100 Bonds, and a $50 Bond.

Jack Dempsey as "Mr. Hush"

The contest generated many telegrams from servicemen who wanted to attend the show and become a contestant. Mothers who had their boys in service also wrote with similar requests. A cookie-cutter letter was generated and mailed in response to every query explaining that during the half-hour warm-up immediately preceding the show, Edwards chose the contestants directly from the studio audience. Tickets could be obtained through the National Broadcasting Company and everyone who attended the show had an equal chance to be a contestant.

When Ralph Edwards saw his final "Mr. Hush" Hooperating as 17.8, he knew he had something that negated his anti-giveaway notion. People flew to California from Maine in an effort to obtain a ticket for the broadcast and perhaps an opportunity to name the mystery voice. "People flew in from all over America, wearing crazy hats and carrying signs to gain my attention when I was selecting contestants from the audience," Edwards later recalled. "When I saw all the greedy hands go up in the audience to get a crack at the 'crackpot,' I realized we had an enormous agent for good if we opened other mystery contests to our radio listeners benefiting the March of Dimes, the Heart Association, etc." Edwards and his crew began plotting another contest on a grander scale.

Chapter 7
The Mrs. Hush Contests:
Clara Bow and Martha Graham

Hollywood celebrities participating on a radio quiz program was not uncommon during the forties. In December of 1945, Jack Benny initiated an essay contest prompting radio listeners to compose the closing half of, "I Can't Stand Jack Benny because..." For the promise of a share of $10,000 in Victory Bond prizes, the response was overwhelming. The final count was between 250,000 and 300,000 letters. This was a precursor to the stunts to come on *Truth or Consequences*, one of which would ultimately involve Jack Benny himself.

On the broadcast of January 19, 1946, one of the evening's guests was a little blind girl who was also a patient at a Hollywood hospital where she was undergoing treatment for the after-effects of polio. The little girl sang a song, accompanied by program organist Buddy Cole. She also talked about her stay in the hospital and said she was learning to read Braille. Ralph Edwards announced that if the listeners of the program would help, the little girl might have the gift of sight. Listeners were instructed to put a dime or more in an envelope and mail it to Ralph Edwards in behalf of the child. If the total of dimes mailed in on behalf of the little girl reached the amount of $25,000, to be used in the March of Dimes fight against infantile paralysis, the child would be sent to the Eye Bank, where the best surgeons in that field hoped to bring back her sight. The initial examinations had been made and the child was believed to have an eye defect, which could be cured. First, she must finish her treatment for polio, however, and meanwhile, all of the dimes sent in her name will be going to help other little polio victims.

Auld Lang Syne Chorus, broadcast of December 27, 1947.

Blowing Bubble Gum contest, broadcast of September 13, 1947.

The results of the fundraiser exceeded their expectations. This was when Edwards proposed something much bigger to the March of Dimes. Avoiding lottery laws, Edwards decided to open the next contest to the general public as a sure-fire way to benefit deserving causes. This would pave the way to a series of on-air contests that would bring millions for charity. Hoping to reprise the "Mr. Hush" contest with a mystery woman and applying the same essay contest recently concluded on the Jack Benny program, Edwards and producer Al Paschall began investigating the legalities of charitable contribution from qualifying participants.

C. Roy Smith, the First Assistant Attorney General of the State of California, reviewed state laws to ensure the contest would not be discontinued on the grounds of a violation of law. "It appears that your proposed Mrs. Hush program is not objectionable from the standpoint of state law, providing that eligibility for participation in the contest is not contingent upon the payment or contribution of any sum whatever and such fact is announced over the air during each broadcast of the program." Michael D. Fanning, Postmaster of Los Angeles, California, reviewed the rules of the proposed game and on January 23, 1947, informed Ralph Edwards: "If the letter-writing contest winners have their opportunity to identify 'Mrs. Hush' and fail to do so correctly and thereafter persons are selected at random from the studio audience to attempt to supply the correct identification, and a consideration such as a contribution to the March of Dimes is exacted from those so selected, the plan at that time would be regarded as a lottery and matter relating thereto unacceptable for mailing under Section 601, Postal Laws and Regulations."

Howard J. London, Radio Director of the National Foundation for Infantile Paralysis, in Washington D.C., contacted Al Paschall on January 23 via telegram with the following: "March of Dimes fund raising committee definitely approves Mrs. Hush plan with condition that at least 80 percent of contest letters contain March of Dimes contributions. If non-contribution letters run higher adjustment in setup will be necessary. Do not feel this will happen inasmuch as we are paying for all letters. Think this factor should be included in approval. The first week will tell the story."

On January 20, Howard J. London told producer Al Paschall via telegram: "Just been advised by the Hyde Park Post Office that they cleared FDR, so see no reason why we couldn't clear Mrs. Hush through the Hollywood office."

The entire contest was thought out by the National Broadcasting Company, the advertising agency, and the sponsor and producers of *Truth or Consequences*,

Organist Buddy Cole

Ralph Edwards and Al Paschall

with the stipulation that no specific dollar amount would be requested, to avoid any accusations of lottery or chance.

The subsequent "Mrs. Hush" contest began on the evening of January 25, 1947. Listeners who heard the voice of an unnamed woman and thought they could identify her could send their letters to "Mrs. Hush, Hollywood, California." (Further diggings unearthed the box number was 2549.) Listeners were instructed to complete in 25 words or less the following sentence, "We should all support the March of Dimes because..." The letter must be accompanied by a contribution to the March of Dimes but the amount they sent would in no way affect the entry. "Let your heart be your guide," was included in the instructions. In the upper right-hand corner of the letter, radio listeners were instructed to print their name, address and telephone number. Make sure the phone number was legible and be at the telephone when called. From one penny to a $100 bill, submissions and donations poured into the Mrs. Hush office. Donations of all denominations were accepted. An estimated ten percent of the submissions were disqualified because listeners did not legibly write their name and phone number with readable penmanship.

It was also explained to radio listeners that two weeks from January 25, the writers of the three best letters would have a chance to answer a telephone call from Ralph Edwards and have a chance to identify Mrs. Hush. The prize for identifying Mrs. Hush was a 1947 Ford Sportsman Convertible automobile, a Bendix washer, and a round-trip ticket to New York City for two with a weekend reservation at the Waldorf-Astoria Hotel. Who could not resist mailing a donation to the March of Dimes for a chance at that?

For every week contestants could not identify the voice of Mrs. Hush, three more prizes were added to the pot. It was requested of the radio audience not to include the name of Mrs. Hush in their letters – that would be reserved for the phone call broadcast "live" on the air.

Because the East Coast broadcast was not taped for playback a couple hours later for the West Coast, radio listeners on the West Coast were instructed to be at the phone during the time of the East Coast broadcast, in case they were to receive the call. Only one attempt would be made to reach the listener. On the technical side, before the radio contestant went on the air, a representative of the radio program sought verbal permission to re-enact the on-air conversation for the West Coast broadcast.

For the slogan contest and the choosing of the contestants, the letters were judged by Federal Judge J.F.T. O'Connor, Roy Nastgner, head of the Los Angeles County Chapter for the National Foundation for Infantile Paralysis, and Dr. Vierling Kersey, Superintendent of the Los Angeles City Schools. Entries were judged on the originality, aptness of thought, and sincerity. It was specified that Mrs. Hush was a famous person and could be located from anywhere in the country; not necessarily from Hollywood. On the January 25, 1947, broadcast, Mrs. Hush read the following four-line jingle:

> "Two o'clock and all is well;
> Who it is I cannot tell;
> Queen has her King, it's true,
> But not her ribbon tied in blue."

A celebrity guest did assist with the January 25 broadcast, actress Louise Arthur, and it was clarified on the air that she was not Mrs. Hush. For the February 1 broadcast, it was specified that any letters received through February 4 would be considered for the February 8 broadcast when Ralph Edwards phoned the first three lucky contestants. Letters received after February 4 and through the next week would be used on the contest for February 15, etc. Contestants were allowed to submit as many letters as they wanted to throughout the life of the contest. The first of the calls would be placed on February 8 but on the broadcast of February 1, three more prizes were added to the pot: a $1,000 full-length silver fox coat (provided by I.J. Fox), a Columbia Trailer, fully equipped and sleeps four, and a $1,000 diamond and ruby Bulova watch.

Prizes on display for the Mrs. Hush contest.

Every company donating a product or service for the jackpot had to coordinate with Al Paschall, Production Manager for *Truth or Consequences*, so that the proper reference to the company was mentioned over the air. Regrettably for the donors, nothing could be said that would resemble a paid commercial. Most references stated the company name and the product, and where the company was located. For products such as appliances and automobiles, contestants receive a gift voucher good for that item to be delivered from the nearest authorized dealer. Numerous companies attempted to take advantage of what could be considered free publicity and advertising, and many were rejected due to various reasons both practical and legal.

The first three contestants in the contest, phoned during the broadcast of February 8, 1947, failed to identify Mrs. Hush, so three more prizes were added to the pot. These included a Tappan Range, a Jacobs Home Freeze Unit packed with Birdseye Foods, and a 1947 RCA Phonograph-Victrola combination with 100 records. Edwards teased the radio listeners by stating the voice of Mrs. Hush was heard from "Shangri-la," an undisclosed location somewhere in the United States. The February 15, 1947, broadcast originated from the Golden Gate Theater in San Francisco, but that did not interfere with the scheduled phone calls. Once again, the voice of "Mrs. Hush" remained unidentified and once again three more prizes were added to the pot: an electric refrigerator, a vacuum cleaner with accessories, and a week's vacation for two in Sun Valley with air transportation both ways.

Prizes on display for the Mrs. Hush contest.

The program resumed in Hollywood with the February 22, 1947, broadcast. After three phone calls, spread throughout the half-hour broadcast, interlaced between commercials and consequences, "Mrs. Hush" was again unidentified and three additional prizes were added: a Brunswick billiard table installed in the winner's home and complete with all sporting accessories needed to play the game; a $1,000 art-carved diamond ring designed by J.R. Wood; and a complete Hart Schaffner Marx wardrobe of clothes for each adult man and woman in the winner's family. There was a guest during this broadcast, Miss Claire Dodson, an Earl Carroll showgirl, who assisted Ralph Edwards by entertaining one of the contestants.

The "Mrs. Hush" contest truly became a national sensation. In Times Square in Manhattan, newsstands were selling tout sheets at a dollar apiece. Large signs were displayed on the street offering tip sheets with the identity of "Miss Hush" for one dollar. On buying the envelope with "Miss Hush," printed on the front in heavy 36-point type, one found that all the clues were reprinted and carefully worked out on a single mimeographed sheet. The sheets, however, only stated "suggested identification" for legal purposes and when the identities proved false, a new one cropped up the next week.

The Singapore Bar in Chicago had a $1,000 bet that the voice was Spring Byington, which of course the bar owner lost when a contestant guessed Byington on the air and this proved to be wrong. Office pools, by many accounts, were very popular. People dropped their guess and a single dollar into the pool, with the hope of winning the pot.

The contest was discussed by disc jockeys, used as a point builder for comedian gags, made front page on publications known to have an "anti-radio" policy, written up in *Time* and *Newsweek* two weeks consecutively, received two-page coverage in *Life*, and was featured briefly in studio newsreels. Mail supposedly reached 180,000 letters in one day (the highest the contest ever drew) and collected almost $600,000 for the March of Dimes.

The voice of "Mrs. Hush" was not identified on the broadcast of March 1, 1947, and three more gifts were added for next week's program: an Oil-O-Matic burner completely installed with a year's supply of fuel, a Piper Cub airplane, and free maid service for one year. Due to a faulty line connection, at 8:54 p.m., the "Mrs. Hush" portion stopped momentarily and the two words, "has her," were lost over the air. In what was becoming an expectation with weekly radio listeners, "Miss Hush" was again unidentified the week following. Again, three additional prizes were added to the pot: a 144-piece china set, a typewriter, and a complete house-painting job inside and outside with Sherwin Williams paint.

Finally, on the broadcast of March 15, the voice of "Mrs. Hush" was identified. Mrs. William H. McCormick of 243 Water Street in Lock Haven, Pennsylvania, a residential section of Castanea Township, located along the Susquehanna River, answered her telephone and provided Ralph Edwards with her guess... Clara Bow. Mrs. McCormick's winnings, valued at the time between $17,590 and $18,000, included: a 1947 convertible car, an electric washer, round-trip plane ticket for two to New York City with a week and a suite at the Waldorf-Astoria, a $1,000 full-length Silver Fox fur coat, a house-trailer fully equipped for four people, a $1,000 diamond and ruby wrist watch, a home-freeze-unit stocked with frozen foods, a Tappan gas range, a 1947 RCA Victor console radio-phonograph with 100 records, a refrigerator (Electrolux), a full-size home-billiard table with all equipment and installation, a furnace with a year's fuel supply to complete the home-heating unit; a 144-piece china set, free maid service for one year, complete house-painting job inside and out with Sherwin Williams paint, a typewriter, an all-Metal airplane, a week's vacation for two at Sun Valley, Idaho, with transportation both ways, a $1,000 diamond ring, an electric vacuum cleaner with all the attachments and a complete Schaffner Hart Marx wardrobe for every adult member of the immediate family.

When newspaper reporters paid Mrs. McCormick a visit and asked her what she planned to do with the prizes, the contestant explained how she planned to divide her winnings with her neighbor, Mrs. A.H. Timms, and her sister, Mrs. William Harmon, both of whom helped identify Mrs. Hush. Following the identification, there was a pick-up from Las Vegas, Nevada, for two special guests. Clara Bow (Mrs. Rex Bell) told the story behind her silent contribution to the cause, every week broadcasting via remote from an auto park near her Las Vegas home. Her husband, Rex Bell, and their two children, George and Toni Bell, never knew their mother was Mrs. Hush until this very evening. The entire family was heard on the program. The actress formerly known as the "It" girl then told how she kept her "Mr. Hush" identity from her family, including the nearest neighbor who almost surprised her just when she was starting out to the "Shangri-La" where she made her broadcasts. Ralph Edwards told Clara Bow that he was sending her a special award, as a way of saying thank you: a golden statuette, n behalf of the National Foundation of Infantile Paralysis, to be bestowed to Clara Bow as a result of the letters and contributions to the March of Dimes from contestants who sought to identify "Mrs. Hush." An estimated total of $400,000 was raised as a result of the contest, according to a number of trade columns, but when the exact amount was finally calculated, weeks following, the total reached $550,000. According to a representative of the March of Dimes, this was the largest single radio contribution ever received by the March of Dimes Fund... topping the January 30, 1942, Presidential March of Dimes fund appeal, and the famous all-star January 23, 1944 March of Dimes campaign that made headlines across the country. More than one million letters were sent in by contestants, each with a donation.

Clara Bow delivering her lines from a secret location.

McCormick also experienced the setback radio contestants experienced after winning a nationwide radio contest. The quiz show contestant received multiple visits from the local press, unwanted solicitors and "every whip-switch when the telephone rings because people feel that they have given me sufficient time to recover and now they want to hear all about it," she wrote to Edwards in a letter. "Well, they will. It was an out-of-this-world Magic Carpet trip with the way made smooth, with everything and everybody so much nicer than two mortals could reasonably expect." McCormick asked producer Al Paschall for two requests as mementos: autographed pictures of both Paschall and Edwards, and a sound recording of the broadcast she appeared on. Her request was honored.

Within a month of winning the contest, the McCormicks sold the trailer to an ex-GI for $2,000. The "distributor" agreed to hold the airplane in storage for sixty days while she sought someone interested in purchasing it from her. She sold the plane for $2,100 to the East Penn Flying Club in Pennsylvania. Sherwin-Williams agreed to do two exteriors of the house instead of one interior and one exterior. She donated the pool table to a local club. She sold the Tappan gas range and the Silver Fox coat. They kept the car, accepting a sedan instead of a convertible, receiving a check for the difference in dollar value, which she later referred to as "a honey." The local jeweler in Lock Haven handled delivery of the $1,000 ring and was shocked to discover the ring was not worth $1,000. When this was brought to her attention by the jeweler, she agreed to allow the company to pay her the difference in the form of a check. She accepted the equivalent of a cash annuity value for the maid service, which totaled $1,200. By May she found herself traveling about nearby towns as a guest speaker, talking to Civic Clubs and Rotary Clubs, telling of her Hollywood trip and her experiences. "It's amazing the way people continue to be thrilled," she wrote to Al Paschall, "so I succumb to these invitations."

She took advantage of the vacation trip. "Our stopover at the Grand Canyon was a great success," McCormick later wrote to Ralph Edwards. "Since I prefer nature on a cozier scale, I am glad I don't have to look at it every day but to look at it once was a great privilege. The place was lousy with bankers who, oddly enough, seemed very keen about including us in cocktails, dinner, and the evening. The income tax was their meat, of course, and they thought our first move should be to try to get a special ruling inasmuch as we have a Congressman handy."

Mrs. William McCormick, who correctly identified the voice of Mrs. Hush as Clara Bow.

Among Al Paschall's unofficial assignments over the years was mailing out Christmas cards to past jackpot winners. On January 6, 1948, Mary McCormick wrote to Paschall, thanking him for the Christmas card and providing an update regarding her new lifestyle, including her new duties as Lock Haven's first woman member of the Board of Education. Having learned of Mrs. Subbie, the winner of the second Mrs. Hush contest, McCormick remarked, "I hope Mrs. Subbie proves to be a more convenient winner than I was. Perhaps she can afford to keep everything and with no splitting up to do she and you can have plain sailing." Paschall wrote back explaining, "We are having our selling and distribution problems with Mrs. Subbie the same as you. Like yourself, she is a very charming and interesting person and easy to work with. I am happy that she won."

During the broadcast of March 22, Mrs. William McCormick and her husband were guests on the quiz program. Having won the Mrs. Hush contest the week prior, she and her husband were flown to Hollywood for the broadcast. In front of the microphone, they talked about what they planned to do with the prizes. The McCormick family included three sons (the oldest was 14, the youngest was 18 months). The boys were back home listening to the broadcast.

The "Mrs. Hush" contest also served as a clever marketing ploy to promote the radio program. Numerous periodicals covered the contest, hoping to convince their readers to tune in and try to guess the identity of the mystery woman. Columnists attempting to prove their intellect, offered their own theories. Rex Bell returned to the program a couple years later to help participate in another stunt. In a closing chapter: In the fall of 1948, the telephone bell jangled in the Hollywood home of Ralph Edwards just a few days before he embarked on a *Truth or Consequences* tour, which would bring Edwards and his troupe to the Sports Arena for a broadcast. A feminine voice on the other end of the wire asked to speak with Ralph Edwards and began teasing, "What's my name?" and "Can't you guess who this is?" Edwards did not know and after being taunted for several minutes without learning the identity of the caller, he became exasperated and was about to hang up when the woman volunteered: "I'll give you a clue – Two o'clock and all's well." It was not until the woman recited this jingle that Edwards recognized the voice on the other end of the wire as that of Clara Bow, whose identity baffled the entire nation two years ago. "I'm a fine one not to know the voice of my own 'Miss Hush' when I hear it," Edwards laughed.

> Columnist Paul Gallico, in his syndicated column, wrote in 1947, "A strange, new and astonishing passion seems to be developing in the United States via the radio – the cult of listening in to one-half of a telephone conversation. Why they cannot filter through the really interesting portion, the other half, I do not know. It probably has something to do with the FCC, or maybe they are afraid that some uninhibited lady or gent will from his or her end of the telephone voice his real opinion of radio, but such as it is, the performance has a tendency to drive the listener quite nuts. But the *Truth or Consequences* incident is not an isolated case. Nightly disk jockeys – in our metropolitan area, anyway – urge their listeners to call them up. Then they answer the telephone while they are on the air and let you in on half of it."

Martha Graham and the Quiz Show Controversy

Following the success of the first "Mrs. Hush" contest, it seemed only logical for Ralph Edwards to reprise the contest. On the evening of October 18, 1947, Edwards, having spent the preceding two weeks bantering the radio audience with the announcement of a new contest, the voice of a new "Miss Hush" was introduced for the first time, again described as being picked up from "anywhere in the United States," and was a well-known American celebrity. She delivered a jingle with clues as to her identity:

"Second for Santa Claus, first for me,
Thirteen for wreath, Seven for Tree.
Bring me an auto, a book and a ball,
And I'll say 'Merry Christmas' in Spring, not in Fall."

Script conference with Ralph Edwards

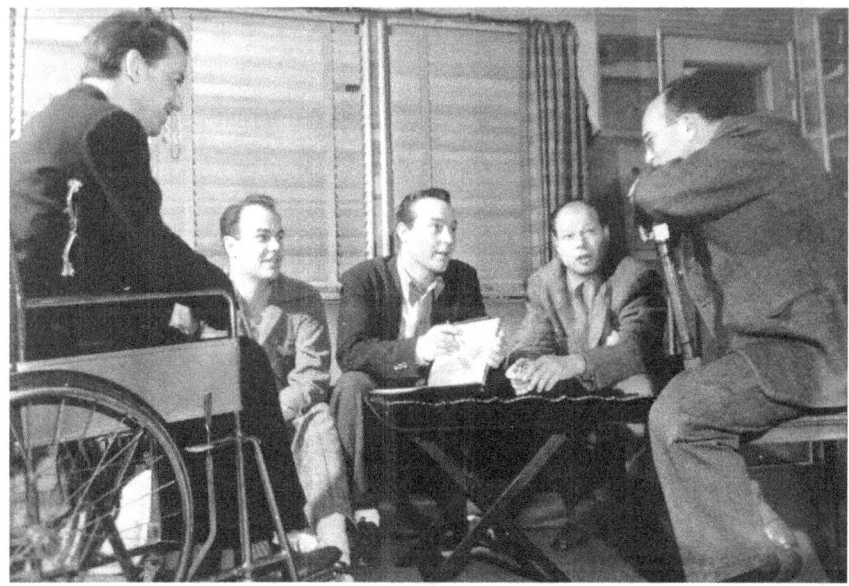

Script conference with Ralph Edwards

Listeners were instructed to try and identify Miss Hush, (now "Miss" and not "Mrs.") and be ready to answer when the first telephone calls to listeners were made two weeks from tonight on the same program, Eastern Standard Time. In order to be eligible to receive a telephone call starting November 1, listeners were told to mail a letter to: "Miss Hush, Hollywood, California." The rules of the contest were the same as the previous contest.

One week later, on October 25, the voice of Miss Hush was heard again, repeating the same jingle. On the evening of November 1, *Truth or Consequences* featured the first three telephone calls. Contestant number one was R.C. Collette of 1400 N. Sycamore, Hollywood, California. He named Elsa Maxwell as "Miss Hush." He was incorrect. So were the next two callers, who incorrectly guessed Maude Adams and Spring Byington.

On the evening of November 8, three more phone calls were made but only one of the three people was at home at the time the phone calls were made. Again, "Miss Hush" was not identified. As a result of the two dead calls, producer Al Paschall made sure going forward that contestants were notified on the phone earlier in the day to stand by their phones for a chance to identify the mystery voice. On November 15, three more telephone calls were made; three more incorrect guesses including Tallulah Bankhead and Sister Elizabeth Kenny. With each passing week, three more expensive prizes were added to the pot.

By this time, the American Federation of Radio Artists, also known as AFRA, intervened. The union sent a message to the office of Ralph Edwards, in Los Angeles, stating that "Miss Hush" was required to be a member of AFRA because she was doing radio performances. The union was mindful of the fact that Miss Hush's identity was kept a secret and therefore sent a stand-by application for membership, to be signed by "Miss Hush," if she should happen not to be a member already. AFRA added a warning that in any event, no matter her identity, "Miss Hush" was to be paid for all performances and union dues should be submitted.

On the evenings of November 15 and 22, more phone calls were made and every guess was incorrect. Charlotte Greenwood and WAC Col. Mary Halloran were among the incorrect guesses. By this time, the identity of Miss Hush was becoming an obsession for radio listeners. Columnist Jo Bradley Reed substantiated: "Almost everywhere you turn there's a mention of the most-talked about woman in America – Miss Hush. We've hardly been able to work this week for answering questions about Ralph Edwards' *Truth or Consequences* program. They range from 'Where do I send my letter?' to 'Let's go together on this. I bet you radio editors are in on the know.' We only wish we were. We could use a little of the till, now valued at more than $22,000. While we'd like to see the March of Dimes campaign get a big boost, we hope by the time this column hits the streets someone will have identified the mystery woman who has been interrupting our work schedule for weeks. Weariest of the contest are Hollywood mail clerks. At last count they were sorting an average of 10,000 letters to 'Miss Hush' daily. Reports from New York are the news and magazine stands are publishing cards which list best guesses."

Actor Paul Lukas ordered his secretary to figure out the clues. Kirk Douglas bought a copy of *Who's Who Among Women* and read the entire book. Set workers at RKO Studios wanted to win something, knowing the chances that any of them would receive a phone call, set up a "Miss Hush" betting pool. A radio station manager in Oklahoma City reported that a man next to him at a funeral leaned over and whispered, as the casket was being lowered, "Hey, do you know who is Miss Hush?"

Angela Lansbury prepares to be a celebrity guest on the program.

In Canton, Ohio, the "Miss Hush" contest couldn't end too soon for the librarians. The local newspaper, *The Repository*, reported the librarians being deluged with telephone calls, direct questions and requests for aid in "looking up" long-lost names. By the fifth week, when someone phoned the library for information about almost any American woman, the librarians started asking, "Is this a Miss Hush question?" If the answer was yes, they apologized and explained that they had too many similar requests to add another on the pile. For patrons being served, librarians faced the challenge of assistance when many of the patrons phrased their inquiries in an oblique sort of way, hoping to conceal the track they were following. Public libraries in Los Angeles reported people actually lining up to get access to the *Who's Who*, an uncirculated reference guide, which was in hot demand. "Nobody is going to be happier than the staff members at the Appleton Public Library when the identity of radio's mysterious Mrs. Hush is revealed," a reporter wrote for a Wisconsin newspaper. "The library telephone rings dozens of times a day as radio listeners seek answers to quiz questions."

In Columbus, Ohio, Budd Sweeney, quizmaster of WHKC's *Housewives' I.Q.* was conducting his own "Mrs. Hush" contest by phoning one person per day in the hopes someone would provide the correct answer: "Who is the chief librarian of the Columbus Public Library?" One dollar was added to "the teapot fund" every day an incorrect answer was provided and the kitty grew to more than $100.

In Ohio, a reporter named J.D.R. for the *Canton Repository* attempted to decipher the clues as to the identity of Miss Hush, theorizing the solution as Polly Rutherford. Glenn Ford's wife, Eleanor Powell, was on a performance tour during the time of the contest. Because she was not publicly accessible during the weekly radio broadcasts, many theorized Powell was Miss Hush. One wild and false rumor that was quickly debunked was Evangeline Booth, former general of the Salvation Army. "If Evangeline Booth is 'Miss Hush,' her voice has certainly changed since the last time she addressed a Los Angeles audience," stated Lt. Col. Russell E. Clarke, a local Salvation Army head in Hollywood, California.

Tout sheets, which were flourishing on a number of New York newsstands, were reporting Evangeline Booth, which seemed at the time the most likely solution to the mystery. A sign on a newsstand at Sixth Avenue and 40th Street read, "Who is Miss Hush? Answer and complete explanation, $1.00." Bill Alexander of the *Chicago Star* warned people about the tip sheets being sold in the streets for $1.00, claiming that she was born on Christmas Day, was over the age of 30, and if those tips did not make sense of the weekly clues provided by the elusive "Miss

Hush," the Salvation Army was about to begin their annual drive. "Personally, we think the voice begins to cinema actress Jean Arthur," Alexander offering his own theory. "Reason? Just because it sounds like her. This info, worth $19,860 in prizes, is free to all *Star* subscribers." In New York, similar tip sheets were being sold, also suggesting Evangeline Booth.

For a few days, this "tip" was the hottest news to circulate the radio grapevine. Shortly after the newspapers ran with the suggestion that "Mrs. Hush" was Evangeline Booth, the Salvation Army ultimately went public and requested that inquiries regarding Booth be limited to the radio contest because hundreds of phone calls were tying up their switchboards. Ralph Edwards issued a public statement that Booth was incorrect and suggested people instead invest their dollar by sending it to the March of Dimes.

In Portland, Oregon, a woman wrote to the *Oregonian* proposing Flora Juliette Cooke, called "the grand old lady of education," as the mystery woman: "In regard to Miss Hush, here is what I have dug up instead of washing my windows which are badly in need of same, and such a nice day." *Coronet* magazine backed the same theory. When newspapers across the country theorized that her voice was not live, "substantiated" by a tape expert who claimed the voice of Miss Hush was provided via tape recording, the same kind that Bing Crosby was using, plus filter, according to a columnist for the same paper. "In case Miss Hush is about Miss Cooke's age, 82, it would be only sensible to use tape (a) because a woman that old, if she is in frail health, could hardly be depended upon to dash to a studio or remote control point every Saturday night, especially if she lives in a place where she might be kept indoors by blizzards, and because (b) if she lives in a city, neighbors who recognized her voice could easily watch her residence and see if engineers entered the place or if she left the house every week before the broadcast. If Miss Hush is Miss Cooke, who lives in crowded Chicago, the chances that she broadcasts live on the show are just about zero."

One columnist suggested Nellie Revell, who used to be on the network coast to coast three times a week, and her voice was known to millions. Mrs. O.G. Tyler of Oregon wrote to her local newspaper suggesting Frances Perkins. In Lock Haven, Pennsylvania, a local newspaper reporter for the *Pittsburgh Press* interviewed the former "Miss Hush" contest winner, Mrs. McCormick, who believed she knew the identity of the present "Miss Hush." Because of winning the earlier contest, she was not allowed to enter the new one. To the newspaper reporter, however, she did not hesitate to withhold her guess: Mary Garden, former world-famous opera star and now a vocal advisor in a Hollywood movie studio. Citing her reasons was because Miss Garden was single, made her professional debut on Friday the 13th, and took 20 curtain calls. McCormick did not mind passing along her clues to the newspaper but she refused vehemently to give advice on problems arising from winning the contest.

A display of prizes on stage for the Miss Hush contest.

According to one newspaper, McCormick admitted to having to divide her treasure trove with her sister, Mrs. William H. Harman, Jr., and a friend, Mrs. A.B. Timms, both of whom helped her solve the quiz last spring. Dividing prizes like an automobile, an airplane, a trailer, maid service for a year and three vacation trips was not an easy job. The women sold the articles they could not use and deposited the money, along with the $1,200 for the maid service, in a bank to be divided later. But after choosing the gifts each wanted, there was still the matter of a furnace, a diamond and ruby wristwatch, and a silver fox coat to be settled. The Internal Revenue Department solved another problem for them. It ordered each of the women to pay income taxes on about $4,000 worth of prizes.

Theories began appearing in print that "Miss Hush" was disguising her voice. Ralph Edwards addressed the issue by clarifying that she was indeed using her natural voice, without filters or any other mechanical contrivance. He insisted she was delivering her lines live from an undisclosed remote source. Cynics chose to ignore Edwards and insisted "Miss Hush" was transcribed. A long discussion in KGW's engineering room revealed the theory of a sound engineer: if Miss Hush broadcast live, then there was a low-pass filter in the circuit. Such a filter would pass only low frequencies, making her voice much lower than it was. The absence of the letter 's', which is a high frequency sound, in her speech, indicated a filter was used. Second, a disc recording could be used without announcing the Miss Hush portion was a transcription, since FCC rules said no electrical transcription announcement was required if a transcribed portion of a program was one minute or less. No needle scratch was heard when Miss Hush spoke, however.

The Public Library in Los Angeles and the library at UCLA phoned the producer of *Truth or Consequences* to state that people were standing in line to check out the reference book, *Who's Who*, which remained on the shelf as uncirculating reference. In Atlanta, Georgia, the reference department of Carnegie Library was kept busy. While the Hush family provided peak interest with radio listeners who thought they had the solution to the clues, the library staff was kept busy the remaining 38 weeks with a rash of lesser radio contests from other radio programs. "At least we outlasted New York City," said Miss Carrie Williams, head of the department. "The public library there closed its doors to all contestants long ago."

"We got so we were suspicious of all telephone calls," quoted Isabel Erlich, first reference assistant. "If someone asked another name for a syrup pitcher, we knew they were doing a picture puzzle. Nearly all the questions about history, songs, plays and people were for contests. And the quotations! But the one we weren't expecting was on abbreviations. The first time a call came for about a dozen we gave them readily, thinking we were helping a stenographer. But not fifty stenographers all wanting the same thing at five-minute intervals." As a result, many public libraries across the country suffering from the same effects of radio quiz programs were forced to limit their telephone service to short, factual information needed for a serious purpose. Reference departments were often understaffed and their first duty was to help those who were physically in the library, seeking assistance. According to Erlich, one day 377 people wanted to use the Current Biography set and as many waited their turn, they argued at the top of their lungs over the relative merits of everyone from Sister Kenny to Margaret Truman. "The phone calls were the worst trial," Erlich added. "They jammed the line so that our regular customers couldn't get us. One man who wanted the address of CARE, the European relief organization, said he got the busy signal for two days."

The mail, according to an NBC Press release, jumped from 3,000 letters the first week to an average of 15,000 per day. Mail addressed to the radio program was handled by an outside agency; all clerks were college graduates. Two employees at the radio station in Hollywood were temporarily relocated to help assist with the task of sifting through the incoming mail, deciphering which letters were addressed to *Truth or Consequences*, and which needed to be routed and delivered to other departments. Regardless of the statutes specified on the program, many people sent telegrams while others sent special deliveries. Columnist Marcia Winn in the *Chicago Tribune* reported that librarian Mrs. Mildred King was inundated with numerous people rushing into the library at noontime to research questions pertaining to the Miss Hush contest.

When Aline Mosby of the United Press questioned Ralph Edwards regarding the identity of "Miss Hush," he took a moment to address the commotion. "It's reached a point of frenzy," he explained. "My phone rings constantly. Somebody has to guess next week. I can't stand the strain…" The December 8 issue of *Time* magazine misquoted Edwards of saying: "Master of Ceremonies Ralph Edwards was desperately sick of the whole stunt. It had all started out as just a burlesque of giveaway programs, but 'Well, to my chagrin, people took it seriously. It's got out of hand. I wish we could start all over again from scratch." The statement was taken from part of the general conversation he had with a *Time* reporter in a telephone interview from his Norman hotel. "We were talking about giveaway prize contests in general," Edwards later defended, "and I said many of the radio quiz programs maintained the interest of the audience only because of the prizes they gave away. I also said that unless these prizes were given away intelligently or else for a worthy cause, it would be better for the radio industry if everybody would start their quiz programs over again from scratch."

In late November, on a radio comedy program, Jack Paar offered a take-off on the "Miss Hush" contest. Jack Dempsey, "Mr. Hush" on the radio program two years prior, was repeatedly hounded by people on the street – and reportedly at one time a crowd – who wouldn't believe he did not know who the current Miss Hush was. Only three people knew the answer to that question: Ralph Edwards, producer Joe Kay and engineer Al Paschall. Lewis Titterton, vice-president of radio of Compton Advertising, the agency that handled the program, reported the agency was being swamped with a number of phone calls, letters and telegrams but would not clarify how many exactly. The agency responded to each one personally, verifying they did not know her identity.

Ralph Edwards found himself the victim of a scam when a woman registered in a hotel in Shreveport, Louisiana, under the name of "Miss Hush." She explained that she had been doing the broadcasting from a farm nearby, but that the fire destroyed the house and she now needed a secret hideout. The hotel manager readily obliged and went to great extremes to make sure his honored guest had every possible comfort. "The bill," the manager was told, "is to be sent to Ralph

Edwards in Hollywood." Edwards received the bill and immediately launched an investigation, which proved the woman was a phony and was merely trying to capitalize on the nation's interest in the contest.

On November 27, columnist Ben Gross reported that "an enterprising Brooklyn gent – whose initials are E.F.M. – in a letter to this column, offers to disclose the identity of the mysterious 'Miss Hush,' for a cash consideration of $1,000. And he wishes it known that if he fails to name the right person, he will refund, 'without question, the money paid to me.' This is the latest in the list of rackety schemes which have arisen in the wake of the radio's most publicized guessing game. Ralph Edwards warns the public against all such schemes."

On the evening of November 29, the voice of "Miss Hush" was again heard and all three contestants failed to identify. Three new prizes added to the pot were Universal Electric blankets for every room in the house, an Electrolux vacuum cleaner, and Art Craft Venetian Blinds for every window in the house. Realizing that the contest could continue for weeks – possibly months – Edwards and the producers agreed to provide additional clues on the same evening. Her last name, the announcer explained over the air, had something to do with "crackers," and her vocation compares with one of the reindeers in St. Nick's Christmas team. This was almost a dead giveaway.

Martha Graham

Word on the Street is Martha Graham

Famed Hollywood columnist Jimmy Starr, against good principles, was reportedly the first person to break the news publicly – before the identity was revealed on the quiz program. Within 24 hours of Starr's syndicated column appearing in print, newspapers across the country began reporting the leak. Walter Winchell debunked the possibility that "Miss Hush" was Faith Baldwin in his column, then reported that "25 out of 25 persons in different sections of Los Angeles offered to tell us her name: M.G., which some radio columns in the East published days before. Miss Hush has the first handle as George Washington's wife. All I know is that's a heckuva way of sneaking into Hooper's Exclusive Gentleman's Club."

A reporter for the *Herald Express* in Los Angeles, California, conveyed in his December 3 column, "My phone has been ringing almost constantly with requests for the identity of radio's Miss Hush, personally, I think it is Martha Graham." The December 4 issue of the *Buffalo News* reported: "Sorry to spoil your party by naming Martha Graham as Miss Hush. Actually, we know no more about it than you and that name could be completely wrong. We're just guessing, same as you, so don't let it ruin your Christmas." Ralph Mahoney of *The Arizona Republic* commented on his December 4 "Tune In" column, "A lot of Phoenicians will have more than a cursory interest in *Truth or Consequences* Saturday. According to the telephone calls received by *The Arizona Republic*, everyone and his brother who listens to the program believes Miss Hush is Martha Graham, famous interpretive dancer."

The December 6 issue of *The Herald Leader* in Menominee, Michigan reported: "If ever a program was getting advance tips on the possibility of a boost of its Hooper rating, *Truth or Consequences* certainly has been doing so. It's all because of the Miss Hush stunt with plenty of folks indicating their intention to tune in NBC tonight to see if her identity is guessed in accordance with the widespread but unverified reports that she is Martha Graham, dancer." In Eau Claire, Wisconsin, *The Telegram* reported the same statement, verbatim. So did the *Palladium Times* in Oswego, New York, giving one to wonder if this was a press release deliberately sent out to local newspapers across the country. There was nothing Dave Alber/, in charge of the radio program's publicity campaign, could do to squash the rumors that were circulating in print, but could he have created such a leak?

A columnist for *Variety* remarked: "Jimmy Starr didn't make any friends or enhance his reputation as a snooper by divulging the identity of 'Miss Hush' in his pillar. It took him long enough to catch up with it as most of Hollywood guessed the lady's name more than a week ago. The charity angle must have meant nothing to him, the fact that the longer the contest runs the more money is collected for the March of Dimes. It's a safe guess that every columnist knew about 'Miss Hush' long before he did but sacrificed the 'scoop' in the interest of one of the most worthy charities of our time."

On the evening of December 6, *Truth or Consequences* reached what was probably the largest rating to date as a result of what many correctly predicted: someone was going to guess the identity of "Miss Hush." "With all of the hints given in preceding programs and especially with those revealed last on Saturday's broadcast," Al Paschall said, "it is more than likely that one of the three winning letter writers will give tell just who 'Miss Hush' is." The radio program originated that evening from the University of Oklahoma's south campus, sponsored by the campus American Legion Post 303. It was the first time that the quiz show would be presented at a university or college. (The American Legion post sponsored the appearance and arranged for two shows, besides the regular Saturday night broadcast. All performances would be held in the South Campus auditorium, which seated 7,500.) Press and newsreel agencies throughout the country, smelling the big break that the identity would be disclosed, made elaborate arrangements for the complete and immediate coverage and transmission of the news.

If no one guessed the correct name, additional hints given by "Miss Hush" herself would have been provided, but the contest never had to go any further. The first of what would have been three phone calls stuck pay dirt. Mrs. Ruth Annette Subbie, housewife, age 45, of 1712 Frederick Place, a narrow street on the West Side of Ft. Worth, Texas, identified "Miss Hush" as Martha Graham, the professional stage dancer. Edwards congratulated the contestant, hoping she would make a personal appearance on the radio program next week, and reminded the radio listeners of the cumulative prizes Ruth Subbie would soon be receiving, estimated at a value of $21,500. Later in the program, from 8:55 to 8:57 p.m., a live pickup from the New York apartment of Martha Graham, where the dancer and the NBC engineer who conducted her pickups during the contest, Harry Grelck, explained how they managed to keep her identity a secret even from members of their own families and friends.

Once the answer was out, Ruth Subbie's neighbors – apparently in tune with the program – began streaming into the house. Traffic was jammed in the 1700 block of Frederick Place. It seems when the fateful telephone call came, Mrs.

Subbie was listening to the radio in the living room. Her husband, Casimir, who traveled for an oil well chemical company in Texas and Oklahoma, was lying asleep, in the bedroom. The telephone was at his side. When the bell jangled, Mrs. Subbie said, she ran for the bedroom, suspecting that it might be the call she wanted most.

Within minutes following the quiz program, a neighborhood radio dealer contacted Subbie and rushed her off to a local radio station, to introduce her as the winner. Mrs. Subbie appeared on WBAP-820, the station she was listening to when Ralph Edwards called, in an exclusive interview with newscaster Larry Dupont. This wound up a hectic day for the middle-aged housewife which included being fitted for a complete new Hart, Schaffner and Marx suit and topcoat and receiving a Luscombe airplane. In the interview, Subbie stressed the fact that she was not a "professional" in the contest field but had been working at it several years as a hobby. "A hobby," she added, "that is particularly suited to a housewife."

The letters and the dimes poured in.

During the local broadcast, Subbie admitted with pride that she honestly worked the personality of Martha Graham, together with a number of others out of the little "Second for Santa" verse several weeks before the news columnists found her. At first, Subbie was not fully convinced it was Graham that Edwards had in mind, until the week prior to the phone call, when Graham gave the clue, "Well, I think I'll eat a cracker and go to bed." It would later come out that Ralph Edwards was initially upset at the 45-year-old Texas housewife, spending much time talking her out of making any mention on the air that she was a habitual contestant of radio contests.

To please officials at the AFRA, who insisted "Miss Hush" had to be a member of the union, Edwards and crew registered her anonymously.

Ruth Annette Subbie receiving her prizes.

"Since I already had the dancer idea from Clement Moore's poem *The Night Before Christmas*, which originates the eight reindeer; the Graham-Paige car; notations after the word 'wreath' of her many wonderful achievements and successes in the creation and presentation of the dance; and 'ball' taken out of the word ballet – the word Cracker was the magic word to me which spun around in my mind and came up immediately with Graham cracker," Subbie explained. "Then I knew I had her."

After the interview on WBAP, she was given a box of Duz as a remembrance. The local radio dealer, however, had ulterior intentions. Before the local radio station completed the interview with their new local celebrity, the radio dealer presented her with an additional prize -- a portable radio valued at around $37.

Hours later, when local newspaper reporters asked Mrs. Subbie how she figured out the now-nationally famous Martha Graham, the contestant confessed that she had not known of the dancer until a week prior. She first "ran across" Graham, she said, in a book of biography after scanning volumes of "Who's Who in America" and "Famous American Women." Subbie was an ardent participator in contests for almost two decades. In previous contests she won a round-trip vacation to San Francisco and a $100 cash prize.

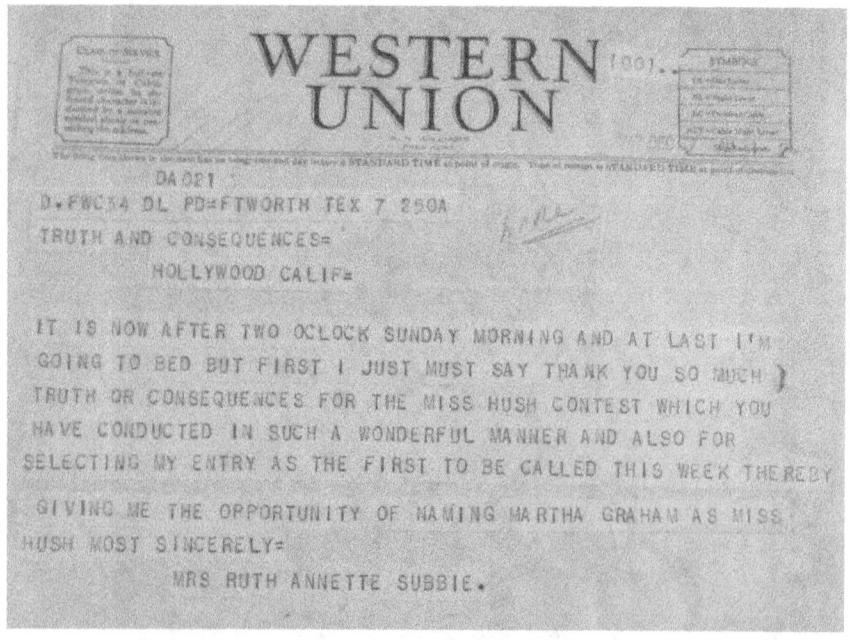

Telegram from Ruth Annette Subbie to Ralph Edwards.

Local coverage of her success was nothing compared to the national coverage she would receive by morning. Her personal life certainly went public that evening. If radio listeners did not know who Martha Graham was, they certainly knew who Ruth Subbie was. Newspaper reporters asked questions, photos were taken of her for the papers, and she would not get to bed until close till three in the morning. In a classy move, she took a moment and thanked Ralph Edwards for the contest. Time-stamped 2:50 a.m., she had Western Union send a telegram addressed to Ralph Edwards in Hollywood, California.

Ruth Annette Subie signs officially as recipient of the prizes awarded.

Rather than tout Ruth Subbie's success in the trade columns, newspapers were quick to point out that Ruth Subbie would be plagued with the trouble of income tax on her winnings, a possible $5,000 – roughly one-quarter of her winnings. In Washington, an Internal Revenue spokesman said the fact that Ruth Subbie planned to share her winnings with members of the family did not alter the fact that the prizes are to be regarded as income to her, and therefore taxable. Under Texas law, the income of a married couple was divided equally between them for taxation purposes.

Some cried foul as a result of the "leak" in newspapers across the country. Mrs. Elizabeth Mullin of 31 West Main Street, Hummelstown, Pennsylvania, told a reporter for the *Harrisburg Telegraph* that she came within a telephone call of winning the prizes. "My guess was going to be Martha Graham," she explained. "There was so much talk about who Miss Hush was that I was convinced that was who she was. I was notified by a Los Angeles NBC studio employee in a phone conversation earlier that afternoon that I was on stand-by because I was third on the list."

Two days following the conclusion of the broadcast, on December 8, *Variety* reported: "It would have been more surprising if the lady in Fort Worth had not tabbed the voice as that of Miss Graham, who had been identified in columns and tips by other sources."

List of prizes
1. 1947 Buick Super Convertible from the Howard Automobile Company.
2. Bendix Home Laundry with washer, dryer and automatic iron.*
3. Round-trip ticket for two via United Airlines to Honolulu and a suite of rooms for two weeks at the Matson Lines Royal Hawaiian Hotel.
4. $2,000 Columbia House Trailer, fully equipped. **
5. $1,000 diamond and ruby Bulova wristwatch.
6. RCA Victor radio phonograph combination plus a new 1948 RCA Victor Television receiver and a library of 100 Red Seal records.
7. I.J. Fox $1,500 full-length Beaver fur coat.
8. Luscombe Silvaire all-metal airplane from Dallas, Texas.
9. $2,000 in cash.
10. $1,000 Popular Mechanics Home Workshop with a library of Popular Mechanics Instruction books.
11. Servel Silent Gas Refrigerator.
12. Sherwin-Williams cover-the-earth trademark paints will paint your house inside and out.
13. Hart Schaffner and Marx suit and topcoat for every adult man and woman in the family.
14. Tappan Gas kitchen range.
15. 13-cubic foot Jacobs Home Freezer, product of Jacobs Wind Electric Company, Minneapolis, filled with Birdseye Frozen Foods.
16. $1,000 J.R. Wood and Sons Art-carved diamond ring.
17. Fitzgibbons Steel Residence Heating boiler to heat your entire home complete with tank saver to furnish year-round domestic hot water.

18. Houseful of Willett golden burl solid maple furniture to completely furnish your dining room, two bedrooms and living room.
19. Universal Electric Blankets for every bed in your house.
20. Electrolux Vacuum cleaner with all attachments.
21. Art-craft Venetian blinds throughout your entire house.

Prizes offered and rejected because they were "too small" were a pressure cooker, and a year's subscription to the Candy of the Month Club. A Remington Model 7 Typewriter and a weekend at the Waldorf were set among the next prizes to be added to the pot had the contest continued an additional week. Had the contest continued, additional prizes slated were a Knabe Piano, the Servel Silent Gas Refrigerator, and a Piper Cub airplane. (The latter two became prizes for later contests.)

Oops! A radio flash about the "Miss Hush" contest stated that the total prizes were valued at $22,500 – "The largest prize in radio history." The press release was incorrect, however, but many newspapers ran with the story anyway. The Celotex Corp. prize (they donated the house, property and exquisite furnishings won by the sender of the "Arrest Cancer, It's Wanted for Murder" slogan) was larger. The house cost $10,000; the lot $1,500, the furniture $18,500. In short, $30,000.

* Described as a "Bendix Home Washer, Mangle and Iron" on the broadcast of October 25, the Bendix Company submitted a complaint about the use of the word "mangle" in reference to their give-away and requested that the article be called the Bendix Automatic Home Ironer in future broadcasts.

** It was requested by the manufacturer in advance that when a mention of the trailer was made on the radio program, donated by the Columbia Trailer Company, to add "of Glendale, California," since there was some confusion in the past with other trailer companies of the same name. This was at the request of E.R. Shaw, President of the Columbia Trailer Company.

Within a week of Mrs. Subbie winning the contest, the Fort Worth post office experienced another headache during the Christmas rush period. Her mailing address had been given out over the radio and reprinted in multiple newspapers across the country. The Subbie mailbox at 1712 Frederick bore the brunt of a daily avalanche of letters from all over the United States and three from foreign countries: Italy, England and Scotland. Most of the mail was congratulatory in nature, but some letters asked for more. There was an offer to invest $5,000 in a farm in Pennsylvania, a Colorado mother wrote in that her home could use the free paint job Mrs. Subbie had coming, and another woman offered Mrs. Subbie to relieve her of the Buick convertible, "because my car is falling apart." One woman in Oklahoma City, however, was willing to compromise. She said she would accept Mrs. Subbie's old washing machine and refrigerator in view of the fact that the Fort Worth housewife has won new ones.

Until she and her husband departed for Hollywood to appear on *Truth or Consequences*, Subbie's phone rang almost incessantly since she won the contest. People reportedly walked into her house without knocking, one claiming they paid her a visit "just to get a look at you."

None of the smaller trinkets appear to have been mailed to Subbie, for fear of getting lost in the mail. It was the duty of the companies that manufactured the products and services to follow through with delivery. Among the first items she received were the two suits and two topcoats from Hart Schaffner and Marx which Casimir (her husband) and she wore when they went out to California to attend the radio broadcast. The Buick Super Convertible was the next item to be delivered, yellow in color, provided by the Sanford Webb Motor Company in Fort Worth, and both the diamond and ruby Bulova watch and the J.R. Wood and Sons diamond ring were, as Mrs. Subbie confessed in a letter to Al Paschall, "perfect."

By January 5, however, she wrote a letter to Paschall explaining that while most of the prize people had contacted her to arrange for delivery of promised products and services, five had yet to contact her. These included the Columbia Home Trailer, the RCA Victor Radio and Television, the Servel Silent Gas Refrigerator, the Tappan Gas Kitchen Range and the Electrolux sweeper. She confessed that she did not have need for many of the prizes and had intentions of selling them – especially considering the income tax she had to pay. Mr. R.J. Wickel of the Fitzgibbons Steel Residence Heating Boiler had contacted her via letter, offering her $250.00, in lieu of the boiler heating unit, which she gladly accepted knowing that the Internal Revenue in Dallas was going to have a field day with her winnings.*

After contacting Charles Steinglass, the attorney for the quiz program, Subbie was appreciative that, combined with his expertise on the subject, and the $2,000 check, helped to keep the Internal Revenue at Dallas at bay. She received only the Buick Convertible and the four articles of clothing before January 1, allowing her to break down the rest of the prizes as income for the next calendar year. As allowed under the State of Texas because of the Community Property Law, Casimir Theodore and Ruth Annette Subbie, Sr., filled out a joint return for their winnings. The Sanford Webb Motor Company and the A. Davis Clothiers provided both the wholesale and retail values of the items. Since Procter & Gamble paid the wholesale price, she sought Steinglass' advice on which she was to list on her income tax return.

	Wholesale	Retail
Buick Convertible	$2,093.36	$2,662.09
1 man's top coat	$38.50	$70.00
1 ladies' top coat	$33.00	$54.75
1 man's suit	$38.50	$68.50
1 ladies' suit	$29.00	$49.75
	$2,232.36	$2,905.09

Ruth Annette Subbie on stage to receive her prizes.

* This was the same Mr. Wickel who was singled out by Ralph Edwards to be the recipient of the one-half piece of the $1,000 bill which precipitated the deluge of books sent to him by radio listeners, and for which Edwards still retained a middle front row seat reserved for him by a slip cover enstamped with "Mr. Wickel."

Because the pyramid of prizes, which she won, were donations to the March of Dimes, a charitable drive, there was an allowable $5,000 deduction. This did not stop Ruth Subbie from selling a number of other items. She drove the car for a few months and later sold it. She took one short trip in the Columbia Home Trailer, then sold it. She took possession of the Bendix Home Washer and mangle, but not the dryer. She had no need for it and wanted to keep her winnings low enough to ease her tax situation. She never accepted the trip to Honolulu. She kept the Servel Silent Gas Refrigerator, the Sherwin-Williams paint job, the jewelry, the furniture, the electric blankets, the Electrolux Cleaner, the venetian blinds, the Tappan Gas Kitchen Range, and RCA Victor Radio Phonograph combination and Television receiver and 100 Red Seal records. With the assistance of Al Paschall, Subbie was able to convince Maurice W. Rybeck, advertising director at the I.J. Fox Company, to personally split the $1,500 beaver coat into three coats of $500 each, for herself and her two daughters. The arrangement was made personally over the phone with I.J. Fox, who gave no hesitation for her special request. (Little did either of them know that it would be one of Fox's last phone calls – he died a few days later.) She kept the Jacobs Home Freezer filled with Birdseye frozen foods until the food was exhausted, then she sold it. She sold the Luscombe Silvaire Airplane and before receiving the Popular Mechanics Home Work Shop with a library of Popular Mechanics Instruction books, she already had a prospective buyer.

On the evening of December 13, 1947, Ruth Subbie, along with her husband, appeared on *Truth or Consequences*. She and her husband arrived by plane to California with four days at the Knickerbocker Hotel, and all expenses paid by the quiz show. Edwards announced that over 700,000 letters had been received and over $600,000 had been sent into the March of Dimes as a result of the contributions. (One early source reported $350,000 raised, with an average of 50 cents per donation. Columnist John Crosby reported that the Miss Hush contest comprised 90 percent of the mail received by NBC's Hollywood office.

Following her appearance on *Truth or Consequences*, Subbie told reporters, "I listen to my radio every day while I am doing the housework, and I make it a habit to enter every contest when I hear about. Then I also buy women's magazines and submit entries to all contests announced in them." She said she entered her first contest eleven years prior and won an electric roaster.

Ben Gross of the syndicated column, "Radio Listening In," questioned whether the radio contest was fair. "The critics of the competition argue that Miss Graham was not widely enough known to have served as the mysterious Miss Hush," Gross wrote. "Certainly, no one should doubt that the contest was conducted in a meticulously honest manner. But it was supposedly designed for the participation of as great a number as possible… the inhabitants of the smallest crossroads settlements as well as the sophisticates of the metropolitan centers. Was Martha Graham the ideal choice for such a competition? In the opinion of this reporter, the answer is an emphatic 'no.' Although she had appeared in many recitals, has a devoted group of disciples and has received considerable publicity in newspapers and magazines, she is still essentially the idol of a limited cult. Artists, writers, connoisseurs of the modernistic dance and other intellectuals know her very well. But until Saturday night, when her name was spread from coast-to-coast on *Truth or Consequences*, the overwhelming majority of Americans had never heard of her."

Ralph Edwards and the sponsors of the program might have realized this themselves. This might have been why, on the evening of November 29, when it seemed that the contest might run on for many more weeks, Martha Graham gave such clear clues as to her identity that no radio writer could afford to ignore them. Many hesitated for the benefit of the charity angle, but others sought the glory of a scoop. So it was not surprising that during the week leading up to the revelation, columns throughout the country practically spelled out the correct answer to the puzzle. This also killed any chances for schemers and con men to profit from the quiz program.

A few days following the conclusion of the "Miss Hush" contest, Mrs. Dorothy Oliver of 166 Pleasant Street in Marblehead, Massachusetts, won first prize in a national soap contest, conducted by the Proctor & Gamble Company, the same company sponsoring *Truth or Consequences*. She won $26,000 in cash, surpassing the total of the Miss Hush contest winnings, but news of her winning was overshadowed by newspaper columnists across the country who, caught up in the fervor of the chase, chose to cover the Miss Hush contest instead.

As for *Truth or Consequences*, the second Hush contest was a success. According to the *Union Sun Journal*, the program hit a growth spurt in the Hooper program report, jumping up to tenth from fifteenth. The program had the normal rating of 15.2 percent on October 18, when Miss Hush was first introduced. The December 6 broadcast had 26.7 percent according to Hooper (26.8 according to *Printer's Ink*). The funds raised by both "Miss Hush" contests raised more than $1,000,000 for the fight against polio. (Edwards decided on the March of Dimes because of his dearest friend, Mel Vickland, with whom he roomed in his early days in radio. They married at the same time and each was the father of three children. Vickland was stricken with infantile paralysis a few years later and was paralyzed from the hips down ever since. Vickland was a radio singer at the time but ever since the tragedy, he was a member of Edwards' writing staff.)

With all the publicity Martha Graham received as a result of the contest, it was only natural that she receive offers from three film studios to appear in movies and/or sign over the screen rights for a biographical picture about her career. She rejected all of the offers, insisting that her career should remain on the stage.

Variety took to praise days after the contest ended. "If the radio industry were to make a showmanship award for 1947 its choice would have to fall on Ralph Edwards. You may argue that his 'Miss Hush' contest is not new, being a continuation of what he has done twice before, but we challenge you to name a more outstanding stunt. Last year, we believe, the most talked-of device was Jack Benny's 'humming quartet,' and the year before it was Fred Allen's Senator Claghorn. This year, or more accurately the first half of the 1947-48 season, would have been devoid of anything spectacular had not Edwards revived, shall we say, the 'Hush' gimmick with its bountiful giveaway. True it didn't take a lot of doing nor was it creatively a killer-diller but it must be admitted that he far outdistanced the field in hyping a facet of show business that has shown signs of fraying around the edges. We might even say that in all our years of radio we know of no stunt or exploitation device that has whipped up the interest generated by the late 'Miss Hush' contest. Yeah, we know about the Orson Welles Martian scare of some years ago but it came and went, so to speak... We have no plaques to give away, Ralph, but the industry-at-large owes you some kind of an award for perking up lazy dials. And we know of not one in the industry who begrudges him the success that crowned his efforts. He's that kind of a guy, believe us."

Not to be outdone, Dauphin County employees in Pennsylvania had their own "Hush-Hush" contest to add further stimulus to the already exciting activity in connection with their annual Christmas party on Monday, December 22. County employees were asked to guess the identity of the person described in a rhyme which was liberally distributed among all the county employees. To add the touch of the recent nationwide radio contest, the rhyme was read daily at 11 a.m. over the Courthouse by the telephone operators. Each day an additional clue was provided to help listeners identify the mysterious person. At the party, names of those attending would be drawn from a hat and the person who identified the identity of "Hush-Hush" would receive a prize given by the committee in charge of the arrangements. If guessed incorrectly, another contestant was drawn from the hat until a winner was declared.

Left to Right: Bill Goodwin, Jack Benny, Ralph Edwards and Eddie "Rochester" Anderson.

Chapter 8
Hubert Smith and a Christmas to Remember

It became an annual tradition on *Truth or Consequences* to offer Christmas-themed "consequences." Capturing the magic and good will of the season, Ralph Edwards departed from the norm on the broadcast of December 15, 1945. As a special Christmas feature, the evening's guests were three children all under six years of age. One of the children was a Negro child who said that the father in his family was a Pullman Porter or "Red Cap." The children were asked how they planned to celebrate the holiday, the type of decorations on display in their home, and what they wanted for Christmas. Ralph Edwards recited the story of the Nativity with a flavor of Christmas music and the singing of carols. Following the touching narrative, Edwards made reference to Santa Claus and the jolly old man arrived in person, on stage, to take the children into his confidence and assured them that they would get the gifts they wanted come Christmas. (Of course, Edwards had the power to arrange delivery of the very same gifts on Christmas Eve.)

For the broadcast of December 22, *Truth or Consequences* arranged for a solider taken direct from his ship of debarkation in California, to be flown to his home in Wayne, Michigan, just in time to walk in upon his family during the broadcast.

Transportation was arranged from the airport to the soldier's home and the family reunion was picked up by mobile unit, as he stood on the street just outside his own house. The quiz program arranged with a neighbor of the soldier's family to borrow the radio from the soldier's home, to hide the engineer who was attending to the pickup of the soldier's report, and to be sure that the family was at home on that particular evening at that particular time. Edwards explained all this on the air for the benefit of the radio listeners, and then switched to Wayne, Michigan, where Ed Bailey, the engineer on the pickup, arranged for Al Teale, the lucky soldier who received a trip home for the holidays, to be broadcast coast-to-coast.

During the eight-minute segment, the audience listened in to the soldier's first reactions to getting home as he stood outside his home and then finally on the perch from where he described seeing his wife and child through the window. The microphone he used was hidden in a large bouquet of flowers so that when he did surprise his wife, her first remarks were caught over the air without her seeing the microphone. There was then a two-way conversation between the soldier, his wife and his child, and Ralph Edwards. For the concluding part of the homecoming, the engineer came into the open and Christmas Carolers (part of Ralph Edwards' arrangements) were on hand outside to serenade the couple on their reunion. The soldier then told his wife of the gifts which *Truth or Consequences* had him bring home: a Sentinel Radio, to replace the one which the neighbor was instructed to borrow (to keep the wife from listening to the broadcast and ruining the surprise); an order for delivery of a Bendix washing machine; all kinds of gifts for the child; and a variety of things for the house. Then, in the two-way conversation, Ralph Edwards gave the soldier a gift of his own… a $500 Victory Bond.

Fan mail poured in to the program, exceeding that of the Mr. Wickel stunt from 1944.

"Our family listens regularly to *Truth or Consequences* and enjoy it immensely. However, I feel that a special commendation should be given you for Sunday night's performance wherein you had the children on stage and told them the story of Christmas. I am what some people call a 'hard-boiled banker,' but I must confess that I have come to the conclusion that we have tried everything else and the world still experiences conflict. Perhaps if we tried more of the type of entertainment, which you featured Sunday night, a different feeling would take place in the hearts of men and then we could look forward to a more lasting peace."

—Stephen H. Fifield, Vice-President of the Barnett National Bank, Jacksonville, Florida

"This letter is to thank you and those responsible for your Christmas broadcasts overseas, especially appreciated in Japan. My son who is in the Army in Nagoya, wrote me how the boys enjoyed these programs, and they all think you are 'swell.' Thank you again."

—Elsa M. Johnson, Croton Falls, New York

"After listening to your program last night, I felt it my duty to write you and tell how both my wife and I enjoyed your splendid reading of the Birth of Christ and the Christmas season."

—Jesse M. Pouch, Sr., of the Pouch Drapery and Upholstering Company, Anderson, Indiana

Al Teale greets his wife at the door.

Al Teale and his wife.

The Teale family gather after the surprise reunion and radio broadcast.

Christmas carolers outside the Teale home.

A year later, Ralph Edwards reprised his story of the Nativity for the broadcast of December 21, 1946. As with the prior rendition, one of the children was a Negro child and Ralph Edwards mentioned that color, race and creed made no difference to Santa Claus. This time, the children not only received appropriate gifts, but their parents received special merchandise as well. Added to the scheme, all of the children in the studio audience received toys. Ralph Edwards narrated what he hoped would be an annual Christmas tradition, accompanied by music and carolers, about the "Birthday of Jesus." But the stunt he pulled off during the Christmas of 1947 topped them all.

It was the evening of December 20, 1947. *Truth or Consequences* recently concluded another "Miss Hush" contest, Edwards tricked contestants into taking two live seals home for the night (for a $500 prize of Easter Seals) and following a steady stream of DUZ commercials, Ralph Edwards delivered a holiday message that set the stage for the remaining 23 minutes of the program, with no commercial interruption. "Yes, it's here again. For the past week you've been going over that gift list and maybe most of your purchases, but now on the threshold in the big week of the year, with wreaths in the window, holly on the door, with a jolly old man with the long white whiskers fattening up his reindeer for the big trip down... There's no denying it, Christmas is here!" Edwards proclaimed. "And come Thursday morning, the bells will be ringing in all the churches, the kids will be laughing in all the houses and most everyone in their own way will be celebrating the reason for Christmas, the doctrine of peace on Earth, goodwill toward men. And... we got to thinking what an ironic thing it is that many of those who helped give peace the real meaning of the word, will be doing their celebrating from a bed or a wheelchair in a veteran's hospital. And I wonder if each one of them can know and feel in their hearts just how grateful we are. So fellas in hospitals all over the country, this next consequence is for you."

For the holiday season, Ralph Edwards and Ed Bailey, the producer of the program, established a special three-way set-up from the Long Beach Naval Hospital, in Long Beach, California, with a pick-up from several locations in Greeneville, Tennessee. Through this three-way set-up, a wounded veteran in the hospital, Hubert Clark Smith, known to his friends as H.C., found himself a contestant on the radio quiz program.

Born in 1927, Hubert was a native of Greeneville, Tennessee. When he was old enough to enter service during the War, he asked his parents for permission. They hesitated at first but later figured it would be better to volunteer than wait to be drafted. He joined the Navy where he spent three years working on a minesweeper and on the USS Monongahela, an auxiliary oiler. His service in the war ended prematurely when Hubert and a friend hitched a ride back to the Naval Base and the driver of the vehicle hit a utility truck that was working on the road. The force of the crash caused Hubert to hit his head on the roof of the automobile, breaking his neck. Before the automobile came to a standstill, Hubert's body had been thrown from the car and found on the pavement. He was promptly discharged from service and returned to the United States as a patient of the Long Beach Naval Hospital. He was paralyzed from the neck down and doctors gave him one chance in a million that he would ever get better. While most of America was sitting by the fire with their family and enjoying good health, Hubert, at the age of 19, was among the many war casualties who were lying in a hospital bed. And he was a long way from home, family and friends from Greeneville.

Hubert Clark Smith

"I knew I was to be on the program, but of course I didn't realize to the extent I would be involved," Hubert recalled in an interview with Chuck Schaden in 1988. "I had a previous call from one of Mr. Edwards' associates that they would like for me to be a contestant on the program."

His appearance on the radio program was the result of weeks of scheming and planning. The question he was supposed to answer correctly was "Why is a lazy husband like a Model T Ford?" Hubert was unable to answer correctly. The answer Edwards was looking for was "Because both are shiftless." As a consequence, Hubert had to go along with the joke of pretending that he was wandering the streets of Greeneville on Christmas Eve. A number of engineers were stationed in Greeneville to broadcast live from the old George R. Lane Store, traffic sounds from Main Street, cut-ins from the high school Christmas party, and the ringing of the bells of Asbury Church. Hubert was able to exchange brief conversation with friends providing warm wishes.

Among his high school friends was Robert Parks, who reminded Hubert about the explosion they made in Mrs. Rhymer's chemistry class. Hal Neas mentioned the big football games they used to play. Bill Gammon told how he and Hubert used to shoot firecrackers in the study hall. Mr. Gilland, the principal at Chuckey-Doak High School, told Hubert that, "We're thinking of you all the time. The gang's all here with a happy tear in their eyes for you. Hurry and get well and Merry Christmas."

In Asbury Church, Ida Ripley was playing the organ and Rev. M. Guy Fleenor, spoke: "I have always thought about and preached about the joy of giving and how much more blessed it is to give than to receive. But tonight, I find genuine reason for joy in receiving… in receiving back into our midst one of our dearest friends, H.C. Smith. And whether by radio's miracle or in our dreams, H.C. has never left our hearts… and prayers that went with you into war will bring you back to us again to share the peace you have helped make possible."

By this time, Hubert Smith was trying to hold back the tears. With friends in Tennessee to back him, Hubert led them in singing a rendition of "Silent Night." But the best was yet to come. He heard from his grandparents but he had yet to hear from his mother and father. As it turned out, they were in the Long Beach Naval Hospital, surprising the unsuspecting lad. Hubert was crying in a manner that he was almost speechless. This followed with a reunion with his girl, Lila Morrell, two years his senior, who he would later marry. During the program she told Edwards and the radio listeners that she was an operator for the Inter-Mountain Telephone Company, "but the number that I want best is H.C."

In arranging for Hubert's reunion, Edwards was able to talk to Hubert's mother into flying to California. She had never flown before and she was scared to death the entire time. She and her husband operated the Greeneville Bus Station for 50 years and on the program, Edwards explained how he arranged to have their employer hire substitute workers in order for Hubert's parents to come to California.

Near the end of the program, Edwards addressed all the servicemen in all the military hospitals. "This is your moment, too, fellows," he said, "because your parents and wives and children and sweethearts, in their minds and hearts, are thinking that they, too, are there with you. And that's what your hometown is thinking right now, too, boys. Small towns. Big cities. That's what they're thinking, and don't think it is just at Christmastime, either. It's every day. It's just that with all this talk about peace on Earth at Christmas time, we wanted you to know in this special way that the peace you fought to give us… we are going to fight to keep."

The holiday offering prompted a number of letters from radio listeners – supposedly hundreds, if not thousands. One letter was addressed simply to "H.C." – no state, no city, no hospital name, no nothing, just H.C. –sent from the post office in Greeneville and it went directly to Hubert's hospital bed in Long Beach, California. No delay. No dead letter office. No "Return to Sender" stamped on it.

"I received a number of cards and letters and some of the people, local groups in California, visited me and gave me gifts," Hubert later recalled. "Of course, a few months later, more or less as people went on with their daily activities, I didn't hear anything more until a number of years later when a record was released to individual stations for reruns and again I started receiving a number of phone calls." The reruns Hubert Smith recalled were probably as a result of a follow-up on *The Ralph Edwards Show* in the early fifties.

Fred Carney, the sound engineer who arranged for the connection at the military hospital that evening, later recalled that in all the years he worked on *Truth or Consequences*, "The one which touched me most deeply was that in which a paraplegic boy in Long Beach was reunited by a three-way remote with his hometown friends and in his hospital room with his mother, father and girlfriend. The boy even heard carols sung in the church where he had attended. There were tears in my eyes, in the engineers and in the eyes of the other patients."

A total of 1,003 complimentary letters, cards and telegrams were received following the 1947 Christmas program. A sample best representing the overall consensus from radio listeners, and the types of people who submitted their feedback, is reprinted below.

"I have just heard one of the most inspiring programs I have heard in a long time. It was your wonderful program this evening. When you took that soldier boy back to his home town by radio and then – that reunion with his parents and sweetheart. I just wanted to thank you for this heart-warming program and wish you a most joyous Christmas."

—G.C. Robberson, First Methodist Church, Ashland, Nebraska

"I served in the Armed Forces during the First World War, was at one time Chairman of the State of Washington Hospitalization Committee, was for 12 years adjutant of Seattle Post No. 1, the American Legion. In World War II, I was a Field Director of the American Red Cross, and should be immune, but the program which took us to the Long Beach Hospital, and to Greenville, Tennessee, brought tears to the eyes of both my wife and myself."

—Harry Weingarten, The Northwest Camp & Hospital Council, American Red Cross

"Your program has just gone off the air and I have such a lump in my throat that I can hardly think straight enough to write you this letter. I have never been so impressed in all my life as I was from the fine thing you did tonight. I am sure all veterans join me in saying thank you very, very much."

—Edwin F. Strasser, Commander, Richard Lahmer Post 5178, V.F.W.

"Probably I feel the more deeply about this tonight, since I must now go ahead with my preparation for the final rites for G.I. Charles F. Webb, set for tomorrow afternoon. His father came this evening with Charles' sister from Decatur, Illinois, and brother from Manly, Iowa. And they told me so many things about the young fellow, who in '44 celebrated Christmas in the States, and was killed in action, in the aftermath of the Battle of the Bulge, in Belgium, January 23, 1945. I do not think I needed this evening's extra 'spur' to make of tomorrow's service one of real appreciation of the service and sacrifice so many of our fine young men rendered to help bring understanding and peace to our troubled world, -- but be sure, I just can't fail now!"

—Benjamin T. Schwab, Minister of the Congregational Christian Church, Madrid, Iowa

Hubert C. Smith 1947 broadcast three 78 rpm phonographs of Christmas Show.

Following the radio broadcast, Hubert Smith partially recouped from his injuries. Both surgery and physical therapy helped improve Hubert's condition. He remained a quadriplegic for the remainder of his life and required assistance in daily activities. He needed a walker to get around until the day he died. Hubert did in fact marry Lyla Morrell, who remained his lifelong partner in marriage until her death from cancer in 1973. After he returned home in the late forties, Hubert attended Tusculum College and majored in mathematics and accounting, with hopes to become a CPA. His dream was never realized and he settled with managing a large farm in the small community. Through physical therapy Hubert overcame his handicap and was able to walk using a special walker, drive around using a special vehicle around the farm and ran his own business raising Angus beef on the farm. "Despite his injuries, he was a great example of determination and positive attitude," his sister-in-law, Mary Hartman, told the local newspaper, upon his death in 2006. Following his death, Hubert C. Smith left the majority of his money to the local College for an endowed scholarship fund under his name. The scholarship continues – every year Mary Hartman receives numerous cards and notes from students.

Santa Claus stunt from December 13, 1947.

For Christmas 1947, Mary A. Lyons of Los Angeles, nicknamed "The Christmas Box Lady," was presented this package labeled "Do not open until Christmas, 1948." She returned to the program a year later, opened the package and found inside another box labeled, "Do not open until Christmas, 1949." She returned to the program every year until the broadcast of January 2, 1951, when she received her prize.

Mr. and Mrs. Harry Dewey volunteered to drive 3,000 miles in three weeks in order to win a new car. The Deweys were unaware at first that their "trip" consisted of going around the block by their Los Angeles home, and had three weeks to accomplish the task.

Chapter 9
This is Your Life, Lawrence Tranter

In the aftermath of World War II, there were many ex-G.I.'s recuperating from battle wounds in military hospitals; a percentage emotionally paralyzed, despairing of readjustment to civilian life. Having tapped the resources of *Truth or Consequences* to assist in the war effort, there was now a fresh opportunity to help in a post-war era. Little did Ralph Edwards know that a "good gesture" act for one particular contestant, physically crippled, would ultimately lead to the creation of another successful radio/television program, *This is Your Life*.

"Shortly after the end of World War II, General Omar Bradley, impressed by our bond efforts, asked if we could help with the disabled veterans, particularly the paraplegics," Ralph Edwards later recalled. "The hospital doctors told us many were afraid to go home for fear they wouldn't be accepted and properly cared for." Known as the "invisible wounds of war," the result of prolonged exposure to combat-related stress, many of the wounded were depressed and reluctant – ashamed – to have family and friends see them in their debilitating condition. Edwards had multiple discussions with Al Paschall and the idea men to create a means by which the radio program could offer a second chance for veterans to advance their lives beyond a hospital bed, and double as a public service message to radio listeners from coast-to-coast.

Producer Al Paschall

Producer Al Paschall

A paraplegic at Birmingham General Hospital in Van Nuys, California, Lawrence Tranter, was selected as the first honoree. (It was at the suggestion of a doctor at the Rehabilitation Department of Veterans Hospitals, that a soldier paralyzed from the waist down be selected.) The doctors and psychiatrists were in full support that the radio program try to encourage paraplegics to talk about their past and welcome their new future. The public needed to know the reason why the wounded, in both heart and body, were fearful of returning to their home and native communities because they felt a lack of acceptance. "We selected a paraplegic soldier from a Navy hospital in California, researched his story, and had him brought to our stage in Hollywood in a wheel chair," Edwards later recalled. "We decided to present a young ex-Marine, Lawrence Tranter, of Murray, Utah, on *Truth of Consequences* and surprise him with a show of love and pride from all his family and school pals, his boss at the drug store and his favorite teacher."

On the evening of April 27, 1946, 21-year old Lawrence Tranter, weighing a mere 91 pounds, confined to a wheelchair, paralyzed from the waist down as a result of wounds he suffered on Luzon, appeared on stage as a contestant. Mentally, prior to the radio broadcast, he was close to death. Physically, he wasn't much better. His only control was over his fingers, which he could move freely. As usually happened when a special contestant had been "set up" in advance, he couldn't answer the question and therefore had to pay the consequences: an emotional revisit of his past. One by one, old friends, family and neighbors, were reunited with him on stage – beginning with the chief clerk of his draft board. The profile of a returning hero was dramatized through a series of dramatic flashbacks with leading events and personalities who played a part in Tranter's life from his high school days, through his induction into service. One scene dramatized the day of his birth. The appearances of friends and family were a complete surprise to Tranter. Mrs. Louise Erickson of the Murray, Utah, draft board at the time when he was inducted in 1943, spoke to him in behalf of the late Mrs. Glen Howe, who was chairman of the board when Tranter was called, but had since died. Mr. Varion Morteson, the high school principal who gave Lawrence his high school diploma spoke praise of the student who impressed his teachers. Irving Olsen, Junior Madsen and Orlan Parker, friends who Lawrence used to "gang up" at Hammond's Ice Cream Parlor back in Murray, Utah, recollected Lawrence's job as a soda jerk in 1940. Lawrence's brother (Leonard) and sister (Mildred), made an appearance. Mildred was now married and had a young daughter. Dr. Warren Shepherd, the physician who brought Lawrence into the world, back in 1925, re-enacted Lawrence's first day on Earth. Frank and Lorene Tranter, father and mother, reunited with their son.

After the reunion on the stage, Lawrence was given a glimpse of his future… While Lawrence was in the hospital recovering, he was studying watch repair and had often said that he would like to make a life business of repairing watches.

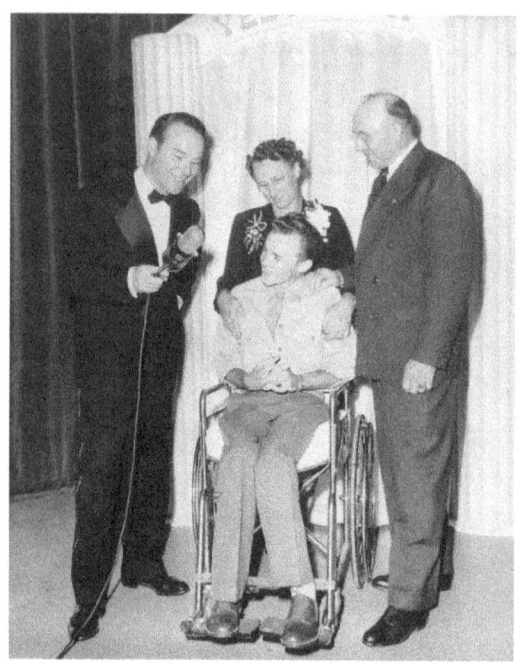

Lawrence Tranter with parents Frank and Lorene.

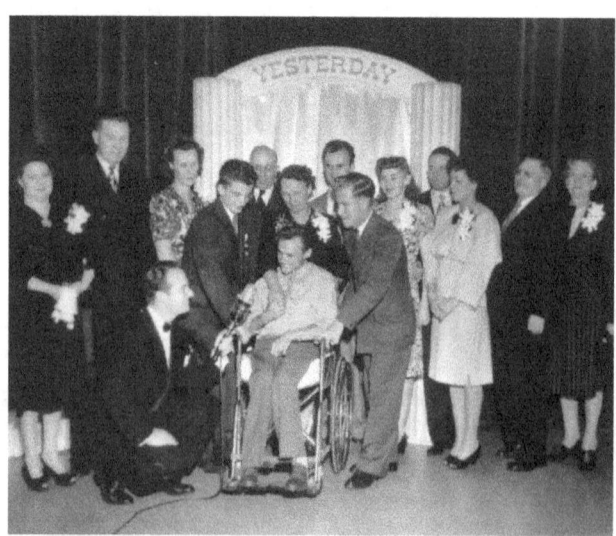

Lawrence Tranter with friends and family on stage.

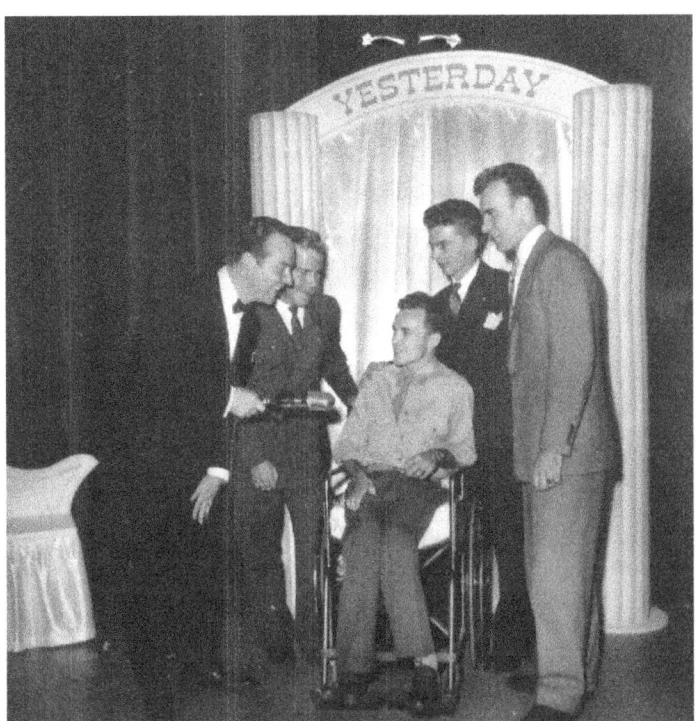

Prior to the broadcast, Ralph Edwards made arrangements with the Bulova Watch Company, located at 630 Fifth Avenue in New York City, for Tranter to receive complete free training, plus a regular weekly salary, while attending the Joseph Bulova School of Watchmaking for Servicemen in New York. John H. Ballard and Arde Bulova, along with their associates, through the Bulova Foundation, had established the school for people like Tranter. Alex Cohen, in charge of public relations at Bulova, helped work out the arrangements for this radio broadcast. A place to live would be provided for Lawrence during his attendance at the Bulova School. He was also asked to choose the city in which he would like to open his own business for a jewelry store and watch repair shop... And that store would be set up for Lawrence Tranter, completely stocked with the merchandise he needed to open business, all the tools of the watch-repairing trade, and rent paid for one year in advance for the store. Meanwhile, until arrangements for Tranter's trip to New York's Bulova School were completed, he was provided a few days to spend in Hollywood with his family and friends who came to visit him for the radio program. (Edwards closed the ceremony by informing "the gang from Murray, Utah" to be guests at a private supper at the expense of *Truth or Consequences* – and, so that Lawrence would not be late for any of his "future appointments," he received a pullover wristwatch.)

In New York, the Joseph Bulova School of Watchmaking had been established to teach a craft to veterans who needed a new field in which to earn a living. Since Tranter had not yet recovered sufficiently from his injuries for the hospital to allow him to travel to New York immediately following the program, Gen. Omar Bradley and the Veterans' Administration requested the Bulova School to open a branch at Tranter's hospital. Once he was well enough, he would go to New York and complete his studies. Between tears of joy, the war veteran accepted the proposition. And, according to two separate accounts from staff members who were involved with the surprise consequence, there wasn't a dry eye in the audience.

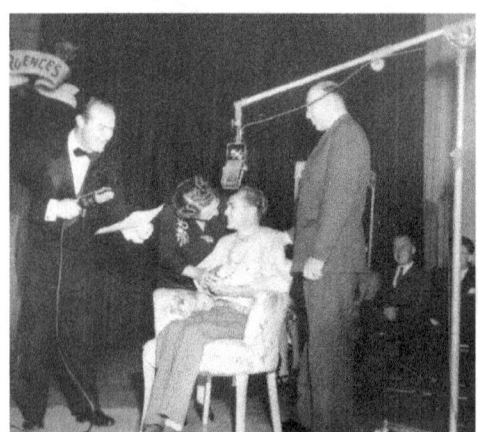
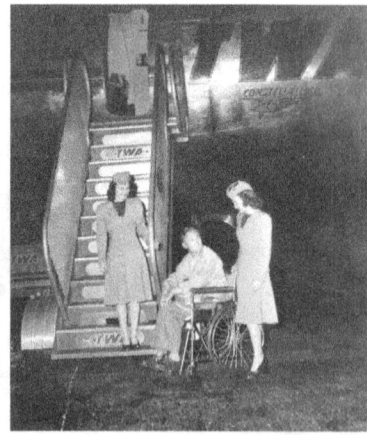
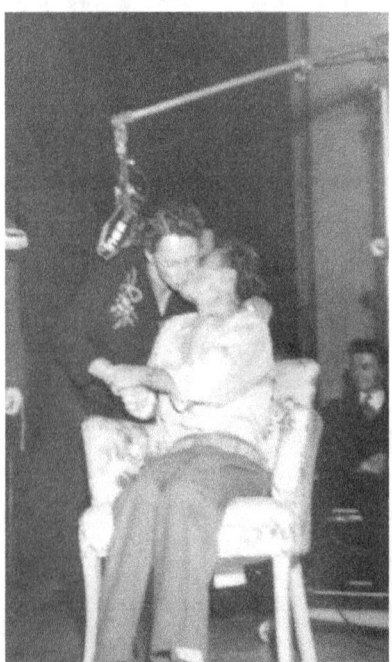
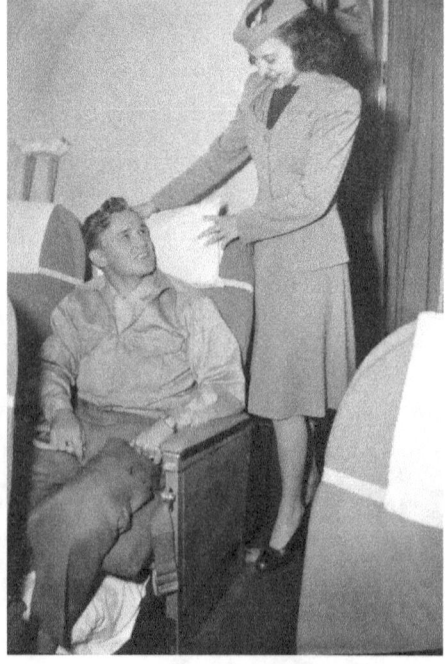

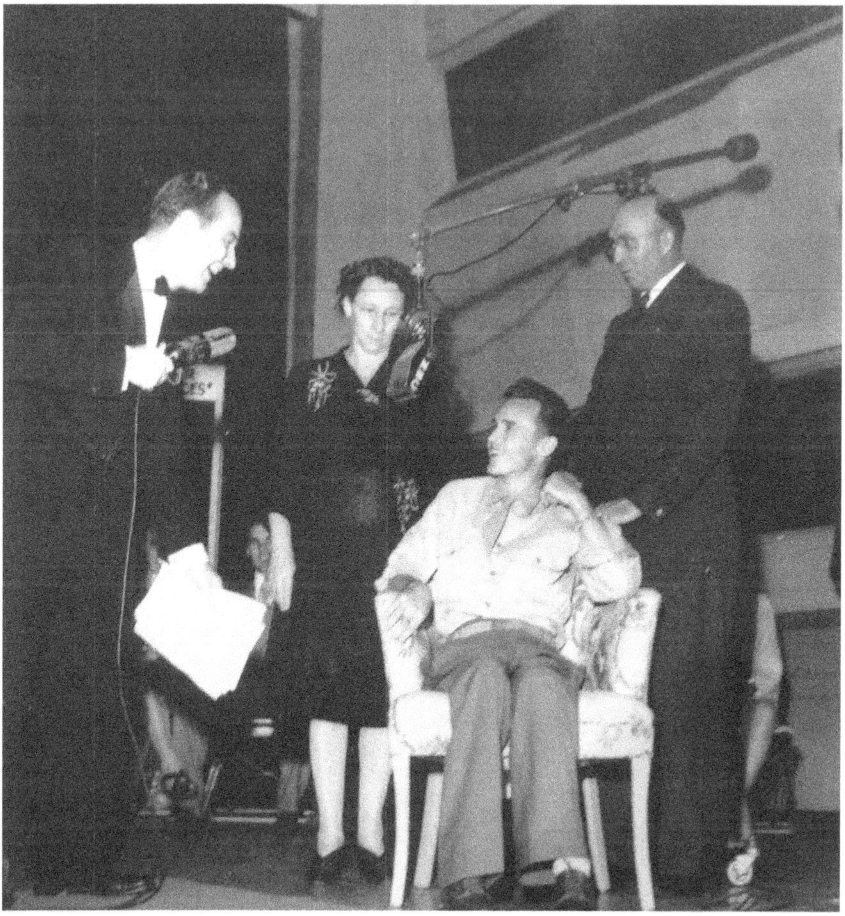

This is Your Life, Lawrence Tranter

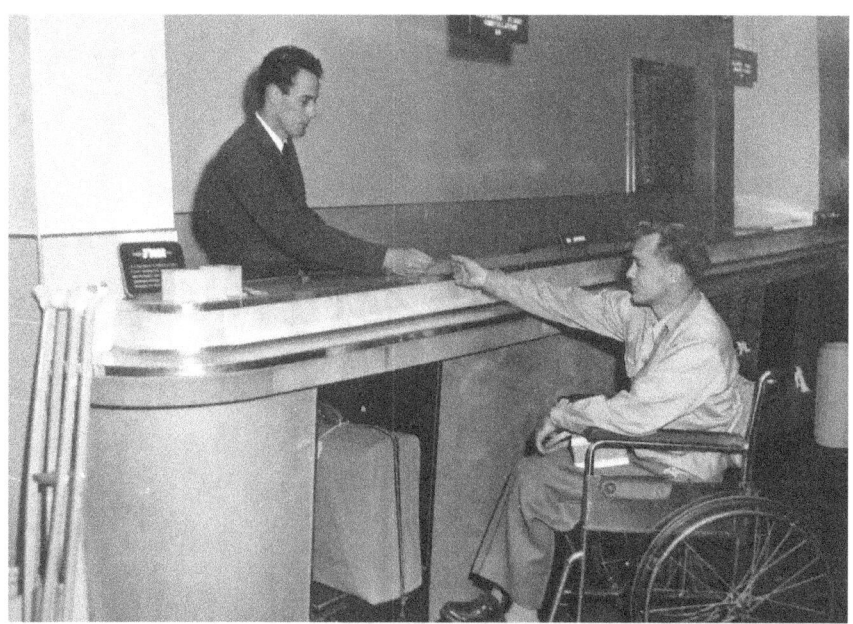

 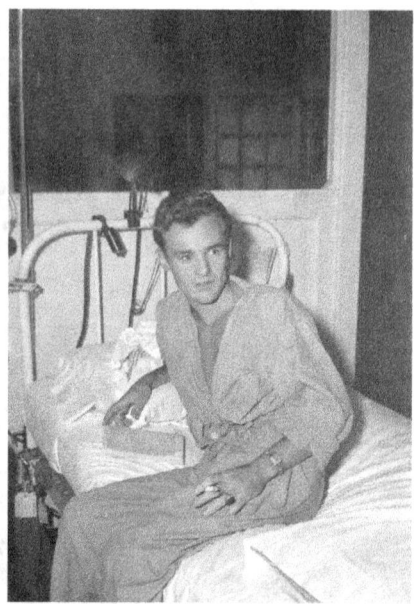

Lawrence Tranter

Edwards closed the act with these words: "This is a great example of what an industry can do to help the disabled veteran. Boys paralyzed as Lawrence Tranter or otherwise disabled in battle. The Veterans' Administration hopes other industries will set up similar rehabilitation programs for veterans in hospitals. Training courses such as this help speed the recovery of these disabled G.I.'s and it may start them on a new career as it did Lawrence. Those boys didn't forget you, folks. Let's not forget them."

On *Truth or Consequences*, surprising a contestant with family relatives was done a number of times, especially for soldiers stationed at training bases during the War who longed to see their mother, wife and/or children. The war might have been declared over, but the urgency of family reunions was still essential. Emotions rose on stage and in the studio audience, attesting Edwards succeeded beyond anything he and his crew expected. If there was any question whether the quiz program succeeded in delivering a public service message, there could be no doubt by the letters, telegrams and feedback, numbering in the thousands.

"I have been advised by our Radio Director, Mr. Brechner, of your help in preparing the *Truth or Consequences* radio broadcast of April 27 involving a patient from the Birmingham Veterans Hospital. This outstanding broadcast, which I thoroughly enjoyed, was a fine contribution to our Medical Rehabilitation

Program. Will you please accept my thanks and extend my appreciation to Mr. Al Paschall and other members of your staff who helped prepare this worthy broadcast."

—Omar N. Bradley, General,
U.S. Army, Administrator of the
Veterans Administration

"I listened to your very fine program on April 27, 1946, and I want to express my great appreciation to you for your fine work in the rehabilitation of Lawrence Tranter, Murray, Utah. This young man, according to your introduction, served in the Philippines and was wounded there while taking part in the Liberation of the Philippines... The great deed that you have performed in his rehabilitation and of other young men deserves great praise and I hope that you and others will continue the good work for the men who have given all they had for humanity."

—Joseph P. Hyman, National
Commander of the National Society
– Army of the Philippines

"I listened to *Truth or Consequences* Saturday night and still can't get the show out of my mind. I've heard many human interest spots before, and during the war had occasion to handle a number of them myself, but can honestly say that I have never heard anything done so well."

—Warren Lewis of the National
Broadcasting Company

Ralph Edwards did not forget Lawrence Tranter. Almost two years later, on the evening of April 24, 1948, the same chair was wheeled up to a microphone on the *Truth or Consequences* stage. Tranter had begun a new interest in life. He became mentally stimulated because he had found something to occupy his alert mind and supple fingers. He learned a trade and improved physically. Tranter had completed his course and put on 45 pounds. Edwards moved over to Tranter's microphone to bestow his promises: a lease for the store which Tranter then signed; a check for the first year's rent; an inventory of the stock guaranteed in writing; and a $1,000 check to open the store's bank account from John Ballard and Arde Bulova of the Bulova Foundation. Edwards then informed Tranter that a group of Salt Lake

City jewelers had formed a committee to help him with the number plate for his store: 4881 South State Street, in his hometown of Murray, Utah.

With the formalities over, Edwards walked back to his own microphone and said, "Oh, Lawrence, there's just one more thing. You can't get in the store without a key. Here's the key, fellow... come and get it. Remember, two years ago they said you'd never be able to get out of that wheelchair. This is the future, Lawrence. This is your key to the store. Come and get it." Slowly, Tranter rose from the chair. Leaning on a large table, the ex-Pfc. made his way across the stage, slowly walking, and took the key. "I had purposely encouraged this to demonstrate the tremendous rehabilitation that had taken place in the boy's previous physical and psychological deficiencies," Edwards later explained. "The audience stood and applauded." Tranter could now get along with crutches.

It was during this broadcast that Tranter had a surprise for Ralph Edwards. He announced that he had gotten married four months earlier, and introduced his wife, Dorothy. She was the lovely red-haired lady who served as his nurse at the Bulova School of Watchmaking. Together they stood on stage for the official presentation of his diploma from the Bulova School of Watchmaking, made by former head of the Veteran's Administration, Chief of Staff of the Army, General Omar Bradley, speaking from Washington, D.C.:

"Hello, Lawrence. I'm going to step out of my job as a soldier for just a minute this evening to back to those days when we were working for you in the Veterans' Administration. I like to recall them because they were busy and productive days when we could do a little for those of you who did so much for us. Tonight, as you leave the Bulova School, as you put the hospital behind you to take your place as a business man in your home town, you are helping to prove what millions of veterans everywhere have claimed when they say to the American people, 'Give us the chance – give us the opportunity – and we will make good.' Lawrence, the burden of proof is not so much upon you as it is upon us, the American people, to whom you have come back. For it is up to us to show you that democracy is the measure not only of a man's personal freedom, but his economic opportunity as well. If only we will remember that this great country of ours is peopled by young men like you, men and women with the spunk and courage to make it an even better place in which to live, we will make democracy mean a great deal more to our children – yes, and to the puzzled people who live tonight in nations around the world. Again, congratulations. My good wishes to you and Mrs. Tranter for a full and happy lifetime."

Ralph Edwards thanked General Bradley and then spoke the works he was to repeat many times to millions of radio listeners: "This is your life."

Behind the scenes, the Decker Jewelry Company, wholesale jewelers, supplied the opening stock for the store. As promised on the broadcast, Tranter was given a completely-stocked jewelry store, including electric sign, all interior fixtures, window trims, a watchmaker's bench, a safe, interior work, and other necessities. The merchandise itself, the bill of goods, was given to Lawrence Tranter. The Bulova Watch Company agreed to underwrite his credit, but Tranter had to pay for the merchandise. His stock, like any business, was to be paid for out of his profits, since, of course, he would be selling the goods and realizing the difference between the wholesale and retail price. Edwards explained this to Tranter on the evening of his initial consequence and reminded on the evening of his return to the program, and Edwards himself agreed to underwrite his credit to the extent of $500. When it was discovered that $500 would not even complete window dressing for one of the two display windows, the Murray City Chamber of Commerce got involved and explained to Edwards that tentative dates set for the grand opening of the store had been pushed back to ensure the store would be fully furnished as promised on the program. As a result, Bulova extended Tranter with $2,000 worth of credit.

Once business commenced, his first customer was Herbert B. Maw, the Governor of Utah.

This is Your Life

The Lawrence Tranter broadcast was so overwhelming that Ralph Edwards discussed the proposal of doing a weekly "good gesture act" covering the life of an exceptional individual who deserved more than verbal gratitude. On the evening of September 7, 1946, *Truth or Consequences* featured a consequence imposed on Lester Hansen, who was asked to "act" in a little dramatization in which he was assisted by radio actors Jack Moyles and Ivan Green. The dramatization portrayed the actual heroism and experiences of the veteran, but the contestant was not aware until he read the "script" that he was acting out his own story. For his efforts as an actor and in recognition of his exploits during the war, Lester received a $1,000-diamond engagement ring (and wedding band to match) to give the girl he was marrying soon; a complete wardrobe for civilian life including two Hart Schaffner Marx suits and top coats; and all-expenses-paid for equipping his new car (he already had the car) so that he would be able to drive it without using his disabled limbs. *Truth or Consequences* arranged this special equipment for the car through consultation with the vet's hospital.

Lester Hansen, 28, was paralyzed from the hips down. An artillery lieutenant in the war, Hanson was wounded in the back in a battle on Biak Island, a dot in the Pacific Ocean off New Guinea. After two and a half years spent in army hospitals at Walla Walla and Los Angeles, he was discharged from the army as a major. In 1947, he was 28 years old, busy laying out a doctor's career for himself. He was living in Los Angeles with his wife, Ethel, whom he married less than a year prior after meeting her in the Walla Walla hospital, where she served with the Red Cross. Doctors were puzzled by Hansen's ailment, saying they knew no reason why he could not walk, except that nerves had been shocked. And, they claimed, another great shock might undo the damage and enable Hansen to walk again.

Two days later, on October 6, 1948, an audition disc was recorded (never aired) focusing on the life of Lester Hansen, a paralyzed war veteran from Spokane, Washington. Hosted by Harry Von Zell, who would obviously be replaced by Ralph Edwards when the radio program premiered in November, the demo was played back for potential sponsors. Hansen played the role of a "surprised" guest, with full understanding that his demo could convince a sponsor and a network to feature a similar program on a weekly basis.

Ralph Edwards

The first radio broadcast of *This is Your Life* aired on the evening of November 9, 1948. Sponsored by Philip Morris and broadcast over NBC, the premiere episode was modeled after the Lawrence Tranter show, which was the forerunner of *This is Your Life*. Paul Jackson, a paraplegic, was chosen to be the first "victim" of the new radio program. Jackson was wounded and buried in the snow in the Battle of the Bulge. A medic tripped over him and saved his life. Jackson never knew who the medic was so Edwards and his crew ran down the files and presented to Jackson the young man responsible for saving his life. For his future, they provided complete equipment for a gun shop in a place he was starting in Tulare, California.

Future highlights on the radio program included a tribute to Ada Nelligan, a wardrobe mistress in many Broadway shows, who encouraged many youngsters who became great stars. She was beside herself with joy and tears when the following stars appeared to personally thank her and reminisce: Barbara Stanwyck, Joan Crawford, Maurice Evans, and Al Jolson (who brought Ada on stage in the "Passing Show" to take a bow when he sang "Girl in the Gingham Gown"). For her future, the radio program paid off the mortgage on her house.

Harry Steffel came about as a result of Ralph Edwards' proving there was a show in anybody. He took an unbiased member of the audience out into the street and had her select any passerby. The result a week later was the very moving story of an immigrant and his devotion to America.

Barney Ross was one of the deepest of stories, having fought his way up from the ground. He watched his father shot and killed in his Chicago grocery store, became champion of three divisions in the fight world, was at Guadalcanal where he played a portable organ one Christmas night in a foxhole and sang "Kol Nidre" while a Catholic priest played a violin. It was told how Barney fought and overcame the dope habit developed through medicine given him in a G.I. hospital. Many greats of the prize ring were present at the show, and Barney and the priest re-enacted the Christmas Night at Guadalcanal.

The story of Major Peter Ortiz, a Major in the O.S.S., was revealed to the American public. What he did behind the enemy lines during the war was impressive. He saved an entire city from destruction by fire when he gave himself up to the Germans. On the radio broadcast, in person, was the French boy who took him to the German Commander. For his future, Ortiz was given a job in the movies, and a plaque in the square of the French city of Cetron for having saved it and its people.

This is Your Life was broadcast on NBC radio for a total of two years, before making the transition to television. So much has recently unearthed through academic study regarding this program that it warrants an independent publication; justifying narrow coverage in this book. Over the years, obituaries for war veterans who were afforded comparable treatment on *Truth or Consequences*, including Hubert C. Smith, asserted they were the inspiration for *This is Your Life*. There were other veterans that followed Lawrence Tranter; paperwork in Ralph Edwards' files, spanning decades, cements claim that Tranter was the muse, and supposedly Mel Vickland was the staff member of Edwards' crew that came up with the idea for *This is Your Life*, following the Tranter broadcast.

Actress Dorothy Lamour assisted with a contestant's consequence and received a plug for her new radio program, *Front and Center*, which aired over NBC during the summer. Photos from the broadcast of July 5, 1947.

Beginning on January 28, 1950, a race began between two contestants to get to City Hall in Los Angeles, with $1,000 prize money. Larry Haynes, a singer, must go around the world via TWA Constellation; Carol Fieldhouse had to use a pogo stick on a course of 24 miles mapped out by the radio producers. Left to Right: Larry Haynes, Ralph Edwards and Carol Fieldhouse.

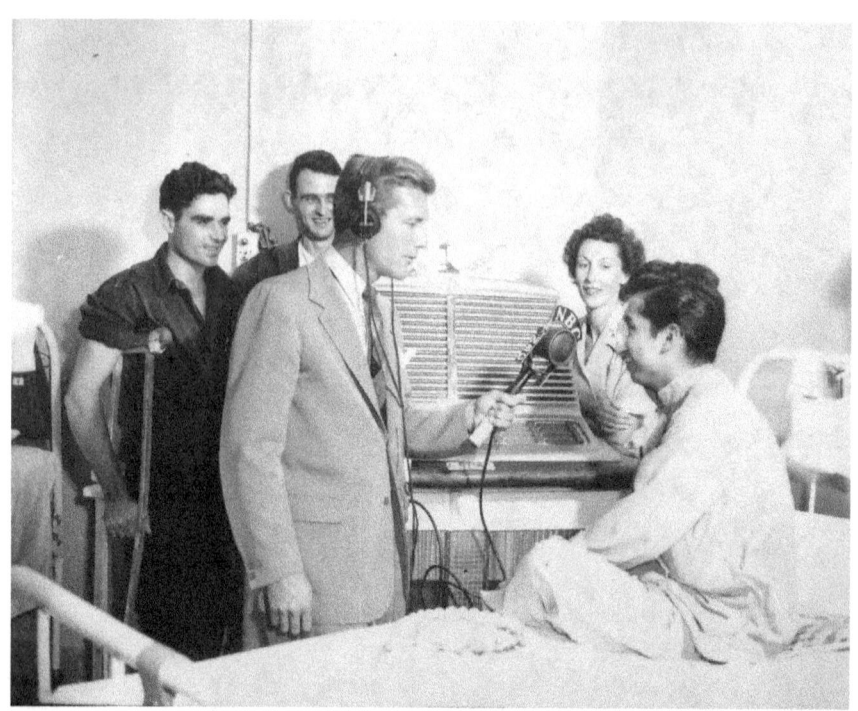

At the McCornack U.S. Army Hospital in Pasadena, California, a Private First Class is having a birthday party, complete with an Aireon Automatic Phonograph Player, with 900 records. (Top) His buddies were present when the gift was given. (Bottom) Executives posing with the Phonograph Player.

Chapter 10
Jack Benny and The Walking Man Contest

> *"Who is the Walking Man? Keep listening to Truth or Consequences for the Walking Man... It may mean a gigantic prize to the one who knows! Who is the Walking Man? Hear all about it next week on Truth or Consequences!"*
> -- Ralph Edwards, December 20, 1947 broadcast

Succeeding triumph of the two Mrs. Hush contests resulted in another – the "Walking Man" contest – quickly culminating in a national phenomenon that, subject to debate among historians, may have been the highlight of Ralph Edwards' career. Bookies sold tip sheets, libraries were swamped with radio listeners trying to look up reference books in search of meanings to the clues, and for eight weeks while the jackpot of prizes piled up, trade columns offered their own theories as to who the elusive Walking Man was. The final revelation made front-page news across the country. The contest would ultimately raise $1,639,000 for the American Heart Association and put the organization in business on a national basis, for which Mr. Edwards would be honored in person by four U.S. Presidents for the millions of dollars for worthy causes raised through the radio program. Other contests would come and go but statistically, "The Walking Man" contest was the crowning achievement for *Truth or Consequences*.

In 1947, the American Heart Association was in dire need of funds to complete its planned reorganization as a national voluntary health agency. Founded in 1924 as a purely professional society of physicians and scientists, it had neither the manpower nor facilities to organize a nationwide fund-raising drive. On learning these facts, Edwards obtained approval from Proctor & Gamble to name the Heart Association as beneficiary of a contest he would conduct over the air.

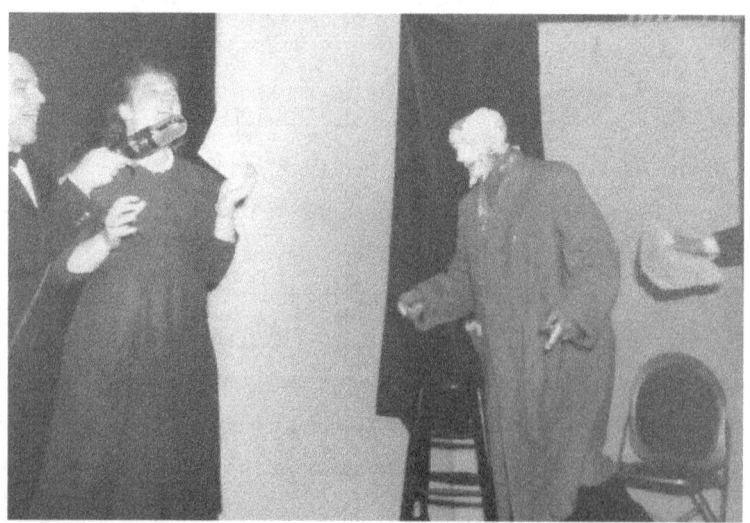

Contestant receives a custard pie in the face.

The second Miss Hush contest raised over $350,000 for the March of Dimes but inside talk had it that the polio drive people, fearing the reaction to the newspaper tips leaking Miss Hush's identity, did not want a repeat for the next contest, hence why Ralph Edwards chose the American Heart Association for "The Walking Man" contest. During the second Miss Hush contest, some theorized that there would not have been any future giveaway contests on *Truth or Consequences* because of NBC's ruling to charge off the product plugs of the donors against the program's own commercial time. An end to the multitude of free product plugs on NBC stanzas was promised when the network sought to put in effect a proposed censorship and broadcast practices code early in 1948. NBC outlined several stringent regulations designed to make scriptwriters and producers think twice before inserting a Studebaker or Bulova wristwatch reference. According to the proposal, NBC would charge off the airtime for the free plugs against the regular commercial time. If used on a comedy program, the loss of commercial time would be rated from the beginning of the gag to the ending. NBC executives feared the practice of free plugs would eventually get out of control and mean revenue loss to the network. One such example was the Bulova watch outfit, known for snagging plugs on many top-rated shows in return for a few gift watches to producers, script writers, actors and quiz show contestants, was getting advertising dirt cheap.

In the Hollywood studios on the evening of December 20, 1947, shortly after Ralph Edwards and his crew finished production of the Hubert Smith holiday offerings, Edwards made the first announcement of a new contest. Added to the excitement was the sound effect of a man's footsteps heard over the microphone; footsteps of a man walking, and Ralph Edwards asks the audience, "Who is the Walking Man?" On the evening of December 27, the sound of "The Walking Man" was again dramatized for the benefit of the radio audience.

On the evening of January 3, 1948, from the Hollywood Studios with a two-way set-up to the home of Jack Dempsey, a contestant named Jack Bayuth, of Tulsa, Oklahoma, was tricked into forcing his way onto a residential scene, without realizing that he was being sent to the home of the ex-boxing champ. Announcer Charles Lyon relayed the events as they occurred. Jack Dempsey, naturally, was in on the gag. The entire consequence may have been strategic – clarifying for the benefit of the radio audience that the former Mr. Hush was at his home at the time they heard "The Walking Man," ruling him out of the list of possible candidates.

Contestant Jack Bayuth forcing his way onto the home of Jack Dempsey.

Now the details of the contest were finally revealed. Ralph Edwards recited the riddle, told in rhyme, which had provided the necessary clues to identifying "The Walking Man," described as a well-known American male – not a female.

"Bing – Bong – Bell! It's ten and only one can tell.
Master of the Metropolis, fits his name quite well."

To enter the contest, radio listeners were asked to write a letter to "The Walking Man, Hollywood, California," completing in no more than 25 words the following statement: "We should all support the American Heart Association because…" Contestants were instructed not to provide their solution to the mystery – that was to be reserved for the phone calls. With the completion of the statement, listeners were instructed to include their name, address and telephone number in the upper right hand corner of their letter. They were to include a contribution to the American Heart Association. The judges of the letters would not see the financial contribution, because the amount of money donated was not taken into consideration. Only the closing half of the statement was being judged.* The winners of the three best letters each week would be telephoned and asked to give their guess at the identity of "The Walking Man."

* The nationally famous company, Reuben H. Donnelley, was in charge of judging winners of eligible participants, opening envelopes, extracting the money and depositing it. Names at Chicago payoff: Fred Arkus and Wynn Nathanson.

(This particular qualification was no different from the prior "Miss Hush" contests.) According to statistics, 9.5 percent of the contestants did not submit their letters as instructed. Some failed to include their phone number. Others did not provide their mailing address on the envelope or the letter. Others did not print legibly for the judges to read.

The first of the listeners would be called during the broadcast of January 17, giving contestants two weeks to send in their initial donations. Letters received by Monday of each week would be judged in the contest for the following Saturday; those letters received after Monday would be held over for the next week. Listeners could continue to submit letters every week, provided they followed instructions and made another donation to the American Heart Association. Any amount was accepted.

Announced on the evening of January 3 were the first three prizes, meant to entice even the casual listener into mailing their contribution: a Bendix Home Laundry (washer, dryer and automatic ironer), a $1,000 diamond and ruby wrist watch, and a four-door Cadillac car. For each week the contest continued, three new prizes would be added to the pot. All listeners who were telephoned during the contest would receive a set of sterling silver flatware, regardless of whether they won the contest or not.

Ralph Edwards and Jack Benny for publicity photo.

On the evening of January 10, Edwards repeated the jingle and then announced the next three prizes added to the pot: a Tappan Kitchen Range, a 16mm picture sound projector and screen with a complete reel for the picture *I Walk Alone* (and arrangements for the winner to receive film for one moving picture for each month during an entire year), and two weeks paid vacation for two in Sun Valley, Idaho.

On the evening of January 17, three more prizes were added to the pot: a vacuum cleaner with attachments, a 1948 console FM and AM radio-phonograph combination television set, and a $1,000 diamond ring. Also, the first three telephone calls were placed to contestants. All three guesses were incorrect: Harry Truman, Louis B. Mayer and J. Edgar Hoover. New clues in the contest were added: the whinnying sounds of a horse, the howling of wind, rushing of water, and growling noises of cats and dogs.

On January 24, three more prizes were added to the pot: a Servel Refrigerator, Art-Craft Venetian for every room in the house, and a Sherwin Williams paint job inside and out for the entire house. Three more telephone calls were placed and three incorrect guesses included James E. West, Boss Ed Crump of Memphis, Tennessee, and the third contestant did not provide an answer. (They hesitated too long.)

 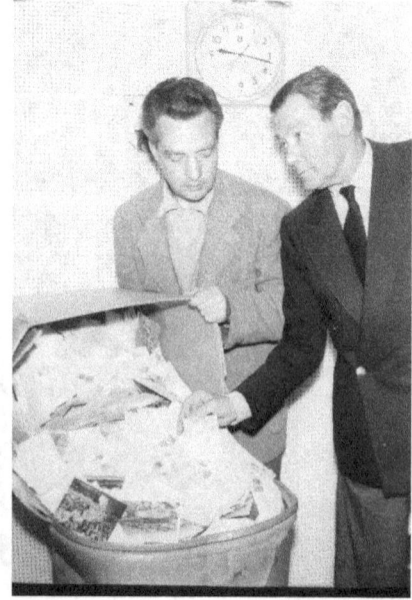

Actor Herbert Marshall and Ed Bailey looks over the mail that poured in to NBC.

On the evening of January 31, Herbert Marshall and Henry J. Kaiser were among the incorrect guesses. The third contestant did not answer his phone and missed out on the opportunity. All of the contestants were notified in advance by telegram to be ready for the phone call and instructed on what time the call would be placed. The contestant who failed to answer his or her phone would not receive a second chance. Prizes added to the pot included a complete wardrobe of women's clothes for every season in the year (Fay Foster design), a new 15-cubic foot Coolerator home freezer filled with Birdseye Frozen Foods, and a Luscombe Silvaire Standard 65 airplane made in Dallas, Texas.

On the evening of February 7, Richard Dix, Edward J. Baker and Bing Crosby were among the incorrect guesses. Added to the pot were three more prizes: complete installation of "Pomona Space-Rite" tile in the kitchen and bathroom, complete Ida-O-Pine furniture for both the living room and dining room, and a $2,400 Normel Trailer coach equipped with modern kitchen and sleeping quarters for four.

On the evening of February 14, Walter Huston, Eddie Cantor and Winston Churchill were among the incorrect guesses. Ralph Edwards provided new clues through the magic of sound effects such as the sounds of gunshots and the statement: "Go back to your field -- will you walk again next week?" Prizes added to the pot were a Remington noiseless typewriter, an outboard motor boat and a $1,000 full-length Persian lamb fur coat.

On the evening of February 21, *Truth or Consequences* originated from New York City, instead of Hollywood, California, because Edwards was attending the current dance recital presented by Martha Graham, the former Miss Hush. James Petrillo, Robert E. Hannegan and Joe Louis were among the incorrect guesses. Prizes added to the pot included two years' supply of Lady Pepperell Sheets, $500 worth of electrical equipment for the winner's home (equipment chosen by the winner and installed free of charge) and a brand new piano. The clue added to the contest was the whistling of *Annie Laurie*.

By this time, the question regarding who is "The Walking Man" became a national sensation. "It's the most expensive gag in history," criticized columnist Walter Haight. "A billion and more man, woman and child hours have gone into the game. If you don't believe it, ask the libraries. Men are staying home from work trying to figure it out. Women are piling dirty clothes in the corner and serving picnic lunches instead of dinner. Kids are skipping school."

On the evening of February 28, Alvin C. York (Sgt. York of WWI), Andy

Varipappa, and Bulldog Drummond were among the incorrect guesses. The last guess referred to the radio actor, Ned Weaver, who played the role on radio and whose footsteps were heard on the weekly program. Edwards added another clue by informing the radio audience: "Remember we say the Walking Man, not the Waking Man, or the Laughing Man" and "Listen to the squeak of his shoes – doesn't the squeak tell you anything?" A third clue was provided: "Bing-Bong-Bell, when do bells ring Bing-Bong-Bell?" A violin fiddler played the scales during the delivery of the rhyme. Prizes added to the pot included electric blankets (one for every bed in the winner's home), three Coronado suits for every male member of the winner's family, and an electric sewing machine.

During the week of February 23 to 27, Jack Eigen, a disc jockey at WINS in New York, brought down the wrath of Ralph Edwards (among others) on his head for revealing the identity of "The Walking Man" on his radio broadcasts. A number of newspaper columnists and radio broadcasters had, on occasion, learned the identity but refrained from publicizing it because of the charity angle. Eigen attempted to justify his actions by proclaiming "freedom of the press," but after pressure from his employer, Eigen offered a public apology. As a result, however, Edwards and his staff had to make the hard decision whether or not to include radio contestants from the state of New York, fearing unjust and unfair practices to contestants. The decision was ultimately made to randomly select contestants without bias, as it had been done weeks prior, since radio listeners of Jack Eigen could have phoned friends in other states. A winner to the contest was expected on the evening of February 28, as a result. To Edwards' surprise, no one guessed correctly.

On the evening of March 6, 1948, "The Walking Man" was correctly identified as radio comedian Jack Benny. The winner of the contest was Florence Hubbard, a widow, of 40 North Waller Avenue in Chicago, Illinois, where she was employed as a "dress checker" in the Carson-Pirie-Scott department store, commonly referred to as Carson's. After the identification of Jack Benny, Ralph Edwards said, "Jack, you can stop now… the contest is over… Jack, you can stop walking now." The sound effect ceased and Jack, over the microphone remarked, "Thank goodness. My feet are killing me."

Nothing has been found to verify whether Florence Hubbard, on the broadcast of March 6, took a wild guess, an educated guess based on the clues, or heard the rumor leaked as a result of Eigen's radio broadcasts. More than likely she read about it in the morning papers, which were among the many across the nation that was "leaking" the news.

Jack Benny

Florence Hubbard

One week following Florence Hubbard's good fortune, she appeared as a special guest on the program. The 68-year-old told the story how she became interested in the contest because the proceeds of letters entered went to the American Heart Association. Her late husband was a physician who died of heart disease in 1935. She sent in scads of entries, an estimated 30 letters to the contest over a period of eight weeks, with each a contribution of one dollar. She paid tribute to her employers, the Carson-Pirie-Scott Department Store in Chicago, and told how they gave her a luncheon and had the store stylist outfit her in a complete new wardrobe for her trip to Hollywood, with their compliments.

The week following the conclusion of the contest, after his interview with Mrs. Hubbard, Ralph Edwards publicly thanked a number of individuals on his radio program, including the sponsor, Procter & Gamble, "for being so humanitarian in their thoughts, allowing us time for the contest and entering so wholeheartedly into the selection of the American Heart Association for the recipient of the contributions." Edwards also thanked Dr. Charles A.R. Connor, president of the American Heart Association, the Los Angeles Branch of the Reuben Donnelly Contest Company, and to the three finalist judges, Superior Court Judge Thurmond Clarke, Dr. Howard F. West (past president of the American Heart Association), and Mrs. Joseph S. Hook, President of the 10th District California Congress of Parents and Teachers.* At the conclusion of the broadcast, Edwards took a quick moment to ask Mrs. Hubbard where she worked, purposely providing free publicity to her employers for allowing her a leave of absence to California.

An announcement was made on the program that *Truth or Consequences* was given the *Radio Mirror* magazine award for the Best Quiz Program on the air, according to a *Radio Mirror* listeners' poll. Ralph Edwards hinted that a new contest would begin soon but provided no details or dates, suggesting it might be the "The Laughing Lady." The next contest, however, would be "Microphone X," inviting the radio listeners to guess the mysterious sound and where it originated. (Edwards originally planned to have Greta Garbo as "The Laughing Lady" but when he approached the actress, her business representative politely explained

---

* Public relations names in connection with the Walking Man contest and the founding of the American Heart Association: Rome Betts, Henry Bernay and Dr. Sullivan.

that she never heard of Edwards or the Walking Man and "the one and only time I ever listened to the radio was to hear President Roosevelt declare war against the Axis.")

"I can hardly believe it happened to me," Hubbard told a reporter for a Chicago newspaper. "I came home Saturday from work, wet from the rain, hungry and tired. I took a hot bath and just had an opportunity to get into a bathrobe when the telephone rang. It was conductor Ralph Edwards of the *Truth or Consequences* program, sponsors of 'The Walking Man' program. He asked me who was 'The Walking Man' and I replied: 'Jack Benny.' Mr. Edwards congratulated me and told me I was the winner."

Her interview was legit (as evidenced by reviewing the script, which featured questions by Edwards and a notation for Mrs. Hubbard to respond.)

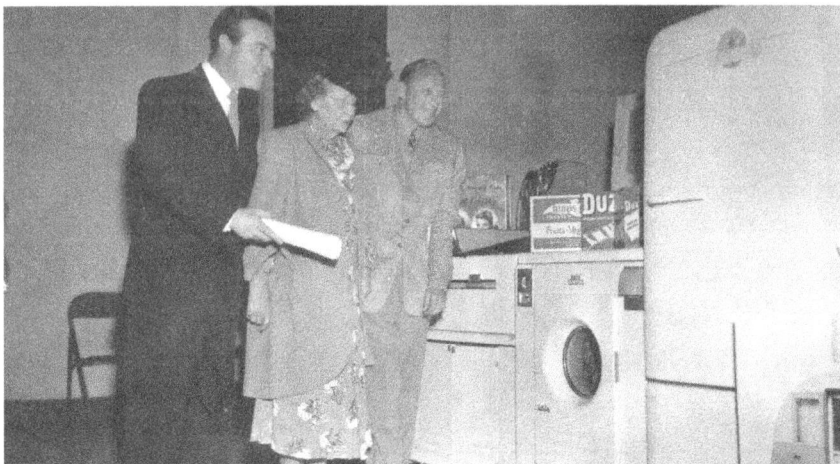

Florence Hubbard meets Jack Benny in person when she arrived at the studio to receive her prizes.

Hubbard Schedule

Florence Hubbard arrived Friday morning, March 12, via The Chief, Drawing Room E, car 190, at 8:30 a.m. She was greeted by Fred Carney, members of the press, John McEnroe of NBC and a friend of hers, Mrs. Madeline Miller. She was taken directly to the Knickerbocker Hotel. There, she was interviewed by Virginia Marmaduke, feature writer for the Chicago Sun, for an exclusive, and who remained with Ms. Hubbard during her entire stay on the coast. At noon, Ms. Hubbard lunched with Sue Clark and *Radio Life*. Sue Clark brought the winner back to the hotel. At 2:00 p.m., she met with Al Paschall at the *Truth or Consequences* office, as they went over the list of prizes. After the meeting, working out the technical and signing disclosures and legal forms for acceptance of the prizes, she met Ralph Edwards for a script rehearsal for the radio broadcast.

At noon on Saturday, she met Jack Benny and his company for a rehearsal of his Sunday program. She was treated to lunch and dinner by Ralph Edwards, personally, and attended the broadcast for *Truth or Consequences* that evening. On Sunday morning, Al Paschall picked her up from the hotel and took her to the studio for the Jack Benny broadcast. On Monday morning, Evie Byrd picked her up at the hotel for her appearance on the *Breakfast in Hollywood* show. Late that afternoon, she and her nephew met with Al Paschall to finalize more paperwork for the prizes. She then visited Paramount Studios and was the guest of Walter Seltzer, an employee of Hal Wallis Productions, who donated the motion-picture projector and screen.

Sometime during the end of the week she would leave for San Francisco and be the guest of the Sew Gem Company and tour northern California to see the Redwoods. She left on Thursday, March 25, to return to Chicago.

List of Prizes

Bendix Home Laundry
$1,000 Ruby and Diamond Bulova Watch
Four-Door Cadillac Sedan
Tappan Gas Range
16mm Motion-Picture Sound Projector and screen with print of Hal Wallis film, *I Walk Alone*, plus delivery of a picture a month for one year.
Two-week vacation, all expenses paid, to Sun Valley, Idaho
$1,000 Diamond Ring
Electrolux Vacuum Cleaner

1948 RCA Victor Console FM and AM radio-phonograph and television set all in one cabinet
Servel Silent Gas Refrigerator
Art Craft All-Metal Venetian Blinds
Sherwin-Williams house painting inside and out
Complete woman's wardrobe for every season of the year, designed by Fay Foster, including beachwear, play clothes and street dresses
15 Cubic Foot Coolerator freezer filled with Birdseye food
Luscomb Silavire Airplane
Kitchen and Bathroom tiled completely.
Dining room and two bedrooms filled with Ida-O-Pine furniture
$2,400 three-room Normel Trailer coach
Remington Rand typewriter
14-foot Aluma-craft boat complete with outboard motor
Full-length new look Persian lamb coat

> A critic for *Variety* magazine remarked in his April 5, 1948, column, "Every season is made noteworthy by an incident, character or even a punch line. Year's best yock in our book was delivered by a non-pro, Mrs. Hubbard, who won 'The Walking Man' contest. Her show-stopper was, 'I'm lonely but loaded.'"

Summary

The system was set up carefully to ensure the least number of people were in on the gag. Even Mary Livingstone did not know Jack Benny was The Walking Man. Neither did his scriptwriters. Every Saturday evening Benny was hidden away with an NBC engineer in the Laurel Canyon home of producer Al Paschall. The engineer set up the microphone and floor mat to ensure the sound came through perfectly. No recordings were used. Today, listening to 1948 recordings, one would question whether the audience really heard Jack Benny walking – or someone else. Edwards was a stickler for accuracy and honesty. The sound of a man walking really was Jack Benny, and the comedian supplied his own shoes.

Topping Edwards' own mark of eight weeks to a contest, the radio competition raised more than $1,500,000 for the American Heart Association and staggered mailmen with over 2,000,000 letters for an average contribution of 70 cents per letter.*

The mail department provided an accurate count and it was evident that "The Walking Man" contest outdrew all prior "Miss Hush" contests. By May of 1948, C.E. Hooper revealed a startling statistic that Ralph Edwards was already aware of: *Truth or Consequences* was the second highest rated evening program, falling behind *Fibber McGee and Molly*, especially during the months of January and February as a result of "The Walking Man" contest. As expected according to Crossley (another ratings system), the *Truth or Consequences* radio program, when the contest was blown, millions turned off their sets after learning who "The Walking Man" was. The week following the conclusion of the contest, ratings dropped. Many radio producers believed their programs were worth the cost factor when they paid off better than one Hooper point to each $1,000 of program cost. After the success of *Truth or Consequences*, radio producers started wondering if the answer came from contests with immense giveaways.

The end of the second "Miss Hush" contest attracted an estimated 25,000,000 listeners, which was a husky figure on any night and an incredible one on Saturday nights. The normal Hooper rating for *Truth or Consequences* was about 13, shot up to 26.7, an all-time high for a quiz and stunt show. "The Walking Man" contest brought in an estimated 1,100,000 letters, 100,000 more than "Miss Hush." So many in fact, that it comprised 90 percent of the mail received by NBC's Hollywood office, which testily informed Edwards in writing that he would have to handle his own mail after this. It was too much for the network to handle.

According to inter-office memos at CBS and NBC, the "Miss Hush" and "The Walking Man" contest set a bad precedent, claimed a growing number of radio executives. The *Truth or Consequences* "hooplas," with their spectacular rating and publicity payoffs, touched off the most widespread prize contest and giveaway epidemic on record. "Most feel it's approaching the critical stage, that it's unhealthy for radio advertising in general – an artificial stimulant to listening and buying; that it's giving people a feeling that radio's a big lottery, and it isn't helping to raise broadcasting standards," reported *Variety*. A great bulk of the

---

* *Time* magazine reported that 114,000 letters were received in a single day, a week before the contest ended.

merchandise given away was donated by manufacturers for free advertising, which Ralph Edwards accepted with open arms. The only exception was medicine and drugs since the weekly sponsor for *Truth or Consequences*, Procter & Gamble, was a drug manufacturing firm (promoting their popular product, Duz). The sponsor also had to approve all the prizes before they were officially accepted.

Mrs. Ruth Annette Subbie, winner of the "Miss Hush" contest, was asked by newspaper reporters who she thought the "Walking Man" was. She suspected Boris Karloff. But it was no surprise that someone won the contest that evening. Like the "Miss Hush" contest before, word leaked out in trade columns that Jack Benny was the mystery man. The day after Mrs. Hubbard won the contest, one columnist in Chicago remarked in his column: "Her answer, Jack Benny, was the one hundreds of Chicagoans had been ready to give since a local newspaper 'broke' the secret of the 'Walking Man's identity." After all, the Chicago papers (both *Sun* and *Times*) were reporting Jack Benny as the most likely candidate in the Saturday morning papers. (In the Friday paper, a columnist named Handy Andy theorized it was one of two people: Jack Benny or Peter Lorre.)*

Aline Mosby, United Press Hollywood correspondent whose column was syndicated across the country, broke the news on March 4. "It isn't anything definite," she reported, but having heard a sound of a squeaky violin on the broadcast of February 28, she called up a guy who owned a violin and started putting the clues together. "Might be Jascha Heifetz, the concert violinist," he told Mosby. So she went as far as to contact Benny himself. "You know, people have been stopping me on the street and writing letters asking me if I'm the Walking Man," Benny admitted. "Oh, and Mary said something about it. I suppose we should have put the clues together, but we never listen to the program." Mosby went so far as to reveal her possible solutions to the clues, leaving readers of her column to figure out the most obvious answer to the question that plagued radio listeners from coast-to-coast. Mosby wasn't the only person who pointed the finger at the Pride of Waukegan.

---

* The suspected article that may have tipped off Hubbard was in the Sunday, May 6, 1948 issue of the *Chicago Daily Tribune*. Columnist Larry Wolters reported word on the street was Jack Benny. Following the conclusion of the contest, Edwards acquired a clipping of this article and pasted it in his scrapbook, adding a notation in his own handwriting: "Rotten journalism, darned poor citizenship."

C.E. Butterfield of the Associated Press reported: "As was the case last Saturday, the wiseacres are predicting it may be the last time for the stunt. They figure all the clues seem to point to Jack Benny." A newspaper in Cleveland, Ohio, listing the evening's radio programs, remarked: "8:30 – WTAM, Truth or Consequences: Look for the "Walking Man" to be identified as Jack Benny during tonight's show." Jeanne Ring of the *Bangor Daily News* in Bangor, Maine, admitted that "I know the answer to the national puzzler." She then began listing movies Jack Benny starred in, among other tips, but avoided mentioning Jack Benny's name directly. Larry Wolters of the *Chicago Daily Tribune* reported the morning of the broadcast, "Too many of these aspirants are thinking of calling *The Tribune* to get the answer. So far as we know only Edwards and perhaps an NBC technician or two and The Walking Man himself know the identity. A dozen or two persons have guessed wrong up to now. This week many people are suggesting that the clues point to Jack Benny."

Jeanne Yount of the *Oregon Journal* offered harsh criticism. "Nothing but double-crossing clues for eight or nine weeks," she wrote. "Then all of a sudden the sponsor or somebody orders 'get rid of it' and Edwards as good as gives it away. It's not fair to those who wrote the best letters early in the contest or to the many who tried to ferret out the answer by logical deduction. Many of the clues wouldn't ever make sense to a professional detective." Yount criticized the sound clues provided each week to help listeners identify the "Walking Man," claiming, "the whole thing was a design for confusion from start until Edwards decided to finish it and instead of building good will, quite possibly will work just the opposite."

L.M. McCall of Wichita Falls, Texas, told reporters that he was notified by the quiz program that he would be one of three people given a chance to identify "The Walking Man" and to stay by the phone that Saturday night. Regrettably, he was not the first person phoned. "I knew the answer was Jack Benny," McCall told reporters. "It was in the newspaper earlier that week. I told all my friends to listen to the broadcast and hear me win the jackpot. Those could have been mine."

According to newspaper columnist Ed Sullivan (years before he became a major television personality), the contest put a strain on the relationship of Jack Benny and Mary Livingstone.

On the third Saturday night on which he came home late, Mary Benny said to her husband: "Jack, I'm getting fed up with this every week. What's the alibi this time?" She looked at him with the curious glint in her eye that husbands accept as the last calm before the storm. "I haven't any alibi, Doll," said Jack weakly. Jack pledged not to tell even his wife the truth. Every Saturday afternoon, Jack Benny drove from the house to play "The Walking Man" for the quiz program. As a result, he was late for dinner each Saturday night, and as Sullivan described, "He was rapidly getting himself into a peak of trouble with the irate missus. The tension started easing about two weeks ahead of the formal revelation. At that time, in Los Angeles, enterprising hawkers were peddling handbills in the street, price $1, giving a regular racing sheet rundown of the possibilities. Mary bought one of them, saw that Jack was high on the list of probabilities. From then on, when he came home late Saturday nights, she just looked at him coldly but stopped bawling him out."

Indirectly, Mary Livingstone played a hand in the contest. According to one Chicago newspaper, on one evening, Benny found himself without leather heels and out of desperation, had to borrow a pair from his wife, to make the sound effect.

"I got a call from Mickey Rockford, of MCA, to rush to NBC to discuss something he couldn't divulge over the phone," Jack Benny later recalled. "He met me and told me to follow him to an office. He unlocked the door, looked up and down the corridor, entered quickly and beckoned me in. When I saw Ralph Edwards alone in the place, I figured that it was one of Ralph's contests, and it was.... 'This is the only time I'll ever talk to you, Jack,' said Ralph. 'From now on, we can't ever be seen together.' Then he gave me my instructions and I had to pledge I'd never reveal our secret to a soul."

"It was funny at Hollywood parties," Benny laughed. "Van Johnson is a nut on mystery contests, and this contest really drove him batty. One night, at the Billy Goetz house, Van was sitting with me and saying how exasperated he'd become at his failure to identify 'The Walking Man.' He wouldn't talk about anything else. 'Ding, dong, bell,' reasoned Van, 'must be a church. Do you think it's Winston Churchill, Jack?' I said it probably was. Weeks later, after the announcement, I met him at a party. Van looked at me and whispered: 'You no-good louse.'"

Jack Benny's radio writers started suspecting that it was their employer and laid a Saturday trap for him instigated by Mary's brother, Hilliard. (Benny's program was written every Saturday afternoon.) Hilliard and Sam Perrin, pretending they'd left their cars at home, asked Jack to have dinner with them after the program was drafted and then drive them home. Throughout dinner, Jack couldn't look at his watch. Then he drove them home, and after dropping off Perrin, he drove away very slowly. Once around the corner, Benny tore at high speed up to the house in the Hollywood hills, reaching his destination moments before he was needed for the broadcast.

"If a motorcycle cop had grabbed me, I'd have been a dead pigeon," Benny recalled. For fear of tipping off contestants, the Benny program following Ralph Edwards' announcement could not be written in advance. On Saturday afternoon, the scriptwriters for Jack Benny's radio program completed the regular Sunday night program. A few hours later, Ralph Edwards named the winner and the writers called for an emergency meeting. With the exception of the Phil Harris spot, they had to write a whole new program. They finished it at 2 a. m. Sunday. Among the jokes was comedy stooge Dennis Day who asked Jack if he was "The Walking Man," indicating he was the last person in the country to find out. The program was built around Benny's "Walking Man" character and made full capital of the lighter side of the contest. Tradesmen in multiple newspapers and magazines agreed that it was one of Benny's funniest shows of the season.*

On the evening of March 14, Florence Hubbard made an appearance on *The Lucky Strike Program*, starring Jack Benny. Her radio appearance was courtesy of her employer. After winning the contest, she told Ralph Edwards over the phone that she would come to Hollywood only if her employer would give her the time off. Considering the publicity value to the department store, there was no hesitation. Jack Benny and his writers rated a low curtsy from the trade for his hastily thrown-together show that featured Florence Hubbard. Mistakenly referred to with the wrong prefix as "Mrs. Florence Hubbard" in newspapers (remember, she was a widow), she spent the remainder of March in Hollywood at the expense of the producers of *Truth or Consequences*. She was provided a tour of the Paramount lot and reportedly somebody sold her a ticket for a $15,000 drawing to be held at the St. Timothy Parish. Seems even after winning the contest and all those prizes, she could not resist buying a one-dollar ticket for a drawing. The total estimated value of the prizes she won on the radio quiz contest was close to $25,000.

Ralph Edwards later explained his clues thusly: "Bing, bong, bell" meant three things: the bells ring on Sunday (and Sunday is the day of Jack Benny's program), the chimes of Big Ben and the NBC chimes; "It's ten and only one can tell" refers to a deck of cards, eleventh card being the jack, and J is the tenth letter; "The

---

* In an interview with Ralph Edwards after the contest, Jack Benny said he had been "hoisted with his own petard" because the *Truth or Consequences* show with "The Walking Man" contest had knocked him out of his number one rating.

master of the metropolis" refers to his man-servant, Rochester, who answered the phone after the contest as "Hello, Master, this is Metropolis." Metropolis itself means a central city or a colony or a county seat, and Rochester is the county seat of Monroe County, New York; "Fits his name quite well" meant benny, which in the dictionary is an overcoat. Benny was chosen as The Walking Man because Waukegan is from the Indian of "walk again." The heavy tread of Benny's walk was to indicate that he carried his money in his shoes.

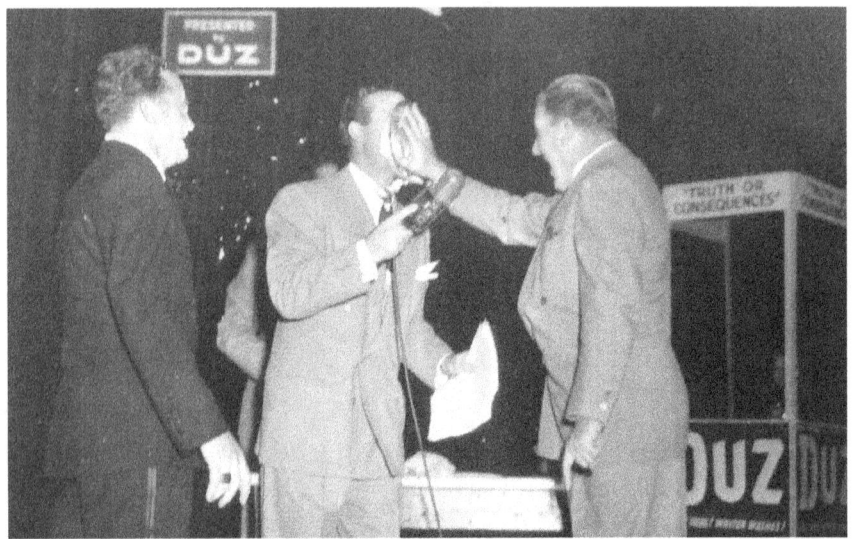

William Bendix slams a pie into the face of Ralph Edwards. From the broadcast of January 17, 1948.

William Bendix sprays water seltzer into the face of a contestant. From the broadcast of January 17, 1948.

Ralph Edwards cleans up from the surprise pie in the face.

Criticisms

One newspaper columnist criticized the contest: "Jack Benny got a million dollars-worth of advertising – which he does not need. Mrs. Florence Hubbard, occupant of a three-room apartment, got more prizes than she knows what to do with. The people of the nation contributed $1,500,000 to a cause to which few of them would have cared to contribute – except for an opportunity to participate in a contest that hinged on the slim chance that they would be called and able to give the answer (which a national magazine and many newspapers had given them). Where is this radio lottery business going to lead us?"

Columnist Tom Manche satirized in his column, "There can be all sorts of mystery characters now. For instance, the next celebrity may take a slug of Pepsi-Cola, then step up to the mike and express himself and another contest is born. Who is Mr. Belch? A beefy male with fat knuckles may be called upon to rap a staccato-like cadence on a piece of beaver board. Who is The Knocker? Or how about giving some toothy harridan a piece of celery, let her masticate same over the network and before you know it, 80,000,000 people will be going crazy trying to think of The Chewing Lady."

"Critical lashings of the give-away craze that has swamped the dials have become more and more frequent. Too much gold is being distributed, is the justifiable complaint, and not enough entertainment," remarked Sid Shalit in the syndicated column, *Listening In*.

Strike It Rich, with the first season on the air, alertly handled by Todd Russell, made no apology to those who cited the manner in which the prizes were spent. A 70-year-old listener wanted and won a new set of molars. A Cherokee Indian needed money to provide a few extra luxuries on his reservation. An elderly Irish lady wanted a chance to win enough to get her back to Ireland for one "last look" before she died. A blind man wanted to contribute what he won to the Industrial School for the Blind because that institution had been so helpful to him. One contestant needed money in order to change his name legally from that of Mussolini. Two females wanted enough loot to send them to Alaska, where they had heard the ratio of men to women was three to one. A 17-year-old girl explained her need for a charm school matriculation. Her brothers – two longshoremen – insisted she was getting to walk and talk like a truck driver.

Naturally, this success attracted imitators. In Cleveland, Ohio, station WJMO promptly started a "Neighbor X" program on which listeners were asked to guess the identity of prominent Clevelanders whose voices were broadcast by transcription. WWDC, an FM station in Washington, started a "Who's Mr. F.M." contest which backfired rather badly. The contest brought in 25,793 letters of which 19,120 guessed Mr. F.M. correctly as Peter Donald. The winner, an employee of the FBI, was selected over the others by virtue of the neatness, originality and logic of the letter. One enterprising radio showman recorded voices of famous people and started peddling to local independent stations a complete program, including radio scripts with clues. All the station had to provide was a master of ceremonies and somebody to open the letters. With the Miss Hush contest concluded, Paul Whiteman began a contest of his own, prizes totaling $22,500, on his daily disk jockey show on ABC. Each day for four weeks a tune would be played while listeners wrote a letter of 25 words or less. *Bride and Groom* waved $10,000 in cash for letters explaining why listeners like the radio program, and sponsor Lever Brothers. (*Bride and Groom* began as a program about marriage but ventured into the giveaway premise and ultimately gave some $600,000 in gifts in 1946.)

In late February 1948, what had been a good-natured rivalry between the contending camps of *Truth or Consequences* and *People Are Funny* took a rancorous turn with the announcement of a new "Raleigh riddle" on the Art Linkletter radio program. Somehow or other the word leaked to the Compton Agency and Procter & Gamble radio executives that the giveaway device too closely resembled the Ralph Edwards format for the "Miss Hush" and "The Walking Man" contests.

A protest was lodged with NBC in New York, which was said to have given its blessing to John Guedel, producer of *People Are Funny*. According to the agency, this setup would follow the same general patter of *Consequences* even to the three phone calls made during the show. Lewis Titterton, radio director of Compton, flew to New York to consult with executives at Procter & Gamble on the demands to be made to NBC.

Following the contest, Edwards contemplated additional contests including "The Walking Lady," "A Baby Hush" and "The Burping Baby." One newspaper columnist in the Naperville, Illinois *Sun* paper joked that the nation could relax again until Ralph Edwards started a new contest, "Who is the Talking Dog?" Prizes would include $10,000 in Confederate currency, a trip to Lisle with all expenses paid, two weeks' vacation without pay, a suit of tar and feathers for every male member of the family from the American Asphalt Roofing company, a 1913 Model T convertible with gas lights, a seven-room house burned clear to the ground, a ten-cent diamond ring from Woolworth's, a two-year supply of mothballs, and an oil-burning lantern slide projector with 100 views of Naperville.

In late March 1948, a proposed exploitation stunt for the *Molle Mystery Theatre* radio program was slated for the junk pile as a result of complaints by Ralph Edwards, who wrote to Niles Trammel, president of NBC, on the grounds that Molle's projected "Shaving Man" contest, a sort of satire of his "Miss Hush" and "The Walking Man" gimmicks, would damage his "Laughing Lady," which was being readied next fall. Molle's "Shaving Man" contest, with a $25,000 giveaway, and a letter gimmick on "Why I like Molle shaving cream," was to have been a gag for publicity and mail pull, with Fred Allen obviously the unknown man to be identified.

Ralph Edwards was not happy when he discovered that experts estimated that no less than thirty other programs have copied the formula or pattern, or both. $50,000 in cash was dangled by *Breakfast in Hollywood*; Drew Pearson offered $20,000; *True or False* offered $25,000; NBC offered $50,000 through a combination of four soap operas, *Joyce Jordan*, *Road to Life*, *Life Can be Beautiful*, and *Pepper Young*; *Stop the Music* offered $13,000 worth of merchandise; a "surprise" award which could be anything from a burnt match to an airplane was offered on *Stop Me If You Heard This One*; and Abbott and Costello offered a $4,000 plane, a trailer, a diamond ring, a two-week vacation, and a baby elephant!

Radio listeners, ignoring the fact that judges did not know the names and address of the letter writers until after the three best letters of each week were selected, started to criticize the lack of interest in their community. When a rumor circulated that Edwards ignored Wisconsin contestants in his "Miss Hush" and "The Walking Man" contests because of a fear of violating Wisconsin lottery laws, Deputy Dist. Atty. John S. Barry in Wisconsin verified this statement publicly for the local newspapers, citing it was not considered a lottery because there was no legal element of chance, which must be present in a lottery.

In May of 1948, Ralph Edwards reversed positions when he was discovered to be "The Mystery Man," for a radio contest in Kansas that benefited the American Red Cross. Multiple prizes were donated by local businesses such as the Coca Cola Company, Charm House Decorators, Charmer Dress Shop, the Burns Publishing, Co., the Jack Burns Jewelry Company, Marshall Bros., and the Goetz Company. The winner was Virgil L. Crew, a night switchboard operator.

The Closing Chapter

Mrs. Hubbard did not have enough space in her three-room apartment for all the prizes. She sold some of the prizes, including the airplane, to help cover the taxes on her winnings. She kept only the television, the fur coat and the sewing machine. The remainder of the prizes, for the most part, had been turned over to her nephew, Harvey L. Davis, in Dallas, Texas, an attorney, for disposal. The money helped pay the taxes – an estimated $8,000 by most accounts. "This isn't going to change my standard of living," Hubbard told reporters. "I'm going back to my $30-a-week job after that Sun Valley, Idaho, vacation they tell me I won." And she did exactly that. She had no need for the automobile, so the Hillcrest Motor Company disposed of the Cadillac and signed a check over to her, payable for $3,800. The Bulova wristwatch was sold for $500. She would not accept the tiles, at the suggestion of her nephew, and instead accepted a check for $400. In exchange for the freezer, she accepted a check for $468.25 from The Coolerator Company. The Normel trailer was not delivered at her request and instead, a check covering the wholesale price of $1,908.03 was provided. In lieu of the sheets, she was offered the wholesale price of $153.83. The men's suits were valued at $180. It was agreed that Westinghouse pay her $500 instead of delivery of product. Because Ms. Hubbard lived in an apartment, Sherwin-Williams understood her situation and instead provided a check for $1,000. In the question of dollar value for prizes, a number of companies attempted to provide a check for the wholesale value, not retail. This was often negotiated between her nephew and the reps for those companies. Within a year she received 47 marriage proposals by letter, telegram and phone. "I didn't bother to answer any," she said. "I'm not in the market for a husband."

In February 1951, Ralph Edwards received a visit from three Southern California girls who formerly had heart trouble but who had been cured because of discoveries by medical science. They personally thanked him in the names of 500,000 high school and elementary children suffering from rheumatic fever. They were Madeline Feeney, Carroll Ray King and Margaret Hopkins.

In October 1957, Ralph Edwards was presented with a Gold Heart Award, the highest honor of the American Heart Association. The citation marked the tenth anniversary of "The Walking Man" contest, which helped launch the Heart Association as a national health agency. The citation accompanying the Gold Heart Award read as follows: "His *Truth or Consequences* radio program, through its "Walking Man" contest in 1948, created nationwide awareness of the heart problem and brought forth public contributions exceeding $1,500,000. In providing funds so vitally needed to launch the American Heart Association as a national voluntary health agency, he performed an act of public service without parallel in the annals of mass communication."

Mrs. Hubbard had no children and was living in Dallas at the time she passed away in 1978 at the age of 100. On the side of her house, near the front door, was a sign: "The House that Ralph Edwards Built."

Florence Hubbard meets Jack Benny in person when she arrived at the studio to receive her prizes.

Chapter 11
Truth or Consequences, New Mexico

"Howdy partners! Pull up a cactus, pull out a Phillip Morris!"

"We're going to make a lot of noise, blow a lot of horns and open up the city."
– Ralph Edwards

In February 1950, aware that *Truth or Consequences* was soon to reach a ten-year milestone, Ralph Edwards and his idea men, and the producers of the radio quiz program, sought a novel means of celebrating. Prior anniversary broadcasts featured an all-star celebration but this time they wanted to do something legendary. Already they had recognized the achievements of war veterans, set the bar for the sale of War Bonds, and created a national phenomenon with "The Walking Man" contest. That was when Ralph Edwards gave serious consideration to an idea proposed by Al Simon: Why not find a town or city in America that would be willing to change its name to that of the show and do the anniversary broadcast from that city?

To commemorate the 10th anniversary of the radio program, a unique proposal was made. The quiz program offered $1 million in publicity to the first town willing to officially change its name to Truth or Consequences. "We were searching for a way to celebrate *Truth or Consequences* ten years on the air," Edwards later recalled.

"One of our idea men, Al Simon, asked, 'What if a town changed its name to Truth or Consequences?' Amazingly enough, our staff found several towns eager to do it."

Half a dozen towns vied for the opportunity. The Denver Chamber of Commerce offered a suburb, the small town of Martin City, Montana, population 600, put itself in the running, and another in St. Helens, Oregon. Bob Zimmerman, a United Press correspondent at Santa Fe, was responsible for suggesting Hot Springs, New Mexico. Contacted by Sue Clark, publicity agent for the program, Zimmerman pointed out that Hot Springs was a health resort, with a historic reputation for the Apache leader, Geronimo, soaking in the mineral springs, and was constantly being confused with Hot Springs, Arkansas.

Hot Springs, New Mexico, is the high desert country of southwest New Mexico, ringed by rugged buttes and mountains. Bayonet-bladed yucca plants dot the landscape. The sun shines 318 days a year, on average, and the air is clean. Hot Springs advertised itself as the recreational paradise of the Southwest because of its proximity to two large dammed lakes on the Rio Grande, forming the greatest mass of water in New Mexico. A typical rural settlement in 1940, Hot Springs quadrupled in population from 2,000 to 8,000, within a decade. It was a flourishing agricultural, cattle-raising and oil-drilling center. It was the location of the recently completed Elephant-Butte Dam, an important source of power and water for the surrounding areas. Its warm springs were known for healing powers, and several hospitals, including the Carrie Tingley Hospital for Crippled Children, were situated there.

Even with its warm and dry climate, and medicinal mineral baths, the city suffered from low tourism as a result of much needed publicity. The city was nestled in the mountains along the banks of the Rio Grande and had more to offer the health seeker and the sportsman than advertised in pamphlets and newspapers. The deciding factor, which appealed to Ralph Edwards, was the presence of the Carrie Tingley Hospital for Crippled Children, which opened in 1937, named for his wife by then Gov. Clyde Tingley. Children were sent from all over the state suffering the effects of polio, as well as other crippling diseases. Edwards, ever the philanthropist, had someone in his office contact city officials.

On March 9, producer Ed Bailey phoned Joe Bursey, following up on a letter mailed to the secretary of the New Mexico Tourist Bureau, and it was Bursey who suggested Bailey contact State Senator Burton Roach, who was also serving as secretary to the Chamber of Commerce. When Roach discovered the phone call was not in jest, but a legitimate business proposal, the Senator called a conference with the City Council. A straw vote was taken the next day for the name change with a 12 to 1 outcome in favor.

The City Council wanted to talk the proposition over with a program representative so Bailey flew to Hot Springs on March 12 to meet with city officials, explaining the publicity angle the city would receive from the program. "I am not trying to sell you anything," Bailey told the councilmen. "We can't even commit to ourselves that we will mention the town's name on the air even once a month. But we will mention it from time to time." After two days of conferences it was decided to submit the proposal for the name change to the people. The man who spearheaded the most enthusiastic support for the name change was Burton Roach, who promised to move mountains if it was necessary to make it happen.

Many times over the years, Ralph Edwards has been credited for the name change from Hot Springs to Truth or Consequences. It should be noted that while his fulfilled promises exceeded even Ralph Edwards himself, then a veteran showman with a long-standing love for the state, it was Burton Roach who really carried the ball, with the cooperation of the vast majority of his fellow townsmen. It was Roach who took the incidental scoffing and ribbing; took it smiling because he figured he was right.

Roach was a resident of New Mexico for more than 25 years, he was before that Sheriff of Potter County (Amarillo), Texas. He was in the cattle business, had a wide acquaintance and his friends voted him into that office by an overwhelming majority. In New Mexico, he soon took over management of the Ladder ranch, one of the largest in the state, near Hillsboro. In 1936, he was elected to the Legislature, as a member of the House. Two years later, he was elevated to the State Senate and, when the management of the Chamber there was left vacant a couple of years back, he took it.

On the evening of March 21, 1950, at a regular recess meeting of the city of Hot Springs, fifty-five people attended the council meeting, including Burton Roach. Hot Springs wasn't a particularly good name for the town, Roach explained, except for singing praises of its mineral baths. Too many towns across the country laid claim to similar bragging rights. Hot Springs, Arkansas, boasted larger size by comparison. South Dakota also had a Hot Springs; Mississippi had Holly Springs; Texas had Mineral Wells, and so on. It was pretty confusing and, as Roach explained, the name of Hot Springs, New Mexico, meant nothing in the national picture.

City Council met on March 21 to vote for the name change from Hot Springs to Truth or Consequences. Ed Bailey, radio producer, is seated at top left between the calendar and window. Senator Burton Roach is seated with his back towards the camera in the dark suit, second from lower right. Nills Kjellstrom, the attorney for Hot Springs, is seated at the bottom left.

Supported enthusiastically by Mayor G.J. Mims and State Sen. Burton Roach, on a show of hands 54 favored the change and one opposed. Jack Morgan, a resident in town, stated he would not have invested money in a court had he known the possibility existed of a name change. He cited Montgomery Ward with having trouble shipping his merchandise to Hot Springs if the town changed names. "Here was a man talking about building Hot Springs and still he sends his money out of town," Paul Tooley reported in his newspaper. "This man and another who opposed the change are not members of the chamber of commerce." J.W. Scott, a resident of the town, began voicing his disapproval among the streets of town, following the meeting. Andy Anderson, another resident, said he was glad the town was changing the name. "I've been wanting to move to another town, now I can do it without getting out of my room."

In a letter addressed to Ralph Edwards, it was explained that all legal formalities would be taken to assure the legal change, and that the undersigned pledged their support. In return for the honor of changing the city's name, Edwards and his crew promised to broadcast the radio program from the city on the evening of

R.S. Kaiser (left) was a resident of Hot Springs who opposed the idea of the name change. Postmaster Joseph D. Tafoya is pictured on the right.

April 1, with all the attendant national publicity that such an event would inspire. "We are enlisting the huge publicity facilities of NBC on both coasts to work with my Hollywood and New York press representatives to focus the spotlight of the nation on what we happily hope will be Truth or Consequences, New Mexico," Edwards wrote in a letter. "You may be assured we will make your city our city and mention it whenever possible on the air and at times try to slant constructive stunts towards the city."

With this matter taken care of, Ralph Edwards, on the evening of March 25, 1950, told his estimated 19,000,000 listeners throughout the nation: "We are announcing the biggest thing that has ever happened to *Truth or Consequences*. Listen, everybody, across the nation. I have a letter in my hands from Hot Springs, New Mexico, a beautiful city of some 8,000 people, located in the middle of the Rio Grande Valley, on U.S. highway 35. A letter from the mayor, J.G. Mims, of Hot Springs, New Mexico, and countersigned by eight councilmen of Hot Springs, the state senator, representative, and other officials." Edwards informed the audience that he and the entire *Truth or Consequences* gang would journey to the small town to officially dedicate the city and put Truth or Consequences on the map. Edwards also informed the radio audience that the entire crew would arrive a few days early to go fishing and take a motor boat ride on beautiful Elephant Butte Lake, the third largest body of impounded water in the world, 44 miles long, behind the dam where largemouth bass reside. Edwards also took a moment to acknowledge the Carrie Tingley Hospital for Crippled Children. "We feel it's a perfect tie-up and are proud to think that this particularly wonderful city will be the city known as Truth or Consequences." Edwards closed his dedication over the mike with the remark, "That lollypop really grew into something big, didn't it, Alvin Robinson? It grew into a city and doggone if we aren't thrilled clear down to the tips of our toes." (Robinson was the first contestant on the very first broadcast of *Truth or Consequences*.)*

The town citizens had about a week to prepare not just for the upcoming election, but for a parade, celebration dinners, and election campaigns prompted from both supporters and those who opposed. A number of roundtable discussions were held over radio station KCHS. In those discussions, a majority felt that the large volume of publicity which the town would receive would warrant changing the name. Among the staunchest supporters was Paul O. Tooley, owner and editor of the *Hot Springs Herald*, the weekly newspaper. "At first I was opposed to changing the name of this town to Truth or Consequences," he wrote in his editorial a week before the election. "I think the name is silly, but it seems it takes something silly in this age to get along. I am of the opinion that the name doesn't mean too much. Even if it is changed, the schools will continue to teach the same courses, the bank will operate as usual, in fact very little will be changed."

One week later, Tooley reported in his column: "Tomorrow, probably, is the most important day in the history of Hot Springs. Personally, I am for it. It is too good an advertising deal to pass up. Many of those who have been against the proposal are now for it, after they understood what the deal was. Here are a few items to consider, if the change is made: It still will be Hot Springs High School, all mail addressed to Hot Springs will be delivered here, present printed matter can be changed with a 35-cent rubber stamp, it will not be necessary to change deeds and abstracts until property is sold, it still will be the *Hot Springs Herald*, in fact, the only change will be the name of the town. I have checked all these angles and pass it along for the consideration of the readers of this column. Regardless of how you feel about the idea, cast your vote tomorrow."

"When people of other towns oppose changing the name of Hot Springs, it can be for two reasons only," Tooley continued. "They are lacking of information on what actually lies behind the move, or fear that Hot Springs will grow to the

---

* Edwards and his staff arrived via plane at the new Truth or Consequences Municipal Airport, dedicated March 26, the day following the radio broadcast.

point of menacing the businesses of other towns. I really believe this is true with Albuquerque. I hope their efforts bear fruit, the right kind of fruit. I think this is a local problem and it doesn't behoove other editors to stick their noses in our business and that goes for the Santa Fe New Mexican who approves the plan."

After careful review, it was estimated that if the city was mentioned only once a month on the *Truth or Consequences* radio program, it would mean about $2,736,000 in advertising annually. "As a whole," the local newspaper reported, "the offer made Hot Springs is bigger than the national debt, if anything can be bigger."

Senator Burton Roach sent 500 copies of the *Herald*'s extra to all members of Congress. Father A. Burgmeier, pastor of Our Lady of Perpetual Help Church, who told his parishioners that the offer made Hot Springs to change its name was providential because it gave the town an opportunity to help humanity. The local newspaper featured numerous advertisements each bearing the word "Welcome" and a photograph of Ralph Edwards, showing public support for the name change. This included the Trailways Café on 128 Broadway, Owston's Jewelry across from the bank, The Holland Shop on Main Street, the Geronimo Bus Lines, the Sav-Mor Market on Highway 85, the Hot Springs Coal and Feed, the Hot Spot Grocery and Market, Thomas Davenport Real Estate and many others.

On March 31, the day before the scheduled radio broadcast, the citizens of Hot Springs went to the polls with open minds and cast their ballots for whichever they considered would be for the betterment of their city. As one citizen described the effect it seemed to have, "The whole town seems to be jumping up and down." By a vote of 1,294 to 295, practically six to one, Hot Springs voters Friday elected to change the name of the city to Truth or Consequences. Nine minutes and 40 seconds after the polls closed, an extra edition of the *Hot Springs Herald*, retitled the *Truth or Consequences Herald*, was on the streets carrying the election returns.* Burton Roach succeeded in what would ultimately become the largest publicity campaign for the city in history. "It became an almost holy cause," as described by columnist Thom Boger. "The result was rated by some as another personal victory for this big, ex-cowboy."

* Numerous references cite the newspaper remained the *Truth or Consequences Herald* for many years, but this is inaccurate. The newspaper would revert to the original title of *Hot Springs Herald* with the next edition. Proving that the printed page cannot be taken as the gospel, the March 30, 1950 issue of *Radio Daily* incorrectly stated a Texas town would be renamed Truth or Consequences.

The first resident of Hot Springs, New Mexico, to cast his vote was Omaray Isaac. Presiding over the voting as election judges were C.W. Hatchet (left) and Mr. Carter.

The official declaration is signed by the City Council.

As a result of the nationwide broadcast, letters, telegrams and telephone calls poured in on weary secretaries and other citizens. Besides the chamber of commerce, hardest hit was Roy Stovall, appointed by Edwards as "Public

Relations Director" for *Truth or Consequences*. "I think this is the smartest action my people could have ever taken," Mayor Glen Mims said to the press. "Now the whole United States will know of our fine facilities, our ideal climate, our excellent fishing, our health-giving water and sunshine, and the many other wonders that we have to offer."

Meanwhile, Bailey and his production crew located to the Buckhorn Bar, temporarily office for maneuvering and storing the electronic equipment necessary to make the radio broadcast happen. Skeptical town citizens who went to the bar to get a drink and discuss the news of the week, were reportedly motivated into voting in favor of the name change when they saw all the equipment stored along the wall, realizing the promise of a radio broadcast and a moment of fame was genuine.

Left to right: Sue Clark, publicity director for the radio program; Ralph Edwards; Senator Burton Roach; and Nils Kjellstrom, city attorney.

Tickets for the radio program were put on sale on Monday, March 27. There were 460 bleacher tickets at $3 each and those were sold out in about 1.5 hours. The five, three and two dollar tickets also sold out an hour later. On Thursday, March 30, the $10 tickets (for the best seats in high school auditorium) were put up for sale. By Thursday evening, the total number of tickets available was 1,530 and all but 200 were sold before the close of day.

Saturday morning, a fishing party tried its luck on the same lake, and later Edwards was introduced into the Sierra County Sheriff's posse – a ceremony which involved his being forcibly relieved of his city clothes and properly garbed in the posse uniform, complete with ten-gallon hat, badge, gun and holster. Edwards wore the uniform to lead the hour-long parade, which was the big event of Saturday afternoon. Ten thousand people lined the parade route to see Ralph, a series of impressive floats, bands, mounted riders and a group of local and visiting dignitaries, including Congressman John Miles of New Mexico and the Mayors of El Paso, Texas, and Juarez, Mexico.

The parade welcomed Ralph Edwards and his crew, starting 2 p.m. Saturday, featuring floats sponsored by local business houses. By some accounts, 10,000 people lined the parade route. Edwards personally offered a 72-piece Fine-Arts Sterling Silver set valued at $350.00 for the best float. Second place was a choice of any Westinghouse appliance such as a mixer, roaster, waffle-iron, vacuum cleaner, electric comforter, and many others. Third place was a set of matched Halliburton luggage, "precision made to last a lifetime." While in town, Edwards was honored at a dinner at the Country Club, given a fish fry at Elephant Butte Lake and honored at a western style barbecue.

"We took a plane load of press for the show originating there," Edwards recalled. "I was met by a man who came up to me and said, 'Ralph Edwards? H.B. Huckabee – Chief of Police, Truth or Consequences, New Mexico.' I knew then that we were really there."

A $10 ticket for Saturday's broadcast was offered for the best window display of Procter & Gamble products. To the high school boy and girl whose window paintings were judged the best, Bulova "Academy Award" watches, and to the winner high-over-all would also get a $10 ticket and $5 and $3 tickets to the runners up. Edwards and Bailey were the judges for these events. The local newspaper, the *Hot Springs Herald*, featured numerous advertisements from local businesses welcoming Ralph Edwards. All featuring the same publicity photo of the game show host and the word "Welcome" in large print.

Almost 10,000 people were reported to have lined up along the two-mile parade route and marveled at the bigness of the parade, which was arranged on short notice. The lengthy procession was led by Ralph Edwards, who was initiated into the Sierra County Sheriff's Posse earlier that day, by undressing him on Broadway and presenting him with the Posse's regulation uniform, and mounting him on a Palomino stallion. Edwards rode with the Sheriff's Posse Auxiliary. The float entered by Johnson's Drive 'N' was awarded the sterling silver. Other winners were the high school junior class float (Westinghouse) and the Gage Continental Divide Indian Trading Post float (Halliburton luggage). Miss Jo Ellen Jennings and Alerico Torres were awarded the watches for the best high school window paintings. Roy Stovall, parade marshal, thanked everyone publicly for making the parade possible.

The Saturday following the election, the Hot Springs National Bank began cancelling its checks under the new name of Truth or Consequences National Bank. A huge sign at the entrance to the town was posted. Many business establishments in the downtown district had special window decorations welcoming Ralph, the program and the change of name.

To christen the event even further, Mr. and Mrs. Thomas Passmore (the former Dorothy Mott of Wills Point, Texas) named their newborn baby Ralph Edwards Passmore in his honor on Friday, the day that the town was voting to change its name in honor of the tenth anniversary of the radio quiz show. The baby was born on Wednesday, March 29, at approximately 4 p.m., weighing seven pounds, five ounces. The couple had resided in Hot Springs for four years prior to the birth. Thomas Passmore was employed at the Bullock Grocery.

Dorothy Passmore and her baby boy, Ralph Edwards Passmore, greeted by Ralph Edwards.

The Anniversary Broadcast

The broadcast of April 1 over NBC may have caused a number of radio listeners to wonder if the entire program was an April Fools' joke. Edwards assured the town citizens that the plan was no gag. "I have my own reputation and show to protect and I want to go along and make this town one of the greatest health centers in the nation." During the broadcast, the christened town of Truth or Consequences was made official via ceremony – a bottle of mineral water was broken over the head of State Senator Burton Roach, as a representative of the city during the broadcast. The Woman's Club, represented by Mrs. Walter Knox, placed in charge of the Truth or Consequences Museum of relics and props used during the ten years of the broadcast was given a 72-piece set of Fine-Arts Sterling Silver for club use. W.A. "Skinny" Davis was presented the "County Seat" which turned out to be an overstuffed chair which he sat in and found to be a "hot seat" to place at the entrance of one of the drug stores in town. "There was an electric cord connected to the chair," Davis later recalled. "The problem was someone forgot to turn on the electricity. So I faked the shocks and went along with it the best I could." Later, Davis received a letter addressed "Hot Seat Davis" from San Bernardino, California.

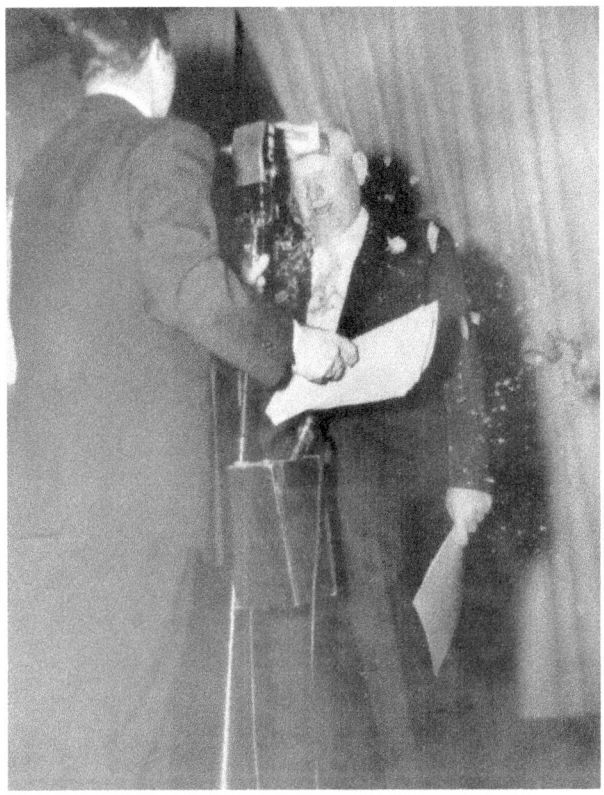

A bottle of mineral water is broken over the head of State Senator Burton Roach during the ceremony.

Mrs. Walter Knox of the Knox Drug Store receives her consequence during the radio broadcast to take charge of a new museum displaying props from radio broadcasts of the past ten years.

The town citizens lined up to see Ralph Edwards in person during the welcoming parade.

One of the many floats during the parade.

Popular Henry Gardey, World War II veteran, was dubbed City jester for one year, and got off to a good start by presenting to Edwards $1,000 in Chinese money before his departure for Hollywood Sunday. Early Tuesday morning, a pine coffin was found deserted near the cemetery. The box, filled with old bones, revealed the legend: "Hot Springs, born December 1916, died March 31, 1950" and an envelope addressed to "the next of kin" containing a joker from a deck of cards. Although Mr. Gardey swore he had nothing to do with the prank, every indication pointed to him.

Mrs. Beulah Shirk, co-owner of radio station KCHS; Paul Tooley, editor and publisher of the *Hot Springs Herald*, and Mrs. Arletta Coleman, editor and publisher of the *Sierra County Advocate*, were jointly presented with two large billboards to be placed at either end of the town, welcoming travelers to Truth or Consequences, New Mexico.

Sent out to Elephant Butte Lake to bring back an elephant and not expecting to find anything but mountain goats, Herb Lett not only surprised the audience, but himself, by returning with a live elephant, which had been transported by van from the Clyde Beatty Circus in Hollywood to take part in the show. Soon after the broadcast, Lett received numerous letters asking if the elephant was truly real.

Herb Lett brings the elephant into the auditorium for the radio broadcast.

Roy K. Stovall, a well-known cattleman, was placed in charge of distributing signs showing the distance to Truth or Consequences, New Mexico, and souvenir tickets. At a later date, he would appear on the radio show originating from Hollywood with snapshots of his signs, posted across the continent. Just minutes after the broadcast, Stovall received phone calls from Vancouver, Canada, asking for a sign, and another call from the wife of a close friend, Fred Olander, dispatched from Kansas City, Missouri.

It was estimated, according to the *Hot Springs Herald*, that he received approximately 400 letters, wires and calls from every state in the union. One of his consequences was that he place a sign in Cairo, Egypt, and Wednesday he promised that one would be erected there by Sunday evening. Monday he received a call from Williams, Arizona, agreeing to place one in the bottom of the Grand Canyon, four wires and numerous letters asked for signs for Grand Central Station in New York, and Notre Dame requested two placards to be placed at either end of their famous stadium. A very nice letter from a gentleman in Maine ended with a cartoon entitled, "Sucker."

The successful attempt to plant a road sign in the Grand Canyon took the contestant to restricted land owned by local natives. A permit was required along with an almost hazardous trek through unbearable temperature.

The Rev. O.L. Dennis*, pastor of the First Baptist Church; the Rev. F.J. Seddon, of St. Paul's Episcopal Church; the Rev. Father A. Burgmeier, of Our Lady of Perpetual Help Catholic Church; and the Rev. Harvey Carrell, pastor of the Methodist Church, representing a cross-section of the city's religious faction, were also interviewed on the broadcast. Due to the limited time on the air, more contestants had to be interviewed after the broadcast. The radio audience was unaware of these additional stunts. Orville Pickett paid the consequences by performing his interpretation of a hula dance, complete with grass skirt. A gentleman from Albuquerque was hit in the head with cream pies every time his wife told a joke and got the audience to laugh. A local young lady and a sailor from Missouri recently sent back to the states from service, blindfolded and outfitted in football helmets, participated in an apple biting contest.

*The sermon topic of Rev. O.L. Dennis on Sunday, April 2, given at the regular church service in the First Baptist Church, was about the name change. His sermon was also delivered over radio station KCHS at 11:30 a.m.

The radio broadcast of April 1, 1950 in Truth or Consequences, New Mexico.

Technicians setting up the equipment for the remote radio broadcast over NBC.

> *Truth or Consequences* established itself as a longtime Saturday night stalwart on NBC, but Procter & Gamble at the time was questioning the wisdom of continuing with the program, according to an inter-office memo in the last week of March, suggesting "it has outlived its audience impact." This is ironic when you consider the New Mexico celebration and the fact that relations between Edwards and the sponsor were solid (as evident by Edwards presiding as emcee over "Dividend Day" at the Procter & Gamble plant in Long Beach, California, in late February). Local residents made sure DUZ was on display as window store dressing, and on a number of parade floats. Philip Morris, the sponsor of *This is Your Life*, was somewhat apprehensive over the program's rating pull and started considering sponsorship of *Truth or Consequences* should the drug manufacturer drop sponsorship.

Following the broadcast, thousands of letters and telegrams poured into *Truth or Consequences*. A majority of the letters and wires requested information on the care of arthritics through use of mineral waters. Others asked about working conditions there, and still others were eager to become tourists. In his 9 p.m. news broadcast, originating in San Antonio, Texas, Austin Williams, noted news commentator, stated: "If there's anyone in Truth or Consequences, New Mexico, listening to this broadcast, I want to extend to you the heartiest congratulations from myself and staff on your recent achievement. Jack White, mayor of San Antonio, is with us in this salute. He would greatly appreciate receiving cards and letters from those of you listening to this program."

Other wires received are reprinted below:

"Please convey to Ralph Edwards my congratulations on this tenth anniversary of his radio program, *Truth or Consequences*, which has achieved such high standards in entertainment and public service. A bountiful harvest is in store for your city from the seeds of good will that he sows."

—Fletcher Bowron, Mayor of Los Angeles, California

"All Alexandria's citizens listen to *Truth or Consequences* on KSLY on Saturday night. So it's a pleasure for me to congratulate Ralph Edwards, the show, and your fine city on its new name, Truth or Consequences, New Mexico. We always tell the truth, but it would be fun to play Ralph Edwards' consequences. With my sincere congratulations goes a cordial invitation for all to visit Alexandria, in the 'heart of Louisiana.'"

—Carl B. Close, Mayor of Alexandria, Louisiana

"Congratulations, a splendid idea. Hello to Ralph and all the gang."

—Leo C. Williamson, Mayor of Williamsport, Pennsylvania

"On behalf of the entire staff of WOAI, we are pleased to send warm congratulations to you and citizens of your town on change of name to Truth or Consequences. Hope you're all listening to my 10 p.m. news Saturday night. Sincerely."

—Austin Williams, WOAI, San Antonio, Texas

"Congratulations on your new and distinctive name from the only city in the world called Pocatello. It is our hope that your future will be as evenly and successful as your radio program namesake. As for your christening, we hope you will tell the truth and not have to pay the consequence."

—J.L. Craig, Jr., Executive Secretary of Pocatello, Idaho, Chamber of Commerce

"Congratulations on your new name, Truth or Consequences, wishing you best always."

—Henry V. Diefenbach, General Manager, WGKV, Charleston, West Virginia

"Congratulations on your name change to Truth or Consequences. But keep an eye on that man, Ralph Edwards."

—Arthur R. Meehan, Mayor of Spokane, Washington

"You and your administration are to be heartily congratulated upon accomplishing two forward steps today through your efforts. Continental Air Lines puts Hot Springs on the air map. Saturday Ralph Edwards gives you nationwide publicity. You are building well. May God bless you in your efforts."

—Charles R. Keyes, former Hot Springs Chamber of Commerce Secretary

Mayor J.G. Mims gives Ralph Edwards the key to the city.

Additional telegrams offering congratulations came in from the mayor of Raleigh, North Carolina, the mayor of Grand Rapids, Michigan, the mayor of Terre Haute, Indiana, and the mayor of Wilmington, Delaware, among others. Of the 10,000 inquiries received during the two weeks following the radio broadcast, Mr. Stovall discovered he was called everything from a "screwball" to "Royball," and received letters addressed to "Put-her-on-the-map Chief," "Keeper of the Signs," "The man in charge of putting Truth or Consequences on the Map" and "Unusual Signs." One letter came addressed to "People Are Funny, New Mexico," another "Truth or Consequences, Duz, New Mexico," and one addressed to "Threw the

Consequences, New Mexico." An advertising agency in Portland, Oregon, notified they were inserting, along with some other of their neighborhood businessmen's ads, a sign pointing south and reading, "Follow the birds to Truth or Consequences, New Mexico." William E. Strobo, of Quebec, Canada, wanted to place a mileage sign at the crossroads of the Kent House, former residence of the Duke of Kent, father of Queen Victoria, and the historical Shrine of St. Anne de Beaupre, where thousands of tourists visit yearly. Douglas T. Koki, of Honolulu, Hawaii, offered to be the representative in charge of posting signs on the island.

Hours before the radio broadcast, Ralph Edwards sent Senator Burton Roach the following telegram:

TONIGHT MARKS THE GREATEST VISUAL ENDORSEMENT OF A CITY TO THE NATION IN THE HISTORY OF TELEVISION OR ANY OTHER MEDIUM I KNOW OF. I AM THRILLED BEYOND WORDS AT THE PROSPECT OF AMERICA SEEING FIRST HAND THE GLORIOUS HEALTHFUL BENEFITS OF YOUR CITY AND MEETING IN PERSON THE FRIENDLY PEOPLE WHO ARE ITS CITIZENS AND WHEN TONIGHT'S SHOW IS OVER WE HIT THEM AGAIN NEXT WEEK WITH MORE OF THE SAME. AFTER TONIGHT IF THERE IS ONE PERSON IN THE UNITED STATES WHO IS NOT AWARE OF TRUTH OR CONSEQUENCES, NEW MEXICO, AND WHAT IT HAS TO OFFER, HE WILL HAVE TO BE THE WORLD'S LONELIEST HERMIT.

SINCERE BEST WISHES FROM THE TRUTH OR CONSEQUENCES GANG, BARBARA AND MYSELF, RALPH EDWARDS

Upon receipt of a letter from Ralph Edwards, on Monday, April 17, the city council passed its first order of business a resolution assuring Ralph Edwards of the council's intention of cooperation. "We are gathering our guns for the Truth or Consequences, New Mexico, attack on the nation which began with heavy artillery on April first," Edwards wrote.

Not everyone was as enthusiastic about the name change. The town's postmark needed to be revised to suit its new name, and local stores hoisted new signs proclaiming themselves as "Truth or Consequences" establishments. When Mayor T.B. Williams contacted the New Mexico congressional delegation in connection with the delay of the postal department in changing the name of the post office, V.C. Burk, Deputy Postmaster General advised the mayor that the proposed name was "three words too long." Local leaders quickly strategized "pressure" that would be brought to effect the change since there was no longer any legal city of Hot Springs any longer.

The town of Truth or Consequences received additional publicity while the story of the "refusal" appeared in papers across the nation. A. Johnson in Denver, Colorado, wrote: "Since I am a resident of Hot Springs, New Mexico, away from home, I naturally made a point of listening to the broadcast, *Truth or Consequences*, Saturday, April 1. At the time I left there, the movement to change the name of Hot Springs to Truth or Consequences had already been started, and as I had been out of touch with the home town for over two weeks, the broadcast was the only means I had to finding out if the people of Hot Springs had actually decided to change the name. To me is was a question that went far beyond the publicity concerned in the change… I got a great thrill from hearing the voices of acquaintances and friends on the program, and as I listened, the thought came to me that I had left Hot Springs but can never return to Hot Springs. It will be a different name on the map, but I still have the consolation that the same people and the same places will always be there."

Sign near Fresno, California, publicizing the newly-renamed New Mexico town.

By the first week of May, the treasury department authorized the Hot Springs National Bank to alter its articles of association to show that its main offices was in Truth or Consequences. The department of commerce approved a change in the code name on U.S. Weather Bureau circuits to DUZ for Truth or Consequences. Originally it was HSP.

Meanwhile, photographs evident of the 1,200 mileage placards and 50 metal signs dispatched since the April 1 broadcast began pouring in. Signs had been placed in Venezuela, South America; Dallastown, Pennsylvania; Grand Central Station, New York; Fresno, California; Oklahoma City, Oklahoma; and two in Houston, Texas – one in the lobby of Glen McCarthy's fabulous Shamrock Hotel and the other on the hotel lawn.

A proposed museum was in the works, spearheaded by Mayor T.B. Williams. A plaque in memory of the late Frank Winston was to be erected in the museum, as a memorial to the foresighted citizen who started the State Bath House, originally planned to become the site of the new museum. Edwards proposed sending props from the radio program for display. By April of 1951, the museum was open for business, located in the rear of the Chamber of Commerce building. Among the items on display was a baby bottle used on the first radio broadcast of *Truth or Consequences*, as well as original lollipops on the same. The "Beetle Derby Maize" prop represented one of the most complicated stunts performed on the radio show. Various awards given to Ralph Edwards were mounted and hung on the wall, as well as numerous pictures made during various broadcasts. An elephant sweater to cover the body, a tam o' shanter, four booties and the tail and trunk covers represented three weeks of work by Mrs. Susan Jarvis, a contestant on one of the broadcasts, when she volunteered to knit a sweater for a friend of Ralph Edwards. The friend was an elephant over eight feet tall and weighing 8,000 pounds. The seven, one dollar bills paid to the first contestants on the first broadcast of *Truth or Consequences* were also on display. The jester's cap, presented to Hank Garday on April 1, 1950, was on display. Another item concerning Garday was the can which was "Bill's home away from home." Bill was the frog captured from the waters of Elephant Butte Lake, that was taken by Garday to the Jumping Frog contest at Angel's Camp, California. Bill was christened "Elephant Butte Bill" and came in 10th place.

Four weeks after the radio broadcast, using press releases provided by Ralph Edwards' office, the *Hot Springs Herald* published a souvenir edition of the *Truth or Consequences Herald*. Photos of Ralph Edwards and his staff heavily illustrated the factoids that made up the 15,000 copies, which sold for 25 cents each. "I honestly feel that the voters of Truth or Consequences, New Mexico, have made a great move that will prove beneficial to suffering humanity over the nation," wrote Paul O. Tooley in his editorial. "Today, we have voted to change our name to Truth or Consequences. It's a silly name for a town, but then my own name is a bit on the odd side. But we don't have too odd a name. Look at Muleshoe, Texas; Six Mile Run, Pennsylvania; Ahgwahching, Minnesota; Lukachukai, Arizona; and Pushmataha, Oklahoma."

A Hot Button Issue

On June 1, City Attorney Nils T. Kjellstrom ruled that the legality of the election changing the name of the city could not be questioned, following the filing of a suit one week prior by Attorney Douglass K. FitzHugh, in behalf of J.W. Scott, alleging that there was not sufficient notice given to voters in calling the special election on March 31. He claimed that a public notice in newspapers was required by law, two weeks before the election.

By mid-June, petitions were circulating about town asking Congressmen John E. Miles and A.M. Fernandez to introduce or cause to be introduced, a bill in the Congress that would give the city of Truth or Consequences, New Mexico, a post office. Mayor T.B. Williams was the first to sign the petitions and 1,000 names were sought. The petitions were sponsored by the mayor, city council and the chamber of commerce. It was believed that the post office department was about ready to change the name when a nuisance suit was filed in an attempt to show the election was illegal. Regardless of technicalities, the election was considered legal and the petition urged immediate action on the proposed bill. It was cited on the petition that numerous businesses were being financially handicapped by the refusal of the post office department to give the town an official designation, prompted, in some cases, for mail to be turned back and not be delivered as required by postal regulations.

On August 29, an injunction suit of J. W. Scott, a reformed Texan, in district court, challenging the legality of Hot Springs changing its name to Truth or

Consequences, was heard before Judge Charlie Fowler. Burton Roach said the postmaster general in Washington had told the New Mexico delegation in Congress that the post office department would not make any changes until the suit was out of court. Fowler gave equal attention to the attorneys representing the conflicting parties, and after hearing testimony and many legal citations of similar cases, Fowler took the case under advisement, pending study of the decision. "This is a city without a legal name today," quoted columnist Rick Raphael of the *Hot Springs Herald*. "The whole crux of the argument centered around publication of the official calling of the election in the *Hot Springs Herald* for two weeks prior to election day. Scott, through his attorney, Douglass K. FitzHugh, says that the required time of notice was not complied with. But under cross-examination, he admitted that he had voted in the election." When asked how he learned of the election, Scott claimed he heard about it in the streets and added, "I never read the newspapers."

The Sierra County Courtroom was jammed with spectators representing both sides of the controversy. But there was no 38th Parallel down the line of benches as proponents of both names intermingled. The day-long trial involved FitzHugh, armed with nearly three dozen law volumes, citing similar cases in nearly every state of the union and the District of Columbia, taking up the better part of four hours. FitzHugh then spent 45 minutes to sum up his side of the debate. "Although the legal point was before the bar, persons close to the controversy gave additional light," Raphael observed. "Basically, the name change is being fought by a group of older persons."

"They can't stand the idea of our town being tied up with anything connected with Hollywood," one long-time resident said. "They firmly believe that everyone out there is living in sin."

On the afternoon of Tuesday, September 26, Judge Charles Fowler handed down a decision stating the vote of March 31 was illegal. Fowler pointed out in his decision that citizens were battling a time element when the vote was made. Fowler explained that the election was not lawfully called at the city council meeting and that there was not sufficient legal notice of the election as required by law. Shortly after, the city council followed the guidebook and decided to hold another election, this time on November 7, re-submitting the question to the people. On the evening of October 16, the city council met to proceed with some degree of satisfaction, and make the selection of November 7 an official date for the election. One vote marred an otherwise quiet session. Jack Morgan voted no to the date and also cast a negative vote on the election proclamation before walking out on the council. In connection with the proposed date of the election, Morgan objected to the vote because of lack of money in the general fund. "I ain't going to stick my neck out," he said. Burton Roach said businessmen had pledged $1,600 to defray costs of the election but that costs would be small since it was being held with the general election. Mayor Williams explained that every effort to follow the letter of the law would be made so that the election would stand to avoid confusion in the future.

For the second time in a year, residents of Hot Springs went to the polls and decided to change the name to Truth or Consequences. The vote was 1,262 for and 732 against. The second election had virtually the same number favored but opposition more than doubled. Amongst the opposition was J.W. Scott, represented by Douglass K. FitzHugh, who complained that the second election could not be held on November 7 and that the city was without funds to defray costs of the election. Judge J.E. Scoggins of Las Cruces heard the case for Judge Charles Fowler and found that Scott was without authority to bring the case and it was dismissed. Hot Springs, New Mexico, was officially Truth or Consequences, New Mexico.

With the voting made official, the long-awaited order to change the name of the Hot Springs post office to Truth or Consequences post office arrived on January 8, courtesy of postmaster Joe D. (Dutch) Tafoya, who immediately informed Senator Burton Roach who was then attending the state legislature in Santa Fe. Congressman John Dempsey was given credit for bringing about the post office change. Data of both elections, court suits and other information were forwarded to the postmaster general in Washington who studied these before reaching a decision on the change.

The name change not yet effected did create minor confusion found through tidbits in newspaper briefs such as the January 20 issue of the *Modesto Bee*, detailing how Joe D. Kinsey, Jr., missed a date with his father in Hot Springs, Arkansas, by at least one day and a third of the way across the U.S. The young manager of a ranch at Sebring, Florida, arrived by plane on January 19 from San Angela, Texas. Not until he registered at a hotel did he discover he was in the former town of Hot Springs, New Mexico. The airlines picked him up the next day to take him to the correct town.

On Thursday, March 1, 1951, the Hot Springs post office officially became the Truth or Consequences post office when Mayor Thomas B. Williams, during opening ceremonies at 10:00 a.m., using a pair of gold plated scissors, clipped a yellow ribbon to mark the name change. It was a climax of a struggle of almost a year by a progressive element of the city to get the post office to recognize the name selected by a majority of the voters in two elections. By noon that day, the post office had already cancelled more than 20,000 pieces of mail and Postmaster Joe D. Tafoya was busy with a heavy influx of mail. The first official cancellation of the new name was made by Mayor Williams as Postmaster Tafoya looked on. (It wasn't until a few years that the sign outside the post office changed from Hot Springs to Truth or Consequences.)

> Citizens who would not let the matter drop, insisting the name change was a farce, led by E.M. Van Sant and R.H. Middleton, who attempted to have the town of Williamsburg vote on May 23 to change its name to Hot Springs. Middleton said he was hopeful to retain the name of Hot Springs in the vicinity so that he would not lose all 25 years of buildup for the name. One lone dissenter marred an otherwise unanimous ballot when the city of Williamsburg, an active suburb of Truth or Consequences, voted to change their name to Hot Springs. The count was 62 to 1. The May election of 1950 was later voided when the city of Truth or Consequences was temporarily forced to change its name back to Hot Springs, defeating the purpose of the Williamsburg vote. After Hot Springs resolved the problem a short time following, Williamsburg did not hold a second vote.

The Fiesta

Truth or Consequences received an immense amount of publicity since it changed its name. Ralph Edwards not only gave the little town the million dollars in publicity as promised, but thanks to his continued interest in the town citizens, and the annual Fiestas, he provided untold value to the resort city by seeking to attract visitors. The Edwards returned each year which was marked with celebration including the annual Fiesta, carnivals, rodeos, beard contests, animal costume contests, junk boat races, jeep races, speed boat races, golf and tennis tournaments, fiddle contents, and celebrity stage shows. Ralph and Barbara Edwards contributed heavily to the Carrie Tingley Hospital. Whenever Ralph

Edwards learned that a major Hollywood studio was discarding used sound equipment and sound stages, Edwards arranged for the equipment to be donated and shipped to the schools at Truth or Consequences. It was estimated at one time that Ralph Edwards spent up to $12,000 a year on the Fiestas. He brought celebrities to New Mexico, paid for hotel rooms, parties, prizes for contests, and so on. In doing so, Edwards became an adopted son and something of a local hero.

The annual Fiesta celebration became a tradition in Truth or Consequences, attracting folks from neighboring states. Out-of-state tourism flourished. Beginning in 1954, a beauty contest was held, crowning one lucky female "Miss Truth or Consequence." Barbara Floyd was the first to be crowned in 1954; Charlotte Musser in 1955; Nancy Carter in 1956 and Sue Barnett in 1957. There was also a Fiesta Queen. Teresa Benevidez was the first in 1954; Norma Smith in 1955; Beverly Sikes in 1956 and Janice Phillips in 1957. Beginning in 1958, Miss Truth or Consequences was dropped and there was just the Fiesta Queen – a tradition that still holds true to this day.

Ralph and Barbara Edwards at the annual Fiesta.

After a few years, Edwards and the city council of Truth or Consequences proved the cynics wrong. "I remember one day when Ralph Edwards and Ed Bailey showed up at one of my Scout meetings," recalled Mike Tooley. Scout Troop 78 invited Edwards to their meeting. After the Country Club dinner, he visited the troop and they were elated. "I was about nine years old and my father invited Ralph to come have dinner at our house. My father was the editor of the *Hot Springs Herald* and Ralph accepted the invitation. They remained good friends. Years later when my father went to California, he paid a visit to Ralph Edwards' home and got the full tour. I remember him telling me about Ralph's impressive collection of wine downstairs. We were kind of mesmerized by the whole thing. All these Hollywood people would show up and walk all over town and mingle with the town folk."

Over the years, Ralph Edwards and Ed Bailey built a core of new friends. W.H. Edens, Jr. arranged for the roof of the interstate airway communication station building at the local airport to feature the words "Truth or Consequences" painted in white. Pilots could easily spot the sign on the roof from the air.

When Ralph Edwards learned that the local high school needed a new stage, sound and lighting equipment, he contacted the movie studios in California and used equipment that was going to be replaced with new equipment was shipped to the high school – at the expense of Ralph Edwards. When the high school needed sufficient football, basketball and volleyball equipment and suits, he contacted the Wilson Company, the sporting goods wholesaler, to supply hundreds of dollars of athletic equipment. This was not unexpected to those who knew or worked with Edwards. He paid his employee's hospital bills, bought their Christmas turkeys and threw parties for their birthdays and weddings. He cultivated outside friends whenever he traveled and he called his employees "family."

The Financials

When the quiz program returned for another national broadcast in April of 1951, the April Fools' Day weekend fooled the town: the city formerly known as Hot Springs ended up at least $6,800 in the red. The Albuquerque Chamber of Commerce felt sympathy for *Truth or Consequences* and wrote to the governor about it. President Don Woodward explained that the entire state benefitted from the publicity, following the Edwards broadcast, and asked that the Tourist Bureau chip in to pay the cost. The Fiesta actually provided a profit of $3,600, but the sheriff's posse lost money on the rodeo and went into the red by $2,700. The Chamber of Commerce ultimately paid one-third of the debt, but not all of it.

The Second Election

A bone of contention for many years, a group of "concerned citizens" opposed to the name of Truth or Consequences tried too many times to get an election called on the name but failed. Numerous petitions had been presented but city commissions declined to call an election. In late 1963, they succeeded in bringing the subject up to debate during a meeting with the city commission, creating a heated discussion that led to scheduling of an election. The election was not on the agenda and after the regular meeting Mayor Robert M. Holcomb asked for other matters to come before the commission. Charles Ragsdale mentioned the name change since all five commissioners were present. Commissioner William I. Buhler passed out a prepared statement which brought about a lengthy discussion. On a final vote, Commissioners Ed English, Ragsdale and Holcomb voted to call an election while Commissioners Buhler and Frank Luchini abstained. Holcomb took Luchini and Buhler to task for abstaining on important matters.

On Monday, January 13, citizens of Truth or Consequences had to decide if the name should remain as it was or be changed back to Hot Springs. Votes were cast at five different polling places in the city. A heavy Hot Springs vote was expected since the Committee for Hot Springs was organized and active for many months. The Organization for Truth or Consequences got underway about three weeks before the election and was backed mainly by business leaders. An estimated 6,000 citizens turned out for the election and Truth or Consequences again won.

There are year-round residents who seem reconciled to the name, despite occasional grumbling, but decades and generations later opposition eventually conceded. Members of the police department, identifying the town while calling on official police business, are sometimes questioned whether it is a joke. They have to explain, briefly, the history of the name. Most residents, however, simply refer to the town as "T or C" – which seems to defeat the purpose of the name change. Members of the Chamber of Commerce, over the years, say the name change was never a mistake. Millions of tourists have poured into the town as a result of the publicity. "It is of economic benefit to us," Lois Reaver, executive director of the Truth or Consequences Chamber of Commerce, remarked in 1989.

For decades a lone dissenter continued to protest the name change, regardless of the growth both in population and commerce, including tourism that continues to wander through town every day. The Chamber of Commerce has officially reigned firm

Closing Addendum

A number of events marking the city's progress have been observed during the Fiestas. In 1964, Ralph Edwards helped to celebrate the opening of a state park at Elephant Butte Lake by participating in dedication ceremonies held during the Fiesta that year.

In 1965, the New Mexico Cattle Growers' Association awarded Edwards his own "Truth or Consequences" private brand. Joe Pankey and his son, Ruben, both members of the Association, saw to it that Edwards received his own branding iron, made by H.H. Ellis of Truth or Consequences, New Mexico.

In 1971, after earlier unsuccessful attempts, the Rotary Club launched a drive to raise funds for a museum to house memorabilia from the rich history of the town and Sierra County. William Buhler, president of the Sierra County Historical Society, was the driving force behind the project. Money was raised through a variety of sources and projects. Many people in the community volunteered their time and services. Contractors, painters, plumbers, carpenters and electricians all gave freely. The Hot Springs Woman's Club donated funds they had been collecting for several years to build a clubhouse. These funds went for the Community Meeting Room of the Museum. Originally, the museum was to occupy the Dr. White office building on Main Street next to the natural spring known as Geronimo Springs. It soon became apparent that more room would be needed, so three adjacent buildings were purchased and rebuilt for the museum. In May 1972, the Geronimo Springs Museum was officially opened. The Sierra County Historical Society was created to manage the museum.

Edwards' dedication to the Geronimo Springs Museum was a highlight of the 1972 Fiesta. Ralph and Barbara Edwards were major contributors to the building of the museum, having purchased two of the three adjoining buildings to allow expansion to the museum, which would also include a wing devoted to Ralph Edwards and *Truth or Consequences*. The Ralph Edwards wing opened in 1974, telling the story of the town's name change and the annual Fiestas and putting many of Ralph Edwards' mementos on display. Barbara joked that it was worth the money to have a place to put all those mementos so she could finally get them out of the house.

A special Educational Wing of Carrie Tingley Hospital was officially opened by Ralph Edwards and Gov. Bruce King of New Mexico during the 1973 Fiesta.

On the evening of May 1, 1998, during the annual Fiesta at Truth or Consequences, New Mexico, a re-creation of the April 1, 1950, radio broadcast of the quiz show was performed by the Truth or Consequences Community Theater and their friends. The re-creation and concept was orchestrated by Paul Tooley, reprising his role as the editor of the *Hot Springs Herald*, as he did 48 years prior. The cast of performers are reprinted below.

April 1, 1950	**May 1, 1998**
Harlow Wilcox	Charles Kuhne
Ralph Edwards	Gerald Keith (Boland)
Ed Bailey	Larry Woods
Sen. Burton Roach	William (Bill) Kohler
Mrs. Knox	Betsy Bauer
Hank Gardney	Charlie Bauer
Arletta Coleman	Mary Allton
Paul O. Tooley	Paul O. Tooley
Beulah Shirk	Jeane Darland
W.A. Davis	Thomas (Tom) Novak
Mrs. Herbert Lett	Grita Wortman
Mr. Herbert Lett	Fred Wortman
The bald headed man	Ralph Crispell, Sr.
Postmaster Tafoya	Eddie Montoya

Applause and Props by Marty Novak.

Window display arranged by Claude Owens, owner of Owens' Market Basket, to surprise Ralph Edwards and his crew when they arrive in town.

Chapter 12
The Longest Golf Course in History

Following the April 1 radio broadcast, on the way back to Hollywood from Truth or Consequences, NM, Edwards and his idea men came up with a publicity stunt that would make newspapers across the nation. What would happen if someone was given the consequence of hitting a golf ball from Los Angeles, California, to Truth or Consequences, New Mexico? A golf course was presently under construction in the town formerly known as Hot Springs and publicity for both the town and the radio program would almost certainly be ensured. After returning to the West Coast, and ironing out the details (including insurance), Edwards and his men sent out free tickets for his show to golf clubs around the Los Angeles area.

On the evening of April 15, Edwards, during the course of the warm-up before the show, asked if there were any golfers in the audience. Four men raised their hands and were asked to come on the stage. Among the candidates was a 43-year-old real estate salesman named Al Baker, selected for both strength and character to participate in a pie-throwing stunt. Little did Baker realize what providence had in store for him and if he had the gift of prophecy, he would have rejected that ticket handed to him days before at Griffith Park. During the program, four men and Edwards were lined up and Baker was told that one of the men on stage had a $100 bill in his pocket. If Baker hit him in the face with a pie, he would collect the money. Baker hit the wrong man (It was Edwards who had the bill in his pocket) so Baker was forced to take the consequence.

Armed with golfing equipment furnished by Wilson Golfing, which included a brand new set of clubs, bag, and at least 18 dozen golf balls, Al Baker was told that he had to hit a golf ball from NBC in Hollywood to the town of Truth or Consequences, New Mexico. The distance was 823 miles (or 1,448,480 yards) and par over this, the world's largest golf course, was set at 25,000 strokes. If Baker completed the course, he would win a complete set of Wilson clubs, a Columbia Mountaineer trailer, and a brand new Nash Ambassador Airflyte sedan. If he completed the course under par, he would receive an additional $500. Baker was considered a top-notch golfer, a member of Local 47, a member of the Musicians' Golf Club, a former saxophone player and former member of Abe Lyman's orchestra, and recently supplemented his income by being a stuntman for numerous films starring Alan Ladd, Donald O'Connor and in Ingrid Bergman's *Joan of Arc*. Numerous newspapers reported Baker was an "unemployed musician" at the time and if this fact was correct, anyone unemployed would have taken on the challenge.

Al Baker with a caddy helping to assist with the task.

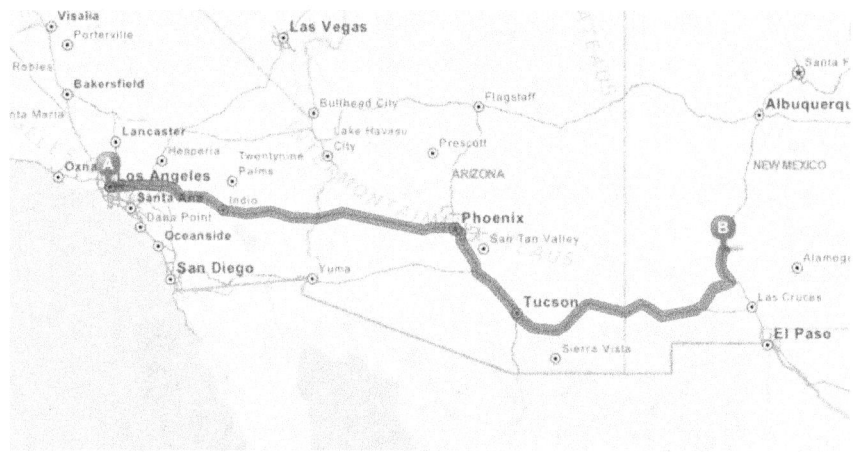

Baker's travel expenses were paid by the sponsors of the radio program, including lodging and food. Following the broadcast, the exact route, mapped out by Arch Arnold, was reviewed and approved by Baker. When asked how long it would take to complete the course, Baker theorized it would take about four weeks. Every week along the route, via NBC remote, courtesy of local affiliates along the route, Baker reported on his progress. The entire trip, as he would eventually discover, would last about six weeks.

On Sunday, April 16, at 10:15 a.m., Baker hit the first ball down Sunset Boulevard and Vine Street to commence a golfing adventure that has never been experienced by any man since. If he played the course in par or better, he would be richer by approximately $6,000 in prizes and cash. Climbing into the trailer that was to be his home for the next six weeks, the golfer who would make nationwide papers took after his ball.

Baker was accompanied by chauffeur-escort John Benson, a staff member of Ralph Edwards Productions, who clocked the strokes and verified the authenticity of the game. Baker's route through California would pass through San Bernardino, Palm Springs, the Coachella Valley and Brawley. Crossing into Yuma, he would pass through Gila Bend, Tucson, Benson, Willcox, Lordsburg, Deming, Hatch and finally Truth or Consequences. When Baker got tired of walking, he hopped on the running board of the car and rode to the next stroke. For relaxation and sleep, he had the trailer, decorated with banners to promote the radio program. Armed with spare golf balls, loose cash, numerous caps and a pair of sunglasses, Baker was prepped with the necessary bullet points for local press coverage along the way.

The route took Baker through the center of every major town on the map. The turf along the route was the asphalt pavement. On the road, he used a putter so as not to get too much loft on the ball and thus encounter such hazards as windshields. Out in the county along the highways, he used woods and irons. Playing out of Banning, California*, where the pavement had high curbs and a downgrade and a stiff tail wind blowing, he hit a ball that by actual measurement rolled two miles before it stopped.

By the second day, April 17, Baker made his way northeast to Pasadena, avoiding the major freeway, Route 210. Much to the amusement of motorists, Baker was knocking the ball eastward along Walnut Street, which ran parallel with the 210, while off-duty Motorcycle Sergeant Gerald E. Wright tried to untangle traffic jams. The *Pasadena Star-News* reported the earliest statistic: 221 golf strokes from Hollywood to Pasadena. Baker lost seven balls down sewers. By April 18, in the heat of Tuesday afternoon, Baker went through Monrovia via Foothill Blvd. to the wide-eyed amazement of many local residents. Stating he got his second wind

* This statement was reprinted in numerous local newspapers during the course of the game citing the two-mile hit out of Brawley; another claiming the same downhill from Whitewater, California, road between Indio and Blythe.

along about the time he arrived in the city, Baker told reporters to sit back and relax and follow the reports weekly on the quiz program. "Be thankful you are not in my shoes," he told reporters. "I hope to eventually take home the prizes offered."

Al Baker practicing his golf swing.

Progressing East from East Foothill Blvd to Huntington Drive and to West Foothill Blvd, Baker worked his way to Azusa. On April 19, the Azusa Police Department cooperated in entertaining the visitors on the Civic Center Lawn. Azusans gaped while tired and grateful contestant Baker leaned back in an armchair under a beach umbrella and gulped refreshing orange juice, resting momentarily before continuing his long journey down "the Main Street of America" that led him to fleeting fame and probably a lot of blisters. Under the supervision of Chief Kendrick, a detail composed of Captain Fred Williams and Policeman Bob Torrance, conducted Baker as he putted down Foothill Blvd., through the center of town. Opposite the city jail, the police surrounded the perspiring golfer. They provided him with an easy chair. Chief Kendrick personally poured iced orange juice for him. Captain Williams personally guarded the ball so no souvenir seekers would steal what would become a valued piece of memorabilia. Policeman Torrance produced a towel to wipe the sweat from Baker's brow. Lucky Lager, a local brewery, produced a couple of cases of thirst quencher for the desert roadway. (Perhaps Azusa wanted to get a plug over the airwaves as a result of their hospitality.) Scotty Maxwell and Cliff Wynn of the Wynn Oil Company, local manufacturer of Wynn's Friction Proofing Oil, provided Baker with the new Nash Ambassador sedan that the golfer would receive as a partial reward if he completed the trek. On April 20, Baker was seen whacking a golf ball down the middle of Highway 66 behind the police escort. It was reported the number of strokes totaled 777. Staying on Foothill Blvd., he passed through Fontana around 8:15 a.m., playing golf towards San Bernardino and Colton.

On April 21, Baker stopped for a short rest at the corner of Mt. Vernon and I Streets in Colton, California. He was presently at 920 strokes. Supposedly the day before, April 20, Baker was hitting the golf ball through the streets of San Bernardino. Columnist Chuck Shelton of the *Azusa Herald* witnessed the stunt in the streets and remarked in his column, "I don't think there's any question in anyone's mind that the world is getting crazier. When that bird went through town Tuesday morning, clouting a golf ball down the road as part of a stunt sponsored by the *Truth or Consequences* radio show, I figured that was just about the durndest [sic] waste of human energy I ever ran across. That guy, just to provide a little publicity for a zany radio production, has set out to chop divots in the pavement all the way from Hollywood to a town in New Mexico. As I say, I couldn't imagine any endeavor less productive in the history of mankind than the one I was witness to Tuesday a.m. Then I got to thinking about some of our political candidates, and I realize that every day I get a stack of mimeographed verbiage that represents, in its way, just about as much value to mankind as a golf game between Hollywood and New Mexico."

"The fellow who rode along in the trailer in the Truth or Inconsequentials [sic] caravan, and who managed the publicity for the cross-country golf match, asked the *Herald* if we would like to have the golfer, whose name I didn't get, slice a drive off his nib lick right in front of the Bank of America and send the ball crashing through the plate glass window. 'We've got plenty of insurance,' he told us. 'Azusa's a good town to pull a trick in, because of its famous name. Imagine breaking into the bank with a golf ball.' Our lack of enthusiasm for the gag was all that kept the Bank of America from getting it right in the face!"

Columnist Dave Underhill of the *Herald News* (Klamath Falls, Oregon), shared the same opinion in his column: "Remember the days of many college boys who swallowed gold fish alive, just for the fun of it? Well, here is an item about ten times as nutty." It didn't take long, however, for newspaper and radio columnists to soon realize the stunt was meant to be serious and so would the remainder of their editorials.

By April 22, Baker had progressed southeast, avoiding the San Bernardino National Forest, bidding goodbye to Redlands, headed for Palm Springs. Capt. Frank Freeman of the State Highway Patrol also kept his eye on the ball. Baker was reportedly going along Highway 99 at a speed that averaged between two and three miles an hour. Over the next four days, he progressed through Riverside where local residents lined the curbs on Highway 99 to watch Al Baker. (It took him approximately 1,200 shots from Los Angeles to Beaumont.) On the evening of April 22, Baker reported in via remote on *Truth or Consequences*, letting the public know he was just reaching Palm Springs.

Caddies en route were being provided by the States of California, Arizona and New Mexico in the persons of Highway Patrolmen who escorted the party for safety reasons along the road. Sometimes the official police vehicles, sometimes a motorcycle, sometimes the familiar white-painted patrol car, followed Baker as he chopped away uphill along Highway 99 from Redlands Friday afternoon, reaching a point about 3 ½ miles west of Beaumont before stopping for the night, resuming his journey Saturday morning en route to Palm Springs. The group stayed at El Rancho in Beaumont overnight after digging their way through steak dinners at the Rusty Lantern. Baker said the greatest difficulty to date was the backwards progress he constantly encountered either when his uphill shots did not carry to the crest of the grade or when a truck or car coming westward socked his little white pill closer to the point of starting than from where he had teed off. One of the more sensational features of the gag, according to John Benson, was that very few people along the route paid much attention to what was going on. Southern Californians, he said, appeared to accept even the most unusual incident during a day as commonplace and not noteworthy.

Baker stayed over at the Sun Tan Lodge, in Palm Springs, soon after his arrival to town and delivering his report on the radio broadcast. Baker drove off Sunday, April 23, after leaving a party in his honor Sunday morning, reaching Shadow Mountain Club in the evening where he was put up for the night by Cliff Henderson. Baker had taken 1,823 strokes to that point.

He drove through Indio on April 24, Monday morning, clipping his 2,000th stroke in front of Roosevelt School just before 5 p.m. The photo in the newspaper showed him ready to tee off just at the city limits on Highway 111 and Monroe, while John Benson held a parasol above Baker to shade him from the sun.

By April 28, 11 days and 2,024 strokes later, reached Brawley, California. While in town, Baker was one of the guest speakers at the Soroptimist Club meeting at the Planters Hotel. Other guests included John Benson of the radio program, Dick Andrus of the Pittsburgh Paint company, Maxine Dottson and Zella Clayton of Brawley, Irene Bradford was chairman of the program and Neil Eldridge, acting president, presided. Baker told of several amusing incidents that have happened to him since leaving Los Angeles, of the minister who met him on the highway with a card with three scriptures written on it for him to look up in the Bible, a woman who baked a cake in the shape of a golf ball, a little boy who brought his ball back to him, and the dog that ran off with the ball.

On Saturday, April 29, he worked his way south to El Centro, where he attended the 10th Annual Tomato Festival. Lovely Maxine Dottson was honorary queen and reigned over the festival. Visitors were given all the free tomatoes they could eat and dinners were served in the big tent by members of the Niland Women's Club. A square dance competition was part of the festivities, as well as Al Baker broadcasting on the radio show that evening, reporting his score of 3,200. Ahead of him lay the "big sand trap" (the sand dunes) between the valley and Yuma. Friday, when Baker progressed into Brawley, having covered the first 200 miles, he reached 3,042 strokes. Benson said Baker was on his seventh dozen of golf balls. Balls lost in the open cost Baker a stroke, but Benson said no stroke was charged for all those lost down the sewers of Los Angeles. Members of the

Truth or Consequences golf club are anxiously awaiting Baker's arrival in New Mexico. When he sinks the ball in the first hole of the new golf course overlooking Elephant Butte Lake, the course will be dedicated. Friday evening Baker stopped play about eight miles south of Brawley. He marked the spot and resumed play Saturday morning. He was scheduled to arrive in El Centro sometime during the afternoon. An escort by the California Highway Patrol was protecting Baker and the passing motorists as Baker golfed along to New Mexico.

When Baker passed the Barbara Worth Resort and Country Club on Highway 80 Sunday, April 30, he noticed several duffers vainly searching for lost golf balls in the drainage ditch which parallels the long No. 7 hole. Baker knocked his ball down the center of the highway and started off for the next shot. "Ha, ha," he yelled at the boys into the ditch, "I found my ball."

He crossed the Arizona border and reached Yuma on May 2, 17 days and 4,205 strokes after starting the game. He drove his ball over the Colorado River Bridge in the early morning, and stopped over in Yuma to have his car serviced before continuing his game.

Following Yuma, Baker traveled East through the Fortuna Foothills, parallel with the Gila River, travelled through Gila Bend, stayed south of Phoenix and on Tuesday, May 9, spent the night in Casa Grande. By that time, John Benson figured Baker had a total of 6,627 strokes, and they were a little more than half way to their destination. While Baker was in town, the Casa Grande Junior Chamber of Commerce presented him with a Gila monster. Don Kinser, son of Mrs. J.E. Kinser of Casa Grande and a member of the Arizona State Highway Patrol, was assigned by the State Highway Department to escort Baker across Arizona. They left Casa Grande en route east about 9:30 Wednesday morning.

On May 12, Baker arrived in Tucson, staying at the Westerner hotel, with 542 of his 823 miles completed. His score was presently 7,472. Fred Briggs, manager of the Westerner Hotel, heard about Baker's up-coming arrival and provided free hotel accommodations for both Benson and Baker, and took advantage of the publicity by posing for a comical photo with the manager bathing the feet of Al Baker. By this point Baker was on his 11th dozen golf balls. He was still averaging three hits per mile. Baker remained in Tucson for a couple days to recoup from the desert heat, taking time to appear on the Saturday night (May 13) broadcast via the local NBC affiliate in Tucson, meet up with a new caddy from the quiz show, and partake in a scheduled golf tournament at the Randolph Park Municipal Golf Course. He played against 18 Tucson opponents on May 14, selected by the

Chamber of Commerce, for an 18-hole route. The competition began 9:30 Sunday morning. Caddies were furnished by local high school beauties from The Sunshine Model Club. The match at the Randolph was arranged through the co-operation of Dell Urich, pro at the municipal course.*

While in Tucson, Baker participated in two radio interviews on local KVOA. The first was with Fred Gerletti along the side of the road, and later by Jim Hayes in the studio. Back in Hollywood, on the evening of May 6, 1950, Ralph Edwards told the listeners of *Truth or Consequences* that Al Baker was in Gila Bend, Arizona, having completed 424 miles in 5,855 strokes, averaging 1,300 strokes per 100 miles. A studio contestant, Carl Yokum (spelled Carl Yoakum in one newspaper), was asked to guess the exact number of strokes he thought Baker would use between Gila Bend and Tucson, Arizona, a distance of 126 miles. The contestant guessed 1,672 strokes. Yokum missed the number of strokes by 55 (or 54, according to one source but the math comes to 55); Baker actually used 1,617. On May 13, because he missed more than 13 points of the correct number of strokes, Yokum was assigned the consequence of joining Al Baker to caddy for him. On the evening of May 14, Carl Yokum of Los Angeles, flew in to Tucson. (Yokum was paid ten cents for every stroke Baker made during the week and would ultimately be rewarded with $200.40, after trekking 148 miles.) On May 15, Baker, Benson and Yokum took off towards Benson and points east.

The troupe reached Benson by Thursday, May 18, where Lyn Hargrave, President of the Chamber of Commerce, presented the keys to the city to Al Baker. By this time he used up 8,078 strokes and 12 dozen golf balls, with five being used between Tucson and Benson. "Believe me," Baker stated, "This golf course is well-trapped." Throughout the week-long sojourn, Yokum stayed out of the spotlight when reporters came to interview Baker. The golfer wore a tee shirt, with Truth or Consequences emblazoned on the front and back in big, red letters. Yokum wore the same shirt. This was possibly to let people know they were not crazy. In seriousness, the custom shirts were used for radio and newspaper publicity, especially when newspaper reporters took photos. While in Benson, the men were the guests of Richard Lopshire at the Rotary on Tuesday evening.

* Seventeen of the eighteen players named to compete against Baker: Ed Conway, Col. Lawrence M. Thomas, deputy commander at Davis-Monthan Air Base, James F. Houston, James C. Grant, Billy Bell, Jr., Charley Lamb, Harry Chambers, Jack O'Dowd, Eddie Belton, Ricki Rarick, Fred Gerletti, Joe Niemann, Max Klinger, Tom Valdespino, Mac Beaudry, Jack Eyman and Steve Ribble.

Yokum, however, expressed disappointment for the lack of attention, reportedly complained on much of the route, and he quickly developed sunburn. "When I quit hurting," Yokum said to one reporter for the *Denver Post*, who gave him two minutes of attention, "I think I'll enjoy it too." Yokum was quoted in one paper as being forced to perform "community service" and mistook the consequence as a punishment. When his week-long task expired, he took the first flight back to Los Angeles. His name was never mentioned throughout the remainder of the trip, and after the men reached their destination.

By this time, Baker had already passed through Riverside, Palm Springs, Indio, Coachella, and El Centro, California; Yuma, Gila Bend, and Tucson. From Benson the last part of their journey would venture east to Willcox and across the New Mexico border. On Saturday, May 20, Al Baker and John Benson arrived in Lordsburg, New Mexico, where they were greeted by a parade with a high school band taking part.

Progressing east, they arrived in Deming on Monday, May 22, where they were entertained at an exclusive dinner. Working north towards Truth or Consequences, they arrived in Hatch shortly before noon on Wednesday, honored with a dinner by the Valley Chamber of Commerce. Baker was greeted by signs reading: "Hatch, N.M., the friendly little city of trees and flowers welcomes Al Baker on route to our neighboring city, Truth or Consequences, New Mexico." Hatch, by all accounts, went all-out to extend Baker a welcome. "Baker's cross-county trek was telling on him yesterday as he plodded between Deming and Hatch," reported the Associated Press. "To that time, he used 10,480 strokes and 16 dozen golf balls. Chet Iden, president of the Truth or Consequences County Club, plans to challenge him to a nine-hole game. Then he can rest." Hatch was located 38 miles south of Truth or Consequences.

The Arrival

A delegation of citizens from Truth or Consequences with signs on their cars welcoming Al Baker to Highway 85, first met the golfer at Hatch. He worked his way north towards the village of Williamsburg, adjoining Truth or Consequences, where he and John Benson met with a delegation in celebration. Benson later recalled how every town along the route gave them police protection voluntarily. (In San Bernardino, the police inspector thought the idea of driving the ball to Truth or Consequences was a great idea and asked Benson if he could get on Ralph Edwards' program sometime.) Some of the best police protection along the entire route of Baker's cross-country golf game was attributed to the Sierra County Sheriff's Posse, John Benson told a reporter for the *Hot Springs Herald*. They met up with the Posse twenty-three miles out of Truth or Consequences, down the highway on Thursday afternoon and there were six Jeeps along the route to help retrieve the balls. Stock was getting low and Baker was aware of the risk of a delay if he needed to acquire additional golf balls. The Sheriff's Posse was divine as the road was lined with thousands of cars and many enthusiastic spectators were trying to grab a ball for a souvenir. They were prevented from doing so by the men in uniform. According to Benson's recollection, not a single ball was lost within town limits (although one souvenir hunter almost got away with one). As a kind gesture, one of the Sheriff's Posse offered to get them a fresh box of golf balls, at his expense, if the call of duty was needed.

Arriving in Truth or Consequences on Thursday evening, the golfer celebrated in traditional fashion by enjoying a bath in the hot springs, eating local food, receiving free drinks in local bars and resting for two days before officially concluding his long-distance game on Saturday afternoon, for the radio broadcast.

Saturday afternoon, people lined the route Baker took through the city, escorted by the Sierra County Sheriff's Posse, in completing his course through the downtown streets from atop Carrie Tingley Hospital hill, out Date Street, and then west to the Country Club (now presently located along Ralph Edwards Drive). Through traffic was re-routed over other streets and traffic halted at the west end of Main Street was only delayed for five minutes while Baker was traversing the distance between Carrie Tingley Hospital and the Broadway-Main intersection. On each of his drives through the city there were loud cheers to greet and congratulate him on his accomplishment, and a spontaneous rousing welcome greeted him when he made his last drive onto the country club green.

On the afternoon of May 27, at 5:00 p.m., exactly 42 days since he teed off from Hollywood, California, Baker arrived at the Truth or Consequences Country Club. Five thousand people were lined up along the streets, waving flags and displaying signs of congratulations from their porches, and along the ninth fairway and the surrounding green waiting for Baker to make that last shot. The golfer played up to the green and was ten feet from the pin. By this time, the program was on the air and Baker had to stall for a while as he had lines to read on the broadcast. Finally, at a signal from the announcer, he stepped up to his ball and dropped the ten-footer to complete the longest golf course in history – both for time and distance. Instantly, a tremendous roar and cheer came from the gallery – a great ovation to a tired and gallant golfer. The goal was the first hole of the new Truth or Consequences golf course overlooking Elephant Butte Lake, and the course was dedicated when Baker arrived. At 5:42 p.m., live on the air, with a perfect putt he sank his ball in the cup of the 9th hole of the new country club golf course.*

The broadcast included also the official welcome of the city made by Dr. T.B. Williams, mayor, who told Baker the city was his and the mayor hoped Baker would stay for a long while and enjoy the fine mineral baths they were known for, as well as some lake fishing. Senator Burton Roach, manager of the Chamber of Commerce, likewise gave his greeting of welcome and expressed appreciation for the fine publicity Baker, in carrying out his consequence assigned him by Ralph Edwards, had given the city.

Al Baker, a muscular outdoorsman of slightly more than five feet was in top notch physical condition upon his arrival. After about 36 hours rest after his arrival and some relaxing indulgence in hot mineral baths, was also in top-notch spirits, having earned his right to a real celebration. Also partaking in the celebration was John Benson, and Dick Gottlieb, production director for the radio show; the latter of whom flew to Truth or Consequences on Thursday to meet Baker and Benson and prepare for the broadcast Saturday evening. NBC producer Greiner and engineer Joe Kay handled the technical hookups. Gottlieb had charge of the six minutes of the broadcast that was made from the country club. Others in town for the broadcast were Carl Gruener, NBC producer, Joe Kay, engineer and Norma Hambay of the Gila Bend Trading Post, Gila Bend, Arizona. Taking part on the radio program were Mayor T.B. Williams, who officially welcomed Baker and dedicated the golf course; Burton Roach, manager of the Chamber of Commerce; Dick Gottlieb, Al Baker and John Benson.

Upon his arrival Thursday evening, Baker, John Benson, and Dick Gottlieb were guests of honor at a covered dish dinner given by the American Legion in the new Legion Hall. Each of them gave short talks expressing their warm thanks

---

*The ninth hole on the course was the closest to the parking area, road and clubhouse, which is why this particular hole was chosen. Sandwiches and cold drinks were sold at the club house. Hole number one was located on the opposite side of the golf course. While advance publicity cited hole number one, for practical purposes, hole number nine was chosen instead.

for the kind reception they were receiving in Truth or Consequences. Baker mentioned, "I hear some of you still calling the town Hot Springs. Isn't this the town that I knocked a golf ball to – Truth or Consequences?" His answer from the audience was a resounding applause. Legion spokesmen agreed with him. "It takes a lot of courage to knock a ball all the way from California, especially when there is so much desert to cross, so hats off to Al Baker, for the fine job he did of it."

Baker was extravagant in his praise of people encountered all along his route, stating that he never knew people could be so wonderful. He expressed particular appreciation for the full cooperation and courtesy extended him by the State Police of California, Arizona and New Mexico. "All along the route people were wonderful and demonstrated real hospitality," he explained. For many people along the route, Baker posed cheerfully for pictures, as well as local photographers. It was estimated that he shook hands with more than 1,000 people – half of them during the last day of the course.

"The people of Truth or Consequences seemed to be more sincerer in their reception than any other town. But, I think I was just about as proud to see them as they were to see me." Baker admitted in the *Hot Springs Herald* that the contest was a grueling affair and that he was proud it had been completed. "I cannot begin to thank the people of Truth or Consequences for what they have done for me. I appreciate so much the many compliments they have given me."

Looking back at the adventures Baker and Benson had during their trip, the men were greeted by Gov. Dan Garvey of Arizona. In Brawley, Baker finished third in a moonlight golf tournament. In Tucson, he beat 18 different members of the golf club 2 up. (He beat the president of the club 3 up.) During the first week, Baker became alarmed at the loss of seven pounds of weight. However, he gained that amount back later which he attributed to the fine steaks along the route. Then he added that he got the best steak on the entire trip in Truth or Consequences at the Ritz. "My biggest trouble was people and dogs picking up my golf balls," Baker remarked. "One afternoon an owl swooped down and picked one up. Everybody wanted those balls and each time I lost one, it cost me a stroke. We figured out that I lost over 100 that way."

Baker's trailer was another center of attraction in Truth or Consequences, as the thousands of spectators looked it over, noting the multiple thousands of signatures that had been inscribed on the big sign that told who and where it was going.

Al Baker won the $500.00 in cash, a complete set of Wilson clubs, a Columbia

Mountaineer trailer, and a Nash Ambassador Airflyte sedan. Estimated total was $6,000. He also made many friends. He was made honorary Deputy Sheriff of Yuma County; and in the days that followed he received mail from all over the country.

The final score? Al Baker went the distance with 11,469 swings, bettering par by 13,531 strokes. He was on his 19th and final box of golf balls when he arrived in Truth or Consequences; having used up a total of 222* golf balls, beat, strayed or stolen, and having a reserve of but six balls when he finished his assignment. Seconds after Baker sunk the final ball on the green of the course, some spectator made a dash for his ball hoping to acquire a souvenir, but Baker was too fast for him. Grabbing it from the cup, Baker announced emphatically, "That one is mine."

Following the broadcast on Saturday evening, the guests were entertained by city and Chamber of Commerce officials and enjoyed an outdoor barbecue. On Sunday, Dick Gottlieb, production manager for *Truth or Consequences* and liaison officer between the show and the city, was escorted on a fishing trip up Elephant Butte Lake by Robert B. Smith, president of the Chamber of Commerce, who demonstrated the three methods of fishing practiced on the lake. On Monday morning, Chamber of Commerce manager Burton Roach saw the NBC men, including Gottlieb, off on the 7:18 a.m. Continental Air Lines plane. Al Baker and John Benson left for Hollywood in the Nash Ambassador with the house trailer, retracing their route they travelled to get to New Mexico. Along the way, on Monday afternoon, the two men stopped overnight in Lordsburg to make a short return call to especially thank the Elks Club, which royally entertained them on May 20 during their trip east.

Only after the conclusion of the golf game did it become known that Al Baker was also a real estate dealer and just before his golfing trek sold 20 new homes in Lakewood, California, a new community near Los Angeles. The town was composed of 35,000 acres and already had churches of all denominations, schools, a country club, and all other things that go to make up a good town. A press release claimed that Baker's real estate business was in connection with the large G.I. project that was now under construction in that state. Baker told reporters that he might event write a book about his experiences. (If he wrote of his six-week adventure, it was never published.)

* It remains a challenge to verify the exact number of golf balls used during Baker's trek. Newspaper columns reported one of two numbers, 208 and 222. The latter number was chosen because it was repeated more often than 208.

Radio Editors Award, broadcast of February 11, 1950.

Radio Editors Award, broadcast of January 4, 1947.

Public Schools Week Award, broadcast of April 17, 1951.

Chapter 13
The Truth or Consequences Fiesta

True to his word, Edwards and his idea men continued to find excuses to send contestants to Truth or Consequences, New Mexico, to create additional publicity for the city. A Frenchman was sent to kiss the hands of all the ladies. A grocer from Buffalo, New York, delivered a can of milk to a customer in Hollywood, with a convenient stop-off at Truth or Consequences, New Mexico. Louis Laurent was labeled the "official greeter" for the city and was sent tails, stovepipe hat and all, to perform his official duties. One of the most surprising stunts that backfired was when Edwards dubbed Joey Benjamin as taxi ambassador, sending him to downtown Hollywood and told him to hail a taxi and ask to be taken to Truth or Consequences. Joey wound up, not at the studio as he expected, but at Truth or Consequences, New Mexico.

For the 1951 Fiesta, an Elephant Hunt was commissioned. To qualify as a contestant, all eligible had to register for a hunting license with the Sheriff's Posse Headquarters of the Chamber of Commerce, beginning March 30, kicking off the three-day Fiesta. A live elephant was hidden within a radius of five miles of the city. All shooting was to be done with a camera and no one under 21 was permitted to participate. The winner was the first to shoot the elephant with a camera. The elephant bore a clock on his back, showing the time the picture was shot. To make it more difficult for the contestants, horses, cars and other means of transportation were barred. All hunting had to be on foot. Contestants were divided into two groups. The first was made up of those living within a 25-mile radius of the city; the other group, those living beyond the area. A partial list of prizes included a television set, $500 in cash, a 72-piece Fine Art Sterling Silver set, a gas range, a food freezer, luggage, books and watches. For a day or two, town residents theorized that a stuffed elephant would be used. As it turns out, the Horne Bros. Circus, which wintered in New Mexico, had agreed to ship a real one. It was not full size, agreed upon in advance by the Chamber.

The Fiesta would climax a three-day Sierra County Sheriff's Posse Rodeo staged by Beutler Brothers of Elk City, Oklahoma, with prize money amounting to $1,750. The annual rodeo was moved up from September to highlight the weekend celebration. Edwards had a staff of 45 people flown in to Truth or Consequences for the eleventh anniversary of the radio program, his second remote broadcast. During the broadcast from the high school auditorium, Edwards made his appearance out of a chute on the back of a donkey. A cowhand, who preferred his name not be given, tried his hand at riding a Brahma bull while blowing up a top balloon. For his effort, he received a movie camera. Mrs. Viola Keith of Truth or Consequences took part in the show by trying to bridle an obstinate horse before a cowboy could throw his steer. She was successful and was rewarded with a gas range. Mrs. E. W. McDaniel of Truth or Consequences agreed to the consternation of her husband, to try riding a bull. One of the guests on the program was Governor Mechem, whose introduction brought a rousing ovation. Another celebrity who attracted out-of-town visitors was Johnnie of Philip Morris commercial fame.

The tradition continued in 1952. Ralph Edwards flew in on Friday, March 28. After serving as guest of honor for the Saturday morning breakfast, Edwards rode in the parade, attended the dedication of the new city administration building, followed by the radio broadcast from the high school auditorium. Edwards arranged for celebrities to attend the Fiesta including Carolina Cotton, Marshall Thompson, Harry Carey, Jr., David Brian and Adrian Booth, the latter of whom had been playing opposite Gene Autry in cowboy Westerns. A large tank containing hundreds of minnows was centered at the Chamber of Commerce. The person guessing the closest number of minnows received an 18-foot home freezer. Edwards announced the winner over the air during the broadcast.

Ralph Edwards in Sierra County Sheriff's Posse Uniform.

In 1952, a contestant suddenly found her soldier husband from North Carolina on the stage with her. The contestant was Mrs. Wesley Little whose husband was stationed at Fort Bragg. The former Jeanne Phipps got close enough to the answer to her question that she was awarded the prize which included a pipe set, a can of tobacco, a pair of men's house slippers and other items for a man. When she protested that all of the prizes were for a man, Edwards explained that they also had furnished the man. At that point of the program, Mrs. Little's husband walked from the wing of the stage. He was a corporal with the Army and stationed at Fort Bragg, North Carolina. He was in New York with 19 other men of his battalion making a movie when he was selected for the trip. On Saturday morning, he was flown into El Paso and met with local residents there who kept him under guard in the home economics room at the high school until time for him to appear on the radio program.

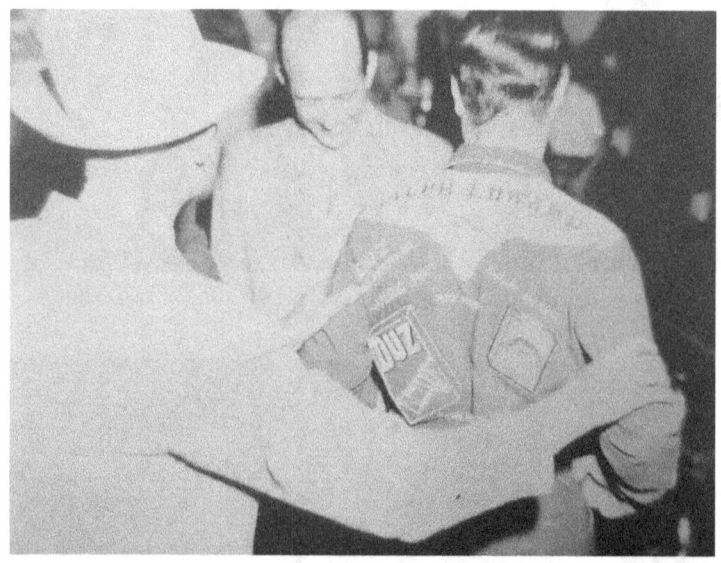

Jayne Mansfield attending one of the annual Fiestas.

Steve Dunne attending one of the annual Fiestas.

At the 1953 Fiesta, an Old Fiddler's Contest became a permanent part of the program. Entries came from Colorado, Oklahoma, Kansas, Texas and New Mexico. The winner over 26 other contestants was Mrs. Susie Snodgrass, age 86, of Hutchinson, Kansas. As one of the stunts on the 1953 broadcast, Edwards conducted a contest in which letters were written on "Why My Father Should Be Mayor of Truth or Consequences During the Fiesta." Fourteen-year-old Lynn Higinbotham of Sunburst, Montana, wrote the winning letter, and her dad, R.L. Higinbotham, was honorary mayor during the event. She accompanied him on the trip and had the pleasure of seeing him act in his honorary capacity Saturday morning when he led the parade through the main street of the town.

Edwards kept the town and his radio audience guessing with a "Mystery Man" contest in which it was necessary to guess the identity of a hooded and masked celebrity. On the mask were the clues, "A star, a bell, a shout; put them together, you've found me out." He arrived from El Paso on April 2 and toured the town in his mask and hood. Bill Perry, accountant and bookkeeper for the REA, was the first to guess the identity and got a $1,000 certificate from Speigel mail order house in Chicago when he named the mystery man as Hoot Gibson. (The show was recorded in Truth or Consequences and later broadcast over NBC.) Gibson arrived on Thursday afternoon before the show and was hooded until he appeared on the show Saturday night. Gibson remarked that he was glad the thing was over and that all he had to eat during the time was five sandwiches and 24 cups of coffee. Gibson was under the custody of Posseman Earl Coalson from Thursday until after the radio show.

Harold Tucker, a Chicago car salesman, appeared on the March 19 show and missed a question, causing him to hitchhike to Truth or Consequences leading a deodorized skunk on a leash. Thirteen days later he arrived, two days ahead of the Fiesta and said the skunk had actually helped his hitch hiking. Enough people knew of the stunt that they recognized him when they saw the skunk. He made many stops en route, and at Albuquerque found it necessary to buy a dog license for the skunk! Tucker received $500 and a 21-inch television set for his part in the stunt. The skunk was disposed of at Truth or Consequences in a Chinese auction.

In the spring of 1954, $1,000 was safely buried in New Mexico. Not a death was required to bury it. No mayhem, no broken bodies, no spilled blood was involved when it was hidden. No intricate map, no creepy dangerous formula was required to find it. Searching for it was as safe as walking down a city street – in Truth or Consequences, New Mexico. A couple weeks before the Fiesta, Edwards told the radio audience of the hiding of treasure somewhere within what was now the city limits of Truth or Consequences, New Mexico. He introduced "Loco Louie," a crazy old prospector who knew the location of the hidden treasure, and sent him, along with his favorite burro, to Truth or Consequences several days before the fifth annual Fiesta. Once there, "Loco Louie" roamed the streets announcing clues to the whereabouts of the hidden treasure. Local citizens and visitors from out of town had to figure out the clues to locate the hidden treasure and receive the $1,000.

Several weeks before the 1954 ceremonies, Edwards launched a contest asking couples to write a letter on "Why we want to get married at the Fiesta in Truth or Consequences, New Mexico." The winning couple received an all-expense round-trip to the Fiesta, along with two friends who they selected to accompany them. They were married at the Fiesta as desired, and as part of their honeymoon would attend all the Fiesta events as guests of honor.

Throughout the years, Ralph Edwards was the big drawing card of the event and his services were entirely free. He received no recompense of any kind from the Fiesta for broadcasting his radio program live from the event. In fact, the Edwards group was out several thousand dollars each year in order to make the broadcast in New Mexico. It was decided in 1953 that all net profits of the Fiesta would be given to the Arthritis and Rheumatism Foundation. The same thing was to be true for the following years.

Ralph Edwards and his wife Barbara returned to the city every year for the Fiesta, for more than thirty years, spending dinner at the homes of locals who they friended, attending dedication ceremonies, riding in the parade, and influencing a number of Hollywood celebrities to attend the event to help build publicity for the town. In the earliest years of when Edwards was diagnosed with Alzheimer's, he still made the trek to Truth or Consequences, New Mexico.

Ralph Edwards and Bob Barker at one of the annual Fiestas.

Actor Billy Barty clowning around with Ralph Edwards while attending one of the annual Fiestas.

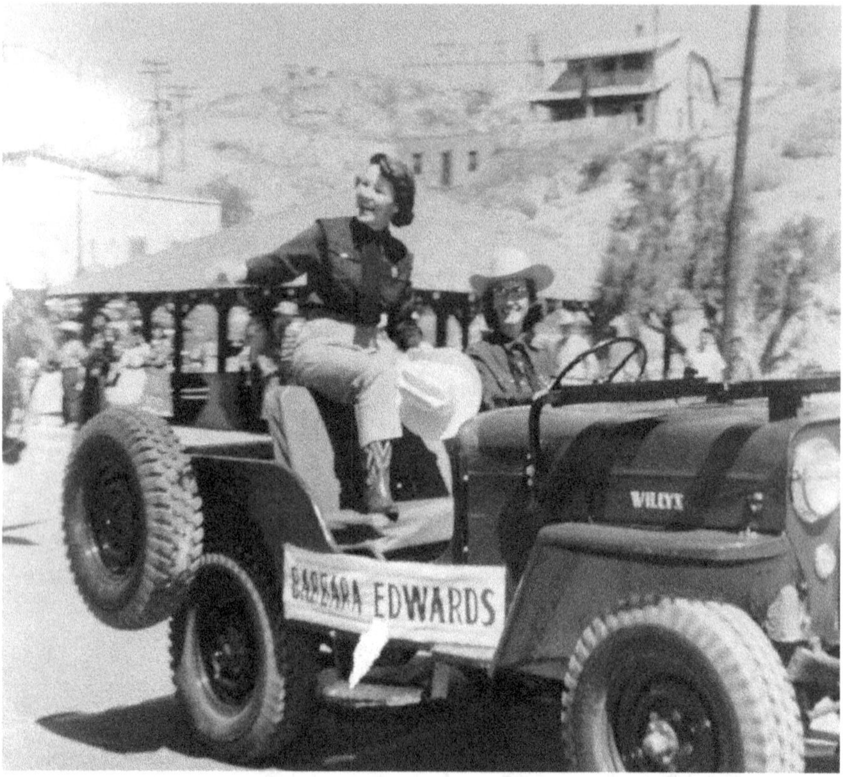
BARBARA EDWARDS
WILLYS

MILLING CO.
GREAT BEND, KANSAS
KANSAS WHEAT FLOUR SINCE 1877
H RALPH OR WE'LL GAMBLE ON
CONSEQUENCES
ALTERNATE
NEW MEXICO
US
85
NEW MEXICO
US
85

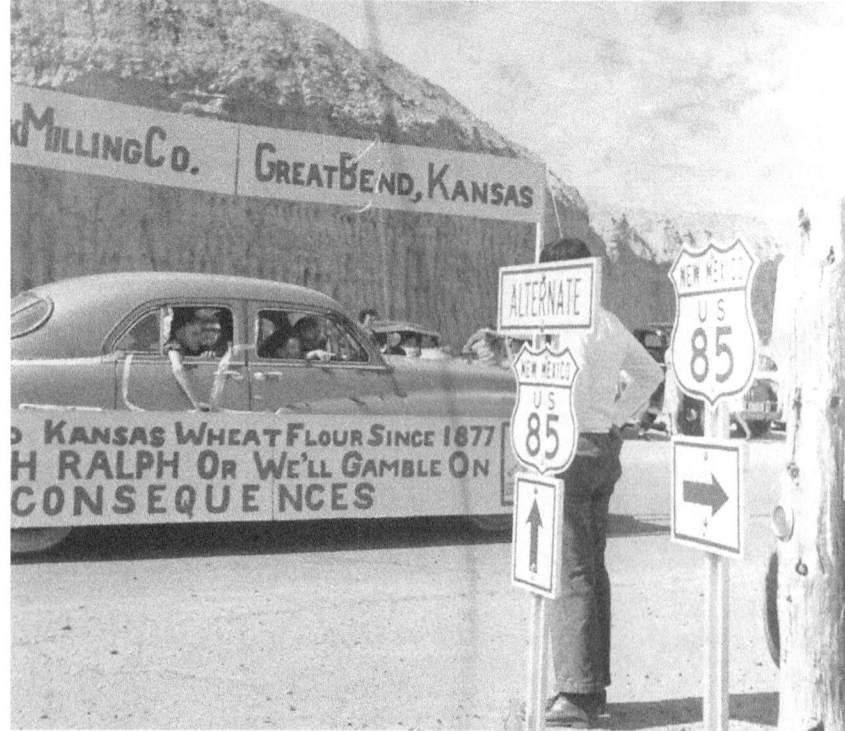

Chapter 14
Additional Consequences

"There are enough morons who'll listen to anybody who'll give away three refrigerators and 800 feet of garden hose... but radio must be either a medium of entertainment or a medium blessed by lottery."
—comedian Fred Allen, November, 1948

"A contest is always exciting," Ralph Edwards told Milwaukee columnist Bea J. Pepan. "I know. I've listened to playbacks of my own show and while I can't say I've always liked how I sound on the air, I honestly feel myself getting excited when those phone calls are put through." But comedian Fred Allen did not share the same opinion. In October of 1948, Allen bonded his listeners up to $5,000 to insure their attention against the current "giveaway" craze. It seemed like a novel idea for Allen to combat the inroads on his Sunday audience by *Stop the Music*; that of insuring his listeners against the loss of prizes should they be called on the phone while tuned in to his program. (The idea was unique, but not new, having been done back in the 1930s when Horace Heidt was riding high with *Pot o' Gold*.) Allen was prompted because of a recent study suggesting giveaway shows were gaining more attention than comedy, variety or discussion shows on the networks.

It all began when Fred Allen found his Sunday night comedy show buffeting the competition of a musical question game, *Stop the Music*. Many listeners, it seemed, were more interested in taking one chance in 20 million at winning a prize than they were in listening to the mighty Allen's quips. "I think his open feud with *Stop the Music* did the show an incredible amount of good," Edwards defended. "I never even thought about the show before I heard Fred's opening program this season in which he touched the whole thing off. But Fred piqued my curiosity and I'll warrant a lot of other listeners likewise. What Fred should have done, in my opinion, was ignore it. It's the smartest thing you can do in politics or show business."

"For the last ten years, Ralph Edwards, the emcee of *Truth or Consequences*, has been getting people to drive golf balls across the country, or to get into bed with a seal at the corner of Hollywood and Vine, or to get dumped in a tank of water. Why do people submit voluntarily to these indignities?" questioned columnist John Crosby. Meanwhile, the stunts kept coming and Ralph Edwards shared a laugh, along with the listening public.

Ralph Edwards parked in front of his house in California.

By 1949, the Edwards family had adjusted to fame and fortune, and the price to pay. Ralph and Barbara were careful about facts that appeared in print – especially asking to review any article or photo spread about the household – for fear of kidnapping and other crimes. For security purposes, Ralph Edwards made sure the address of his production company appeared in print more than his home address. When Hollywood tour guides began offering brochures listing his residential address, he protested in writing to have his name and address removed.

"Ralph's office was on the second floor of a two story building on Hollywood Boulevard and for years he hired an elderly man to run the elevator," recalled Ben Alexander. "For years also, Ralph had been playing a dual role while riding up and down each day. When he wore his toupee, the old gentleman recognized him as Ralph Edwards – the businesslike star of the *Truth or Consequences* show. But when he doesn't wear his toupee, Edwards slouches in the back of the elevator, makes snide remarks about 'Ralph' and tells how the famous Edwards is a no good bum. To this day, the old fellow still believes that there are two Edwards – Ralph, who has a fine crop of hair, and his brother Jack, who's bald as an eagle."

By 1950, in Latin America, Puerto Ricans had their own version of the radio quiz program titled, *El Patina… Se Cae*. Broadcast from San Juan, one episode featured a contestant who missed his question and as a consequence was supposed to leap from the top of the broadcasting station's four-story building. The $100 prize was part of the deal. While 3,000 spectators stared, the contestant made his dive into a fireman's net and pocketed the prize. Ever since, listeners in Puerto Rico were arriving at the radio station offering to jump without even a net for that $100 prize.

Comedian Jerry Colonna making one of two appearances on the quiz program.

 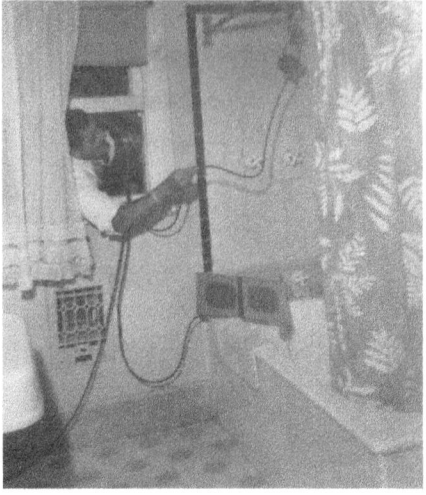

Remote pick-up from the Hollywood home of Mr. and Mrs. Owen Winston Day, where Mr. Day thought his wife was in the bath tub. When he finally gets the door open, Joe Kay of the *Truth or Consequences* engineering staff, walks out. The wife's voice originated from the Hollywood studio through special hook-up!

Dusty Rhodes and the Traffic Island

Envy the man who could make a goose who lays a golden egg out of the man who bites the hand who feeds him. That is what happened in late 1946 when Ralph Edwards thought he put one over on "Dusty" Rhodes, an amateur herpetologist, who faced "consequences" extending a number of weeks… before he got revenge against Edwards.

On the evening of September 14, 1946, a veteran named Dusty Rhodes, of Brooklyn, New York, answered his question incorrectly and accepted his consequence: to live on Traffic Island at Hollywood Boulevard and La Brea Streets, one of the busiest street corners in Hollywood. If Rhodes stayed on the island, he would receive $3 an hour for every hour that he held out and would be given a chance to report his progress on every Saturday night broadcast. He was supplied with enough food to last him three weeks and Ralph Edwards said would he would call it a deal if Rhodes stayed on the island for three weeks (which would net the contestant $1,512). The contestant was told that he would be observed and entertained every minute of his stay on Traffic Island. (The Traffic Island stunt was dedicated to a drive for public safety.) Also, he was given a bamboo fishing rod and a suit of long white underwear to raise as a distress signal should he decide to give up. A tent, bed and blankets were placed at the Island. Dusty Rhodes, a lanky ex-GI who once lived in a quiet Hollywood hotel and lectured on snakes, agreed under one condition: he insisted on having his pet snakes with him.

Traffic Island

Nineteen hours a day, during the hours Dusty wasn't sleeping, thousands of people crowded around his tent on the island. Edwards was true to his word, providing clowns, dancing girls and movie stars to entertain him. The press excitedly recorded his every move. And every week Dusty talked on the radio from his traffic island. Dusty could have been a comedian, providing ad-libs that were both witty and funny. He was so good Edwards cracked, "It's almost Dusty's show, not mine."

"I was a natural on the radio," Dusty told Aline Mosby, United Press Hollywood Correspondent. "Big-time radio announcers told me my voice, my timing, my ad-libbing was perfect. I threw the cracks at Edwards as fast as he threw 'em to me."

On the broadcast of September 21, Ralph Edwards told the radio audience that anyone who wanted to write to Dusty Rhodes could address him simply: "Dusty Rhodes, Truth or Consequences, NBC, Hollywood, California." Actor Keenan Wynn, opening a new theater, the El Patio, on October 1, was a guest on the broadcast, asking Rhodes to attend the grand opening. Since Rhodes could not leave his station, Wynn left a pair of binoculars with which he could watch the play by climbing to the top of a palm tree on Traffic Island – the El Patio Theater was just across the street. Meanwhile, Dusty talked to spectators, read and responded to his growing fan mail, sold autographed pictures of himself to tourists and gave the money he raised to the Sister Kenny Polio Foundation. He even showed the crowd his snakes.

Dusty Rhodes passing the time in his private island. To cross the street he required a raft.

After three weeks, on the broadcast of October 5, Dusty folded his tent and reported to the studio to collect his fee. The Mayor of Los Angeles, Fletcher Bowron, presented Dusty with a citation of merit from the Mayor's office and from the Police Department of Los Angeles, on behalf of the work being done to encourage safety among drivers. During his stay on Traffic Island, Dusty had been shouting at careless drivers and using his hands to help direct traffic. He exposed careless drivers and careless walkers alike and in many cases they returned to thank him for helping them prevent accidents. And Dusty collected his money: $1,500 in pennies. Because of his heavy load of pennies, Dusty was provided a cab from the Reliable Cab Company of Hollywood to take him "anywhere he likes." Dusty chose Brooklyn, New York. The audience howled. Taken aback, but not for long, Edwards dispatched one of his men to join the Dusty entourage and arranged for Dusty to bestow gifts to various folks across the country, on route to the East Coast. The 46-year-old contestant smartly stretched his good fortune. He took eight weeks to get to New York. He lived in the best of hotels, costing the radio program $7,000. On the broadcast of October 12, Steve Evans, the cabdriver, joined Dusty via remote from Oklahoma City. Edwards tells Evans that he will take a calf named "Clarence" from Oklahoma City to Chicago, in the cab, to keep Dusty company.

In New York, Edwards gave Dusty one last gag. To bring back a plate of Atlantic Ocean water to Hollywood... without spilling a drop. The Brooklyn man was deluged with wires from well-wishers offering him advice. Most of them advised him to freeze the water, forgetting that salt water doesn't freeze easily. Dusty finally hit on his own plan. He extracted the salt from the water, froze the liquid, preserved it in dry ice, and set out for the Golden State. For that, he collected an additional $500.

Despite his popularity with listeners, Dusty's career in radio was temporary. Four agents promised to get him on the air. His fame was short-lived. His checkbook was broke. He called the agents. Their deals never quite came through. Dusty checked out of his fancy hotel and disappeared. He moved to a cheap hotel in nearby Pasadena. Hollywood wondered for an hour what happened to him. Then it forgot. Dusty couldn't go back to snake lectures. He sold his snakes long ago, believing fame was his destiny. He took jobs washing dishes.

For a year Dusty lived in disillusioned oblivion. It seemed as if he had to "die" to get back into print. Another man named Dusty Rhodes – a movie stunt actor – jumped off San Francisco's Golden Gate Bridge. Some columnists mistook the stuntman for the contestant on *Truth or Consequences*. Rhodes phoned Edwards to assure him that he was still alive, and Dusty found out that the radio show was swamped with phone calls from his worried fans who feared the worst.

Ralph Edwards and Dusty Rhodes.

The Sunkist Summer Tour

In the summer of 1947, Ralph Edwards convinced Pat Clark, a journalism student at the University of California, and whose home was in Philadelphia, Pennsylvania, to take a consequence that would be documented through newspaper accounts across the country. On the evening of June 14, 1947, Clark missed his question and as his consequence, traveled east, touring for three weeks and visiting from 15 to 17 major cities in the United States; and in each city, he had to squeeze orange juice for all the families named Edwards. Newspapers would proclaim his upcoming arrival and anyone named Edwards was welcome to attend the breakfast at the expense of *Truth or Consequences*. Armed with a big truck of California Sunkist oranges, a road map, and a list of cities and dates, Clark was informed that his truck would be refilled as many times as necessary. Accompanying him was quiz show rep Roy Rector, to help Clark fulfill his promise. In one of the cities, Clark cooked an entire breakfast for families named Edwards, in addition to squeezing orange juice. Somewhere, he was told, he would find a fellow named Edwards who had his prize waiting for him, a $1,000 bill. The stunt concluded in July when, in New York, he succeeded in fulfilling his stunt and was awarded the prize money.

The crate was specially designed to hold a capacity of 5,106 oranges. Because of the tremendous weight of that many oranges, it was necessary to insert a center drum into the barrel. The actual number of oranges was 4,026.

Lizabeth Scott Goes Back to High School

On the evening of January 10, 1948, actress Lizabeth Scott took part in a stunt by serving as the real date for a student at Fairfax High. She went to the ROTC ball at Fairfax with the student after his "date" called off the original date and Ralph Edwards learned the boy had no girl to go with. Producer Hal Wallis, whose movie *I Walk Alone* was about to be released theatrically, co-starring Scott, took advantage of the free publicity on the quiz program with this special offer. In June of 1952, actor Aldo Ray participated in the same stunt for a female contestant. Lizabeth Scott was on that same broadcast, to participate in an "intimate" movie star stunt with a male contestant. The two agreed to switch stunts should the sex of the contestants accidentally be switched prior to the broadcast.

Lizabeth Scott discusses her participation in the stunt with Ralph Edwards.

Actress Lizabeth Scott meeting the contestant for the first time. When asked over the air what he thought about his consequence, the young man responded, "I would have preferred a blonde."

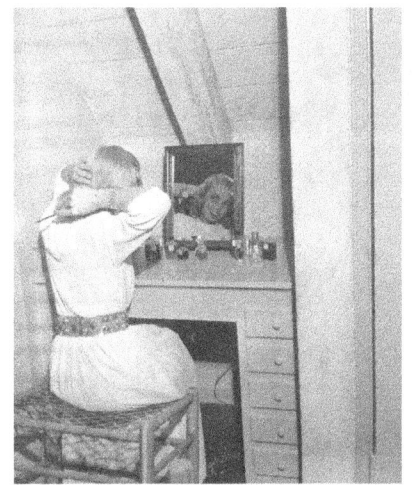

Margaret McGinn, the Irish Mother

On the evening of May 8, 1948, a special Mother's Day feature involved contestant Tom McGinn, who was surprised by having his mother flown from Shannon, Ireland, on a TWA plane to spend Mother's Day and a two week vacation with her children in the United States. Tom had not seen his mother since he left Ireland over ten years ago. She was the mother of 15 living children and she told how she was contacted by a story in a newspaper in Ireland. The story asked her to contact Radio Erin and arrangements for the flight were immediately made. Tom received a movie camera and a sound projector to record his mother's visit with him.

The story of the sixty-four-year old Irish mother, Mrs. Margaret McGinn, brought to America's shore for the first time since 1906, was considered by many as the best of the season. Once decided that an Irish mother was what was needed for the Mother's Day program, the complex wheels of *Truth or Consequences* organization began to turn as Al Paschall, the production manager, contacted Radio Erin and asked them to select a mother who had a son in Los Angeles whom she had not seen in several years. This was accomplished by the simple expedient of advertising in the Irish papers for just such a lady. Many applicants applied and from all of them, Mrs. Margaret McGinn was selected.

She was the mother of sixteen children, was on her way to the town pump for a bucket of water and stopped in a small shop to buy a paper. The front page story caught her eye and she became so excited over the possibilities, she forgot about the water, even leaving her bucket at the paper shop. Two days later, when she was notified that she was the one selected for the trip, she was rushed through the formalities of obtaining a passport and checking with customs.

While all of this was taking place in Ireland, it was necessary to make sure that the son attend the program on the night scheduled. This was accomplished by contacting the next door neighbor who, after being sworn to complete secrecy, vowed that she would have him there hell or high water.

When Mrs. McGinn was taken by car from her home in Ireland, it was her impression she was to return later to pack her things and say goodbye to her husband Joe. However, it was necessary to rush her to a TWA plane for the trip to America. As she drove by her husband's place of employment, she called to him, "Good-bye, Joe, I'm off to America." As Mrs. McGinn laughed, "Sure and I'll bet he's still just standing there looking." Mrs. McGinn didn't let the fact that she would not be able to return home for her things alter her plans one bit. She boarded the plane with the clothes on her back for a trip half way around the world. This oversight was immediately remedied by the *Truth or Consequences* crew who supplied her with fresh outfits from head to toe.

Meanwhile, Thomas McGinn of Los Angeles, the son, was brought to the show by the neighbor, still with no idea at all of the big surprise in store for him. He was picked from the audience and seated on stage with the other contestants. When his turn at the microphone came, his "consequence" was to talk to his mother in Ireland by long-distance telephone… or so he thought. Actually, of course, he was merely talking over an interphone to his mother who was backstage pretending to be in Ireland. At the conclusion of the call, Ralph Edwards asked Thomas if he thought his mother had changed much in the twenty years since he had seen her. Thomas replied she sounded much the same as he remembered her. "Well," said Ralph, "Do you think she would look like this lady who is walking on stage right now?" The back curtains parted and into the spotlight walked Mrs. McGinn. There was a gleeful reunion on stage followed by two weeks of visiting in Mrs. McGinn's suite at the Knickerbocker Hotel in Hollywood, all provided by Ralph Edwards and *Truth or Consequence*. Mrs. McGinn summed up the whole adventure very nicely when she remarked, "Sure and it was a great day for the Irish."

Roy Rogers, "King of the Cowboys," was a friend of Ralph Edwards and made frequent appearances on *Truth or Consequences*.

Actress Celeste Holm took part in a stunt ad libbing the lines of a drama.

Putting Hollywood on the Map

On September 3, 1948, more than 400 celebrities, business and public officials attended the Hollywood Chamber of Commerce luncheon celebrating the fact that Hollywood attained official recognition of a Hollywood postmark. The event climaxed 14 years effort on the part of the Chamber of Commerce, businessmen, and public officials to give Hollywood an official status. Hollywood existed but all mail displayed the Los Angeles postmark because Hollywood had no official postal recognition. A quarter-of-a-million pieces of mail were picked up daily in Hollywood, but go out with a Los Angeles postmark. At the luncheon plaques were presented to a number of individuals, including Los Angeles Postmaster Michael D. Fanning, and Ralph Edwards. As a gag on his quiz program, Edwards began the circulation of a petition to put Hollywood on the map. "Add the power of radio," proclaimed *Radio Daily*, "While the Hollywood Chamber of Commerce worked for 14 years to get Movietown its own postmark, Ralph Edwards, via a *Truth or Consequences* stunt, swung the deal in something like two months."

On the evening of June 19, contestant Eddie Carideo, of Los Angeles, agreed to tour the country during the summer and attempt to get enough people to sign a petition to get Hollywood on the official Rand McNally map and in the files of the Post Office Department. Carideo's challenge was to get one million people to sign his petition and to return to the quiz program in the fall with news of his tour. The route he was to follow through the summer was mapped out for him. He would end his tour at Washington, D.C., where the petition would be presented to the Postmaster General, who would then authorize a Hollywood Sub Station Postmark, in addition Rand McNally would include Hollywood on their latest maps. If he succeeded in getting the one million petitions, he would get $2,500 in cash. In real life, Carideo was a substitute mail carrier!

Los Angeles, California (June 21-22)
San Francisco, California (June 25-26)
Salt Lake City, Utah (June 28)
Denver, Colorado (June 30, July 1-4)
Kansas City, Missouri (July 6-7)
Omaha, Nebraska (July 9-10)
Des Moines, Iowa (July 12-14)
St. Paul, Minnesota (July 16-17)
Milwaukee, Wisconsin (July 19-21)

Chicago, Illinois (July 23, 24)
St. Louis, Missouri (July 26)
Louisville, Kentucky (July 27-28)
Indianapolis, Indiana (July 29-31)
Cincinnati, Ohio (August 2-4)
Detroit, Michigan (August 6-7)
Cleveland, Ohio (August 9)
Buffalo, New York (August 11)
Syracuse, New York (August 13-14)
Boston, Massachusetts (August 16-21)
New York City, New York (August 23-25)
Philadelphia, Pennsylvania (August 27-28)
Pittsburgh, Pennsylvania (August 30-31)
Baltimore, Maryland (September 1-2)
Washington, D.C.

Carideo was generously supplied 4,000 BB Ball Pens, from the BB Ball Pen Company, with which the one million signatures would be inscribed in the giant petition books. Roy Rector of *Truth or Consequences* accompanied the contestant, verifying all of the signatures were legit, keeping tabs on the actual count of signatures, and as contact for local newspapers and radio stations who were notified in advance of Carideo's arrival. Jack Melvin was the advance man for handling timely publicity, while Gene Juster, the program manager for the quiz program, attempted to set up in advance some stunts for the contestant's visit. Local radio stations used their news features and local morning programs to promote the event and encourage listeners to come out and sign the petition. The 23-city tour was occasionally featured in local newspapers, along with various accompaniments such as five girls, known as the Pen-Quints, local residents chosen to help Snyder secure signatures. A judge reviewed photos of all the Pen-Quints and the most beautiful was given a free trip to Hollywood, and a screen test at RKO-Radio Studios.

During the broadcast of June 26, a Los Angeles tire salesman, William Snyder, received two sealed envelopes with consequences enclosed (three smaller sealed envelopes were inside each envelope, progressing down in size). The first one contained a $100 bill; the second a ten-week vacation at home, plus a hammock to insure the tops in relaxation, and pay while he vacationed; the third

Jerry Colonna took part in a stunt about the song, "My Honky Little Donkey and Me." As a special "gift," Ralph Edwards presents Colonna with a real live donkey on stage. Broadcast of January 24, 1948.

Phil Baker, host of radio's *Take It or Leave It*, was a guest on November 23, 1946.

Frank Sinatra was in the NBC studio warming-up for his performance on *Your Hit Parade*. A female contestant was sent to Sinatra to collect a "kiss" from him. She received what she asked for.

envelope, which the contestant chose to open although he had his choice to keep the first envelope and not open any more, assigned Snyder to replace contestant Carideo, who was now on the first lap of his visit to 23 cities in the U.S., in the all-summer tour trying to get one million signers on a petition to get Hollywood on the official postal maps.

Because contestant Snyder chose this third envelope, he now traded his consequence with contestant Carideo. Carideo came home and spent ten weeks on vacation lounging in a hammock, "with pay," while William Snyder started out to replace Carideo and have a chance at the $2,500 prize… if he acquired one million signatures by the time the quiz show returned to the air for the fall.

On the season premiere of August 28, 1948, William Snyder returned to the radio microphone to report on the progress. The contestant did not get the one million signatures assigned to him and he protested over the air that the possibility of getting the number of signatures in the time allotted him was impossible, and unnecessary. Citing postal regulations requiring only half a million signatures, Snyder felt the necessary task was accomplished. This statistic was reported to him by one of thousands of people who came out to sign the petition. He was correct in his assumption and was told by Edwards that only 500,000 signatures were actually required, but the "million" was specified to "confuse him." (Behind the scenes, Edwards confessed that "one million" was more exciting to the American public, and agreed to provide Snyder with a consolation prize.) Actually, Snyder acquired a total of 630,322 signatures. A check for $2,500 was also mailed to Eddie Carideo, the contestant who started the signature project and then traded his "consequence" with Snyder.

The Beetle Derby

One of the most expensive stunts Ralph Edwards had on *Truth or Consequences* was that which gave a new car to the first of four drivers reaching Detroit. This was no ordinary race. The automobiles had to follow the direction taken by beetles in boxes. Known as "The Beetle Derby," the contest required live beetles to be caught and used for the life of the contest. When Fred Carney was considering the possibility of carrying through such a stunt, he asked one of the secretaries in Ralph Edwards' office if there were any beetles in the Hollywood Hills where she lived. She suggested to study their ways and find out how they lived. Then she brought some to him. But by the time Edwards was ready to do the stunt, there had been a hot spell and all the beetles had died. Carney was forced to advertise for the bugs, paying a dollar a beetle… and kids brought them to him.

"The Beetle Derby" commenced on the evening of September 18, 1948. The automobile race was planned to carry over through two or three weeks. The contest consisted of four contestants who were on the program that evening: Jasper Spencer, Johnny Asher, John Benson and Charlie Range. All four agreed to drive a car from Hollywood, leaving at 9 a.m. Monday morning, with their destination being Detroit. Each driver was accompanied by an official representing *Truth or Consequences*, who oversaw that the drivers did not do more than eight hours driving per day, that they obeyed all traffic regulations and speed laws, and that they follow the beetle in their car. Each car was equipped with an ordinary beetle and a plastic box. As the driver entered a new state, he slipped a map of that state into the beetle's box and then follows the route taken by the beetle. Once in another state, the driver could not go back into a previous state even if the Beetle heads back for the state line. At the end of the race, the winning driver received his choice of four prizes:

1. A brand new Kaiser car and $250 cash.
2. A brand new television set and $1,000 cash.
3. A Columbia Trailer complete with refrigerator, and $100 cash.
4. A projector and screen, and a complete set of tires and tubes, plus $500 cash.

The Beetle Derby in action.

The driver to come in second gets his choice of prizes not chosen by the winner; the third chooses between the two remaining prizes and the fourth gets what was left. Also, the driver who gets the best mileage per gallon of gas received a bonus of $200. If, at any time during the race, two drivers of Kaiser cars meet in the same town, each driver received a $200 bonus. If, at any time, the four drivers hit the same town at the same time, each driver received a $500 bonus. All expenses were paid during the trips. Drivers tonight drew straws to see what they would drive: Spencer and Benson drove Kaisers; Asher and Range drove Frasers.

On the evening of September 25, contestant John Asher provided an update courtesy of station KOA in Denver, Colorado. Asher reported how his beetle named Tyrone guided him to Denver. He and the beetle were having a great time at NBC radio stations along the way and at one time, he and Jasper Spencer, another driver in the contest, met. Back in the Hollywood studio, Ralph Edwards reported on another contestant, Charlie Range. With his beetle named Willie, the two were presently in Elko, Nevada; Jasper Spencer was last heard from in Trinidad, Colorado. Spencer's first beetle, named Percy, died but it had since been replaced with another now named Percy. John Benson, spoke for himself from the Hollywood studio for his beetle never took him outside of Hollywood. His first beetle, named Please, also died. His new Beetle was named No, Thank You, but proved no better at guiding his driver.

On the evening of October 2, Edwards reported that John Benson finally got out of California and was now in Mexico City, Mexico; John Asher was in New Orleans; Charles Range was in Boys Town, Nebraska; and Jasper Spencer was in Chicago, Illinois. Courtesy of radio station WMAQ, Chicago, Jasper Spencer reported how he was averaging 22 and a half miles per gallon. He also hoped to win the Derby.

On the evening of October 9, a special pickup from the steps of City Hall in Detroit, Michigan, the winner of the Beetle Derby was broadcast, where Mayor Eugene I. Van Antwerp, presented Jasper Spencer with the key to his new Kaiser car, the prize for winning the derby. Bob Leslie, announcer at station WWJ in Detroit, was the emcee and announced the points where other Beetle Derby contestants ended the race at 6 p.m., October 8. John Asher was in New York City, and Charles Range in Moscow, Michigan. Range got the prize for the best mileage. Spencer said his faithful Beetle, Percy, died the night before the awarding of the prize, and told of when he met John Asher in Kansas, receiving a bonus of $200, as does Mr. Asher. At the conclusion of the broadcast from Detroit, Spencer was surprised by his wife when she appeared in person to congratulate her husband.

The Breakdown

Charlie Range (Jack Wormser, *T or C* rep)
30 radio broadcasts ranging from five minutes to one hour, including two Transcontinentals.
2 Television Broadcasts
Stories and pictures in 39 different newspapers

Jasper Spencer (Bill Card, *T or C* rep)
56 radio broadcasts
27 Radio Stories (news broadcasts, etc.)
46 newspaper stories
26 pictures

John Benson (Bill Hawes, *T or C* rep)
22 radio broadcasts
18 newspaper stories
pictures in 12 newspapers

Johnny Asher (Jim Chadwick, *T or C* rep)
40 radio broadcasts
25 newspaper stories
18 newspaper pictures

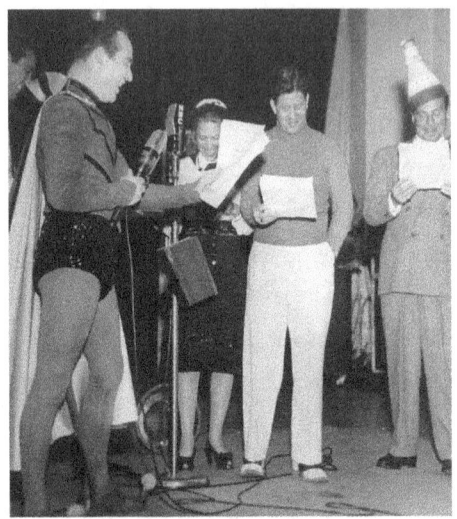

Rudy Vallee was among the numerous celebrity guests that attended the "Sixth Birthday" celebration honoring the quiz show on the evening of March 23, 1946.

Basil Rathbone feeds Eddie "Rochester" Anderson cake on the evening of March 23, 1946.

Mama and Papa Hush

Throughout the 1948-1949 season of *Truth or Consequences*, Ralph Edwards revived the "Hush" contests with a series of "Mama and Papa Hush," a married couple who shared the chore of reciting clues to their identity, in rhyme. On the evening of October 16, 1948, for the first time in the history of the mystery voice contests, given from time to time on the program, the first person telephoned in the contest identified the mystery voices: Mrs. Mildred R. Liebermann, 6034 Columbia Street, St. Louis, Missouri, was the lucky winner as she named actors Kitty Carlisle and Moss Hart, her producer husband, as Mr. and Mrs. Hush.

The St. Louis housewife received a number of prizes valued at $7,000: a $2,000 all electric kitchen; a $2,000 mink coat (or its cash equivalent); a television and radio-phonograph combination; a $1,000 diamond and ruby wristwatch; and a complete solid maple living room furniture set, plus Spinet piano. Moss Hart and Kitty Carlisle were heard from the Statler Hotel in Boston, Massachusetts, that evening. Heard twice prior on the program, the couple's voices originated from their New York apartment on October 2, and the Taft Hotel, in New Haven, Connecticut, on October 9. The NBC engineer, Perry Alexander, was thanked on the air for helping them arrange for their mobile hideouts.

Ralph Edwards explained that in all of the Hush contests, the program always maintained "standby personalities" to use for a new contest in the event that the first was solved during the early weeks. The arrangement was made so that the worthwhile organization to get the proceeds from listener contributions would realize substantial sums to carry on its good work. On the same evening "Mama and Papa Hush" were identified, a new contest was launched, with proceeds to continue going to the Mental Health Drive. The same rules applied. Listeners were instructed to send in letters to "Papa and Mama Hush, Hollywood, California." The voices of the second "Papa and Mama Hush," speaking from somewhere in the United States, was heard in the form of the following clue:

> "If Two and Three our Number be
> Then we are Four – Yet we are Three!
> But when Time goes on and Life's begun
> Five and Two are then about One!"

"Mama" read the first two lines and "Papa" read the last two lines. The person who identified the new "Papa and Mama Hush" would receive the prizes to date, with three new prizes added each week the contest continued to run. Additional clues provided over the weeks, added to the jingle, were:

"We are not the parents of famous children."
"Good night, Ernest..."
"My star is your eye."
"We have merrily picked our way along life's way."
"Yes, my lifetime buddy."

Every week, three or four new prizes were added to the pot: a 10-year supply of the sponsor's product (DUZ), a two-week vacation for two in Sun Valley, Idaho, and a new 1949 Nash car, scheduled for unveiling on November 22 (October 16); $2,500 in U.S. Security Bonds, a three-year supply of tires and tubes for one car, a 16mm sound and silent picture projector and camera; and a trip to Washington for the president's inauguration with a week stay at the Statler Hotel (October 23); a Stromberg radio phonograph combination, a Spinet piano, and a $2,000 Hot Point all-electric kitchen (October 30); a $1,000 diamond ring, a Maple furniture set for the living room, a $1,000 men's wardrobe, and a $1,000 woman's wardrobe (November 6); a $1,500 tractor and equipment for a farm home, a one-year supply of food including meat for a family of four, and a complete power tool workshop (November 13); a $1,000 diamond ruby wrist watch, a $1,000 Gil portrait for the winner or any member of his family by Ray Hoff, and a $1,000 gift certificate for Spiegel mail order house items (November 20); a dozen pairs of ladies shoes and matching handbags, a complete house painting job inside and out, and a complete home laundry unit (November 27); a vacuum cleaner with all the attachments, Venetian blinds for the entire house, and a fox fur coat (December 4).

Incorrect guesses included Mr. and Mrs. Eddie Cantor, Henry Luce and Clare Boothe Luce, and Dr. Francis Griffith and his wife, Irene Dunne (October 23); Bing Crosby and Dixie Lee, Dorothy Stickney and Howard Lindsay (of *Life with Father* and *Life with Mother* fame), and Mr. and Mrs. Lewis Stone (October 30); Mr. and Mrs. Sullivan who lost five sizes in the war, Gov. and Mrs. Earl Warren of California, and Mr. and Mrs. Harold Lloyd (November 6); Mr. and Mrs. Earnest Kidder Lindley (Washington correspondent of *Newsweek* magazine), John Boettigr and Anna Roosevelt, and Mr. Norman Chandler and wife (publisher of the *Los Angeles Times*) (November 13); Fredric March and Florence Eldridge, Ronald and Benita Colman, and Mr. and Mrs. Ernest Hemingway (November

20); Mr. and Mrs. Dwight D. Eisenhower, Mary Pickford and Buddy Rogers, and Mrs. and Mrs. Ernest Orlando Lawrence (November 27); and Mr. and Mrs. Buddy DeSylva, Gov. Thomas E. Dewey and wife, and Gen. Jonathan Wainwright and wife (December 4).

There were no "Hush" calls on the evening of December 11, 1948. Ralph Edwards informed the audience that the contest ran long enough and no new entries would be accepted after midnight. Next week, December 18, the entire program would be devoted to phone calls for contestants to identify "Mama and Papa Hush." On the evening of December 18, Mama and Papa Hush were identified as the dance team of Veloz and Yolanda, who spoke in behalf of the Mental Health Drive, explaining the clues used during the contest.

The first person telephoned made the correct identification: Oscar Keith of 8931 West Delaware Parkway, Munster, Indiana. His family was $30,000 richer, giving Uncle Sam a merciless 34 or 35 percent tax from the jackpot. Keith admitted to reporters that his 1948 income amounted to $3,600. Being put in the $30,000 bracket only complicated matters. Keith gave credit to his wife for working out the clues. They had four children. Linda, age 6, Sharon, age 8, Larry, age 4 and Daryl, age 3. They had lived in Munster's Independence Park subdivision for four years, having formerly resided at 4840 Carey in East Chicago. Oscar toiled away at the Harbison-Walker Refractories, the East Chicago brickyard, where he hauled brick in wheelbarrows from the kilns to the storage racks.*

Oscar Keith was 34 at the time, his wife was 31. She had leafed through hundreds of references at homes and libraries to select the correct answer. She had the radio tuned in to the program at the time her husband was talking on the telephone to a friend just released from a hospital. Hundreds of calls were handled by the Times Office telephone exchange and the operator interrupted Keith's phone conversation with "an emergency call is coming through from Hollywood." Oscar took the call. Mr. Keith was asked if he could identify Mr. and Mrs. Keith and he did – correctly. Mrs. Keith's penchant for radio contests paid off.

Keith didn't have to shovel snow from the walks of his home that weekend. Following the broadcast, neighbors, friends, relatives, newsmen, photographers and radio representatives beat a path to his door. The contest letter submitted,

---

* Ironically, Keith's brother, Claude Keith of East Chicago, one of the first to congratulate Oscar was an employee of Lever Brothers – a competitor of the soap firm which showered wealth on Oscar's household.

Keith explained to everyone who asked, was one of five they submitted during the life of the contest. Hoping to turn down a third of the prizes, it was his intention to lower the prize income to $20,000 to affirm an acceptable tax bracket. The tax, according to Wilbur Enders, Lake County internal revenue chief, was based on prize value listed by the contest sponsors. A lower tax would be computed at the prices Keith sold some of the prizes. It all came under the "willing buyer, willing seller" tax statute. It was also Keith's option to request delivery of the prizes after January 1. This would establish a 1949 tax year and provide months of convenience to re-organize the total value of the prizes.

Horror star Boris Karloff, disguised as a swami, arrived at the door of a female contestant, Mrs. O'Sullivan, who was tricked into believing it was her husband in disguise, and kissed the actor many times.

Veloz and Yolanda phoned the Keiths the day after the broadcast to offer a year of free professional dancing lessons. Oscar and Mary said that with four children around the house, they wouldn't have much time for terpsichorean pleasures. Sharon and Linda like to dance and they would share the prize.

A contestant named Bob Dyer is sent out into the streets with a real-life kangaroo named "Bouncing Betty" and told to collect girls who will leap through life with him. He received $10 for every girl who returned with him to the studio.

In an official release dated early December, Edwards made a plea for the print media to restrain their pride for philanthropy. "In the past," said Edwards, "the divulging of the identity of the 'Hushes,' when a columnist or other person had solved it, had no pronounced effect upon the contest because the newsbreaks coincided with the more obvious clues given to bring the contest to a close. The grave danger of publicizing the name at the outset of the contest, however, would seriously injure the real purpose of the competition, which is to bring funds to the most needy, but least-financed charity in existence. We would like for the contest to last long enough to give the drive enough funds to do a real difference. Therefore, I am making humanitarian aspects to all media to consider the names of Mr. and Mrs. Hush of the contests but not to divulge the clues."

To ensure the accuracy of statements regarding the National Health campaign, the staff psychiatrist of The National Mental Health Foundation, Dr. Dallas Pratt, provided commercial copy for use on the quiz show. Dr. George Stevenson of the National Committee for Mental Hygiene also reviewed the copy. The contest ultimately raised more than $500,000 for the Mental Health Drive.

The Whispering Woman

On the evening of January 15, 1949, "The Whispering Woman" was heard for the first time, from her hideout "somewhere in the United States," and whispered the following clue referring to her identity:

> "I'm a cake,
> My coat is white,
> My father owns the stock,
> Half of mine is light."

Rules for entering the contest were similar to prior contests: listeners were instructed to write 25 words or fewer to accompany the statement: "We should all support the American Heart Association because..." Their name, address and telephone number had to be printed clearly in the upper right hand corner, addressed to: The Whispering Woman, Box W, Hollywood, California. Contestants were encouraged (but not required) to send a contribution to the American Heart Association. The contribution was to be sent to another address: Box A (A for American Heart Association), Los Angeles, California. On each broadcast, beginning January 29, the writer of the three best entries that week would be telephoned. Each person phoned had a chance to ask one question that could be answered by "The Whispering Woman" with a simple "yes" or "no" answer, serving as clues to identify "The Whispering Woman." Listeners were then held on the line and given about five minutes time to consider the answer before making their identification.

The first caller each week received a new car, the 1949 Kaiser Deluxe, even if they did not identify "The Whispering Woman." The car would be assigned through a local dealer, provided the contestant was willing to pay for the expenses to have the automobile driven to the local dealer from the factory. The second prize-winner each week received another valuable prize, differing on each broadcast. The person who identified "The Whispering Woman" would receive $25,000 in cash, the biggest one-time cash prize ever given on the history of this series. The letter voted as the best of the week was chosen as the first to be phoned, followed by the second and third, respectively.

The pirating of program ideas was indulged freely. The award of a pyramiding jackpot was borrowed, an entire program built around it, and *Stop the Music* was among the more popular on the airwaves. *Stop the Music* was an instant hit and was followed almost immediately by *Sing it Again*. By 1950, the "Phantom Voice" on *Sing it Again* was stumping radio listeners who tried to crack the clues. The most logical solution to that mystery, based on the clues, was Edgar Bergen, which more than one contestant guessed over the span of the contest, which was incorrect. Realizing that a jackpot of prizes was almost futile as a result of stiff competition, Edwards instead chose a cash prize.

The first of the phone calls was on the evening of January 29, establishing clues that she is over 40 years of age and had no children. Second listener received a Stromberg-Carlson radio-television set combination. Listeners incorrectly identified "The Whispering Woman" as Billie Burke and Ginger Rogers. On the evening of February 5, clues established that she did not play in silent movies and that she has never achieved fame in the world of sports. Listeners incorrectly identified her as Alice White and Louella Parsons. Second caller received an electric Laundromat and clothes dryer. On the evening February 12, clues verified she attained fame as a singer and that her husband has never been an Academy Award winner. Incorrect guesses include Kate Smith and Marion Anderson. Second caller received a Victor camera and projector for motion pictures.

On the evening of February 19, 1949, the mystery voice was identified as motion-picture star and concert artist Jeanette MacDonald. The first listener phoned, Miss Merle Ford, home economist and retired college professor, of Chicago, Ill., identified MacDonald and received the $25,000 cash prize, the Kaiser automobile, and a free trip to California to appear on next week's broadcast. Miss Ford thus became the winner of the "biggest cash prize ever offered to one person on this program," proclaimed Ralph Edwards. Over the air, Edwards explained how the jingle pointed to Jeanette MacDonald. The white coat on the cake referred to icing, which meant, "I sing." The line, "Dad owns the stock," hinted at the song, "Old MacDonald had a Farm," thus supplying the singer's last name. The "half mine is light" referred to the "ray" in the last name of MacDonald's husband, actor Gene Raymond. While the clues were being explained to some 15,000,000 radio listeners, bedlam broke loose in the lobby of Miss Ford's South Side hotel. Hundreds of well-wishers joined newsmen and promoters in a clamor to see the jackpot winner. Then, blinded by photographer's flash bulbs, she emerged smiling from an elevator. Hundreds of people crowded into the Broadview Hotel. From the hotel she was whisked to television station WBKB for a *Sun-Times* spot news broadcast. She said she had no idea what she would do with her $25,000 windfall. When asked about her present job and income, she ducked the question. "One thing is certain," she answered, "this is the most money I ever made in a week."

The hideout of "The Whispering Woman" each week was a Wilshire Boulevard apartment, belonging to a production man on the show, but even he did not know who was using the apartment each week!

Merle Ford was a home economist and former schoolteacher, described by one newspaper columnist as a "middle-aged spinster." She answered the phone call from Hollywood in her room at the Broadview Hotel at 5540 Hyde Park Blvd in Chicago, where she had been living for the past six months. She kept missing the call; her phone ringing every few minutes. After she answered the phone, Edwards permitted Miss Ford to ask the mystery voice one question. "Have you ever appeared with the Metropolitan Opera?" When MacDonald, a movie soprano, answered "no," Miss Ford immediately guessed her identity. She had only two potential guesses and the answer helped eliminate one of them.

Merle Ford admitted that she researched the project when the clues were first announced on January 15. In technical libraries she studied books on heart diseases. In the public library, she had studied the biographies of prominent women. Then she entered the contest by writing three letters urging public support of the American Heart Association. On Monday, following the Saturday broadcast, the sandy-haired textile produce expert explained her interest in heart work was first aroused through her public school work as an adviser in home economics teaching. She visited schools for the handicapped, which brought her in close contact with children suffering effects of heart disease, some of whom were recovering from rheumatic fever.

"I couldn't help but marvel at the way children can be rehabilitated despite damaged hearts," she remarked. A more personal connection with heart disease came from two deaths in her immediate family, both heart cases. At the age of 52, her father died after a heart attack some years prior in the family home of Maryville, Missouri. Her brother died at 48 a few years later in the Canal Zone. Her mother was completely helpless for a year and a half as a result of a stroke. "Of course I wanted to win the contest if I could," she told reporters. "But even if I hadn't, I would have been glad I had contributed to the heart cause." She hoped her newfound fame would lend emphasis to her plea that everybody join in the work to stamp out heart disease, she added. "In my work as a home economics teacher in public schools, I often saw the wonderful work of rehabilitation being done among children suffering from heart ailments."

Be it $25,000 or $25, the first thing most women think of when they get their hands on some extra money is – a new hat. Having accepted an invitation to California to appear on *Truth or Consequences*, that is exactly what Merle Ford did. She also purchased a new pair of shoes. She appeared as a guest on the broadcast of February 26, accepting her $25,000 cash prize, and thanked Ralph Edwards for the wonderful contest. While on stage, she also met Hollywood screen actors Gregory Peck and Rod Cameron, and had her photograph taken with them as a souvenir from her trip.

The prize-winning answer ended a month-long contest, which netted the American Heart Association an additional $500,000 for the current fund drive. The same association benefited by "The Walking Man" contest, which was won by another Chicago native.

Singer Joan Edwards made a guest appearance three times on the quiz program. The two photographs above are from her 1946 appearance which involved contestant Roy Anderson trying to sell a recording to the singer.

The Laughing Boy

Kicking off the 1949-1950 season, *Truth or Consequences* initiated a new "Telephone Feature" for citizens living anywhere in the United States. A person was chosen at random from the phone book and telephoned during the week. Those segments were later played back as a weekly feature on the quiz program. During the conversation, "The Laughing Boy" would carry on a zany conversation with the lucky recipient of the phone call. (For legal purposes, the person telephoned was also asked for permission to record the conversation.) On the broadcast following the original telephone call made, the recorded conversation of "The Laughing Boy" and the listener was presented while the listener had a chance to overhear the recording. Then they were given a chance to identify the voice and receive $2,500. If they did not guess correctly, they received a 72-piece set of sterling silver. Each week that "The Laughing Boy" remained unidentified, he called someone else, giving new clues to his identity. The prize remained $2,500 and was not cumulative.

The first phone call was broadcast on the evening of August 27, 1949. The female contestant was unable to identify him. On the broadcast of September 3, the contestant incorrectly guessed W.C. Fields; on September 10, Charlie Ruggles. During the broadcast of September 17, "The Laughing Boy" struck up a conversation about a recipe for Swivel Meatloaf. Mr. and Mrs. J. Halett of Alburg, Vermont, were telephoned and their incorrect guess was George Rector. A resident of Chico, California, was the contestant on September 24, and incorrectly guessed George Mardikian, the famed restaurant owner. "The Laughing Boy" joked that he was a plumber who wanted to repair the leaking sink.

"The Laughing Boy" impersonated a banjo teacher on the broadcast of October 1, a pinecone collector on October 8, and a maker of wigs and a designer of coiffures on October 15. Incorrect guesses were Robert Lewis on October 1, Chic Johnson of the Olsen and Johnson comedy team on October 8, and on the evening of October 15, the woman who was called during the past week could not be contacted. She did not answer her telephone although the call was attempted throughout the entire broadcast. Thus, she forfeits her privilege of trying to identify the "Laughing Boy."

On the evening of October 22, Mrs. Lincoln Kilbourne, 3647 14th Street, Milwaukee, correctly identified "The Laughing Boy" was Milton Berle. The comedian's "voluntary services" to solicit funds for the Cancer Drive last year were mentioned as Edwards thanked Berle for cooperating in the contest. Mrs. Kilbourne confessed that a clue provided by Ralph Edwards, week prior, that "Laughing Boy is a famous American who you have all seen and heard," suggested Mr. Television himself. (Another clue, not provided on the program, was that Berle's latest motion-picture, *Always Leave Them Laughing*, was due for theatrical release in late November.)

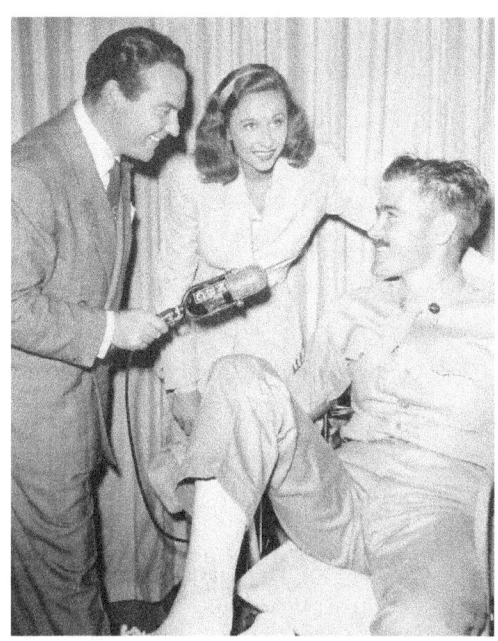

Sgt. Richard Suchanek, a 23-year-old war veteran of deQuincy, Louisiana, participated in a stunt choosing an actress to play a small role in an up-coming movie. Actress Vera Ralston participated in the stunt.

Actress June Clayworth, currently filming *Beat the Band* (an RKO picture with Ralph Edwards in the cast) participated in a stunt with Frankie Carle, piano-playing orchestra leader.

Otto the Great

Receiving more coverage in newspapers than "The Laughing Boy" was "The Great Otto," whom Ralph Edwards entered in the breakers between the English and French coasts. He was certain he could crack the record set in 1936 with his Catalina Crawl, which was not to be confused with a new wrestling hold. The *Truth or Consequences* stunt performed on an international scale was picked up by the Associated Press and carried in most newspaper dailies. The yarn, about a California sea lion swimming the English Channel, was the result of a consequence handed out to Burt Kennedy, who missed his question. Kennedy was the son of the old vaudeville team known as The Dancing Kennedys, had been appearing in bit film roles in Hollywood, and was slated to rejoin his brother Ken's band as a vocalist in the winter. But first, he had a consequence to fulfill.

Contestant Burt Kennedy being assigned his consequence.

On the evening of September 24, 1949, Burt Kennedy of Hollywood, California, was assigned the "trainer" for "Otto the Great," better known as "Pierre Cilion," to swim the English Channel. Radio listeners could not see or hear "Otto the Great" but the contestant was sent backstage to consult with Otto, through an interpreter, and then the contestant returned to report that he and Otto would start on their way whenever Ralph Edwards was ready. Edwards told the listening public that Otto would make trial swims in the U.S. during the next few weeks and then leave with his trainer, contestant Burt Kennedy, via TWA for Calais, France. The contestant would get one dollar for every minute Otto the Great beats the time of the current Channel swimming record. (The fastest time for a human swimmer was made by Czechoslovakian Vencelas Spacek, who made the 19-mile Channel crossing in 10 hours and 45 minutes in 1926.) The joke was on Kennedy – "Cilion" was really a "sea lion." The seal was borrowed from Marineland of the Pacific, located in Hermosa Beach, California.

Contestant Burt Kennedy with Otto the Great.

On the broadcast of October 1, the contestant who agreed to act as a trainer for Pierre Cilion, also known as "Otto the Great," said he and Pierre were now ready to board a TWA to fly to France. The two practiced swims made by Pierre in the Missouri River and again at Jones Beach, New York. On the broadcast of October 8, there was an attempt to contact Calais, France, where Kennedy was waiting with Pierre Cilion to start their historic Channel Swim. Ralph Edwards announced that he would report on Pierre's swim next week. "It is too bad that the pickup from Calais failed to come through," Edwards said over the air. Allen Adair, famed British sports announcer, was waiting in Calais to report.

On the evening of October 15, Burt Kennedy made an appearance on the quiz program, having just returned from his part in the English Channel swim of the sea lion. Kennedy received $361, figured on the basis of one dollar per minute, for every minute the swimmer cut off the record Channel Swimming time. Pierre Cilion made the entire swim in five hours and four minutes.

Pierre in Paris, preparing to swim across the English Channel.

Pierre Celion successfully swam the English Channel from Calais to Dover. Twenty-two newsmen followed in the boat behind. The French were changing government that day but Pierre got the headlines and the change of government second banner.

The City of Redondo Beach had a tremendous welcome home day after the event. The seal was borrowed from Marineland of the Pacific, located in Hermosa Beach, California.

Mr. Heartbeat

A new contest was inaugurated in March of 1950, inviting listeners on the phone to identify "Mr. Heartbeat," heard only through the radio speakers by the beating

Contestant Herb Holland agreed to be sent by the program to the Arctic Circle, joining the latest gold rush now in progress.

Herb Holland prepares for his airport departure to the Arctic.

of his heart, and a number of clues including: "Please, Ease, Sneeze, Freeze." With momentum thinning for the mystery man contests, so did the cash prize: $10,000. The first three callers on the evening of March 25, 1950, guessed incorrectly: Alben Barkley, Bing Crosby and Arthur Godfrey. Contestant Margaret Maher, manager of the Blair Convalescent Home, was among the lucky callers on the first broadcast. For $10,000 cash, she was asked by Edwards if she could identify "Mr. Heartbeat." Her guess was Arthur Godfrey. As a consolation prize worth several hundred dollars, she received a 48-piece set of Fine Arts Sterling Silver. After the broadcast, the phone in her home was kept busy for several hours as family relatives phoned to comment on her luck – and to give her "inside tips" on who they thought "Mr. Heartbeat" was. When a local newspaper reporter in Kansas City, Missouri, asked her about the contest, she remarked: "Nobody can tell me from now on that the selection of people being called on those radio quiz shows is a put-up deal."

Like the contests that preceded, newspaper columnists were quick to provide their own theories, almost always incorrect answers, for the benefit of their readers. One newspaper columnist theorized that the clue: "If I knew you were coming I'd have baked a cake," might refer to a star in the motion-picture, *The Uninvited Guest*. After ten weeks, the identity of "Mr. Heartbeat" was identified. After a woman in Sioux Falls, South Dakota, said it was the "King of the Hoboes," and a New Orleans man guessed A.B. Chandler, Dorothea Ziegler of 735 20th Avenue, San Francisco, confessed she was "a lover of poetry," and guessed Edgar A. Guest. Dorothea Ziegler, age 80, a former Western Union telegrapher, lived in a rented room with her adopted daughter. When asked if she was a regular listener to the program, Ziegler confessed that she was not, but that she sometimes "cut in" on Saturday nights. "They make too much noise to suit me and I get tired of it sometimes. But they sure have a good time and I guess I'm going to myself now."

The "Mr. Heartbeat" contest raised an additional $400,000 for the American Heart Association.

Grandma Hush

One year later, on the evening of March 6, 1951, the voice of "Grandma Hush" was first heard. In the hallowed tradition of the radio giveaway, three prizes were added to the pot each week contestants failed to guess the identity. Statistically, "Grandma Hush" was a sign of the times: newspaper columnists ran with publicity provided by NBC press releases, but their columns were filled with reports of other quiz programs and the prizes offered. "Grandma Hush" received only a fraction of newspaper publicity compared to prior "Hush" contests. The largest amount of letters received in a single day was estimated to be 3,000.

In direct competition, Ralph Edwards chose to revert to the format of bestowing a jackpot of prizes, accumulating every week the mystery voice remained unidentified. The "Grandma Hush" contest operated much like all of the previous 'Hush' contests, with every contestant completing the statement, "We should all support the National Arthritis Foundation because..." Although not a requirement of the contest, entrants were encouraged with each entry to send contributions, mailed to "Grandma Hush, Truth or Consequences, New Mexico." The first callers were on the evening of March 20 and the contest ran nine weeks until the correct answer was provided. Incorrect guesses included Hedda Hopper, Adela St. John, Grandma Moses, Billie Burke, Gloria Swanson, Emily Post, Gertrude Berg, Irene Castle, Mrs. Woodrow Wilson, Mae Murray, Josephine Hull, and Marlene Dietrich, among others.

Producer Ed Bailey

On the evening of May 15, Mrs. Oliver Hopkins of 318 Woodland Avenue, Birmingham, Alabama, won the $33,000 jackpot when she identified the voice of "Grandma Hush" as that of Mrs. George M. Cohan, wife of the late songwriter, who died in 1942. She had two boys, Olive and Dave, and her husband was a traveling show salesman.

Her winnings included a ten-day Caribbean cruise for two with a week in New York, $1,500 worth of merchandise from Spiegel, $1,500 diamond ring, two Bulova wristwatches, a Westinghouse Laundromat, refrigerator, dryer and deep freeze, a 16mm Bell & Howell camera, a silver service for twelve, maid service for a year, a 1951 Nash convertible, a $500 rug, a year's supply of frozen food, $600 worth of power tools, two sets of luggage filled with clothes, 18 pairs of shoes, and a $1,000 U.S. Savings Bond.

Hopkins was a well-known club worker and served the past year as president of Edgewood PTA. Her first task was to figure out her income tax on the gift merchandise and then see what was left. She kept most of the kitchen appliances, and the trip to New York and the Caribbean.

The initial goal was to raise $25,000 for research and treatment funds. By the time the contest concluded, the quiz show raised $400,000 for the National Arthritis and Rheumatism Foundation.

The Rules of the Game, It's Only Business (Enter Philip Morris, Pet Milk)
By 1950, producer Al Paschall and director Ed Bailey were receiving two or three proposals from potential prize donors every week. Robert Gould, the Sales Promotion Manager of Mobo Toys, Inc. in New York City, proposed a stunt on the quiz show around their products. The proposal involved flying a contestant to Boston, having them ride the Mobo Bronco over the entire route covered by Paul Revere (Charlestown, a section of Boston, to Concord), and then flown back to Hollywood to reappear on the quiz program. The Mobo Bronco was an all-steel horse that actually galloped. Primarily a children's toy, its rugged construction allowed grown men that weighed over 200 pounds to ride it without difficulty. The proposal was rejected by Ed Bailey.

Peter C. Goldsmith, President of the Foto Murals of California, proposed seascapes, mountains, deserts and other full-size wall murals or window-size "muralettes," which supposedly looked like the real thing. The product, as Goldsmith proposed, would be used for a stunt to fool contestants residing in dingy hotel rooms with no view to believe they were somewhere else. The proposal was rejected by Ed Bailey.

In January of 1950, Bob Farr wrote to Ralph Edwards: "You probably don't remember me but I worked at CBS before your *Truth or Consequences* days when you were at WABC, New York. I am an electronic engineer now with RCA in Camden, New Jersey. I have just returned from Korea where I was sent as a technical consultant to the Signal Corps. The reason I am writing is to tell you the good news that you have the 'hottest show in radio.' Last spring, some of us at RCA Victor Labs invented a machine to measure the temperature of sound. Simply, it consists of a converter that takes sound, converts it into electronic impulses, and then turns the electric impulses into measurable heat. Just for fun we tried out about 50 different radio shows on the sound-temperature machine and *Truth or*

Consequences had the highest average heat of all – or about 148 degrees Fahrenheit. So you do have the 'hottest show in radio'."

In May of 1951, in Omaha, Nebraska, confidence men pulled a "Truth or Consequences" on Mitchell Wolski, 2917 Castelar Street, to the tune of $40. It was only after Mr. Wolski suffered the consequences that he learned the truth. Detectives said he told them he received a telephone call shortly after he arrived home at midnight. A man's voice said, "This is the *Truth or Consequences* radio program. Please go into your living room and play three popular records on your phonograph and wait for developments." Mr. Wolski said he thought it was rather late, but heeded the call. While listening to the music, he heard a door slam. He investigated and found two men in his kitchen. They told him, he said, they were from the radio program and asked him to return to the living room and play some more records. Though baffled, Mr. Wolski complied. A short time later he went back to the kitchen. The two men had left, taking with them $40 he had left on a table when he reached home.

Fred Carney was the production manager for *Truth or Consequences*.* Assisted by Ed Bailey, director of the program, Carney was responsible for setting up the stunts and assembling the props – including live animals. "I learned that nothing was impossible," Carney commented in a press release. "It may be difficult, but it is possible. There was once we couldn't use our 'prop' and had to substitute a stunt. We always have a spare set, a floater we call it, just in case of an emergency. The prop was a zebra. We were going to have it accompany a contestant to the Zebra room. It came to the studio in the company of a donkey to which it was greatly devoted. The zebra kicked so when being taken from the wagon we didn't dare have him on the show."

In late March 1950, sponsorship headaches plagued the future of both *Truth or Consequences* and *This is Your Life*. Philip Morris was sponsoring the radio version of *This is Your Life* on NBC; reportedly dissatisfied with the Wednesday evening time slot on the network, and CBS was initially reluctant on finding a day and time slot more suitable with the sponsor. (The network eventually found a suitable time slot and the last few weeks *This is Your Life* was on radio, it aired on CBS instead of NBC.)

* Carney came on the show as an assistant to Al Paschall, production manager. He stepped up when Paschall could act only in a supervisory capacity because of the many details he had to handle on Edwards' new radio program, *This is Your Life*.

In May, Procter & Gamble continued the rising trend of dropping radio (in this case, *Truth or Consequences*) for the video version. Ralph Edwards had final say and held up the decision until he determined if the quiz program, both radio and television, could be sold to a single sponsor. Philip Morris wanted to sponsor the television series but not the radio counterpart. It was Edwards' hope to use audio from the television series for the radio program, saving money for the same sponsor. If the radio program was sold to one sponsor and television to another, then the two would be entirely separate productions. MCA, in the meantime, was offering the television program to a number of advertising agencies, using the pilot that had been filmed weeks prior. Procter & Gamble made a firm offer for the television series, rumored not negotiable.

"Known as the sharpest buyer of broadcast time and respected for its comparative research in media returns, P&G's choice undoubtedly will affect other advertisers," quoted *The Hollywood Reporter*. CBS and NBC fought bitterly for *Truth or Consequences*, but CBS won out because of availability of time more acceptable to Philip Morris. During the first week of June, the deal was finalized for the quiz program to move to CBS, both for radio and television, under sponsorship of Philip Morris. The cigarette firm would not continue sponsorship of *This is Your Life*, which is why the radio program concluded by the end of the month. Edwards kept his promise and decided to go along with the sponsor who bought both the radio and television version of *Truth or Consequences*.

In 1950 and 1951, in a countermeasure to the CBS talent raids, NBC signed celebrities to long-term contracts and in the fall of 1951, signed Ralph Edwards in what NBC called a $6,500,000 contract, in return for committing himself to the network exclusively for radio and television for the next five years. Edwards focused on a new program, *The Ralph Edwards Show*, causing the quiz show to idle for a season after Philip Morris dropped sponsorship.

During the last week of May 1952, Pet Milk signed a contract sponsoring *Truth or Consequences* on radio, dropping *Fibber McGee and Molly*, despite their consistent rating in the top ten, making the first time in 15 years that the comedy team had been without a bankroller. Pet Milk wanted to promote their product to an audience that did not frequent Jim and Marian Jordan, and saved money: *Fibber McGee and Molly* cost $10,000 a week and were requesting $13,000 for the new season, with no options – *Truth or Consequences* cost $7,000 a week, with the option of dropping sponsorship every 13 weeks. Throwing a favorable carrot toward the sponsor, Edwards proposed numerous ways of incorporating the product into the stunts.

During Pet Milk sponsorship, a recipe using the trademarked product was highlighted as "recipe of the month." From the Harvest Gold Peach Pie to the Frozen Pineapple Dessert, the recipes were incorporated into many of the stunts contestants had to endure on the stage.

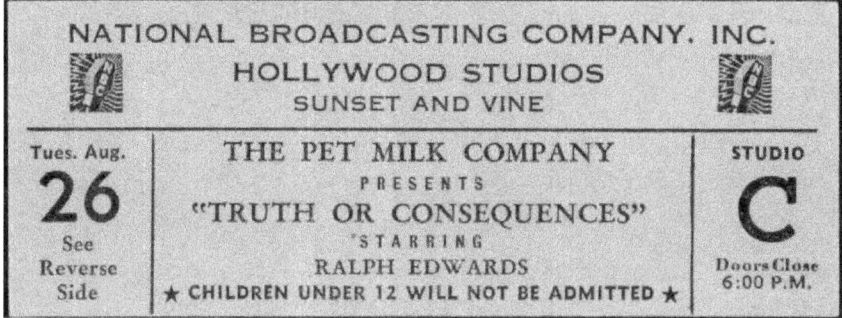

Admission ticket to the August 26, 1952 broadcast.

In 1952, Amana Refrigeration, Inc., struck a deal to provide gifts such as this 12-cubic foot Amana freezer on *Truth or Consequences*, at no cost to the radio producers, in exchange for the free advertising generated as a result of the product being mentioned over the air by name. More than a dozen were given away on the program within two years.

The Harvest Gold Peach Pie Treasure Truck

On the broadcast of October 8, 1953, the Harvest Gold Peach Pie Treasure Truck stunt premiered, operated by National Van Lines, visited 32 cities across the country, stopping at designated points in each city so that the citizens could visit the truck, talk with the Harvest Gold Peach Pie Man, and choose a key from a gigantic replica of a Pet Milk cylinder. If the key unlocked a secret door to an immense replica of a "Harvest Gold Peach Pie" in the truck, the holder of the key received fabulous prizes valued to at least $5,000, including a $1,500 gift certificate to be used in ordering merchandise from Spiegel Mail Order Catalogue in Chicago, a Westinghouse washer and dryer; a 21-inch Stromberg-Carlson TV set, a Tappan Gas Range, a $500 Wright Air Conditioner; and a Bulova Wristwatch (men's or women's, as the case may be).

The quiz program was used to promote the up-coming city on the itinerary where radio listeners could expect to find the truck. The idea was to get as many people as possible to visit the Treasure Truck and choose keys. The truck traveled from Long Beach, California, to New York City. A contestant on the premiere program of the season, Gilbert Fishman, known as "The Duke of Catalina," was chosen to be the Harvest Gold Peach Pie Man, who rode in the truck to dispense keys.

On the broadcast of October 15, Fishman reported via KOB in Albuquerque, New Mexico, mentioning that nobody had yet chosen the lucky key. He told of his reception everywhere along the way, especially reporting on a visit to the Children's Hospital in Truth or Consequences, New Mexico, where a little boy in a wheelchair had the honor of throwing pies at the pie man. (When nobody gets a lucky key, a pie is thrown at the pie man.) From Pet Milk and the *Truth or Consequences* program, all of the patients and nurses and doctors in the Children's Hospital received a Harvest Gold Peach Pie for dessert.

On the broadcast of October 22, the first winner was announced: Mrs. Rose Isner, homemaker, of Clarksburg, West Virginia. The winning key was put back in the box of keys and a duplicate prize was set up for the next winner. Fishman received a $1,000 U.S. Savings Bond because a winner was found, and would receive another $1,000 should another winner come forth. Reporting from station WAVE in Louisville, Kentucky, Fishman told of his recent cross-country travels.

On the broadcast of October 29, from the NBC studios in New York City, Fishman was interviewed by staff announcer Mel Brandt, revealing how he completed his trip but that there were no additional winners. His $1,000 Savings

Bond, however, was locked inside the Harvest Gold Peach Pie and he had to go through the 26,000 keys to find the one that opened it.

Cross Country Trip

Marine Cpl. Donald Mainland, a 21-year-old native of Racine, Wisconsin, had to suffer the consequence of breaking the cross-country bicycle racing record. Corporal Mainland shoved off from Santa Monica on Friday morning, May 15, 1953, hoping to pedal the 2,910 miles to New York City in less than 20 days, 7 hours and 29 minutes. "I hope to trim the time by about five days," he told reporters on the takeoff. "With a little luck I think I can make about 200 miles in a 10-hour day. I'll sleep in motels and eat in restaurants along the highway." The stunt was sponsored by the *Truth or Consequences* radio program, which began with the broadcast of May 14.

For most of the pedaling, Mainland used an Italian road bike with eight speeds forward, but in the car that would accompany him would be two American racing bikes, one with a low gear ratio for climbing mountains and another with a high gear ratio for flat lands. To get in shape for his long-distance attempt, Mainland, a communications man in the Third Marine Division, pedaled as much as 100 miles a day over the mountainous roads at Camp Pendleton in California. "I guess I'm one of the few Marines who works harder off duty than on," he joked. Along for the trip was his wife, Ruth, and a Marine buddy, Sgt. Sam Scherr, as well as the publicity man representing the radio program.

Along the trip from Santa Monica, California, to New York City, a transcribed conversation for the radio program reported on their progress. A few miles west of Albuquerque, New Mexico, Mainland had run into some thorns and needed some tire repairs. Weather also played a factor in his attempt to beat the record: rain in California and snow in Arizona.

Every week on the quiz program, an update was provided by Cpl. Don Mainland and Sgt. Sam Scherr. On the evening of May 28, for example, the men were in Indianapolis, providing an update of their cross-country status, which began two weeks prior. On the broadcast of June 11, the cross-country bike race was over and a new record set. Marine Cpl. Don Mainland and Marine Sergeant Sam Scherr, who sat it out on a stationary bike, broke the record for a cross-country bike run. They told of their experiences and Edwards thanked Sunkist Frozen Orange and Lemonade Juice for supplying them with all the Vitamin "C"

The official trailer that tagged along for the tour with Cpl. Donald Mainland.

Cpl. Donald Mainland, age 21, on his bicycle.

they needed during the ordeal, and Abbey Rents for supplying them with their living equipment and to Schwinn bicycles for supplies.

Mainland's record breaking coast-to-coast cross-county trip was upheld for eleven years until the next contender beat the record. Weeks following the *Truth or Consequences* stunt, Mainland raced in Japan's Keirin circuit and returned to Wisconsin to own and operate Pioneer Manufacturing, his own bike manufacturing company, later supplying the 1972 Olympic frames and Schwinn Superiors during the eighties.

Chapter 15
The Television Program

> *"We always have had the problem of making our stunts understandable to the radio audience, which couldn't see what was happening. The studio audience always got a bigger kick out of the program than did listeners. There won't be that problem with television."*
>
> – Ralph Edwards

On the evening of July 1, 1941, Ralph Edwards agreed to host a one-time experimental telecast of *Truth or Consequences* over WNBT in New York City, sponsored by Procter & Gamble, paying what came to the equivalent of $9 for each commercial. On the same evening, *Uncle Jim's Question Bee*, another radio program, made its television debut courtesy of the Ruthrauff & Ryan advertising agency, proudly proclaiming itself the first advertised/sponsored television quiz program in history. It was first by about one hour, Ralph Edwards and *Truth or Consequences* being a later offering on the same evening. Compton used the time slot to ensure camera close-ups of Ivory Soap, but the late schedule of 10:30 p.m. questions how many viewers were watching the experiment. According to *Variety*, the evening consisted of "dullish, slow-paced, unedited, time-ignoring telecasts" and that "television was able to offer all who were mechanically equipped to see the strange spectacle of an adult citizen told to perform a hula-hula dance... May destiny preserve this nation from the terrible example of smart-aleckism which, with the aid of television if ever organized nationally, this kind of drunk-while sober behavior represents."

Historically, the first use of television as a prop on a coast-to-coast radio show was Edwards' introduction of video for a stunt on the *Truth or Consequences* radio broadcast of May 27, 1944. The husband of a contestant was disguised in NBC's television studios and performed before the camera for direct relay to the stage of *Truth or Consequences* radio show. The stunt made for much confusion on part of the wife and probably did for the unseen audience, the large majority of which, of course, had never seen television in action, and probably wondered what was going on. The pioneer spirit on the part of Ralph Edwards, naturally, forecast his acceptance of television. After all, what other radio program was so made-to-order for sight-and-sound broadcasting?

Ralph Edwards sharing a laugh for the television version.

In 1949, Edwards televised his radio program for Procter & Gamble, as an experiment, over KNBH on Los Angeles. The kinescope facilities at that time did not project the show favorably, as a result of faulty equipment.

Throughout 1950, Ralph Edwards commissioned three television pilots. The first was filmed on February 27, 1950, funded by Procter & Gamble, included such

---

* The April 12, 1950, radio broadcast of *This Is Your Life*, featuring the life of Emma Crooks Gilbert, was filmed for telecast on the evening of April 19, 1951.

stunts as a water tank, a ballet, kissing a cow, the notorious hot seat, and a good gesture act. Jerry Fairbanks, the former head of NBC's fledgling film department and now in charge of his own production company, was responsible for filming. A few weeks later, *This is Your Life* was filmed. The pilots were shot on industry standard 16mm format.

Understanding that catching a contestant's expression was shot on chance, the camera crew could easily ruin an elaborate stunt despite the fact that every element from the point of view of staging and direction was carried out perfectly. It was decided that the man at the helm who could direct the operators and assistants should be the first cameraman, also known as director of photography, which at the time was considered an unorthodox procedure since the normal function of the cameraman was to light the set. An intercom system was built, designed exactly like the intercom system used during a live show. The operators, assistants, grips and soundmen could talk freely to each other on one circuit.

Deciding live television was too limited in its scope, with short takes under perfect conditions, and kinescopes (poor-quality recordings made by pointing a film camera at a TV camera's electronic viewfinder), Fairbanks convinced Edwards and Paschall to use two or more cameras to shoot simultaneously on the action. Contestants were spontaneous, unrehearsed and chosen out of the audience. For this reason, the three-camera system was set up to film the quiz show, pre-dating Desi Arnaz and *I Love Lucy*, which has often been credited for being the first television program to be filmed with the three-camera system. Through this process, they shot 30 minutes of completed film in 30 minutes. Jerry Fairbanks had a reputation for putting a show on film as cheap as a live telecast, reportedly $6,500 a program. Acceptance, however, was still at the discretion of the sponsor, following feedback from a test audience.

By February 1950, Fibber McGee and Molly were already on film and producers were reviewing the footage and polishing it up for presentations to viewers in the fall. Bob Hope's $40,000 appearance on the Frigidaire show for Easter was the first in a series he would do on holiday shows, preparatory to his television debut. Frank Sinatra was scheduled to make his television debut with Bob Hope and the singer started to negotiate for a show of his own on television. Kate Smith had signed a five-year contract with NBC to do a daily hour-long variety show for TV. Garry Moore's new CBS show would be seen and heard at the same time. The industry was still in its infancy, but all telltale signs indicated that radio celebrities wanted to conquer television.

"I'm not ready to give up radio yet," Edwards said in a press release. "Television has made people entertainment conscious. As soon as the novelty wears off, a lot of them will go back to radio for their entertainment." Procter & Gamble apparently agreed with Edwards; negotiations with Philip Morris in the spring of 1950 included a potential television version, as well as the radio program. When the cigarette company signed on the bottom line, they quickly commissioned two pilot films.

On June 17, 1950, the two pilots were put before the cameras – again using the three-camera system. Fairbanks convinced Ralph Edwards and Al Paschall that the pilot films, unlike the one put before cameras earlier in the year, should not be shot on 16mm stock. This was the generally established process since TV studios were equipped only with 16mm electronic projectors. Predicting that 35mm electronic projectors would be installed in all television stations in a relatively short span of time, he convinced Edwards and his troupe to experiment with the pilot by shooting on both 35mm and 16mm, at the same time. Both were later projected on a closed circuit and the difference in quality, as seen by the home viewer, was much better from 35mm, despite the fact that the difference in production cost was much more. Even the union labor scales for operators, assistant cameraman and film cutters were higher. The actual raw stock cost approximately three times as much and lab processing was increased threefold. According to some sources, producer Al Simon was responsible for suggesting 35mm, but interoffice memos suggest Fairbanks was responsible.

"Although both shows will be three times as difficult to produce for a video audience, I think the results will be three times as good as ears-only shows," Edwards told the press shortly after completion of the two pilots. "Not long ago, we tested both of them with a three-camera technique that permits editing afterward. With *Truth or Consequences*, we found our principal problem was keeping each contestant within range of the cameras while reacting spontaneously to his consequence. However, the difficulty was counterbalanced by the fact that, with a camera, we will not have to make essentially visual consequences audible, too. You listeners at home will actually see what is going on. With television's *This is Your Life*, we can bring much more graphic detail to you by actually picturing scenes of major events. In addition, I think actually seeing the person we're talking about will make *This is Your Life*, a more absorbing show on TV."

Prizes for the first of the two pilots included a $25 Savings Bond, a Bulova wristwatch, a $50 S.B. & Evans lighter, a 72-piece Fine Arts Sterling Silverware, and a Black Evans bag. To win the prizes varied, contestants had to knit a sweater for an elephant, perform a stunt using a telephone booth, a shooting gallery, and a Minstrel family. The second pilot offered a Westinghouse television set, a $50 Savings Bond, and $100 cash. Games included paperhangers, a soldier's baby blonde, and another elephant sweater with contestant Susan Jarvis, carried over from the first show.

"At first, it was hard for me to remember that I could be seen and therefore didn't have to interpret the act for the audience," Edwards later recalled. "For fourteen years I had been the 'Aren't We Devils' guy on radio. On TV I could let the acts speak for themselves."

Following the completion of these pilots, and approval from Philip Morris, *Truth or Consequences* made its television debut on September 7, 1950, hosted by Ralph Edwards. Adjusting to a visual medium, the quiz program allowed for slapstick acts, a bridegroom chase, a blindfold square dance, water tanks, a hypnotist, the Easter Bunny, a car wash, acrobats, family reunions and of course, pies in the face and seltzer bottles. Hollywood celebrities who made guest appearances included Hope Emerson, Ruby Keeler, Dolores Costello, Bryant Washburn and the Keystone Cops. Beginning in February 1951, a picture identification contest began, asking viewers to submit postcards for a possible chance to identify a series of photographs. Judges who chose the postcards were Tony Curtis, Jeff Chandler and Shelley Winters. The winner was featured on the March 22 broadcast: Mrs. Charles Huber of 129 South Ridge Street, Crown Point, Indiana. The program spanned only one season, 39 episodes, as a result of a business decision from Philip Morris to drop sponsorship at the conclusion of the season.*

One highlight of the series was a contestant selected from the audience and told to spend a week in San Francisco with "Harvey," the six-foot imaginary rabbit. Motion-picture cameras concealed within the hotel filmed the contestant's arrival and his registering at the desk. The camera caught the confusion among the people at the desk as the contestant discussed the situation with his imaginary companion. CBS reviewed the footage before each episode aired on the network and Ralph Edwards and his crew quickly discovered that censorship was more predominant than the radio counterpart. A toilet seat had to be removed from a "wooden wedding" stunt for one episode; a couple seconds of footage had to be excised as a result of a horse conducting business on stage.

---

* The Biow Company, representing Philip Morris, was billed for one 35mm print and two 16mm prints for each episode. Edwards himself received one 35mm print and one 16mm print.

The second television version aired from May 18, 1954 to September 28, 1956, sponsored by Old Gold Cigarettes, now with Jack Bailey as emcee replacing Ralph Edwards. With the success of *This is Your Life*, Edwards chose to hire someone to host the television version of *Truth or Consequences*. Stunts included a tin whistle symphony, a family reunion with a ventriloquist and his daughter, a snake charmer, a dog duet, kissing the mayor, musical pigs, movie star for a day, a fake rajah, a hunt for uranium, and a race in hammocks. Hollywood celebrities making guest appearances included Vincent Price, Jack Carson, Tab Hunter, Tony Martin, Mala Powers, Olsen and Johnson, Terry Moore, Piper Laurie, Lauritz Melchior, Jimmy Durante, Zsa Zsa Gabor, Johnny Weissmuller, Connie Haines, Jack Palance, Marilyn Maxwell, and Rhonda Fleming. In April of 1955, Jack Bailey had a contestant, George Ashworth, hitch-hike to Truth or Consequences, New Mexico, with a horse. Beginning with the broadcast of January 18, 1955, the "Sleeping Beauty" contest began, inviting viewers to guess the identity of the mystery woman. She was correctly identified after eight weeks, on the broadcast of March 8, 1955. A picture puzzle contest gave $9,000 to one lucky contestant. A total of 124 television broadcasts were filmed and telecast.

Nina 'Honeybean' Waver as the 1955 Sleeping Beauty.

The final evening telecast of *Truth or Consequences* aired from December 13, 1957 to June 6, 1958, with Steve Dunne as the emcee. Twenty-six half-hour episodes were filmed but only twenty-five were telecast. Dunne undoubtedly received the role because he filled in for Jack Bailey for three consecutive broadcasts of the prior television series. The sponsor for the first eighteen episodes was Sterling Drugs, hocking Phillips' Milk of Magnesia, Bayer Aspirin and Fletcher's Castoria. The program was sustained for the remaining seven telecasts. Stunts included a knife thrower, a hot seat shower, a suitcase race, an act performed by Rosemary Clooney and Jose Ferrer, a lion tamer, the reunion of five generations, a telephone reunion with Steve Dunne's father, an amateur comedian performing for Lou Costello, the reunion of a barber shop quartet, cross country swimmers (contestants had to be swimming constantly, alternating on resting and sleeping, taking three weeks to make the trip), a kissing test with John Forsythe, and a *Maverick* Man-in-the-Moon Reunion featuring James Garner. One contestant had to shoot a large-sized paper heart and out came her serviceman husband. A contestant's wife, sawed in half a la magician style, was reading the directions on how to get her together again.

Understanding that the "golden" acts from radio were not always of contemporary value, and competing against variety shows, Edwards' production company allocated additional money to ensure Hollywood celebrities were featured in every broadcast: Ernie Kovacs, Roy Rogers, Cesar Romero, Eva Gabor, Jacques Bergerac, Jon Hall, Buster Keaton, Brian Donlevy, Dennis Day, Frankie Laine, Zsa Zsa Gabor, Jimmy Durante, Jack Costanzo, Jon Provost, Jock Mahoney, Linda Darnell, Peggy Lee, and even Ralph Edwards himself.

Chapter 16
The Jack Bailey and Bob Barker Years

The Jack Bailey Years

The Pet Milk series expired on the evening of April 15, 1954, marking the last of the original radio productions. Weeks prior, in February 1954, Old Gold informed Fred Allen that sponsorship of his *Judge for Yourself* program would be terminated upon completion of the 39-week cycle in the latter part of May. Old Gold bought *Truth or Consequences*, sharing sponsorship with Toni and Paper Mate, although Ralph Edwards would not appear on the television program because he was tied down by *This is Your Life* for Hazel Bishop. Jack Bailey was signed to take over this chore. The television series premiered on May 18, 1954 and nine months later, in March of 1955, audio from the Jack Bailey television series would be edited down for NBC radio, under various sponsors.

When *Truth or Consequences* returned to radio in March of 1955, the majority of the radio broadcasts from the final season consisted of audio tracks from the television program, hosted by Jack Bailey. Carryover contests, public service announcements, announcer opening and closing, and sponsor commercials were voiced specifically for the radio program. Stunts that were visual in nature were narrated by radio announcer Arch Presby. The fake Maharajah stunt, for example, featured contestant Erwin Porter, who had "reservations" at the Knickerbocker Hotel in Hollywood, who is greeted by the unsuspecting manager of the hotel, Harry Bradley. Jack Bailey interrupts the stunt just when the manager is at his wits end as the Maharajah has his entourage of strange animals and a harem, etc., being brought into the lobby. Arch Presby filled in for the benefit of the radio audience. Contestants on the television program, Porter, included, were reminded that descriptions and vocals were just as important as visuals because the stunts would be broadcast on radio, not just television. *

Jack Bailey

The "Horse Hitchhike" stunt was originally taped from the Butler Bros. Rodeo in Truth or Consequences, New Mexico, where contestant George Ashworth and "Ermintrude," his horse, hitch-hiked to the rodeo and was heard singing "I'm an Old Cow Hand from the Rio Grande." The spot also tied in with a plug for the movie, *Strange Lady in Town* (1955). Originally telecast on April 19, 1955, the radio broadcast aired on May 11.

* Steve Dunne was the host for two episodes, August 29 and September 5, 1956, because he filled in as a substitute for the Jack Bailey television series.

A highlight of the series, recorded specifically for the radio version, was "The Snoring Man Contest," which began on the evening of May 18, 1955, and ran until June 15. The contest was first announced on the evening of May 4, using two weeks advance publicity to build up the latest contest. The radio contest aided the United Cerebral Palsy Fund. Listeners were asked simply to send in a 25-word or less completion to the following sentence: "We should all support the United Cerebral Palsy because..." Contributions could range from dimes to dollars. The amount of the contribution made no bearing on the decision which contestants would be phoned on the program. The sentence they provided would be judged and those considered outstanding were considered for the phone calls. Listeners were instructed to include their name, mailing address and phone number on the entries, but not their guess as to who "The Snoring Man" was. Entries were mailed to: "The Snoring Man, Hollywood 51, California." The person who correctly identified "The Snoring Man" would get fabulous merchandise prizes plus a check for $1,000 (donated by the Paper Mate Company) signed with a famous Paper Mate pen. Each week "The Snoring Man" remained unidentified, three more prizes were added to the jackpot, referred to on the program as the "Treasure House of Prizes."

The voice of "The Snoring Man" was served as he talked and snored, all in his sleep, making the voice difficult to recognize. Every week, host Jack Bailey repeated a riddle which provided clues to the identity.

"I'm a Sport – Hit me high.
I make Monday's game gay.
Tho I end in a tie,
I'm in front all the way."

Jack Bailey told the radio audience that "The Snoring Man" was one of the most colorful personalities in America and that radio listeners heard him often "and many have seen him." On June 15, "The Snoring Man" was identified as Spike Jones, the famous orchestra leader. The winner was Mrs. Frances Sheldon of Burbank, California, who happened to be the first person who phoned that evening. The solution to the riddle was explained thus: "I'm a Sport" – a Sport is a City Slicker and Spike Jones' band was known as the City Slickers; "Hit me high" – one always hits a railroad spike "high"; "I make Monday's game gay" – Spike Jones plays music on a washboard and Monday is traditionally "wash day"; "Tho

I end in a tie" – railroad spikes end in rail "ties"; and "I'm in front all the way" – Spike Jones "fronts" a band.

Mrs. Sheldon's prizes included the $1,000 check, a 1955 Nash Rambler, an automatic washer and dryer, a deep freeze, a gas range, $500 worth of groceries, a 54-piece set of china, a 72-piece set of sterling silver, a home power tool set, an electric fryer, razor and attachments for all men in her family, a 21-inch TV set, $300 string of pearls, two wrist watches, and a merchandise certificate valued at $250 in merchandise. She appeared as a guest on the next week's broadcast (June 22), explaining how she used some of the clues to figure out who "The Snoring Man" was.

Highlights of the radio program, which consisted of audio excerpts from the television counterpart, included The Great Zaccinni, who "is shot from the mouth of a cannon," involving a contestant whose wife thought her husband was being shot into outer space. (Mr. and Mrs. Harold Blanchard were the contestants.)

For the broadcast of June 1, 1955, Marjorie Ellis Land, Western Editor of *Charm* magazine, took part as a contestant and later spoke about the way the program was helping those less fortunate by giving trips, merchandise, etc. to many who needed the prizes. She also mentioned the importance of the United Cerebral Palsy Fund which was aided by "The Snoring Man" Contest. Joe Allison, another contestant, was provided the consequence of putting together a car in a top-floor workshop across the street from the studio. If he gets the car put together, and down on the street, the car was his. He completed the project in less than two weeks, using a derrick to get the car out of the upstairs workshop, after it was completed.

For the broadcast of June 29, 1955, a female contestant, Mrs. Webb, is told to deliver a lecture about "Indian" heads on a totem pole. Unknown to her, the pole was made of the disguised heads of her husband and other relatives. The July 6 broadcast saluted the Elks national convention with 150 delegates in the studio audience and with Elks as contestants. Voice actor Paul Frees did an impersonation of Charles Boyer for one of the stunts on the evening of July 13. John McCullough, Assistant Chief of Police of Burbank, California, put in an appearance on the evening of October 5. When a contestant was asked to view several "criminals" in a "lineup" and to suggest plans for their rehabilitation, the contestant had no idea that McCullough was in on the stunt and that the criminals were actually actors and the lady's husband in disguise. On October 12, contestant John E. Gaston, a retired ambulance driver, met a number of people who came on the program to honor him because he helped save their life during his 21 years of service. On the evening of October 26, Billy Outten, famous high diver, internationally known for his diving feats, assisted in a stunt.

NBC, applying a similar tactic to "Operation Tandem" in 1950, offered sponsors the chance to fund programs in the "Top-Ten Plan," so named because they were supposedly the top ten programs, on the network, in the Nielsen Ratings. These included: *One Man's Family* (night shows), *Fibber McGee and Molly* (night shows), *The Great Gildersleeve, Dragnet, People Are Funny, Truth or Consequences, NBC Radio Theatre, Biographies in Sound*, and *National Radio Fan Club*. The plan started officially on October 1, 1955. Sponsors that participated in the Top-Ten Plan were RCA, Anahist, Curtis Publishing, Crowell-Collier, Brown & Williamson, Carter Products, Look Magazine, General Motors, and Paper Mate. The audio version of *Truth or Consequences* was sponsored by these companies, promoting ReaLemon-Puritan (May 9 to August 1, 1956), Curtis Publishing (November 2, 1955 only) and the Buick Division of General Motors (November 2, 1955 only).

In the fall of 1955, a new carryover contest was introduced: "The Thing." The sound of something physical was played and replayed over a period of four months until someone correctly guessed what "The Thing" was. On October 19, 1955, a contestant incorrectly guessed "a key and door latch," and Jack Bailey told her she was real close. But it would not be until November 2 that Mrs. Bertie Stephens, Rt. 1, Box 202-B, Mt. Vernon, Alabama, correctly identified "The Thing" as a pair of doorknobs. The wife of a farmer, Mrs. Stephens was also a ward attendant in the Colored People's Hospital in Mt. Vernon, Alabama. She worked out the sound by piecing together a list of clues that were provided.

Her prizes included a Westinghouse Laundromat and Dryer, $500 worth of groceries from IGA Food stores, a Stromberg-Carlson television set, a Tappan Gas Range, an Amana Food Freezer, men's and lady's Bulova watches, Presto Steam Iron, a Presto Coffee Maker, a Presto Cooker-Fryer, a Presto Electric Cooker, $250 Merchandise Certificate from Spiegel, Inc., a 12-piece set of Fine Arts Fine China, an Electronics Geiger Counter, two Mohawk Carpets and cushions, an electric shaver and Shavex, a $500 Savings Bond from Wildroot, Amelia Earhart Luggage, and a check to cover transportation and vacation for two in Las Vegas, from Universal Agency in Hollywood, California. Full retail price of all the prizes was $4,769.

A special consequence on the broadcast of November 9 was a salute to the Ground Observer Corps and the part played by the men and women in our nation's security. Special guest was Col. Owen Clark, Air Force Project Officer, Ground Observer Corps, who explained the functions of the Ground Observer Corps. Then, a contestant named Mr. Murray, a pilot, agreed to pit his flying skill against the Ground Observer Corps for an entire week. On the same broadcast, a "fake holdup" involved contestant Blaine Gailing, assistant cashier at the Wilshire & 15th Street Branch of the Bank of America, in Santa Monica. He rides with his boss, Stanley Sundell, Manager of the Bank, who is "apprehended" by actors who pose as cops and ask him to open the trunk of his car. Inside the trunk, without his knowledge, were machine guns, revolvers, rifles, ammunition and several sacks of bank money!

Celebrity Guests (Radio Broadcast Dates)
May 4, 1955, Prince Michael Romanoff
June 22, 1955, Joe Besser
July 20, 1955, Boris Karloff
August 10, 1955, Tab Hunter
October 12, 1955, Maxie "Slapsie" Rosenbloom
October 19, 1955, Mala Powers
December 7, 1955, Piper Laurie
December 21, 1955, Olsen & Johnson
January 11, 1956, Terry Moore
February 8, 1956, Dan Duryea
February 29, 1956, Zsa Zsa Gabor
April 11, 1956, Tab Hunter
June 27, 1956, Zsa Zsa Gabor
July 6, 1956, Linda Darnell
August 1, 1956, Arlene Francis
September 12, 1956, Marilyn Maxwell
January 13, 1957, Jimmy Durante

The final broadcast of the Jack Bailey radio program concluded on October 3, 1956. This would have been the final season of the radio program if it had not been for NBC's decision to revise the radio program one last time, this time with Bob Barker.

The Bob Barker Season

"Remember this name, you'll be hearing a lot about him. Ladies and gentlemen, Mr. Bob Barker!"
– Ralph Edwards

A daytime version of the television program premiered on December 31, 1956, sponsored by Lever Brothers, General Foods, Lehn & Fink, American Home, Sterling Drugs, Miles Laboratories, and Alberto-Culver. Telecast in the evening hours prior, this was the first time *Truth or Consequences* aired five days a week, and during daytime hours. Produced in Hollywood, the new version of *Truth or Consequences* became the first program to be broadcast in all time zones from pre-recorded videotape. This technology, which had only been introduced the previous year, had been used only for time-delayed broadcasts to the West Coast.

Bob Barker

The long-running success this show achieved for a full decade, hosted by Bob Barker, marked his big break in television. While in high school, Barker announced football on the public address system. A teacher told him that he did a pretty good job and should consider a career in radio. Fresh out of the Navy, following World War II, Barker put on his uniform and the wings of gold, and went to the local radio station in Springfield, KTTS. "I was sent in to see the manager of the station," Barker later recalled, "and it might be said that my Navy uniform made an instant hit. Turned out the manager was an old pilot, a flying buff. We starting talking about flying and the Navy and wartime experiences. And we just sat there and exchanged stories. We just talked and talked. Finally, when there was a pause in the conversation, I said, 'You know, the reason I came here today is that I'd like a job.' And the station manager said: 'Oh, of course, Bob. Of course. When would you like to start?' He didn't even ask me to do an audition."

Barker did stints in Springfield, Missouri, and Palm Beach, Florida, before migrating to Hollywood. His first gig in town was hosting a radio program for the Southern California Edison Company, *The Bob Barker Show*, in which audience members were called upon to help with on-air demonstrations of appliances in "electric living centers." In due course, Barker moved out to Los Angeles, where he continued to work in radio. When Ralph Edwards sold the quiz program to NBC, he began searching for potential emcees in Hollywood and New York, conducting auditions.

"I was looking desperately for an emcee for the new daytime version of *Truth or Consequences*," recalled Edwards." I had just picked up my daughters, Lauren and Chris from ice-skating, and we had the car radio on. Suddenly I heard some fellow on that radio station getting lots of laughs from a room full of people somewhere on the fringes of Los Angeles. I couldn't tell exactly where. This was a fresh, fine emcee. I told the girls to listen for the emcee's name and the station call letters, but all we heard was the name 'Bob.' On Monday morning our switchboard girl finally rang me on the line. 'I have a Bob Barker on the line.' I invited Bob to drop by and see me at his convenience. In 20 minutes he was there, a very young and handsome Bob Barker. We gave him a couple *Truth or Consequences* acts to do and all agreed Bob was terrific. But how would he look on camera? So my agent, Berle Adams, had Ernie Ford introduce Bob during the warm-up of Ernie's show, and whatta ya know, Bob looked great on camera. One week later he started *Truth or Consequences* five-days–a-week." Asked later what impressed him about Bob Barker, Edwards remarked: "Bob sounds like Jack Benny doing audience participation."

Bob Barker

The story of Barker racing over to Edwards' office has been told many times over the years, with variations. The general consensus among all variations was that 20 minutes after Ralph Edwards finished his phone call with Bob Barker, the young protégé was knocking on his front door. In reality, Barker's wife initially received a phone call from an inquiring Edwards, Barker returned the call on Sunday afternoon and offered to come right over, and Edwards insisted he come over to the office on Monday. Barker's visit with Edwards was not only pleasant, but Edwards discovered they had a lot in common. After a number of screen tests, Barker was hired with a four-week clause. Out of the eleven people voting in the original hiring meeting, including network executives who had a share of interest in the program, only one vote was in favor of Barker – Ralph Edwards. "This guy is your man," Edwards informed the board. "You give him four weeks and see if you don't agree."

Bob Barker's starting salary was $750 per week, plus $25 additional for every 15-minute segment broadcast under commercial sponsorship. His contract, dated December 28, 1956, commenced on December 31, 1956, initially for 260 consecutive weeks, divided into 20 successive periods of 13 consecutive weeks. The phone call informing him that he had the job was five minutes after noon on December 21. Every year on the anniversary of that phone call, and that time, Edwards and Barker drank a toast to their long and enduring friendship. Since the untimely passing of Edwards, Barker continued the tradition and takes a moment to pause and thank him.

Among the highlights of the daytime version, hosted by Bob Barker, was a guest appearance of Jack Dempsey on the premiere broadcast. On another broadcast, contestants Jerry Morton and Ed Armbruster, entered a tank, which traveled from Los Angeles to New York. One of them, exchanging shifts, had to keep swimming all the time, the length of the route.

In a simian reunion, a monkey named Beulah was reunited with her three-year-old niece. What started out to be a funny gag went too far when the two four-legged creatures were expressing their love too strongly on camera.

On one broadcast, a mother and her five-year-old son was selected from the audience. The youth was taken backstage and placed into a soundproof booth. The mother, it was explained, would have a chance to win some money. Her son was going to be asked how much she paid for the various items of his clothing, and she would win whatever he said. It would figure that the mother could potentially win as much as four or five dollars. The child came out on the stage and Barker knelt down to ask him how much his mother paid for the jacket he was wearing. "One thousand dollars," the boy shouted. The audience exploded into laughter, the mother picked up her little hero and smothered him with kisses, and Barker remarked, "I have no more questions."

A contestant sat on an ostrich egg for two weeks at the Los Angeles Home show waiting for the egg to hatch. Unfortunately, it was broken before it hatched. One contestant had to make an overcoat from scratch so, starting with shearing the sheep, continued through all the processes of cloth making until the coat was finished. One contestant had a pretty sticky consequence when dumped into a bathtub filled with Jell-O.

Pat Morris, USC coed, was told she could keep $100,000 placed on a table if she could pick it up while under the influence of hypnotist Arthur Ellen. She failed, but was given many consolation prizes. One man allowed himself to be dressed in baby clothes and pushed in a baby buggy down the sidewalks of New York City. A man was offered $1,000 if he could go to sleep in the noisy pressroom of the New York Journal. A doctor was on hand to see if he really was asleep. He could not succeed.

During the Bob Barker years, the granddaddy of big prize contests came up with a unique twist to "Mr. Nemesis," brought to life in the person of a mystery personality whose correct identity would net the lucky contestant additional prizes such as a Studebaker car, $1,000 in cash, a trip for two to the Riviera Hotel in Las Vegas, a $2,000 nutria fur stole, and an Esther Williams swimming pool… provided they could guess the identity of "Mr. Nemesis." A clue to his true identity was found in a riddle:

"I was lonely till I lost three.
Scores of stores, but only one you see.
A thousand steps will lead to me."

The contest generated over two million entries and cards were selected at random and one telephone call made each program day. "Mr. Nemesis" traveled the country in disguise for a number of weeks until one lucky viewer correctly guessed his identity: Lon Chaney, Jr.

During Barker's run as host, one consequence repeated many times was "Barker's Box." Four drawers each containing a different prize; a $10 bill, a $20 bill, a $50 bill, and a surprise that contestants sometimes feared.

Ralph Edwards and Bob Barker celebrate the 25th anniversary in February 1965.

The Radio Counterpart

Physical slapstick was the meat and potatoes for the medium of television and the radio program, broadcasting audio from the television counterpart, suffered from this disadvantage. Many pay-offs contained dreams-come-true for deserving people. Families were reunited. Servicemen after taking part in some innocent stunt were rewarded by having their wives and children flown in to appear on the program and provided with an all-expense-paid vacation for the family plus arrangement made for the servicemen to enjoy a furlough which they could spend with their family. Announcer Arch Presby provided commentary to describe the action.

The radio program was heard five-days-a-week, Monday to Friday, beginning April 29, 1957. Prizes varied from a $25 U.S. Savings Bond, merchandise and certificates for purchase from department stores, clothing, furnishings, and payment of an old harrying debt which has troubled the contestant for many months, and so on. Some carry-over stunts allowed jackpots to grow with accumulating prizes. Charities for many carry-over stunts were now children's homes and orphanages. Like the season prior, a number of carry-over contests were created specifically for the radio audience, allowing them to write in and participate. The contestants were selected at random, not by judges. One such contest was "Mr. Whisper," in which a well-known personality whispered clues to his identity. The Mr. Whisper contest began with the first episode of the season, April 29. The first phone call was made on May 6.

Ralph Edwards was a special guest for the April 29 debut, introducing the new emcee, Bob Barker, an audio track from the December 31 broadcast. The feature stunt in the season premiere concerned construction Driver Chief Bert Smith, who spent three and a half years in a Japanese prison camp during World War II. His wife was brought to the coast for a reunion with him.

The May 2, 1957 broadcast was taped in Truth or Consequences, New Mexico, where the Eighth annual Fiesta was in progress. Ralph Edwards was a guest on the radio and television broadcast, along with Bob Barker, and actor Jimmy Brown, cast member of television's *The Adventures of Rin-Tin-Tin*.

Through the latter half of the fifties, television ultimately dominated the spotlight and radio programming faded. NBC had difficulty selling sponsorship on radio compared to television, and the final radio broadcast of a seventeen-year run concluded on the morning of August 30, 1957.

In September 1966, the television program made the move to nighttime, syndicated by Metromedia. The success of *Truth or Consequences*, no doubt credited to the persona of Bob Barker, would continue until 1975, spanning more than 1,700 telecasts. Barker established a signature sign-off at the conclusion of each episode with the phrase, "Hoping all your consequences are happy ones."

The Final Head Count

Truth or Consequences reached the pinnacle of success when modern-day pop culture spoofed the quiz programs in humorous light. In December 1948, issue number 127 of *Action Comics* depicted Superman as a contestant on radio's *Truth or Consequences*. Throughout the funny pages, Edwards subjects Superman to a number of tasks – cleaning Lois Lane's apartment, bringing an inch of rain back to the studio (an inch of rain by a meteorologist definition), and revealing his true identity on a chalk board. (The ingenious man of tomorrow writes with such incredible speed that the board melts from the terrific friction.) Ultimately, Edwards is subjected to his own consequence, becoming a shoeshine boy for 1,000 pairs of shoes.

A 1950 Merrie Melodies cartoon called *The Ducksters* featured Daffy Duck as the host of a radio game show called *Truth or AAAAAHHHH!*, with Porky Pig as the contestant. A parody of *Truth or Consequences*, Daffy asks near-impossible questions, subjects Porky to near-fatal consequences, spoofs the "Miss Hush" contest by referring to it as "the Miss Shush" contest, cries "Aren't we gruesome?", spoofs Procter & Gamble, the real sponsor, with a make-shift commercial for Eagle Hand Laundry… "If your eagle's hands are dirty, we'll wash them clean!" During the cartoon, Porky is crushed by the Rock of Gibraltar, rained upon by 600 gallons of Niagara Falls, pounded with a mallet, threatened with a buzz saw, blown up by dynamite, and thanks Porky for being "a great sport." (At one point, Daffy tells Porky, "Listen, Mac, you got 32 teeth… would you like to try for 16?") Ultimately, Porky wins $26 million dollars and three cents. He immediately contacts the president of the Ajax Broadcasting Company and discovering the purchase price is $26 million and three pennies, purchases the studio. Daffy quickly discovers he is put on the opposite end of the spectrum and facing imminent death, shouts, "Have you got a doctor in the balcony, lady?" (The last line spoofing another radio quiz program, *Doctor I.Q.*)

On George Carlin's 1969 debut album, *Take-Offs and Put-Ons*, the character Congolia Breckinridge appears on a quiz program called *Truth or Penalties* (although at one point Carlin says *Truth or Consequences*). Because she has too little time to buzz in, when she is invited to pull back the curtain, an empty stage is revealed. The host then announces, "We were going to reunite you with your sister, whom you haven't seen in 27 years, but you blew the question, so we sent your sister back to Maine."

A 1977 *SCTV* comedy sketch featured the quiz show as a news item on *The SCTV Evening News* when the host, Bert Parks (played by Dave Thomas), angry and tired of hosting the show, loses it and throws a bottle of acid in the face of a female contestant, then pulls out a gun and shoots the studio audience.

During the fourteen years *Truth or Consequences* aired on radio, about 150 people got a pie in the face; most of them got more than one.* Ralph Edwards was pied at least 8 times, not always scripted. About 115 people got squirted with seltzer, not counting Edwards (who usually got it by accident).** This doesn't include the many contestants who were squirted with hoses, drenched in shower baths, soaked by buckets or shot each other with water pistols – one of whom picked up her bucket of "ammo" and threw it on Edwards. About 50 people were dunked into a giant water tank (one contestant ended up in the tank 8 times over the span of a month). Edwards himself made it into the tank twice (pulled in once by a contestant he was trying to help out, and pushed in once by the staff – the latter of which was scripted, by the way). About 54 people were given a hot seat, and two (who happened to be fire chiefs) were given a hot foot. Over 100 contestants were surprised by reunions with loved ones – one mother was flown from Ireland to surprise her son on the show, and an Italian brother and sister were brought together who hadn't seen each other in 42 years.

Today, with more than three major networks available to the masses, quiz programs require national sensationalism and expensive gimmicks to gain the interest of the American public. Legal eagles and insurance companies shy away from such proposals, influencing producers away from the notion of reviving quiz programs. A sad statement of the times in an environment where talk shows and reality-themed programming (very cost-effective) pave the way to the shape of things to come. *Truth or Consequences* was produced during an era where everybody wanted to pay the consequences and accept nationwide public humiliation in exchange for the promise of a new car or cold hard cash. Who wouldn't want to see that today?

---

* Shaving cream was always used for the pie filling during the pie throwing acts.

** In 1965, Edwards remarked, "Many people remember the days we threw pies and squirted seltzer. They think we did it often because they remember it. Actually, it happened only once or twice a season." This conflicts with the statistic above, but since most recordings of the radio program are not known to exist, and no notations on the scripts can verify the exact number, the count remains questionable.

EPISODE GUIDE

Notes about the Episode Guide

The information contained in this episode guide was compiled from a decade of research and a number of sources from archives both on the East and West Coast. With the majority of the radio broadcasts not known to exist in recorded form, radio scripts formed the primary source of information. Sadly, a small percentage of radio scripts were not available at the time this book went to press. In the case of one University archive, whose mission statement is focused on preservation, the institution temporarily misplaced a few boxes of radio scripts. Withholding this publication for an additional year in the hopes that the University would correct their oversight, and the gaps filled in to the author's satisfaction, a second trip to the same archive only resulted in semi-satisfaction: only a few boxes were found but a number of radio scripts that are supposedly stored and preserved were still misplaced. Having devoted a decade of research, intermittently between other projects, it was decided not to hold back publication an additional year in the hopes that the University would fulfill their solemn oath, for information that would total less than one percent of what had already been compiled.

Due to limited space, it was impractical to list every contestant who appeared on each and every radio broadcast. In most cases names of contestants were written on the radio scripts, and waiver agreements, and penmanship was not always clear and concise. As a result, a small percentage of contestant names in this book may be spelled incorrectly. When spelling was questioned, multiple people were consulted to verify the best possible answer. The selection of stunts and contests described in the episode guide were selected based on details historians might be seeking to narrow down their search: live animal stunts, on-going contests, elaborate stunts, etc.

Because all of the contestants signed a waiver before appearing on the program, granting permission for their name (and their residential address) to be made public, and because all of the radio scripts consulted for this book are available to the public in various archives across the country, and because most contestants granted permission for their names to appear in local newspapers at the time, names of contestants printed in this book are already considered public knowledge and are provided for the benefit of family relatives seeking metadata for genealogy purposes.

Unless otherwise stated, the radio broadcasts originated from New York City on NBC until the broadcast of March 17, 1945, when the program originated from the NBC studios in Hollywood, California.

March 23, 1940 to July 27, 1940
Selected CBS stations – Procter & Gamble, 9:45 to 10:15 p.m., Eastern
Limited number of stations in the New England area including WABC in New York; WDRC in Hartford; WPRO in Providence; and WROC in Worcester. For the early broadcasts, the "Consequence" was referred to as "the Ivory Antic."

August 17, 1940 to June 28, 1941
NBC Red Network – Procter & Gamble, Saturday from 8:30 to 9:00 p.m. Eastern

July 5, 1941 to June 24, 1950
NBC Red Network/NBC – Procter & Gamble, Saturday from 8:30 to 9:00 p.m., Eastern

September 5, 1950 – May 29, 1951
CBS – Philip Morris, Tuesday from 9:30 to 10:00 p.m. Eastern

June 17, 1952 – September 9, 1952
NBC – Pet Milk, Tuesday from 9:30 to 10:00 p.m., Eastern *

September 18, 1952 – June 18, 1953
NBC – Pet Milk, Thursday from 9:00 to 9:30 p.m., Eastern *

June 24, 1953 to September 16, 1953
NBC – Pet Milk, Wednesday from 9:30 to 10:00 p.m., Eastern *

September 24, 1953 – April 15, 1954
NBC – Pet Milk, Thursday from 9:00 to 9:30 p.m., Eastern *

March 23, 1955 – October 3, 1956
NBC – Multiple Sponsors, Wednesday from 9:30 to 9:55 p.m., Eastern
Effective September 28, 1955, Part of Top-Ten Participation Plan.**
Effective January 4, 1956, Wednesday 8:00 to 8:30 p.m.

April 29, 1957 – August 30, 1957
NBC – Multiple Sponsors, Monday thru Friday, 10:05 to 10:30 a.m.

Procter & Gamble Products
Ivory Soap commercials from March 23, 1940 to March 27, 1943
Duz commercials beginning April 3, 1943
As of February 1945, network commercials for Duz with hitch-hike for Ivory Soap
As of June 1945, network commercials for Duz

---

* SEGO, a subsidiary of Pet Milk, carries show on some stations.
** Sponsors participating in this Top-Ten Participation Plan:
    Buick Division of General Motors Corp. November 2, 1955 only.
    Curtis Publications, November 2, 1955 only
    ReaLemon-Puritan, May 9 to August 1, 1956

As of November 1945, network commercials for Duz

Cut-In for Velvet Skin (local)

As of April 1946, network commercials for Duz with trailer for Drene

Cut-In for Velvet Skin (local) and Prell (local)

As of September 1946, network commercials for Duz and Drene

Cut-In Prell (local)

As of October 1946, network commercials for Drene

Cut-In for Prell (local)

Cut-In for Velvet Skin

As of November 1946, network commercials for Duz

Cut-In for Prell (local)

Cut-In for Velvet Skin

Trailer for Drene

As of February 1, 1947, network commercials for Duz

Cut-In for Prell (local)

Cut-In for Velvet Skin

Trailer on repeat program only – Crisco

As of March 1, 1947, network commercials for Duz *

Cut-In for Press (local)

Cut-In for Velvet Skin

Trailer on repeat program – Crisco

Trailer on early program – Spic & Span

As of September 6, 1947, trailer for Drene added to the broadcasts

As of January 1949, network commercials for Duz

Trailer for Drene

Procter & Gamble Contract Terms with Compton Agency and NBC

August 17, 1940 to June 28, 1941, 46 weeks

July 5, 1941 to June 27, 1942, 52 weeks

September 12, 1942 to June 26, 1943, 42 weeks

July 3, 1943 to June 24, 1944, 52 weeks

(Summer interval July 3 to August 21, 1943)

July 1, 1944 to June 30, 1945, 53 weeks

* DUZ singers referenced during the 1947-48 season: Helen Rogers, Del Porter, and Boe Walker.

(Summer interval July 3, 1944 to September 2, 1944)
July 7, 1945 to June 29, 1946, 52 weeks
(Summer interval July 14 to September 1, 1945)
July 6, 1946 to June 28, 1947, 52 weeks
(Summer interval July 13 to August 31, 1946)
July 5, 1947 to June 25, 1948, 52 weeks
(Summer interval July 12, 1947 to August 30, 1947)
July 3, 1948 to June 25, 1949, 52 weeks
(Summer interval July 3 to August 21, 1948)
July 2, 1949 to June 24, 1950, 52 weeks
(Summer interval July 2 to August 20, 1949)

Organist
Bill Meeder (March 23, 1940 to June 26, 1943)
Johnny Gart (August 28, 1943 to July 7, 1945)
Buddy Cole (September 8, 1945 to April 15, 1954, *with exceptions listed below*)
Howard Jackson (October 8, 1949)
Sammy Prager (January 8, 1953)
Gaylord Carter (September 16, 1953)

Announcer
Mel Allen (August 17, 1940 to March 20, 1943, *with exceptions listed below*)
Paul Jones (February 1, 1941)
Ed Herlihy (February 15, 1941)
Dresser Dahlstead (March 8, 1941)
Frank Barton (March 15, 1941)
John Grover (March 22, 1941)
Ford Pearson (March 29 and April 12, 1941)
Ralph Powers (August 23, 1941)
Ed Herlihy (June 6, June 13 and June 20, 1941)
Ken Roberts (July 19 and July 26, 1941)
Ed Herlihy (June 20, 1942)
Todd Russell (November 18, 1942)
Ed Herlihy (February 20 and March 27, 1943)
Cliff Engle (April 3, 1943 to June 26, 1943, *with exception listed below*)
Petie Worth (May 8, 1943)

Clayton "Bud" Collyer (August 28, 1943 to December 4, 1943)

Lamont Johnson (December 18, 1943 to February 12, 1944)

Clayton "Bud" Collyer (February 19 to April 8, 1944)

Lamont Johnson (April 15, 1944)

Clayton "Bud" Collyer (April 22 to July 7, 1945)

Jay Stewart (September 8, 1945 to July 6, 1946)

Harlow Wilcox (September 7, 1946 to June 24, 1950, *with exceptions listed below*)

Clayton "Bud" Collyer (November 2 and November 9, 1946)

Ed Bailey (May 10 and May 17, 1947)

Johnny Pawlek (May 17, 1947)

Clayton "Bud" Collyer, Joe Walters and John Holbrook (September 5, 1950 to May 15, 1951)

Harlow Wilcox (May 22, 1951)

Art Gilmore and Jay Jackson (May 29, 1951)

Ken Carpenter (June 17, 1952 to September 16, 1953)

Harlow Wilcox (September 24, 1953 to April 15, 1954)

Arch Presby (March 23, 1955 to August 30, 1957)

Sound Man

Ted Slade (responsible for Beulah)

Engineer

Hal Flood (September 12, 1942 to June 26, 1943)

Johnny Pawlek (September 8, 1945 to July 6, 1946)

Larry Lawrence (June 17, 1952 to September 30, 1952)

Ed Pawlek (September 24, 1953 to April 15, 1954)

Producers/Directors

Herb Moss (September 12, 1942 to June 26, 1943)

William Burch (September 8, 1945 to June 26, 1948)

Al Paschall (September 8, 1945 to September 30, 1952)

Joe Daly (June 17, 1952 to September 30, 1952)

Ed Bailey (June 17, 1952 to April 15, 1954)

Ed Bailey (April 29, 1957 to August 30, 1957)

Assistant Producer

Charles Lyon (April 29, 1957 to August 30, 1957)

Writers
Bill Davis (September 7, 1946 to July 5, 1947)
Bill Burch (September 7, 1946 to July 5, 1947)
Bill Hawes (September 7, 1946 to July 5, 1947)
Paul Edwards (September 7, 1946 to July 5, 1947)
Ralph Edwards (June 17, 1952 to September 30, 1952)
Paul Edwards (June 17, 1952 to September 30, 1952)
Bill Davis (September 24, 1953 to April 15, 1954)
Bill Burch (April 29, 1957 to August 30, 1957)
Cal Howard (April 29, 1957 to August 30, 1957)
Bobby Laher (April 29, 1957 to August 30, 1957)
Bill Reed (April 29, 1957 to August 30, 1957)

Audition: A recording was made on March 20, 1940, as a demo, not for broadcast.

Episode #1, Broadcast of March 23, 1940
Stunts: Suck Lollypop, Describe Man in Audience, Put Baby to Sleep, and Kitchen Band

Episode #2, Broadcast of March 30, 1940
Stunts: Sound Effects, Romeo and Juliet, Break a Date, and Play on Violin
Anne Gans of Brooklyn, New York, has to play the drums to "Hold That Tiger," and roar like a tiger at key moments in the song.

Episode #3, Broadcast of April 6, 1940
Stunts: One Man Drama, Make a Date with Man in Audience, Five Nice Things, Sing with Bell & Racket, and Tongue Twister

Episode #4, Broadcast of April 13, 1940
Stunts: Hold Tongue & Sing, Describe Woman's Hat, Recite Alphabet, Purchase Night Shirt, and Tell Jokes

Episode #5, Broadcast of April 20, 1940
Stunts: Crew Cracker & Whistle, Describe Ideal Man, Tie a Tie, and Drum Sole
Three known contestants include **Ginger Manners**, an actress from Brooklyn, New York. **Mr. Yale Ruben** of Milford, Connecticut, who manages the

Wayside Furniture Shop in New Haven, has to whistle Yankee Doodle Dandy. Another contestant, **Marge Brennan** of Woodlawn, New York, a stenographer by profession, has to describe her ideal dream man.

Episode #6, Broadcast of April 27, 1940
Stunts: Vocal Scale, Chinese Sentences, Commercial Consey, Mary Lamb, and Sell Backscratcher

Contestant **Johnny Jones** must reach the lowest musical notes his voice could reach and sing the scale do-re-me-fa-so-la-ti-do, reaching a high note by the end, then deliver a campaign speech in the same manner. **Mildred Sachs** of New Jersey, confessed housewife of five children by profession, has to perform a stunt involving speaking different languages.

Episode #7, Broadcast of May 4, 1940
Stunts: Laundry List, Ask for Sweetheart's Hand, Dog & Cat Fight, Crying Baby, and Tongue Twisters

Jean McKinney of New York City must read a men's laundry list as if she was the conductor of a commuter train. **T. Tetrald** of Fall River, Massachusetts, and **Miss Walwick**, must imitate a cat and dog fight with Walwick playing the role of the cat. **Mr. Balsamo**, another contestant, must imitate the sound of a crying baby and Ralph Edwards will not give him a bottle until the contestant cries loud enough.

Episode #8, Broadcast of May 11, 1940
Stunts: Hog Calling, Bawl Yourself Out, Describe Fight, Electric Horse, Tooth Pulled with Laughing Gas, and Hula Dance

John Lloyd Raywood of Melbourne, Australia, has spent two months in America and found himself the unwilling contestant on the radio quiz program. **Charles Purcell** of Newark, New Jersey, has to play the role of a hog caller. A short contestant had to ride an electric horse. One contestant who needed to have a tooth extracted, agreed to have it removed on stage by a professional dentist, while under the influence of laughing gas.

Episode #9, Broadcast of May 18, 1940
Stunts: Hillbilly Band, Palm Reader, Busy Phones, and Dog Duet

Beginning with this broadcast, the series moved from the CBS Playhouse No.

2 to the Barbizon Plaza Hotel. **Ruth Michaelson** of Providence, Rhode Island, has to play the role of a fortune teller and read the palm of a man and deliver his fortune. The man in the audience chosen to participate was Burgess Pool. **Michael Mayo** of Ware, Massachusetts, has to sing "I'm A Hillbilly, By Cracky," to the tune of "I Like Mountain Music."

Episode #10, Broadcast of May 25, 1940
Stunts: Barber Chair, Goldilocks, Broken Record, and Sell an Icebox
J. Rateenbury of New York City has to pretend he was standing in front of a barber chair and impress the producer getting a shave, by singing "Down by the Old Mill Stream." While singing, the contestant received a real facial massage. A woman had to deliver the fairytale of Goldilocks and the Three Bears to an imaginary class of students while the sound man delivered surprises in key sections of the story, from whistles to cow bells. Another contestant has to sell an icebox to an Eskimo.

Episode #11, Broadcast of June 1, 1940
Stunts: Imitate Trains, Marshmallow, O-Wa-Ta-Goo-Siam, Sing Song While Pushing Bells, and Laugh Different Ways
Dorothy Ogden of Philadelphia, Pennsylvania, pretends to be a disloyal husband returning home at 3 a.m. in the morning, after spending a night out with the boys. Radio actress **Jean Colbert** is hired to play the role of the wife who caught her husband coming home and the contestant has to make excuses – with marshmallows in her mouth at the same time. **Mrs. Leon Fisher** of Holyoke, Mass., is dressed like an American Indian and provided words to deliver as an Indian war cry, unaware the words, when repeated fast enough, say something different.

Episode #12, Broadcast of June 8, 1940
Stunts: Sip Soup, Recite in Key to Organ, Whoa Fish, Bathtub, and Tarzan
Dorothy Klein of Brooklyn has to play "The Anvil Chorus" while sipping soup. **William Burns** of Custer, Pennsylvania, performs a rendition of "Singing in the Bathtub" while pretending to take a bath in hot water. When he gets to the final two lines of the song (lyrics provided on paper by Ralph Edwards), he is required to sing the song as if the water turned cold as ice. **Harold Wyckoff** of New York City has to deliver the Tarzan yell with a banana in his mouth.

Episode #13, Broadcast of June 15, 1940

Stunts: Father's Day, Sing Dixie, Quints, Sell New York Back to Indians, and Happy Birthday

Rose Watras of New Britain, Connecticut, has to pretend to be an expectant father in the hospital, waiting for the news. **Mary Ruth Bertram** of Shavertown, Pennsylvania, has to sing Dixie and when the bell rings three times, perform a tap dance sequence. **Charlotte Schilling** of New York City has to sell New York back to the Indians, and Smiling Bear, a full-blooded Hopi Indian, participates in the stunt.

Episode #14, Broadcast of June 22, 1940

Stunts: Diogenes, Blindfold, Cuckoo Clock, Massage, and First Date

Honey Ehleis of Brooklyn, New York, has to sing a song while receiving a massage from **Harold Reilly** of the Reilly Health Service in Rockefeller Center. **R.V. Boley** of Denville, New York, has to describe their first date by answering a series of embarrassing questions.

Episode #15, Broadcast of June 29, 1940

Stunts: Lecture on Health, Propose to Self, Movie Stars, Buggy Ride, and Snore

Mrs. Harry Desmond of Marion, Massachusetts, has to pretend to be "The Voice of Health," lecturing on the radio and read a prepared speech. She has to pretend she has hay fever while delivering the speech. **Mrs. C. Connevy** of Poughkeepsie, New York, pretends to be at a Hollywood party and imitates celebrities while reading a poem.

Episode #16, Broadcast of July 6, 1940

Stunts: Sing Menu, Spanking, Birdies, Nightmare, and Read Backwards

Jesslyn O'Connell of Worcester, Massachusetts, has to sing a menu taken from a real local restaurant. Two contestants have to act out the role of mother and son and with a wooden paddle, spank the bad little boy who ran away from home. **Mrs. E. Louise Hill** of Hartford, Connecticut, has to jump in bed and act out the role of suffering a nightmare complete with yells, moans and screams.

Beginning with this broadcast the program originates from the new CBS studio annex on East 52nd Street in New York.

Episode #17, Broadcast of July 13, 1940
Stunts: Bull Fiddle, Double Talk, Hypnotized, Wash Face, and Meet a Ghost
Manny's Music Store in New York City provides a bass fiddle, all six feet of it, for a contestant, **Agnes Loomis** of Rye, New York, who is forced to play the instrument and sing "Put On Your Old Gray Bonnet." **John Roberts** of Providence, Rhode Island, pretends to be hypnotized and follows any command shouted out from the audience. The voices shouted out from the audience, however, are "planted" by the radio producers.

Episode #18, Broadcast of July 20, 1940
Stunts: Squeeze Horns, Make Up Poem, Husband Wife, Jump over Candlestick, Hold Nose, Tap Throat, and Describe Milking a Cow
Grace D. Beaumont of Amherst, Mass., must play "There's No Place like Home" with a number of horns attached to a flat board. **Gordon McMillan** of Hartford, Connecticut, has to explain in well-chosen words, how to milk a cow. Whenever the occasion presents itself, the contestant must use the word "faucets."

Episode #19, Broadcast of July 27, 1940
Stunts: Peanut Butter, Broomstick, Animal Imitations, Rhumba, and Torn Trousers
Jerrie C. Maloney of Hamden, Connecticut, must eat a peanut butter sandwich while the organist performs "O Sole Mio." When a specific music cue is delivered, the contestant must go out and sing. **Mrs. R.G. Calder** of Tuckahoe, New York, must pretend a broomstick is her faithful lover and subject a lovemaking sketch on the stage with the broomstick.

Episodes #20 & 21, Broadcast of August 17, 1940
East Coast Stunts: Suspend Apple, Proposal, Adverbs, Seal, and Bedroom Band
West Coast Stunts: Suspend Apple, Proposal, Bedroom Band, Seal, and Trains
Contestants must imitate a sad and happy train, complete with whistle, bite an apple suspended on a string, fake a marriage proposal, attempt to sell papers using different adverbs (sleepily, stupidly, romantically, sinisterly, etc.), mimic a seal calling for its mate, and perform a band in the bedroom.

Episodes #22 & 23, Broadcast of August 24, 1940

East Coast Stunts: Balloon, Crystal Ball, Beetle, Chinese Laundry, and Hammond Sing

West Coast Stunts: Lollypop, Crystal Ball, Chinese Laundry, Drum Solo, and Five Nice Things

Contestants include **C. Cachicame** of Brooklyn, New York; **Miss Ethyle Reveenman** of Providence, Rhode Island; **John Seymour** of Georgetown, Colorado; **Rose Davis** of Newark, New Jersey; and **G.E. White** of Arcadia, California. The classic lollypop stunt was a favorite of Ralph Edwards.

Episodes #24 & 25, Broadcast of August 31, 1940

East Coast Stunts: Washboard, Poem, Two Horses, Mistaken Identity, Watermelon, and Chicken Feathers

West Coast Stunts: Sound Effects, Whoa Fish, How to Swim, Apple Tree, Watermelon, and Tongue Twisters

Episodes #26 & 27, Broadcast of September 7, 1940

East Coast Stunts: Babbling Brook, Diogenes, Sell Song, and Family Feud

West Coast Stunts: One Man Drama, Alphabet, Ideal Man, and Nightgown

Episodes #28 & 29, Broadcast of September 14, 1940

East Coast Stunts: Laugh Cry, Good Wife, Cheerleader, Back Seat Driver, Hookey, and All You Know

West Coast Stunts: Sing Menu, Describe Hat, Backseat Driver, Electric Horse, and Crying Baby

Episodes #30 & 31, Broadcast of September 21, 1940

East Coast Stunts: Gramophone, Western Union, Advice, Peanut, What's Wrong, and Oh Please

West Coast Stunts: Broken Record, Western Union, Husband-Wife, Bathtub, and Milk a Cow

Episodes #32 & 33, Broadcast of September 28, 1940

East Coast Stunts: Piano Mittens, Flirting, Sneezes, Reducing, and Garbage Collector

West Coast Stunts: Sip Soup, Ask Father, Dog Duet, Nightmare, Make Love to a Broomstick, and Tarzan

Episodes #34 & 35, Broadcast of October 5, 1940
East Coast Stunts: Button Tongue, Fried Egg, Train Talk, Single-Minded, Feed Pie, and Inaudible Sounds
West Coast Stunts: Wash Face, Hog Caller, Cheerleader, Kitchen Band, Bawl Yourself Out, First Date, and Vocal Scale
Broadcast originated from the Food Show in Omaha, Nebraska. All of the stunts performed on stage were proposed by radio listeners. Each stunt used on the program paid out $10 to the radio listener who submitted the proposal. The grand prize winner, indicated by the "sensitive applause meter" was **Rose Jensen**, who proposed a contestant play a song using kitchen utensils. She won $25 prize money. In later radio broadcasts the prize money would be $20.

Episode #36 & 37, Broadcast of October 12, 1940
East Coast Stunts: Banjo, Narration, Strange Interlude, Roller Skates, and Tongue in Cheek
West Coast Stunts: Cry Baby, Blindfold, Beetle, Barber Shop, and Movie Stars

Episode #38 & 39, Broadcast of October 19, 1940
East Coast Stunts: Emily Post, Blind Date, French, and Pants in Barrel
West Coast Stunts: Violin, Mistaken Identity, Describe Fight, and Pants in Barrel

Episode #40 & 41, Broadcast of October 26, 1940
East Coast Stunts: Duck for Apples, Witch, Man Phones Wife, and Initiation
West Coast Stunts: Duck for Apples, Witch, Marshmallow, and Initiation

Episode #42, Broadcast of November 2, 1940
East Coast Stunts: Hawaiian, Clock Whistle, Donuts, and Dog House
There was no West Coast broadcast as a result of a speech by **General Hugh Johnson**.

Episodes #43 & 44, Broadcast of November 9, 1940
East Coast Stunts: Treadmill, Loves Me Not, Three Bears, Bird in Gilded Cage, Elevator Man, and Snow White Story
West Coast Stunts: Banjo, Treadmill, Donut, Buggy Ride, and Propose to Self

Episodes #45 & 46, Broadcast of November 16, 1940
East Coast Stunts: Bass Drum, Muscle Builder, Dishes, and Church
West Coast Stunts: Happy Birthday, Diogenes, Chinese, and Feed Pie

Episodes #47 & 48, Broadcast of November 23, 1940
East Coast Stunts: Dentist, Boots Horns, Old Maid, and Mental Giant
West Coast Stunts: Hillbilly Band, Good Wife, Break Date, Milking, and Double Talk

Episodes #49 & 50, Broadcast of November 30, 1940
East Coast Stunts: Ticklish Drivers, Clothes Wringer, Greased Pig, and Snow White
West Coast Stunts: Piano Mittens, Underwear, French, and Waiting at Church
Broadcast originated from the Palace Theatre in Cleveland, Ohio.

Episodes #51 & 52, Broadcast of December 7, 1940
East Coast Stunts: Grocery List, Onions Laugh, Milking, Ice Box, and First Letter
West Coast Stunts: Grocery List, Onions Laugh, Marshmallow, Ice Box, and First Letter
Broadcast originated from the Wardman Park Hotel in Washington, D.C.

Episodes #53 & 54, Broadcast of December 14, 1940
East Coast Stunts: Spell Horn, Western Drama, Women Lecture, Punching Bag, and Broken Record
West Coast Stunts: Punching Bag, Oh Please, Clothes Wringer, Dog House, and Tie A Tie

Episodes #55 & 56, Broadcast of December 21, 1940
East Coast Stunts: Pie, Turkey, Rolling Pin, Santa Claus, Pump Tire, and Seven Dwarfs

West Coast Stunts: Pie, Turkey, Rolling Pin, Santa Claus, Seven Dwarfs, Pump Tires, and The Letter "G"

Episodes #57 & 58, Broadcast of December 28, 1940
East Coast Stunts: Typewriter, New Years, Fish a Man, and Men Shaving
West Coast Stunts: Dentist, Limburger, Break Dishes, Men Shaving, and Resolutions
Broadcast originated from the Fox Theatre in Detroit, Michigan.

Episodes #59 & 60, Broadcast of January 4, 1941
East Coast Stunts: Limburger, Seesaw, Telephone Call, Pogo Stick, Surrealist, and Lees Po
West Coast Stunts: Jump Rope, Narration, Telephone Call, Seesaw, Animal Imitations, and Lees Po

Episodes #61 & 62, Broadcast of January 11, 1941
East Coast Stunts: Kick Pants, Auction off Hubby, Ice Talk, Jump Rope, and Snores Talk
West Coast Stunts: Gramophone, Spanking, Rhumba, and Quints
Ralph Edwards made his first announcement of the "Truth or Consequences Party Book," a radio premium giveaway, beginning with this broadcast.

Episodes #63 & 64, Broadcast of January 18, 1941
East Coast Stunts: Song Switch, Mind Reader, Bouncing Chair, Baby Act, and Marshmallow
West Coast Stunts: Girdle, Baby Act, Bounding Chair, Husband's Noses, and Surrealist
The mind reader act went over extremely well. Questions included during this broadcast included: What animal can touch its ear with its nose? (Elephant) What NYC Fire vehicle cannot go up a one-way street? (A fireboat) What seven letters read the same upside down? (O, I, S, H, X, Z and N) What planet is definitely known to be inhabited? (Earth)

Episodes #65 & 66, Broadcast of January 25, 1941
East Coast Stunts: Kitchen Band, Girdle, Pie Throwing, Laughs, Elephant, and Driving Lesson

West Coast Stunts: Peanut Butter, Chinning Man and Wife, Women Lecturing, Driving Lesson, Elephant, and Man in Moon

Broadcast originated from the Fox Theatre in St. Louis, Missouri. A female contestant has to perform music using kitchen tools such as pots, pans and wooden spoons. The classic husband-wife pie-throwing contest was performed on stage. And just to surprise the audience in a stunt Edwards would reprise again on the radio program, an elephant is brought to the stage (Rosie in "Jumbo"). A man (as his consequence) had to wash the elephant while singing "I Dream of Jeannie with the Light Brown Hair." The act went off perfectly. But in order to get the elephant, Edwards and his crew had to engage the entire troupe that went with him: a camel, a mule, and two Great Danes, and pay all their transportation from New York to St. Louis, and the return trip.

The soundman made an error and missed the Beulah cue at the beginning of this episode.

Episodes #67 & 68, Broadcast of February 1, 1941

East Coast Stunts: Grapefruit, Chinning, Recipe, Husband Noses, Man in Moon, and Name

West Coast Stunts: Button Tongue, Blind Date, Mind Reading, and Pie Throwing

Broadcast originated from the Taft Auditorium in Cincinnati, Ohio.

Episodes #69 & 70, Broadcast of February 8, 1941

East Coast Stunts: Hammer Saw, Roast Pig, Clothes Line, Cave Woman, and Three Blind Mice

West Coast Stunts: Swimming, Lion Tamer, Balloons Barefooted, Apple over Table, Laugh Cry, and Paging Names

Episodes #71 & 72, Broadcast of February 15, 1941

East Coast Stunts: Swimming, Lion Tamer, Balloons Barefooted, Apple over Table, Train Dispatcher, and Karloff Giggles

West Coast Stunts: Letter "Z," Recipe, Clothes Line, and Cave Woman

Broadcast originated from the Hippodrome Theatre in Baltimore, Maryland.

Episodes #73 & 74, Broadcast of February 22, 1941

East Coast Stunts: Railroad, Ping Pong, Armored Man, Cherry Tree, and Page

West Coast Stunts: Saw Hammer, Roast Pig, Ping Pong, Cherry Tree, and Trunk

Episodes #75 & 76, Broadcast of March 1, 1941

East Coast Stunts: Mush, Baby Answers, Handwriting, Bronco Busting, Frank Fay, and Cucumber Cream

West Coast Stunts: Musical Typewriter, Roller Skates, Flirting, Bronco Busting, Mixed Songs, and Sneezes

A contestant has to sing "Oh Where Has My Little Dog Gone," but sing only the letters indicated on paper as they type it on a typewriter. Actor **Frank Fay** makes a guest appearance for one of the stunts.

Episodes #77 & 78, Broadcast of March 8, 1941

East Coast Stunts: Washing, Shave Barber, Corset, Red Riding Hood, and Spoon in Mouth

West Coast Stunts: Babbling Brook, Fish a Man, Ice Talk, and Reducing Belt

Broadcast originated from the Paramount Theatre in Los Angeles, California. A female contestant has to put about a quarter of a glass of water into her mouth and fully describe a babbling brook, answering four questions from Ralph Edwards.

Episodes #79 & 80, Broadcast of March 15, 1941

East Coast Stunts: Blow Ball, Fred Allen #1, Cinderella, Letter "Z", and Pat a Cake

West Coast Stunts: Corset, Fred Allen #1, Adverbs, Tongue in Cheek, and Peanuts

Broadcast originated from Station KPO in San Francisco, California. East Coast broadcast included blowing a ping pong ball across the table, a Fred Allen parody, a Prince Charming stunt involving Cinderella's shoe, singing all the names that start with Z in the phone book, and playing pattycake with real cakes. On the West Coast, the organist missed a cue at the end of the show. Stunts included singing in a corset, the Fred Allen parody, selling papers using different adverbs, and rolling a peanut with your nose. Riddles included: What two whole numbers multiplied equal 31? (1 x 31) and What is the first number to contain the letter a. (One thousand)

Episodes #81 & 82, Broadcast of March 22, 1941
East Coast Stunts: Standing on Head, Cat and Dog Sip, Argument, Lift Voices, and Forty-Niner
West Coast Stunts: Train Dispatcher, Audience Occupation, Auction off Hubby, Lift Voices, and Jump Marshmallow
Broadcast originated from Station KPO in San Francisco, California. A contestant sang "Oh, My Darling Clementine" while standing on his head. Another contestant puts a lollypop in their mouth and delivers train stops through a megaphone just as a train conductor would.

Episodes #83 & 84, Broadcast of March 29, 1941
East Coast Stunts: Trunk, Jump Marshmallow, Cow, Chorus, and Toothache
West Coast Stunts: Blow Ball, Kick Pants, Cow, Vain, Pat-A-Cake, and Name
Broadcast originated from the Orpheum Theatre in Minneapolis, Minneapolis. A female contestant had to describe how to milk a cow, with her hands tied behind her back. It would have been normal to hear the instructions except that she was unaware that a real cow had been brought on stage. The cow got restless and the stunt ended up in an impromptu rodeo.

Episodes #85 & 86, Broadcast of April 5, 1941
East Coast Stunts: Pencil, Bridal Shower, Hawaii, Vain, Tongue Lashing, and Cackle
West Coast Stunts: Recite in Key, Treasure Hunt, Red Riding Hood, and Hawaiian
A contestant has to sing "My Bonnie Lies Over the Ocean" while maintaining a pencil between their upper lip and nose. Another contestant has to deliver a speech while **Bill Meeder**, the organist, strikes notes of various pitches,

cueing the contestant to change the pitch of their voice. Switch to Hollywood, during tonight's program, for a few words by **Mrs. James Hays**, winner of the Grand Prize in the Ivory contest.

Episodes #87 & 88, Broadcast of April 12, 1941
East Coast Stunts: Bells, Water Pistols, Treasure Hunt, 2041, Harp, and Laugh Louder
West Coast Stunts: Bells, Cluck Whistle, Hokey, and Shave
A contestant has to play a song using a number of bells, with musical notes corresponding specific bells.

Episodes #89 & 90, Broadcast of April 19, 1941
East Coast Stunts: Barker, Carving, Telephone, Eggs, Rope, and Chicken Feathers
West Coast Stunts: Stand on Head, Tongue Lashing, Telephone, Three Way Mary, and Chorus
Broadcast originated from the Wisconsin Theatre in Milwaukee, Wisconsin. A contestant has to pretend to be a circus side show barker, a fast-talking spieler, promoting such displays as a bearded lady, a sword swallower, a shimmy dancer, a midget and a horse that talks sense. Another contestant has to demonstrate the proper technique of carving a turkey, with a real roast turkey on a table, and such implements as a saw, a hammer, a chisel, nails, two pieces of rope, a pair of goggles, a fishing pole, a broom and a dustpan.

Episodes #91 & 92, Broadcast of April 26, 1941
East Coast Stunts: Spring Song, Frank Fay, Sound Table, and Ankles
West Coast Stunts: Speech-Woman, Carving, Argument, Ankles, and Tank
A contestant has to dance to Mendelsohn's "Spring Song," wearing snow shoes, a shimmering silk veil, and a garland of roses for their hair. Actor **Frank Fay** makes a surprise appearance for one of the contestants in this broadcast.

Episodes #93 & 94, Broadcast of May 3, 1941
East Coast Stunts: Wrestling, Speech-Woman, Johnny, Three Way Mary, Bathtub Boat, and Chew the Rag
West Coast Stunts: Spring Song, Water Pistols, Rope, Eggs, and Count Again
Two female contestants, complete with ten-gallon hats and red handkerchiefs, must use water pistols to settle a verbal battle. Just in case they run out of ammunition, each are supplied with a pail of water. A male contestant has

to pretend he is wrestling against another opponent – the invisible man. A contestant has to deliver a speech, "Why I Should Be Elected Dog Catcher," switching back and forth from being the speaker and the heckler, at the sound of a bell.

Episodes #95 & 96, Broadcast of May 10, 1941
East Coast Stunts: Sing Fast, Two Proposals, Jekyll & Hyde, Sip Soup, and Water Bags
West Coast Stunts: Sound Table, Draw Songs, Cinderella, Dummy Dance, County Fair Band, and Jekyll & Hyde.
Dancing to the tempo of "Turkey in the Straw," a contestant pretends to be a farmer who travels to the city, falls in love with a window store dummy, and dances with a real mannequin on stage. Another contestant has to sing the lyrics of four songs under 30 seconds and is paid one dollar for every second remaining when completed… provided they finish the task under 30 seconds.

Episodes #97 & 98, Broadcast of May 17, 1941
East Coast Stunts: Sniffs, Imitate, Pig Latin, Conover Model, Tank, and Husband-Mule
West Coast Stunts: Conover Model, Swan Song, Pig Latin, and Movie
Broadcast originated from the Ritz Theater, New York City. The contestant participating in the Conover Model stunt had to travel from the Ritz Theatre, at 48th Street and Broadway in New York City, to an NBC Studio in Radio City to phone their spouse back later in the broadcast. The spouse, unable to enjoy the program they came to watch from the studio audience, was provided with a complimentary copy of the radio broadcast at a later date. Actress **Agnes Moorehead** played a supporting role for the Conover Model stunt.

Episodes #99 & 100, Broadcast of May 24, 1941
East Coast Stunts: Dummy Dance, Sing Dishes, Mrs. Fry, and Horse Race
West Coast Stunts: Wrestling, Sing-Howl, Adjectives, Water Bags, Sing Fast, and Beauty Secrets
Broadcast originated from the Earle Theatre in Philadelphia, Pennsylvania. Two contestants must use a towel to dry as many dishes as they can within a set time. Two hundred dishes were provided on the tables for this stunt. The

contestants had to sing "Here We Go 'Round the Mulberry Bush" while performing the task.

Episodes #101 & 102, Broadcast of May 31, 1941
East Coast Stunts: Sing Chinese, Husband Donkey, Clear Throat, and Recording
West Coast Stunts: Sing Chinese, husband Donkey, Clear Throat, Recording, and Hat Poem
The first four contestants answered correctly onstage! The husband with a donkey stunt went over well with the audience. Questions on the East Coast included: How much does it cost to wash a 5-foot by 5-foot window at one cent per square foot? (50 cents – both sides). What is the antonym of synonym? (Antonym) On the West Coast, a question was asked, "What three states have four letters?" (Utah, Iowa and Ohio)

Episodes #103 & 104, Broadcast of June 7, 1941
East Coast Stunts: Bounce, Ticklish, Electric Horse, Soldier, Beauty Secrets, and County Fair Band
West Coast Stunts: Carmen, Ticklish, Imitate, Simon, and Band
After a pillow is tied to a contestant's bottom, the unwilling victim is forced to bounce on the stage like a rubber ball, without the use of their hands, singing "Funiculi Funicula." The Ticklish stunt involves a married couple talking about the serious side of marriage. During the stunt, the couple each use a feather to make the other smile and laugh. The one who held out longer without hysteria won an extra dollar and the loser had to spend ten days in a strait jacket.

Episodes #105 & 106, Broadcast of June 14, 1941
East Coast Stunts: Dog Duet, Simon, Carmen, Bald Heads, Blow Horn, and Rope
West Coast Stunts: Bounce, Soldier, Bags, Bald Heads, Jack Be Nimble, and Blow Horn
Broadcast originated from the Earle Theatre in Washington, D.C. A contestant is asked to sing "Believe Me If All Those Endearing Young Charms" on stage, while holding onto a dog's leash. The dog was trained to howl when someone sings. A contestant gets a phone call from a soldier out at Fort Ord in Monterey, California, unaware the soldier is a family relative.

Episodes #107 & 108, Broadcast of June 21, 1941

East Coast Stunts: Bag Race, Massage, Hope Chest, and Alphabet

West Coast Stunts: Massage, Hope Chest, Coffee Pot, and Locked Out

Two contestants compete in a race to blow up small, brown paper bags, repeating rapidly three times before each burst, "A quick biscuit, a mixed biscuit, and a biscuit mixer." **George Morrison**, assistant to **Harold Reilly** of the Reilly Health Service in Rockefeller Center, teaches a contestant how to give a massage.

Episodes #109 & 110, Broadcast of June 28, 1941

East Coast Stunts: Animal Crackers, Coffee Pot, Drum Duet, Telephone, Rope and Broken Record

West Coast Stunts: Animal Crackers, Baby Answers, Drum Duet, Telephone, Garbage Collector, and Laundry List

Contestants must pull animal crackers out of a box, one at a time, imitating that animal as they eat the cracker. Another contestant must dress like a baby, with rattle, and throw crying temper tantrums.

Episodes #111 & 112, Broadcast of July 5, 1941

East Coast Stunts: Broken Record, Marriage, Calisthenics, Walk Plank, Laundry List, Drafted, and Rope

West Coast Stunts: Cymbals, Marriage, Calisthenics, Walk Plank, Laundry List, and Drafted

Ralph Edwards opens the broadcast welcoming eleven new NBC affiliates, broadcasting *Truth or Consequences*: Raleigh and Asheville, North Carolina; Charleston, Columbia, Florence and Greenville, South Carolina; Rochester and Syracuse, New York; Bristol and Kingsport, Tennessee; and Norfolk, Virginia. A contestant has to sing "Bicycle Built for Two" and pretend to be a broken record every time Ralph Edwards snaps his fingers. He deliberately leaves the contestant singing the closing line, "Goodnight Everybody," for a lengthy period of time.

Episodes #113 & 114, Broadcast of July 12, 1941

East Coast Stunts: Hobby Horse, Dark, Quartette, Squadron, Lollypop, and Tie a Tie

West Coast Stunts: Hobby Horse, Dark, Sell New York, Squadron, Single-Married, and Mary Lamb

Two contestants race stick horses, wear jockey caps, and swing whips while singing "Yankee Doodle Dandy" on an improvised race track. The lights are turned off in the studio as a woman is asked to feel a man's face and describe him, his age, weight, and whether he would be eligible for marriage… until the lights are turned on and it turns out to be a woman who switched places with the man before the light returned.

Episodes #115 & 116, Broadcast of July 19, 1941

East Coast Stunts: Popcorn, Ideal Man, Hellzapoppin', See What I Mean, Rope, and Tie a Tie

West Coast Stunts: Popcorn, See What I Mean, Sob Story, and Pillow Fight

A man is blindfolded and driven from the Ritz Theatre to an unknown location where he is to describe and guess where he was taken to. He thought he was on the Albany night boat but instead found himself on the stage of Wintergarden Theatre where *Hellzapoppin'* was playing. The stunt was distinguishable enough for the East Coast listeners, but it was decided between broadcasts not to use it for the West Coast as it did not fare as well as expected. Announcer **Ken Roberts** helps assist with the stunt. The West Coast broadcast is the earliest broadcast known to use the phrase, "Aren't We Devils?"

Episodes #117 & 118, Broadcast of July 26, 1941

East Coast Stunts: Trains, Jewish, Sob Story, Hellzaswitch, Tie a Tie, and R to W

West Coast Stunts: Laundry List, Jewish, Calisthenics, and Pendulum

Reprising last week's stunt where a contestant is blindfolded and taken to a different part of the city, announcer **Ken Roberts** assists in the same stunt with a different location. Radio commentator **Abe Lyman** is a guest on the program, reading a Jewish newspaper, written in Yiddish. A female contestant returns to the stage to read the same paper and decipher what she thinks it says. The R to W stunt was done multiple times during the first two years of the quiz program. This involved a contestant delivering a prepared speech, pronouncing the letter R as letter W.

Episodes #119 & 120, Broadcast of August 2, 1941

East Coast Stunts: Laundry List, Bashful Sailor, Husband Wife, Pendulum, Tie a Tie, and R to W

West Coast Stunts: Bull Fiddle, Bashful Sailor, Steal Boyfriend, Guess Snores, Aluminum and Jack Be Nimble

Martin Lewis, editor of *Movie-Radio Guide* magazine, presented a trophy from the magazine to Edwards for his radio program. A contestant is asked to return to the program next week to face their consequence, but in the meantime visit their tailor during the week, rent an outfit of top hat, white tie and tails, paid for by the game show. Next week they are to appear at Grand Central Station to meet "a lady you will never forget." **Helen Mueller**, a beautiful Conover model, participates in the "Bashful Sailor" stunt.

Episodes #121 & 122, Broadcast of August 9, 1941

East Coast Stunts: Weather Vane, Steal Boyfriend, Horse Payoff, Pillow Fight, Whoa Fish, and Hat Poem

West Coast Stunts: Dive for Coins, Barter, Mouth, Horse Payoff, Bubble Gum, Tie to Tie, and R to W

A contestant must stand on one leg and act like a weathervane, speaking like a northerner (Eskimo with teeth chattering) to a Southerner, with each direction he is facing. Another contestant must dive for coins – three silver dollars in the bottom of a pan of water. He can keep the coins if he retrieves them using his mouth. The conclusion of last week's set-up is broadcast remotely from Grand Central Station and involves a horse!

Episodes #123 & 124, Broadcast of August 16, 1941

Both Coast Stunts: Seal, Clear Throat, Ankles, and Throw Pie

First anniversary show and a large birthday cake is on stage to prove it. Beulah cue botched at the beginning of the East Coast broadcast. A lady in the audience kibitzes with **Mel Allen** during the commercial break. Ralph Edwards reprises his favorite stunts from the past year, including a woman who is asked to mimic Edwards by repeating three different sentences – but forgets to clear her throat like he did at the beginning of the third sentence, forced to repeat the stunt again and again.

Episodes #125 & 126, Broadcast of August 23, 1941

East Coast Stunts: Bull Fiddle, Hoax, Mouth, Electric Fan, O-Wa-Ta-Goo-Siam, and Call to Dinner

West Coast Stunts: Flypaper, Tongue Twisters, Shoe Paddle, Hellzaswitch, E.R., and R to W

Broadcast originated from the Hippodrome Theatre in Baltimore, Maryland. A contestant has to sing "Daddy" as a real hep-cat, pretending to be the number one Jitterbug, using a six-foot bass fiddle as an instrument. A contestant, wearing gloves, slaps his hands onto flypaper and has to sing "The Hut Sut Song" while playing the banjo.

Episodes #127 & 128, Broadcast of August 30, 1941

East Coast Stunts: Dive for Coins, Movie Star, Barter, Job Hunter, and Tongue Twisters

West Coast Stunts: Brick Wall, Memory Test, Lip Reading, Phoning a Movie Star, and Bubble Gum

A contestant has to fetch silver dollars from a pan of water, while singing "Way Down Upon the Swanee River." This was the same stunt performed on August 9 but now with the addition of the contestant singing a song and humming under water. Another contestant has to eat his way through a wall of bricks – bricks of ice cream, that is.

Episodes #129 & 130, Broadcast of September 6, 1941

East Coast Stunts: Rope, Tongue Twisters, Recite in Key, E.R., Brick Wall, Tie a Tie, Five Nice Things, and Call to Dinner

West Coast Stunts: Grapefruit, Job Hunter, Shout Proposal, Trapeze, Meet a Ghost, and E.R.

A contestant must climb a rope hanging from the ceiling, while singing "For I'm a Jolly Good Fellow." While the contestant climbs, large fans start blowing wind against the contestant. Another contestant must deliver a speech on "Level Thinking" while changing key in his pitch whenever a musician off the side strikes a different key on the piano. Another contestant must sing "Drink to Me Only with Thine Eyes" while eating a grapefruit with a spoon.

Episodes #131 & 132, Broadcast of September 13, 1941

East Coast Stunts: Flypaper, Bladeless Knife-Phone, Calisthenics, Guess Snores, Count Them Again, and Bubble Gum

West Coast Stunts: Out Laugh-Out Cry, O-Wa-Ta-Goo-Siam, Electric Fan, Bladeless Knife-Phone, and Jack Be Nimble

A customer is blindfolded and randomly selects a phone number from the New York Telephone Directory. Their instructions are to call the number and convincingly sell them a bladeless knife without a handle. A knife without a blade, and it does not have a handle. They get a bonus if they succeed in selling the item. Two contestants are selected to spend the broadcast on stage, in separate chairs, on a special platform. Whenever Ralph Edwards yells "laugh" during the program, both of them were instructed to jump up and down and laugh as loud as they can. Whenever Edwards yelled "cry," they were to jump up and down and cry.

Episodes #133 & 134, Broadcast of September 20, 1941

East Coast Stunts: Pie Earing, Elephant #2, Funny Picture, Wrestler, Tap Dancer, and Pat Back

West Coast Stunts: Kisses, Wrestler, Elephant #2, Sponge, Come In, and Laugh Louder

Broadcast originated from the State Theatre in Hartford, Connecticut. The West Coast broadcast may have been the first use of a child contestant. The "Jumbo" elephant stunt from a prior broadcast was reprised. The elephant was used for the West Coast but the East Coast used a seal instead. A female contestant is supposed to receive three kisses on stage… candy kisses.

Episodes #135 & 136, Broadcast of September 27, 1941

East Coast Stunts: Kisses, World Series, Sponge, Columbus Circle, Race Horse, and Come In

West Coast Stunts: Syphons, Cheese, Columbus Circle, Hide Man, Minding the Twins, and Come In

A number of gentlemen have to sing "My Bonnie Lies Over the Ocean" and every time they mention the word "Bonnie," they squirt each other in the face with water from seltzer bottles. A contestant is taken out of the theatre and to New York's famous Columbus Circle where they have to deliver a real speech atop an Ivory Soap box. A microphone and an engineer captured the event to broadcast from location.

Episodes #137 & 138, Broadcast of October 4, 1941
East Coast Stunts: Age to Youth, Saw Man, Sailor, Whack, Count Again, and Laugh Louder
West Coast Stunts: Imitate Wife, Frame, Sailor, Funny Picture, and Laugh Louder
A contestant must sing "When You and I Were Young Maggie," starting out as a feeble old man, and ending as a blubbering baby. The changes must be gradual. A wife is convinced to saw her husband in half while he is lying in a long wooden box. While the wife is off stage, the husband is instructed to pretend the saw is really cutting him, complete with loud moans and agonizing wails.

Episodes #139 & 140, Broadcast of October 11, 1941
East Coast Stunts: Imitate Wife, Frame, Aquarium, and Dummy
West Coast Stunts: Age to Youth, Saw Man, Dummy, Whack, and Alphabet
Radio actress **Elsie May Gordon** participates in the "Imitate Wife" stunt where a husband has to answer questions from his hen-pecking wife (played by Gordon). In another stunt, a woman is taken off stage into a sound booth so the audience can be let in on the joke: she will return on stage to phone Mr. Fish and ask what he does, what he had for dinner, and where he lives. What she does not know is that she is phoning the local Aquarium.

Episodes #141 & 142, Broadcast of October 18, 1941
East Coast Stunts: Cut, Rodeo, Hag Voices, Hide Woman Switch, and Hammer Balloon
West Coast Stunts: Egg Race, Sell Hats, Hot Potato, Hide Man Switch, and Tap Dance
Two contestants must race to the finish line, walking backwards, with a spoon in their mouth. There is an egg in each spoon. Each contestant must recite the Humpty Dumpty poem while they walk backwards. In another stunt, a contestant is taken to Madison Square Garden where a rodeo is underway, to ride a wild bronc that happens to be a hobby horse. Radio announcer **Al Frazin** participates from the rodeo.

Episodes #143 & 144, Broadcast of October 25, 1941
East Coast Stunts: Hammer Balloon, Sell Hats, Whack, Slide, Egg Race, and Football
West Coast Stunts: Music Switch, Aquarium, Cut, Slide, Quick Imitate, and Bat Back
Broadcast originated from the Stanley Theatre in Pittsburgh, Pennsylvania. Contestants are blindfolded and provided a hammer to bust balloons, to the tune of "The Anvil Chorus." A married couple has to impersonate a saleslady selling hats at a hat shop, changing voices and impersonating various customers in a sketch.

Episodes #145 & 146, Broadcast of November 1, 1941
East Coast Stunts: Hammock, Ghost, Telephone Frame, Read Bumps, Paper Bag, and Quick Imitate
West Coast Stunts: Hag Voices, Hammock, Write Play, and Read Bumps
Radio actress **Ethel Owen** participates in the "Hag Voices" stunt, playing the role of three women, with the husband (the contestant) choosing which voice comes closest to his wife. The husband believes his wife is backstage providing one of the voices, but because all three voices were insults, they were all from Owen. But what if the husband thinks one belongs to his wife? In another stunt, a man is forced to dress in a sheet and pretend to be a ghost. Outside in the street, in front of the theatre, he is shouting "boo" and trying to scare passersby.

Episodes #147 & 148, Broadcast of November 8, 1941
Both Coast Stunts: Hut Sut Horn, Plant Mike, Picture Lap, Sammy Kaye, Globe, and Quick Imitate
A contestant is taken by taxi over to the Essex House overlooking Central Park to sing "I Don't Want to Set the World on Fire" with **Sammy Kaye** and his Orchestra. As would be expected when planting a hidden microphone in the ballroom, the East Coast broadcast did not fare as well as the West Coast. The sound quality was very poor in the room. For the West Coast, the microphone was placed differently to provide better sound for the same stunt.

Episodes #149 & 150, Broadcast of November 15, 1941
Both Coast Stunts: Flautist, Column, Parrot, Quick Imitate, and Corn on Cob

A contestant sings a song just like a famous operatic soprano, with one of the music world's leading flautists, **George Purcell**. A contestant believes he will carry on a conversation with a parrot that has been all over the world. While the contestant is off-stage to get into the same costume worn by the trainer, the audience is filled in on the joke: the bird has never been around the world and cannot speak a word of dialogue. In another stunt, a man phoned a soldier in Iceland to sing him a song, unaware the recipient on the opposite end of the line was his girlfriend in Des Moines, Iowa.

Episodes #151 & 152, Broadcast of November 22, 1941
East Coast Stunts: Piano, Arthur Murray, Call Names, Canal Zone, Bathtub, and Football
West Coast Stunts: Piano, Arthur Murray, Column, Canal Zone, Bathtub, and Jug Solo
A contestant must play "Oh Believe Me If All Those Endearing Young Charms" on a piano, while singing the lyrics, unaware that the piano is out of tune. Another contestant must instruct the audience how to properly waltz on stage, unaware that one of the members of the audience is **Arthur Murray**, the world's greatest authority on popular dancing. Another contestant talked with a soldier in Panama.

Episodes #153 & 154, Broadcast of November 29, 1941
East Coast Stunts: Apple Tree, Beauty Parade, Western Union, Salami, and Bathtub
West Coast Stunts: Mockingbird, Beauty Parade, Western Union, Drops, Call Names, and Seven Dwarfs
A contestant must sing "In the Shade of the Old Apple Tree" while substituting various words with various musical instruments. While another contestant delivers a speech, "There's No Place Like Home," three bathing beauties walk past him in an effort to distract him. The bathing beauties were **Miss Lillian O'Donnell** (Miss Westchester of 1939), **Miss Irmgard Dawson** (Miss Miami, Florida of 1940) and **Miss Pat Donnelly** (Miss America of 1939).

Episodes #155 & 156, Broadcast of December 6, 1941
East Coast Stunts: Ice Skating, Bathtub, Mike Howe, Saw Pie, and Marshmallow

West Coast Stunts: Ice Skating, Xylophone, Mike Howe, Salami, Marshmallow, and Jug Solo

Heine Brock, the famous trick ice-skater, participates in a stunt where a contestant is taken to Madison Square Garden, where he or she is fitted in an outlandish costume and asked to appear in the 1942 Ice Follies! The audience at the Garden were filled in before performance time as to the nature of the act.

Episodes #157 & 158, Broadcast of December 13, 1941

East Coast Stunts: French Horn, Chloe, Beau Brummel, and Poor Bachelor

West Coast Stunts: Balloon Shoes, Beau Brummel, Fast Recording, Chloe, and Marshmallow

A contestant is asked to take off her shoes and jump over a candle, reciting "Jack Be Nimble." When Edwards tells her to "take off your shoes and jump over them," he is referring to the shoes, not the candle, and wants to see if she follows instructions specifically. Another contestant has to recite "I Am the Best-Dressed Man in America" 100 times while dressed in a big pair of balloon pants, satin vest with horses on it, and a plug hat with a geranium growing out of it. During the stunt a cameraman snaps a picture and the contestant discovers his photo will appear in the Hart, Schaffer & Marx Fashion advertisement in next week's newspaper, illustrating to men "How Not to Dress."

Episodes #159 & 160, Broadcast of December 20, 1941

East Coast Stunts: Professor Sooey, Fast Recording, Major Bowes, and Santa Claus

West Coast Stunts: Professor Sooey, Santa Claus, Major Bowes, Poor Bachelor, and Seven Dwarfs

A contestant believes they are trying out for a role at the Metropolitan Opera, singing the vowels of the alphabet in key. They are unaware that Professor Sooey, acting as judge behind the stage, is nothing but a real live pig sitting in a wheelchair.

Episodes #161 & 162, Broadcast of December 27, 1941

East Coast Stunts: Neckties, Obstacles, Harmony, Dr. Smith, Seven Dwarfs, and Marshmallow

West Coast Stunts: Lost Consequence, Obstacles, Re-Propose, Dr. Smith, Hot

Licks, and Seven Dwarfs

Four male contestants are asked to remove their neckties and replace them with ones with embarrassing designs. To look inconspicuous among the audience, the men are asked to wear long fake beards throughout the broadcast. In another consequence, Edwards sends a man down to the NBC soda shop, wearing a red carnation. Another contestant is sent down there a few minutes later to throw a pie into the face of the man wearing the carnation. The victim's wife is then handed a pie and instructed to throw it into the face of the man who threw the pie.

Episodes #163 & 164, Broadcast of January 3, 1942

East Coast Stunts: Eggs, Town Hall, Dog Show, Lost Consequences, Seven Dwarfs, and Marshmallow

West Coast Stunts: Eggs, Remote Band, Bed Time Story, Moose Call, Marshmallow, and Seven Dwarfs

The announcer opens the broadcast with a recap of 1941: "We give you the man who in 1941 locked a contestant out of the theatre, broke up a Broadway show with another contestant, walked a man into a ten-foot tank of water, and had 137 custard pies tossed into 14 innocent faces." A five-year-old boy, **Bobby Hookey**, participates in a bed-time story stunt. Hookey was reported by *Newsweek* as "the youngest star ever to have his own weekly network program." Hookey provided song and talk for his own radio program, *Rocking Horse Rhythms*, and got his start on *The Horn and Hardart Children's Hour*.

Episodes #165 & 166, Broadcast of January 10, 1942

East Coast Stunts: Slendro Massager, Dumbo, Bed Time Story, Play Back, Elevator Operator, and Hot Licks

West Coast Stunts: Slendro Massager, Dumbo, Dog Show, Ring Bell, Marshmallow, and Seven Dwarfs

The machine called the "Slendro Massager" used in the first stunt was borrowed from a MacLevy Slenderizing Salon in New York City. It vibrates the contestant into shedding weight and the contestant must sing "A Pretty Girl is Like a Melody" while using the machine. In another stunt, a man is taken off stage into a private dressing room to put on a rigged flying suit complete with wings, to see if a man can fly like the elephant *Dumbo*.

Episodes #167 & 168, Broadcast of January 17, 1942

East Coast Stunts: Jap Dishes, Embassy, Model Date, Presser, Moose Call, and Suspend Apple

West Coast Stunts: Jap Dishes, Embassy, Spray Donkey, Suspend Apple, and Seven Dwarfs

A contestant is given the chance to blow off a lot of steam by participating in three dish-breaking sessions. The first two requires him to shout at his wife when smashing dishes, but the fun is discovering how the contestant reacts as he smashes the third set, after reading what is written on the back of the dishes: "Made in Japan." One of the contestants is asked to sing a song without laughing, unaware that three men – her husband included – will parade past her, dressed like bathing beauties.

Episodes #169 & 170, Broadcast of January 24, 1942

East Coast Stunts: Girdle Race, Remote Band, Sabu, Postal Telegraph, Remote Band, Bird Cage, and Vacuum Cleaner

West Coast Stunts: Girdle Race, Sabu, Postal Telegraph, Model Date, Hot Licks, and Vacuum Cleaner

A contestant gets to take a Harry Conover Model out on a date, **Miss Ona Toth**, starting off at the Stork Club, greeted by the famous host, **Sherman Billingsley**. Another contestant is instructed to send a coded telegraph to a stranger, asking if they love her and would they kiss her, signed Cuddles. What she does not know is that the recipient is a three-year-old.

Episodes #171 & 172, Broadcast of January 31, 1942

East Coast Stunts: Jump Over Shoes, Maternity, X-Ray, Birthday Cake, Maternity, Vacuum Cleaner, and One Man Drama

West Coast Stunts: Play Back, Maternity, Buttons, X-Ray, Maternity, First Date, and Wash Face

Broadcast originated from the Taft Auditorium in Cincinnati, Ohio. A contestant is taken by taxi to a Cincinnati Maternity Hospital on Auburn Street and instructed to find the Chief Nurse on duty and convince her that he is a five-day-old baby who strayed from his crib. A hidden microphone set up in the hospital broadcasts the event as it happens. One of two female contestants participate in an X-Ray stunt, the winner crowned "Mrs. Cincinnati."

Episodes #173 & 174, Broadcast of February 7, 1942

East Coast Stunts: Dempsey, Telephone Bark, Relinquish Consequence, Telephone Bark, Husband's Knees, Saw Hammer, First Date, and Babbling Brook

West Coast Stunts: Dempsey, Remote Love, Telephone Bark, Husband's Knees, Vacuum Cleaner, and Babbling Brook

Two contestants are blindfolded and forced to feed each other blackberry pie. To ensure they do not make a mess on each other, great big towels are placed around their neck. A contestant is encouraged to listen to the voice of a special guest, located offstage. The special guest is the heavyweight champion, **Jack Dempsey**.

Episodes #175 & 176, Broadcast of February 14, 1942

East Coast Stunts: Pneumatic Hammer, Now Listen, Hi Low Jack & A Dame, Cupid, Spray Donkey, First Date, and Babbling Brook

West Coast Stunts: Cinderella, Pneumatic Hammer, Indications, Cupid, Cinderella, Valentine, and Vacuum Cleaner

Beginning with this episode, in cooperation with the Treasury Department, the prize structure changed. All contestants who answer their questions correctly will be awarded with $15 in U.S. Defense Stamps. If the contestant misses the question and has to take the consequences, they receive $5 in U.S. Defense Stamps and five cakes of Ivory Soap. Radio listeners who submitted the best consequence of the evening receives a $25 U.S. Defense Bond. Behind the scenes, the producers of the program made specific notes that the Pneumatic Hammer and Cupid stunts went over extremely well.

This broadcast features the famous Cinderella stunt in which a contestant receives an outfit chosen by the fashion designer, **Sophie Gimbel**, a wardrobe from Saks Fifth Avenue in Beverly Hills, California, and treatment from Antoine, the world-famous hair stylist, and **Robert De Long**, the Hollywood makeup artist.

Episodes #177 & 178, Broadcast of February 21, 1942

East Coast Stunts: Dog Fight, Prison, Washington, Head, and Diaper

West Coast Stunts: Dog Fight, Prison, Washington, Head, Bird Cage, and Vacuum Cleaner

A contestant is encouraged to talk to the owner of a movie theatre, over the phone, and convince the manager that she can get in for free – but she cannot use the words "theatre" or "movie." What she does not know is that the phone call is not placed to a movie theatre, but to a prison warden.

Episodes #179 & 180, Broadcast of February 28, 1942
East Coast Stunts: Cinderella, Ham Sandwich, Rosko, Gorilla, Roller Skates, Alphabet, and Remote Love
West Coast Stunts: Diaper, Rosko, Relinquish Consequence, Gorilla, Roller Skates, and Alphabet
The Cinderella stunt in this episode involves **Christian Jungst**, the world-famous hair stylist, Miss Diane, a makeup artist from the Helena Rubinstein Salon, a manicurist and a seamstress. For another stunt, an R.A.F. Officer was a contestant. A contestant has to change the diaper of a baby – in this case the baby is **Dave Ballard**, seven feet, seven inches tall and 390 pounds.

Episodes #181 & 182, Broadcast of March 7, 1942
East Coast Stunts: Murphy Bed, Grimderella, Arsenic & Old Lace, Black Eye, Love Birds, and Alphabet
West Coast Stunts: Arsenic & Old Lace, Grimderella, Murphy Bed, Black Eye, Love Birds, and Read Menu
This broadcast marks the only time Ralph Edwards was ill and had to miss the broadcast. The opposite of the Cinderella stunt of last week, a female contestant must dress in men's clothes, with a barber and makeup man unglamoring her. Another contestant is taken over to the Fulton Theatre on West 48th Street to take a curtain bow as one of the twelve corpses in *Arsenic and Old Lace*.

Episodes #183 & 184, Broadcast of March 14, 1942
East Coast Stunts: Chinese Theatre, Last Mile, Mother & Daughter, and Hen Party
West Coast Stunts: Chinese Theatre, Twinkle, Hang Clothes, Mother & Daughter, and Ham Sandwich
A contestant is taken to a legitimate New York Theatre on Broadway to play the part in a stage play, delivering his lines to the King as he hands over the message. Only after the contestant leaves is the audience let in on the trick: he is being sent to the famous Canton Chinese Theatre deep in the heart of

Chinatown. Another contestant sings "I'd Climb the Highest Mountain" on the stage with a 150-pound ball and chain to each foot.

Episodes #185 & 186, Broadcast of March 21, 1942
Both Coast Stunts: Bite Dog, Shower, London, What Am I Doing?, Visit from Mother, Shower, Spring, Brooklyn Fan, and Read Menu

During the broadcast there was a remote pick-up from England, between an Irish boy in London and an Irish girl who was a contestant. Remote was broadcast from 8:32 to 8:34 p.m. and on the repeat show from 11:12 to 11:14 p.m. **Harry Hutchinson** was the Irishman in London for both broadcasts. It was announced that this was the Second Anniversary show and to celebrate, Edwards and crew made sure one of the contestants (a serviceman) received a visit from his mother.

Episodes #187 & 188, Broadcast of March 28, 1942
East Coast Stunts: Stand-In, Telephone Scott, Peel Potatoes, Twinkle, and Shoot Japs

West Coast Stunts: Last Mile, Visit from Mother, Telephone Scott, Hi-Low Jack and a Dame, and Shoot Japs

Broadcast originated from the Marine Base in Quantico, Virginia. This was the first episode to be broadcast from a Service Camp. The crew of the quiz show is in Virginia to attend the premiere performance of 20th Century Fox's new movie, *To the Shores of Tripoli*, dedicated to the United States Marines. In acknowledgement, all of the contestants on this broadcast are Marines. One contestant failed to answer his question correctly and as his consequence, peel enough potatoes to feed an army.

Episodes #189 & 190, Broadcast of April 4, 1942
East Coast Stunts: Camel, Roxy, Easter Egg, Hope Emerson, Spring, and Read Menu

West Coast Stunts: Camel, Roxy, Easter Egg, Hope Emerson, and Spring

A contestant sang "The Campbells Are Coming," substituting the word "Campbells" to "Camels," and ultimately comes face to face with a real live camel on stage. In an effort to lay an egg, a contestant is sent to the Roxy Theatre by cab, where they are to participate on the floor show by delivering the worst jokes they can come up with.

Episodes #191 & 192, Broadcast of April 11, 1942

East Coast Stunts: Balloon Sing, Christen Boat, Skunk, Hookey, and Babbling Brook

West Coast Stunts: Skunk, Metropolitan, Deep in Texas, and Twins

A contestant is asked to call someone a skunk and before he can perform the task, finds himself sitting next to a real live skunk. After the audience calms down and observes the man making love to the skunk, he is instructed to take the animal down to the audience and offer it as a fur neck piece to the first girl he meets. (The skunk was de-scented, but the contestant and audience did not know that.)

A married couple find themselves singing "Deep in the Heart of Texas" and smacking their hand in tempo in the right spot. To complicate their task, a rope is tied to each of their wrists and two husky fellows hold the rope to prevent them from clapping. Edwards proposes suspending an egg between their hands so they could aim for it, and the men were secretly instructed not to hold them back, allowing them to crush the hardboiled egg on cue. On top of the five dollars of Savings Stamps and five cakes of Ivory Soap, the contestants receive an extra dollar for every clap they managed to perform.

Mr. Edward Johnson, General Manager of the Metropolitan Opera is in attendance and tries out a female contestant for the possibility of signing her up. She is asked to sing a high "C" and hold it long enough for him to gauge her performance. Only after he approves and signs her to a one-year contract does the woman discover Mr. Johnson is of the Metropolitan Casualty Insurance Company, and she won a free year of accident insurance. "With a voice like that," Edwards says, "you're liable to get hit in the head." The "Metropolitan" stunt is done for the East Coast the next week.

Episodes #193 & 194, Broadcast of April 18, 1942

East Coast Stunts: Metropolitan, Fry Egg, Life Begins, and Sword Swallower

West Coast Stunts: Balloon Sing, Fry Eggs, Life Begins, and Sword Swallower

A husband stands at an electric stove, playing the role of a housewife, to fix breakfast: toast, eggs and coffee. His wife is invited on stage to play the role of the husband, henpecking for her breakfast. **Mel Allen** and Ralph Edwards play the role of the two children in the sketch. The husband burns the food and as a result, is forced to eat his meal. (He is taken off stage and not allowed to eat the food, regardless of what the radio audience is told.)

Inspired by a book, *Life Begins at Forty*, a male contestant is brought on stage and dressed as a baby; complete with baby hat, baby bottle and three-cornered pants. Forty mothers from the Mother Club in Greenwich Village School in New York come out on stage and they put the contestant in a baby carriage. They take the baby downstairs to the Soda Fountain and buy them all a soda. He is given money to buy the soda but as Edwards remarks, after the contestant is off the stage, "he will look pretty silly to the hundreds of other people watching… but, that's the price you pay."

Episodes #195 & 196, Broadcast of April 25, 1942
East Coast Stunts: Lip Switch, Announces Contest, Make Laugh, and Twins
West Coast Stunts: Christen Boat, Lip Switch, Announcer Contest, and Love Insurance
As one of his consequences, a contestant had to take part in an Announcer's Audition with **Milton Cross**, **Ben Grauer** and **David Ross**. Each of the three men demonstrate the ease of reading such lines as "Buy now and save!" and "It floats." (Referring to Ivory soap.) When the contestant is ready to deliver his line, he discovers he is to read, "Strict Stephen slickly snared six sickly silky snakes. Slim Sam swam over the sea. Swim, Slim Sam, Swim! Swim Slim back to me." The audience judged the announcers and determined the best announcer. Because each of the announcers were employed on competitive quiz programs, Edwards provided a generous moment for each of them to name the quiz show they work on.

Episodes #197 & 198, Broadcast of May 2, 1942
East Coast Stunts: Maypole, Gas Substitute, Love Insurance, Knives, and Spring Tonic
West Coast Stunts: Dishpan, Hookey, Gas Substitute, and Kisses Wife
Because everyone is adjusting to the new gasoline rationing, a contestant is provided with something that is promised to take the place of gasoline… a horse! If she doesn't want to take the horse home with her, she will be given a free buggy ride home to avoid the crowded subway.
A contestant is asked to roll his pants up and play the role of four-year-old **Bobby Hookey** of the *Horn and Hardart Children's Hour*. The real Bobby Hookey walks out on stage and the two perform a duet together, "If You Knew Susie."

A contestant is asked to light a loaded cigar and smoke it while singing "I Don't Want to Set the World on Fire." Edwards is curious to know if the contestant can finish the song before the cigar explodes in his face. After the stunt, the contestant discovers the cigar was not really loaded after all.

Ralph Edwards makes a reference to the birth of his first child on both broadcasts.

Episodes #199 & 200, Broadcast of May 9, 1942
East Coast Stunts: Dishpan, My Gal Sal, Husbands Legs, and NBC Tour
West Coast Stunts: Make Laugh, Tarzan, My Gal Sal, and Knives

A contestant is asked to kneel with his head over a pail of water. An NBC pageboy brings in a regular guided tour on stage and every time a woman asks a question, the contestant is to dunk his head in the pail of water and shout, "I love it!" If a man asks a question, he can stay where he is. If he fails to dunk his head when a woman asks a question, he will be paddled from the rear. The entire audience is instructed not to inform the studio-guided tour why the contestant dunks his head in the water. One of the women in the tour was a plant, designed to ask multiple questions after a couple minutes of honest questioning: "May I ask a question, sir?" and "Could I get a couple of tickets to *Truth or Consequences*?" and "Can I write in right away" and "Can I be sure you'll take care of me?" and finally "Who shall I write to?"

The script for this broadcast indicates that if the NBC pageboy was not granted permission to be broadcast over the air, with permission from the American Federation of Radio Artists, announcer **Pete Donald** was to temporarily take over as the page.

Episodes #201 & 202, Broadcast of May 16, 1942
East Coast Stunts: Cigar, Pie Problem, Tarzan, and Dive Bomber
West Coast Stunts: Maypole, Pie Problem, Duck Chick, and Dive Bomber

A stunt originally involving **Rudy Vallee** had to be replaced with a "Tarzan" stunt. The wife is asked to go behind the stage so **Mel Allen** can tell her the name of a famous person of fiction or history to represent. Then she would return to the stage to convey to her husband the character she is imitating. She gets an extra $10 if he succeeds in solving the identity in sixty seconds. While she is off the stage, the husband is informed who she is supposed to imitate and if he can guess anyone other than Tarzan, watching her tear her hair out in desperation, he will win $11.

Flipping a coin to determine who gets to be the target, the husband of a married couple sits cross-legged, Indian-style, with a football helmet and catcher's mask on, and a raincoat draped about him. As he sang "Singin' in the Rain," on a steeplejack chair, his wife dropped water balloons on him. For every balloon that struck its mark, she received $5.00 extra. What was not revealed during the broadcast was that the coin Ralph Edwards flipped was rigged so the husband would become the victim, not the wife.

Episodes #203 & 204, Broadcast of May 23, 1942
East Coast Stunts: Sing Paddle, Mud Pack, Daddy Dear, and Kisses Wife
West Coast Stunts: Sing Paddle, Mud Pack, Daddy Dear, and Guess Where
The husband is required to remember the words of the old song, "Pack up Your Troubles in Your Old Kit Bag." When Edwards yells the word "sing," the husband must talk the words. When Edwards says "talk," the husband must sing the words. Every time the contestant misses a word, or sings/talks the lyrics incorrectly, his wife gets to spank him with a paddle.
A sailor gets a chance to have a date with a famous Harry Conover cover girl model, about to appear on magazine covers and advertisements coast-to-coast. One of New York City's finest barbers, **Mr. Sol Spizza**, gives the sailor a neck trim. A gentleman shines his shoes. A manicurist takes care of his face with a mudpack. When the model arrives, she finds him wearing an apron, missing shoes and a mudpack on his face... and she takes him off stage to the Stork Club in that same condition! (As soon as he arrives at the Club, he will be able to take off the haircloths, mud pack and have his shoes returned.)

Episodes #205 & 206, Broadcast of May 30, 1942
East Coast Stunts: Jump Bills, Follow Leader, Small Town B.U., Sugar Escort, and Cook Roast
West Coast Stunts: Jump Balls, Mirror Man, Small Town B.U., Laundry List, and NBC Tour
A wife is called on stage and has to cook and prepare an outlandish dish named by her husband, who remains seated in the audience. What she doesn't know is that her husband is in on the gag and has the recipe all written out in advance. He is placed right down into the giant kettle and everything his wife puts in will fall on him. The kettle is so high that she will have to reach up to throw the ingredients inside. A microphone at the bottom of the kettle will

pick up her husband's voice. She has no idea he is inside and thanks to the microphone, and a speaker, will believe he is still sitting among the audience. The recipe includes a pinch of salt, two quarts of sawdust, a bushel of beet tops, another pinch of salt, a tumbler of water, then the tumbler itself, two old overshoes, and finally two large flounders.

Two women are asked to ring eight bells, four per contestant. Each rings a different note to "do-re-mi-fa-so-la-ti-do" and a few are tied to their ankles. They are then asked to ring certain bells in a certain order to play a song.

At the beginning of this broadcast, Ralph Edwards thanks the listening audience for answering the plea he made on last week's broadcast. "I wanna say thanks to every one of you who wrote and pledged to share your car with friends and neighbors. Gee, we got thousands of pledges – from you, and you – and I've sent 'em to the War Production Board in Washington. We'd like to see more of those pledges, too. Just write on a penny postcard, 'I pledge to share my car with my friends and neighbors.' Sign it, and sent it to me, Ralph Edwards, care of the National Broadcasting Company, New York City. Do it, friends, won't ya? It means a lot."

Episodes #207 & 208, Broadcast of June 6, 1942

East Coast Stunts: Town Band, Celebrity, Furlough, and Seal in Tub
West Coast Stunts: Town Band, Celebrity, Husband's Legs, and Seal in Tub

This broadcast originates from the home of **Daniel A. Doyle** of West Townsend, Massachusetts, a contestant who was on the program May 30. Last week Mrs. Doyle was attending *Truth or Consequences* and missed her question. She said she was from a small town. Edwards asked about her neighbors, the size of her front parlor, and eventually finagled an invitation from her to come up and meet the folks. The entire staff of fourteen people moved in over the weekend and the radio program was broadcast from her front parlor. Her neighbors and friends became contestants.

One contestant had to wash the dishes before Townsend's famous 29-piece brass band performs a song. The contestant's wife led the musicians. One contestant must go into Mr. Doyle's bathroom and croon to the object of his desire… not a bathing baby, but a real live seal. Cadwalider is the seal's name and when people sing, the seal loves to join them!

Reprising a scene from *Our Town*, a contestant played the role of a small-town boy in love with the beautiful neighbor girl, working up enough courage to tell her at the corner drug store soda fountain. The role of the beautiful girl is played by Hollywood actress **Martha Scott**, who makes a guest appearance on the program.

Episodes #209 & 210, Broadcast of June 13, 1942
East Coast Stunts: Permanent Wave, Guess When, June Bride, Woman Wrestler, and Fill in Word
West Coast Stunts: Permanent Wave, Mask, June Bride, Woman Wrestler, and Inhale
In mailing out tickets this week, the producers went through thousands and thousands of weekly requests and picked out as many couples as they could find who were going to get married this month. One couple was asked questions, separately, to find out how much they know about each other. Questions included "Have you kissed any other girls?" and "When is her mother's birthday?" Correct answers gave the bride a credit slip for a pair of shoes for the bride, a lovely handbag, etc. Incorrect answers gave him a scooter to get out of town when the mother-in-law arrives, a catcher's mask, and a ball and chain. After the game, the couple wins three round-trip tickets to Niagara Falls… so they can take the mother-in-law with them.
One male contestant is sent backstage to get into a ballet costume. He is told he will do a ballet dance with Madame Babette Tyana, a famous dancer. In really, Tyana is a professional woman wrestler, known as the strongest woman in the world. Together, they perform "The Aftermath of the Fawn."

Episodes #211 & 212, Broadcast of June 20, 1942
Both Coast Stunts: Whittle, Girl in Port, Whipped Cream, and Picture Tank
Broadcast originated from the Naval Training Station in Norfolk, Virginia. Contestants during this broadcast were servicemen. Instead of the usual prizes, this episode rewarded servicemen $15 cash for the truthful answer, instead of $5 in War Stamps.
Since every gun pointer knows it is his job to keep his eye on the target, they bring out a branch from an apple tree and hand the contestant a jackknife. He is to sing, "Don't Sit Under the Apple Tree with Anyone Else But Me." He is instructed to keep whittling and singing, without taking his eyes off the branch. Chief Petty Officers are instructed to keep guard of his eyes and report if he deviates. Meanwhile, Ralph Edwards and **Ed Herlihy** start

a sketch that involves two men getting into a fight, shooting a gun, and a bloodcurdling scream... all over a beautiful woman. The contestant did not falter but he did nick his finger when the gun went off. As Edwards checked in on the contestant, a terrific crash from a sound effects record is played and Edwards made it appear as if a runaway car was about to crash on them... and the contestant almost looked over. In the final attempt to make him lose the game, **Miss Kay Gammon**, known as Miss Knoxville of 1941, walked on stage in a bathing suit and promises to give the sailor a kiss if he was willing to lose the $5 wager.

Episodes #213 & 214, Broadcast of June 27, 1942
East Coast Stunts: Bob for Apples, Resuscitation, Audience, and Soldier Frame
West Coast Stunts: Bob for Apples, Resuscitation, Audience, Soldier Frame, and B-Flat
Broadcast originated from Camp Robinson in Little Rock, Arkansas. Contestants during this broadcast were servicemen. Instead of the usual prizes, this episode rewarded servicemen $15 cash for the truthful answer, instead of $5 in War Stamps.
Sergeant Dick Rau had to lay on the floor on his stomach while another Sergeant used his back to practice artificial respiration. This was performed while Rau had the opportunity to talk to his girlfriend, back home, on the phone. He was not allowed to tell her he was on the quiz program.
Miss Anne Mahaffey, a famous model from Little Rock, is told to go into the back room with a Private, to rehearse a romance scene on stage. Since love is blind, both will be blindfolded. While in the back, Edwards informs the audience that another Private will be forced to wear a blonde wig. The contestant from the back room comes out, blindfolded, and discovers that he is caressing the hair of a beautiful girl and talks romance to her... not realizing who it really is.
At the conclusion of this broadcast, Edwards informs the audience that he and his crew are going to spend part of the summer entertaining servicemen throughout the country, spending two weeks in Hollywood to take part in the new RKO picture, *Sweet and Hot* (later re-titled and released as *Seven Days Leave*), and a week of Summer stock up at Holyoke, Mass.

Episodes #215 & 216, Broadcast of August 16, 1942

Both Coast Stunts: Watermelon Bugle, Make Blush, Visit from Sweetheart, and Pass the Key

Sponsored by the U.S. Government, *Victory Parade* was a short-lived radio program that aired over NBC during the summer of 1942. As part of the weekly offerings, various talent of radio from **Red Skelton** to **Fanny Brice** donated their time to remind radio listeners of the importance of purchasing war bonds. On the evening of August 16, Ralph Edwards and crew agreed to participate from Mitchell Field on Long Island, with a *Truth or Consequences* presentation. While these two broadcasts (East and West Coast) were not broadcast as part of the *Truth or Consequences* season, Edwards' production company considered these as official entries in the series, which is why they retain the official consecutive numbering system.

Episodes #217 & 218, Broadcast of September 12, 1942

Both Coast Stunts: Wedding Guest, Eight Candles, M.C. Switch, and WAAC Girdles

A female contestant is sent to the beautiful Grill Room of the Hotel Astor on Times Square, where there is a wedding going on. She is the unexpected guest who takes no part in the ceremony and sits quietly until the Justice asks if anyone has an objection to the wedlock. She is then instructed to jump up and shout her objection, "The Groom likes to roll up his pants legs and go barefooted in the rain." A microphone is planted in the floral arrangement, and what the contestant does not know is that actors were rehearsing a scene in a play at the time she appears. The Bride and Groom are nothing more than two window store dummies. With the lights low and escorted inside moments before she is to make her startling announcement, the stunt was sure to be pulled off.

A contestant switches places with Ralph Edwards moments before an NBC Guided Studio Tour enters. The contestant is to pretend he is the host of the radio program and Edwards the contestant. If he can successfully carry off the show without any guests of the guided tour catching on to the switch, he receives an extra $25 War Bond.

Episodes #219 & 220, Broadcast of September 19, 1942
East Coast Stunts: Bicycle, Greased Rope, Hostess, and Pants
West Coast Stunts: Bicycle, Grandfathers Clock, 26 Pies, and Hostess
In these days of gas rationing, a married couple must demonstrate their contribution for the war cause. A husband peddles a bicycle down Broadway in New York while his wife rides with him... on the handlebars. Several NBC engineers wait down at 48th and Broadway with a pack transmitter, to broadcast the two singing "Bicycle Built for Two," while coming down the street.
A contestant is instructed to put on a pair of overalls over his clothes and climb up a rope to grab a purchase order for a $25 War Bond. If he can perform the task while singing "The Daring Young Man on the Flying Trapeze," he will be awarded the Bond. What he does not discover until he starts his task is that the rope is greased half way up to the end. The upper half of the rope proves a challenge.

Episodes #221 & 222, Broadcast of September 26, 1942
East Coast Stunts: Grandfathers Clock, 26 Pies, Mass Consequence, Tony Galento, and California Chocolates
West Coast Stunts: Greased Rope, Mass Consequence, Pants, Cabbage Head, Dixie Cup, and Tongue Sandwich
Broadcast originated from the Capitol Theatre in Washington, D.C. where Edwards and his crew were on stage for one full week. A husband places his head through a hole in a wooden screen, with a sheet over his head, while his wife is sent to the prop room, marked "Torture Chamber." She is told to select a handful of items for which she can hit her husband in the head. While she is off stage, the husband is escorted out and a head of cabbage is substituted. The husband is instructed to shout "ouch" every time the head of cabbage is struck. She is then told she will win money for each time she hits her husband in the head. Grapefruit, an old shoe, a horseshoe, and a sledge hammer... in that order. Question: How far will she go before she hesitates using the more dangerous props?

Episodes #223 & 224, Broadcast of October 3, 1942

East Coast Stunts: Allied Chorus, Bench Phone, World Series B.U., Remember Names, and Giovanni

West Coast Stunts: Allied Chorus, Horse Phone, World Series B.U., Remember Names, and Giovanni

The first contestant failed to answer correctly and must sing "Over There" with participants from Russia (**Mr. Efrim Vitis**), China (**Lee Ling Ai**) and Brazil (**Sampayo Brandao**), to show the strong unity and friendship "that exists among all of us who are allies."

A St. Louis baseball fan and a New York Yankees fan agree to wager the outcome of the World Series this week. The loser agrees to push a baseball across the four bases with their nose, in the darkened baseball stadium, while singing "Take Me Out to the Ballgame." Results will be reported next week.

Also in this episode is a horse race with two men and two women, originally planned to be a barrel race until horse costumes were made available.

Episodes #225 & 226, Broadcast of October 10, 1942

Both Coast Stunts: Run Scale, Million Kisses, World Series, and Adopted Family

In a follow-up from last week's wager, **Raymond Bastow** of Springfield, Massachusetts, and **Harry Kushins** of St. Louis, Missouri, meet again and Bastow has to push a baseball across the four bases with his nose, in the stadium at St. Louis, while singing "Take Me Out to the Ballgame."

Lucille Lambert, Conover cover girl, billed as "a West Coast girl taking New York by storm," makes a guest appearance in this episode in a stunt involving lipstick and a dishpan full of water. Edwards invited the radio listeners to perform the same stunt in their living rooms.

Episodes #227 & 228, Broadcast of October 17, 1942

East Coast Stunts: Bucket Brigade, Egg Baby, and Rodeo

West Coast Stunts: Bucket Brigade, Egg Baby, Remote Control, and Foreign Orders

Broadcast originated from the Rhode Island Auditorium in Providence, Rhode Island. A contestant named "Cyclone," known in real life as Mr. Butler, is introduced as the "world's greatest cowboy" while riding his horse, Thunderbolt… a little old donkey. He has to sing "Git Along Little Doggies" while riding atop the donkey and before the song is over, dozens of donkeys are put into the arena, many joining in the vocals. Mr. Butler won the grand prize of a $25 War Bond for his participation in the rodeo.

Episodes #229 & 230, Broadcast of October 24, 1942
East Coast Stunts: Service Romeos, Giant Post Cards, Junior Cover Girl, and Foreign Orders
West Coast Stunts: Bond Salesman, Hand Spray, Letter to Hitler, House Wives Trio, and Age 7 Reactions
A woman is asked to participate on stage with a number of servicemen in a musical sketch. (Organ music performed by **Bill Meeder**.) When she hears "Anchors Aweigh," the sailor has the spotlight, and the girl. When the organ plays "From the Halls of Montezuma," the Marines have landed. When the organ plays "The Caissons Go Rolling Along," the solider takes over. The soldiers are reminded that romantic build-ups need to be the condensed version.
Efrim Vitis, the Russian singer who appeared on the program last week, returns for the same stunt, "Foreign Orders," in which a wife has to interpret what he is saying in Russian. Her husband is prepared on stage to take the consequences. Grapefruit, a bowl of whipped cream and a paddle is on the table. She has three chances to win the $5 by interpreting what Mr. Vitis is asking her to do. If she misses all three, her husband gets the prize money.

Episodes #231 & 232, Broadcast of October 31, 1942
East Coast Stunts: Candle Procession, Pig Milk Race, Halloween, and Adopt Pilot
West Coast Stunts: Candle Procession, Pig Milk Race, Halloween, Adopt Pilot, and Dark, Isn't It?
The first Halloween victim of the evening is asked to blow out the candles in the torch procession of the spooks – 25 members of the audience in the front section each holding a lighted candle. They slowly parade by her and for every candle she blows out, she receives a 25 cent War Stamp. For each one missed, the spook holding the candle gets the War Stamp. And she must sing, "I Don't Want to Set the World on Fire" during the entire stunt. What she is not aware is that the fifth person has an enormous candle, the ninth person has a battery flashlight (a fake candle) and the last person has a candelabra with six candles on it.

A married couple are invited on stage for a Halloween stunt. The husband is placed into a wooden box, the lid locked, and chains secured to ensure that he cannot escape. There are hundreds of holes on the lid so he can breathe. The wife is told to go backstage and get into the Little Bo Creep costume and hat, unaware that her husband was quietly removed from the box, escorted to the clients' booth above the stage, furnished with a microphone. Every time the wife, blindfolded, stuck a spear into the box, she could hear her husband scream from the speaker inside. She walked on eggshells and was told it was broken glass. A hairnet brushed her face and she was told it was spider webs. The lamb she was supposed to have next to her was a lamb chop.

As a public service reminder, a young couple must face the consequence of adopting a boy for the duration of the War. "He is one of thousands of boys who because of some minor defect such as not quite enough schooling, a minor operation, his teeth… or some similar reason has been turned down by the Army or Navy Air Services. The American Flying Services Foundation, a voluntary non-profit organization, rehabilitates these boys… fixes up their minor defects… physical or scholastic or what now… to enable them to become flyers. Ten thousand boys have sought assistance of the A.F.S.F. This organization has a plan whereby families or clubs or schools or any organized group or individual can donate $100 towards rehabilitating a pilot applicant. This club or family may have a picture of the boy… his history… may write to him and get a play by play account of how he makes out in the War."

A young couple is asked to become "Air Parents" of a young boy, **Erich Ericson** of Brooklyn, New York, who is introduced on stage. After the formal introduction, they are told to go back stage and get acquainted. The couple really wasn't required to adopt if circumstances would not allow, but Edwards explained that the quiz program would pay the $100 applicant fee if they chose to adopt during the War. "I know they will find as much pleasure as all the other families and clubs who have donated through the American Flying Services Foundation and adopted a young man who would be a pilot and fight for the country he worships." Just for participating, the couple win $5.00 in War Stamps and five cakes of Ivory Soap.

For the West Coast broadcast, Edwards provides the listening audience with an update regarding the War Bond Consequence of last week. The mother of a soldier boy, Mrs. Brenner of New York, whose son was at Camp Shelby, Mississippi, was instructed to provide a thirty-second speech that would sell over $10,000 in War Bonds by telephone. If she accomplished her task in raising that much money, the quiz program would give her a trip with all-expenses paid to visit her son at his service camp. Not only did she hit the $10,000 mark, but the total pledges were $108,976.00 in War Bonds. (In the weeks that followed, a special mention was made that KGIR in Butte, Montana, successfully raised over $50,000 of this figure as a result of the broadcast.) As a result, Mrs. Brenner gets to see her son at his camp in Mississippi. Mrs. Brenner herself was a member of the American Women's Voluntary Service and it was revealed that she had a second son in the service in Honolulu, and she was given the opportunity to call him on the phone. "So now a good many more weapons can be made to crack the axis with the money you pledged," Edwards told the listening audience. "Thanks for your loyalty."

Episodes #233 & 234, Broadcast of November 7, 1942
East Coast Stunts: Dunk Donut, Meeder Stand-In, Chimp, and Mimic
West Coast Stunts: Dunk Donut, Bench Apple, Chimp, and Mimic
Broadcast originated from the Stage Door Canteen in New York City. For the East Coast broadcast, a man must bite into an apple tied to a string hanging in front of him at mouth level. He is handed a concertina, a musical accordion-like musical instrument, and must sing "Wait Till the Sun Shines, Nellie," while trying to bite into the hanging apple. He receives a dollar for every bite he can get out of the apple. But he could not stop singing or playing the musical instrument. The bench he sat on was electronically controlled and jiggled all over when they turned on the switch. For the West Coast broadcast, a woman is selected for the stunt.
A bachelor selected from the audience has to borrow another man's girlfriend to escort to nightclubs and hotels in New York City, while the girl's boyfriend has to pay the checks with money furnished by the radio producers, and care for the bachelor's hat and coat. This included a trip to Jack White's Club 18, to Leon Eddies, The Hurricane, The Stork Club and The Rainbow Room. They will be photographed in all these places and photos sent to the International News Service to appear in newspapers throughout the country. The couple were photographed dancing at the Lincoln Hotel to Harry James music, the Roosevelt Hotel dancing to Guy Lombardo's music, and to Vaughn Monroe's music at The Commodore. The contestant agrees to the scheme and then

discovers the girl is a chimpanzee named Guinevere, dressed up like a girl, and the trainer, **Harry Lander**, is the boyfriend. After the contestant leaves, Edwards tells the listening audience that there was no real chimpanzee. The monkey was Carzong, the famous movie ape who called himself "The Human Ape." (In real life his name was **Pat Welch**.) He's been fooling people on stage for more than 20 years and makes it almost impossible to tell that he is really human in the costume.

Famous impersonator **Al Bernie** is a guest on this program, imitating **Charles Boyer**, romantically playing the role to a female contestant who is blindfolded and has to identify the Hollywood celebrity in order to win a large prize. "A lovely face… your chin… so strong… so beautiful…" Bernie remarks in character. "And those cheeks… like Baldwin apples… glowing, radiant, and so appealing… And your lips… your lips… so soft… so tempting… may I kiss you, my dear? Just one kiss." (Her husband really kisses her for that part of the stunt.)

Episodes #235 & 236, Broadcast of November 14, 1942

East Coast Stunts: One Man Band, Railroad B.U., Marseillaise, and Ring Bell

West Coast Stunts: Murder Stand-In, Railroad B.U., Marseillaise, Maiden's Prayer, and Football Scores

Broadcast originated from Baker Field, Manhattan Beach, New York. Two Americans, a soldier and a sailor, along with a British soldier in the U.S., a Russian (Mr. Sitiv) in Washington and a Chinese (Mr. Yang) in London – all participate in a three-way conversation supposedly speaking to the people of France. "Last Saturday night, a few hours after American and British troops landed on the shores of North Africa, President Roosevelt delivered by shortwave a message of hope and inspiration to the men and women of France. To echo the sentiments of our great leader, we hope to bring to the French people a message to show them that the people of America and the United Nations are solidly joined with them in their struggle to regain their liberties and free institutions." With a French interpreter, the soldier and sailor speaks to the free men and women of Europe. The men were provided with a one-page script to read: "Frenchmen everywhere, this is an old American game called *Truth or Consequences* that is broadcast once a week to people all over America. Tonight it comes to you from New York City. Three contestants chosen from our audience, an American soldier and sailor, and a British Air Craftsman, have missed a question and now must perform a consequence… an act!

A female contestant, single, is ordered backstage to speak into a crystal ball and tell the spirits what kind of serviceman she would like to go out with on a date. The ball had a hidden microphone and as the speakers revealed her request, brown eyes, broad shoulders, etc., servicemen in the audience came up on stage. During the stunt, she asked for "a fighting man who is romantic. One who can thrill me with his kisses." She goes out on a date, at the expense of the radio producers, to watch the floor show at the Rainbow Room and dance to the music of Del Casino's orchestra… an answer to a maiden's prayer and with five men!

Episodes #237 & 238, Broadcast of November 21, 1942

East Coast Stunts: Alarm Clocks, Canada B.U., Railroad, and Director Frame

West Coast Stunts: Water Balloon, Canada B.U., Railroad, and Love Teaser

A female contestant, **Miss Florence L'Hommedieu** of Roselle, New Jersey, from last week's radio broadcast, won a trip on board the New York, New Haven & Hartford Railroad, famous for their crack engineers, winners of safety records in the enormous task of transportation. This week at the same time, she receives the chance to ride in the engineer cabin operating one of their modern steam engines. Here, she will turn on the throttle, pull the whistle, and actually drive that engine down the tracks. And she will sing "She'll Be Comin' Around The Mountain" and punctuate the song with loud bursts from the train whistle.

A female contestant must deliver a real live turkey to the John Inglis plant in Canada next week, a turkey named Oswald, and dance the turkey trot on stage of the CBC Playhouse in Toronto. Next week the program will originate from the CBC Playhouse. Until then, the contestant is provided with a crate and must take care of Oswald and make sure he is fed a daily diet of correct food.

For the East Coast broadcast, singer **Hildegarde** was a celebrity guest. A number of alarm clocks are set off ringing at the same time, spread throughout the theatre. If a contestant (a sailor) can find them and turn them all off within 30 seconds, he will get to escort Hildegarde to the Persian Room where she is singing at the Hotel Plaza, and have dinner with her at the same hotel. The sailor must also sing "Got a Date With an Angel" at the same time he sets out to find the alarm clocks. When the sailor is ready to set off on his task,

Hildegarde remarks, "You won't forget to come back?" He wasn't able to fulfill his mission but he still went out on the date with Hildegarde. The sailor is sent off with a package he not supposed to hand her until after she sings her song at midnight. What he did not know was that the package contained a dozen more alarm clocks, all set to go off at midnight while she sings her song.

Episodes #239 & 240, Broadcast of November 28, 1942
East Coast Stunts: Turkey Trot, Casting Contest, Wives' Noses, and Maiden's Prayer
West Coast Stunts: Turkey Trot, I'm Joe, Ring Bell, and Wives' Noses
Broadcast originated from the stage of the CBC Playhouse in Toronto. The contestant from last week's broadcast has traveled to Canada with Oswald, the turkey, to deliver him to the Sperry Gyroscope war plant in the United States, and to the people of the John Inglis plant in Toronto, Canada. The contestant must also hop around the dance floor, gobbling like a turkey, in tempo to "Turkey in the Straw." Canadian bagpipe music is performed by six musicians to the stage for the stunt. **Joe Johnson** was one contestant, **Ann Rochelle** from New York was the other.

Repeatedly throughout the entire broadcast, contestants are required to call a man and tell him his wife was a great date the other night. The final contestant, unaware of the earlier phone calls, is required to visit a specific address and introduce himself as "Joe," the name of the man who kept identifying himself when he called the stranger. (A member of the quiz show contest went along to make sure the contestant did not get beat up.) The contestant is also paid enough money to take the phone victim to dinner and a show, when they can make it… besides the regular prize money.

One contestant is encouraged to eat thirty-five feet of spaghetti as he sings, "There's a Long, Long Trail A' Winding." In actuality, it was thirty-five pieces of spaghetti, each a foot long. A 25 cents War Stamp is awarded to him for every foot he eats. He could eat more than one at a time. And he could not use his hands.

Episodes #241 & 242, Broadcast of December 5, 1942
East Coast Stunts: Ice Follies, Bear, Wire Flowers, and Water Balloon
West Coast Stunts: Sing and Write, Bear, Wire Flowers, and Director Frame
In the beginning of this episode, five male contestants are sent to Madison Square

Garden where they are to pretend to be the Dionne Quintuplets. **Nora McCarthy**, the woman who taught the real Dionne Quintuplets how to ice skate will teach them to ice skate as well… during the 1943 Ice Follies, in front of 17,000 spectators. The men are dressed in costume complete with skirts and hoods. Pillows are tied to their waist and if they fall during training, horns inside will honk. They are also instructed to sing "Ta-ra-ra-Boom-de-ay," as the Quints might sing it. Towards the close of the episode, the live performance is broadcast via remote.

Episodes #243 & 244, Broadcast of December 12, 1942
East Coast Stunts: Bond Salesman, Hand Spray, Seven Days Leave, and Hat Trick
West Coast Stunts: One Two Three, Christmas Stocking, Record Wife, and Seven Days Leave
- **Mrs. Siering** of New York was given 30 seconds to sell $50,000 worth of War Bonds. Should she do succeed in the challenge, she would receive a free round-trip visit to her son in Fort Logan, a new outfit and a free phone call to anyone in the United States. She ultimately sold $540,345 worth of Bonds.
- Three male contestants are asked to roll up their sleeves, put on shower caps and slide their faces and arms through the holes in walls facing each other in the form of a triangle. Each are assigned a number from one to three. Every time Edwards asked a question from the audience, if the answer was three, numbers two and one would spray seltzer on three, and so on. The questions were cleverly plotted: How many shower caps do you see on stage? Which man on stage do you feel sorry for… one, two or three?
- A female contestant, with a boyfriend stationed at camp, agrees to sacrifice her nylon stocking, because Edwards cannot find a Christmas stocking to fill with presents. (She is provided a sheet for privacy to take off the nylons.) Presents for the stocking included a Ronson cigarette lighter, an EverReady Flashlight, a Seaforth Commando Shaving Kit, a box of Fifth Avenue candy bars, a year's subscription to *Newsweek* magazine, a Bulova Serviceman's wristwatch and a portable radio, among other gifts.

Episodes #245 & 246, Broadcast of December 19, 1942
East Coast Stunts: Sing and Write, Christmas Stocking, Kiss Clear Throat, and Silent Night
West Coast Stunts: Bugler, Upside Down Cake, Kiss Clear Throat, and Silent Night

Having entertained the Marines at Quantico, the soldiers at Little Rock, the sailors at Norfolk, and the Airmen at Mitchel Field, the *Truth or Consequences* tour arrived to broadcast from the Coast Guard Station in Manhattan Beach, California.

A serviceman is asked to write a letter to his girlfriend and they will give him $1.00 for every line written. Before collecting the money, he has to read the letter out loud for all to hear.

Four Coast Guardsmen, who are also members of the singing organization at Manhattan Beach, are asked to sing "Silent Night" for all the servicemen listening in to this broadcast.

In the "Short Pants" stunt, a serviceman is asked to run around the auditorium yelling "Merry Christmas to You," while Edwards looks for a poem, "Ah, the Quiet of the Night," which he misplaced.

Episodes #247 & 248, Broadcast of December 26, 1942
East Coast Stunts: McDonald Tank, Bench Apple, Bloodhound, and Auction Wife
West Coast Stunts: Finish Song, Bloodhound, Madeline Pearce, Round-Up, and Mouth

A male contestant was given an overcoat and handed $10 to spend anywhere he wanted in Radio City... including the Rainbow Room. No one knows where he went. His wife is handed the leash to a real bloodhound, which has the scent of the overcoat they gave the husband. She is to set out and find her husband. The husband returned but not with the wife. Half-way through the broadcast, the husband returned to the program... solo. He is handed a bloodhound and set out to find his wife.

Episodes #249 & 250, Broadcast of January 2, 1943
East Coast Stunts: Spaghetti, I'm Joe, Fort Logan Remote, Round Up, and Dark, Isn't It?
West Coast Stunts: One Man Band, Auction Wife, First Consequence, and 12 Seltzers

A portion of the program originates from Fort Logan, Colorado, where **Mrs. Siering** was sent to visit her son as guest of Procter & Gamble, for selling more than $50,000 worth of Bonds. (Reference to the broadcast of December 12, 1942.)

A husband and wife participate in a fake auction. The husband is instructed to go back to the soundproof room and think up good sales points for a combination dishwasher and fireless cooker. What he does not know, when he returns blindfolded, is that the machine does not exist. Instead, his wife stands on the stage and will attempt to auction her off. The audience is instructed not to go over 37 cents, to make it tough for the husband to accomplish his goal. During the stunt, the husband, blindfolded, is asked how long it is guaranteed, if it will rust, and how she will stand up under heat and water.

Reprising the very first consequence ever done on the program, a sailor boy is invited up on stage to answer the boss of a grocery store while sucking on a lollypop and handling a basket of eggs. He is subjected to a number of questions such as "What is the meaning of this?" and "What will your doctor say about this?" The contestant wins $5 and ten cakes of Ivory soap for his participation.

Episodes #251 & 252, Broadcast of January 9, 1943

East Coast Stunts: Night Court, Flyer's Test, and 12 Seltzers

West Coast Stunts: Night Court, Kazotsky, and Uh

In the "Night Court" stunt, a married woman agrees to be taken by taxi to one of the Night Courts in New York City. She would be seated by the judge, right with him on the bench, and would help him pass judgment on some of the law violators who are brought before him. Later in the broadcast, they would tune into the program to hear what she has to say to some of those arrested. Her husband agrees to play the gag by dressing up like a hobo, with applied makeup, and appear in court as one of the accused. What she does not know is that the Night Court is fake. The radio producers rented a hall with benches, tables, jury box and everything required to make it look as if it were a real court. The audience roars when she is asked to impose a sentence on her husband, unaware of who he is, and asked by the judge, "What would you do with a case like this?"

A female contestant is handed a baby rattle and bottle and asked to sit down on a rocker. She must rock a 12-month-old baby to sleep and discovers the baby is none other than **Madeline Pearce**, a famous baby impersonator for radio programs originating out of New York City.

Episodes #253 & 254, Broadcast of January 16, 1943
East Coast Stunts: Kangaroo, Income Tax, Answer in Song, and Throw Pie
West Coast Stunts: Kangaroo, Two Heads, and Income Tax
As a consequence, one contestant has to sing "Swanee River" but instead of using words to the song, Edwards asks the contestant to use the answers to questions as substitute lyrics... and they have to fit the melody. With organ music from **Bill Meeder,** the contestant has to answers such questions as "Where do you franken the strible?" and "What are you doing for your hair?"
Another contestant has to hurry over to a boxing arena, put on a pair of trunks and gloves and a catcher's mask for facial protection, and go up against the prize fighter, Kid Killem, mentioned by name in numerous sports columns including **Cas Adams** of *The Herald Tribune,* **Harold Parrot** of *The Brooklyn Eagle,* **Ed Van Every** of *The Sun,* **Barney Nagler** of *The Bronx Home News,* **Milton Gross** of *The New York Post* and many other newspapers. Imagine the contestant's surprise when he discovers the most talked about "Kid Killem" was nothing more than a kangaroo!

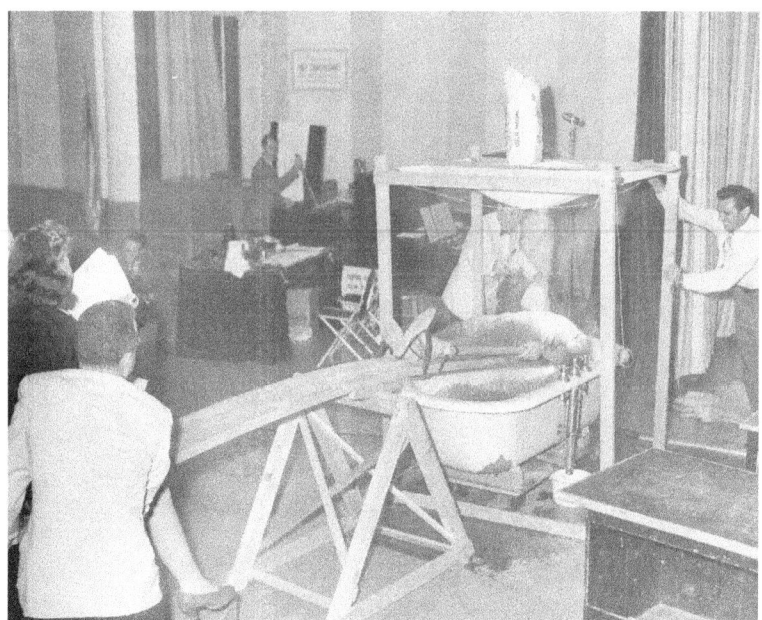

Prop wuth flour above, water below, contestant 'Makes some dough.'

Episodes #255 & 256, Broadcast of January 23, 1943
East Coast Stunts: Running Gag Aria, Greatest Guy, and Send Penny
West Coast Stunts: Flyer's Test, Coincidence, and Question Consequence

In an effort to pull a gag on Ralph Edwards, the cast and crew set the clocks back two minutes so the program would open with Ralph Edwards in the audience trying to wind up his selection of volunteers.

The first contestant of the evening is asked to step into a soundproof room off stage and sing the first few bars of the song "Il Bacio" for the entire program. If they keep up the music, they receive $50. If Edwards checks on her at any time and finds she stopped, she loses the game.

When government copper was scarce, Edwards dreamed up a consequence for a housewife who had a son in the Marines. **Mrs. Dennis J. Mullane**, mother of 17-year-old **Private Harold Mullane**, serving in the U.S. Marines, failed to answer her question and as a consequence she agreed to help the government's drive to put copper pennies into circulation. Listeners were asked to send in their pennies to Mrs. Mullane, to exchange for War Bonds for her son so he would have some financial security to come home to after the war. The result would ultimately total more than 300,000 pennies, or $3,000 in cold copper cash.

Episodes #257 & 258, Broadcast of January 30, 1943

East Coast Stunts: One Two Three, Penny Review, Hidden Songs, and Phone Booth

West Coast Stunts: Answer in Song, and Impromptu Drama

Mrs. Dennis J. Mullane is back on the program to thank the listeners for their overwhelming contributions in pennies. Her son, **Private Harold Mullane** of the U.S. Marines, is also brought to the program, rushed over from the Marine's Camp Lejeune at New River, North Carolina, to join his mother on the program. To prove they actually did receive the pennies, which exceeded expectations, and that the newsreels and newspapers were not kidding, under special guard, attendants brought in casks of pennies and coins and poured them into containers in front of the microphone. Radio listeners heard the sound of 300,157 pennies being dropped. Mullane then said that he would like to turn over every fiftieth penny to buy sport equipment for the Marines on Paris Island. With the remainder he is going to buy War Bonds and after the war complete his education.

Episodes #259 & 260, Broadcast of February 6, 1943

East Coast Stunts: Punctuation, Record Wife, Merry-Go-Round, and Valentine Cards

West Coast Stunts: Punctuation, Remember, Merry-Go-Round, and Valentine Cards

For the benefit of young children listening, schoolteachers were forced to take a consequence. A little story is read out loud and the contestants must supply the proper punctuation. If the teachers make a mistake, little children brought to the stage were allowed to jump up and yell, "Nea! Nea! You missed it!" The story contained a total of 29 punctuation marks.

Episodes #261 & 262, Broadcast of February 13, 1943

East Coast Stunts: Buy Girdle, Stage Directions, Hello, Victory Book, Expectant Father, and Yes or No

West Coast Stunts: Buy Girdle, Goulash, Hello, and Expectant Father

An update was delivered regarding the penny contest: as of this afternoon a total of 326,362 pennies have been received.

A serviceman and expectant father has to explain to the radio audience exactly how to put a diaper on a baby. His explanation of the time-honored dressing technique must be done using military terms such as "flanking movement." To help assist, the Private is provided with a life-sized doll, a diaper and some safety pins. As a consolation prize, he is given an entire layette for the baby including undershirts, baby stockings, safety pins, sweater, bootees, mittens, baby bonnet, a crib, a high chair, a playpen, and ten different toys.

Episodes #263 & 264, Broadcast of February 20, 1943

East Coast Stunts: Use Your Head, Telephone Bathtub, Grandma Fights, and Welders

West Coast Stunts: Sweetheart, Telephone Bathtub, Grandma Fights, Welders, and Two Songs

Ed Herlihy delivers the Ivory Soap commercial in rhyme, with organ accompaniment to "When Lights Are Low."

Two servicemen sing two songs for a fantastic prize.

Episodes #265 & 266, Broadcast of February 27, 1943

East Coast Stunts: Sweetheart, Pull Horse, Ventriloquist, and Potato Girl

West Coast Stunts: Use Your Head, Pull Horse, Ventriloquist, and Help Old Lady

Broadcast originated from the stage of the Roxy Theater in New York City. An announcement is made that *Truth or Consequences* will begin a two-week engagement at the Roxy Theatre in New York City. The payment Edwards receives for his daily performances will be used to take care of the show expenses on tour. Two weeks from tonight, March 13, the first actual War Bond performance of *Truth or Consequences* will take place at Pawtucket, Rhode Island. Admission to the broadcast – and all broadcasts on the tour – will involve the purchase of a War Bond and the price of the Bond will determine the position of the seat in the audience. From Pawtucket the show will go to Buffalo. "Come out and play *Truth or Consequences* when we come by your way and help Uncle Sam buy more bullets and bombs with your purchase of War Bonds."

The first contestant of the evening has to go into the audience and find a nice-looking man and propose to him. Then she has to sing to him, "Let Me Call You Sweetheart." With every word she says and sings, the vowels must all sound like "er." What she sings sounds like "Lert Mer Cerl Yer Swerthert…"

A ventriloquist named **Jay Marshall** and his wooden dummy, Johnny, are guests on this broadcast. A female contestant is asked to walk backstage and talk to the wooden dummy and give him some good motherly advice on what to look for in a girl. While the contestant is backstage, Marshall is instructed not to use his talents as a ventriloquist. He is supposed to sit here with Johnny on his knee and pretend to make Johnny talk. Actually, the voice of the dummy will be the voice of her husband, sitting in the audience, with a hidden microphone.

A contestant named Mr. Peterson was sent outside the studio to pull a buggy, with a harness around his chest and neck, while his girl, Miss Carlson, and Clarence the horse, sit inside the buggy. A remote broadcast was picked up towards the end of the program for the audience to hear how the stunt turns out.

Episodes #267 & 268, Broadcast of March 6, 1943

Both Coast Stunts: Rosie the Riveter, Tug-O-War, Soldier's Sister, Talk Fast, and Carry Over

A male contestant who knew the lyrics to "Rosie the Riveter" is asked to sing to a real lady riveter, **Helen Barber**. Rather than have the lady take time off from her job, the producers took a microphone right to her War Plant where she is working, the Eastern Aircraft Division of General Motors in Terrytown, New York.

Three married couples must play a game of tug-of-war. Husbands on one side, women on the other, and in the middle a shower of water that will soak anybody who passes the line. (Originally it was a mud puddle but the producers questioned the mess that would be required to clean up.) The women had an advantage: they were hidden behind a screen and were assisted by three stagehands to help pull the men into the shower. The contestants sang "Row, Row, Row Your Boat" during the contest.

Episodes #269 & 270, Broadcast of March 13, 1943

East Coast Stunts: Carry Over, Baby Editor, Send Bride, Many Voices, and Bumpsadaisy

West Coast Stunts: Carry Over, Phone Book, Address Book, Many Voices, and Apples Over Table

Broadcast originated from Pawtucket, Rhode Island. $504,000 worth of Bonds were sold in exchange for admission to attend the performances. Last week the quiz program ended before a consequence could be completed. A contestant with his head and neck sticking through a screen with 10 seltzer bottles staring him right in the face was not able to complete the task. So he traveled with the crew to Pawtucket to finish the consequence.

A wanna-be musician is invited on the stage to take the consequence of auditioning for orchestra leader **Woody Herman**, who is listening on his phone at his home in Hollywood, California. The contestant talks to Herman briefly on the phone before his demo.

Geek trivia: The first of many radio broadcasts on the coast-to-coast War Bond tour. Superstitions aside, the train that took the cast and crew to Pawtucket was number 13. This broadcast aired on the 13th. There are 13 stops on the War Bond tour. And Ralph Edwards was born on June 13, 1913, 13 minutes after 9.

Episodes #271 & 272, Broadcast of March 20, 1943

East Coast Stunts: Little Indians, Trust Balloons, Whip, and Address Book
West Coast Stunts: Little Indians, Hide Phone, Whip, and Poor Bachelor

Broadcast originated from Buffalo, New York. $811,725 worth of Bonds were sold in exchange for admission to attend the performances. Hoping to play a trick on a famous psychiatrist, Dr. N.U. Spaper, Edwards has a contestant phone the doctor and make him think he is a four-year-old boy who has called him to tell him what is wrong with the way his parents are bringing up children. The contestant tells the doctor that children should not have to go to bed early, etc. What the contestant does not know is that there is no such doctor. Instead, he will be talking to the City Editor of the *Pawtucket Times* newspaper. (The doctor's name was N-ew-spaper, get it?) They also had a photographer take a picture of the contestant dressed as a baby so it will appear in the local paper following the broadcast.

A contestant is sent off stage to the soundproof room to get in disguise. If he can identify what famous historical figure he is supposed to be, he receives $10. His hint is the song "Ten Little Indians," with three little Indians holding seltzer bottles!

Episodes #273 & 274, Broadcast of March 27, 1943

East Coast Stunts: Saw Tank, Toledo Scales, Coincidence, and Hide Phone
West Coast Stunts: Saw Tank, Toledo Scales, Phone Bride, and Strong Man

Broadcast originated from Toledo, Ohio. $1,025,455 worth of Bonds were sold in exchange for admission to attend the performances. Two gentlemen suffer the consequences of dressing in bathing suits and suffering a wet conclusion in water tanks. In another stunt, two ladies are placed on a scale and another contestant has to guess their combined weight. For every pound they miss, they will receive that many whacks with a paddle on the spot they usually use for sitting down. The ladies sing "Keep Your Sunny Side Up" while they spank in tempo.

A mention was made of the second *Truth or Consequences* party book being available.

The East Coast performance was conducted for the benefit of the studio audience, but not broadcast over the network as a result of a speech by **Major General Campbell**.

Episodes #275 & 276, Broadcast of April 3, 1943

East Coast Stunts: Jeep, Question Consey, Phone Bride, Strong Man, and Fit for Pigs

West Coast Stunts: Jeep, Old Sweetheart, Pass the Ammunition, and Fit for Pigs

Broadcast originated from the Taft Auditorium in Cincinnati, Ohio. $7,548,475 worth of Bonds were sold in exchange for admission to attend the performances. A soldier and a girl fail to answer a question and are asked to ride on a real Army jeep, as they sing "Bumpy Road" while the Jeep drives around the stage. Towards the end of the broadcast, there was a mention that the April issue of *Reader's Digest* features an article written by **Beatrice Schapper** giving the inside facts about *Truth or Consequences*.

Ralph Edwards during his usual preshow audience warmup before the live broadcast.

Episodes #277 & 278, Broadcast of April 10, 1943

East Coast Stunts: Bird Cage, Old Sweetheart, Drop Tank, and Mountain Climber

West Coast Stunts: Sing for Ham, Mountain Climber, Bird Cage, and Choose Hats

Broadcast originated from Indianapolis, Indiana. $10,619,425 worth of Bonds were sold in exchange for admission to attend the performances. The crew of the quiz program pooled their ration cards to purchase a ham, highly valued and prized during the war. The ten-pound ham is suspended from the ceiling and a contestant can go home with the meat if she sings for it. The louder she sings, the lower the ham will come down. If she sang loud enough, she would be able to reach out and grab the ham. The song she sung was "My Hero." (Originally the script called for the contestant's choice of songs. The other option was "My Melancholy Baby.")

A wife agrees to go off stage to the desk and sign a release, which permitted her to have a hat for free of charge. On stage, a dozen hats are displayed on a table to choose from. Her husband is taken to a special section of the stage where a big shower nozzle is aimed at his face. There are 12 automatic controls for turning on the shower, one under each ladies' hat on the table. Every time his wife picks up a hat, she automatically trips a control, which shoots out water in his face. The joke is to see how undecided a woman is when it comes to choosing a hat. And yes, he was soaking wet when the game concluded!

Episodes #279 & 280, Broadcast of April 17, 1943
East Coast Stunts: Two Hammocks, Governor, Music Lesson, and Choose Hats
West Coast Stunts: Two Hammocks, Governor, Faults, and Mud Girl
Broadcast originated from Topeka, Kansas. $3,408,864 worth of Bonds were sold in exchange for admission to attend the performances. Announcer **Cliff Engle** jokes that the title of the quiz show tonight should be "Kansas takes the Konsequences" or "Topeka Tells the Truth."

A contestant is given the opportunity to imitate the Governor of Kansas, **Andrew Schoeppel**, and is sent backstage to get into the Governor's outfit to properly play the part. When the contestant returns, he is told to convince a man on stage into believing he is the real governor. What the contestant does not know is that the man on stage is the real governor! **Frank J. Warren**, Mayor of Topeka, also makes an appearance on this program.

Episodes #281 & 282, Broadcast of April 24, 1943
East Coast Stunts: Jail, Jump Rope, Easter Corsage, and Totem Pole
West Coast Stunts: Jail, Bumpsadaisy, and Send Bride
Broadcast originated from Denver, Colorado. $6,118,129 worth of Bonds were sold in exchange for admission to attend the performances. A male contestant is provided an American Indian costume, complete with head dress, and asked to identify one of the faces on a Totem Pole as a family relative. The man is

instructed to act like an Indian and make love to one of the faces on the pole, acting out the scene. In another stunt, two men are blindfolded and asked to bite apples suspended from above, while singing "Old MacDonald Had a Farm."

Episodes #283 & 284, Broadcast of May 1, 1943
East Coast Stunts: May Dance, Apple Over Table, Requests From Camp, and Sack

West Coast Stunts: May Dance, Pear Tones, Requests From Camp, and Sack

Broadcast originated from Camp Farragut in Spokane, Washington. $7,518,830 worth of Bonds were sold in exchange for admission to attend the performances. At the United States Naval Training Station at Farragut, Idaho, 53 miles away from Spokane, America's second largest naval base, sailors were listening. The producers of the program placed a microphone in one of their barracks, and a loudspeaker, so the radio listeners could hear what the sailors out at Farragut were saying, and they were given a chance to request anything they wanted. It was up to the radio listeners to fulfill as many of their requests as possible. **Seaman Paul Stielmacker**, having been in boot training for four weeks, asked for a girl to sigh. **George Gilbert** asked for his girl to be called up and he receives an update on how she was doing. Bill Lang wanted a message delivered to Hitler. (You can guess what that was.) **Gordon Haason** wanted his mother to know he is doing well. All of their requests were fulfilled.

Six men were sent out at the beginning of the quiz program, three dressed as little boys and three dressed as little girls, to dance the May Dance around a Maypole. The Maypole was located at one of Spokane's busiest intersections, Wall and Riverside Avenue. Local radio announcer **Rod Klise** reported on the event as it was happening live, via remote. At the conclusion of the stunt, a big white wagon marked "Booby Hatch" and six white uniformed men with big nets rounded up the boys and girls.

One female contestant wins a beautiful pair of $25 ultra-smart shoes from Spokane's famous Arthur Schuline Shoe Store. Her order is marked $18.75 because it is actually a War Bond. It will be worth $25 in ten years. It will be left at the Shoe Store and in ten years she can go in and claim her $25 shoes.

Episodes #285 & 286, Broadcast of May 8, 1943
East Coast Stunts: Auction Pants, Who's Boss, Mother's Day, and Choose Hats

West Coast Stunts: Auction Pants, Who's Boss, Mother's Day, and Baby Editor

Broadcast originated from Seattle, Washington. $32,112,625 worth of Bonds were sold in exchange for admission to attend the performances. A married couple went over to the Paramount theatre in Seattle with the assignment of raffling off his pants for War Bonds. Another contestant went along to be the auctioneer. First auctioned off was the tie, then the coat, and then the audience had to bid for his pants. What the audience did not know was that he wore underneath an old-fashioned, knee-length, striped bathing suite.

Petie Worth was the announcer who introduced the two contestants to the theater audience. By remote, the broadcast offered an update to the total raised in the auction.

Episodes #287 & 288, Broadcast of May 15, 1943

Both Coast Stunts: Husband's Noses, Airplane Jump, Soldier Dog, and Mrs. Courtley

Broadcast originated from Portland, Oregon. $109,915,391 worth of Bonds were sold in exchange for admission to attend the performances. The sale of War Bonds was so monumental that a representative of the United States Treasury, **Wilbur Carl**, Deputy Administrator of the Oregon War Savings Staff came on the program to report the news.

A male contestant meets an attractive model from Portland, **Patsy Bauman**, who sits next to him while holding a little poodle dog. The contestant's girlfriend is phoned long distance and while he speaks to her, the model is to speak lovingly to the little poodle dog. He is instructed not to tell his girlfriend where he was or that the gorgeous girl sitting next to him has a poodle dog on her lap. For his participation, he received $5.00 and a big red box of Duz.

Episodes #289 & 290, Broadcast of May 22, 1943

East Coast Stunts: Motorcycle, Mind Reader, Help Old Lady, and Milk Goats

West Coast Stunts: Motorcycle, Mind Reader, and Milk Goats

Broadcast originated from the Capitol Theatre in Salt Lake City, Utah. $1,579,650 worth of Bonds were sold in exchange for admission to attend the performances. Announcer **Cliff Engle** announced Ralph Edwards as "that touring toreador" and "that wacky wanderer," and Edwards himself appeared on stage to thank the audience for their generous contributions. "Here at the foot of the Wasatch Mountains, Salt Lake City has really dug down deep for Uncle Sam's War Bonds.

The broadcast concludes with a female contestant winning a beautiful $25 pair of Ultra Smart Shoes from Salt Lake's famous Paris Department Store. The order, handed to the contestant, is marked $18.75 and the order is actually a War Bond. "It will be worth $25 in ten years," Edwards explains. "We'll leave it at the show store and in ten years you go in and claim the $25 shoes." (Similar prize given away during the broadcast of May 1.)

Episodes #291 & 292, Broadcast of May 29, 1943
Both Coast Stunts: Papoose, Broken Telephone, Lullaby, and Water Boy
Broadcast originated from San Francisco, California. $4,101,000 worth of Bonds were sold in exchange for admission to attend the performances. A contestant is asked to dress like an Indian, headgear and all, and go down to the nearest cigar stand with a cigar lighter and offer to light people's cigars and cigarettes as they walk by. In other words, he became a living cigar store Indian. Strapped on his back is a real live Papoose. Instead of a baby, what is really strapped to his back is **Kayo**, the famous midget who has imitated babies in movies for many years. Imagine his surprise when, later in the stunt, the baby pulls out a cigar and lights one up and refers to a woman on the street as "babe" and asks her if she has a date!

Frank Jones is instructed to trick other contestants to walk through a door rigged with a bucket of water that would fall on them when they open the door and pass through.

In another stunt, Edwards introduces a female contestant who gave birth since her husband left for service. **Mrs. Kenneth Beyer** of San Francisco was selected from the audience and she is given a chance to let her husband see his child for the first time.

Episodes #293 & 294, Broadcast of June 5, 1943
East Coast Stunts: Girdle Hammock, Lullaby, Own Drama, and Slim Summerville
West Coast Stunts: Girdle Hammock, California Florida, Lullaby, Slim Summerville, and Name Sweethearts
Broadcast originated from the Municipal Auditorium in Glendale, California. $2,058,088 worth of Bonds were sold in exchange for admission to attend the performances. A female contestant is instructed to call up one of Hollywood's

famous movie stars and try to get a date to go with him for an ice cream soda. Edwards will not disclose the name of the celebrity, but she has to act like she knows who he is. **Slim Somerville** is on stage in an isolated phone booth, prepared to play the game. The contestant, unaware that he is in the studio, enters another booth to place the call. She does not guess correctly but she does get a kiss on the brow after the stunt comes to a conclusion.

Episodes #295 & 296, Broadcast of June 12, 1943
Both Coast Stunts: Pump Balloons, Four Service Men, and Bond Cities Seltzer
Broadcast originated from Oakland, California. $1,210,000 worth of Bonds were sold in exchange for admission to attend the performances. Two female contestants pretend to be garage attendants pumping up tires. They are told to pump as fast as they can so the balloon wrapped around the competition's neck will blow up in size and burst. First balloon to burst loses the game. What they do not know is that the tubes and contraption is rigged and they do not realize that they are blowing up their own balloon!
Four service men are performing a rendition of "Marching Along Together" but are not all in the studio. A Marine, a Soldier, a Sailor and an Airman. The private sings at the microphone in the Oakland Auditorium while a Soldier (**Corporal Technician Anthony Lantone**) in the Tank Corps, riding in a tank, sings with him. Then they tune in to a War Ship by remote control and a Sailor (**Seaman L.D. Gilmore**) on board joins the singing. Then an airman (**Sergeant Bill Boebel**) with a microphone high above will join.
This broadcast marked the close of the *Truth or Consequences* War Bond tour. The total raised was $188,481,082.79.

Episodes #297 & 298, Broadcast of June 19, 1943
Both Coast Stunts: Song Situation, Farm B.U., Write Daddy, and Call Mayor
Broadcast originated from the Golden Gate Theatre in San Francisco, California. A young girl who recently learned to write is brought up on stage to write a special letter to her father in recognition of Father's Day. As a present for her father, the girl is handed a $500 U.S. War Bond to help with her education ten years from now. While her father is away fighting overseas, Edwards comments, he wanted to make sure that the little ones have a chance for a democratic education.

Angelo Rossi, Mayor of San Francisco, California, helps assist with a stunt. A contestant was told to go offstage and help the operator call a number at random and act like Mrs. Rossi, the wife of the Mayor, to "tell him just what you think of this city, the people in it, and him." In a similar stunt *Truth or Consequences* did on **Governor Andrew Schoeppel** of Kansas a few weeks prior, the citizen who answers the phone is the Mayor himself.

The entire cast and crew are performing four shows a day at the Golden Gate Theatre in San Francisco, for an entire week.

Episodes #299 & 300, Broadcast of June 26, 1943

Both Coast Stunts: Hog Caller, Set on Eggs, Calf Kiss, Barnyard Quartette, and Milk Cows

Broadcast originated from the farm of **Joe Rose**, last week's contestant, at The Rose Brothers Farm in Pleasanton (Livermore Valley), California. Because Rose missed his question last week, his consequence was to play host on this week's broadcast. The quiz show is performed in the shade of Rose's big barn, with the bottom of a hay wagon used as a stage. Sailors and Seabees from Camp Parks, just down the road, and flyers from down Livermore Way where the servicemen were earning their wings, hear the airplanes overhead during the broadcast.

Spectators had to apply at the City Clerk in Pleasanton, and the price of admission would be some small farm commodity such as a head of lettuce, a bunch of beats, a half dozen of eggs, etc. The food would be donated to a children's home or some other worthy cause.

Contestants and spectators were seated on bales of hay, plows, barrels, hay wagons and all sorts of farm equipment. A hog-calling contest was held to see who could stir up the pigs the most and win a prize. Film actress **Ellen Drew** participated in a contest where a married couple had to figure out who was kissing whom. The husband, blindfolded, was kissed three times. The first from his wife, the second from the actress and the third from a little calf! The actress pitched her new radio program, *The Hollywood Theatre of the Air*, and thanked all the farmers for listening. "All of us in Hollywood know how important the farm work is toward winning the war."

A contestant is instructed to perform "Down by the Old Mill Stream," making as loud a noise of any particular animal or fowl as he chooses. Six children (three boys and three girls) are taught how to milk a cow and with six cows, perform the "milk pail symphony." They sing "Toreador" during the game and if they have enough milk in their pails to fill a quart milk bottle, they win a special prize.

Episodes #301 & 302, Broadcast of August 28, 1943
East Coast Stunts: Met Star, Oaken Bucket, and Movie Actress
West Coast Stunts: Met Star, Oaken Bucket, Movie Actress, and Send Movie

A contestant who claims he can sing is tricked into playing the role of Figaro in "The Barber of Seville," and that he might win an audition at the Metropolitan Opera House. But little did the contestant know until it was too late that he was being sent to the Metropolitan Barber Shop on Sixth Avenue. His audience consisted of three barbers, one manicurist and whoever was there to get a Saturday night haircut. A real orchestra was out on the street to perform the music. **Milton Cross** was the announcer on location.

A contestant is instructed to make love to Hollywood actress **Joan Blondell**, with **Miss Jean Colbert**, who makes a specialty of imitating Blondell. Because the contestant wasn't ardent enough with his love making, the lights were turned out and the couple were blindfolded. The real Joan Blondell walked out on stage and replaced the imitation. The sailor discovers after the lovemaking scene that he really was making love to the actress! (A mention of her **Gypsy Rose Lee** play, *The Naked Genius*, was opening soon in New York.)

A Private in service is instructed on stage to act out a number of scenes for a movie camera including hugging an imaginary person and saying, "I wish I had you in my arms," waking up when the bugle blows, smiling and throwing kisses at the camera… and then discovers the film will be developed as a mini-movie for his mother, along with a movie projector and a screen, so she can see her son at all times. Radio actor **Bill Zuckert** is featured briefly in this stunt.

Episodes #303 & 304, Broadcast of September 4, 1943
East Coast Stunts: Messenger Boy, Piano Upside Down, Close Call, and Send Movie
West Coast Stunts: Messenger Boy, Piano Upside Down, and Close Call

A contestant is provided the coat of a messenger boy and told to act like a Western Union Messenger Boy and deliver a telegram to Mrs. Grace Dalrymple at the Hotel Astor in Times Square. For every cent she tips him, they will give him a dollar. What the contestant is not aware of is that Mrs. Grace Dalrymple is really the six-foot-two actress, **Hope Emerson**. And at the time of delivery, a concealed microphone (engineer in the other room) will pick up a terrific domestic battle between Mrs. Dalrymple and her make-believe husband, played by radio actor **Ward Wilson**. The contestant receives no tip and instead is convinced to romance her in her attempt of making her husband jealous. How will the contestant perform? (The script originally called for **Gale Gordon** to play the role of the husband, but for reasons unknown Ward Wilson was his replacement.)

Episodes #305 & 306, Broadcast of September 11, 1943
Both Coast Stunts: Heckler, Hypnotize, and Returned Sailor

A contestant is sent over to the Capital Theatre, two blocks away from Radio City, to attend the stage show featuring **Horace Heidt** and his Musical Knights. When **Henry Russell**, his featured vocalist, is scheduled to sing the song, "Git Along Little Dogies," the contestant who has a reserved seat in the tenth row, equipped with a hidden microphone, is required to howl like a dog. If he succeeds in making Henry Russell laugh on stage, the contestant receives an extra $15. A remote pickup is featured later in the broadcast. After the contestant leaves, Edwards informed the audience that the gag is on him. The entire audience and Heidt and Russell are expecting the contestant. When the howling gets too bad, they are going to call the contestant up on stage to howl while Russell sings, and fifty real live dogs will come running out on the stage yelping and barking.

Earlier in the week, tickets were sent out for railroad transportation to New York and expenses paid to a typical American family who had a son stationed overseas. (Historically, this was the first time Edwards imported contestants to *Truth or Consequences*.) He asked the parents about their boy and explained that while he cannot reveal their son's location, he provided a means of communication so they could talk to him tonight. They hand a phone to the parents and after a bit of chat, the son walks onto the stage as a surprise. The family is handed $100 to spend and have a pleasant evening in New York City.

Episodes #307 & 308, Broadcast of September 18, 1943
East Coast Stunts: Recipe Lyrics, Small Tank, Mary, and Pin Up
West Coast Stunts: Recipe Lyrics, Small Tank, Mary, and Follow Sounds

Two men are chosen from the audience to perform a high dive act, the second unaware that the first man is Mr. Foster, one of the country's most famous trick high-divers. Mr. Foster appeared in the Aquacade at the World's Fair. When they come back on stage, they will be instructed to dive from the ceiling into a small tank of water on stage. Imagine the surprise of the audience – and the second contestant – when Mr. Foster successfully makes the dive! The radio audience was in on the gag, as was Mr. Foster, but the audience in the studio did not!

By remote, Ralph Edwards is able to talk to the boys of the St. Alban's Hospital on Long Island, and they are able to talk to him. A sailor, **Gunner's Mate Mickey Costa**, sings "Wait for Me, Mary" into a telephone, while his fiancée, **Mary Barnish**, was listening at her home in Lilly, Pennsylvania. Sailor Costa was suffering from shrapnel wounds in his arms and legs. Edwards asked the listeners to go out and purchase War Bonds and write in to *Truth or Consequences*, providing the producers of the program the amount purchased and the serial number of the Bond. If $1,000,000 was pledged, Sailor Costa would to be given a $1,000 War Bond to be used to marry Mary.

Episodes #309 & 310, Broadcast of September 25, 1943
East Coast Stunts: Glee Club, Springfield Mayors, Victor Mature, and Gramophone
West Coast Stunts: Glee Club, Springfield Mayors, Victor Mature, and Fire Net
Broadcast originated from the Municipal Auditorium in Springfield, Massachusetts. Admission to show was through the cash purchase of U.S. War Bonds. The bigger the bond, the better the seat. Total raised was $45,160,000 including $2,000,000 in "E" Bonds. This was not the figure quoted by Edwards on the program, because the total was still being worked on at the time of broadcast.
Hollywood actor **Victor Mature** appears on the program. He was billed on the program as: "a member of the United States Coast Guard for the past year and four months. During that period he has really been places and seen things in this war. His last assignment was with the North Atlantic convoy and though censorship doesn't allow us to mention the ports in the active combat zone that he visited, I can say that he was part of the vast convoy system that has been and still is protecting our boys through the dangerous waters leading to the war fronts… Fourteen days ago he returned from sea duty and because of his brilliant record as a fighting serviceman, the United States Treasury requested his services in behalf of the Third War Loan Drive."

A female contestant responsible for keeping the service boys happy at the U.S.O., the Canteens and various other organizations is treated to a date with a serviceman for an ice cream soda and a movie, *Seven Days Leave*, featuring Victor Mature and Ralph Edwards, unaware who she is really going on a date with. Wait till she recognizes him on the big screen!

A contestant is provided one minute to talk about his local business to the nation – free publicity – if it wasn't for the local Springfield Glee Club who was also told to use that same minute to try out a musical number, "The Rangers Song," from *Rio Rita*.

Celebrity guests also included **Deputy Mayor J. Albin Anderson** of Springfield, Massachusetts. A contestant was told to go offstage and help the operator call the Mayor of Springfield to "tell him just what you think of this city, the people in it, and him." What she doesn't realize, and the audience is let in on, is that she is talking to the Mayor of Springfield, Illinois, **John Kapp**. After the stunt, on stage, she meets the real Mayor in person.

Episodes #311 & 312, Broadcast of October 2, 1943

East Coast Stunts: Link Trainer, Ralph's Remote, Seal, and Hose
West Coast Stunts: Link Trainer, Ralph's Remote, and Seal

On stage was a training device of the Army Air Force, known as a Link Trainer. It does everything a real plane does except fly. A female contestant is asked to go climb into the cockpit. **Lt. Albert Travis** of the Air Forces Training Aids Division provides instructions how to operate the ruder, the wheel, and other technicals and she simulates the way she should fly a plane. On the West Coast broadcast, **Major John A. Dodds** of the U.S. Army is the trainer.

An update about **Mickey Costa**, who sang "Wait for the Navy" on the quiz show two weeks ago, has raised $4,001,837 in U.S. War Bonds and Stamps. (The final total would eventually come to $4,449,195.)

Episodes #313 & 314, Broadcast of October 9, 1943

Both Coast Stunts: Jingle Jangle, Baby Care, Soldiers Christmas, and Three-Piece Band

Details remain unknown at this time. **Victor Mature** returns to the program partly as a public service announcement. Mature, it is reported on the air, was helping to aid women enlisting as a WAC. One female contestant is blindfolded and brought onto the stage. She follows the orders given to her and proposes to a solider... unaware of who is standing in front of her.

Episodes #315 & 316, Broadcast of October 16, 1943
East Coast Stunts: Alligator, Madeline Carroll, WAC Act, and Sing Type
West Coast Stunts: Alligator, Madeline Carroll, and WAC Act

A Private had to start singing in a normal voice. Then WACS from different WAC centers throughout the country, via remote, were brought in over the radio to drown him out. Remote broadcasts were courtesy of stations WRC in Washington, D.C., WMAQ in Chicago and NBC in Hollywood.

A merchant seaman is asked which are more romantic: American girls or English girls? Which play harder to get? He gets his chance to prove it by proposing marriage to an English girl and then an American girl. So he doesn't get influenced, the contestant is blindfolded. What he doesn't know at first is that the famous film star, **Madeleine Carroll**, better known as "the First Lady of the Merchant Marines," plays the role of both women!

Episodes #317 & 318, Broadcast of October 23, 1943
Both Coast Stunts: Roy Rogers, Depot Hoax, Ghost Host, and Russian Song

Boy contestant was asked to pretend he is a cowboy like **Roy Rogers**. If he can sing "Pistol Packin' Mama" like Rogers does, he will get three tickets (for the boy and his parents) to the rodeo that night at Madison Square Garden. The boy is dressed in a ten-gallon hat, chaps, vest, and gun-belt with pistols. Then they bring out Roy Rogers' guitar for accompaniment, then they introduce Rogers himself (with reference to Republic's *King of the Cowboys*), and they sing a duet. The boy and his parents all exit with Roy Rogers to attend the rodeo. (The same act was performed for the West Coast broadcast, but the tickets were for the next day's performance.)

A contestant is dressed up to play the part of "Honorable Willard Cranston" and be escorted to Grand Central Station. One hundred extras have been hired to mill around, passing the word that Honorable Willard Cranston is due any minute. The contestant is told that when the reception calls for a speech, he is to deliver what is scripted in his hand, with the closing remark, "If flyversant is boint... who will condle the three-gant?" The results are broadcast via remote.

A contestant, **Albert Cudner**, is given the consequence of haunting a house next week, promised to play the role of "Gus the Ghost," modeled after the famous Gus the Ghost in the *P.M.* comic strip and will serve as "ghost host" from coast-to-coast.

Episodes #319 & 320, Broadcast of October 30, 1943
Both Coast Stunts: Ghost Host Payoff, Skeleton, Close Shave, Witch Date, and Bear

Edwards explains that the broadcast originates from a deserted old haunted house on the outskirts of a little town called Cos Cob, Connecticut. The guests huddled together are all seated on dusty boxes, old bedsprings, and bleachers that were built in the living room and ladders that were brought in. The mystery house has been rumored to be haunted for years and the locals tell tall tales of blood and murder.

Albert Cudner, a contestant from last week who was to be ghost host for this broadcast, appears in person, and is asked to put on a ghost sheet and little eye glasses over the sheet just like Gus the Ghost, and wander the eighteen rooms of the big old house to haunt every one of them, yelling and moaning in each room. He is provided a guide and a flashlight. He will receive a dollar for every room they hear him wailing. Cudner is unaware that in one room a man waits to spray the ghost with a seltzer bottle.

A woman is asked to open a closet and meet the man of her dreams... which turns out to be a skeleton. Because a story about a giant headless barber circulated around the town, a contestant is asked to go into a dark room with a lit candle and sit in a barber chair, tilting his head back on the chair, singing "I Aint' Got No Body." What the contestant doesn't know is that a seven-foot carnival giant, **Dave Ballard**, with his coat buttoned above his head to make it look as if he was headless, will quietly walk into the room with a shaving mug and a wooden razor in his hands.

A woman is blindfolded and told to feed a peppermint stick to a boyfriend. She puts one end of the stick in her mouth, unaware that the boy is switched for a real live (domesticated) Brown Bear!

Episodes #321 & 322, Broadcast of November 6, 1943
East Coast Stunts: Fire Net, Telephone Seltzer, Guadalcanal, Handcuffed, and Adverbs

West Coast Stunts: Type Song, Telephone Seltzer, Guadalcanal, and Handcuffed
Broadcast originated from New York City and from Camp Elliot, California. A female stenographer is asked to type the lyrics to "Row, Row, Row Your Boat" as men sing it, while she has to sing "The Farmer in the Dell."

One female contestant discovers the hard way that the phone is really a seltzer bottle.

A soldier is asked to go out on a date with a beautiful girl, **Dorothy Mitchell**, to Toots Shor's famous restaurant, with $25 to splurge. But the girl confesses that she is handcuffed to her father, who is sitting next to her. The boy is asked if he doesn't mind the family tagging along and the youth agrees. Then he discovers father is handcuffed to his wife, who is handcuffed to Cousin Wilbur, who is handcuffed to Aunt Emma, and so on. Twelve members of the family! The boy still agrees to go along so he is told to pocket the $25 and the quiz show will front the entire bill.

To promote 20th Century Fox's latest picture, *Guadalcanal Diary*, starring **William Bendix**, **Preston Foster** and **Lloyd Nolan**, and because November 10 was the 168th Anniversary of the founding of the U.S. Marines, the movie is premiering in Philadelphia on the same date. The son of a Marine is asked on stage to sing the praises of his father's service, and sing the song, "From the Halls of Montezuma." The boy's performance is backed by the United States Marine Band from the fleet Marine Force Area, 3,300 miles away at San Diego, California, via remote. The boy is surprised when movie star Preston Foster comes out on stage and helps assist.

An announcement is made about a waste paper collection contest for school children that starts November 8 and closes November 15.

Episodes #323 & 324, Broadcast of November 13, 1943
Both Coast Stunts: Inflation, Phony Symphony, British Baseball, and Time Capsule

A lady is asked to sing "The Italian Street Song," accompanied by sixty people who cannot properly play a musical instrument.

Two women are sent backstage to a soundproof room to speak one word, and only one word, repeatedly. One woman is told to say "everything" and another is told to say "DUZ." They tune in to the room from time to time to make sure the women are not out of breath and still saying the same word over and over.

A British soldier, who knows nothing of baseball, is told to sit next to a movie screen and watch the two baseball teams and deliver the play-by-play report. A contestant is told to mess up his hair and stick out his tongue and clap his ears to pose for a photograph, which is tossed into a collection of assorted knick-knacks such as chewing gum, a baby's three-cornered pants, a lock of his hair… all placed into a time capsule to be sealed in a tube. The capsule will be buried to let people know 1,000 years from now what 1943 was like. The time capsule was sent out to the manager of Station WOW in Omaha, Nebraska, **John Gillen**, who will make sure it is buried approximately in the geographical center of America. "Just think," Edwards tells the contestant, "you'll probably be a museum piece at the 'Believe-It-or-Not' exposition in 5,000 A.D."

Episodes #325 & 326, Broadcast of November 20, 1943
East Coast Stunts: Pawn Shop, Paper Doll, Aviation Cadet, and Thump Melons
West Coast Stunts: Pawn Shop, Type Corn, Aviation Cadet, and Thump Melons

A woman is blindfolded and asked to tell which melons are ripe, unaware that two of them are not melons – they are bald-headed men!

A wife is asked to rush down to the local pawnshop and purchase a hat, a coat, a tie, pair of pants… a complete suit for her husband. She is provided $50 and for legal and security reasons, an escort to guide her way. She is told to talk the pawnshop owner down in price and what money she saves, she keeps. Her husband gets the suit. As soon as she is off the stage and out of the theater, her husband is rushed on stage and told to go behind a screen and take his clothes off. This will be the only suit available for purchase in her husband's size, which will be rushed down to the pawnshop. The husband, meanwhile, is placed in a barrel with suspenders and will wait for his wife to return with the purchase of his clothes. The pawn shop owner is an actor in a real pawn store and broadcast remote in the middle of the episode is the wife's frantic attempt to knock the price down for the suit. The pawn shop owner remarks, "You talk as if your husband was really over a barrel for a suit."

Guest was **Aviation Cadet C. B. Thompson**, a full-fledged flyer who phoned his mother in Paris, Texas, telling her that Procter & Gamble was paying her expenses to and from her son's graduation from the Army Flying Corps. To top the evening, Edwards hands Thompson two tickets to the new Broadway musical, *What's Up*, so he can take a buddy or a girlfriend along.

Edwards makes a reference to performing four shows a day of *Truth or Consequences* at the Capitol Theatre on Broadway in New York. **Clayton Collyer** makes an announcement that the December issue of *Radio Mirror Magazine* has a full color picture of Ralph Edwards, suitable for framing, and an article by Edwards about the importance of purchasing War Bonds.

Episodes #327 & 328, Broadcast of November 27, 1943
Both Coast Stunts: Eric Blore, Sound Sing, Phone in Key, and Husband Chair
A contestant is to pretend he returned home from a day's work driving a taxi, and is served by a butler, actor **Eric Blore**, known for playing a butler in many Hollywood movies. Blore appears moments before curtain time in the Ziegfeld Follies over at the Winter Garden Theatre.
A contestant is provided a free friendly phone call to his wife, back at home. He is not to tell her where he is but must carry on a conversation. As **Johnny Gart** performs a musical note at the organ, the contestant is to talk in the musical key that is provided. He is to act like nothing is wrong and see how the wife reacts.
Announcement of the winner of the Waste Paper Contest which was announced on the November 6 broadcast. Total amount collected by all school students was 42,761,829 pounds. **Mr. Norman Greenway**, member of the Executive Committee of the Paper Consuming Industries of America, and one of the contest judges announced the winner. The Moore School, District 81, Linn Co., Missouri, a rural school with only 12 students. Their collection amounted to 274,000 pounds, an average of over 22,000 pounds per pupil. The winning school of each state will receive a special Scroll Award from the War Production Board. On December 11, the program will originate in Moore School in Missouri, the students to be the contestants.

Episodes #329 & 330, Broadcast of December 4, 1943
East Coast Stunts: Water Song, Telepathy, Mirror Scream, Grandma Sings, and Type Corn
West Coast Stunts: Water Song, Telepathy, Mirror Scream, and Grandma Sings
Eight men lie down on their stomach, heads overhanging the edge of the stage, facing the audience. Each is assigned a number from one to eight. Above them are eight bells, each providing a different music note on a scale. A rope from each bell is tied around their forehead so when they lower their heads,

the bells ring. They are provided numbers that should make the song, "The Wind and the Rain in Your Hair." And to give it a realistic touch, directly under each face is a tub filled with water. In jerking their heads downward to ring the bell above them, they will submerge their noggins in 12 inches of water. Numbers eight and four were lucky – they were not needed in the song!

Two seamen are sat in chairs, facing each other. Using a metronome, they are required to hold their breath for 15 seconds and scream at each other. When they are blindfolded, one of them is removed and the other is screaming at himself in the mirror. The question is to see how long it takes him to discover he is screaming at himself.

Episodes #331 & 332, Broadcast of December 11, 1943

East Coast Stunts: Pretend Marriage, Missouri Mule, Play Teacher, and Teacher's Pet

West Coast Stunts: Political Speech, Spelling Bee, Missouri Mule, and Teacher's Pet

Broadcast originated from the Moore School in Brookfield, Missouri, the winning team in the scrap paper drive. **Leo Walsh** is asked to sing "Let Me Call You Sweetheart" to a beautiful woman standing outside the schoolhouse window. The contestant is blindfolded and had no idea that the face sticking inside from the window was a mule. He even had to kiss her.

Ronald Lester Noah, one of the students, helped Ralph Edwards participate in the first DUZ commercial. Fifth grade student **Richard Schaffer** had to dress up in wig and costume to play the role of the teacher, giving another student a talking to for having been a bad pupil. The real teacher plays the role of the bad pupil, sitting behind a screen, and Richard has no idea who he is really scolding.

Two screens are set up with three girls sticking their heads through, and three boys on the other side. Armed with seltzer bottles, the children participate in a spelling bee. If the girls get it wrong, the boys get to squirt the girls, and vice versa. Words included "valedictorian" and "schizophrenia." The students participating are **Donald Noah**, **Tommy Lewis**, **Patsy Schaffer**, **Joan Smith** and **Evelyn North**. Teacher's pet, **Lyle McCollen**, is dressed like a pet dog.

Episodes #333 & 334, Broadcast of December 18, 1943

Both Coast Stunts: Diaper Pig, Husband vs. Edwards, Lady Ralph, and Sailor Husband

Broadcast originated from the Golden Gate Theatre in San Francisco, California. A contestant must pin a diaper on a baby pig, confined in a pen. While performing the stunt, the contestant must sing "Rock a Bye Piggy." His first problem is catching the pig.

A husband is placed into a glass shower stall with fake pipes and faucets, six of them. Two dollars is placed in a box and the lid closed. The wife comes out and is told to open the box and take out the $2.00 that is inside. The husband is instructed, without the wife knowing, that if he can convince her not to open the box, he gets $20.00. The question is whether she will accept the word of her husband or Ralph Edwards! And the husband cannot tell the wife that the faucets and pipes are dummies.

A soldier, along with five others, is lined up behind a wall with only their pants legs showing. His wife is supposed to recognize which one is her husband. If she does, she wins $100. She fails so they have each men snore like they are asleep. She still fails. When a beautiful model walks by and the men are instructed to whistle, the wife spots the correct man!

Episodes #335 & 336, Broadcast of December 25, 1943

Both Coast Stunts: Quartette, Bedtime Story, Home, Sailor Kibitzes, and Christmas Stocking

Broadcast originated from the Oak Knoll Hospital, a naval hospital in Oakland, California. (Ward #44 to be exact.) This broadcast was mapped out to entertain soldiers who were unable to make it home for Christmas. "They were too busy fighting a war and getting fixed up to go back and fight some more, so tonight America comes to them," Edwards explains.

Three nurses and a soldier sing "Jingle Bells," with the soldier dressed like a nurse and the quartette wandering throughout all the rooms and wards serenading the men from cot to cot.

Armed with a Christmas stocking, a soldier is told to dress like Santa Claus and deliver gifts to soldiers in the hospital. The stocking is filled with such gifts as a cigarette lighter, a cigarette case, bedroom slippers, writing paper, a clock, a razor, ten dollars, a fountain pen, a pencil, a comb and brush set, cigarettes, a picture frame, etc.

Five men must tell a bed-time story, making it up as they go along, and every time Edwards rings the bell, the next soldier must pick up where the last left off, until the fifth one signs off with "And they lived happily ever after."

A sailor in the hospital is asked by Edwards "What do you suppose your mom is saying right now? I guess they'd be sitting around the Christmas tree, don't you think, looking over the gifts? I imagine she's saying, 'What do you suppose Joe is doing right now?'" At that moment, his mother speaks the same line and the sailor discovers his mother, father, girlfriend and brother are in the hospital, flown in from Texas at the expense of the quiz show. The family sings "Silent Night" to close the broadcast.

Episodes #337 & 338, Broadcast of January 1, 1944

Both Coast Stunts: Women Hillbillies, Only Truth, Soldier's Family, Husband Baseball, and Hold Breath

Broadcast originated from Radio City in San Francisco. Three women are christened "The Corn Fed Cacklers," known as a new Hillbilly Trio, and handed musical instruments: a washtub with a string attached to it, a fiddle, and a banjo. They are asked to sing "My Darling Nelly Gray" with clothespins on their nose.

A Private in the Army is invited on stage to take a "very cute girl" out on a date and splurge on her. The quiz show producers will even provide the money for the night out. The Private agrees, unaware that she is **Diane McKay**, a six-year-old. When Diane says she promised her little sister she could tag along for ice cream sodas, Edwards agrees and brings out Diane's sister, **Doreen McKay**, one of San Francisco's most glamorous models.

Episodes #339 & 340, Broadcast of January 8, 1944

East Coast Stunts: Piano Lap, Read Head, Great Lady, and Venetian Blind

West Coast Stunts: Piano Lap, Read Head, Great Lady, Venetian Blind, and Help With Props

Broadcast originated from Radio City in San Francisco. A female contestant is instructed to play "I'm Called Little Buttercup" on a piano while **Moyles and Benny Walker** put on a scene with Moyles trying to prevent a gate crasher, Walker, from entering the theater and raising loud volume. His distractions are to see if the female contestant would continue playing the piano regardless of the distraction.

A housewife is blindfolded and asked to identify her husband from the bumps on his head. Three men are on stage, sitting on stools, one being her husband. When she is blindfolded, the two strangers are asked to step aside and her husband continues to move from one stool to another to see if she notices any difference. She is also asked to tilt their heads back one by one and kiss each of them, unaware of the gag!

Episodes #341 & 342, Broadcast of January 15, 1944
Both Coast Stunts: Water Fan, Hidden Husband, Wash Shirts, Girdle Situation, and Alphonse Gaston

Broadcast originated from Phoenix, Arizona, at the request of the U.S. Treasury Department. Ralph Edwards and the crew were helping assist with the Fourth War Loan Drive. Entry to the broadcast was through the purchase of a War Bond. Their appearance in Phoenix netted approximately $915,475 in sales.

A contestant is asked to sing "April Showers" while he sprays a seltzer bottle into an electric fan, which sends the spray back in his face.

A housewife is asked to accompany a male contestant in a long-distance phone call. Because it is not urgent war business, they agree to "pretend" to play long-distance. In reality, her husband in the audience has a third phone and he will do all the talking while the actor in on the gag mouths the words. She will think the stranger on the stage is trying to romance her, asking to kiss her when he gets closer, and the actor, hearing every word her husband says, will inch closer to her. The trick is to see how long it takes for her to react to the improper invite.

A soldier and a sailor must knock each other over with kindness and politeness. **Sergeant McClean** and **Jerry Bucham** were the contestants, who try to win the contest by convincing the other to walk through the door and receive whatever is on the other wise. The two contestants, suspecting something foul, attempt to be too kind to each other to convince the other to be the victim… unaware that two beautiful women are on the other side, **Janice LaPrade** and **Betty Speakman**.

Episodes #343 & 344, Broadcast of January 22, 1944
East Coast Stunts: Fat Man, Ice Cream Rock, Mama Doll, and Bathing Beauty
West Coast Stunts: Fat Man, Upside Down Texas, Mama Doll, and Bathing Beauty

Broadcast originated from Dallas, Texas, which was the second stop on the Fourth War Loan Drive tour. A total of $1,828,500 in the sale of War Bonds was purchased.

A 260-pound contestant is sent out to make house calls of housewives in Dallas and collect fat. Fat contains glycerin, which makes bullets. It also makes surgical dressings, antiseptics and drugs. If he collects his weight in waste kitchen fat from Dallas housewives by the end of the show, he will get a $100 War Bond. A remote phone call is placed towards the end of the program to check on his status.

A contestant is provided a phone call to his wife and every time Ralph Edwards taps him on the shoulder, the contestant is to tip a Mama Doll forward so it says, "Ma-Ma." The contestant is instructed not to tell the wife what the doll is, or that he is on a quiz show. When the doll fails to work, Edwards has a model, **Dorothy Hoover**, come out on stage and she says more than "Oh, Daddy" and "Ma-Ma!"

A male contestant is dressed up like Miss Rocky Mountain 1944, complete with blonde wig. He is provided company with two bathing beauties, Miss Peach Festival of 1944 and Miss Rose Arbor of 1943. He and his indiscretions are then exposed to his wife.

Episodes #345 & 346, Broadcast of January 29, 1944

Both Coast Stunts: Frank Sinatra, Elephant Fable, Louis XIV Chair, and Mayor Switch

Broadcast originated from Memphis, Tennessee. A total of $2,891,225 in the sale of War Bonds was purchased.

A contestant is asked to put on a bowtie and hang on to the mike stand, hair falling idly over the right eye, and croon "You'll Never Know" or "Paper Doll" like Frank Sinatra would. Edwards asks all grandmothers in the audience to squeal like all the young girls do when Sinatra sings.

Recalling the Aesop fable of three blind men who each felt different parts of an elephant got into a terrible argument because they all insisted it was something different. One felt the trunk and thought it was a snake, and so forth. Three women were blindfolded and when they were brought back out on stage, they were asked to guess what the object is by touching it. And a real live elephant, courtesy of its trainer, was brought on stage for the stunt!

A contestant is asked to pretend to be **Walter Chandler**, the Mayor of Memphis, while a second contestant is sent outside to find a man off the street and convince him that the imposter is the Mayor of Memphis. While the contestants are outside, Edwards explains that the real Mayor is dressed in shabby clothes and walking outside to be the first man picked up – a joke on the contestants!

For the East Coast broadcast, the show ran over and as a result, the Bulova commercial and the NBC Chimes were not heard.

Episodes #347 & 348, Broadcast of February 5, 1944

Both Coast Stunts: Maternity, Rhett Butler, Hat Penalty, Mother's Lullaby, and Sing in Mood

Broadcast originated from Atlanta, Georgia. A total of $1,163,575 in the sale of War Bonds was purchased.

Mrs. Seegers, mother of a serviceman, whose consequences was to sing a lullaby that she used to sing to her son, a background chorus composed of 150 voices from the combined churches of Atlanta, hummed along with the contestant. Afterwards, Edwards tells her, I'm sure if your son is listening, his heart is warm. And even if he isn't, I'm sure he must feel the love you and his country hold for him."

Two male contestants are dressed up like Rhett Butler and Scarlett O'Hara from *Gone with the Wind*... complete with hoop skirt, bonnet and umbrella. They are sent out to Peachtree Street with Rhett calling out for Scarlett, and Scarlett teasing him by shouting, "You can't find me, Rhett!" An engineer with a microphone is out in the street capturing the scene while Ralph Edwards places a call to the local police department to report "suspicious looking characters."

Episodes #349 & 350, Broadcast of February 12, 1944

Both Coast Stunts: Welder Cinderella, Cigar Seltzer, Hiccup, and Drummer

Broadcast originated from the Mosque Theatre in Richmond, Virginia. Total sales of War Bonds generated was $576,215. This was the last of a five-week tour which grossed a total of $7,374,990 worth of War Bonds sold. **Barry McKinley** and his orchestra supplied music on this show.

Reminding radio listeners that tens of thousands of women are doing assembly line in war plants throughout the country, getting grease on their nose and paint on their hands, Ralph Edwards wanted people to remember how charming American women can be. A female contestant, a working girl in overalls and grease, becomes Cinderella for a night. A crew of beauty and fashion experts, including **Francis Church** of Elizabeth Arden, and **Arnold**, the famous hair stylist, prey on the first contestant of the evening and return towards the end of the broadcast with a Cinderella.

One contestant is strapped to a chair and hung from the ceiling, armed with a seltzer bottle, pretending to be a pilot operating a machine gun. Another contestant, smoking a cigar, is forced to wear a raincoat and a shower cap and if his cigar is extinguished, the other contestant wins $5.00.

Drummer **Willie Farmer** allows a female contestant to take over part of the band and play music with a bunch of old dishes, glasses, pots, pans and all kind of instruments.

Episodes #351 & 352, Broadcast of February 19, 1944

East Coast Stunts: Husbands Bark, Sailor Actress, Lock, Crowded Booth, and Girdle Race

West Coast Stunts: Husbands Bark, Sailor Actress, Lock, and Crowded Booth

Broadcast from New York City. Celebrity guest is actress **Constance Bennett** who participates in a stunt involving a sailor who expresses how much he loves her, according to a script he is provided. Unaware who he is talking to, the sailor delivers such statements as "I would swoop you up and dash you away on my trusty horse" and "If I were just close enough to hold you in my arms."

Because husbands are known for being in the dog house, three husbands are put into a big dog kennel in the middle of the stage, with three little windows for them to stick their heads out of. Each husband is required to bark like a dog and the blindfolded wives must identify their husbands. But what the women don't know is that the men are replaced by real dogs, trained to bark on cue.

A man is asked to mail an envelope to the Mayor of his hometown, without asking any questions. The mail chute is located outside the studio. When he returns, later in the program, Edwards rewards the contestant with a special lapel pin, the emblem of the sealed heart and drawing the lapels of the coat together, Edwards puts the emblem through the lapels. It turned out to be a Yale Lock, which firmly seals the lapels of the coat together. It is impossible to get the coat off the contestant with both lapels locked together. As for the key? The contestant mailed it to the Mayor of his town. When he gets home, he will have to call the Mayor's office to get the key.

Episodes #353 & 354, Broadcast of February 26, 1944
East Coast Stunts: Feature Story, Upside Down Texas, Mairzy Doats, and Song Concentration
West Coast Stunts: Feature Story, Ice Cream Rock, Mairzy Doats, and Song Concentration
Broadcast originated from the Adams Theatre in Newark, New Jersey. (At one point, the program switched to the Editor's office of the *Newark Star Ledger*.) A female contestant is asked to take a yellow envelope over to the City Editor of the *Newark Star Ledger*, and sell him, sight unseen, the two romantic pictures of a famous playboy caught in the act with a beautiful girl on his lap. After she leaves the stage, her husband is asked to come on stage and with a beautiful model, poses for the photographs. Later, when the wife is handed the sealed envelope, she will not suspect that the photos are of her husband. If the photos are printed in the next edition, she receives an extra prize. (For the West Coast, the stunt was performed with permission of *The San Mateo Times*.)
A contestant is strapped into a specially-built harness and hung upside down from the ceiling. He is asked to sing "Deep in the Heart of Texas," delivering each line backwards. Cymbals are attached to his ankles because when he comes to the part of the song where he is to clap his hands, he will clap his feet together.
Editor **Victor Hammerslag** of the *Star Ledger* receives a visit from the contestant, courtesy of a remote pick-up and announcer **Clyde Kittel**.

Episodes #355 & 356, Broadcast of March 4, 1944
Both Coast Stunts: Steam Roller, Sniff Roses, and Fred Allen
A contestant is asked to remove his trousers and put on a pair of winter underwear, and a big wooden barrel to wear as a skirt, which has suspenders on it. The wife is handed her husband's trousers and the couple are sent outside the studio in Rockefeller Plaza where a steamroller in the streets is operating. Her mission is to convince the operator of the road equipment to press her husband's trousers while he is on the street wearing the barrel. **Ed Herlihy** is the announcer in the streets, reporting what is happening. (The West Coast

broadcast ran over unexpectedly so the outcome of the Steamroller stunt was not broadcast except on the East Coast.)

Edwards: Now let's have our next contestant. Bring up a man. What's is your name, please?

Allen: Fred Allen.

Edwards: Fred Allen... and where are you from?

Allen: Boston.

Edwards: What is your occupation, Mr. Allen?

Allen: I'm in the gasoline business.

Edwards: You sell gas?

Allen: No, I'm usually out looking for it.

Edwards: Somehow I got the idea you were in the egg business.

Allen: I used to be, but I got too fat. I was overshooting the nest.

Edwards: Well, that's interesting. Just seeing the sights of New York? And you just dropped in to *Truth or Consequences* for a little fun, eh?

Allen: I was on a 55-cent tour of Radio City. I must have gone in the wrong door.

Edwards: What will you do when you leave here?

Allen: I'll go home to Portland.

Edwards: I thought you lived in Boston.

Allen: Please, Mr. Edwards, I'm very nervous. You're confusing me.

Edwards: I don't mean to do that. Just in a little closer to the mike, please. No, that's too close.... back a little.

Allen: I don't seem to get the hang of this.

Edwards: But we do have a question for you, Mr. Allen. Miss it and you'll pay the consequence... By the way, you're no relation to that Fred Allen on the air, are you?

Allen: I'll tell you after the consequence.

Edwards: Okay, here's your question.

[Trick question to be provided]

Edwards: You haven't told the truth, so you must pay the consequences. Well now, what consequence shall we give you, Mr. Allen?

Allen: I'll take the one where you take a model to the Stork Club with all expenses paid.

Edwards: Mr. Allen, the country has been hearing your tones for many years now. You're specialty is putting people to sleep. Why, in some sections you're known as the coast-to-coast, Sunday Night Sandman.

Allen: Well, thank you…

Edwards: Yes, "Old Gravel Voice," they call you. And tonight we want you to continue your nocturnal offerings. You're going to read a bedtime story to three little children… three lovely little kiddies. You will be "Uncle Fred" to them and read the story of "Peter Rabbit." Now run off stage for a second, get into your slippers and long white night gown and bring back the story of "Peter Rabbit."

The three little boys (age six) selected for the stunt are three tough little kids from the Boys Club, 110th Street Branch. While **Fred Allen** is off stage, Edwards instructs the boys to be as ornery as they can. "When 'Uncle Fred' starts reading the story of 'Peter Rabbit,' we want you to go to work on him," Edwards instructs the youths. "Climb on his shoulders, put raisins in his ears, glue on his fingers so the pages of the story book will stick to his fingers. Take his shoes off, stuff an egg in his mouth… anything. And if you can succeed in breaking him up before he finishes the story, we'll give you boys a little prize."

The boys sit quietly and act like good little boys until Allen enters, dressed in slippers, long flannel nightgown and nightcap. Allen was then introduced to the three boys, Mac, Robert and Charlie, and then sat on the sofa with the boys on each side. Allen is instructed to win $5 if he completes the reading of the story. As Allen read, accompanied by music, Edwards asks "Uncle Fred" if he wants any raisins, followed by glue, a clothes pin, molasses, an egg, all while Edwards remarked, "Now boys, I wouldn't pour that molasses in those slippers…" By the time the stunt concludes, Allen is referring to the boys as "foul cherubs" and refers to them by name as "Dynamite" and "Formaldehyde." The stunt concludes when Edwards answers the phone and tells the recipient that Mr. Allen will not come to the phone. "He says you're a jerk," Edwards tells the voice on the other end of the phone. "He says to go soak your head in a pail of mud." When Allen asks who was on the other line, Edwards explains, "The Texaco Company," which is Allen's weekly sponsor.

Before Fred Allen leaves the stage, he thanks Edwards for the swell contest. "I just want to say you've treated me with all the dignity and respect a man of my reputation deserves." Allen invites Edwards over to his program tomorrow night. When one of the children ask Allen for a hug and kiss, and the comedian bends down to assist, the child smacks the comedian in the face with a custard pie.

Episodes #357 & 358, Broadcast of March 11, 1944
East Coast Stunts: Pull Tub, Test Eggs, Oklahoma, and Fluoroscope
West Coast Stunts: Pull Tub, Test Eggs, Oklahoma, Fluoroscope, and False Alarm

- Three men are dressed in old-fashioned bathing suits as if they were going to Atlantic City forty years ago and sit in a tub of lukewarm water. There were wheels on the bathtub and it was pulled across stage by two donkeys. The men had to scrub with soap and literally take a bath in public. With a crowd of people in the hallway, a few planted by Edwards and his staff, spectators could be heard saying, "Don't you guys ever bathe at home?" and "Why don't you put the donkeys in, too?"
- The sixth floor at Radio City had two big theatres separated by a big hall. *Abie's Irish Rose* was the feature for the evening. The bathtub stunt on the East Coast was witnessed by people leaving the theater, following the conclusion of *Abie's Irish Rose*. For the West Coast show, people were milling about getting ready to go into *Abie's Irish Rose* for the second production. The stunt was put on in the second theater so the contestant's bath was not as private as they initially thought.
- Four eggs, three raw and one hard-boiled, are strapped around the head of a contestant, with one on his forehead, one at the back of his head, and one on either side of his head. The contestant has to choose which one is hard-boiled and in order to do so, he has to smash each egg he thinks is the correct one. (All four eggs were raw. No hardboiled.)

Episodes #359 & 360, Broadcast of March 18, 1944
Both Coast Stunts: Dentist Chair, Oklahoma Remote, and Police Car

Broadcast originated from New York City with a remote pickup from Tulsa, Oklahoma. A contestant, a dentist by profession, is made to wear a rubber apron and a shower cap and sit in a dentist chair, directly below a bulging water balloon. With marshmallows crammed into his mouth, the contestant must laugh (as if he has been treated to laughing gas) every time Edwards, playing dentist, asks a question. If Edwards cannot understand what the patient is saying, he pumps the chair higher and higher, applying more pressure on the balloon filled with water. As the contestant answers questions, Edwards continues to add more marshmallows.

Last week, two contestants in the studio audience, **Mrs. Louise Osborne** and **Mrs. Edith Sheridan** of New York City, were asked if they wanted two tickets to see *Oklahoma*. They said "yes" and thought they would be going to see the stage musical. Instead, they were handed two tickets to Tulsa, Oklahoma, and broadcast via remote the two contestants tonight tell how they have been helping raise money for the Bond Rally, while they are on stage in the Delmar Theatre in Tulsa.

From Oklahoma, **Robert S. Kerr**, Governor of Oklahoma, told that the two contestants Edwards sent raised another $500,000 in War Bonds. There was a Bond rally going on through the day at the Municipal Auditorium. One hundred men from the Rainbow Division of Infantry stationed at Camp Gruber, Oklahoma, were guests and **Corporal Allen Funt** led them in singing.

Episodes #361 & 362, Broadcast of March 25, 1944
East Coast Stunts: Can-Can, Mock, Sleep Baby Sleep, Camels, Post Office, and Hitler Pie
West Coast Stunts: Can-Can, Mock, Sleep Baby Sleep, Hitler Pie, and Post Office
Two male contestants dress in big bonnets, blond wigs and fluffy can-can dresses. They perform with empty tomato cans tied to their shoes. A Navy Air Crewman, who has not seen his newborn child, gets the surprise of his life after he plays a stunt. His wife was in on the stunt from the beginning.

Episodes #363 & 364, Broadcast of April 1, 1944
Both Coast Stunts: Purse, Barber Chair, Vaughn Monroe, Equal Rights, and Palm Read
A man is instructed to be the unwilling victim of a barber's chair, while trying to romance the manicurist. What the contestant is unaware of is the man playing the barber, complete with shaving cream, is the real-life husband of the manicurist.

Singer and orchestra leader, **Vaughn Monroe**, participates in a stunt where a female contestant is handed a trumpet and told to instruct a member of the audience how to play the musical instrument. What she is unaware of – and the audience is let in on – is the fact that the man she instructs is trumpet player is Vaughn Monroe.

Episodes #365 & 366, Broadcast of April 8, 1944

Both Coast Stunts: Flopsy Mopsy, Hope Chest, and Water Fight

Ralph Edwards introduced **Harry Von Zell**, who will take over Edwards' spot on the show as emcee for a brief spell. Edwards was drafted and is scheduled to leave the show in four weeks. **Eddie Cantor** is a celebrity guest in this episode for the Flopsy Mopsy consequence.

Episodes #367 & 368, Broadcast of April 15, 1944

Both Coast Stunts: Molasses Money, Camel, Dinah Shore, and Quick Sounds

Celebrity guests include **Jack Benny** and **Dinah Shore**. **Harry Von Zell**, still feeling his oats, assists Ralph Edwards as emcee. A contestant is given the chance to pick up as many dollars as he can in a given period of time – with his hands tied behind him and molasses spread over his face. Dinah Shore assists with the stunt. In another consequence, a soldier beats Ralph Edwards to the punch on the quick sounds stunt during the West Coast show. The West Coast Show has a Betty Wright Announcement.

Episodes #369 & 370, Broadcast of April 22, 1944

Both Coast Stunts: Sleep Sheep, Boxer's Teeth, Call Home, and Close Mouth

Contestants **Harry Foreman** and **Paul Doran** are provided with old fashioned night dress and night cap and ordered to bed. If the men are able to fall asleep on stage before the close of broadcast, they will each be paid $1,000. In order to verify the men are truly asleep and not faking, a doctor from the audience is asked to verify. To ensure the men do not fall asleep, Hawaiian musicians and dancers are brought on stage.

Episodes #371 & 372, Broadcast of April 29, 1944

East Coast Stunts: Circus, Oldsmobile, Leap Frog, Seeds, and Close Mouth

West Coast Stunts: Circus, Wife, Oldsmobile, Leap Frog, and Closed Mouth

Radio announcer **Clyde Kittel** escorts a blindfolded contestant to Madison Square Garden where the circus is being performed. She does not know she is at the circus, but told to dramatize for her husband verbally, professing her love. Announcer **Ed Herlihy** is heard over the air via remote pick-up. Only after the blindfold is removed does she discover she was making love to a chimpanzee in front of the audience.

Episodes #373 & 374, Broadcast of May 6, 1944
East Coast Stunts: Without a Shift, Hiawatha, Come as You Are, and Tickle Announcer
West Coast Stunts: Without a Shift, Hiawatha, Come as You Are, and Piano Toes
This was the final broadcast for **Harry Von Zell**, as the question of drafting Ralph Edwards for the U.S. Military was resolved. A contestant is told to say "Without a Shirt" every time the music stops playing, while at the same time Ralph Edwards asks questions. For every time the contestant remembers, he is paid one dollar. For every time he forgets, he loses a dollar. The last question is "What is the tune **Johnny Gart** is playing?" At that point the music stops and the contestant must quickly decide to answer the question or remember to say, "Without a tune." In another stunt, a contestant is asked to remove his shoes and play "Tiptoe Through the Tulips" on the piano using only his toes. The program closes with a contestant, paid $5 and a box of DUZ, if they tickle the announcer as he closes off with the signature, "This is the National Broadcasting Company."

Episodes #375 & 376, Broadcast of May 13, 1944
Both Coast Stunts: Reducing Diet, Mother's Corsage, Come as You Are, and Goodnight Seal
Last week three women were instructed to phone a friend and ask them to appear on *Truth or Consequences* one week from that night, they would receive $100. **Mrs. Walter Lennstrom** of Richmond Hill, Long Island called **Mrs. J. Leroy Lennstrom**, her sister-in-law; **Mrs. G. Avallone** of New York City phoned **Rose Avallone** of the Bronx; and **Martha Luyster** of Sea Cliff, Long Island, phoned **Frances Hedden** of Brooklyn. All three women won the prize money. In another stunt, the mother of a serviceman is brought to New York City to spend Mother's Day with her son.

Episodes #377 & 378, Broadcast of May 20, 1944
East Coast Stunts: Charlie Spivak, Thought Waves, and Glass of Water
West Coast Stunts: Charlie Spivak, Thought Waves, and Tickle Announcer
One of the consequences involved a pick-up from the Paramount Theatre with **Charlie Spivak** and his orchestra. A male contestant is put into a dress and escorted to the Paramount, with a member of the production crew, to perform on stage. According to Edwards, Spivak needed a female vocalist for his stage

performance and Edwards does not want to disappoint the trumpet player. Considering this stunt was performed on both coasts, Charlie Spivak was probably in on the gag.

Episodes #379 & 380, Broadcast of May 27, 1944
Both Coast Stunts: All Day Sucker, Hammer Pie, Television, and WAC Recruit
As a public service announcement, during this broadcast **Claudia Suesse** is sworn in as a WAC on the program, by **Major Lucille Van Bolt**. Suesse received $50 as a gift from Procter & Gamble. Following the gift, an announcement about WAC recruiting was made.

Episodes #381 & 382, Broadcast of June 3, 1944
Both Coast Stunts: Cargo Net, Carol Thurston, and Tin Whistle Symphony
This broadcast originated from the Academy of Music in Philadelphia, Pennsylvania. This broadcast kicked off the start of the "E" Bond tour. All admissions to the show were made through a purchase of a war bond in the Fifth War Loan campaign. The larger the purchase, the better the seats in the house. Actress **Carol Thurston** was a celebrity guest on this broadcast, assisted by the Philadelphia Symphony Orchestra. Edwards announced over the air that a total of $2,500,000 in bonds were sold.

Episodes #383 & 384, Broadcast of June 10, 1944
Both Coast Stunts: Pump Balloon, Earphone Interview, Inside Drum, and Prayer
Broadcast originated from the Kiel Auditorium in St. Louis, Missouri. Continuing with the current War Bond drive, the audience gained admission with the purchase of a War Bond. A contestant named Mrs. Stewart appeared on the program and was told that if listeners purchased $1 million worth of bonds within the next week, her son would receive a $1,000 War Bond from *Truth or Consequences*.

Episodes #385 & 386, Broadcast of June 17, 1944
Both Coast Stunts: Honor Father, Horse and Buggy, and Amateur Comedian
Broadcast originated from the Music Hall of Cleveland Public Auditorium in Cleveland, Ohio. An announcement was made on this program that **Private Dallas Stewart**, the young man who was promised a $1,000 War Bond if his

mother's on-air plea would generate at least $1 million in bond sales, was the lucky recipient of the prize.

Episodes #387 & 388, Broadcast of June 24, 1944
Both Coast Stunts: Xylophone Nose, Boston Tea Party, Lie Detector, and Sears Sing
Broadcast originated from Boston, Massachusetts. In recognition, two men are asked to reconstruct the Boston Tea Party, with scripted dialogue. This party, however, involves two infants in Boston pretending to have tea. Complete with miniature chairs, tables and toy dishes, the men are dressed in baby clothes and bonnets and quarrel over who has the prettiest dress.

Episodes #389 & 390, Broadcast of July 1, 1944
Both Coast Stunts: Bathtub, Nylon Present, Talk to Self, and Three Grannies
Broadcast originated from Raleigh, North Carolina. A man and woman are instructed to act out a scene from a movie – a pie fight that turns into calamity on the air. In another stunt, a contestant is sent out into the street to soak in a bathtub, situated next to a fire hydrant, and sing "How Dry I Am." This was the final program of the season.

Episodes #391 & 392, Broadcast of September 9, 1944
Both Coast Stunts: Hawk Saw, Bake Biscuits, Reflex Syphon, and Fish Wife
This broadcast concerned a "Honeymoon Cruise." Edwards recruited fifty brides and bridegrooms from the ranks of servicemen and war workers. Following the broadcast they boarded an excursion boat for an all-night trip up the Hudson. The cruise consisted of a dance band for their enjoyment, including a wedding supper and breakfast the following morning before the boat docked. Edwards devised this plan so as to give uniformed men and war workers a brief honeymoon, who otherwise would not be able to have one. Edwards arranged for marriage ceremonies for a few of them, following the show, providing ministers, etc., basically everything but the ring.

Episodes #393 & 394, Broadcast of September 16, 1944
Both Coast Stunts: Money Hose, Elsie Manager, Telephone Fund, and Valet
Broadcast originated from New York City, with a remote broadcast from Halloran Hospital. **Clyde Kittel** interviews **Tony Ventriglia**, a soldier wounded on

New Guinea, who told of marrying an Australian girl. He made a recording and also sang on it, which will be sent to his wife in Australia. The sponsor sent the transportation to his wife and surprised him on the air by bring her to Halloran.

Episodes #395 & 396, Broadcast of September 23, 1944
Both Coast Stunts: Cinderella Baby, Guy Lombardo, Heartbeat, and Pearl
A contestant thinks he is telephoning **Guy Lombardo** to tell him, from what he thinks is a safe distance, that he cannot stand Lombardo's music. What he did not know, of course, was that the gentleman standing next to him, listening to his every word irately, was Guy Lombardo himself.

Episodes #397 & 398, Broadcast of September 30, 1944
East Coast Stunts: Goldfish, Double Talk, and Mink Coat
West Coast Stunts: Goldfish, Double Talk, Mink Coat, and Bouncing Fiddle
Celebrity guest is **Al Kelly**, famous double-talk artist. On this show a $2,000 genuine mink coat from I.J. Fox was given away to a contestant (two, one for each broadcast).

Episodes #399 & 400, Broadcast of October 7, 1944
Both Coast Stunts: Sliding Staircase, Trade Jobs, and Symphony Message
Broadcast originated from Cincinnati, Ohio. Among the celebrity guests was **J.J. Rowe**, a banker in Cincinnati, famous locally for his contributions to the American Red Cross and as chairman of Community programs.

Episodes #401 & 402, Broadcast of October 14, 1944
Both Coast Stunts: Roy Rogers, Three Voices, and $200 Hat
Broadcast originated from New York City. Celebrity guest was **Roy Rogers**, who was in the Big Apple to perform at a rodeo going on at Madison Square Garden. Contestant **Mrs. Harold (Mary) Kinneman** was told a famous movie star backstage would sing a few notes. She must identify the singer or pay the consequences. Rogers sang a few notes of "Home on the Range" but she could not identify him. Roy Rogers was introduced and they sang a duet of "Pistol Packin' Mama" with Roy sitting on a stool and Mrs. Kinneman, wearing a sombrero, riding an Everlast electric horse. The Madison Square Garden rodeo was plugged on the program thru October 29. For the repeat

show for the West Coast, the first contestant chosen, **Louise De La Vigne**, correctly identified Roy Rogers. (She admitted on the air that she knew it was him because she listened in on the East Coast broadcast earlier in the evening!) Edwards had a difficult time as he kept mispronouncing her name. Because De La Vigne confessed she cheated, **Mrs. Ernest (Lena) Allen** was then chosen as her replacement in the consequence.

Episodes #403 & 404, Broadcast of October 21, 1944
Both Coast Stunts: Sound Effects, Milk Shower, Frankie Carle, and Duncan Phyfe

Broadcast originated from New York City. For a brief spell, the program switched to a general hospital in Richmond, Virginia, where **Pfc. Raymond Kenney** of New York City and a member of the 77th Division was recovering from wounds he received. Kenney wished to hear **Frankie Carle**, bandleader and pianist, and the real Carle appears on the program to play to him. Edwards then informed Kenney and his friend that they would be presented with the first Plymouth car to come off the assembly line.

Episodes #405 & 406, Broadcast of October 28, 1944
Both Coast Stunts: $300 Pie, Milton Berle, and Tuba Lesson

Celebrity guest was **Milton Berle**, who participated in a consequence for a lucky contestant. The wartime commercial asks people to save their fats for the war cause. Tricky question asked during this broadcast, "What is the most intelligent animal?" (Answer: man) An organ cue was missed at the beginning of the West Coast broadcast.

Episode #407, Broadcast of November 4, 1944
East Coast Stunts: Egg Note, Wickel Payoff I, Opera Star, and Thump Heads

In the audience was **Rudolph J. Wickel**, of Verona, New Jersey. The show has been searching for someone named Wickel since last April. He was told there was a box containing $1,000 buried in an empty lot in Holyoke, Massachusetts. He was to take a train there and pick it up. Because the Wickel stunt could not be repeated for the West Coast, the East Coast broadcast was recorded and played back for the West Coast broadcast.

Episodes #408 & 409, Broadcast of November 11, 1944

Both Coast Stunts: Spin Contestant, Wickel Payoff II, and White Christmas

Edwards embarrassingly reported that two residents of Holyoke, Massachusetts, dug up the money which had been buried for Mr. Wickel, before the contestant arrived at the scene: **Joe Roy**, a 32-year-old medically-discharged serviceman and his 14-year-old brother-in-law, **Henry Hartell**. The successful diggers appeared on the program. Mr. Wickel also appeared on the program, and said he was glad a war veteran had gotten the money. He was also given a check for $1,000 without the name of the bank on it. If Mr. Wickel finds the bank, he would receive the money.

The program switched to Rome, Italy, from 8:49 to 8:56, for a two-way conversation with **Electrician's Mate First Class Edward B. Dander** of Auxiliary Route 27, Albany, New York. Dander told of his experiences overseas and sang "White Christmas," accompanied by **Corporal Harris Martin** of Nashville, Tennessee, on the harmonica. Edwards informed Dander that all his Christmas shopping had been done for him and he was being given a $500 War Bond. (Following the broadcast, Edwards would ultimately receive a lot of postcards and letters from listeners suggesting the harmonica player should have received a prize as well for his participation.)

Episodes #410 & 411, Broadcast of November 18, 1944

East Coast Stunts: Register Horse, Wickel Payoff III, Seltzer Accompanist, and Chicken Every Sunday

West Coast Stunts: Register Horse, Wickel Payoff III, and Seltzer Accompanist

Rudolph J. Wickel makes his third appearance on the program. Mr. Wickel presents the check he received on last week's program to his bank in Verona, New Jersey, and was paid in Confederate money. He was given a safe containing $1,000 and told that if he could figure out the combination, he could have the money. (He is to appear again next week to report on the progress.) **Sammy Prager**, accompanist for many famous singers, also appeared on the program.

Episodes #412 & 413, Broadcast of November 25, 1944

Both Coast Stunts: Tuba Payoff, Conover, Wickel Payoff IV, and Pie Woman

Rudolph J. Wickel reports that he opened the safe but had only found one-half of a $1,000 bill. He was given a clue where the other half of the bill is – the clue is a talking parrot. He was told to report on next week's program. **Harry Conover**, Head of the Model Agency, was a guest celebrity on the program.

Episodes #414 & 415, Broadcast of December 2, 1944

Both Coast Stunts: Honest Frame, Lights Out, Wickel Payoff V, and Admiral (Frame)

Program originated from the Navy Pier in Chicago, Illinois, where the Navy exhibits "Pacific Theatre," being held in the interest of the Sixth War Loan Drive. From New York City, Mr. Wickel said he had not found out from the parrot where the other half of the $1,000 bill was. Edwards said it was around the parrot's neck (but the parrot is now in Chicago) and he would mail it to Mr. Wickel, enclosed in a book. Then, without Wickel aware of the joke, Edwards asked everyone listening to the radio program to send books to Mr. Wickel, which would ultimately be turned over to the Victory Book Committee to be sent overseas. The address reported on the air (and in newspapers) was 35 South Prospect Street, Verona, New Jersey.

Episodes #416 & 417, Broadcast of December 9, 1944

Both Coast Stunts: Russian Chorus, Bald Heads, Wickel Payoff VI, and Love Tunnel

Rudolph J. Wickel appeared on the program and said that a total of 9,373 books had arrived so far. He found the other half of the $1,000 bill in a book titled "Blood, Sweat and Tears." This was Mr. Wickel's last appearance on the program. He was told there would always be a special seat reserved for him at the radio broadcasts, should he choose to watch the staged stunts.

Episodes #418 & 419, Broadcast of December 16, 1944

East Coast Stunts: Trolley, Tears, Don't Travel, and Revolving Door

West Coast Stunts: Trolley, Tears, Serial Number, Chicken Every Sunday, and Moustache

Pfc. Robert Smart appeared on the program. He is traveling to Asheville, North Carolina, for Christmas. Radio listeners were urged to call and give him their reservations for the trip in connection with the "Don't Travel" campaign.

Episodes #420 & 421, Broadcast of December 23, 1944

Both Coast Stunts: Christmas Tree, Chimes, Dizzy, and Screen Test

A special Christmas broadcast with a switch to an Army base in Rome, Italy, from 8:36 to 8:42. **T/Sgt. William Wahlert** of St. Louis, and of the Special Service Division of the Army, sang "Silent Night," accompanied by chimes from St. Thomas Episcopal Church in New York. **T/Sgt. Howard Dalberg** of Public Relations of Air Force Headquarters in Italy is announced. (The producers of the program sent each boy at the church a billfold containing a $100 bill.) From New York, **Richard Harvey** (mentioned by name) rang the chimes at St. Thomas Episcopal Church.

A WAVE is handed a script from the motion picture, *Here Come the Waves*, directed by the producer-director, **Mark Sandrich**, with radio actor **Joseph Julian** playing the opposite lead. For her consequence she receives a two-week visit to Hollywood, after the war is over, with all-expenses-paid and a traveling outfit to be created by **Edith Head**, designer for Paramount Pictures. The grand-prize winner was the soldier in Rome, Italy, who sang.

Engineers were unable to contact Rome for the repeat show. That segment was quickly replaced by **Pvt. Buddy Marino** (in studio) from Los Angeles, formerly with Harry James, who sang "Silent Night" with chimes from St. Thomas just as in the first show. **Specialist 3rd Class Margaret Sullivan**, WAVE, enacted the part of *Here Comes the Waves* in both the first and repeat performance of the show.

Episodes #422 & 423, Broadcast of December 30, 1944

East Coast Stunts: Penn Station B.U., Hold Under Water, Faint, Diving Suit B.U., Penn Station Payoff, and Evening Clothes

West Coast Stunts: Same as East Coast but without Evening Clothes stunt

There was a brief pick-up from Penn Station, North Carolina, during the broadcast, when a woman was provided a $100 bill and instructed to go down to Penn Station, find a soldier or serviceman, ask their name, where they are from, and other questions. Then she was instructed to kiss the soldier, hand them the money and wish them a happy 1945. For her participation, she received a $25 War Bond and a big red box of DUZ.

Actress **Hope Emerson** is a guest celebrity, participating in the Faint stunt.

Episodes #424 & 425, Broadcast of January 6, 1945

East Coast Stunts: Serial Number, Conference Call, Delicatessen B.U., and Diving Suit Payoff

West Coast Stunts: Peanut Butter Address, Conference Call, Diving Suit Payoff, and Delicatessen B.U.

Julius Benson, owner of the Trafalgar Delicatessen Store, 70th Street and Columbus Avenue, New York City, appeared on the program to help with a stunt. His consequence is to attend with a major gala – a grand opening with movie stars, limos and host **Milton Cross** to promote the event. In another stunt, a contestant who put on a heavy diving suit last week, with microphone inside, is instructed to sing, "Don't Fence Me In."

Episodes #426 & 427, Broadcast of January 13, 1945

East Coast Stunts: Seltzer Description, Dramatic On, Delicatessen Payoff, and Barber College B.U.

West Coast Stunts: Seltzer Description, Dramatic On, Delicatessen Payoff, Barber College B.U., and Revolving Door

Mr. and Mrs. Julius Benson were on the program from their delicatessen store where a "grand opening" was being held. **Milton Cross** was the emcee from that point, introducing **Carl Ravazza**, singing band leader, and his orchestra; **Lee Bowman**, movie star; **Mr. and Mrs. Arthur Murray**, dancing instructors; **Harry Conover**, head of the model agency; and **Earl Wilson**, columnist of the *New York Post*.

Episodes #428 & 429, Broadcast of January 20, 1945

Both Coast Stunts: Pull Cork, Barber Shop Payoff, and March of Dimes B.U.

Bobby Riggio, a 10-year-old infantile paralysis victim, appeared on the program in connection with the March of Dimes. Edwards offered to give him a $1,000 War Bond if listeners would send $10,000 in dimes to Bobby, to be turned over to the March of Dimes campaign.

Episodes #430 & 431, Broadcast of January 27, 1945

Both Coast Stunts: Melting Ice B.U., Janet Blair, and March of Dimes Payoff

Actress **Janet Blair** makes a celebrity appearance in this broadcast. Switch to Washington to hear **Bobby Riggio**, who appeared on the program last week. Announcer **Don Fisher** presented young Bobby with the $1,000 War Bond because $79,642 worth of dimes was sent in for the March of Dimes.

Episodes #432 & 433, Broadcast of February 3, 1945

Both Coast Stunts: Fill in Dialogue, Melting Pot Payoff, Jane Froman, Kiss Boss, and Pork Chops

Singer and actress **Jane Froman** made a guest appearance on this broadcast, which required a switch to the Copacabana Night Club, replayed by announcer **Ben Grauer**, who was on location. A male contestant is dressed as Lolita, Froman's newest songbird discovery, and sent over to the Copacabana to perform on stage. The contestant is supplied a blonde wig, stockings, evening shoes and evening gown with built in curves. The contestant sings "Dance with a Dolly."

Episodes #434 & 435, Broadcast of February 10, 1945

East Coast Stunts: Dress Aloft, Marie MacDonald, Elephant String Payoff, and Question Gift

West Coast Stunts: Dress Aloft, Marie MacDonald, and Elephant String Payoff

A husband and wife participate in an unusual contest. She ties a string around her husband's neck, with a small elephant charm, and instructed to go outside of the studio and shout "Look at me folks! I've got an elephant on a string!" Outside Rockefeller Center, she is unaware that her husband is switched with a real-live elephant around the corner!

Singer and actress **Marie McDonald** makes a celebrity appearance on this broadcast.

Episodes #436 & 437, Broadcast of February 17, 1945

Both Coast Stunts: Find $100, Carole Landis, Husband's Head, and Fire Tank

One of the stunts required a pickup from the Broad Hurst Theatre, where actress **Carole Landis** participated in a telephone conversation with a serviceman, who believed he was phoning a woman named "Carole" to call off a date for another serviceman. On the East Coast, the serviceman was **Sergeant Jack Donahue**; on the West Coast, Yeoman Millan. In another stunt, the wife of serviceman **John M. Benton**, is instructed to call her husband on the phone. He was an American prisoner in a Japanese camp in Manila and is back in the United States. She was surprised by the news and Edwards informs her that when John gets home, there will be a few things he missed in his years of confinement: a complete wardrobe of new clothes, overcoat, pajamas, bedroom slippers, and a standing order at a local drugstore for an ice cream soda every night for an entire year.

Episodes #438 & 439, Broadcast of February 24, 1945

Both Coast Stunts: Beauty Shop Quartette, Pie Direction, Diamond Record, and Dummy Model

Beautiful Conover model **Jesse Charles** participates in a stunt on this broadcast, involving what the contestant believes is a wooden dummy. In another stunt a serviceman makes a record for his sweetheart, proposing marriage, unaware that she is in the studio. After the ruse is revealed, he receives a diamond ring of the famed designer, **J.R. Wood**, to give to her before the close of the broadcast.

Episodes #440 & 441, Broadcast of March 3, 1945

Both Coast Stunts: Opera Scene, T or C Hat, Dummy Model Payoff, and Quiz Kids

A contestant is instructed to put on a Lord Fauntleroy outfit to participate in a quiz contest to see if he is smarter than four children, a fraction of his age. While the contestant is backstage getting into costume, the audience is let in on the ruse: the four children are members of *The Quiz Kids*: **Richard Williams, Harvey Fishman, Pat Conlon** and **Joel Kupperman**.

Episodes #442 & 443, Broadcast of March 10, 1945

East Coast Stunts: Itchy Nose, Piano Recital, T or C Hat Payoff, MacBeth, and See Answer Seltzer

West Coast Stunts: Itchy Nose, Piano Recital, T or C Hat Payoff, Wolf, and See Answer

Husband and wife contestants provide howls of laughter for the audience when the husband has his left arm tied behind him, his right arm attached to string. His wife is instructed to tickle his nose and should he avoid scratching his nose, wins a prize. If he attempts to scratch his nose, the string will release a box of soap flakes on his head. Provided with shower curtain and towel, the man tries his best to resist pulling the string, unaware that the box is really filled with handfuls of $1 bills.

Episodes #444 & 445, Broadcast of March 17, 1945

East Coast Stunts: Wolf, Soldier's Kiss, Rudy Vallee, and Birthday Cake B.U.

West Coast Stunts: Find Baby, Soldier's Kiss, Rudy Vallee, Birthday Cake B.U., and Cigarette Lighter

The radio program moved to Hollywood beginning with this broadcast. The series would no longer originate from New York City on a regular basis.

The first contestant is asked to dress like a baby, given a large bottle, and ordered to take the Sunset bus home. In another stunt, four Marines do a kissing scene with guest **Chili Williams**, the popular pin-up girl known as "The Polka-Dot Girl." Another contestant is instructed to imitate Rudy Vallee by singing "Vagabond Lover" and serenade a woman in the audience... unaware that the woman is really **Rudy Vallee** in drag.

Episodes #446 & 447, Broadcast of March 24, 1945

East Coast Stunts: 5 Soldiers Phone, Birthday Cake Payoff, and Empty Stadium Payoff

West Coast Stunts: 5 Soldiers Phone, Birthday Cake Payoff, Empty Stadium Payoff, and Cake Seltzer

In what might be considered the most simplistic stunt on the program, a sailor is put on stage and told, "If you can tell me exactly how much money you have on your person tonight, I will double that money and give you twice the amount." This stunt, which took an average of 75 seconds of airtime, was restaged multiple times in 1945 for servicemen seated in the audience.

A contestant shows up on the program with a cake, four feet high and ten feet wide. She was told last week that if she baked a cake that large and brought it to the studio the next week to feed the entire audience, she would be paid $250. This was in recognition of *Truth or Consequences* celebrating a birthday.

Episodes #448 & 449, Broadcast of March 31, 1945

East Coast Stunts: Me Seltzer, Boy Scout, Circus Home, Wife Lecture, and Throw Eggs

West Coast Stunts: Me Seltzer, Boy Scout, Circus Home, Wife Lecture, Throw Eggs, and Cigarette Lighter

Actress and singer **Frances Langford** is a celebrity guest on this broadcast. Langford appeared on the program to promote *Radio Stars on Parade*, her latest picture. One of the servicemen in the crowd is selected to perform on stage with Langford, singing "Melancholy Baby." In another stunt a contestant is asked to light their cigarette lighter and if it lights on the first try, they get $100.

Episodes #450 & 451, Broadcast of April 7, 1945

East Coast Stunts: $500 Tank, OWI Proposal, Old Man Ralph, Circus Payoff and Make Up Consequence

West Coast Stunts: $500 Tank, OWI Proposal, Old Man Ralph, and Circus Payoff

Actor and singer **Dick Powell** is a celebrity guest on this broadcast, in conjunction with his latest film, *Murder, My Sweet*. The lights are dimmed out and a scene from the movie is shown on the big screen. Powell delivers his lines as if he was lopping them in the studio. The female contestant has to recite her lines, using a script, to lip sync the role played by **Claire Trevor**.

Episodes #452 & 453, Broadcast of April 21, 1945

Both Coast Stunts: Yes Rose, Claire Trevor, Find a Place, and $500 Tank No. 2

Actress **Claire Trevor** makes a guest appearance on this broadcast, cross-promoting *Murder, My Sweet*. A contestant on the program, **Norris Darnell**, was a discharged veteran who has been unable to find a job or a place to live. He and his wife have had a rough time and Edwards appealed to the listening audience to find them an apartment or house and to send furnishings, linens, dishes, clothing, etc. Anything the couple cannot use will be turned over to the Army and Navy Emergency Relief.

Episodes #454 & 455, Broadcast of April 28, 1945

Both Coast Stunts: Jack Up Husbands, Find a Place, Model Phone, Melon Ball Head, $500 Tank No. 3

Ralph Edwards presents the above-mentioned couple (**Mr. and Mrs. Norris Darnell**) with the key to their new five-room apartment with rent paid for one year. Norris tells of getting a job with the Naval Supply Depot in San Pedro as a result of last week's broadcast.

Episodes #456 & 457, Broadcast of May 5, 1945

Both Coast Stunts: $500 Tank Payoff, Raffle Husband, Andrews Sisters, Kiss Mule, and Place to Live Payoff

The Andrews Sisters are celebrity guests on this program, billed as "three fat ladies from the circus." **Mr. and Mrs. Norris Darnell** are again on the program, say they are ready to move into their new home, completely furnished and equipped. The excess gifts were used to furnish hospital ships, troop ships, dormitories for servicemen's wives, and USO recreational centers.

Episodes #458 & 459, Broadcast of May 12, 1945

Both Coast Stunts: Airplane B.U., Overall Eggs, Airplane Payoff, Instrumentalist, and Triple Talk

War Bond Stunt: Edwards asks listeners to buy an "E" Bond and send a postcard to *Truth or Consequences* with the serial number and date of purchase of the bond. When a total of $1 million in "E" bonds has been recorded, *Truth or Consequences* will give an airplane to an air corps ground crew soldier who appeared on this program. For Mother's Day, the same soldier wrote a letter to his mother which was read on the program, after which the soldiers' mother appeared in person as a Mother's Day surprise.

Episodes #460 & 461, Broadcast of May 19, 1945

Both Coast Stunts: Telephone Pie, Airplane Payoff, Imitate Lovers, and Cross-Country Payoff

Ralph Edwards presents the soldier with airplane because listeners responded to last week's play with over $1 million worth of War Bond purchases.

Episodes #462 & 463, Broadcast of May 26, 1945

Both Coast Stunts: Three Blind Mice, Speed Up Record, Nurse Date, and Life Story Pie

In an Army nurse stunt, Edwards provides 15 soldiers to act as chauffeur, dancing partners, dinner partners, and entertainers to take an Army nurse on a date to all the nightclubs in Hollywood (accompanied by a *Truth or Consequences* escort for both security and to pay all bills). Edwards also gives her a bottle of perfume, a wristwatch and a complete wardrobe credit at Saks Fifth Avenue in Beverly Bills.

Episodes #464 & 465, Broadcast of June 2, 1945

Both Coast Stunts: Egg Beater, $100 Lover, and Make Up Lyrics

Celebrity guests include **Tony Pastor** and his orchestra, and actress **Betty Jane Greer**. Greer participates in a stunt involving a soldier, a sailor and a marine. The men are to romance the actress verbally (not physically) and use the word "DUZ." Greer is scripted to call it a tie and all three men are awarded prizes.

Two women are instructed to sit on bikes positioned on stationary stands. Instead of a back wheel, there is a wooden wheel attached to rope. At the end of the rope are their husbands. The first wife to pedal and reel in her husband wins

$25. The husbands are referred to as "old goats" but the women are unaware of the prank – their husbands are not on the other end of the ropes; there are real goats!

Episodes #466 & 467, Broadcast of June 9, 1945
Both East Coast Stunts: Barrel Seltzer, Pig Husband, Take Baby, Photo Frame, and Day at Zoo
A husband is asked to walk across the stage on top of a barrel and when his feet are not touching the barrel, his wife is allowed to squirt him with a seltzer bottle. In another stunt, a soldier is instructed to call his girlfriend and ask her to take care of his "baby" until he is out of service. The prize is an automobile, a "baby car," but he cannot mention the word "car." In another stunt, a customer is instructed to spend one hour behind bars at the Griffith Park Zoo as a new exhibition. His prize, should he fulfill the stunt, is a $100 War Bond.

Episodes #468 & 469, Broadcast of June 16, 1945
East Coast Stunts: Fill in Speech, Twins, Beards, Day at Zoo Payoff, and Courtesy
West Coast Stunts: Fill in Speech, Twins, Beards, and Day at Zoo Payoff
In a "Courtesy" stunt, Ralph Edwards instructs all of the listeners to pay close attention to the good will of every man, woman and child on the street and contact their local NBC affiliate next week to report on that person. The local affiliates will judge the submissions and the winner from each station will win a $25 War Bond.

Episodes #470 & 471, Broadcast of June 23, 1945
East Coast Stunts: Imitate Plane, Long Lost Cousin, Calm Woman, Cigarette Lighter, and Courtesy Payoff No. 1
West Coast Stunts: Imitate Plane, Long Lost Cousin, Calm Woman, and Sailor's Money
Broadcast from the Civic Auditorium in San Francisco, California, for the benefit of the 7th War Loan Drive. Admission for audience members required a purchase of a War Bond.
Two cousins, who have not seen each other in 30 years, meet up in a pre-arranged stunt.

Episodes #472 & 473, Broadcast of June 30, 1945

Both Coast Stunts: Joan Edwards, Courtesy Payoff No. 2, and Home Town

This broadcast featured a three-way conversation between **Pfc. Alfred Phelps** in Honolulu and Ralph Edwards in Hollywood, and people from Phelps' hometown of Salem, Oregon. During a conversation between Edwards and Phelps, the private was reminded of his small town and the folks he saw along Main Street: **Vernon Perry**, druggist; **Pat Thatcher**, barber; **Mr. and Mrs. Phelps**, his parents; **Rev. Standard**, his minister; **Charles Sprague**, editor and owner of the local paper, *The Statesman*; an unnamed school friend called "Curly"; **Jean Roland**, his girl; his brother **Bob Phelps**, of the Merchant Marine and his brother's wife **Frances Phelps**. One by one, the good folks extend their heartfelt encouragement and Phelps is given an opportunity to briefly chat with each one of them. This provided him the sounds of his hometown without having to leave the military base in Hawaii. **Don Johnson**, cheerleader at Salem High School, led the good people in the school cheer.

Edwards reminded the listening audience that **Alfred Phelps** was "just one of millions of GI's from one of thousands of home towns" who spent a bit of his Saturday evening back on his Main Street, through the magic of radio. In the next mail to Phelps would go pictures of his home town, and the people there in his honor tonight, taken by a photographer in Salem. He would also receive a recording of his "consequence," a solid gold 14-karat, 21-jewel Bulova wristwatch, and $100 in cash. To his family, a recording of his "consequence," pictures of the evening's gathering, and a complete set of fine table linen to use the first day Phelps comes home to have a piece of cake his mother talked about.

Singer **Joan Edwards** makes a guest appearance on this broadcast, participating in the first stunt on the broadcast.

Episodes #474 & 475, Broadcast of July 7, 1945

East Coast Stunts: Tell Jokes, Phone Frame, $500 Beard, and Turtle Soup

West Coast Stunts: Tell Jokes, Phone Frame, $500 Beard, and Kiss Sheet

Last broadcast of the season. A contestant named **Sidney Cowles** was challenged to grow a beard during the summer and return in the fall when the program returns after a summer hiatus.

Episodes #476 & 477, Broadcast of September 8, 1945
Stunts: Teeter-Totter, Soldier Reunion, Beard, and Add and Sing

Sidney Cowles is present with the beard he began to grow last July when the program went off the air for the summer. Edwards bought the beard for $500 and Cowles expects to have his beard shaved off tonight… But Edwards takes only the right half of the beard and invites Cowles back next week for another installment collection.

About eight minutes into the program, the program switched to Honolulu, where the NBC correspondent, **Jim Wahl**, has contestant **Private Armand "Andy" Andereck** from Kankakee, Illinois, ready to play *Truth or Consequences*, surrounded by a group of convalescent patients in a G.I. hospital. Andereck has a two-way conversation with Edwards in Hollywood and with Mrs. Andereck and two children in Kankakee, Illinois. Four minutes later, the program reverted back to Hollywood for the remainder of the broadcast.

Episodes #478 & 479, Broadcast of September 15, 1945
Stunts: Link Trainer, WAC Act, and Beard No. 2

Sidney Cowles, with half of his beard, is back on the show. Tonight the beard is left untouched but Cowles is sent to The Trocadero Theatre in Philadelphia, Pennsylvania, to have an evening of food and fun at the expense of Ralph Edwards.

Episodes #480 & 481, Broadcast of September 22, 1945
Stunts: Furniture Auction, Nylon Love, Beard No. 3, and Horse Shoes

Sidney Cowles is still a half-bearded man. Cowles decided tonight to leave the beard with Ralph Edwards, and Edwards takes the beard with Cowles attached… It looks as if both Sidney Cowles and beard will be a guest for the week at the Edwards home!

Episodes #482 & 483, Broadcast of September 29, 1945
Stunts: Lombardo, Hitch Hike, and Identify Kiss

Sidney Cowles is absent from the program tonight. Edwards announced that he took both Cowles and beard home with him last week but after one night of watching Cowles sleep on the Edwards bed, raid the Edwards ice box, and select for his personal use Ralph Edwards' best ties, the radio host made Cowles a clean-shaven man again and sent him to his own home. **Guy Lombardo** participates in a stunt.

Episodes #484 & 485, Broadcast of October 6, 1945
Stunts: Right Button and Tokyo Act

Contestants on this broadcast are stationed in Tokyo, Japan, where the program switched over at 8:37 p.m. and **Sergeant Roger F. Von Roth** presided as emcee of *Truth or Consequences* as broadcast from Tokyo. Ralph Edwards remained in Hollywood, where the program reverted back seconds before 9 p.m. to close the program.

Episodes #486 & 487, Broadcast of October 13, 1945
Stunts: Self-Control, Santa Claus Movie, and Plant Wallet

A contestant is taken off stage to do something strenuous, long enough for Edwards to tell the audience that while the contestant is away, they put a wallet containing fifty dollars into his coat. After the contestant returns and sits in the audience will someone, a plant, run into the audience to claim their pocket was picked and his wallet stolen. In another stunt, a woman watches a film of Santa Claus on the big screen and interacts with him, unaware the bearded man in the red coat is her husband.

Episodes #488 & 489, Broadcast of October 20, 1945
Stunts: Telescope B.U., Bendix Spot, Write Me, and Telescope Payoff

William Bendix, star of radio's *The Life of Riley*, participates in a stunt for this broadcast. Program included a pickup from the roof of Radio City in Hollywood. One of the female contestants is escorted to the roof by announcer **Bob Williams** to witness scenes taking place in the rooms of the Hotel Plaza just across the street. Of course, the contestant's husband has been "planted" in one of the rooms – with a life-size dummy!

This broadcast brings the first announcement of the part which the *Truth or Consequences* show will again play in selling Victory Bonds for the Eighth War Loan Drive. Announcements in regard to the coming "Victory Loan Drive" concerns mention the fact that Ralph Edwards is out to uphold his record for selling "E" Bonds and that he considers this the greatest of all the Bond drives. Once again, the radio program will go on a Bond Tour through many of the nation's cities. And in each city, by checking with one of the local committees, citizens may find out how to see *Truth or Consequences* and the entire gang. Admission will be the purchase of a War Bond – or a Victory Bond. For details, listen to future announcements on this program or check with your local committee. Among the cities on the Bond Tour schedule:

Schedule

October 29, Wichita, Kansas

October 31, Des Moines, Iowa

November 3, Omaha, Nebraska (two radio broadcasts)

November 6, Salt Lake City, Utah

November 7, Reno, Nevada

November 19, Detroit, Michigan

November 20, Flint, Michigan

November 21, Milwaukee, Minnesota

November 24, Chicago, Illinois

November 26, Tulsa, Oklahoma

November 27, Dallas, Texas

December 3, Spokane, Washington

December 4, Seattle, Washington

December 5, Portland, Oregon

Intervening broadcasts originated from Hollywood. Originally scheduled was Oklahoma City and Los Angeles, but the tour never reached the two cities.

Other Bond Pulls

Mary (*T or C* appeal) $5,117,962

Mrs. Siering (*T or C* appeal) $501,000

Mrs. Stewart (*T or C* appeal) $1,300,000

Cos Cob, Connecticut (personal appearance, October 30, 1943) $119,000

Pennies (*T or C* stunt) $3,300

Jasper (personal appearance, Alabama) $158,000

Theatres (Strand & Waterbury, personal appearance, Connecticut) $209,000

Polo Grounds (personal appeal) $800,000

McCreery's (advertised personal appearance) $1,500,000

Total $9,708,262

Episodes #490 & 491, Broadcast of October 27, 1945

Stunts: Sailor Baby, and Fill In Dialogue No. 2

Special Victory Bond plan announced by Ralph Edwards as part of this program – in collaboration with a Navy Day tribute. One of the contestants is **Chief Yeoman 2nd Class Clarence Gethers**, who has just returned to the States after many months overseas. Edwards also presented Gethers' wife and baby on the program – without forewarning Gethers. However, after the surprise reunion of the Gethers family, the father mentions he had not seen his baby daughter since she was three weeks old. Edwards announced that Mr. and Mrs. Gethers and Baby Sharon are to have a "Dream Week" in Hollywood with a suite at the Hollywood Knickerbocker. Then, in one week, the seaman father is due to ship out again on the Battleship Texas to keep up the job of holding the peace. However, Edwards is giving everybody listening to the program a chance to secure that peace as soon as possible so that fathers and husbands will be able to get home to stay.

In honor of baby **Sharon Gethers**, Edwards is asking listeners to buy an extra Bond and to drop a postcard to: Sharon, c/o *Truth or Consequences*, NBC Hollywood, California, telling of the amount of the extra Bond thus purchased. And if the total reaches one million dollars in "E" Bonds by the next *Truth or Consequences* broadcast next week, the producers of the program will give Sharon a $1,000 Victory Bond to insure her future education.

Edwards announces that tomorrow, October 28, *Truth or Consequences* leaves on its eighth tour for the U.S. Treasury, selling Victory Bonds this time.

Episodes #492 & 493, Broadcast of November 3, 1945

Stunts: Glow Worm, Pie Cup, Service Couple, and Okinawa Idol

Program originates from Omaha, Nebraska. **Sergeant Fred Van Coute** participates in a stunt that, unbeknownst to him, involves his wife. For his prize the serviceman is granted temporary leave so he can spend time with his spouse, with permission from **Colonel Lincoln Mallory**, who also appears on the program.

Episodes #494 & 495, Broadcast of November 10, 1945

Stunts: Public Bath, Violin, and Aeronca

Edwards asks listeners to buy E Bonds in honor of Air Force Pilot **Major Griffith Williams** and his bride, **Barbara Williams**, who are on the program. Major

Williams tells of his experiences in Japan and his 22 months in a concentration camp in Germany. His bride is briefly interviewed, so Edwards says that if $1,000,000 worth of E Bonds are purchased in honor of the Major and his wife (buyers mail a card to *T or C* to announce such a purchase and results will be announced next week on the program), they would be awarded a private plane; the Bonds must be purchased during the week.

Episodes #496 & 497, Broadcast of November 17, 1945
Stunts: Tokyo Act, Give $50, Two Cigars, and Husband Escort
Program from Hollywood with a pickup from Tokyo, Japan. In Hollywood, **Major Griffith Williams** and his bride are back as guests. The amount of Bonds bought in their honor reached the million-dollar mark and the plane is actually on the stage today waiting to be admired by the winners. The Major and his wife thank Ralph Edwards when speaking briefly on the program.
From 8:33:40 p.m. to 8:57:15 p.m., the series switched to Tokyo. G.I. contestants walked up to the microphone and told from which towns in the United States they came from. In a two-way set-up with Hollywood, the Hollywood studio audience is asked if there is a person from the same town as the G.I. in Tokyo. If there is such a person, the G.I. in Tokyo receives a $25 Victory Bond. If the two contestants know each other, the G.I. gets $50. The Hollywood contestant receives a $25 Bond for taking part.

Episodes #498 & 499, Broadcast of November 24, 1945
Stunts: Séance, and Homesick
Broadcast from the Auditorium Theater in Chicago, Illinois. Listeners are asked to buy Bonds in honor of one of the wounded veterans at a nearby Chicago hospital. If $1 million worth of Bonds are bought in his honor before the next broadcast a week from today, the veteran's mother and father get a trip to Chicago and a two-week stay, plus a trip back home, all at the expense of the *Truth or Consequences* program.

Episodes #500 & 501, Broadcast of December 1, 1945
Stunts: Marriage Rehearsal, and Band Leaders
Taking part in the program are well-known orchestra leaders: **Stan Kenton, Will Osborne, Charlie Barnett, Mike Reilly, Alvino Rey, Matty Malneck** and

Mrs. Pabst, the Blue Ribbon Girl, leads a band of volunteers (left to right) Charlie Barnett, Matty Malneck and Alvino Rey.

Xavier Cugat. A woman in the studio audience is told that she will get to conduct an impromptu orchestra made up of volunteers from the audience, anybody who can play an instrument. The woman is then asked to leave the studio while the orchestra assembles so that she may make a "grand entrance" for her "conducting" – of course, she does not realize that seven of the nation's best-known orchestra leaders are the "volunteers."

Episodes #502 & 503, Broadcast of December 8, 1945
Stunts: Recite Backwards, Give $50, Switch Love, Tramp for a Day, and Sell a Bond

This program includes a special two-way telephone conversation between a contestant in Hollywood and **Ted Gamble** in Washington, D.C., plus an extra Victory Bond talk by Mr. Gamble from Washington. Program is a tribute to the NBC Victory Bond Day. The Hollywood contestant, **Mrs. Albert Miller**, is told to sell a Victory Bond via telephone to an "unknown person at the other end of the telephone line." The contestant, of course, does not know that she will attempt to sell the Bond to Ted Gamble, National Director of the War Finance Division of the United States Treasury. This segment was broadcast from 8:51 p.m. to 8:58 p.m. Following the conversation, Gamble makes a special Victory Bond talk and reads the "Distinguished Service Citation" awarded to Ralph Edwards by **Fred Vinson**, Secretary of Treasury. The Citation is in recognition of Edwards' participation in all the Bond campaigns. Edwards is credited with selling or having singularly caused the purchase of more "E" Bonds than any other individual in the entertainment world.

Episodes #504 & 505, Broadcast of December 15, 1945
Stunts: Tramp for a Day, Wife Chaperone, and Kids' Christmas Nativity

This program includes a special Christmas feature for children and the evening's guests are three children all under six years of age. One of the children is a Negro child who says that the father in his family is a Pullman Porter or "Red Cap." The children are asked what they want for Christmas. Ralph Edwards tells them the Bible story of the first Christmas and has his story flavored with Christmas music and the singing of carols. Finally, in a lighter vein, he talks with them about "Santa Claus," who arrives to take the children into his confidence and assures them that they will get the gifts they want. (Of course, Edwards has the power to arrange delivery of the very same gifts on Christmas Eve.)

An unusual contest followed the Christmas feature. The Victory Bond plea is included, even though the Corporation and Financial Institution Bond purchases have closed in the current drive, but the E Bond (also known as the People's Bond) campaign continued through December 31, 1945.

Episodes #506 & 507, Broadcast of December 22, 1945
Stunts: Hot Seat Picture, Telephone Aunt, and Home for Christmas

Truth or Consequences has arranged for **Al Teale**, a soldier taken direct from his ship of debarkation in California to be flown to his home in Wayne, Michigan, just in time to talk to his family during the broadcast. Transportation has been arranged from the airport to the soldier's home and he is picked up by a mobile unit in Wayne, Michigan, as he stands on the street just outside his own house. The quiz program arranged with a neighbor of the soldier's family to borrow the radio from the soldier's home, to hide the engineer who is attending to the pickup of the soldier's report, and to be sure that the family is at home on this particular evening at this particular time. Edwards explains all this and then the switch to Wayne, Michigan, is made: **Ed Bailey** is the engineer on the pickup.

From 8:48 p.m. to 8:56 p.m., there is a two-way conversation between the soldier, his wife, and his child after the surprise reunion in Michigan (Wayne) and Ralph Edwards in Hollywood. Also picked up over the mike was the audience listening in getting the soldier's first reactions to getting home as he stands outside his home and then finally on the perch from where he describes seeing his wife and child through the window. The microphone he uses is hidden in a large bouquet of flowers so that when he does surprise his wife, her first remarks are caught over the air.

For the concluding part of the homecoming, Christmas Carolers are on hand outside to serenade the couple on their reunion. The soldier then tells his wife of the gifts which *Truth or Consequences* sent: a Sentinel Radio, to replace the one which the neighbor was instructed to borrow (to keep the wife from listening to the broadcast and thus catching on to unusual happenings that evening); an order for a Bendix washing machine; toys for the child; and a variety of furnishings for the house. Then, in the two-way conversation, Ralph Edwards gives the soldier his own gift, a $500 Victory Bond.

Episodes #508 & 509, Broadcast of December 29, 1945

Stunts: Old Songs, Rose Bowl, Baby Sitters, and Crackpot Consequence No. 1

Program inaugurates the "Crack-Pot Consequence" – every person who appears at the microphone tonight until the contest ends has a chance to win at end of the show: a Bendix Washer, a dozen pairs of Nylons, and a new Mercury Sedan Coupe. To take part in this "Crack-Pot Consequence," all of the contestants of the evening sit around a long table; in front of every person is a different kind of sound effect: a whistle, a bird-call, a fight gong, a chime, and many other sounds. Then, the voice of a famous person is broadcast and the contestant who thinks he recognizes the voice and the name of the owner makes "noise" with his or her sound effect. The first person to recognize the voice writes the name on a slip of paper and hands it in. Ralph Edwards read the answer publicly and gave the prizes if the answer was correct. If incorrect, the prizes hold over for the next week. No one guessed correctly. The radio pick-up of "Mr. A" (**Harry Adelman**, USC Captain, Rose Bowl) originated from a dressing room at the Hollywood Bowl. This was not known to the contestants nor to the public. For the West Coast broadcast, an "Old Songs" stunt was performed and ran overtime.

Episodes #510 & 511, Broadcast of January 5, 1946
Stunts: Snatch Purse, First Off Line, Army Nurse Family, and Crackpot No. 2
Nobody won the Crack-Pot Consequence on this broadcast. Prizes were held over for the next week. In addition to last week's prizes, the supply of Nylon hose is now extended to a two-year supply. Also added to the pot was a Knabe Grand piano, an I.J. Fox $1,000 Silver Fox full-length coat, a round-trip ticket to New York, and a weekend at the New York City Waldorf Hotel. The pick-up of the mystery man (now referred to as "Mr. Hush") originates from his private home in Hollywood – unknown to contestants or to the public.

Episodes #512 & 513, Broadcast of January 12, 1946
Stunts: Bawl Out Police, Front Row Kiss, Speak Love, and Crackpot No. 3
The "Crack-pot Consequence" was carried over for the next program, plus an additional number of prizes, as contestants failed to identify the mysterious voice of "Mr. Hush." Today the voice of Mr. Hush is picked up from The Forum, Wichita, Kansas.

Episodes #514 & 515, Broadcast of January 19, 1946
Stunts: Telephone, Doctor, Blacken Gloves, and Crackpot No. 4
Tonight's guest is a little blind girl who is also a patient at a Hollywood hospital where she is undergoing treatment for the after-effects of polio. The little girl sings a song, accompanied by program organist **Buddy Cole**. She also talks about her stay in the hospital and how she is learning to read Braille. Ralph Edwards announces that if the listeners to this program will help, the little girl may have the gift of sight. He instructs listeners to put a dime or more in an envelope and mail it to Ralph Edwards in behalf of the child and if the total of dimes mailed in behalf of the little girl reached the amount of $25,000, to be used in the March of Dimes fight against infantile paralysis, the child will be sent to the Eye Bank, where the best surgeons in that field hope to bring back her sight. The initial examinations have been made and the child is believed to have an eye defect that can be cured. First, she must finish her treatment for polio, however, and meanwhile, all of the dimes sent in her name will be going to help other little polio victims.

The Crack-Pot Consequence is again held over with many added and lavish prizes. Nobody has yet to identify the mysterious voice known as "Mr. Hush." Tonight, Mr. Hush is picked up from the Lennox Hotel in St. Louis, Missouri. The origin of Mr. Hush is at no time announced; he is heard as if coming from a small room near the studio, where the rest of the broadcast is being given.

Beulah was not connected to the mike in this episode, by accident, and not heard over the air properly.

Episode #516, Broadcast of January 26, 1946

Stunts: Brooklyn Texas, Drama, Carroll-Old Ladies, and Crackpot No. 5

The voice of "Mr. Hush" is identified by contestant **Ensign Richard Bartholomew** of Fayetteville, Arkansas, who recognized the voice of Jack Dempsey. After the identification has been made, Ralph Edwards discloses that **Jack Dempsey** has been heard speaking from New York tonight. Dempsey then comes on the air in a two-way pick-up from New York to congratulate the winner. The East Coast broadcast was played back for the West Coast so West Coast listeners would hear the outcome of the contest.

Ensign Bartholomew's prize, an accumulation of five weeks' give-away prizes includes: a $1,000 diamond ring, a $1,000 silver fox fur coat, a $1,000 diamond-and-ruby wrist watch, a 1946 Mercury car, an RCA-Victor radio phonograph console with 100 records, a Bendix washing machine, a two-year supply of Nylon stockings, a piano, a gas range, a refrigerator, round-trip ticket to New York by plane with a weekend at the Waldorf Astoria hotel, two weeks paid vacation for two at Banff Springs Hotel in the Canadian Rockies, one-year maid service, and a complete wardrobe for a man. The entire winning is estimated at approximately $13,500.

A new contest begins, titled the "Heathcliffs Contest," with a two-way pick-up between New York and Hollywood with contestants **Claude Cope** from New York and **Bob Pepper** from Hollywood. At points of origin, each contestant is presented with half of a thousand-dollar bill. Edwards then instructs the contestants that they are to start early tomorrow morning; the California contestant headed for New York and the New York contestant headed for Hollywood. The route of travel is outlined for the two contestants who, hereafter, are to be known as the "Heathcliffs." The method of travel is not limited – they are told to make the trip to "get to their rendezvous the best way they can" – the idea is to meet somewhere between coasts, in front of a Chop Suey house. As the two pass through each town, they must seek a Chop Suey house and must stop briefly in front of the restaurant and scream "Heathcliff" – thus, eventually they will meet in some American city. When they meet, and match the bill halves, they will have the thousand-dollar bill to spend. Meanwhile, along the way, each contestant must stop in a local NBC station on the *Truth or Consequences* broadcast night and telephone to the program. Thus, listeners will keep in touch with their progress. And to look the part, each must dress during the entire trip in hip-high boots and stove-pipe hats.

According to an inter-office memo, the second commercial during the broadcast had terrible sound as a result of the engineer falling asleep!

Episodes #517 & 518, Broadcast of February 2, 1946
Stunts: Tommy Riggs, Heathcliff No. 1, and March of Dimes
Guests include **Ensign Richard Bartholomew**, the lucky winner of the Crackpot Consequence last week; and **Tommy Riggs**, just out of the Navy and creator of the radio character, Betty Lou. Ralph Edwards talks about the "Heathcliff" contest and the Heathcliffs phone in while the program is in progress. There is a special pick-up from the Los Angeles Children's Hospital, where a little infantile paralysis patient, **Janice Wesly**, sings a song for the listeners. Ralph Edwards then announces that if the listeners send in dimes, writing that they are sending the dimes in behalf of little Janice and other children like her, those dimes will be tossed into a huge hospital laundry bag in Janice's room. When there are enough dimes to fill the bag (and Ralph Edwards hoped those dimes will fill the bag before the next broadcast for this program), Janice will receive a $1,000 Savings Bond. The dimes, of course, will go to the March of Dimes fund.

Episodes #519 & 520, Broadcast of February 9, 1946
Stunts: Girl in Every Port, Jack Carson, Heathcliff No. 2, and March of Dimes Payoff
Celebrity guest is actor **Jack Carson**. Announcement is made that little **Janice Wesly**, polio victim in last week's broadcast, received $53,900 worth of dimes for the infantile paralysis fund. The dimes went to the Infantile Paralysis Fund and Janice received a $1,000 Savings Bond. Program includes a two-way pick-up between the Hollywood studios and the Los Angeles Children's Hospital,

where Janice was a patient. She told Edwards that the laundry bag was full of dimes and Edwards told her that she won the Savings Bond.

Episodes #521 & 522, Broadcast of February 16, 1946
Stunts: Eccentric Husband, Round Robin, and Heathcliff No. 3
The ongoing contest grows in interest when the Heathcliffs report from Indianapolis and Detroit. This means they will have to retrace their steps because they evidently overshot each other and passed by without each other's knowledge somewhere between the vicinity of Indianapolis and Chicago.

Episodes #523 & 524, Broadcast of February 23, 1946
Stunts: Cheerleaders, Spirit Wife, Man of Letters, and Heathcliff No. 4
Celebrity guest is author **Sinclair Lewis**. On this program, the Heathcliffs both call in from Chicago; they found each other. In the two-way telephone conversation between Chicago and Hollywood, **Bob Pepper**, Hollywood contestant now in Chicago and **Claude Cope**, New York contestant, also in Chicago, explain how at one time during their attempt to contact each other, more than 20 people were in front of a Chicago Chop Suey house yelling "Heathcliff" in an attempt to cash in on the $1,000… or perhaps just to confuse the real "Heathcliffs." The two contestants were told to put their two halves together of the $1,000 bill. They discover that the two halves do not fit. Edwards tells them that he sent letters to them along the way explaining that an error had been made in presenting the wrong halves of $1,000 bills to them. Moreover, the correct halves of the bill had been included with the letters and mailed to the contestants. The letters had been addressed to the Heathcliffs in care of "Any Chop Suey restaurant in Los Angeles, Oakland, San Francisco, etc. …" listing all the cities scheduled on the original route mapped out by Ralph Edwards. Now the two contestants are instructed to retrace their steps and to check all the Chop Suey places they passed – the letters will be held for them and when each Heathcliff gets his letter, he will find that the half of the bill in the envelope with the letter fits the half they have been carrying. Thus, for all of the extra trouble the wandering Heathcliffs have encountered, each will now have an entire $1,000 bill instead of just being allowed to divide the original bill in half. On their new attempt to find the letters addressed to them, the Heathcliffs must yell "Heathcliff has come back" as he reaches the Chop Suey place. Chop Suey houses along the route are being notified by

radio to hold the letters wherever they may now be. Again, the contestants are instructed to telephone to the program next week and every week thereafter until they get their correct halves of the $1,000 bill together.

Ralph Edwards makes an appeal for interest in National Brotherhood Week. He says American teamwork won the war but that this teamwork must be maintained through peace as well.

Episodes #525 & 526, Broadcast March 2, 1946

Stunts: Wrestling Bout, Mole Hill, Cat and Dog Hospital, and Heathcliff Payoff

This broadcast originated from Hollywood and features the last episode in the cross-country march of the two "Heathcliffs." **Bob Pepper**, Hollywood contestant, tells how he and the New York contestant, **Claude Cope**, tell of their cross-country adventure. Pepper says he found his letter with his half of the bill in St. Louis, at a Chop Suey house. Ralph Edwards announces that the New York contestant has wired and that he has his bill matched also; thus, the Heathcliff contest is ended.

A special guest on tonight's program is **Mr. Vivian D. Corbley**, National Adjutant of the D.A.V. (Disabled American Veterans), presents Edwards, in behalf of the grand work done on his program for veterans, with a special citation. Edwards acknowledges the citation with thanks in behalf of his program, and of all the veterans who have helped from time to time, to make the broadcasts the success they have been. It is then announced that the serviceman on today's program is being reunited with his wife and child tonight, through the efforts of Corbley, who arranged the trip for the family and who personally escorted them to California. Corbley then gives the servicemen a lifetime membership in "D.A.V.," and tells him that his suite has been reserved by the *Truth or Consequences* show for the serviceman and his family, so that the family will enjoy their time together at the Hollywood Hotel with all expenses paid. The serviceman's wife and son are brought forth on the program to surprise the serviceman.

This broadcast also provides a special part in which a contestant (another serviceman) receives a one-year service of a Diaper Service Co. in Hollywood for his baby in return for his part in a consequence (the contestant had to answer questions about babies).

Another contestant is the wife of an amateur boxing contestant; the names of contestants were not used when the wife is sent to the Hollywood Athletic

Club, where she is told to report a "play-by-play" boxing match in progress there. Towards the end of the broadcast there is a brief pick-up from the Hollywood Athletic Club of Los Angeles, where the wife attempts to describe the "Masked Marvel." She does not know that the match is a "hoax" and that the "Masked Marvel" is her own husband.

Episodes #527 & 528, Broadcast of March 9, 1946
Stunts: Mole Hill Payoff, Hospital House, Contestant M.C., and Golden Wedding
Celebrity guest tonight is **Cliff Nazarro**, a doubletalk artist. He appears as a male contestant who was interviewed by a female contestant. Of course, she does not know that she will have to interview a doubletalk artist and the resulting confusion is one of the funniest stunts on the program. For her trouble, the woman gets a big red box of DUZ and a 14-karat gold, 21-jewel Bulova wristwatch.
There is also a tribute to **Mr. and Mrs. George Nye**, contestants who were celebrating their golden Wedding Anniversary – 50 years. The surprised couple almost break out in tears when their children and grandchildren are brought out from backstage to take part in the surprise. An anniversary cake with 50 candles is brought on stage during the show as a special gift to the couple. After the program, the entire family goes to a Golden Wedding Party at Billingsley's, Hollywood's new restaurant, and then an entire week in the bridal suite at the Hollywood Plaza Hotel… all at the expense of the quiz program.
This broadcast includes a two-way pick up from a Hollywood home, where the husband of the family has been rushed blindfolded on a stretcher after being told that he would receive $500 if he could tell where he was after his arrival. The man fails to identify his destination as his own home! He did receive a $100 savings bond and a box of DUZ for his participation.

Episodes #529 & 530, Broadcast of March 16, 1946
Stunts: Filibuster (Seat in Congress), Pal Pie, Hidden Mike, and Irish Lady
This broadcast includes a special pickup from Milwaukee, Wisconsin, and salute to the 100th anniversary which the city of Milwaukee is celebrating this year. Beginning 8:42 p.m., the program switched to Milwaukee, to the home of **Mrs. Jane Getter**, of 4045 Stowell Avenue*, where, without her knowledge but with the corroboration of the rest of her family, a microphone

has been hidden by the NBC engineers. At the request of Ralph Edwards from Hollywood, listeners all over the country are invited to sing out their names, one for each home listening, and the name that carries over the air is the name of the person whose home the "hidden microphone" is located. Of course, Mrs. Jane Getter's home is the name that was broadcast. A two-way conversation between Mrs. Getter and Ralph Edwards ensues and Mrs. Getter is informed that she will receive a Sentinel Radio and a big red box of DUZ as a gift. Also, she finds that the quiz program invited about 75 of the Getter friends to a party at her home. All arrangements including food have been provided by the quiz show. Family and friends are congratulated upon living in Milwaukee, the "100th Anniversary City." Edwards fills in a few facts about Milwaukee.

The program returned to the Hollywood studios at 8:48 with an Irish touch and salute to St. Patrick's Day.

Episodes #531 & 532, Broadcast of March 23, 1946

This was a special "Sixth Birthday" celebration honoring the quiz program. The celebrity contestants included **Jack Benny, Eddie Cantor, Phil Harris, Dinah Shore, John Charles Thomas, George Montgomery** (husband of Dinah Shore), **Eddie "Rochester" Anderson, Rudy Vallee, George Burns, William Bendix, Basil Rathbone, Charlie Cantor,** and announcers **Ken Carpenter, Harlow Wilcox, Jimmy Wallington, Truman Bradley** and **Don Wilson.** (Most of the celebrities had a weekly program over NBC.)

The announcers were brought into the studio in a huge baby buggy managed by Eddie Cantor, who announced that the baby buggy contains his "five sons," the five Cantor boys, whom he proceeds to introduce by using their actual names followed by the "surname" Cantor – the "boy babies" join Cantor in singing "One-zy, Two-zy" and then receive lollipops for the performance. Other celebrity guests participate in special gag stunts as their consequences. At the close of the program, every celebrity contestant is presented with a gold engraved Bulova wristwatch.

---

* Yes, her residential address was reported publicly over the air and in local newspapers in Milwaukee.

Episodes #533 & 534, Broadcast of March 30, 1946

Stunts: Steam Bath, Easy Street, and D.A.V. Drama

Celebrity guests are two impersonators of female characters on the air, **Cliff Arquette**, star of the program, *Glamour Manor*, and **Bill Comstock**, who does the impersonations of "Tizzy Lish." Another guest tonight is **Mr. Vivian D. Corbley**, National Adjutant of the Disabled American Veterans, who accompanied the small son of a disabled veteran on the program, from their home, so that they may spend time with the disabled hero. This was done at the expense of the quiz program with the cooperation of the D.A.V., in recognition of the service the soldier has done for his country. He also presents Edwards a special citation from the D.A.V. in recognition of the work in which Edwards and his program were doing for disabled veterans. (The vet tonight gets two weeks with his family at an exclusive Hollywood hotel, all expenses paid.)

Another feature of this evening's program is the "Easy Street" episode – A woman contestant from Glendora, California, receives a $100 savings bond and finds that the street on which he lives has been officially changed to "Easy Street." New street signs were being erected and the change in name will be in effect by the time the contestant reaches home.

Episodes #535 & 536, Broadcast of April 6, 1946

Stunts: C.O.D., Barber Shop Quartette, and Foreign Serviceman

A group of men are selected to perform on the program as a "barbershop quartet." Each contestant in the quartet receives a gold wristwatch and a box of DUZ. Another feature is a Western Union stunt: a contestant who works for Western Union is told that during the coming week, a delivery chauffeur in a seven-passenger town car will call for him, take him to the office and to make all of his deliveries by Western Union, returning him home at the end of the day. This will be ongoing every day for a week. Incidentally, the first telegram he would have to deliver Monday morning would be one to Ralph Edwards, so Edwards may see that he is really "on the job" with delivery.

Episodes #537 & 538, Broadcast of April 13, 1946

Stunts: Wife's Dresses, Poems, and Cancer Art

A special part of the broadcast is arranged to give a bit of short-lived joy to a young victim of cancer, a child who has been given only weeks to live. Ralph

Edwards talks about the fight against cancer and then the program is picked up direct from the child's home in New Jersey. At 8:47 p.m., the program switched to Parkertown, New Jersey, to the home of **"Buster" Leonard Roos**, an eight-year-old boy who at Christmas time was given only three weeks to live because of cancer of the lung. Buster is interviewed in the two-way set-up by Ralph Edwards – an NBC engineer has the equipment in Buster's home so that the child does not have to exert himself needlessly. Buster is told that he is officially proclaimed Honorary Treasure of the American Cancer Society Drive for Funds.

All of the listeners are asked to send contributions directly to: "Buster, Parkertown, New Jersey." If the amount of money reaches $10,000 by next week's broadcast, Buster will receive $1,000 in cash to help with medical bills. (During the interview, Buster says his cousin, **Charlie Roos**, is with him – the cousin does not talk on the air.) At 8:58 p.m., the program returns to Hollywood for the conclusion of the program. As a result of running over, there is no sponsor break towards the end of the broadcast.

Episodes #539 & 540, Broadcast of April 20, 1946
Stunts: Wife Operator, Famous Bed, and Chinese Drama
All of the stunts on this broadcast concern the Easter holiday. An announcement is made that little **"Buster" Leonard Roos**, who was on last week's program, has had his wishes come true for all the things he wanted. Also, he received the gift of $1,000 in cash because the donations sent to him for use by the National Cancer Society reached passed the $10,000 mark.

Episode #541, Broadcast of April 27, 1946
Stunts: Orpheum Laugh, and Bulova School
An announcement is made on the program that the quiz show will go to the Orpheum Theater in Los Angeles for one week, beginning Tuesday. For this location, a "Mr. Welsh" is chosen tonight to be "The Laughing Man" for the show. This contestant must attend every week's performance and must laugh lustily at all the gags and will also be instructed as to the matter of taking other "audience parts" in the show during the week. We will hear more about this contestant on next week's broadcast.

A stunt on this broadcast is in the nature of a unique attribute to all of the youngsters who were inducted into the service and who did their job for their country. **Lawrence Tranter** was the special contestant selected.

After this broadcast, Ralph Edwards received a telegram from **Frances Greene** of *The Atlanta Journal* regarding a mishap during the contest: "The whole town is in an uproar. *The Atlanta Journal* and WSB have your complete history and spread on the program but have checked all files and no clues available anywhere on Laughing Man. Please wire clues collect by noon to me in Tallapoosa Georgia."

The East Coast broadcast was recorded and replayed for the West Coast.

Episodes #542 & 543, Broadcast of May 4, 1946
Stunts: Love Letters, Dreams, Phone Balcony, and Arctic Trip

This broadcast originates from the Orpheum Theatre in Los Angeles, California. In a stunt continuing from last week, the contestant was heard laughing during other stunts, much like a heckler, calling out that he had peanuts and popcorn for sale, etc., and Edwards interviews Mr. Welsh about his "job" as "The Laughing Man."

A contestant named **Herb Holland** has agreed to be sent by the program to the Arctic circle, about 200 miles north of the little gold rush town of Yellow Knife. There, Holland will join the recent migration and the latest gold rush now in progress. When he returns to the program and presents a piece of the free gold, plus proper identification to prove that he really found the gold in the Arctic, he will receive $1,000.

Another feature spot on the show is the use of a G.I. contestant who was told to telephone his wife and his hometown to let her know that he is getting out of the Army. The ex-G.I. has a job lined up in Los Angeles but says he cannot have his wife and children join him now because it has been impossible to find a home for them to live. The ex-G.I. makes the call but does not know that his wife is actually in the studio, speaking to him from another telephone that he cannot see from his booth. The veteran is united with his wife and the two are sent out to sell tickets to a Coliseum Show, which will be given during the coming week. The show will have many radio and movie guest stars and will be used to acquaint the people with the new Roger Young Veterans Housing Program in Los Angeles. If they sell enough tickets, they will receive a home with rent paid for one year by *Truth or Consequences*. (On the East Coast show the veteran is united with his wife; on the repeat show, he is united with his child, also a surprise.) While the couple sell tickets during the coming week, they are provided with a place to live temporarily, all expenses paid, until they get their real home.

Episodes #544 & 545, Broadcast of May 11, 1946
Stunts: Solo Trip, Arctic Report, Housing Act, and Mother's Interview
The radio broadcast originates from the Hollywood studios with a special pick up from Yellow Knife, on the edge of the Arctic Circle, via two-way pick up from Edmonton, Canada, via shortwave. Contestant **Herb Holland** tells about his arrival in the Arctic District and about the "Wildcat Café" in Yellow Knife, where he had his last cup of civilized coffee before heading for the gold country. Ralph Edwards tells Holland that in addition to returning to the *Truth or Consequences* program with a piece of gold, he is also to bring back the May issue of *Reader's Digest* with an autograph by **Mike Mito**, the famous Northern prospector. The issue has a story about Mike Mito. Holland reports that he is in contact with Mike Mito and that he has the copy of *Reader's Digest* safe for autographing!

Back in the Hollywood studio, special guest was **Leonard J. Roach**, Los Angeles County Supervisor for Veterans' Housing. Mr. Roach presents the veteran and his wife (contestants on last week's show) with a key to their new home, with one-year rent paid in advance. Mr. Roach, who speaks approximately one minute, also makes an appeal to all listeners, both locally and nationally, to notify the Housing Administrator in their own communities, if they know of any rooms, apartments, or houses available for veterans temporarily or permanently.

Another special feature is a Mother's Day spot, with a special guest being Ralph Edwards' own mother. Edwards goes to the audience and spends about four minutes interviewing and giving gifts to mothers in honor of the holiday. Free diaper service for one year to the youngest mother, heirloom pearls to the oldest mother, a $500 diamond ring to the mother with the most children, a Sentinel Radio to the mother with the son farthest away, and a dozen red roses and a kiss from Ralph Edwards to his own mother, the "Mother who spanked her son the largest number of times because he was always playing pranks on people!"

Episodes #546 & 547, Broadcast of May 18, 1946

Stunts: Arrest Contestant, Trade Nylons, Arctic Circle Payoff, and Mock Auction

Herb Holland, the ex-G.I. who went to the Arctic Circle to search for gold, is back in Hollywood tonight with samples of the gold, the autographed copy of *Reader's Digest* signed by Mike Mito, the prospector who served as his guide through the Arctic, and a few other "souvenirs" from his jaunt. Holland receives his reward from Ralph Edwards: $1,000 in cash and a five-year subscription to *Reader's Digest*.

Program includes a two-way pick-up from the police station at Sunset and Vine, Hollywood, where **Guy Gott**, contestant from Joplin, Missouri, is taken away by actors who are thought to be real policemen. Gott received a Sentinel Radio and a $25 Savings Bond for his "consequence." The actors who assisted Edwards in the stunt are **Ivan Green**, who plays the "cop" who "picks up" Guy Gott for an offense that was ludicrous, and **Bob Barron**, who plays the police captain at the Station House.

Episodes #548 & 549, Broadcast of May 25, 1946

Stunts: Back to School, Boss' Wife, First Date, and Van Johnson

The "School Day" stunt involves an adult contestant named **Vernon Keene** who is sent to grammar school to take the six grade examinations, held at the close of the current school term. If the contestant passes the exam, he will receive a Kit Camper Trailer. If he fails, he must sit in the corner of Hollywood and Vine during next week's broadcast. And while sitting there, he must wear a dunce cap and shout, "I am a Dunce."

Another stunt involves the getting together of various parties, of an employee and his boss, and of the employee's wife and the boss's wife. That employee's wife has never met the boss nor the wife of the boss… Her consequence is to tell the wife of the boss what she and her husband do not like about the boss. Boss and employee listen and later confronted the wives.

The stunt involving **Van Johnson** is not performed on the East Coast broadcast, and the opening commercial is overlooked. This was corrected for the West Coast broadcast.

Episode #550, Broadcast of June 1, 1946

Stunts: Back to School Payoff, Husband Escort, and $100 Wink

Vernon Keene, the contestant who had to take the sixth-grade exam, confesses that he failed the exam and is sent to the corner of Hollywood and Vine to sit on the dunce stool. There is a two-way pick-up with Ralph Edwards to speak with the 41-year-old contestant who is informed that he receives the Kit Camper Trailer even though he failed the exam.

The Bridegroom Stunt involves a prospective bridegroom who has to appear at his wedding rehearsal, with "another girl," who is handcuffed to his wrist. The price for this stunt will be a wedding gift: a Deep Freeze unit with enough food to stock it completely. Another stunt on the program is for a wife to go around for the next week winking at every man she meets. As motivation, she is informed that one man, a "plant," will hand her $100 if she winks at him.

The repeat show for the West Coast is canceled in order to schedule a special broadcast for the Automotive Golden Jubilee Program.

Episodes #551 & 552, Broadcast of June 8, 1946
Stunts: Tank Water, Detective, Prize Fish, and Back to School Payoff

The "Fishing Consequence" involves a contestant sent to Minnesota via plane in order to take part in a fishing contest. NBC radio station KSTP in St. Paul and Minneapolis, in cooperation with the Minnesota Fish and Game Preserve, has stocked the lakes of Minnesota with 1,000 choice fish. The fish are tagged with numbers ranging from 1 to 1,000. Every fisherman who gets one of the numbered fish receives one item from a long list of prizes. The contestant will have five days to try to catch the fish, after which the contestant will fly to Minneapolis, where he will be matched by a KTSP representative with a rod and reel. If he returns for next Saturday's *Truth or Consequences* broadcast with one of the fish, he will receive a bunch of prizes.

Episodes #553 & 554, Broadcast of June 15, 1946
Stunts: Bicycle Phone, Diary, Frankie Carle, and Prize Fish Payoff

This broadcast includes a special tribute to infantrymen in honor of Infantry Day. The contestant who was sent to Minnesota to catch one of the "numbered" fish last week, returns. He reports that he could not catch one of the 1,000 numbered fish in the Minnesota Lakes so he was finally escorted by **Sam Levitan** of radio station KSTP, Minneapolis, to the mansion of the Governor of Minneapolis. The Governor arranged to have another fish labeled as "1,001"… this fish was then placed in a bath tub on the front steps of the Governor's mansion and there the contestant finally succeeded in catching a fish! For his efforts, the contestant received $560 worth of sporting equipment (portable stove, portable ice-box and camp lamp, a goat skin leather coat, a lawn mower, a year's supply of Pepsi-Cola, a sleeping bag, an outboard motor, a lady's fur coat, two woolen blankets, and a suit of clothes) plus the fish that he caught – stuffed and ready for mounting!

Episodes #555 & 556, Broadcast of June 22, 1946
Stunts: Pick Costume, Five Generations, and $100 Wink

The "Five Generations" spot included on the program are family representatives ranging from a great-great-grandmother, to the two-and-one-half month-old great-great grandson. The oldest grandmother – the great-great-grandmother Lucas, who is 78-years-old; and great-grandmother McGee, the daughter who is 52-years-old, receive special gifts. The great great-grandmother Lucas receives a $500 diamond ring; great-grandmother McGee gets a radio. The other members of the family on the program – with the exception of the two-and-one-half-month-old child – also receive special gifts. For the young great-great-grandson, the gift is "more than special" because he receives a $100 Savings Bond. (The Family represented in the five-generation spot originated in Cumberland County, Tennessee.)

Episodes #557 & 558, Broadcast of June 29, 1946
Stunts: Back to Studio, $100 Wink Payoff, Husband Boyer, and Switch Life

A woman contestant thinks she is talking to **Charles Boyer** but she is really talking to her husband, who has disguised his voice. There is another stunt about a woman being blindfolded and led to think she is being taken to some distant place. In actuality, she merely rides around outside the studio and she is returned to the stage. Wearing earphones, she is unable to tell where she is. Ralph Edwards talks with her, asking her to do various stunts, such as removing her shoes, etc. She does not know she is being observed by the entire studio audience – and for her consequence receives $5.00 and a box of DUZ.

Episodes #559 & 560, Broadcast of July 6, 1946
Stunts: Tune In, Cross Country Quartet, and Switch Life Payoff

Program originates from Hollywood with a four-way set-up in order to carry a "cross-country quartette" including singers from Chicago, Philadelphia, and

New York City, singing with the contestant from California who is in the Hollywood studios. This stunt has grown out of a contest conducted during the past week by Ralph Edwards through the cooperation of three different colleges in the U.S. to choose singers – the fourth member of the quartette chosen from the Hollywood studio audience.

Contestants in this feature are **Lloyd Stone**, an ex-G.I. representing the University of Southern California and chosen from the Hollywood studio audience; **Howard Roy Hill**, representing Northwestern University and partaking in the program from Chicago; **Mario Jacanto**, representing the New School of Music and partaking from Philadelphia; and **Jonas Javna**, representing New York University and partaking from New York City. All singers in the quartet are ex-G.I.s. Accompanying the singers are **Buddy Cole**, the series organist for the *Truth or Consequence* program, and **Perry Botkin**, guitarist. Contestants receive wristwatches and autographed pictures of movie actress **Jeanne Crain**, who "listened in" to act as a judge.

A couple exchanged jobs during the past week; the wife worked in her husband's business office while the husband did the household chores. On this program the couple reports of their experiences in the "new jobs" during the past week and are told they have earned tickets on United Airlines to fly them to Timberline Lodge, in the Cascades, for a week's paid vacation funded by *Truth or Consequences*.

Closing the final broadcast of the season, Ralph Edwards makes an appeal in behalf of the starving people overseas, asking for cash contributions and canned goods to be used by UNRRA (United Nations Relief and Rehabilitation Administration).

Episodes #561 & 562, Broadcast of September 7, 1946

Stunts: Joan Edwards, Wilcox Commercial Stunt, Personal Drama, and Variety Award

Beginning this evening, for the entire season, at least one $25 Savings Bond is given away during every broadcast. Announcer **Harlow Wilcox** is given a phony commercial to read on the air as his "initiation" and he is stopped as he tries to struggle through the reading, then given the correct script. Celebrity guest **Joan Edwards**, vocalist, took part in the stunt imposed upon contestant **Roy Anderson**, who received a $25 Savings Bond for trying to sell a recording to the singer (with a two-way pickup from the Hollywood record shop for this stunt).

Consequence is imposed upon an ex-G.I. contestant named **Lester Hansen**, who is still hospitalized and asked to "act" in a little dramatization in which he is assisted by radio actors **Jack Moyles** and **Ivan Green**. The dramatization portrays the heroism and experiences of the veteran, but contestant does not know until he reads along in the "script" that he is acting out his own story. For his efforts as an actor, and in recognition of his exploits during the war, Lester receives a $1,000 diamond engagement ring and wedding band to match, to give the girl he plans to marry soon; a complete wardrobe for civilian life including two Hart Schaffner & Marx suits and top coats; and all-expenses-paid to equip his new car (he already has the car) so that he will be able to drive it without using his disabled limbs. (*Truth or Consequences* arranged this special equipment for the car through consultation with the vet's hospital.)

At the conclusion of the broadcast, **Jack Hellman**, Hollywood editor of *Variety* magazine, presented Ralph Edwards with the 1946 *Variety* Award for creative showmanship. In making his presentation, Mr. Hellman praised Edwards for his efforts in using his program for both entertainment and "humanitarianism," and listed some of the results of Edwards' Bond campaigns, his gifts to the needy, ill and War Service personnel, etc. In receiving the award, Edwards thanked his listeners, his cast, his writers, producer, sponsor, etc., for making his program possible, and pledged his efforts in continuing any "good work." Edwards makes a mention that hospitalized veterans would get special attention on the program this season.

For the opening show of the season, every contestant is given the chance to make one word out of the two words, "Roast Mules." The contestant who unscrambles the two words to make one word gets $100. Nobody wins. (Each contestant has a chance to win because all contestants are wearing earmuffs so they cannot hear the preceding contestant's answer.) When contestants are called to the microphone, he or she had a chance to make one common English word out of "Roast Mules." The contestants receive the word and the instruction during the warm-up period, about 20 minutes before air-time, and could work on the word until they were called to the mike.

Episodes #563 & 564, Broadcast of September 14, 1946

Stunts: Agreement, Hollywood Traffic Island, Tank Weight, and Surprise Party

Broadcast from Hollywood studios with a two-way set up with Ward 6 at the McCornack U.S. Army Hospital, in Pasadena, California. The other boys in the hospital and the nurses take part in the surprise. The Private First Class who is having a birthday gets a Hart Schaffner & Marx suit along with other gifts to help him with his hobby. His buddies get an Aireon Automatic Phonograph Player, with 900 records – this phonograph to be installed in the ward or in the recreation hall for all the boys to enjoy. A new supply of records will be forthcoming each week for "many weeks."

The "Roast Mules" word game is still being used. Every contestant is given an opportunity to unscramble the word. Every week the game carries over adds another $100 to the pot. Feature stunt is a surprise birthday party for a hospitalized veteran.

This broadcast includes the first of the "Hollywood Traffic Island" stunt – a veteran named **Dusty Rhodes**, of Brooklyn, New York, ready to go to Traffic Island at Hollywood Boulevard and La Brea Streets, one of the busiest corners in Hollywood. If Rhodes stays on the island, he will receive $3 an hour for every hour that he holds out and he will be given a chance to report his progress every Saturday night at broadcast time. Dusty is supplied with enough food to last him three weeks (that will net the contestant $1,512). The contestant is told that he will be observed and entertained every minute of his stay on Traffic Island. Also, he is given a bamboo fishing rod and a suit of long white underwear to raise as a distress signal should he decide to give up. A tent, bed and blankets are at the Island. The Traffic Island stunt is dedicated to a drive for safety. (Dusty was rarely alone as Ralph Edwards sent, over the next few days, clowns, dancing girls and movie stars to entertain him. Rhodes, a herpetologist, insisted on having his snakes with him.)

Episodes #565 & 566, Broadcast of September 21, 1946

Stunts: Service Man's Choice, Faint Door Lock, Traffic Island No. 2, and Dish Washers

A follow-up with **Dusty Rhodes** on Traffic Island. Anyone who wants to write to Dusty Rhodes is instructed to address him simply: "Dusty Rhodes, Truth or Consequences, NBC, Hollywood, California." In today's pickup from Traffic Island, Dusty Rhodes presents a guest who is visiting the Island, actor **Keenan Wynn**. Wynn is opening a new theater, the El Patio, on October 1 and he wants Rhodes to attend the opening. Since Rhodes cannot leave his station, Wynn is leaving binoculars with which he can watch the play by climbing to the top of a palm tree on Traffic Island – the El Patio Theater is across the street. Rhodes tells Ralph Edwards tonight that he is selling autographed pictures of himself to tourists and is giving the money to the Sister Kenny Polio Foundation.

 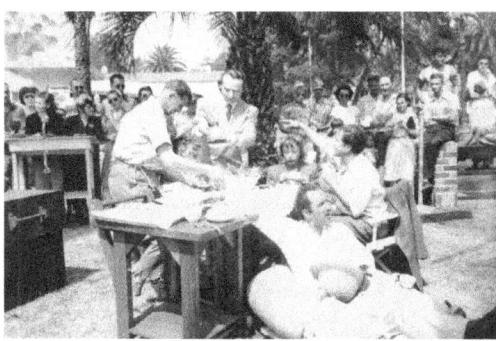

Episodes #567 & 568, Broadcast of September 28, 1946
Stunts: Castaway Queen, Water Commissioner, Traffic Island No. 3, and Rhyme Line
During this broadcast, a "Queen of the Isle" is selected from the studio audience and sent by "tramp steamer" (the "tramp steamer" being a man from the studio audience who carried the "queen" in a washtub) to Traffic Island. The Queen is sent to the Island to prepare **Dusty Rhodes'** favorite dish, "Mulligan Stew." The Queen is contestant **Mary Kinard**.
The "Roast Mules" word puzzle is finally worked out by a contestant, Mrs. Ashby, recently from London, England. She receives $400. The single word made from two words is "somersault."

Episodes #569 & 570, Broadcast of October 5, 1946
Stunts: Speak English, Traffic Island No. 4, Apartment, Traffic Island Payoff, and Speak English Payoff
The guest at Traffic Island is the mayor of Los Angeles, **Mayor Fletcher Bowron**, who presents **Dusty Rhodes** with a citation of merit from the Mayor's office and from the Police Department of Los Angeles, on behalf of the work being done to encourage safety among drivers. During his stay on Traffic Island, Dusty has been shouting at careless drivers and using his hands to help direct traffic. He has exposed careless drivers and careless walkers alike. In many cases Dusty was surprised to discover them returning to thank him for helping prevent accidents. This episode concludes Dusty's stay on Traffic Island and

he is paid off at the rate of $3 an hour for the entire time he was on the island. He was paid, however, in pennies – a total of 151,114 pennies. Then, because of his heavy load of pennies, he is offered a cab from the Reliable Cab Company of Hollywood to go "anywhere he likes" and Rhodes gets even with prankster Edwards by choosing Brooklyn, New York!

Episodes #571 & 572, Broadcast of October 12, 1946
Stunts: Hanky Kid, Describes Football, Dusty Remote, and Diamond Ice
This broadcast includes a pick up from an NBC radio station in Oklahoma City, Oklahoma, where **Dusty Rhodes** talks to Ralph Edwards on route to Brooklyn. **Steve Evans**, cabdriver for the Reliable Cab Company of Hollywood, who is taking Dusty to Brooklyn, New York, also speaks from Oklahoma City. Edwards tells Evans that he will take a calf named "Clarence" from Oklahoma City to Chicago, as a passenger in the cab, to keep Dusty company.
Special guest in the Hollywood studios is **Kenny Baker**, emcee of the *Glamour Manor* radio show. A contestant is told that he will take two hot-water bottles to the *Glamour Manor* show next week and use the bottle heat to melt through a piece of ice which Kenny Baker uses on his show. If he melts enough ice, he can keep the $1,000 diamond ring contained inside. The contestant is **Lt. George Troutman**, who is accompanied by his fiancée, **Dorothy Beavers**. Lt. Troutman hopes to give the ring to Miss Beavers when she becomes his wife.

Episodes #573 & 574, Broadcast of October 19, 1946
Stunts: Diamond Ice Payoff, Write Under Water, Silent Woman, and Peoria Plan
Lt. George Troutman, and his bride of the day, return to the program. The contestant managed to melt through the ice to the $1,000 J.R. Wood Art-carved diamond ring on **Kenny Baker's** *Glamour Manor* show, and the couple married this afternoon. They publicly thank Ralph Edwards for making the ring and the wedding possible!
Special contestant for the broadcast was a wounded ex-serviceman, **Don Fitzgerald**, of Peoria, Illinois. The program features a two-way pick-up from Peoria, where Don's friends, his wife, mother, and father get a chance to talk with Don who is in Hollywood. A request for a job is made over the air and the Peoria businessman offered Don a number of jobs in return. The contestant chooses one with the Caterpillar Tractor Company. Don receives a plane trip back home, leaving from Hollywood tomorrow. And when he

arrives in Peoria, he and his wife will have a house completely furnished, and rent-free for one year!

Dusty Rhodes is also in Peoria, Illinois, still on route to Brooklyn. His cab driver, **Steve Evans**, also speaks briefly telling of their trip thus far.

Episodes #575 & 576, Broadcast of October 26, 1946

Stunts: Calling Dusty, Subtle Date, Silent Woman Payoff, Baby Karloff, and Greyhound

During the broadcast, a telephone call comes in from **Dusty Rhodes** who says he and his cab driver are now in New Orleans, Louisiana. Dusty is not heard on the program, however. The telephone rings and Ralph Edwards, speaking from the studio, merely relates the other end of the conversation to the listeners. In another stunt, a female contestant is provided with a scrapbook of baby photos and asked to look at the face carefully to determine whether he was the gentle type or the criminal type. She later meets the gentleman in the photographs, **Boris Karloff**. (The actor was performing "Gramps" in the play, *On Borrowed Time*, at the El Patio Theater in Hollywood.) For her participation, she wins two free tickets to the play.

Episodes #577 & 578, Broadcast of November 2, 1946

Stunts: Simultaneous Talk, Girl Friend's Mom, Sound Effects Sentence, Little Honey, and Dusty

A service man and his fiancé (**Miss Claire Elbar**) are told that they will receive a two-week honeymoon on the beautiful island of the Dominican Republic, and the Caribbean, plus transportation to and from via Pan American Airways. A honeymoon suite is reserved for the couple during their stay. The stunt, which results in this "gift," consists in part of having the bridegroom-to-be call his future mother-in-law and ask her for a date. The bridegroom-to-be gets a wristwatch to give his mother-in-law after he is married.

Dusty Rhodes, along with the taxi driver from Hollywood, **Steve Evans**, arrived in New York City and appear on the program in person. Ralph Edwards gives Dusty a pie tin filled with Atlantic Ocean water and requests he take it back to Hollywood by taxi… without spilling a drop. If he delivers the tin of water to Ralph Edwards in Hollywood, Dusty will get $500 in addition to the $1,512 he has already received for staying on the traffic island.

The broadcasts of November 2 and 9 originate from New York City, not Hollywood.

Episodes #579 & 580, Broadcast of November 9, 1946

Stunts: Diamond Gloves Gift Choice, Commercial Drama, Italian Football, and Relatives

The "Diamond Glove Gift Choice" stunt involves three female contestants who are given the choice of several gifts: a radio, a wristwatch, a complete set of Encyclopedia Americana, a make-up box, a diamond ring, or a pair of ladies' gloves. What the contestants do not know is that the gloves are Hansen gloves worth $2,000 because each glove of the pair has a diamond band around it! Special guest on the program is **Ray Flaherty**, football coach of the New York Yankees. (The New York Yankees were a professional American football team that played in the All-America Football Conference (AAFRC) from 1946 to 1949.)

Episodes #581 & 582, Broadcast of November 16, 1946

Stunts: Running Sound Effects, Aeronca Cowboy, Dusty Pie Tin Payoff, and Smack Husband

Program returns to Hollywood with this broadcast. The "Aeronca Cowboy" stunt involves an ex-serviceman and cowboy from Texas who gets an Aeronca Champion plane to help him watch his herds and sprinkle his crops from the skies. Estimated value for the plane is $4,475. (The "Aeronca Cowboy" is **Pete Kercher** of Dublin, Texas, just out of the Ninth Air Forces.)

Dusty Rhodes arrived in Hollywood and collects $500 from Ralph Edwards for bringing a pie tin of Atlantic Ocean water via taxi from New York to Hollywood without spilling a drop. Rhodes had the salt extracted from the water and had the water frozen in the pie tin. He also put the bag of salt, which was extracted, on top of the ice so that the Atlantic Ocean water was complete. He received his $500. This also marks the last appearance of Dusty on the program. Incidentally, Dusty's taxi-fare, cash giveaways, etc. cost the radio program $6,427.38, according to Ralph Edwards' announced estimate.

Newspaper article by Aline Mosby, United Press Hollywood Correspondent

Dusty Rhodes is a lanky ex-G.I. who once lived in a quiet Hollywood hotel and lectured on snakes. Nineteen hours a day, thousands of people crowded around Dusty's tent on the island. He entered into the spirit of the thing. He talked to folks. He sold his autographed pictures and gave the money to the polio foundation. He showed the crowd his snakes. Movie stars came to entertain him. His fan mail piled up. The press excitedly recorded his every move. And every week Dusty talked on the radio from his island. He was so good Edwards cracked, "It's almost Dusty's show, not mine."

"I was a natural on the radio," Dusty told Aline Mosby, United Press Hollywood Correspondent. "Big-time radio announcers told me my voice, my timing, my ad-libbing was perfect. I threw the cracks at Edwards as fast as he threw 'em to me."

After three weeks, Dusty folded his tent and collected $1,500 in pennies on the broadcast for the stunt. As a bonus, the radio folks gave him a taxi to take him any place he wanted. Dusty chose Brooklyn, New York. The audience howled. Every week Dusty appeared on the show from location on route to the East Coast. Dusty smartly stretched his good fortune. He took eight weeks to get to New York. He lived in the best of hotels, costing the radio program $7,000. In New York, Edwards gave Dusty one last gag. To carry a plate of Atlantic Ocean water to Hollywood. Dusty did – in the form of dry ice and salt. For that, he won an additional $500.

Dusty's career in radio was temporary. Four agents promised to get him on the air. His fame was short-lived. His check book was broke. He called the agents. The deals never quite came through. Dusty checked out of his fancy hotel and disappeared. He moved to a cheap hotel in nearby Pasadena. Hollywood wondered for an hour what happened to him. Then it forgot. Dusty couldn't go back to snake lectures. He sold his snakes long ago, believing fame was his destiny. He took jobs washing dishes.

For a year Dusty lived in disillusioned oblivion. It seemed as if he had to "die" to get back into print. Another man named Dusty Rhodes – a movie stunt actor – jumped off San Francisco's Golden Gate Bridge. Some columnists mistook the stuntman for the contestant on *Truth or Consequences*. Rhodes phoned Edwards to assure him that he was still alive. And Dusty found out the radio show was swamped with phone calls from his worried fans who feared the worst.

Phil Baker takes a cream pie to the face on the broadcast of November 23, 1946. According to the press release on the back of the photo, Baker was the first of what would become many contestants to receive a pie in the face on the quiz program.

Episodes #583 & 584, Broadcast of November 23, 1946
Stunts: Unruly Son, Good Old Days, Phil Baker, and Delay Answer
Phil Baker, emcee of the *Take It or Leave It* radio program, is a celebrity guest. A married couple participates in the "Good Old Days" stunt, which was performed again with different contestants on December 14.

Episodes #585 & 586, Broadcast of November 30, 1946
Stunts: Pickup Bandbag, Society Women, Husband-Psychiatrist, and Room for Rent
Guest is **"Box Car" Johnson,** known as King of the Hobos, who participates in a stunt involving a serviceman on temporary leave. With no home to stay, the contestant is provided with a box car on the Southern Pacific Lark, en route to San Francisco and Seattle.

Episodes #587 & 588, Broadcast of December 7, 1946

Stunts: Mother-In-Law Travelogue, Sweet Sixteen, and Egg Tour

A student named **Earline Slater** from Franklin High School in Los Angeles was among those students who had no escort to the senior prom. Edwards contacted her parents earlier in the week and arranged for them to take her to the **Guy Madison** movie, *Till the End of Time*, the night before. During the broadcast, the girl was a studio guest and told to wish for a "Cinderella Party Dress, etc." She went to a private dressing room backstage, where she received hairdressing, manicure, etc., including a fitting for the dream dress. Then she was told that her Prince Charming has arrived to escort her to the ball – the prom was later in the evening. Prince Charming was actor Guy Madison and the actor took her to the senior prom. As a final gift before leaving for the prom, Slater received a $500 diamond ring.

Episodes #589 & 590, Broadcast of December 14, 1946

Stunts: No Kiss, Good Old Days B.U. Tank Hamburger, and Women Talk

Celebrity guest is **Myrna Dell**, an actress currently seen in the movie, *Nocturne*. One stunt for two contestants, **Mr. and Mrs. Leonard Platt** of Los Angeles, agreed to live as if they were living in the "good old days" at the turn of the century. If they lived this way for the entire week and returned to the program with a suitable report of their experiences, they would receive a radio phonograph, tickets to the premiere of *Duel in the Sun*, and entertainment in person by several movie stars. They were given appropriate costumes which they donned that evening and must wear all week. They had to churn their own butter, use lamps instead of electricity, etc.

Episodes #591 & 592, Broadcast of December 21, 1946

Stunts: Bowl Rooters, Good Old Days Payoff, and Nativity

Before the traditional Christmas program feature began, last week's contestants returned. **Mr. and Mrs. Leonard Platt**, who lived as if they were back in the good old days, were in costumes to collect. As with last year's holiday offering, no contestants were over six years old. Three children took part. One of the children was a Negro child and Ralph Edwards mentions that color, race and creed make no difference to Santa Claus. The children received appropriate gifts with big special things that they asked their parents for. All of the children in the studio audience received special gifts. Then, Ralph Edwards narrated his annual Christmas story about the "Birthday of Jesus."

Episodes #593 & 594, Broadcast of December 28, 1946
Stunts: Bowl Rooters Valet, Maurice Evans, and Refuse Gifts
This broadcast featured a pick-up from the dressing room of **Maurice Evans**, currently playing Hamlet at the Philharmonic Auditorium in Los Angeles. Another celebrity guest was **Louise Arthur**, actress. In the highlighted stunt of the evening, two contestants received 50-yard-line seats for the Rose Bowl Game. The contestants had been supplied with tickets, pennants, etc. and had been sent to the Rose Bowl on Thursday when the Bowl was empty! The contestants had to pretend they were at the big game, jump up and down while rooting for their teams. Tonight, they receive tickets for the real game. The contestants were **Willard Lind** of Rockford, Illinois, a carpenter, and **Sol Weiss**, of Chicago, a cook.

Episodes #595 & 596, Broadcast of January 4, 1947
Stunts: Hot Seat Jury, Six-Footer, Masquerade, Rose Bowl Playoff, and Try Again
Sol Weiss and **Willard Lind**, contestants from last week's broadcast, were back on the program. The loser, the one who rooted for the losing team after the game, had to be the valet for the other man for an entire week. Both received footballs autographed by the captains and the coaches of both football teams, plus $50 for each one to spend.

Episodes #597 & 598, Broadcast of January 11, 1947
Stunts: Rain Barrel, Return Daughters, Pickles Backward, Win T or C, and Laugh 'Til Off
Louise Arthur, movie actress, returns to the program. A returned veteran participates in a stunt involving his wife and two daughters, whom he has not seen in four years. He thinks he is making a telephone call home and that a record is being made of his voice so that he can send the recording to his daughters. In actuality, his wife is talking to him from a telephone backstage and after he completes his "call," his two little daughters, in person, bring the record to him.

Episodes #599 & 600, Broadcast of January 18, 1947

Stunts: $30 Answer, Remember Relatives Names, Teacher, Muddled-Up, Model Date, Question Answered by Sender, Ralph Volunteers, Dizzy Aunts, and Grand Prize Winner

Mike Kozoll, operator of the Sally Lee Ladies' Ready-to-Wear Shop in Hollywood, is emcee in full charge of the program. Ralph Edwards sits in the front row of the studio audience and heckles his substitute. As a special gag, Kozoll stops regular announcer **Harlow Wilcox** and says since this is his show, he has brought his own announcer. This announcer is **Jimmy Wallington**. Also, the new emcee has brought along another "boy" announcer, **Don Wilson**. Kozoll lavishly gives out gifts to all of his friends and relatives, including $250 and a trip to the Last Frontier Hotel in Las Vegas, Nevada. And Mike Kozoll says it is only fair that Ralph Edwards take over his job for a week. Edwards is promised $1,000 but he must wait on customers, pin up hems, tailor, and do everything else at the Hollywood shop for all of next week, while Mike goes on the special vacation trip to Las Vegas with his wife, **Julia Kozoll**. The wife is on the program tonight, of course, since she is the star contestant and answers all of her husband's difficult questions!

Edwards accepts the job at the store only to have a surprise contestant turn up on the program: **Dusty Rhodes**, who did the Hollywood Traffic Island stunt on the program a month ago. Rhodes is the manager-for-a-week of Kozoll's store while Edwards has to work as an employee!

Mrs. Harold Votaw receives $1,000 because last week on this program she was told she would receive the money if she could name a city in the United States where it was raining at that very minute. She named her old hometown of Indianapolis, Indiana, and the program put through a long-distance call to the police station in Indianapolis. The police station said it was not raining there. During the week, she checked with the Weather Bureau and found that only in the vicinity of the police station was there no rain on last Saturday night during the time of the quiz program. Everywhere else in Indianapolis it was indeed raining. She collected her money.

Ralph Edwards volunteers at the Sally Lee Dress Shop, January 20, 1947.

Mrs. Ann Coon and a disguised Harlow Wilcox on the broadcast of January 18, 1947.

Episodes #601 & 602, Broadcast of January 25, 1947

Stunts: Record Quarrel, Student Teacher, Tin Whistle, Hush Payoff No. 1, and Stop Kiss

The Mrs. Hush contest begins with this broadcast. The voice of a famous American woman is heard on the program. Listeners were instructed to finish in 25 words or less the following sentence: "We should all support the March of Dimes because…" Listeners were also instructed to enclose a contribution for the March of Dimes. The writers of the three best letters would have a chance to answer a telephone call from Ralph Edwards and to identify Mrs. Hush when he phones them. The prize for the first phone call (on February 8) will be a 1947 Ford Sportsman Convertible automobile; a Bendix Washer; and a round trip ticket to New York City for two with a weekend reservation at the Waldorf Astoria Hotel while in New York. If the people who called the first time do not identify the owner of the voice, the contest holds over and three more prizes would be added.

The celebrity guest assisting on today's program in the Studios in Hollywood is actress **Louise Arthur**.

Episodes #603 & 604, Broadcast of February 1, 1947

Stunts: Mrs. Hush, Telephone Frame, Tin Whistle Payoff, No Bark Dog, and Tumblers

Two of the famous Basenji dogs, the bark-less dogs of Africa (Belgian Congo), are used in a contest. Edwards comments upon the growing popularity of these dogs as household pets in this country. (He refers listeners to the January issue of *Magazine Digest*, which has an article about these dogs.) The two dogs used on tonight's program were flown in from the Hallwyre Kennels in Dallas, Texas.

Episodes #605 & 606, Broadcast of February 8, 1947

Stunts: Mrs. Hush, Reducing Belt Drama, Tuba Frame, Adopt Baby, and Watch Stomach

The "Reducing Belt Drama stunt" features two contestants who are presented each with $15 and a set of cards entitling each of them to take a special reducing course of 12 lessons, at Terry Hunt's Health System, on La Cienega Blvd. in Hollywood. Also featured in a stunt is an "Adopt Baby Pig" – the pig is presented to a contestant – pig complete with nursing bottle, etc. The "Watch Stomach" stunt was performed on the West Coast broadcast, not East Coast.

Episodes #607 & 608, Broadcast of February 15, 1947
Stunts: Mrs. Hush, French Question, Always, and Tickle-Cry
Broadcast from the Golden Gate Theatre in San Francisco, California. A beautiful young French woman is instructed to hold $100 bills in her hands and ask three gentlemen, in French, that they can have $100 if they do not kiss her. The men were off stage at the time she was instructed, and the audience has a laugh as the young woman puckers up after each set of instructions – spoken in French.
The "Tickle-Cry" stunt was featured on the East Coast broadcast, not West Coast.

Episodes #609 & 610, Broadcast of February 22, 1947
Stunts: Mrs. Hush, $20 Bill Seltzer, and Clients' Booth Wife
Guest is **Claire Dodson**, Earl Carroll show girl, who assists Ralph Edwards by entertaining one of the contestants. In another stunt, a man is asked if he wants to eat from the Brown Derby for a week and is provided a physical brown derby with a special bowl inside. If he eats from the hat for an entire week, he will receive a 14-carot, 21-jewel Bulova wristwatch, and a $25 Savings Bond. In another stunt, a man is provided a mirror, four feet tall and three feet wide, and instructed to spend the week carrying the mirror in front of him. Every time someone asks what the mirror is for, he is instructed to respond, "My doctor told me to watch my stomach."

Episodes #611 & 612, Broadcast of March 1, 1947
Stunts: Mrs. Hush, Celotex Surprise
Dick Moorman, a war veteran now working and trying to find a place to live in California, dictates a letter to his fiancé back in Long Island, New York... Or so he thinks as he dictates a letter to send for her so they may be married as soon as he gets an apartment or a home for them to live. In actuality, the fiancé, **Gloria Minay**, is the girl to whom he is giving the dictation. She was ably disguised by Hollywood makeup artists who had made her hair blonde and used blue contact lenses to mask her brown eyes. Imagine his surprise when the gag is unraveled, and the couple are reunited on the program. Gloria and her family have been flown to Los Angeles with all expenses paid by

the producers of the program. In addition, after the Hollywood marriage, the couple were sent to Chicago where they will enjoy an all-expense paid honeymoon in a Celotex pre-engineered house built by the Celotex people on Seventh Street next to the Stevens Hotel in Chicago. The trip to Chicago and back will be made on the Super Chief passenger train and when the couple return from their honeymoon, they will find a Celotex House waiting to be put up for them wherever they want to live. The house will be just like the one in which they spend their honeymoon. Ralph Edwards says it may be the very same house and all the furniture to start housekeeping goes with the gift! When the contestant finds that his fiancé is right on the stage with him, he says over the air, "Oh, Christ!"

Episodes #613 & 614, Broadcast of March 8, 1947
Stunts: Mrs. Hush, Reverse Consequence, and Neighbors
Two contestants are provided crackers, which they are to chew in their mouths while performing a scripted drama about Pudge Heffelfinger, who cannot resist the charms of a spy named Penelope Putterpain. In another stunt, a woman is blindfolded and sits on stage throughout the program, listening to every word spoken by the contestants. At the close of the broadcast, the blindfold is removed and she is asked to correctly identify which man seated in the front row was at the microphone after she was blindfolded.

Mrs. McCormick, winner of the Mrs. Hush contest, among the prizes.

Episodes #615 & 616, Broadcast of March 15, 1947
Stunts: Mrs. Hush, Contestant Emcee, and Eat in Derby

The Mrs. Hush contest ends when **Mrs. William H. McCormick** of Lock Haven, Pennsylvania, answered her telephone call from Ralph Edwards and correctly identified silent screen actress Clara Bow. Following the identification of the mystery voice, there is a remote pick-up from Las Vegas, Nevada, for the special guests, **Clara Bow** and her husband, screen cowboy **Rex Bell**, along with her two sons, **George** and **Toni**. The Eat in Derby stunt was performed on the West Coast broadcast only.

Episodes #617 & 618, Broadcast of March 22, 1947

Stunts: Mrs. McCormick, Mothers-In-Law, Community Sing, and Sealed Envelope No. 1

Following a quick segment with **Mrs. William H. McCormick** and her husband, the program features a takeoff titled, "Mrs. Hush's Mother-in-Law," in which mothers-in-law of three contestants are hidden in the studio. They tell their in-laws what they think of them but the in-laws have to identify their respective mothers-in-law. It might be anybody in the studio audience.

Another stunt on this program featured a girl who was sent to the corner of Sunset and Vine to organize a community sing. She received one dollar for every person who joined her singing group. The broadcast featured a remote pick-up from the corner and solicitors could judge the success of the singing.

Ralph Edwards speaks bizarre language for a sealed envelope contest to begin next week.

Episodes #619 & 620, Broadcast of March 29, 1947

East Coast Stunts: Wife's Picture, 49 Kids, Sealed Envelope No. 2, Pie-Cop, and Watch Stomach West Coast Stunts: Wife's Picture, 49 Kids, Sealed Envelope No. 2, Pie-Cop, and Remember Contest

Special stunt on this broadcast is for the benefit of a veteran of WWII, ex-Sgt. **William Sheath** of Arizona, and his wife, who is on the program as a complete surprise to her husband. Ex-Sgt. Heath has his hospital attendant, Mr. Gill, with him on the program. **Jack Albin**, NBC photographer, is on the program to take a picture of the kiss which Mrs. Sheath gives the veteran!

A bachelor contestant receives 50 tickets for the Clyde Beatty Circus, which opens in Hollywood on April 1. Contestant will use one ticket himself and take 49 children from a Los Angeles orphanage with him. A special Tanner Motor Company Bus will provide transportation for the contestant and children.

Truth or Consequences gives the contestant $100 for spending money on peanuts, popcorn, etc. for the children.

This broadcast marked the first time for the "Mystery Envelope" contest. Ralph Edwards shows a contestant a sealed envelope and then pronounces the mysterious sounds, "AF-OO-LA-NISMO-NEE-ARSCO-NEPAR-TED." If the contestant can decipher the statement, he will get the sealed envelope and the right to open it. The contestant fails but he does receive a $25 savings bond.

Episodes #621 & 622, Broadcast of April 5, 1947
Stunts: Helicopter-Love, Sealed Envelope No. 3, Screen Test, and Pretend Man

Broadcast from the Hollywood studios with pickups from a vacant lot and a helicopter. On this program, **Mrs. Lorene Parker**, housewife in Memphis, Tennessee, unravels the mysterious words and gets the envelope in the "Sealed Envelope" contest. The mysterious words are: "A Fool and his Money are Soon Parted." She opens the envelope. Outside of the envelope bears the message, "Check Inside," and inside she finds a baggage check from the Union Depot in Los Angeles. Just as she starts out of the studio to go to the Union Depot, a man suddenly appears, snatches the check, and runs to the studio shouting, "A fool and his money are soon parted!"

Ralph Edwards immediately starts Mrs. Parker in pursuit, with a member of the studio audience to get her a cab to the Union Depot, where she might intercept the stranger before he tries to collect on the check. She is told to return to the program next week to report what happens next. After the contestant has been gone for a while, a "Mysterious Phone Call" comes in for Ralph Edwards. It is a report from a drugstore at Western Avenue and Sunset to the effect that the hooded man just passed in a black sedan headed for Union Depot.

For the helicopter stunt, a prospective bridegroom is interviewed through a pick-up from a vacant lot. The contestant is instructed to get into a helicopter standing in that lot. A pilot flies the prospective bridegroom over his girl's house and will be let down by helicopter to propose again to his love. Later in the program, the pick-up of the proposal is made with an NBC engineer in a mobile broadcasting car, standing by at the bride-to-be's home.

This broadcast had a one-minute tribute to Army Week. Ralph Edwards said the week of April 6 has been set aside as Army Week. He asks everyone to take time out to pay honor to the American soldier, living and dead, who has done his part to perpetuate the American Way of Life. He also urged that we continue to do all we can for servicemen and women who are going back to civilian life.

Episodes #623 & 624, Broadcast of April 12, 1947
Stunts: Wife Hat, Costa Rica, and Sealed Envelope No. 4

Mrs. Lorene Parker returns to the program. She says she received a letter from the Mystery Man telling her to call tonight for a package left at the studio. The package is opened during the program and a recording is played. Radio listeners discover that the Mystery Man is sitting in the audience. The record includes instructions for Mrs. Parker to "jump through the loop" sometime during the week, with reference to the circus. The record also says such a feat will give her the opportunity to share the prize with him, because he knows exactly where the "treasure" is.

A consequence for two ex-servicemen hospitalized at Birmingham General in Van Nuys, California. **Tom Thompson**, of Indianapolis, Ind., and **Louie Bach** of Tucson, Arizona, and their wives who have been brought to the program as a complete surprise to the husbands. Two couples get airplane tickets to Miami, Florida, and a two-week reservation at the luxurious Roney Plaza Hotel in Miami, as their prizes for taking part tonight.

The lady in the hat is Mrs. Harvey, one of the contestants on the broadcast of April 12, 1947.

Episodes #625 & 626, Broadcast of April 19, 1947
Stunts: Celebrity in Between, Continue Story, and Sealed Envelope No. 5

This broadcast includes a two-way set-up from the Clyde Beatty Circus in Los Angeles, where **Mrs. Lorene Parker** "jumps through the loop" in an effort to meet the requirements of the Mystery Man. The voice of the Mystery Man is heard telling Mrs. Parker that he did not refer to the circus loop in Los Angeles but that he meant the "Chicago Loop." The voice is heard over a microphone and Mrs. Parker cannot locate the owner of the voice. However, as one of the circus clowns run from the circus ring, she decides that the Mystery Man was the clown. Mrs. Parker agrees to travel with the *Truth or Consequences* cast for an appearance in Chicago next week.

Back in the Hollywood studio, celebrity guest **Edgar Kennedy** participates in a special stunt with three contestants ranging in ages from 7 to 10 years. The children are **William Porter, Phyllis Hagen,** and **Bob Howard**. The children take part in a rehearsed "continued story" started by Edwards. For their participation, each of the children receive an album, "Let's Have a Party," and are then told that if they, with the help of their other Sunday school members, get ten new members for their Sunday school, *Truth or Consequences* program will arrange for the church and Sunday school to get an Orgatron, a new electric organ which sells for an amount between $1,200 and $1,500. (On the Orgatron will be a plaque engraved with the name of the three children who appeared on this program.) The children are told to have the pastor notify Ralph Edwards next week regarding the outcome of their campaign. This was partly to serve as a public service announcement to encourage radio listeners to help their local church or Sunday school. ("Let's Have a Party" was a Mercury Records release with Ralph Edwards.)

A third stunt had six contestants provided with an all-expense paid round-trip visit to Moscow... Moscow, Idaho, although the contestants think until the last minute that they will be going to Moscow, Russia.

Episodes #627 & 628, Broadcast of April 26, 1947
Stunts: Pie Insult, Balloon Carryover, Husband Box, and Sealed Envelope No. 6

Program originates from both Hollywood and Chicago, with the program from Chicago, direct from the International Amphitheater, where the annual Food Show is in progress; commercials delivered by **Harlow Wilcox** from Hollywood. Ralph Edwards tells about the big Food Show, where the *Truth* *or Consequences* cast is giving two shows daily for entertainment of the crowds who are attending the Food Exhibits and projects. Several of the stunts were on the "food theme" in keeping with the plugs given for the Food Show.

A continuation of the "Mystery Man" consequence in which **Mrs. Lorene Parker** is trying to catch the "Mystery Man" in an attempt to collect a special prize. During this broadcast, the Mystery Man appears suddenly in a box that has been used in another stunt on the stage. Mrs. Parker, who just received two bloodhounds from Ralph Edwards to use and trail the Mystery Man, fails to get her dogs in action in time and the Mystery Man escapes through a rear stage exit. Mrs. Parker says she will trail the man doing the week and return to the program next Saturday.

Episodes #629 & 630, Broadcast of May 3, 1947
Stunts: Midget Baby B.U., Fire Hose, Sealed Envelope No. 7, and Balloon Carryover Payoff

Program originates from the International Amphitheater where Chicago's Food Show is still in progress. (Commercials originate from Hollywood.) Celebrity guest for this program is "Eddie, the Spirit of Mercury." Eddie is the midget famous for being a symbol of the Mercury Record Company. His picture could be seen in music and record stores throughout the United States. Ralph Edwards tells about Eddie and the Mercury Record Booth in the International Amphitheater Building in Chicago, where listeners could meet Eddie. (This was a deliberate advertisement for Mercury Record's "Let's Have a Party" album with Ralph Edwards.)

Also among the guests are **Joe Kelly**, the "Chief Quizzer" of radio's *Quiz Kids* program, with four of the "Quiz Kids" including **Joel Kupperman**, the math expert of the program; **Jerry Rutherford**, ex-G.I. and prospective father; and Mrs. **Lorene Parker** and her "Mystery Man." The feature concerns Jerry Rutherford, who thinks he is carrying a baby around the theater during the entire broadcast but who has Eddie the midget in the perambulator – the prospective father receives a complete layout for his coming baby plus fabulous gifts for his wife and himself, household gifts, etc., for taking part in the stunt.

Joe Kelly and the Quiz Kids do a routine with Mrs. Parker trying to help her catch the Mystery Man. Again, the Mystery Man gets away after giving a clue that the Quiz Kids interpret suggesting the Mystery Man could be found in

Marshall Field's Chicago store. Mrs. Parker is told that the treasure, which the Mystery Man is hiding from her, is $2,000 in cash.

Episodes #631 & 632, Broadcast of May 10, 1947
Stunts: Mother's Day, Polite Pies, Own Present, Spring Fat Man, and Sealed Envelope No. 8

Broadcast originates from the National Air Fair at the St. Louis Arena in St. Louis, Missouri, where the radio show is performing both afternoon and evening for the next nine days until Sunday, May 18. During the program, Edwards and **Harlow Wilcox**, the announcer, make numerous references to the matinee and evening shows at the Air Fair – including an announcement that the *Truth or Consequences* "Mystery Man" will appear in person somewhere in the audience at every performance for the nine days.

Mrs. Lorene Parker and the "Mystery Man" are both on the program. The Mystery Man is heard via loudspeaker and is finally on the stage. He wears a mask and a robe, and disguises his voice. He announces that on next week's broadcast, after his twice daily appearance at the Air Fair shows, he will speak in his natural voice and give every contestant on the show an opportunity of guessing his identity. The first contestant who recognizes him will receive $500 and after he is identified, Mrs. Parker gets the "treasure" of $2,000.

As a special Mother's Day stunt, a St. Louis mother, who thinks her son is in a Service Hospital, agrees to take ten Army sons (who are unable to get home to their own mothers) out to dinner at a special place planned by *Truth or Consequences*. She has never seen the "guests" – as she thinks but is told only that the boys are all from Army hospitals. The surprise comes when the boys come to the stage and she discovers one of them is her own son, having been flown home by the producers of the radio program after being granted a week's furlough to spend with his Mother. (Following the furlough, the boy reports back to the hospital for a final check preceding his discharge. This news is announced to the mother during the broadcast.)

The East Coast broadcast featured a "Spring Fat Man" stunt which caused the program to run over, and one less commercial for Crisco. For the West Coast broadcast, the stunt was not performed. **Ed Bailey** delivers commercials from Hollywood.

Episodes #633 & 634, Broadcast of May 17, 1947

Stunts: Mystery Guess, Own Hot Seat, Red Flannels B.U., Cancer Fund B.U., and Wooden Wedding

Program originates from St. Louis, Missouri, same location as last week's broadcast, with East Coast commercials from Hollywood delivered by **Ed Bailey**; West Coast commercials by **Johnny Pawlek**. Contestant **Edward Nehauser** steps behind a screen to put on a pair of flannels, keeping only his own shoes and socks. He is then instructed to start from St. Louis to Hollywood, wearing the red flannels. If he arrives in Hollywood by next week's broadcast, he will get $500. All of his clothes (including wallet) is taken from him and turned over to his wife. His transportation to Hollywood will be paid by the program.

Special guest on this program is little 14-year-old **Virginia Green**, who was flown to the program from Shannock, Rhode Island. Virginia lost one of her legs because of cancer and tonight asked to have an artificial leg so she could leave the wheelchair. Edwards asks listeners to mail contributions to the Rhode Island Cancer Society. If the amount of money sent in by listeners reached $25,000, the quiz program would arrange for an artificial leg for Virginia. Because Virginia confides that she hopes to be a teacher, Ralph Edwards said that if listeners send in more than $25,000 to the Cancer Society, **Mr. Otto Sieder**, Vice President of the Rhode Island Cancer Society, would personally sponsor a $2,000 scholarship to take Virginia through a teacher's college. Virginia sang on the program.

The "Mystery Man" and **Mrs. Lorene Parker** are on the program. Contestants failed to identify the Mystery Man, so next week's contestants have a chance of winning $1,000. This week's prize was $500 and another $500 has been added. Mrs. Parker will still get $2,000 when the Mystery Man is finally identified.

Episodes #635 & 636, Broadcast of May 24, 1947

Stunts: Hot Licks Band, Cancer Fund Payoff, Object: Wife, Red Flannels Payoff, Find Toupees, and Fish Bowl (East Coast only), and Word in Edgewise (West Coast only)

Program returns to Hollywood beginning with this episode. Ralph Edwards proudly announced that listeners raised the $25,000 with contributions sent to the Cancer Society, after hearing **Virginia Green** on last week's program. Details not provided on the program: Over 19,612 pieces of mail were received in response to the appeal making a total of $26,868.45 or $1.37 average per letter from listeners. Virginia's home was in Kenyon, Rhode Island.

Ed Nehauser, the man who wore red flannels from St. Louis to Hollywood, is in the studio. He receives $500 for the completion of his stunt.

Episodes #637 & 638, Broadcast of May 31, 1947

Stunts: Mother-in-Law Goat, Whistle Tune, Week on Boat B.U., and On the House

Jack and Aline Vrooman, young married contestants (Jack is a war veteran), spends a week on the Truscott, a cabin cruiser and "drydock" in the Los Angeles Coliseum where the Los Angeles Boat Show of 1947 is in progress. Of course, the Vroomans will have very little privacy because the exhibition is open to the public day and night. They will have full provisions of food for the week, comfortable sleeping quarters inside the cabin. Every hour, on the hour, Mr. Vrooman has to ring the ship's bell and run to the ship's bow and shout, "Storm Ahead!" Mrs. Vrooman must rush out every hour on the hour to squirt a bottle of seltzer water over her husband's head when he shouts. If they keep this up for an entire week, day and night, they will win a 17 ½ foot Ventnor Mahogany Speed Boat.

Episodes #639 & 640, Broadcast of June 7, 1947

Stunts: Water Tank Running Gag, Woman "How Do You Do," Husband Answers Wife, Shirts, and Week on Boat Payoff

The "Mystery Man" is identified as **Rex Bell**, movie star and husband of **Clara Bow**, who was the famous "Mrs. Hush" on the same program earlier in the season. The couple who identified the cowboy actor and received the $2,000 prize are **Maude McKenzie** and her husband of Honolulu. (Mr. McKenzie's first name is not given but described as a singer by profession.) **Lorene Parker** is on the program to receive her promised $2,000.

Mr. And Mrs. Jack Vrooman, picked up in a two-way set-up between the Hollywood studio and the Los Angeles Auditorium, are on the cabin cruiser as part of the Los Angeles Boat Show. For living on board the display cruiser for one week, they received the speedboat that accommodates six people, worth approximately $3,000. The Vroomans confess they will spend their honeymoon on the speedboat.

Back in the Hollywood studios, a contestant couple takes part in a screwball "dramatic performance in the Land of ZUD." (That is DUZ spelled backwards). They receive a subscription for one year to the "Cracker of the Year" club. This included Hi Ho Crackers, Cheez-Its, and Crispy Crackers for themselves, plus a carton of crackers of each variety for their close relatives.

The West Coast repeat broadcast was cancelled in order to make room for a special broadcast, a talk delivered by President Truman. Ralph Edwards and his production crew maintained official episode numbers for each broadcast and counted the non-extant West Coast repeat as an actual episode.

Episodes #641 & 642, Broadcast of June 14, 1947
East Coast Stunts: Theremin, Tootsie Rolls, Father's Day, and Orange Juice
West Coast Stunts: Theremin, Tootsie Rolls, Father's Day, Orange Juice, and Live on Boat Resume
In the "Mystery Musical Instrument" stunt, the contestant who guesses the name of the mystery instrument played offstage will receive $100. (The instrument is the Theremin which was used to provide mood music for such movies as *Spellbound*, *Lost Weekend*, *The Red House*, etc.) According to Ralph Edwards, there are only four people in the United States who can play this instrument successfully. On the program is **Dr. Samuel Hoffman**, leading Thereminist, who performs the instrument.
As a Father's Day stunt, one contestant receives a $500 Lionel Train set.
Pat Clark, journalism student at the University of California, and whose home is in Philadelphia, Pennsylvania, agrees to start on a multi-city tour to the East Coast, for three weeks, visiting 15 to 17 major cities in the United States. In each city he must squeeze orange juice for all the families named Edwards. He leaves at once with a big truck of California Sunkist oranges and it each city, this truck will be refilled as many times as necessary. Accompanying him is **Roy Rector**, who is sent out by *Truth or Consequences* to help Clark fulfill his promise. In one of the cities, Clark will be asked to cook an entire breakfast for an Edwards family in addition to squeezing orange juice. Somewhere along the tour, he will find a fellow named Edwards who has his prize… a $1,000 bill!
The repeat show for the West Coast differs only from the East in that listeners were brought up to date concerning the two big stunts, because last week's broadcast was cancelled: the successful guessing of the Mystery Man and the

stunt in which **Mr. and Mrs. Jack Voorman** earned their speedboat. Therefore, on the repeat show, celebrity guests **Rex Bell** and **Clara Bow** step up to the microphone, along with the contestants.

Episodes #643 & 644, Broadcast of June 21, 1947
East Coast Stunts: Tootsie Roll Payoff, Kiss in Bathing Suit, Dear Ruth, Orange Juice No. 2, Hot Seat "C", and Balloons in Hair B.U.
West Coast Stunts: Tootsie Roll Payoff, Dear Ruth, Orange Juice No. 2, Hot Seat "C," Balloons in Hair B.U., and Shirts
Pat Clark sends a telegram from Oklahoma City, reporting on the number of oranges he has squeezed throughout his tour, while looking for his $1,000 bill.
Celebrity guest is **Renee Randall**, talented starlet of *Dear Ruth*.

Episodes #645 & 646, Broadcast of June 28, 1947
Stunts: Balloons in Hair Payoff, Explain Baseball, Big Family Picnic, William Demarest, and Orange No. 3
Pat Clark sent another telegram and reveals he is now in Syracuse, New York, squeezing oranges for people with the name of Edwards.
Celebrity guest is **Fred Haney**, radio sports commentator for all of the Los Angeles Angels of the Pacific Coast League, participates in a baseball consequence with a contestant. Another celebrity guest in the studio is movie actor **William Demarest**.

Contestant falls victim to the stunt with actor William Demarest.

Episodes #647 & 648, Broadcast of July 5, 1947

Stunts: Orange Juice Payoff, Dorothy Lamour, Scavenger Hunt, and Laundry Mark

Pat Clark, the man who toured the country squeezing oranges is back in the Hollywood studio having found the man named Edwards with a $1,000 bill. He was in New York City. The bill, however, was for $1,000 owed for all the oranges used on the tour. Edwards arranged for 1,000 oranges to be brought onto the stage and inside one of them is a $1,000 bill. Pat Clark has to cut each orange to find the money. (He ultimately finds the prize and gets to keep it.)

This episode launched an expensive scavenger hunt in which contestants **Albert and Betty Anderson**, a young Los Angeles couple, have to spend their summer acquiring certain objects specified on a list and return with those items to the first broadcast of *Truth or Consequences* in the fall (September 6). These objects can be acquired through personal visits or through the mail. Objects listed:

1. A cigar partly smoked by Winston Churchill.
2. A band from a hat owned by former Mayor LaGuardia.
3. A hair from Jack Benny's toupee.
4. A salt shaker from Senator Claude Pepper.
5. A hambone autographed by George Bernard Shaw.
6. A schilling or 25 cent-piece contributed by Scotsman Sir Harry Lauder.
7. A copy of the Missouri Waltz, autographed by President Truman and Senator Taft.
8. One of former President Herbert Hoover's collars.
9. A hair from the eyebrow of John L. Lewis.
10. A portion of a sheet worn by Mahatma Gandhi and autographed by him.

Episode #649, Broadcast of September 6, 1947

Stunts: Will 2047, Re-Pose Picture, and Scavenger Hunt

Contestants **Albert and Betty Anderson** were assigned the consequence of securing ten different articles in a scavenger hunt and given the entire summer to collect. For a hair from Jack Benny's toupee, the couple received a $500 diamond ring; for a band from one of the hats of Fiorello LaGuardia, ex-mayor of New York City, the couple get a complete Hart Schaffner & Marx clothing outfit, one wardrobe for each; for a salt shaker from Senator Claude Pepper, the couple get a vacuum cleaner; for a shilling from Sir Harry Lauder, each of the young people receive a Bulova wrist watch; for Mahatma Gandhi's autograph on a "sheet," they received a deep freezer filled with frozen foods (it is explained that Gandhi did not send a piece of one of his famous "wearing sheets" but sent his autograph on a "sheet" of paper, which was acceptable to Edwards); for a copy of the Missouri Waltz, autographed by Senator Taft, the contestants received a Servel Refrigerator. (They attempted to secure President Truman's and Senator Taft's autographs but it was explained that White House regulations did not permit the President to autograph articles, letters, etc.) The couple failed to secure the remaining articles.

Mr. and Mrs. Odell Hatfield, who were observing their 37th wedding anniversary, were asked to pose for a wedding picture just as they posed 37 years ago. The lights are put out "to take the picture" and when the lights return, the Hatfields find that the members of their original wedding party have been brought on stage for the "picture pose" of the original bridal party! The Hatfields receive a 32-piece Sterling Silver set and the entire party is entertained at a wedding supper at Sherman Billingsley's Stork Club.

Mr. and Mrs. Gage, former residents of Texas who teach on an Indian Reservation in Arizona, were asked to take part in a pie throwing stunt in which Mrs. Gage throws a lemon pie at her husband. The Gage couple received $50 for their stunt with a "100-years-to-come" payoff tonight. They are told that if their nearest of kin appears on the program, wherever it may be 100 years from now, will receive $100 if the couple can do the same pie-throwing stunt that the Gages performed. The Gages will leave a provision about such stunt as part of their official will.

Episode #650, Broadcast of September 13, 1947
Stunts: Running Gags, Phantom Shower, Overseas Call, and 3,000 Mile Trip
With a live cut-in to a Los Angeles home, the "husband-in-the-bathtub" stunt is performed. The husband has been instructed to start to the bathroom and to have his wife, who is entertaining a lady friend in the living room, think he is going to take a shower. In actuality, a hidden speaker in the bathroom is tuning in voices from contestants in the studio, so that the wife gets the notion that the bathroom is full of strange people. The husband has been brought the short distance from his home to the studio while **Joe Kay**, radio engineer, is managing the speaker in the bathroom. The speaker is connected to the studio microphone on the stage in Hollywood studios, so the wife's shrieks are heard

from outside the bathroom and the husband's voice reaches his wife's ears. Finally, the farce is explained and the wife is let in on the ruse. The "Bathroom Couple" get a 72-piece set of Fine Arts Sterling Silver.

Mr. and Mrs. Harry Dewey volunteered to drive 3,000 miles in three weeks in order to win a new car. The Deweys are unaware that their "trip" consists of going around and around the block by their Los Angeles home, and will be tuned in each broadcast until the three weeks are up. Ralph Edwards estimates that they will have to drive 214 miles per day if they hope to finish the drive in two weeks. They have three weeks to accomplish the task and complete the drive. Mr. and Mrs. Dewey will take turns driving but nobody else will be allowed to help them. They may stop long enough to pick up friends and neighbors to share the ride from time to time. Mr. Dewey is a carpenter so he will work by day while his wife drives. The Deweys receive food, lunch box, and thermos to take on the trip.

Episode #651, Broadcast of September 20, 1947
Stunts: Grape Juice Goat, Shut-In Remote, 3,000 Mile Trip No. 2, and Mayors
Broadcast originates from Kennewick, Washington, at the home of a young child, who is the lucky recipient of prizes. There are 88 Mayors in the audience because this is Mayor's Day at the Grape Festival in Kennewick. Program switched back to Hollywood momentarily where **Mr. and Mrs. Harry Dewey**, contestants who volunteered to drive 3,000 miles in three weeks around the block, reported on the progress of their trip.

Episode #652, Broadcast of September 27, 1947
Stunts: Ned Sparks, 3,000 Mile Trip No. 3, Public Contestant B.U., and Happy Birthday Payoff
Studio contestant is **Earl Hedrick, Jr.** of Denver, Colorado, brought to Los Angeles by *Truth or Consequences* as a "surprise birthday gift" for his 67-year-old mother. Mr. Hedrick is interviewed briefly in the studio and is then sent to his mother's home as a "Western Union Singing Messenger" to sing "Happy Birthday" to her. Pickups on the program feature (1) from the home of **Mrs. E.R. Hedrick**, 1934 Clark, West Hollywood, California, when Mrs. Hedrick recognizes her son — a two-way set-up between the studio and the Hedrick home for conversation between mother and son; and (2) from the home of **Mr. and Mrs. Harry Dewey**, of 1616 ¾ Maltman Avenue in Los Angeles,

where the Deweys have one more week to drive around the block to bring their total mileage to 3,000 miles in three weeks. The Deweys report that they feel that they can reach the required mileage goal.

John Early, a college student, was interviewed on the program and given a consequence of volunteering to "take a dare" from listeners. Early agrees to try to do whatever listeners create as a dare stunt. Ralph Edwards says he will select the "most dangerous stunt" submitted by listeners and letters sent in next week. Early will do one stunt each week during the next three weeks. If he succeeds in the dares, he will receive $1,500. Radio listeners are asked to submit their dares by writing to "Truth or Consequences, NBC, Hollywood." John Early is referred to as the "Laughing Contestant" because he has been laughing ever since he appeared on the broadcast.

Celebrity guests include **Ned Sparks**, screen actor who just came out of retirement to appear in the **Robert Riskin** production of *Magic Town*; and **Paul Frees**, who impersonates Clark Gable, Charles Boyer and Ronald Colman on the program.

Episode #653, Broadcast of October 4, 1947

Stunts: Wooden Wedding, Mind Reader Son, Public Contestant No. 1, 3,000 Mile Trip No. 4, and Minister

Contestant **John Early** performs his first of three dares. The listener who sent in the selected "dare" received a 72-piece set of Sterling Silver. The stunt which John Early successfully performed was to walk boldly into the dining room of the Los Angeles Biltmore Hotel, wearing the robes of a magician, and pull a tablecloth from beneath a load of food, flowers, etc., while the astonished diners wonder what goes on. Announcer **Charlie Lyon** delivers the play-by-play via remote pick-up.

Mr. and Mrs. Harry Dewey receive a new automobile because they successfully completed the 3,000-mile drive in three weeks.

In the mind reader stunt, a mother meets a perfect stranger, a young man about the same age of her own son, who tells her facts that only her own boy would know (the "Mind Reader" is being prompted by her son, of course). This stunt is done as a salute to National Newspaper Boys Week. The mind reader stunt was submitted by a newsboy listener named **Ronnie Martin**. Ralph Edwards pays verbal tribute, stating American newsboys receive benefits such as educational, athletic and social activity-training, and they in turn grow into leaders among businessmen.

Also on the program are a man and wife celebrating their wooden wedding anniversary and they receive appropriate prizes. An announcement of **Minnie Edwards'** birthday was made on the program. Actress **Virginia Mayo** performs the Drene Shampoo commercial.

Episode #654, Broadcast of October 11, 1947

Stunts: Senator's Wife, Public Contestant No. 2, Fire Chief Hot Foot, and Cute Mama

Broadcast originated from Houston, Texas, with commercials from Hollywood and a cut-in from New York City. Ralph Edwards has been appearing at a benefit show for the Veterans of Foreign Wars, who sponsor a building project in Houston. The program is broadcast from the Civic Auditorium. **Senator W. Lee O'Daniel** of Texas participates on a stunt. The contestant is told to telephone the Senator's wife and tell her exactly what the people think of the Senator. Then, the contestant is told to step aside and give another contestant a chance to talk about the Senator. The second contestant who was listening to the entire phone conversation is Senator O'Daniel in person! The phone call was direct to the Senators wife, **Mrs. W. Lee O'Daniel**.

Following the stunt, the Senator makes a brief one-minute talk in behalf of "Employ the Physically Handicapped Week," pointing out that it is "ability and not disability" that counts in a job. (Also referenced throughout the program was the importance of caring for disabled veterans and other physically handicapped.)

A surprise visit is arranged whereby a disabled veteran is on the program and his wife, and a baby that he has not yet seen, are flown to Houston to be with him. *Truth or Consequences* paid all expenses for the vet, wife and baby and for a hotel stay with a special nurse to care for the baby during the coming week.

From New York City, 42nd and Broadway, radio sports commentator and announcer **Mel Allen** interviews both the "dare" contestant, **John Early**, and the listener who sent in this week's "dare," **Miss Lorraine Ocepa** of Jamaica, New York. Miss Ocepa is garbed in a wedding dress and her dare is that John Early marry her. Mr. Early declines the dare at the risk of losing his chance at the $1,500. Miss Ocepa receives a $500 diamond ring to soothe her breaking heart (she was already presented with a 72-piece Sterling Silver Set for sending in this week's winning "dare"). John Early mentions he will return to Hollywood and he is instructed to make his appearance without fail because Edwards wants to "talk over" the touchy situation with Mr. Early.

The November 20, 1947, issue of the *New York City News* featured the following advertisement: "Please let me give my story of a recent happening, because a lot of wrong things have been said about it. I am the young lady who asked a fellow to marry her on the *Truth or Consequences* radio program. I was not offered $1,500 to marry him. The contestant was offered $1,500. It was more or less his consequence. To all narrow-minded, jealous people: I want you to know that I would do it all over again, so put that in your pipes and smoke it. Signed, Miss Lorraine Ocepa."

Episode #655, Broadcast of October 18, 1947
Stunts: Always Glee Club, Public Contestant No. 3, Remote Water Glass, and Studio Names Tour
In the Hollywood studio, **John Early** confesses that failed to take last week's dare and marry a young woman. Edwards confesses that in agreement with the studio audience, Mr. Early was not unwise by doing the "gentlemanly thing" in refusing to accept this particular dare, so Early will receive another dare next week and thus still have opportunity of winning the $1,500.
Episode includes a cut-in from the home of **Mr. and Mrs. Martin Bridges** of 3116 North Long Avenue, Chicago. A hidden speaker is set up in a home somewhere in America and one member of the family of that home is in on the gag. The radio is turned on and the person who knows about the stunt receives her timely cues. A wife throws a glass of water into her husband's face as her part of the stunt. Radio listeners are given the opportunity to listen in to the calamity.
This episode also marks the first of a new "Miss Hush" contest. Picked up from "anywhere in the United States," Miss Hush, "a well-known American Miss," read a jingle filled with clues as to her identity. Listeners were instructed to submit a letter consisting of 25 or fewer additional words to complete the following statement: "We should all support the March of Dimes because..." The letter must include a contribution to the March of Dimes but the amount

submitted in no way affected their entry. "Let your heart be your guide," Edwards adds.

Episode #656, Broadcast of October 25, 1947
Stunts: Cracker Love, Public Contestant No. 4, and Doctor's Babies
In the "Doctor's Babies" stunt, a retired doctor is faced by three grown men whom he delivered as babies. He is told to identify them and to treat them as he had upon their arrival in this world! Edwards announces that the records of the retired doctor were "researched" by the American Medical Association and through the help of the Medical Association, the three "babies" and their wives are given a dinner party for their prizes. The doctor also receives a wristwatch.
From the Prospect Park Building in Niagara Falls, New York, courtesy of WBEN, Buffalo, announcer **Marshall Dane** tells about the arrangements made for contestant **John Early**, the contestant who dared to go over Niagara Falls in a barrel. Early was undaunted by Edwards' stunt and the local radio station, WBEN, arranged for an announcer to be on hand near the brink of the cataract, for obvious reasons, and the local description went over the NBC network. From 8:41 to 8:42 p.m. John Early spoke from inside a barrel, on board the airplane, flying over Niagara Falls. He wins the $1,500 promised him for taking on the listeners' dares.

Contestants perform "Cracker Love" on the broadcast of October 25, 1947.

Episode #657, Broadcast of November 1, 1947

Stunts: Remote Hot Seat, French Drama Seltzer, and Night and Day Trio

Broadcast from Chicago where Ralph Edwards and the quiz show performs daily at the Chicago Theater for a period of two weeks; with commercials from Hollywood and cut-ins for a stunt in New York City. First of the telephone calls in the new "Miss Hush" contest began. **R.C. Collette** of 1400 N. Sycamore, Hollywood, California, incorrectly named Elsa Maxwell as "Miss Hush." The other two contestants were incorrect and one of them also suggested Elsa Maxwell.

Celebrity guest in Chicago was **Jean Deltour**, French actor, who took part in one of the stunts. Three contestants volunteer to sing "Night and Day." The song to be sung literally "night and day" for two weeks or until the city of Chicago reaches the $5.5 million mark in the Community Chest campaign. They will appear on both *Truth or Consequences* and on the daily radio program, *Welcome, Travelers* (with **Tommy Bartlett** broadcasting from Chicago), singing for the Community Chest. The singers are **Harold Tucker**, **Phil Keith** and **Ward Chase**. Edwards and his crew were in Chicago for two weeks, from October 30 to November 13. During every one of the six performances of *Truth or Consequences* performed on stage, a beautiful orchid corsage was presented to one of the contestants by Edwards and the Chicago florists on behalf of National Flower week.

Episode #658, Broadcast of November 8, 1947

Stunts: Squirtless Seltzer, Crime Doctor Drama, and Night and Day Trio Payoff

Same as last week, the broadcast originated from the Chicago Theater. An update regarding the three men who were singing "Night and Day" for the Community Chest Drive: the drive passed the $5.5 million goal and the singers each received $200 and a Hart, Schaffner & Marx wardrobe.

Program included a birthday salute to the U.S. Marine Corps (172nd Anniversary of the U.S. Marine Corps, November 10).

Three more phone calls were made on the "Miss Hush" contest but only one of the three people were at home at the time the phone calls were made. "Miss Hush" was not identified so the mysterious voice provided extra clues regarding her identity.

Episode #659, Broadcast of November 15, 1947

Stunts: Italian Cow, and Juvenile Jury

Third consecutive broadcast originating from Chicago, with commercials from Hollywood. Feature stunt of the evening involved a Chicago couple, thinking their little boy asleep at home, when actually he was disguised as a little girl so the parents would not recognize their own among the children of the *Juvenile Jury* radio cast. The children who took part were Peggy, Dicky, Robin and Charlie – and "Elizabeth," who is really little **Tommy Albright** of Chicago.

Episode #660, Broadcast of November 22, 1947

Stunts: Home Water Tank, and Parent's Thanksgiving

Thanksgiving spot on the program included a Los Angeles couple, **Mr. and Mrs. Godfrey**, sent out to invite the first young couple they see in the halls of NBC to have Thanksgiving dinner with them. The young couple selected are **Mr. and Mrs. Herbert Baker**, with their two-year-old daughter. Mrs. Baker is the daughter of the Godfreys, who have not seen their daughter or son-in-law for more than two years and, of course, have never seen their little granddaughter. The entire family reunion was on the program as guests of *Truth or Consequences*.

Episode #661, Broadcast of November 29, 1947

Stunts: Bed Bath Race, and Sit on Barrel

The voice of "Miss Hush" is again heard and unidentified. Three new prizes are added to the pot: Universal Electric blankets for every room in the house; Electrolux; and Art Craft Venetian Blinds for every window in the house.

Episode #662, Broadcast of December 6, 1947

Stunts: Goat Cow Guess, and Mother-Cashier

The *Truth or Consequences* program is in Norman, Oklahoma, to entertain members of the American Legion Post 303, and students and faculty members of Oklahoma University. This was the first campus Post to be formed after World War II.

The identity of "Miss Hush" is identified in the first telephone call. **Mrs. Ruth Annette Subbie**, housewife of 1712 Frederick Place, Ft. Worth, Texas, correctly identifies Martha Graham, the famous dancer. Towards the end of the program, Martha Graham speaks from her New York apartment (257

West 11th Street), where the dancer and the NBC engineer who conducted her pickups during the contest, **Harry Greleck**, explain how they managed to keep Miss Graham's identity a secret even from members of their own families and friends. Ralph Edwards announces that Ruth Subbie will be on the program, originating from Hollywood next week.

- Special Oklahoma University guests include **Dr. George L. Cross**, president of Oklahoma University and **Mrs. Dora MacFarland**, Ph.D., a professor of mathematics at the University for 27 years. On one of the spots on the program a student–veteran's mother from California has been brought to Norman to visit her son as a surprise to him.
- The post commander at the American Legion responsible for the contract and arrangements was **Preston J. Moore**, who, a year later, elevated to a state commander. More than a year following the broadcast, he wrote to Ralph Edwards, hoping the radio host would help use his influence to obtain Hollywood talent for a State-wide beauty contest. Edwards' secretary informed Moore that the program could not assist but suggested a couple venues that could help.

Episode #663, Broadcast of December 13, 1947
Stunts: Broken Record Hot Seat, Santa Claus Payoff, and Christmas Question No. 1

- This broadcast features a cut-in from the toy department of a department store near Hollywood and Vine, where a lieutenant just back from Korea is sent to act as the store Santa Claus. His own little son, whom he hasn't seen for over a year, is one of the children who makes an appearance. He only discovers the ruse after the microphone picks up the exchange and his wife step out before him. The lieutenant was still in a wounded Vet Hospital but was on temporary leave for this particular stunt.
- **Mrs. Ruth Annette Subbie**, of Fort Worth, Texas, winner of the "Miss Hush" contest, along with her husband, Edward, are special guests on the program. An announcement is made that over $600,000 was sent into the March of Dimes as a result of the contributions.
- A new type of write-in letter contest was announced: no prizes, no recognition. Listeners were asked to write and answer as briefly as possible (one word was acceptable) the question: "What would you give the world for Christmas if you had only one choice of gifts?" Send your answer to: "Merry Christmas,

Box 400, New York City 20." A contestant on the program said he would like to give the world "peace."

Shortly before her appearance on *Truth or Consequences*, Mrs. Subbie appeared on WBAP-820, the station she was listening to when Ralph Edwards phoned the week prior, in an exclusive interview with newscaster **Larry Dupont**. This wound-up a hectic day for the middle-aged housewife which included being fitted for a complete, new Hart, Schaffner & Marx suit and topcoat, and accepting receivership for a Luscombe airplane. In the interview, Subbie stressed the fact that she was not a "professional" in the contest field but had been working at it several years as a hobby. "A hobby," she added, "that is particularly suited to a housewife." After the interview on WBAP, she was given a box of DUZ as a remembrance.

Episode #664, Broadcast of December 20, 1947
Stunts: Christmas Seals, Christmas Question No. 2, and Remote Christmas

A special Christmas offering broadcast from the Hollywood studios; with pick-ups from the Long Beach Naval Hospital in Long Beach, California, and several different locations in Greenville, Tennessee. Courtesy of the magic of radio, a three-way set up was established for **Hubert Smith**, a Naval veteran, from the hospital where he received a surprised visit from his mother and father, and his fiancée, **Lila Morrell**, and with numerous sounds and salutations from his hometown of Greenville. This included cut-ins from a high school party, the George R. Lane & Co. Department Store; cross-sections of Main Street; and the Asbury Methodist Church. The bells of Asbury are heard ringing and **Ida Ripley**, church organist, opened for the Christmas carolers who sang during the program. Also featured is **Rev. M. Guy Fleenor**, of Asbury Methodist Church, who extends Christmas greetings.

Back at the Hollywood studio, the first announcement of a new contest was referenced as the sound of footsteps are heard over the air and Ralph Edwards asks, "Who is the Walking Man?"

Episode #665, Broadcast of December 27, 1947
Stunts: Husband-Wife Camel, Player's Bench, Christmas Question Payoff, Auld Lang Syne Chorus, and Kiss Ladies

The "Prizeless Christmas Wish" letters are discussed tonight. More than 76,000 letters were received in response to Ralph Edwards' request two weeks prior. The top 10 "wishes" are read, including peace, tolerance, faith, love, and friendship as "one gift" a person might choose to give the world at Christmas time.

Episode #666, Broadcast of January 3, 1948
Stunts: Dempsey Remote, Mop the Floor, and Avoid Consequence
Celebrity guest is **Jack Dempsey**, ex-heavyweight boxing champion of the world, who took part in a stunt with contestant **Jack Bayuth**, of Tessa, Oklahoma. Bayuth was sent to force his way into Dempsey's Home (then located at 5254 Los Feliz Blvd. in Hollywood) without realizing whose home he was being sent to. Announcer **Charles Lyon** appears on the broadcast, delivering a play-by-play from the Dempsey home.
"The Walking Man" is heard tonight and details of the contest were announced for the first time. **Ida Lupino** makes a guest appearance in the Drene commercial.

Episode #667, Broadcast of January 10, 1948
Stunts: Bathing Suits Package, Impediment Drama, ROTC Ball, and Scream to Finish
Lizabeth Scott, movie actress best known for starring in silver screen crime capers, takes part in a stunt by serving as the real date for a high school student at Fairfax High.

Episode #668, Broadcast of January 17, 1948
Stunts: Contestant M.C., Hotel Worker Vacation, and Don't Open 'til Christmas
William Bendix, screen actor and star of the radio program *The Life of Riley*, is featured in a stunt called "Contestant M.C."
Mrs. Gertrude Penn, a maid at The Town House in Los Angeles for eleven years, suddenly found herself a contestant in a modern Cinderella act. **Al Paschall**, production manager, contacted **Jane Bourne**, head of publicity for The Town House, who brought the unsuspecting lady to the program where she was picked out of the audience by the radio show host. In the meantime, Mr. Richter, front desk clerk at the hotel, had been let in on the secret and was all ready for the telephone call from the studio at the time of the broadcast when Mrs. Penn, as her "consequence," was told to call the hotel where she worked and reserve a suite complete with flowers in the room and breakfast in bed.

Needless to say, Mrs. Penn was speechless when she learned that she really had a reservation, and in addition a new wardrobe had been selected for her at Saks Fifth Avenue by the production manager, **Fred Carney**. She spent a wonderful week at The Town House as a guest of the hotel, and with a full week's salary paid by Ralph Edwards.

Episode #669, Broadcast of January 24, 1948
Stunts: Jerry Colonna
As with broadcasts prior and afterwards, three contestants were phoned and no one could identify "The Walking Man."

Episode #670, Broadcast of January 31, 1948
Stunts: Door Prize, Three Wrestlers, and Sinatra Kiss
Celebrity guest **Frank Sinatra** was in the NBC studio warming-up for his performance on *Your Hit Parade*. A female contestant was sent to Sinatra to collect a "kiss" from him. She received what she asked for.

Three professional wrestlers for the broadcast of January 31, 1948.

Episode #671, Broadcast of February 7, 1948
Stunts: $100 Kiss, and Quartette Reunion
The featured stunt of the evening was the surprise reunion of a barbershop quartet, who disbanded 20 years ago. All four members were on the program and

together they sang several numbers. They also received weekend entertainment, all expenses paid, in Hollywood. The four members of the original quartet were: **Thomas Rawlings** of Santa Monica, California; **Carleton Scott** of Birmingham, Michigan; **Joseph Jones** of New York City; and **Herman Smith** of Highland Park, Michigan. The members of the quartet talked about the Society for the Preservation and Encouragement of Barbershop Quartet Singing in America. They told about the fact that President Truman was one of the members.

Episode #672, Broadcast of February 14, 1948
Stunts: Slanguage Rondelay, Animal vs. Men, Quickie Group, and Live Under Water
This broadcast originated from Davenport, Iowa, at the Masonic Auditorium, where the cast was entertaining at the Mississippi Valley Home and Food Show. The commercials were broadcast from Hollywood. Special guest was **Arthur Kronach**, Mayor of Davenport, who took part in a stunt in which a contestant agrees to "run for Mayor" for one week – the contestant unaware that he would run errands for the Mayor.
Another stunt featured Iowa's animals: an Iowa mule, two puppies, and a trained monkey. The monkey appeared with his master and organ grinder, William, who came from Chicago for this personal appearance.

Background for the Broadcast of February 14, 1948
While *Truth or Consequences* was in Davenport, Iowa, Ralph Edwards provided entertainment at the first annual Mississippi Valley Home and Food Show at the Masonic Auditorium from February 13 through 19. Edwards was also invited to act as general manager for radio station WOC during that time. He operated the station in a manner he considered to be in the public interest. This included interrupting local programs for self-creations. Three special programs were arranged. First, Edwards put on the air a program especially for hospitalized war veterans in Rock Island and Scott County institutions, during which he talked by direct telephone wire, to the veterans. The program for veterans brought Edwards in telephone contact with hospitalized men at East Moline state hospital, Rock Island County Tuberculosis sanitarium, and Scott County's Pine Knoll sanitarium. Next, he invited everyone in the WOC area named Edwards, to meet and participate in an informal broadcast from the Masonic Temple, to get

acquainted on the "Edwards Family Hour." His third special event was a broadcast "gripe session" during which listeners aired their complaints on policy, operation and programming.

Among the stunts on the broadcast of February 14 was **Sergeant Bill Brandt**, who had to "live under water for a week." After failing to answer his question correctly, Brandt was forced to wear a hot water bottle, tied to his head, with a $400 camera as a prize. The Moline police sergeant reported for work the morning following the radio broadcast, without his regulation cap. Because of his new head covering, **Chief Harry Fromme** issued an order for Brandt to direct traffic at the corner of Fifteenth Street and Fifth Avenue during two busy hours. Shortly before Brandt's special chores were finished, Edwards drove over to Moline to see if the officer was keeping his promise to wear the water bottle for a week. Edwards did not know about the new ordinance prohibiting left turns at the intersection, and when he made the traffic violation, Brandt halted the quizmaster and gave him a ticket; thus Edwards found his "consequence" had backfired on him. However, Brandt agreed to forget about the ticket if Edwards personally removed the hot water bottle from his head at Edwards' final appearance at the Masonic Temple on Thursday night.

Episode #673, Broadcast of February 21, 1948
Stunts: Cuckoo Time, Own Hot Seat, and Band Leaders Accompaniment
This broadcast originated from New York City today with commercials from Hollywood. Ralph Edwards announces he was in New York to attend the current dance recital presented by **Martha Graham**, the same "Miss Hush" of the recent *Truth or Consequences* contest.
Future stunt of the evening concerned orchestra leaders **Guy Lombardo, Horace Heidt, Frankie Carle, Dick Jurgens, Louis Prima** and **Larry Clinton**. The boys played their favorite instruments. With every one of them playing in his own style, the men do a rendition of "Roses in Picardy." A contestant from Brooklyn, **Mrs. Brooks**, led the orchestra without realizing how famous the orchestra members were.

Episode #674, Broadcast of February 28, 1948
Stunts: Leap Year Kangaroo, Dunk Own Husband, and Ten Dollar Garters
Celebrity guest on this broadcast is **Jim Backus**, who performs his "Hubert

Updike" characterization. In the Leap Year stunt, a contestant is sent out with a real-life kangaroo named "Bouncing Betty" and is told to collect girls who will leap through life with him. He will receive $10 for every girl who returns with him to the program. Feature contestants are **Mr. and Mrs. Bob Dyer** of Sydney, Australia, and they talk about the land down under.

Episode #675, Broadcast of March 6, 1948

Stunts: $100 Bill, and Retired General

The "Walking Man" is correctly identified as Jack Benny. Over $1,500,000 has been raised for the American Heart Association as a result of the contest. The final total would approximate $1,575,000, even though $1.5 million was the "official" number given to the press. The check would be personally handed over to President **Dr. A.R. Barnes** in a ceremony at the Stevens Hotel in Chicago, Illinois, with **William G. Werner**, representing Proctor & Gamble. Special studio guest was **Brig. Gen. Leonard D. Weddington** (retired) who took part in a stunt and put in an appeal to young men to make a career of the Army. **Corporal Hiram Shute** failed to answer his question: "How many successful jumps must a paratrooper make to qualify for combat," (answer: all of them) and as a consequence was ordered to instruct a "civilian" on military tactics. The civilian happened to be **General Weddington**, who saw battle service in both World Wars. Shute was instructed and then sent off stage while Weddington was introduced. Hiram returned and began quizzing the "civilian." After questioning and several sharp remarks by Shute, the Corporal was introduced to his student. After a jovial exchange of words, both the instructor Corporal and pupil General went their ways – both reminiscent of a rare event when a Corporal instructed a General on military tactics.

Episode #676, Broadcast of March 13, 1948

Stunts: Speaker Under Seat, and Telephone Pie

Mrs. Florence Hubbard, winner of "The Walking Man" contest, is a guest on the program and pays tribute to her employers, telling how her late husband was a physician and died of heart disease, how she submitted 30 letters to the contest, each with financial contributions, how her employers gave her a luncheon and had the store stylist outfit her with a complete wardrobe for her trip to Hollywood, and so on. Ralph Edwards tells of a new contest that will soon begin on the same program, joking about the possibility of a "Laughing Lady."

During this broadcast, an announcement was made that the quiz program was given the *Radio Mirror* Magazine Award for the "Best Quiz Program on the Air" in the annual "Listeners' Poll."

Episode #677, Broadcast of March 20, 1948
Stunts: T or C Hat Easter Hat B.U., Easter Seal Boy, and T or C Girl B.U.

This broadcast features a two-way set up from the El Portal School in Millbrae, California, a school for crippled children. The "Easter Seal Boy" stunt was one in which the contestant was not present at the show. Ralph Edwards announced that they had placed a speaker and hidden microphone in a young boy's room and asked all boys listening to the show on radio to say hello; Cerebral Palsy patient **Harold Ferrell**, in his classroom at El Portal School, did as Ralph asked and was surprised to find himself in the conversation. **Roy Rogers** appeared on stage to sing "You Are My Sunshine" with Harold. Harold tells how his classmates are listening in and about the work being done at the school. Harold receives a Home Motion Picture Projection Set to be used in his own home. The El Portal School receives a Motion Picture Projection Set complete with sound facilities. Harold receives a free trip to Cleveland, Ohio, where he will be the guest of Cleveland Indians baseball star, **Bobby Feller**, for an entire week, and meet the entire team. Feller promises to send an autographed baseball. Harold's mother or father will accompany him to Cleveland, all expenses paid. The set-up between the El Portal School and the Hollywood studio is maintained during approximately 20 minutes of the program.

Ralph Edwards began the wrap-up by remarking that earlier in the week Paramount had sent a movie to Harold's home for them to watch – *Cross My Heart*, with **Betty Hutton** and **Sonny Tufts**, and was saying farewell to Harold when there was a knock on the classroom door. Into the room came Sonny Tufts himself, with more movies in hand. Ralph Edwards joined the three celebrities in singing "For He's a Jolly Good Fellow" to Harold and closed with an appeal to the audience to buy Easter Seals and support the National Society for Crippled Children and Adults.

This broadcast starts the recurring "Microphone X" feature in which radio listeners listen to various sounds coming from a microphone hidden "somewhere in the

United States." Contestants must identify the exact spot where the sound originates. The prize tonight moves from $1,000 to $1,500. The jackpot increases $500 for every week the sound and location remains unidentified.

Edwards sets up next week's contest involving ten male contestants who will serve as a girl's "godfathers." Any young lady who fits the description is asked to write or call "Truth or Consequences, Hollywood, 28, California." The description is weight 145 pounds; height 5 feet, 7 inches; brown eyes; blond hair; hips that measure 36 inches; waist measure 28 inches; shoe size 5 ½; no marital status; first name Marie; and must be 25 years of age.

Episode #678, Broadcast of March 27, 1948

Stunts: Dog Summons, T or C Easter Hat Payoff, Mail Foot, and T or C Girl No. 2

Broadcast from the Hollywood home of **Irvine Newman, Mrs. Irvin Newman** and radio actor **Willard Waterman** are heard, with announcer **Charles Lyon**, giving an "on the spot report" of what happens when Mrs. Newman thinks Waterman is an Animal Regulations Officer complaining about her dog. What she finds is her husband in the doghouse in her backyard.

The Easter stunt finds contestant **Mrs. Percy Thayer** of St. Paul, Minnesota, who agrees to wear a real flowerpot with a flower growing in it for a hat. She wore the hat all week and now gets to wear it in the Easter Parade tomorrow. She also receives cash and prizes for her participation.

The "Ten Godfathers" who "manufactured" the *Truth or Consequences* Girl" last week are back and will get another week to find the girl.

Episode #679, Broadcast of April 3, 1948

Stunts: Report Wallet, Kid Cowboys, Mr. Ripley, and T or C Girl Payoff

In connection with the Children's Home all over the nation, **Marilyn Barrows** and **Don Barrows**, a sister and brother from the "Church Home for Children" in Los Angeles, appear as guests on the program to tell how the Children's Home is benefiting them. Their father is dead and their mother is working and cannot afford to care for them. The Barrows children are told that they have been chosen "Junior King and Queen" of the World's Championship Rodeo to be held in Phoenix, Arizona, on April 9. Mrs. Morris of the Church Home will accompany them. **Earlene Wilson**, the grown-up "Queen of the Rodeo," was also a guest on the program and tells the children that she will be their hostess in Phoenix. The children also received a $100 Savings Bond. While at the rodeo, the children will represent all of the Children's Homes of the nation.

Special guest is **Robert L. Ripley**, of the *Believe-It-or-Not* fame, who tells of his coming trip to the Orient. A contestant on the program, **George McMillin**, impersonates Ripley in a stunt without realizing that Ripley is present in the audience. McMillan is given the opportunity to join Ripley on his trip to the Orient. McMillan will receive a salary of $100 per week, plus all expenses paid during the trip, but must secure certain "oddities" such as some of the Oriental "Barking Sand," etc.

The "*Truth or Consequences* Girl" dreamed up on the program of March 20, appears in person as **Marie Peterson** of Seattle, Washington, an employee of Boeing Aircraft. She presents Ralph Edwards with a model of a Boeing plane. The "Ten Godfathers" who dreamed up the girl are also on hand to take over the pleasant task of showing Hollywood to her.

Episode #680, Broadcast of April 10, 1948
Stunts: Paramount Theatre, Bendix Stunt, Ad Lib Drama, and Seal Tie

The program includes a cut-in from the home of **Mr. Duncan Lloyd** and **Mrs. Olivia Lloyd** on Jackson Street in Glencoe, Illinois, where they and their 12-year-old daughter are contestants. Olivia Lloyd does not know that her living room has a hidden microphone and that her words are being broadcast. She thinks she is being telephoned by the program to win a prize but only if she answers her telephone within 30 seconds. Meanwhile, her friends, who are in on the gag, purposely keep her line busy. Columnist **Ben Gross**, two days later, wrote in his syndicated column, "Radio Row is still talking about that woman who became hysterical during Saturday's broadcast."

Mr. Lloyd, the contestant's husband, was an attorney with offices at 135 S. La Salle Street, and agreed to the stunt played on his wife. It required elaborate preparation, including a direct wire from Hollywood to the radio in the Lloyd living room, so she heard only one program that failed to give away the ruse while everyone else in the nation heard another. A radio engineer was smuggled into the attic of the Lloyd home, with microphones concealed near the telephone cabinet and in the living room fireplace so the radio listeners could hear what went on in the Lloyd living room.

In the program received on the Lloyd radio, Edwards announced he was going to call a name at random in a new kind of contest. He then pretended to select at random the name of Mrs. Lloyd, on Jackson Street in Glencoe. She heard him pick up the telephone and place the call. She ran to the telephone, which rang at once. It was a friend, **Mrs. Barbara Crawford** of Evanston, who was in on the secret and telephoned the Lloyd home by pre-arrangement. Mrs. Lloyd, naturally, was frantic. Rapidly she explained the situation to Mrs. Crawford and got her to hang up. Immediately the telephone rang again. This time is was **Mrs. Willard Wheeler** of Glencoe.

"Please!" pleaded Mrs. Lloyd. "Get off the phone. You're costing me money!"

By arrangement with the telephone company, the Lloyd's line was reserved for such prearranged calls between 7:30 and 8 p.m. The callers were kept waiting on the line, and as soon as one call was completed, another was plugged into the Lloyds' line.

This went on for ten minutes. Then the regular *Truth or Consequences* program was switched onto the Lloyd radio and Mrs. Lloyd heard Edwards say: "Now, Mrs. Lloyd, since you've been such a good sport about the whole thing, we're going to see that you receive the gifts anyway." Then the radio engineer emerged from the Lloyd attic and the most "important client from Rockford," with whom Lloyd had been conferring, was introduced as **Richard Loughrin**.

Celebrity guest in the Hollywood studio was **Celeste Holm**.

Mr. Mason, an 82-year-old of Louisville, Kentucky, was the contestant selected in a studio stunt involving a trained seal.

"Microphone X" feature is again unsolved and holds over for next week. At one point, intentionally, the voice of a man is heard through the microphone asking, "How does it sound, Ralph?" and "Okay, Ralph."

Feature consequence was the assignment of a 6,000-mile trip by air from Los Angeles to New York City where contestants **Oswald Sowash** of Burbank, California, is guest of the Paramount Theater, in New York City, for a motion-picture showing of *Saigon*, starring Alan Ladd and Veronica Lake. The trip will be by TWA Constellation with contestants reaching New York in time for the 2:30 p.m. showing tomorrow (Sunday) and getting him back to California at 7:45 a.m. on Monday.

Episode #681, Broadcast of April 17, 1948

Stunts: Quickie Group, $100 Masked Husband B.U., Adjective Letter Remote, Page Author, The Last Fling, and Hiccup Poem

"Microphone X" origination is finally identified tonight by three contestants who divide the $2,000 cash prize among themselves. The winners are **Eiler Jorgenson**, a writer; **James Koby**, an aircraft worker (both of San Diego, California); and **Robert Chalmers**, policeman of Los Angeles. Microphone X is correctly identified as being located in the Statue of Liberty, with the microphone placed in the statue's hand. Engineer **Harry Greleck** of NBC, New York, arranged for the microphone to be installed and supervised for pick-up every week. It was his voice heard on both this broadcast and last week's. The contest was successful enough that a new "Microphone X" contest is announced for next week, with a microphone hidden somewhere else and with next week's contestants eligible to win a jackpot of cash by identifying the origin of the sound picked up by the mike.

Episode #682, Broadcast of April 24, 1948
Stunts: Memorize Names, Cow Symphony, Lawrence Tranter Payoff, and Masked Husband Payoff

The second "Microphone X" contest is held tonight and is worth $1,000. "Microphone X" is placed at the Tomb of the Unknown Soldier and this is properly identified by a contestant on the first go-round: **George Ray** of 624 Orange Street in Toledo, Ohio.

In another "consequence," a contestant is asked to memorize the names of 100 different listed articles while she is being heckled by celebrity guest **William Bendix**, who just "dropped into the studio" following his own broadcast of *The Life of Riley* program on the same network.

Wheelchair veteran **Lawrence Tranter** and his wife, **Dorothy**, of Murray, Utah, return to the program after a two-year absence. Dream gifts consisted of a diploma and $1,000 from the Bulova Watch School of New York in recognition of Tranter's completion of a two-year training as a drawer and watch repair expert in the Bulova School for Veterans. A repair shop with rent paid for over a year, set up in Tranter's hometown of Murray, Utah, was given to Tranter. The governor of Utah has promised to be the first customer. Various additional gifts were bestowed which the young couple can use in starting the business. (Tranter was a guest on the broadcast of April 27, 1946, when he was first told that arrangements had been made for him to enter the Bulova Watch School in New York.)

Program includes a tribute to the Bulova Watch personnel who were doing training work for disabled veterans. In connection with the way veterans were showing supreme courage and fighting their "way back," a special tribute was paid by guest speaker **General Omar Bradley**, Chief of Staff, U.S. Army, heard from Washington, D.C.

Episode #683, Broadcast of May 1, 1948
Stunts: Smith-Jones B.U., Camp Fire Girls, Hong Kong Remote, Whiffenpoof Lamb, and $50 Pie vs. $200

This broadcast included a short-wave report from Hong Kong, China, for four minutes, with **Robert L. Ripley**, currently in the Orient on a special *Believe-It-or-Not* expedition, and with **George McMillin**, contestant on a prior *Truth or Consequences* radio broadcast, chosen at that time to accompany Mr. Ripley on his expedition. A Chinese gentleman sings "McNamara's Band" on the broadcast tonight, which happened to be one of McMillin's many challenges. Also on the list was the acquiring of permanent waves on the beach of Waikiki. McMillan tells the way he had native girls give him his "permanent wave" while he lolled on the beach.

Hollywood studio stunt was a salute to the Camp Fire Girls of America with a contestant, **Mrs. Paul**, asked to talk to a group of Camp Fire Girls of the Los Angeles area. In the group is her son, **Jeffrey Paul**, disguised as a girl. The girls represented on the broadcast received $100 for summer camp funds; Jeffrey Paul received a complete set of *World Book Encyclopedia*, for fooling his mother.

A new $50,000 contest opened to all users of DUZ, with instructions to follow the rules found on entry blanks at local groceries, available Monday morning in all grocery stores. The contest would run for five weeks, with $10,000 in prizes each week.

A soldier is asked to sing the "Whiffenpoof Song," with two live lambs to do the "ba" parts! A new "Microphone X" contest started and the contestants failed to identify the new location of the microphone. The prize for identifying the third Microphone X is a $1,600 trailer.

An announcement is made that the quiz program was awarded a special Health Citation for its service and arranging for medical care, etc., for various needy persons.

Episode #684, Broadcast of May 8, 1948

Stunts: Call Hooper, Irish Mother, McMillin Spot, Smith-Jones Payoff, and Jane Doe

Contestant Mrs. Keller is told to call a certain phone number and ask the usual questions asked on a Hooper Radio Survey. Mr. Hooper says his radio is on and he is listening to the quiz program. Mrs. Keller receives $250 – if Mr. Hooper had been listening to any other network, the contestant would have received no prize. Edwards gets on the telephone, following Mrs. Keller's interview, and explains to her husband about the stunt. The husband knew nothing about the contest until the phone rang.

"Beauty Contest" features **Vera Ralston**, movie star, to serve as a "model." **Sergeant Richard Suchanek**, a 23-year-old war veteran of DeQuincy, Louisiana, currently hospitalized at McCornack General Hospital, Pasadena, California, appears in a wheelchair and is told that he and his ward-buddies (about 40 of them) at McCornack will judge feminine aspirants for a film career, judging entirely from photographs submitted by girls who hear the program and send in their pictures… A 5 x 7 in. or larger, un-retouched photograph, with name, address and telephone number written on the back of the picture. Picture is judged as "the typical American Girl, Miss Jane Doe," and is offered in connection with the movie, *I, Jane Doe*, in which Vera Ralston was currently playing. The winner will receive a trip to Hollywood, all expenses paid, and a contract to perform at a movie at Republic Pictures. All pictures must be received by midnight, May 19. No photos will be returned. They become the pin-up photos of the McCornack Hospital judges. The boys in the ward receive an RCA television set for their Ward as part of the prize for judging the contest. Their decision will be final.

Announcement made about the current DUZ contest. $10,000 in prizes each week for five weeks, second week starts Monday. No details announced over the air. Entry blanks and rules can be found at local grocery stores.

> **The Irish Mother Stunt on the Broadcast of May 8, 1948**
>
> For a special feature, contestant **Thomas McGinn** is surprised by having his mother flown from Shannon, Ireland, on a TWA plane, to spend Mother's Day and a two-week vacation with her children in the United States. He has not seen his mother since he left Ireland over 20 years ago. She is the mother of 15 living children and she tells how she came across a newspaper story in Ireland, asking

her to contact Radio Erin, where arrangements for the flight were immediately made. Tom received a movie camera and a sound projector to record his mother's visit with him.

The story of the sixty-four-year old Irish mother, Mrs. Margaret McGinn, brought to America's shore for the first time since 1906, was considered by many as the best of the season. Once decided that an Irish mother was what was needed for the Mother's Day program, the complex wheels of *Truth or Consequences* organization began to turn as Al Paschall, the production manager, contacted Radio Erin and asked them to select a mother who had a son in Los Angeles whom she had not seen in several years. This was accomplished by the simple expedient of advertising in the Irish papers for just such a lady. Many applicants applied and from all of them, **Mrs. Margaret McGinn** was selected.

She was on her way to the town pump for a bucket of water and stopped in a small shop to buy a paper. The front-page story caught her eye and she became so excited over the possibilities that she forgot about the water, leaving her bucket at the paper shop. Two days later, when she was notified that she was the one selected for the trip, she was rushed through the formalities of obtaining a passport and checking with customs.

While all of this was taking place in Ireland, it was necessary to make sure that the son, who had not seen his mother in 20 years, attend the program on the night scheduled. This was accomplished by contacting the next-door neighbor who, after being sworn to complete secrecy, vowed that she would have him there hell or high water.

When Mrs. McGinn was taken by car from her home in Ireland, it was her impression she was to return later to pack her things and say goodbye to her husband Joe. However, it was necessary to rush her to a TWA plane for the trip to America. As she drove by her husband's place of employment, she called to him, "Good-bye, Joe, I'm off to America." As Mrs. McGinn laughed, "Sure and I'll bet he's still just standing there looking." Mrs. McGinn didn't let the fact that she would not be able to return home for her things alter her plans one bit. She boarded the plane with the clothes on her back for a trip half-way around the world. This oversight was immediately remedied by the *Truth or Consequences* crew who supplied her with fresh outfits from head to toe.

Meanwhile, Thomas McGinn of Los Angeles, the son, was brought to the show by the neighbor, still with no idea at all of the big surprise in store for him. He was picked from the audience and seated on stage with the other contestants.

When his turn at the microphone came, his "consequence" was to talk to his mother in Ireland by long-distance telephone… or so he thought. In actuality, he was talking over an interphone to his mother who was backstage pretending to be in Ireland. At the conclusion of the phone call, Ralph Edwards asked Thomas if he thought his mother had changed much in the 20 years since he had seen her. Thomas replied she sounded much the same as he remembered her. "Well," said Ralph, "Do you think she would look like this lady who is walking on stage right now?" The back curtains parted and into the spotlight walked Mrs. McGinn. There was a gleeful reunion on stage followed by two weeks of visiting in Mrs. McGinn's suite at the Knickerbocker Hotel in Hollywood, all provided by Ralph Edwards and *Truth or Consequence*. Mrs. McGinn summed up the whole adventure very nicely when she remarked, "Sure and it was a great day for the Irish."

Episode #685, Broadcast of May 15, 1948
Stunts: Horn Opera, Two Mothers-In-Law Frame, Horse for a Day, Jane Doe Mention, and Crated Husband
Microphone X is identified today as the Chinese Telephone Exchange in San Francisco, 743 Washington St., Chinatown. Contestant **Louella Hafner** identified the location of the microphone and won the $1,600 trailer house. NBC engineer **George McElwane**, of San Francisco, planted the microphone used in the contest and his voices were heard on the various broadcasts of Microphone X as a voice said, "Okay, Ralph Edwards," "Take it away, Ralph Edwards," etc. The contest winner is surprised to discover her own mother, **Mrs. Fred Rodelle**, of Jamestown, North Dakota, and her mother-in-law, travel to Hollywood for a special visit with her and her husband, **Ed Hafner**, who is also on the broadcast. The mothers have paid entertainment and week-long reservation at the Knickerbocker Hotel.
Special guests are the members of the University of California Glee Club under conductor **Robert Mormon**. The Glee Club sings and takes part in a stunt with contestants. The Glee Club is presented with a giant Coca-Cola bottle and two-year supply of Coca-Cola for their rehearsal room. Also guests on the program are radio actors **Willard Waterman** and **Bruce Cameron**, to take part in a remote-control stunt via two-way pick up from the home of contestant **Mrs. Thomas Tracy**, Budlong Avenue, Los Angeles. **Thomas Tracy**, the husband, is a contestant in the Hollywood studios.

Program also has spot in observation of "Be Kind to Animals" week in which "Jimmy," a horse that draws a junk cart, is on the program and is named "Horse for a Day" in a take-off on the *Queen for a Day* radio program. Horse receives blankets, feed, rest from work, a grooming job, participation in a parade and will be featured in exhibition appearances at various racetracks, etc. (Jimmy's master, "Mr. Malamut," is also on the show.)

Billie Clevenger, chief telephone operator at NBC and personal assistant to Ralph Edwards, appeared in the closing Drene commercial.

Episode #686, Broadcast of May 22, 1948

Stunts: Unscramble Hot Seat, Ripley-McMillin Payoff, Nellie Lutcher B.U., Cancer Act, and Jane Doe Payoff

Broadcast from the Hollywood studios and from the Children's Hospital in Boston, Massachusetts. In Hollywood, the celebrity guests are **Robert L. Ripley**, creator of the *Believe-It-or-Not* Radio program, and **George McMillin**, contestant on the quiz program several weeks ago. The men are back from the expedition and tell about the way the contestant met the requirements for various consequences assigned to him by Ralph Edwards. McMillan presents Edwards with a real head from a headhunter and a 20-foot skin from a boa constrictor.

Sergeant Richard Suchanek and his ward buddies from McCornack General Hospital have selected the winner of the "Typical American Girl – Jane Doe" contest in which Suchanek and his buddies selected a girl from photos submitted. The winner was **Mary Ruth Wade**, an 18-year-old student at a junior college in Lake Charles, Louisiana. She was selected from among 5,000 girls submitting pictures. She would be seen in the movie, *The Plunderers*, now being made by Republic pictures. A contract with the movie studio was the prize.

The remainder of the program was devoted to bringing joy to a child cancer sufferer, broadcast from the Children's Hospital in Boston, Massachusetts. A child cancer victim identified merely as "Jimmy" is interviewed. Jimmy does not know that he has cancer and his identity is not disclosed for reasons that might make Jimmy aware of his condition. Jimmy likes baseball and his favorites are the Boston Braves baseball team. Today, appearing at Jimmy's bedside during the broadcast are **Billy Southworth**, manager of the Boston Braves, and the entire first-string nine players of the team. The boys appear one at a time and talk with Jimmy, giving him autographed baseballs, bats, and a Boston Braves uniform scaled to Jimmy's size. Also, Jimmy will be allowed to go to the game tomorrow (Sunday) when the Braves have designated the day as "Jimmy Day" at the ballpark.

Back in the Hollywood studios, Ralph Edwards asks listeners to send any contributions they wish to be used for cancer research for child cancer sufferers primarily addressing their contributions to: Jimmy, Children's Hospital, Boston 15, Massachusetts. Listeners were instructed not to mention the word cancer when writing to Jimmy. It is not necessary to include any writing with a contribution. If $20,000 is raised through these contributions, Jimmy gets a free television set for his room so he can watch the ballgames that he likes so much.

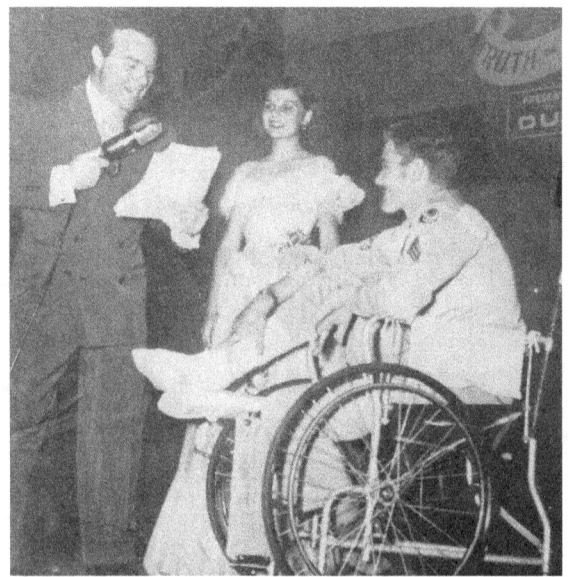

Sgt. Richard Suchanek, from the McCornack General Hospital, meets Mary Ruth Wade.

The Short-Lived Screen Career of Mary Ruth Wade

There was a great bustling at **Mrs. John Guillory**'s home, 508 Clarence Street, where Mary lived while attending McNeese Junior College. When the call came from Hollywood, telling her she won the contest, she was immediately rushed down to the Little Theatre where she was interviewed over KPLC by **Pelham Mills**, along with **Rosa Hart** and columnist **Bill Gabbert**.

While at the Little Theatre, the *Life* photographer, **Mike Rougier**, took pictures to be submitted to the magazine. He outfitted Mary with a complete traveling ensemble the following morning prior to her departure west. Pete's Flower Shop sent her a beautiful orchid corsage. She was again interviewed by KPLC at the Eastern Air Lines Terminal and was seen off by many friends and well-wishers. The plane landed at New Orleans where she was interviewed by radio station WSMB. Minutes following, she boarded a TWA Constellation aircraft bound for Hollywood. At St. Louis, she was handed a bouquet of over two dozen American Beauty roses and greeted by Chicago and Southern Airline officials and **Roger Dann**, the Frank Sinatra of France. In Los Angeles, she was met by **Sue Clark**, Ralph Edwards' secretary, along with **Jim Chadwick**, and **Mort Goodman**, publicity director of Republic Studios. Photos were taken; coffee and sandwiches over a review of her itinerary; and she was checked into the Ambassador Hotel. On Saturday morning, she met with **Maggie Waite**, representing the publicity department of Republic. Mary was presented the keys to a 1949 Mercury, which she had the privilege of using during her entire stay in Hollywood. She was taken by Miss Waite to the Screen Actors Guild office where she registered to qualify for her screen debut. Then pictures were taken of her in a bathing suit and in the costume she would wear in *The Plunderers*.

At four in the afternoon on Saturday, Mary reported to NBC Studios where she began rehearsal for the *Truth or Consequences* radio program, which went on the air in a short time following.

After the radio program, which was photographed by *Life* magazine, *Photoplay* magazine, Republic Studios, and *The Southwest News*, Miss Waite, **Dick Suchanek**, the injured veteran who was the head judge of the contest, Mary and a few others went to Earl Carroll's nightclub. Sunday afternoon Miss Waite drove Mary and **Bill Gabbert** to Santa Monica Beach for dinner. Sunday evening, they attended the *Hollywood Star Preview* program with tickets furnished by Republic Studios. On this program, **Charles Laughton** appeared.

On Monday morning, Mary reported to Republic Studios for shooting of the picture starring **Ilona Massey** and **Rod Cameron**. She played the role of a pioneer girl, marking her only Hollywood screen credit.

Episode #687, Broadcast of May 29, 1948

Stunts: Around-the-World Sentence, Nellie Lutcher Payoff, Class Prophecy Reunion, Cancer Returns, and Pace Floor B.U.

An announcement is made on this program that the amount of money sent in for cancer research reached $16,813.33, with many letters still unopened. Ralph Edwards asks listeners to continue to send in contributions of any amount because the total must reach $20,000 in order for Jimmy, the child on last week's broadcast, to get his television set.

Feature stunt is the "Around-the-World Sentence" in which a contestant in Hollywood telephones an operator and states the sentence: "Don't kid me, I'm wise." This sentence is relayed around the world via telephone to New York, Paris, Rome, Tokyo, San Francisco, and back to the telephone contestant in the Hollywood studios. The sentence came back as "Do not fancy yourself, I see." If the sentence had come back in its original wording, the contestant would have received $500. Now, she only receives a Sterling Silver flatware set.

Another feature stunt is the appearance of **James Love**, a member of the 1927 graduating class at Canoga High School (Cal.) sent out to find as many of the original class members as possible. For every successful prediction of what occupations they chose, Love gets $50.

Guest star is vocalist **Nellie Lutcher**, who made a quick appearance on the program last week. A 70-year-old woman attempts to sing "He Sends Me." The contestant was on the program last week and has had the entire week to practice. She succeeds!

Animal contestant on this broadcast is a huge St. Bernard dog. The dog's mate is expecting puppies and is out at the Jack Weatherwax Kennels. A contestant from the studio is sent with a St. Bernard to visit the kennels and to report back next week about the puppies. If there are more girl puppies then boy puppies, the contestant gets the prize.

Episode #688, Broadcast of June 5, 1948

Stunts: Newlywed Group, Presidential Candidate Namesake, Pace Floor Payoff, No Fade Shirt Payoff, Main of Cotton, and Cross Country Interview

Broadcast originates from Hollywood, with remote broadcasts from Washington, D.C., Cleveland, Ohio, and a Denver, Colorado, where NBC announcers on local stations are placed at certain street corners, one in each of the three cities, to ask a passerby, a woman, to tell her exact age. If the woman answers correctly, the contestant in the Hollywood studio takes a consequence for stating earlier that a woman would not tell her age in public.

Washington, D.C., announcer is **Charles Batters**, who speaks with a woman aged 50.

Cleveland, Ohio, announcer is **Joe Mulvahill**, who interviews a woman aged 46.

Denver, Colorado, announcer is **Starr Yellen**, who interviews a woman aged 55.

Ralph Edwards announced that the funds for Jimmy reached $32,854 and the boy will receive his television set. **Wayne Hogeman**, the contestant, last week sent to accompany a St. Bernard dog to the kennel is back to report that the St. Bernard's mate had more boy dogs than girls, so the contestant loses his prize of $250 and has to live in a specially made "dog house" in his own back yard for one week.

Presidential candidate stunt features real-life contestants named Abraham Lincoln and Thomas Jefferson. Studio audience members receive buttons, "Vote for Abraham Lincoln" and "Vote for Thomas Jefferson." The men must wear these buttons all week, everywhere they go.

Honeymoon couple contestants get a free honeymoon in Eureka Springs, Arkansas, for two weeks but must attend a "Barefoot Dance" while there and also must go without shoes and socks for their other public appearances while honeymooning.

This broadcast features the reappearance of contestant **Bruce Gary**, a war veteran who said he would give the "shirt off his back" to any other veteran. For an entire year, he has been giving the shirt off his back to any veteran who came to him, showed a service button and asked for the shirt. Gary removed his shirt wherever he was and passed it on to the other veteran. The shirts were supplied by the "No Fade Shirt Company." Gary reports that he gave away 313 shirts during the year. He brought back the pins from the shirts and collected $500 for 1,872 returned pins. The shirt company adds another $500 to the prize and Gary gets to keep 50 shirts that he had left over from a supply of 365 shirts provided earlier in the year.

Special guest in Hollywood is the Maid of Cotton, 1948, **Mathilda Nail** of Fort Worth, Texas.

Episode #689, Broadcast of June 12, 1948

Stunts: News Broadcast, Wives Strongmen, Radio Survey Relative, and New Look for Woman B.U.

Contestants are asked to imitate their favorite commentators: choosing from H.V. Kaltenborn, Walter Winchell, and Gabriel Heatter. One of the contestants is a 93-year-old lady. (Ralph Edwards says he thinks this is the first time a 93-year-old lady has appeared on the series.) In the "Radio Survey Relative" stunt, contestant **Bill Jackson** is told to call his relatives and pretend he is taking a radio survey. The calls are all long distance. Actually, the contestant's aunt, **Mrs. Loreen Cox Love,** is in the studio although the contestant thinks he is contacting her long distance. Mrs. Love later appears on the program. In the "Look Girl" stunt, a female contestant must wear a dress made entirely of *Look* magazine covers, for one full week.

Episode #690, Broadcast of June 19, 1948
Stunts: New Look for Woman Payoff, Guess State Intro, Concentration, Put Hollywood on the Map, and Earphones Hoax Sinatra
Program includes four remote cuts from Milwaukee, Wisconsin, for a consequence involving contestants who are given the opportunity to listen to a clue coming direct from the "Mystery State" and if they guess the State correctly, they win a three-week vacation in that State, all expenses paid. The winners are **Mr. and Mrs. Dolan**, for the correct answer was Wisconsin.
Celebrity guests are **Donnie Darnell**, model, and **Frank Sinatra**, vocal star. Sinatra is heard from another studio at NBC, where he is engaging in the warm-up preceding his own weekly radio program, *Your Hit Parade*.
Contestant **Eddie Carideo** of Los Angeles, California, agrees to tour the country during the summer in an attempt to get enough people to sign a petition to put Hollywood on the official Rand McNally map – and also in the files of the U.S. Post Office. As Hollywood now exists, all mail featured the Los Angeles postmark because Hollywood has no official postal recognition. Carideo is to get 1,000,000 people to sign his petition and return in the fall to present his petition on the quiz program. The route he is to follow this summer is mapped out for him. Carideo receives a supply of Ball Point Pens and several petition books to carry with him. If he succeeds in getting the one million signatures, he will receive $2,500. Carideo, in real life, is a substitute mail carrier!
The tour ends at Washington, D.C., where the petition would be presented to the Postmaster General, who would then authorize a Hollywood Sub Station Postmark. In addition, Rand McNally would include Hollywood on their maps. The tour, locations and dates, are as follows:

Los Angeles, California (June 21-22)
San Francisco, California (June 25-26)
Salt Lake City, Utah (June 28)
Denver, Colorado (June 30, July 1-4)
Kansas City, Missouri (July 6-7)
Omaha, Nebraska (July 9-10)
Des Moines, Iowa (July 12-14)
St. Paul, Minnesota (July 16-17)
Milwaukee, Wisconsin (July 19-21)
Chicago, Illinois (July 23, 24)
St. Louis, Missouri (July 26)
Louisville, Kentucky (July 27-28)
Indianapolis, Indiana (July 29-31)
Cincinnati, Ohio (August 2-4)
Detroit, Michigan (August 6-7)
Cleveland, Ohio (August 9)
Buffalo, New York (August 11)
Syracuse, New York (August 13-14)
Boston, Massachusetts (August 16-21)
New York City, New York (August 23-25)
Philadelphia, Pennsylvania (August 27-28)
Pittsburgh, Pennsylvania (August 30-31)
Baltimore, Maryland (September 1-2)
Washington, D.C.

Roy Rector of *Truth or Consequences* accompanied the contestant, verifying all of the signatures were legit, keeping tabs on the actual count of signatures, and as contact for local newspapers and radio stations who were notified in advance of Snyder's arrival. **Jack Melvin** was the advance man for handling timely publicity, while **Gene Juster**, the program manager for the radio program, attempted to set up in advance some stunts for the contestant's visit. Local radio stations used their news features and local morning programs to promote the event and encourage listeners to come out and sign the petition. The 23-city tour featured various accompaniments such as five girls, known as the Pen-Quints. A judge reviewed photos of all the Pen-Quints and the most beautiful was given a free trip to Hollywood, and a screen test at RKO-Radio Studios.

Episode #691, Broadcast of June 26, 1948

Stunts: Foreign Double-Talk, Review Ozark – Hollywood on the Map, Modern Nostradamus, and Burlesque Family Reunion

Program included a remote from McCornack General Hospital, Pasadena, California, where **Louis Peterson**, hospitalized veteran, was given a chance to make several predictions and if more than one-half of his predictions came true before the radio program returned to the air in the fall, he would get a two-week Caribbean trip for himself and his bride. The predictions he makes include:

(1) Democrat candidates for the Presidency and Vice-Presidency will be **Harry Truman** and **Alben Barkley**, respectively. (counted as two predictions)

(2) The majority of the Olympic Games this year would be won by America.

(3) The Stock Market would go down from the present rate and continue to go down for the next two months.

(4) The St. Louis Cardinals will be ahead on August 28 in the National Baseball League.

(5) The New York Yankees will be leading the American Baseball League.

(6) **Ben Hogan** will win the Tam o' Shanter Golf Tournament.

(7) Acres O'Riley will still be in the *Dick Tracy* comic strip.

(8) "Nature Boy" will still be on *Your Hit Parade*.

(9) It will rain in Seattle on August 28. (The veteran's bride is in Seattle.)

In the Hollywood studio, feature contestant is a Los Angeles tire salesman, **William Snyder**, who receives two sealed envelopes with consequences enclosed (three smaller sealed envelopes are inside each envelope, progressing down in size). The first one contains a $100 bill. The second envelope offers a ten-week vacation at home (plus a hammock to ensure the tops of relaxation) and pay while he vacations. The third, which the contestant chooses to open although he had a choice to keep the first envelope and not open any more, assigns Snyder to replace contestant Carideo, who is now on the first lap of his visit to 23 cities in the U.S. in an all-summer tour trying to get one million signatures on a petition. Carideo gets to come home and spend a ten-week vacation, lounging in a hammock, "with pay," while Snyder starts out to replace Carideo and have a chance at the $2,500 prize… if he gets his one million signatures by the time the show returns to the air.

Episode #692, Broadcast of August 28, 1948

Stunts: Launch Program, Television, Nostradamus Payoff, Drive to Airport B.U., and Truman and Dewey

Mr. and Mrs. Albert G. Brain of 265 Hampton Ave., Salt Lake City, Utah, afforded laughs for the 600 people in the audience when she unknowingly hit her husband in the face with a "gooey meringue" pie. Edwards chose her from the audience to open the show. While **Harry Von Zell** gave her instructions and a pie, Mr. Brain was taken backstage. His head was put through a hole in the wall and a curtain was draped in front of him. When the signal was given, Mrs. Brain raised the pie, the studio announcers raised the curtain, and Mr. Brain could have raised a fuss. But he did not when he saw his wife's surprised and apologetic expression. For their entertaining abilities, they received a wristwatch each and a $50 War Bond.

Episode #693, Broadcast of September 4, 1948

Stunts: Reverse Consey Gift, Put Hollywood on the Map Payoff, Mayor Hoax, Drive to Airport Payoff, and Ten Pies

Broadcast from Hershey, Pennsylvania, Lebanon Airport in Lebanon, Pennsylvania, and the NBC Hollywood studios. Ralph Edwards is staging the show at the Hershey County Fair. Program opens with contestant, **Mrs. Bricker**, mother of 14 children being presented with a long list of valuable merchandise and then given the consequence that every prize must be given away to members of the audience – the members stand as she gives away her prizes to find later that every person to whom she gave a gift was a member of her family in disguise.

Feature pay-off is the presentation of a check for $2,500 to **William Snyder**, the contestant who toured the country to get signatures to "put Hollywood on the map." Snyder did not get the one million signatures and he protests the possibility of getting that number of signatures in the time allotted – he is correct in this assumption and is told by Edwards that only 500,000 signatures were actually required but the "million" was specified to "confuse him." In actuality, Snyder acquired 630,322 signatures. A check for $2,500 was also mailed to **Eddie Carideo**, the contestant who started the signature project and then traded his "consequence" with Snyder.

From the Lebanon Airport, **William Forscht**, Mayor of Lebanon, Pennsylvania, is heard welcoming an Ariel Flyer whom is believed to be a famous woman big-game hunter – she turns out to be the mayor's wife, who gets a 72-piece Sterling Silver set for fooling her husband. The Mayor receives a gold watch. **Sid Philips** is the on-the-spot announcer handling the Lebanon interview. (**Bob Grimes** is the pilot who flew in Mrs. Forscht – the pilot is mentioned by name but does not talk on the program.)

Back in Hershey, Ralph Edwards presents his contestants **Mr. and Mrs. George Marsh** of California, who drove their car from Hollywood to Hershey. Last week Mr. Marsh found himself facing a consequence of unusual proportion. He was to drive his wife to the airport –only to find the airport referred to was the airport in Hershey, Pennsylvania! The Marsh couple, who are celebrating their sixth wedding anniversary, get a set of new tires for their car, a projector and screen, a radio-and-television set, and a five-day vacation in Las Vegas.

Episode #694, Broadcast of September 11, 1948
Stunts: Mass Kiss Slap, Orchestra Yiffniff, Know What I Mean Seltzer, President's Cabinet, Boxers, and Clarence B.U.

Broadcast from the Toldeo Sports Arena in Toldeo, Ohio, with commercials from Hollywood and a cut-in from the J.W. Green Auditorium in Toledo. Ralph Edwards appears in Toldeo in cooperation with the Lucas County American Legion. At the end of the program, an announcement is made that *People Are Funny* is presenting the Lucas County Chapter, American Legion, with a movie projector and screen. Members of the Lucas County American Legion are predominant in the studio audience and volunteer for the "New Hungarian Orchestra" stunt in which studio guests are taken by bus, 100-strong, to pretend that they are members of the New Hungarian Symphony at the J.W. Green Auditorium. A woman contestant, **Mrs. Grace DeLisle**, is sent to the Auditorium as the "woman conductor" named Madame Sofia Lezinska. Handling the interview with Mrs. DeLisle at the Auditorium is local announcer **Harley West**. The audience who are victims of the hoax arranged by Lucas Co. American Legion and *People Are Funny* are told they will get to see a special movie feature, *The Saxon Charm*, instead of the "New Hungarian Symphony" concert that they expected – both audience and radio listeners hear the brief "orchestra" spot in which the 100 studio guests pretend to be musicians and in which Mrs. DeLisle actually welcome the audience to the "performance."

Carry-over stunts for next week are: (1) contestant **Maury Robbins**, who will be flown to Los Angeles by TWA, to appear at the door of the Leverton home in Los Angeles to pretend that he is an "old flame of Mrs. Leverton." Mr. Leverton, a salesman, is in Toldeo and is "in" on the stunt and every member of the stunt will be awarded a $100 Savings Bond; and (2) contestant **Mrs. Nellie Thrush** who says she likes "dogs," and who is presented with two "Boxers" who turns out to be young fighters (**Tom Shunk** and **Nolan Buck** – Shunk is known as "The Killer" and Buck as "The Tiger") who will appear in a special card of fights on September 15. Mrs. Thrush has to be there to act as their second in the matches.

Episode #695, Broadcast of September 18, 1948

Stunts: Storeroom Bedlam, Clarence Payoff, and Ann Blyth

Program originated from the Hollywood studios with a pick-up from the home of **Mr. and Mrs. Leverton** in Los Angeles. Also included is a preview of the upcoming "Mr. and Mrs. Hush Contest," scheduled to begin on the broadcast two weeks from tonight. Proceeds of the contest to be used for Mental Health. According to *Variety*, two days following this broadcast, "Let's hope no one breaks into print should they stumble on to the identities because of the worthiness of the cause. It's different with *Stop the Music* and others of that ilk because they're pure commercial."

Actress **Ann Blyth** appears in her mermaid costume to promote her movie, *Mr. Peabody and the Mermaid*, along with **Bud Westmore**, Hollywood makeup artist who carries her because she cannot walk in her costume!

A number of contestants are given various articles and animals to deliver to a certain address, unaware they are all sent to the same address. The stunt uses live animals: A horse, a cat and a string of sardines, a chicken, and a seal (known as "Sandy the Seal" – also referenced as "Sylvia the Seal").

Feature stunt is the start of the "Beetle Derby," an automobile race to carry over through two or three weeks. The contest consists of four contestants who are on the program tonight: **Jasper Spencer**, **Johnny Asher**, **John Benson** and **Charlie Range**, who agreed to drive a car from Hollywood, leaving at 9 a.m. Monday morning, to Detroit. Each driver will be accompanied by a *Truth or*

Consequences man who oversees that drivers do not do more than eight hours driving per day, that they obey all traffic regulations and speed laws, and that they follow the "beetle" in their car. Each car is equipped with an ordinary beetle and a plastic box. As the driver enters a new state, he slips a map of that state into the beetle's box and then follows the route taken by the bug. (The driver may never get out of California because the beetle may never pass the California boundary line.) Once in another state, however, the driver does not have to go back into a previous state even if the beetle heads back for that line. At the end of the race, the winning driver gets his choice of a Kaiser car and $250 in cash; a television set and $1,000 in cash; a trailer complete with a refrigerator and $250 in cash; or a movie projector and screen, a complete set of tires and tubes, and $500 cash. The driver to come in second gets his choice of prizes not chosen by the winner; the third and fourth get what remains. Also, the driver who gets the best mileage per gallon of gas gets a bonus of $200. If at any time during the race two drivers of Kaiser cars meet in the same town, each driver gets a $200 bonus; if at any time the four drivers hit the same town at the same time, each driver receives $500 bonus. All expenses are paid during the trip. Drivers tonight draw to see what they will drive: Spencer and Benson drive Kaiser automobiles; Asher and Range will drive Frasers.

Details
The race ended up in Mexico City, another in Florida, and one did make it to Willow Run, Michigan.

The Breakdown
Promotion during the race is broken down below, also listing the *T or C* rep who went along for the ride to validate the race.

Charlie Range (Jack Wormser, *T or C* rep)
30 radio broadcasts ranging from five minutes to one hour, including two Transcontinentals.
2 Television Broadcasts
Stories and pictures in 39 different newspapers

Jasper Spencer (Bill Card)
56 radio broadcasts
27 Radio Stories (news broadcasts, etc.)
46 newspaper stories
26 pictures

John Benson (Bill Hawes)
22 radio broadcasts
18 newspaper stories
pictures in 12 newspapers

Johnny Asher (Chadwick)
40 radio broadcasts
25 newspaper stories
18 newspaper pictures

Newspaper reprint from Ventura, California: Charley Range, one of four contestants, came through Ventura on the first lap of a "Beetle Derby" tour which may win him a new Kaiser automobile. The new contest launched the four contestants from Hollywood yesterday, following the route set by a beetle on a map of the state. Traveling in Kaisers, the contestants are to follow the routes set by the beetles. At the end of three weeks, the contestant nearest to Willow Run, Michigan, wins a new car. Range's beetle set a course for Santa Barbara. He stopped on route at C. Sweney Motors, where the 1949 Kaiser was on display. Range was accompanied by Jack Wormser, judge and escort for the contest."

Episode #696, Broadcast of September 25, 1948
Stunts: Donkey Serenade, World War I Officer, House Movie Premiere B.U., and Plus Business 'til Finish
Broadcast from Hollywood, with a pick-up of one of the Beetle Derby contestants from station KOA in Denver, Colorado, where **John Asher** tells how his beetle named Tyrone, has guided him to Denver. He and the beetle are having a great time at the NBC stations along the way at one time, he and **Jasper Spencer**, another driver in the contest, met.

Back in the Hollywood studios, Ralph Edwards reports on the other Beetle Derby drivers: **Charlie Range** and his beetle named Willie are in Elko, Nevada; **Jasper Spencer** was last heard from Trinidad, Colorado. Spencer's first beetle, named Percy, died but replaced with another named Percy. Contestant in the derby, **John Benson**, speaks for himself from the Hollywood studios for his beetle has never taken him outside of Hollywood. His first beetle, named Please, died. His new beetle is named No, Thank You, and has proven no better at guiding his driver. Benson and beetle have averaged 21 ½ miles per gallon on gas thus far.

Highlights of the broadcast include contestant **Mrs. Dorothy Cristman**, a vocal soloist rendering "The Donkey Serenade," with a background supplied by the braying of 20 live donkeys right on the stage. One stunt plugging WAC recruiting, involved contestants **Sergeant Maj. Barry Hill**, currently in charge of a WAC recruiting station in Los Angeles, and his ex-Adjutant during World War I, **Harold G. Ferguson**, now a real estate man. Hill does not recognize his old Adjutant.

Episode #697, Broadcast of October 2, 1948
Stunts: Wash Family Laundry, House Movie Premiere Payoff, and Obedient Dog Tank

Ralph Edwards opens the program with a special appeal in behalf of Fire Prevention Week, currently being observed. A contestant named **Jack Woodmansee** is given a consequence of doing the laundry for his entire family, including uncles, sister-in-law, etc. for one week. He gets $13 and other prizes.

An update on the Beetle Derby reports **John Benson** finally got out of California and is now in Mexico City, Mexico; **John Asher** is no longer in New Orleans; **Charlie Range** is in Boys Town, Nebraska; and **Jasper Spencer** is in Chicago, Illinois. Spencer is heard courtesy of WMAQ in Chicago, telling about the royalty treatment he receives from NBC affiliate stations as he has been making his way towards Michigan. He hopes to win the Derby. He is averaging 22 ½ miles per gallon of gas.

Contestant **Myrtle Oleson**, carried over from last week, is heard on this broadcast for eight minutes as a big premiere party for movie stars and other celebrities was held at Oleson's apartment house in Los Angeles, for the premiere of *Apartment for Peggy*. The following guests step before the microphone to say hello: **Anne Baxter**, columnist **Earl Culpsenetter** (Culp's Column); movie actress **Nancy Garland**; **Bob Arthur**, movie personality; **Betty Lynn**, **Colleen Gray**, **Barbara Lawrence**, movie actresses; **Dan Dailey**, **Richard Widmark** and **Cesar Romero**, and the mother and father of Oleson from Barnum, Minnesota, who have not seen their daughter in three years. The entire quiz program is arranging for the parents to spend a week with their daughter, including their stay at a leading hotel in Los Angeles.

The voices of "Mr. and Mrs. Hush" are heard for the first time, delivering a jingle as a clue to the identity of the mystery voices, described as a "well-known American husband and wife."

> Hi diddle diddle,
> The Cat is the riddle,
> The stag won the wings of the Thrush;
> The green rock stood fast
> At the place Redskins passed,
> Now the Redskin is dear Mrs. Hush.

In order to take part in the contest to identify Mr. and Mrs. Hush, listeners are asked to send their name, address and telephone number printed plainly in the upper right-hand corner of a letter in which the listener completes the statement in 25 words or less: "We should all support the Mental Health Drive because…" With every letter, a contribution to the Mental Health Drive should be included. All proceeds from the contest will be used in the Mental Health Drive for that National Committee for Mental Health. The judges for each week: **Dr. Burrell Raulston**, Dean of a medical school at the University of Southern California; **Dr. Elmer Belt**, chairman of the Governor's Public Health Committee, California; and **Mrs. Dora Shaw Haffner**, director of Mental Hygiene for the State of California. The prizes for the first week include a $2,000 all-electric kitchen; a television, phonograph and radio combination; and a $2,000 mink coat or cash equivalent.

Episode #698, Broadcast of October 9, 1948
Stunts: Smash Fender, Doughnut Dunk, and Chicago Cubs Pennants

Ralph Edwards honors National Doughnut Week by having two male contestants blindfolded and feed chocolate covered donuts to each other. Contestant **Mrs. Thelma Johnson** agrees to be happy for an entire week without once losing her temper or raising her voice. Afterwards, in the NBC Hollywood parking lot, Johnson discovers the bumper is destroyed on her new car and one of Edwards' stooges accuses her of careless parking. She somehow manages to keep her temper and wins prizes. (The damaged bumper was later revealed to belong to a different vehicle.)

A contestant named Mr. Rizzio gets a trip by TWA to Cleveland, Ohio, for tomorrow's World Series baseball game. During the game between the Cleveland Indians and the Boston Braves, the contestant must sell pennants for the Chicago Cubs!

From the steps of City Hall in Detroit, Michigan, **Mayor Eugene I. Van Antwerp**, presents **Jasper Spencer**, winner of the Beetle Derby, with the key to his new Kaiser car, the prize for winning the derby. **Bob Leslie**, announcer at station WWJ in Detroit, serves as the emcee and announces the race ended at 6 p.m., on October 8. **John Asher** was in New York City, **Charlie Range** in Moscow, Michigan. Spencer says his faithful beetle, Percy, died last night. Spencer, who met John Asher in Kansas, receives a bonus of $200, as does Mr. Asher because the two Kaiser drivers were in the same city at the same time. Mrs. Jasper Spencer appears in person to congratulate her husband.

No one accurately guessed the identity of Mr. and Mrs. Hush so the pot grows with a $1,000 diamond ruby wristwatch, a solid maple living room furniture, and a Spinet piano.

Episode #699, Broadcast of October 16, 1948

Stunts: Warmup Sing, Milwaukee Tease, and Venus

In the first routine studio stunt of the broadcast, involving a sing-a-long, involves singer **Joan Edwards**.

The first contestant telephoned in the "Mr. and Mrs. Hush" contest identifies the mystery voices: **Mrs. R. Learman**, 6034 Columbia Street, St. Louis, Missouri, is the lucky winner as she names actors **Kitty Carlisle** and **Moss Hart**. Mrs. Learman will receive the prizes to date: A $2,000 all-electric kitchen; a $2,000 mink coat or cash equivalent; a television, phonograph and radio combination; a $1,000 diamond and ruby wristwatch; and a complete solid maple living room furniture set, and Spinet piano. On October 2, Hart and Carlisle were heard from their New York apartment. On October 9, the couple were heard from the Taft Hotel, in New Haven, Connecticut. This week they were heard from the Statler Hotel, in Boston, Massachusetts. The

NBC engineer, **Perry Alexander**, was thanked on the air for helping them arrange for their hideout. Ralph Edwards explains that in all of the Hush contests, the program maintained "standby personalities" to use in the event the first contest is solved during the first few weeks. With such a worthwhile organization to get the proceeds from listener contributions, a new "Papa and Mama Hush," contest begins. Proceeds to continue going to the Mental Health Drive, along with the same rules, as with the prior contest.

New clues identifying "Papa and Mama Hush" are found in the following jingle:
"If Two and Three our Number be
Then we are Four – Yet we are Three!
But when Time goes on and Life's begun
Five and Two are then about One!"

The prizes added to the pot are a 10-year supply of DUZ; a two-week vacation for two in Sun Valley; and a new 1949 Nash car. The new Nash will be unveiled on November 22, 1948.

Episode #700, Broadcast of October 23, 1948
Stunts: Running Gag Clothes, Southern Hospitality, and Milwaukee Tease
Future stunt involves an NBC corridor race between a tall man and a short man with the leaders having to remove an article of clothing every time the pursuer catches up with him.
Contestant **Dale Gehersky** is given a chance to decide what is happening before the network switches to specific pickups – if correct, he receives a prize; if incorrect, he gets a pie in the face. The pick-ups (as if he could accurately guess them) are: (1) from the Los Angeles police station; (2) from the NBC studio where **Frank Sinatra** is rehearsing his radio program, *Your Hit Parade*, which followed this broadcast; (3) from the cashier's booth at Grauman's Chinese Theater; and (4) from the contestant's own home where the voices of his two children are heard.
A woman contestant was provided with a tuxedo-dressed "escort" to the night spots along Hollywood Boulevard. The escort is a live penguin, known as Joe the Penguin of the South Pole.
No one correctly guessed the identity of "Papa and Mama Hush." Four new prizes were added to the pot: $2,500 in U.S. Security Bonds, a three-year supply of

tires and tubes for one car; a 16mm sound and silent picture projector and camera; and a trip to Washington D.C. for the president's inauguration with a week stay at the Statler Hotel. "Papa and Mama Hush" repeat the jingle and add one clue: "We are not the parents of famous children." All listeners phoned get a 48-piece set of Sterling Silver.

Episode #701, Broadcast of October 30, 1948
Stunts: Own Haunted House, Not Husband, and Push Peanut B.U.

Broadcast from the Milwaukee Auditorium in Wisconsin, where the radio cast is making special appearances in connection with the Milwaukee Retail Grocers' Association Food Show (cast gave daily shows since Tuesday, October 26, through October 30, as part of the Food Show entertainment).

Program featured a cut-in from the "Mystery House," which was the home of a contestant, **Mrs. O'Sullivan**. Actor **Boris Karloff**, disguised as a swami, arrives to the door. She kisses him many times and when asked if her husband wouldn't mind her kissing a total stranger, she confesses that she knew it was her husband and replied, "No, I knew it was him all the time… I know those lips." Imagine her surprise when she discovered her mistake and that it was Boris Karloff she kissed!

In a Presidential Election stunt, two contestants, a Republican and a Democrat, agree that the candidate who loses the election will appear on the program next week to push a peanut past the winning presidential candidate headquarters in New York City.

Three more incorrect guesses in the "Papa and Mama Hush" contest means additional prizes added to the pot: a Spinet piano, a Stromberg radio phonograph combination, and a $2,000 Hotpoint all-electric kitchen. Papa and Mama Hush Provide additional clues. Mama says the clues are in the first two lines of the jingle – "Three what? Four what?" Papa says, "As for the numbers, 5 and 2 are then about one – I'd just forget about those."

Episode #702, Broadcast of November 6, 1948
Stunts: Learn Be-Bop Rhythm, Push Peanut Payoff, and Play Pool-Pool B.U.

Russell Jefferson, a 12-year-old African American, demonstrates his ability to sing "Be-Bop" style and tries to teach a lady-contestant how to sing likewise. Jefferson is presented with a Bulova wristwatch for his mother, who has accompanied him to the broadcast, and a $500 Savings Bond for himself to save for his education fund 10 years from now. Edwards ties the stunt with a "Harbor No Prejudice" appeal and praises the talents of Russell Jefferson.

In the carryover contest from last week, the losing contestant agreed to pay off his election bet by pushing a peanut in front of the New York election headquarters of the winning candidate, in front of the Biltmore Hotel. Contestant **Herbert Sherr,** Republican of Milwaukee, is interviewed by announcer **Mel Allen,** who describes the "pushing of the peanut." Incidentally, the peanut is inside a live elephant named Jumbo and the contestant has to push Jumbo down the street. Radio listeners were able to hear the crowds cheering him on, etc. As the contestant pushes the elephant, he sings "I Lost an Election Bet" to the tune of "Farmer in the Dell."

Three more incorrect guesses to the identity of Papa and Mama Hush result in the additional clues: "Two and Three; Four; Three; Time; Five; Two; about." Then Mama Hush says, "Good night, Ernest..." The prizes added to the pot include a $1,000 diamond ring, a maple furniture set for the living room, a $1,000 men's wardrobe, and a $1,000 woman's wardrobe.

Announcement made during the broadcast that the story of *Truth or Consequences* is told in the November issue of *Photoplay* magazine.

Episode #703, Broadcast of November 13, 1948

Stunts: Turkey Thanksgiving, Seal Accompaniment, and Pool-Pool Payoff

Feature stunt is the "mission" assigned to contestant **Jack Root**, a Los Angeles pickle salesman, who agrees to take a trip to the real Turkey (Istanbul, Turkey) for Thanksgiving as part of his consequences.

Pick-up from the Hollywood Athletic Club Swimming Hole, where sports announcer **Gerry Lawrence** describes a pole game being played underwater with contestants. Diving equipment was provided for the contest. The contestants are heard on the air from time to time. The contestants are **Bob Goldstein,** from Los Angeles, and **Lauren MacGowan,** a construction builder from Texas.

"Papa and Mama Hush" pick-up adds another clue. Papa says, "Take the two and three of the first line. How many are two and three?" Mama Hush says, "That's enough homework for tonight, teacher!" Three incorrect guesses made by listeners add more prizes to the pot: $1,500 worth of equipment for a farm home including a tractor, a year supply of food including meat for a family of four, and a complete power tool workshop.

Episode #704, Broadcast of November 20, 1948
Stunts: Dorothy Shay, Parents Pie Thanksgiving, and Turkey Thanksgiving B.U.
Contestant **Audrey Hallett** is led to believe she is telephoning her parents in Lockport, Illinois, wishing them a happy Thanksgiving, and then asks them to throw a pie into the face of a guest in their home. She believes she will win prize money if they do so. In actuality, her parents, **Mr. and Mrs. Elmer Grant**, are in the studio and backstage. Their guest is Mrs. Hallett's husband, **Charles Hallett**. The parents have a one week all-expense stay in Hollywood. "Papa and Mama Hush" pick-up adds another clue. Papa says, "We have merrily picked our way along life's way." Mama replies, "Yes, my lifetime buddy." Three incorrect guesses made by listeners add more prizes to the pot: a $1,000 diamond and ruby wrist watch, a $1,000 Gil Portrait for the winner or any member of his family by Ray Hoff; and a $1,000 gift certificate for Spiegel's Mail Order House items.

Dorothy Shay, a singer known as the "Park Avenue Hillbilly," with contestant Joseph Giuseppe Aquino, a bartender by profession, on the broadcast of November 20, 1948.

Episode #705, Broadcast of November 27, 1948
Stunts: Remote Doorbell Kiss, Perfumed Animals, Turkey Thanksgiving No. 2
Broadcast included a stunt with a cut-in from Brooklyn, New York, the home of **Hyman Siegal**, where announcer **Ed Herlihy** interviews the Siegal

housewife, after **Ray Morgan**, radio actor, impersonates a policeman. **Mrs. Hyman Siegel** gets $250 for kissing the policeman.

Back in Hollywood, contestant **Joseph Koukol** confuses his mother-in-law by guessing the names of animals by the perfume used (animal sprayed with perfume – goat, dog, etc.).

Two of the radio listeners telephoned on the program for the "Papa and Mama Hush" contest were residents of Phoenix, Arizona: **Mrs. R. M. Reynolds** and **A. H. Bowman**. All three guesses were incorrect, adding more prizes to the pot: a dozen pairs of ladies shoes and matching handbags, a complete house painting job inside and out, and a complete home laundry unit. New clues include a reference to the number five in the jingle as "same as five points in a shooting star." Mama Hush also says to Papa Hush, "My star is your eye. Is that right?" Papa says, "Generally right."

Episode #706, Broadcast of December 4, 1948
Stunts: Turkey Thanksgiving Payoff, What's My Name Seltzer, and Kitchen Sink
Studio stunt involves the return to the program of **Jack Root**, Los Angeles pickle salesman, who spent Thanksgiving in Istanbul, Turkey. He tells about giving a box of DUZ to an American correspondent – soap flakes and soap are scarce articles in Turkey.

Three more incorrect guesses as to the identity of "Papa and Mama Hush" add four more prizes to the pot: a ten-year supply of the sponsor's product, a vacuum cleaner with all the attachments, Venetian blinds for entire house, and a fox fur coat. Announcement is made that because of the Christmas rush, in order to cooperate with the Postal Department, there will be only one more opportunity to get letters in to enter the Hush contest: December 11 will be the deadline for dating letters. No calls will be made next week. On December 18, however, as many phone calls as time allows will be made in order to give a chance to as many contestants as possible.

Episode #707, Broadcast of December 11, 1948
Stunts: Mail Christmas Ice, Spike Jones, Ralph Pie, and Give Away Studio Audience
Special guests in the studio are **Spike Jones**, orchestra leader and radio personality, and **Michael D. Fanning**, Postmaster of Los Angeles, who makes an appeal to mail Christmas packages at once for pre-Christmas delivery. Postmaster

also takes part in a stunt in which a contestant, **Boatswain's Mate Cleland Martini**, agrees to send his "girlfriend," **Kathleen Maraia**, in Brooklyn, a block of ice. For every pound of frozen water that is not melted when it reaches the New York City Post Office, where **Postmaster Albert Goldman** will weigh the ice, the contestant and his girlfriend will receive $10. The cake of ice is displayed tonight on the program. A 50-pound cake of ice wrapped in rubber bag over which canvas and other insulation is placed. The Los Angeles Postmaster, accompanied by the contestant, takes the package of ice to the Post Office tonight, for mailing to **Miss Kathleen Maraia**, c/o Postmaster Goldman, New York City.

Feature "giveaway" is the presenting of the entire studio audience of 450 people to one contestant, **Mrs. Urey**. The studio audience will go to Mrs. Urey's home for a party with refreshments supplied by *Truth or Consequences*.

Papa and Mama Hush provide new clues: "You can waltz right into this: Five and Two are in the alphabet but remember to reverse the alphabet for Five and Two are then about One."

Episode #708, Broadcast of December 18, 1948

Stunts: Mail Christmas Ice Payoff, Eddie Bracken, and Delicatessen Cowboy

Actor **Eddie Bracken** makes an appeal on behalf of the Santa Claus Foundation. Anyone wishing to contribute so that needy people may have Christmas cheer this year are asked to send contributions to Santa Claus Foundation, Santa Monica, California.

Ralph Edwards reports on 50-pound cake of ice mailed from California to New York, carried over from last week. Both the contestant and the recipient received $10 for every pound of ice that reached New York. The ice completely melted by delivery. There was, however, $50 for the contestant and his girlfriend – the bill was frozen in the cake of ice.

Papa and Mama Hush are finally identified as the dance team of **Veloz and Yolanda**. The winner is **Oscar Keith** of 8931 West Delaware Parkway, Munster, Indiana. Veloz and Yolanda spoke in behalf of the Mental Health Drive, explaining the clues used during the contest, and how they were heard weekly from their home in Beverly Hills, California.

The Papa and Mama Contest Draws to a Close

While $30,000 richer in prizes, Uncle Sam set a merciless 34 or 35 percent tax from the accumulated jackpot. Oscar Keith admitted to reporters that his 1948 income amounted to $3,600. Being put in the $30,000 bracket only complicated matters. Hoping to turn down a third of the prizes, it was his intention to lower the prize income to $20,000 to affirm an acceptable tax bracket. The tax, according to Wilbur Enders, Lake County internal revenue chief, was based on prize value listed by the contest sponsors. A lower tax would be computed at the prices Keith sold some of the prizes. It all came under the "willing buyer, willing seller" tax statute. It was also Keith's option to request delivery of the prizes after January 1. This would establish a 1949 tax year and provide months of convenience to reorganize the total value of the prizes.

Oscar was 34 at the time of the contest and was talking on the telephone to a friend just released from a hospital. "An emergency call is coming through from Hollywood," the operator said, interrupting Keith's phone conversation. Oscar was asked if he could identify Papa and Mama Hush and he did – correctly. Keith gave credit to his wife for working out the clues. Mary Keith's penchant for radio contests paid off. She had leafed through hundreds of references at homes and libraries to select the correct answer.

The Keiths lived in Munster's Independence Park subdivision for four years in Indiana. Oscar did not have to shovel snow from the walks of his home that weekend. Neighbors, friends, relatives, newsmen, photographers and radio representatives beat a path to his door. To reporters he confessed the contest letter submitted was one of five they submitted during the life of the contest. Oscar toiled away at the Harbison-Walker Refractories, the East Chicago brickyard, where he hauled brick in wheelbarrows from the kilns to the storage racks.*

---

* Ironically, Keith's brother, Claude Keith of East Chicago, one of the first to congratulate Oscar, was an employee of Lever Brothers – a competitor of the soap firm which showered wealth on Oscar's household.

Veloz and Yolanda phoned the Keiths the day after the broadcast to offer a year of free professional dancing lessons. Oscar and Mary said that with four children around the house, they wouldn't have much time for terpsichorean pleasures. Daughters Sharon and Linda like to dance and they would share the prize.

The total list of prizes included a two-week vacation for two in Sun Valley, Idaho; a 1949 automobile; a three-year supply of auto tires and tubes; a 16mm sound movie projector and silent camera; $2,500 in U.S. Security Bonds; round-trip for two to Washington with one-week accommodations and entertainment during the Presidential Inauguration; a Stromberg radio phonograph combination; a Spinet piano; a $2,000 all-electric kitchen including range; living room of maple furniture; complete wardrobe for a man (value up to $1,000); complete wardrobe for a woman (value up to $1,000), a $1,500 farm tractor (which he sold to meet the big tax on the windfall); a year's supply of food including meat for a family of four; complete power tool home workshop; $1,000 oil portrait of the winner or a member of his family; a $1,000 diamond-and-ruby wristwatch; $1,000 worth of gift certificates on a mail-order house; one dozen pairs of ladies' shoes and matching handbags; a complete house-paint job inside and out; a complete home laundry; a ten-year supply of the sponsor's product, DUZ; a vacuum cleaner with all the attachments; Venetian blinds for the entire house; and a full-length fox fur coat.

During the broadcasts, commercial copy for the Mental Health Drive for use on the quiz show was supplied by The National Mental Health Foundation, and checked by their staff psychiatrist, **Dr. Dallas Pratt. Dr. George Stevenson** of the National Committee for Mental Hygiene also reviewed the copy.

In an official release, Edwards made a plea for the print media to restrain their pride for philanthropy. "In the past," said Edwards, "the divulging of the identity of the 'Hushes,' when a columnist or other person had solved it, had no pronounced effect upon the contest because the newsbreaks coincided with the more obvious clues given to bring the contest to a close. The grave danger of publicizing the name at the outset of the contest, however, would seriously injure the real purpose of the competition, which is to bring funds to the needy, but least-financed charity in existence. We would like for the contest to last long enough to give the drive enough funds to do a real difference. Therefore, I am making humanitarian appeals to all media to consider the names of Mr. and Mrs. Hush of the contests but not to divulge the clues."

Episode #709, Broadcast of December 25, 1948

Stunts: Open Christmas Package, and Visit from Santa Claus

Santa Claus is the celebrity guest and tells of wanting to visit the homes of children that may be forgotten on Christmas Eve. Santa says his sleigh with the reindeer travel so fast that he can visit homes across the continent from coast to coast before this broadcast ends. There are numerous pickups from across the country, arranged so that children in the studio and listening audience think they are hearing the same Santa they heard in the studio as he reports "from his sleigh during his coast-to-coast trip. (Santa is actually talking from back stage and in the pickups from the places visited, local radio actors and announcers take over the broadcast in their Santa Claus disguise). The children whose homes are visited receive gifts for which they have asked. Members of their family also receive gifts such as heating systems, washing machines, electric roasters, clothing, radios, etc. The homes visited and from which we hear "Santa" interview the children and other family members are:

San Francisco: Little Susan, who lives on Sacramento Street – has two sisters and four brothers. Her "Mommy" receives a freezer stocked with food, and enough canned goods for all of her cupboards. All of the children receive toys, fruit, candy, food and clothing.

Hammond, Indiana: Little Edward on Schneider Street – has two brothers. His mother receives an electric washing machine and clothes dryer. The children receive all kinds of clothes and toys.

Harlem, New York City: Little Ronald, African American boy, lives on West 116th Street. The New York "Santa Claus" is **Jim Goss**, radio actor, who mentions that his reindeer are taking him along "St. Nicholas Avenue" to the home of Ronald. The child receives toys, candy and clothing. The family receive a complete turkey and sweet potato dinner, an electric roaster, wool blankets for every member of the family, wristwatches for mother and father, and a 72-piece Sterling Silver set.

Back in Hollywood, **Mrs. Mary A. Lyons** of 2520 West 7th Street, Los Angeles, returns from last year's Christmas broadcast with the box she was instructed to hold until this Christmas. She has returned with the unopened box. When she opens it, Mary finds inside another box marked "Do not open till Christmas 1949." She agrees to return in 1949.

Episode #710, Broadcast of January 1, 1949

Stunts: New Year's Calling, Pigskin, Husbands Resolutions, and Rose Bowl Tank

First announcement today about a new contest to begin soon on this program, "The Whispering Woman" contest, which will be similar to "The Walking Man" contest of the prior year.

Celebrity guests include **Hope Emerson**, actress of Broadway and screen, and **Frank Foster**, swimming star and instructor in diving. Feature stunts include a woman contestant who has to carry a live pig (Pigskin) around the stage, etc.; and a special "Help Boy Scout" stunt calling attention to what the average Boy Scout is expected to do. Woman contestant agrees once a week for an entire year to help a Boy Scout across the street, thus emphasizing the way Scouts are usually helping little old ladies across streets. The contestant receives 52 post cards addressed to the program; every time she helps a Boy Scout across the street, she hands him a card which he mails to the program with his name and address. The contestant will receive $5 for every card received and the Scout who sent it in will get a suitable gift. Contestant may thus get $260. Later, on the broadcast of February 12, an update on this contest was provided in recognition of Nation Boy Scout Week and the fact that a Scout who mailed in his postcard received boxing gloves autographed by **Jack Dempsey**.

In another stunt, a contestant has to telephone an unknown party and make disparaging remarks to him. The party phoned is really the contestant's boss, who gives him a raise after he discovers the joke!

Episode #711, Broadcast of January 8, 1949

Stunts: Temperature Hot Seat, Coast Guard B.U., St. Bernard, and Word Association

Feature stunt on the program is referred to as "Operation Lighthouse" or "Operation Ice Cubes" in which contestant **Bob Livingstone**, 4000 Third Avenue, Long Island, NY, agrees to deliver a pail of ice cubes to the Guard Island Lighthouse, in Ketchikan, Alaska. Celebrity guest on the program is **Lt. Commander Robert C. Cannom** of the U.S. Coast Guard, who agrees to "take charge of Livingstone" for the trip to Alaska. (A Saint Bernard dog is on program and takes part in the stunt in which a blindfolded wife thinks her husband is disguised as a St. Bernard, unaware that it is a real live dog.)

Episode #712, Broadcast of January 15, 1949

Stunts: Egghead, Coast Guard Payoff, Stooge Pie Young, and Television Concession

Broadcast includes a pick-up from the Guard Island Lighthouse, 10 miles north of Ketchikan, Alaska, where **Bob Livingstone** reports that he delivered ice cubes to the Lighthouse inhabitants as instructed on last week's broadcast. **Lt. Commander Robert C. Cannom**, U.S. Coast Guard, certifies that the contestant has completed his mission. Lighthouse keepers **Mr. and Mrs. Otto Gibbs** briefly tell of the arrival of Livingstone. Back in Hollywood, Ralph Edwards announces that the U.S. Coast Guard Memorial Chapel Fund will get $200 in the name of Bob Livingstone for assisting the contestant in the Lighthouse stunt.

Another feature is the start of the "Hen Egg-Laying Stunt," with contestant **Joe Greb**, a "frustrated actor" by his own admittance, agreeing to appear on every weekly broadcast until a hen selected for the stunt has laid an egg on his bald head. (The contestant is seated in the studio so that a slide extends from the hen's nest to his bald head). Greb stands a chance of getting $1,000 if the hen lays the egg tonight. Each week the amount of money drops $100 until it reaches zero when it begins to go back up at the rate of $100 a week. This may go on indefinitely.

Celebrity guest on this broadcast is comedian and screen actor **Alan Young**.

Announcement is made on the program that *Truth or Consequences* will make its television debut next Thursday night at 8:30 p.m. over KNBM. Woman contestant wins a television set after agreeing to be hostess to anyone who wishes to go to her home Thursday to watch the show over her new set. Another contestant is given the hot dog concession outside the lady's home for the occasion.

"The Whispering Woman" is heard for the first time, from her hideout "somewhere in the United States," and whispers the following clue referring to her identity:

"I'm a cake,
My coat is white,
My father owns the stock,
Half of mine is light."

Rules for entering the contest are stated in full: listeners write 25 words or fewer to accompany the statement: "We should all support the American Heart Association because…" Mail the statement with name, address and telephone number printed clearly in the upper righthand corner to: "The Whispering Woman, Box W, Hollywood, California." Contestants who wish to send a contribution to the American Heart Association (entry in contest does not require the contribution) can send any amount to another address: Box A (A for American Heart Association), Los Angeles, California. Every contestant phoned will get a chance to ask one question that can be answered by The Whispering Woman in a simple "yes" or "no." These answers serve as clues. Listeners are held on the line and given about five minutes time to consider the answer to their question before making their guess. The contestant who identifies The Whispering Woman will receive $25,000 in cash, the biggest one-time cash prize ever given on the history of the series.

Episode #713, Broadcast of January 22, 1949

Stunts: Egghead, Human Sound Effects, and Same Biography

The feature stunt on the broadcast was the meeting of a mother-in-law and her daughter-in-law who have never seen each other before. They meet when both are contestants describing the same man, the son of one, the husband of the other.

Joe Greb, the contestant waiting for the hen to lay her egg during the broadcast, is back as usual but fails to collect again. $900 would have been his prize had the hen laid an egg.

Episode #714, Broadcast of January 29, 1949

Stunts: Re-Tell Happenings, and Trumpet Water Tank

Celebrity guests include **Tex Beneke**, who "auditions" **Dick Walker**, amateur trumpet player, by making Walker get into a tank full of water. Beneke sings "Cool Water" during the stunt.

The first telephone calls for "The Whispering Woman" contest, establishing clues that she is over 40 years of age and has no children. Every week the first prize winner of the essay (the first to be called on the phone) will receive the 1949 De Luxe Kaiser car, which can be picked up through a local dealer if the contestant accepts an expenses-paid trip to the factory to pick up the car and drive it back home. Second contestant phoned will receive a Stromberg-

Carlson radio-television set. The decision to bestow a single prize to each contestant in "The Whispering Woman" stunt was to offset the tax issue experienced with the recent Papa and Mama Hush contest.

Episode #715, Broadcast of February 5, 1949
Stunts: Husband Hot Seat, and Four Prizes

Two more contestants asked The Whispering Woman questions regarding her identity. Established are the facts that she did not play in silent movies and she has never achieved fame in the world of sports. Second contestant received an electric Laundromat and clothes dryer. The Whispering Woman adds to her riddle by saying a few more words in behalf of the American Heart Association, "Give from your heart, for the heart."

Celebrity guest is **Dennis O'Keefe**, participating in a "Husband Hot Seat" stunt.

Episode #716, Broadcast of February 12, 1949
Stunts: Happy Birthday, Wife Cashier, Help Boy Scout, Oakland Tease, and Fanfare

In honor of Abraham Lincoln's birthday, a contestant sang "Happy Birthday, Abe Lincoln." Celebrity guest was **Helen Groom**, an Earl Carroll Vanities girl.

Questions asked of The Whispering Woman established she attained fame as a singer and that her husband has never been an Academy Award winner. The second contestant won a Victor camera and a 16mm projector for screening movies.

Joe Greb, the contestant waiting for the hen to lay her egg during the broadcast, is back as usual but fails to collect again. $600 would have been his prize had the hen laid an egg.

Episode #717, Broadcast of February 19, 1949
Stunts: Egghead Crackers, Father M.C., and Look Diet

The first listener called tonight, **Miss Merle Ford**, correctly identified The Whispering Woman as **Jeanette MacDonald** and received the $25,000 cash prize, the Kaiser automobile, and a free trip to California to appear on next week's broadcast.

Other stunts include a surprise visit to a father, **Seth Brown**, from his Air Corps son, **Sergeant Joe Brown**, flown from Tokyo with special leave for the occasion. The father is told to act as emcee for Edwards as he interviews his own son in disguise by Hollywood makeup artists.

Joe Greb, the contestant waiting for the hen to lay her egg during the broadcast, is back as usual but fails to collect again. $500 would have been his prize had the hen laid an egg.

The Whispering Woman Contest

Miss Merle Ford was a home economist and retired college professor, described by one newspaper columnist as a "middle-aged spinster." She answered the phone call from Hollywood in her room at the Broadview Hotel at 5540 Hyde Park Blvd in Chicago, where she had been living for the past six months. After a breathless wait of ten minutes, she was given a chance to identify "The Whispering Woman." The prize-winning answer ended a month-long contest which netted the American Heart Association an estimated $1 million for the current fund drive. The same association benefited by $1,500,000 in "The Walking Man" contest, which was won by another Chicago native.

Miss Ford entered the contest by writing three letters urging public support of the American Heart Association. Edwards permitted Miss Ford to ask the mystery voice one question. "Have you ever appeared with the Metropolitan Opera?" When MacDonald, a movie soprano, answered "no," Miss Ford immediately guessed her identity. She had only two potential guesses and the answer helped eliminate one of them.

Edwards explained how the jingle pointed to Jeanette MacDonald. The white coat on the cake referred to icing, which meant, "I sing." The line, "Dad owns the stock," hinted at the song, "Old MacDonald had a Farm." The "half of mine is light" referred to the "ray" in the last name of MacDonald's husband, actor Gene Raymond. While the clues were being explained to some 15,000,000 radio listeners, bedlam broke loose in the lobby of Miss Ford's South Side hotel. Hundreds of well-wishers joined newsmen and promoters in a clamor to see the jackpot winner. Then, blinded by photographer's flash bulbs, she emerged smiling from an elevator. Hundreds of people crowded into the Broadview Hotel. From there she was whisked to television station WBKB for a *Sun-Times* spot news broadcast. She said she had no idea what she would do with her $25,000 windfall. When asked about her present job and income, she ducked the question. "One thing is certain," she answered, "this is the most money I ever made in a week."

On Monday following the Saturday broadcast, the sandy-haired textile produce expert explained her interest in heart work was first aroused through her public school work as an adviser in home economics teaching. She visited schools for the handicapped which brought her in close contact with children suffering effects of heart disease, some of whom were recovering from rheumatic fever. "I couldn't help but marvel at the way children can be rehabilitated despite damaged hearts," she remarked. A personal connection with heart disease came from two deaths in her immediate family. At the age of 52, her father died after a heart attack some years prior in the family home of Maryville, Missouri. Her brother died at 48 a few years later in the Canal Zone. Her mother was completely helpless for a year as a result of a stroke. "Of course, I wanted to win the contest if I could," she told reporters. "But even if I hadn't, I would have been glad I had contributed to the heart cause." She hoped her new-found fame would lend emphasis to her plea that everybody join the work to stamp out heart disease, she added. "In my work as a home economics teacher in public schools, I often saw the wonderful work of rehabilitation being done among children suffering from heart ailments."

Having accepted an invitation to California to appear on *Truth or Consequences*, Merle Ford bought a new hat and a new pair of shoes.

The hideout of the Whispering Woman each week, it was revealed, was a Wiltshire Boulevard apartment belonging to a production man on the show, but even he did not know who The Whispering Woman was.

Episode #718, Broadcast of February 26, 1949

Stunts: Lake Merritt Gondola, Look Diet Payoff, Horse Trade Barrels, and Life of Riley

Broadcast originated from Oakland, California, with a remote pick-up from Lake Merritt across the street, where contestant **Sam Dodson**, pretends to be a "gondolier" with a department store dummy named "Cleopatra." Dodson's mother-in-law, and his minister, the **Rev. Harold Blakeley**, stroll along the lake banks and are heard in the broadcast as they remonstrate with contestant about his unusual behavior. Dodson sang, "I'm a Gondolier" while performing the stunt.

Screen actors **Gregory Peck** and **Rod Cameron** are special guests on a stunt involving wooden barrels on stage. The actors gave an invitation for listeners to attend a benefit performance for the Military Order of the Purple Heart, at

San Francisco Opera House, tomorrow, matinee and evening – special show "What Price Glory?"

An Oakland family named "Riley" (consisting of **Mr. Verne Riley** and wife and daughter) are interviewed and told that they will get an all-expenses paid trip and entertainment for a week's stay in Cincinnati, Ohio, for the premiere of the motion-picture, *The Life of Riley*, starring **William Bendix**. They will be entertained by Bendix and other members of the cast. The motion-picture is based on the NBC radio program of the same name.

During last week's broadcast, contestants Mr. and Mrs. Noble were given copies of the latest *Look* magazine diet. The wife weighed 220 and agreed to lose five pounds by the next broadcast; her husband, who weighed 140, agreed to gain five pounds at the same time. They returned for this broadcast – she lost six pounds; he gained five. They win prizes, cash and new clothes. Mrs. Noble told about the way she would give a substantial sum of the prize money to the Home for Retired Methodist Ministers and Their Families – her father was a Methodist minister who died of heart disease.

One stunt involved guessing the identity of a governor, which turned out to be **Luther W. Youngdahl**, Governor of Minnesota.

In this broadcast, Edwards remarks, "Aren't we diabolical?" and "Aren't we angels?" This was in recognition of the program's ninth anniversary, with **Ed Herlihy** bestowing congratulations from New York.

Episode #719, Broadcast of March 5, 1949
Stunts: Stop Son's Wedding, Dick Haymes, and Baseball Tape B.U.
Celebrity guests include **Phil Harris** and **Elliott Lewis**, featured comedians on the *Phil Harris and Alice Faye* radio program, and singing star **Dick Haymes**.
Herb Butterfield, radio actor, is on the program in the role of the Justice performing a wedding ceremony in a pick-up from the Banquet Room at the Hollywood Knickerbocker Hotel. Contestant **Mrs. Willaford** was sent to protest when the Justice performing a marriage ceremony asks if anyone knows any reason why the couple should not be joined in Holy Matrimony! Mrs. Willaford did the protesting and then found she was attending a "preview" of a wedding of her own son, whose real marriage was planned this summer after he graduated from Northwestern University. The son, his fiancée and her mother were brought to Hollywood for this preview wedding.

Joe Greb, the contestant waiting for the hen to lay her egg during the broadcast, is back as usual but fails to collect again. $300 would have been his prize had the hen laid an egg.

Episode #720, Broadcast of March 12, 1949
Stunts: Income Tax Quartette, Cross Country Pie B.U., Baseball Tape Payoff, and Double Date Telephone

Broadcast from the Hollywood studios with a tape recording made at Wrigley Field during the week, giving a "play-by-play" report of last week's mystery contestant, **James Murdock**, who returns to the program after accepting a "mystery assignment" last week. Murdock has to pretend to be an umpire at an exhibition game in which the Chicago Cubs took part. Cubs were in spring training in California at the time except for five of them, who participated with this stunt. The tape recording was played back with Murdock describing the wrong decisions made by the umpire, the players' reactions, etc. The five Cubs players who were heard on the tape debating the umpire decision each received Bulova watches.

Income Tax stunt involves voice students **Fern Yonker**, contralto; **Nadine Lackey**, soprano; **Bob Lamont**, baritone; and **Gene Kurtsinger**, tenor, who sing the words found on the 1948 income tax filing blank, to the music of the opera, "Rigoletto" by Verdi. Credit for arranging this music is given to **Phil Davis** of the *Truth or Consequences* music staff.

Mrs. G. W. Weston of Cleveland, Ohio, agrees to visit Highway 66 tomorrow morning to relay a pie well-packed in a plastic pie-case, with full instructions on the pie container, to a motorist going east – this motorist takes the pie as far as he is going and then passes it on to another motorist. The aim is to get the pie to New York in time for the grand opening of the Rose Bake Shop in Forest Hills, Long Island, by next week's broadcast. Every motorist who transports the pie gets ten cents per mile. The person who gets to New York with the pie has instructions to take it to the Rose Bake Shop and to heave the pie into the face of the proprietor, **Jack Ross**, during the broadcast next week. If the pie gets into the Bake Shop in time, Mrs. Weston receives $100.

Episode #721, Broadcast of March 19, 1949
Stunts: Mother-In-Law Dinner, Ray Milland, Minneapolis Tease, and Cross Country Pie No. 2

A Los Angeles woman who has never been to a movie picture show will be the guest of Paramount Pictures next week to get a special showing of motion pictures that have not yet been released to the public. Actor **Ray Milland**, along with a plumber of Los Angeles, are celebrity guests for this stunt.

Joe Greb, the contestant waiting for the hen to lay her egg during the broadcast, is back as usual but fails to collect again. $100 would have been his prize had the hen laid an egg.

Announcer **Ben Grauer** interviews guests attending the opening of the Rose Bake Shop: **Dorothy Kilgallen**, New York columnist; **Henry Morgan**, radio comedian; **Candy Jones**, famous Conover model, and **Doris Doe**, opera singer. The pie that went cross-country via relay was scheduled to reach New York in time to be heaved at the proprietor of the new bake shop. Ralph Edwards reports the pie was last seen in Omaha, Nebraska, from whence a man headed for Massachusetts had undertaken transportation of the pie. **E.J. Cristoff** of Cedar Rapids, Iowa, passed the pie on to the gentleman headed for Massachusetts.

Episode #722, Broadcast of March 26, 1949

Stunts: Send Key, Guess Governor, Cross Country Pie Payoff, and Fortune Teller's Son

Broadcast from the Builders' Show at the Minneapolis Municipal Auditorium in Minneapolis, Minnesota, with commercials transcribed and played from Chicago. Special guest is **Luther W. Youngdahl**, Governor of Minnesota, on behalf of the current drive for help in funds needed for care for the mentality ill throughout the country and especially in the state of Minnesota. Governor Youngdahl has recently declared a state-wide concentration on proper care for the mentally-ill.

Special stunts included the flying of **Phil Kruzel**, of the Air Lift in Germany, home for a furlough with his mother. Another stunt involved contestant **Buddy Barnick**, sewing machine dealer and repair man, who was given a letter to mail, with a key included. The key will open the leg iron that is locked on Barnick. Unknown to the contestant, listeners were asked to mail all kinds of keys to him during the week because he had to wait for a letter with the key to unlock his shackles! Buddy Barnick's address provided on the air: 863 Marshall Street, St. Paul, Minnesota.

Three minutes of the broadcast included a remote broadcast from the Rose Bake

Shop in Forest Hills, Long Island, where **Ed Herlihy**, announcer in New York and emcee, interviews **Jack Ross**, proprietor of the Rose Bake Shop, who gets the pie tonight. **Danny Scafuto** of Brooklyn, New York, arrived with the pie after bringing it 900 miles after it was relayed to him in Chicago. He threw the pie into Ross' face, according to instructions, with regard to the plans for proper "launching" of Ross and his new bakery venture. Ross received a television set as a special gift. The man who delivered the pie, in addition to his ten cents per mile transportation pay, received a $50 U.S. Security Bond.

Announcement is made during the broadcast that **Joe Greb**, the contestant waiting for the hen to lay an egg, is in the Hollywood studios. If the hen lays an egg during the broadcast, a bell will ring in the Minnesota studio. The bell did not ring.

This broadcast marks the ninth anniversary of the radio program and **Governor Youngdahl** added congratulations to the many others being extended Ralph Edwards and crew.

Ralph Edwards performed daily at the Builder's Show, 3:30 and 9:30 p.m., except for the evenings of March 26 and April 2, where there was no 9:30 p.m. shows. Instead, the program was heard nationally from KSTP, carried over 150 NBC stations at 7:30 p.m.

On Monday, March 28, there was "Ralph Edwards Day" at the Builders' Show, in honor of the humanitarian who raised more money for charity, research and healing than any other one person. Anyone whose name was Edwards was granted free admission to the Builders Show.

Episode #723, Broadcast of April 2, 1949
Stunts: Milk Container, Milk Cut-In, Re-Tell Joke, Send Key No. 2, and Chamber of Commerce

Broadcast from the Builders' Show at the Minneapolis Municipal Auditorium in Minneapolis, Minnesota, with commercials transcribed and played from Chicago. Ralph Edwards announces that the hen contest continues. The money grows each week, now $200 if the hen lays an egg during the broadcast, and an additional $100 for every additional week. If the hen lays an egg, a bell will be sounded from Minneapolis so radio listeners will know.

Jack Robinson, president of the Minneapolis Chamber of Commerce, was a contestant whose "consequence" was to telephone a phone number that belongs to the president of the rival St. Paul Junior Chamber of Commerce. Jack Robinson tells of the Minneapolis Junior Chamber of Commerce projects, especially the annual children's picnic.

Feature stunts included milking a dairy cow named Susan, by a Minneapolis farmer, and a follow-up with **Buddy Barnick**, who reports getting an estimated 35,000 keys mailed to him to open his leg irons, and he succeeded. Keys were mailed from Canada and Alaska. Edwards tells the contestant that one of the 35,000 keys is the key to a new car. If he finds the key by next week's broadcast, the car is his.

Episode #724, Broadcast of April 9, 1949
Stunts: Soak Feet, Three Children, Send Key No. 3, and Tug O' War Shower
Broadcast from Hollywood, with a cut-in from KSTP in Minneapolis. Contestant **Buddy Barnick** reports that he found the key to his new car among the pile of keys. The words "free car" were spelled backward on the tag attached to the key. During the coming week Barnick will receive a parking lot ticket so he may know where his new car is parked. Address and details to be provided on the ticket. Barnick promised to be back on the show next week to tell where he found his car. Back in Hollywood, when Barnick cannot hear the broadcast, listeners were instructed to send all kinds of parking lot tickets: Buddy Barnick, 863 Marshall Street, St. Paul, Minnesota.

The terms of the hen laying contest have changed. **Joe Greb** is given the opportunity to choose a day and a half-hour next week on which he thinks the hen will lay an egg. If he succeeds, he will win $1,000. Greb chooses Wednesday the 13th, his birthday, from 3:30 to 4:00 p.m.

Feature stunt involved reuniting a sister and her two brothers who were orphaned and separated 40 years ago – brought together through research on the part of the program crew. The three did not know about their relationship until they unfolded the "answer to the mystery" in a little play in which they took part in the roles as "themselves."

Episode #725, Broadcast of April 16, 1949
Stunts: Remove Dinner Table, Easter Bonnets, Send Key No. 4, Drum Lesson B.U., and $1,000 Names

A contestant named McCullough takes part in a stunt in which he selects the best-looking Easter hat. The only hats he sees is one worn by a donkey, another by a goat, and the middle hat by McCollough's own daughter, **Betty Jane Hussin**, who was flown in with her 2½ month old son, **Danny Hussin**, from Green Bay, Wisconsin, to surprise her father at Easter!

Special guest is **Tommy Bartlett** of the radio program, *Welcome, Travelers*, who surprised even Ralph Edwards by appearing at the broadcast. Bartlett said he met the Hussins on the plane flight to Hollywood. Another guest in Hollywood studio was **Dick Shanahan**, musician and instructor in playing drums, who agreed to teach drums to a lady contestant in two lessons. (**Mary Dixon**, the contestant, in turn agreed to teach what she learned to contestant "Jim Cooper," who would appear with her to play the drums next week.)*

Program included a cut-in from the home of **Mr. and Mrs. Douglas Legg**, 1157 Bronson Street, Hollywood, where the Leggs were entertaining prominent guests. Three men from the broadcast were sent over to pretend they were from the Finance Company and came to remove the dining room furniture while a dinner was in progress.

From the Dreske Service and Parking Station in Milwaukee, Wisconsin, two-way setup through WTMJ, for contestant **Buddy Barnick**, who spent the week trying to locate the parking lot where a new Nash car awaits him. Barnick received over 7,000 parking lot tickets in the mail, and finally traced one to a "Key" city – Milwaukee – to the Dreske Service and Parking Station. The building was locked with a sign on the door, "Gone Fishing. Key at 4187 Dalton Ave., Los Angeles." Buddy Barnick will report next week from Los Angeles.

Joe Greb admits that the hen did not lay between the hour of 3:30 and 4 p.m. last Wednesday. He receives a chance to name another day for the coming week when he may win $1,000… if the hen lays during that time. The contestant selects Monday from 4:00 to 4:30 p.m.

Episode #726, Broadcast of April 23, 1949

Stunts: Sealed Lips Seltzer, Husband Recording Disguise, Drum Lesson Payoff, Send Key No. 5, and Torn Laundry B.U.

* Jim Cooper is an alias for famous drummer Gene Krupa.

Contestant **Joe Greb** is back on the program to admit that the hen did not lay the egg on the day he expected her to. Greb receives another chance by choosing a day and hour in the coming week: he again selects Monday from 4:00 to 4:30 p.m., to win the $1,000.

Celebrity guest is **Gene Krupa**, drummer and orchestra leader, who appeared under the alias of "Jim Cooper" with contestant **Mary Dixon**, who spent the week "teaching Jim Cooper to play the drums."

From 4187 Dalton Street, Los Angeles, in the heart of Chinatown, **Buddy Barnick** is on the trail of a free Nash car that he is supposed to get when he finds the car that fits his key. Radio listeners heard **Steven Koe**, a Chinaman who lives at the address, tells Barnick that he must visit "Uncle Charlie" in Canton, China. Charlie made the key to the building where the car is locked!

Dick Powell made a quick appearance to pitch his new *Richard Diamond* program.

Episode #727, Broadcast of April 30, 1949

Stunts: Multiple Consey, Send Key No. 6, Torn Laundry Payoff, and Ralph Edwards Pie

Program is broadcast live from Hollywood, with a recorded portion concerning one contestant and her experience earlier in the week with the man who delivered her laundry. In the Hollywood studios, **Joe Greb** admits that the hen, now named Ermintrude, did not lay an egg during the predicted and time. He chooses another day and time for the $1,000 prize.

Contestant **Bob Stewart** is the winner of a contest conducted by the Los Angeles *Daily News* in which he wrote a letter concerning his "Secret Ambition" – his ambition was to throw a pie into the face of Ralph Edwards. Tonight, Stewart gets the pie and the privilege of tossing it into the face of another contestant bearing the name of Ralph Edwards – this man hails from Temple City, California.

Mrs. Madge Hutchinson was invited back to the program after having appeared on the program last week just at the time that the show had to go off the air. She hears a recorded spot made at the Hutchinson home during the week when **Phil Davis**, one of the "Field Men" for the *Truth or Consequences* program, posed as a laundryman returning Mrs. Hutchinson's laundry – torn in shreds and presented to her. Boy does she complain! Today she is presented with her original laundry, beautifully done.

Two-way set-up with Maurice's Jewelry Store, across the street, where contestant **Mary Wells** receives a surprise appearance from her parents who live in New Mexico. **Jerry Lawrence**, announcer, handles the pick-up from the Jewelry store. Contestant is **H.A. Towery** of Muleshoe, Texas, posing as a detective for this stunt.

Two-way set-up from KZRH, Manila, Philippine Islands, for contestant **Buddy Barnick**, who is on his way to Canton, China. Edwards informs him that he was to go to Canton, Ohio, *not* China! Barnick now has to start back to the States in order to report on next week's broadcast.

Episode #728, Broadcast of May 7, 1949
Stunts: Audience Hot Seat, Vacuum Cleaner Ralph, Braille Drama, Send Key No. 7, and Mother Bouquet

Ralph Edwards visited contestant **Mrs. John Mihld** during the week when he represented himself as a salesman of vacuum cleaners. Wearing toupee, eyeglasses and make-up, Edwards dumped dirt and sawdust all over her living room rug and proceeded to "demonstrate" his vacuum cleaner – but the cleaner would not work and the "salesman" walked out leaving the grime and sawdust. Mrs. Mihld's reaction, all that is not "censored," is played back via recording. In the live studio portion of the program, Mrs. Mihld solves a trick word puzzle and receives a prize.

Actor **John Wayne** takes part in a dramatic sketch with blind contestant **Miss Norma Sharrett**, student at the School for the Blind in Nebraska City. She reads her lines in Braille. She has never met a real movie star in person and Wayne is an answer to one of her wishes to meet one. For her "consequence," she will be sent to the Guiding Eye School conducted by International Guiding Eyes, Inc., for the purpose of training blind people in handling Guiding Eye dogs. When she completes her four weeks' free training, *Truth or Consequences* will present her with her own Guiding Eye Dog.

From Canton, Ohio, a two-way set-up to walk with contestant **Buddy Barnick** and "Uncle Charley Kee" at the Sue Wing Restaurant, 133 Sixth Street, Canton, Ohio. **Charley Kee** explains that the door to Dreske Service and Parking Station in Milwaukee does not require a key to open it. Buddy Barnick is instructed to return at once to Milwaukee to open that lock and get his new Nash car.

Episode #729, Broadcast of May 14, 1949

Stunts: Old Country Relative, Send Key No. 8, and Kilts Water Tank Payoff

Courtesy of radio station WTMK in Milwaukee, a pick-up with **Buddy Barnick** who opens the door to the service station and finds a new Nash – only it is a 1918 model. A note attached to the car instructs Buddy to drive the car to Kenosha, Wisconsin, where he can trade it in for a brand new 1949 Nash. The note is signed by **George W. Mason**, president of the Nash Motor Company.

In the Hollywood studio, contestant **Joe Greb** gets frustrated waiting for the hen to lay another egg. Ten contestants in ten different cities will sit under "local hens" during the time specified by Greb during this coming week. If any one of the ten hens lay during this time, Joe Greb gets his $1,000 and another $1,000 is divided among the ten participants across the nation. Joe Greb specifies a two-hour time period from 11 a.m. to 1 p.m., Thursday, May 19, for the hens to lay. The cities in which the contestants will appear seated in public places such as local store windows, etc., are: Denver, Colorado; Seattle, Washington; Omaha, Nebraska; Salt Lake City, Utah; Indianapolis, Indiana; Buffalo, New York; Boston, Massachusetts; Birmingham, Alabama; New Orleans, Louisiana; and Baltimore, Maryland. Joe Greb is made an honorary member of the National Poultry and Egg Club.

Anna Merrill, of German decent, is told to interview a newly-arrived German girl, unaware at first that she is **Katie Gesler** of Youngstown, Ohio, her niece whom she has not seen in years.

Contestant **Mrs. G.H. Clark** participates in a parade with 20 members of Scottish Post 81, American Legion in Los Angeles. The men are dressed in full Scottish regalia, bagpipes and all.

Episode #730, Broadcast of May 21, 1949

Stunts: Camel Hair Coat, Send Key No. 9, Own Kids Mind Reader, and $5,000 Phone Call

Earlier in the week, movie actress **Ann Blyth**, during an appearance before a large theater audience, selected a number at random from a telephone directory. During this broadcast, Ralph Edwards phones this number and asks the person who answers the telephone to try to answer a question for $5,000 cash. Tonight's question: "Whose face is pictured on a $1,000 bill?" The contestant, **Mr. A.F. Tolley** of Parson, Tennessee, does not know the answer. (Grover Cleveland was the correct answer.) The contestant received a 72-piece Fine

Arts Sterling Silver set of flatware for his cooperation. **(Fred L. Sale**, Assistant Advertising Manager of the Coca-Cola Bottling Company of Los Angeles, attended the broadcast as a member of the audience, along with his brother and his brother's family. Several members of the audience were drawn from a bowl and Sale's niece was among the people who were privileged to have their photo taken with Ann Blyth.)

Several of the studio questions today dealt with the Opportunity Bond Drive, tied in to plug the current drive for sale of U.S. Savings Bonds. Edwards quotes the slogan for the Bond Drive: "Out More Opportunity in Your Future."

One contestant thinks she is arranging to deliver a "camel's hair coat" to an unknown person, only to discover a live camel on stage. She agreed to deliver the camel to her husband at her own home. Another stunt involves contestant name Mr. Wakefield, a businessman with "The Three Mysterious, Mind-Reading Sisters," who turn out to be his own children – three boys dressed as little girls.

With a pick-up from Kenosha, Wisconsin, **Buddy Barnick** sees his new Nash car but the automobile has no key. Meanwhile, he is supplied with a French chauffeur who will drive him about for the next week while he awaits his own car key. The chauffeur, Gaston Etienne, is a French cab driver who is vacationing in the U.S. and speaks only French. Barnick is told that the key will be mailed to him and back in the Hollywood studios, Ralph Edwards again asks listeners to mail keys to Buddy Barnick, 863 Marshall Street, St. Paul, Minnesota. Edwards laughs, "Aren't we maniacal?"

Program ends before the announcement about the outcome of last week's egg-laying contest is made. **Joe Greb**, the contestant who has been waiting for a hen to lay an egg at a specified time, is not on the broadcast. Edwards announces that results of the egg-laying will be given next week.

Episode #731, Broadcast of May 28, 1949

Stunts: Obey Husband Microphone, Four Mask Men B.U., Send Key Payoff, and Pie or Five Dollars

From Minnesota, **Buddy Barnick** reports that he received 12,000 keys through the mail during the week and that the 4,837th key was the one to the new Nash which is now in his possession. Barnick says he is sending the 12,000 keys he received to Ralph Edwards by mail, one key every hour for as long as they last! Edwards informs Barnick that he is being sent a $500 U.S. Opportunity Bond in addition to his new Nash, for being such a good sport. This is the final time the radio listeners hear from Buddy Barnick.

From the Hollywood studio, **Joe Greb** explains that three hens laid eggs at the schedule time: in Seattle (11:01 a.m., Thursday, Pacific Standard Time), in Denver (12:22 p.m., Thursday, Mountain Standard Time), and Omaha, Nebraska (Thursday, 11:01 am, Central Standard Time). The ten men in the ten cities each receive $100 while Greb gets his promised $1,000, plus a radio-phonograph combination and a diamond ring for his wife, and keeps Ermintrude for a pet! This is the last time the radio listeners hear from Joe Greb.

Four masked men are given envelopes, including expense money, and destination for a "visit" they are to make during the week. If they find one another by next week's broadcast, every one of the four men will receive a $100 Mail Order Certificate from Spiegel's Mail Order Stores.

Ralph Edwards makes an important announcement regarding a way in which non-profit charity organization, churches, clubs, etc., may make money for their organizations simply by saving wrappers from DUZ, Ivory Flakes, and Camay Soap. Redeemable at cash value with DUZ and Ivory Flakes each bringing one cent per top and the Camay wrappers one-half cent each. Also, $21,000 additional in prizes for such organizations – "see your local dealers for complete information."

Episode #732, Broadcast of June 4, 1949
Stunts: Observe Model, Four Mask Men Payoff, and Forrest Warren
A transcribed portion from San Diego, California, in the living room of the home of **Forrest Warren**, columnist for the San Diego *Journal*, who wrote in his column of May 17, "I have cancer and I am going to die of it…" The courage of this man who, knowing his fatal illness, continues to write his column and to do all the good things he has been doing all his life – such as collecting funds for children's hospitals, for the Damon Runyon Cancer Fund, for local Cancer Funds long before he knew that he would be a victim of the disease, getting readers interested in underprivileged children, helping and befriending the lonesome men, women and children about whom he happened to hear, getting wheel chairs for local patients and hospitals, etc.

This producers of the program arranged for Warren to realize his dearest wishes: (1) to hear his son, **Bailey Warren**, who as a boy sang for John Philip Sousa, sing again; (2) to see his three dear friends – his first boss, **Fred W. Arnold**, a newspaperman; **Felix Saunders**; and **Walter Layne**, a band-playing friend in the days when Warren thought he might be a musician.

Mrs. Bailey Warren, appearing with her husband, tells how the two turned to prayer when they first realized Warren had cancer and of how they determined to work their "Cross" into help for others through courage and actual work to stop the onslaughts of cancer and other diseases. The 72-year-old columnist is told that the program was arranging for a Forrest Warren Memorial window to be put into the San Diego Methodist Church to remind others of the good one man can do if he wills it. Then, as a special tribute to Forrest Warren, listeners are asked to mail contributions of any amount to: Forrest Warren, San Diego, California. All of the local contributions postmarked San Diego will be used in the San Diego Cancer Clinic; the other contributions will be forwarded to the Damon Runyon Cancer Fund in New York.

Episode #733, Broadcast of June 11, 1949

Stunts: Love Count, Steam Bath, Hospitable Wife, Scavenger Hunt B.U., and Star Masquerade

Transcribed today with insert of taped spot from the Terry Hunt Health System, the Steam Room for Women, for a trick stunt in which a male contestant is sent to the steam room without knowing where he is going.

Report today on the Forrest Warren Cancer contributions – up to yesterday, over $15,000 was received and numerous letters in the hundreds remained to be counted with more pouring in every hour. Listeners were encouraged to continue sending their contributions.

Celebrity guests include actors **Don DeFore** and **Kay Christopher**. Contestant **Mrs. Dell Stabel** is provided a recording machine with all equipment necessary to make recordings which she must play back on next week's broadcast. Her recording assignments are:

1. **Dick Powell** making love to contestant.
2. The head of CBS praising NBC.
3. Digger O'Dell (played by actor **John Brown**) singing "Happy Days Are Here Again."

4. Record of contestant spanking **Red Skelton** during rehearsal of the "Mean Widdle Kid" portion of his radio program.
5. Contestant dressed in a sarong seeking out **Dorothy Lamour** and telling her, "I am the new Sarong Girl."

Episode #734, Broadcast of June 18, 1949
Stunts: Shower, Scavenger Hunt Payoff, Wife Soldier Telephone, and Blindfold Feel Beau

Broadcast features a reunion between serviceman **Wayne Johnstone**, and his wife, and the one-year-old son whom he has not seen since the child was a few weeks old. Johnstone surprises his wife and son by being flown home for a furlough arranged through the program with accommodations and entertainment for the family at the expense of the sponsor.

Follow-up of the woman contestant who was sent out last week to secure recordings of five important people. Radio listeners hear the following recordings: **Dorothy Lamour, John Brown, Dick Powell, Red Skelton**, and the head of CBS. Contestant found a way to accomplish his task by contacting the head of the California Butcher Supply Company instead of the Columbia Broadcasting Company!

Engaged couple stunt with a woman named **Phyllis Byrnes**, who tells about her wedding shower. Every time she mentions the word "shower," her fiancé, **Bill Laffin**, is "showered" with cold water! The couple receive household gifts including Sterling Silver for being "good sports."

Episode #735, Broadcast of June 25, 1949
Stunts: Kiss Model, Impossible Pictures, Grandfather's Clock, Describe Parachute Jump, and Ralph's Seasonal Goodbye

Celebrity guest is **William Cameron Mezies**, producer and director of Hollywood movies, appears to give a "voice and acting test" to a contestant. She passes the test and will be seen with her face on the body of a kangaroo in an animated movie short.

From Paul Mantz Air Services, Lockheed Air Terminal, Hangar Number One, contestant **Edith Sparks** speaks from an airplane in which **Charles Lyon**, NBC announcer and actor, pretends to be "Jack Charles, parachute jumper." Mrs. Sparks thinks that she is in the air and describes her "first plane trip."

In actuality, sound effects plus projected scenery from a movie made from an airplane give her the illusion of flying.

From a "Kissing Booth" on the corner of Hollywood and Vine, a contestant named **Mr. Summons** of Fairfield, Iowa, has lined up 200 people to kiss a girl in a stunt for the Milk Drive. The "girl" turns out to be Minnie, a cow. Contestant receives 50 cents for each of the 200 people who kiss the cow.

Episode #736, Broadcast of August 27, 1949

Stunts: French Poodle, Bathyscope, and Television Frame

Start of The Laughing Boy contest when a person chosen at random is telephoned by "The Laughing Boy" who carries on a zany conversation with clues to his identity. The contestant telephoned is also asked for permission to record the conversation. Phone call is placed during the week and the contestant is contacted by phone during the broadcast and is told to listen to their conversation so that they may identify the voice and receive $2,500. If they do not guess correctly, they receive a 72-piece set of Sterling Silver. The prize remains $2,500 and is not cumulative.

Contestant **Gerald Shumer** is assigned the consequence of walking a French Poodle around the block for one hour every night for the coming week. The French Poodle is still in Paris, France, so the program gives the contestant an all-expenses-paid trip to France with expenses paid while taking care of "Fifi, the Poodle." Contestant will report from Paris on a future broadcast.

Celebrity guest is actress **Shelley Winters**, who appears first on a television screen on the studio stage and later in person.

Program includes outside pick-ups from the corner of Sunset and Vine in Hollywood. **Otis Barton**, scientist for the Hancock Foundation who recently established a depth of 4,500 feet under-seas in a special "Bathyscope," through which he viewed sea plants and animal life and made sketches of these underwater scenes. Barton appears in connection with contestant **Margaret Harvey** who is stationed inside a "Bathyscope" at Hollywood and Vine, proving that she can be 7,000 feet under water. A plane circling over Sunset and Vine, 7,000 feet in the air, features Mrs. Harvey's husband who talks to Ralph Edwards and says he is holding a cup of water over his wife. **Jerry Lawrence** is the on-the-spot reporter.

Episode #737, Broadcast of September 3, 1949

Stunts: Elephant Camel, Explain Cricket, and French Poodle Mention

For the second week in a row, The Laughing Boy is not identified. The contestant thought The Laughing Boy was **W.C. Fields**. (This is funny because Fields passed away three years prior.) Ralph Edwards teases the listeners that The Laughing Boy is a familiar American and that "many of us have heard his voice and have seen his face."

Cut-in for a two-way set-up on Hollywood Boulevard, near NBC. Contestant who thinks his wife is in Minnesota, unaware she has been flown to Hollywood. The husband is seated atop a camel surrounded by dancing girls dressed in Harem costumes (from a Hollywood dramatic and dancing studio). The wife rides around the corner seated atop Jumbo, an elephant. The couple get prizes and free entertainment plus the plane trip from and to Minnesota. She will be flown back to complete her vacation.

Broadcast of September 10, 1949

Stunts: Beep Running Gag, Glass Bottom Boat, French Poodle Payoff, and Polio Remote

Gerald Schumer, the contestant who was sent to Paris, tells about the way he sought the French Poodle named Fifi. According to Schumer, all the Paris girls seemed to answer to the name "Fifi." Schumer brings back the dog, "Fifi," and presents her to Ralph Edwards. Fifi turned out to be a 200-pound St. Bernard! Schumer, in addition to his Paris trip, receives $200.

Pick-up from the glass bottom boat in the Pacific, for contestant **Dorothea Duncan**, who tries to describe the marine scenes she views through the glass. What she does not know is that she is viewing a moving picture film projection made at the Hal Roach Studios, with Dorothea's son, daughter, cousin and husband dressed in fish costumes. She sees the "strange fish" but recognizes the faces of her family. The "fish" talk to the contestant and we hear their voices!

Pick-up from a New York City hospital room of polio victim **Sidney Moody** of Plainfield, New Jersey, whose life was saved when an iron lung and other necessary treatment apparatus was flown to him when he was struck by infantile paralysis while returning from Europe. Moody makes an appeal on behalf of the National Foundation for Infantile Paralysis. If funds are not supplemented, the operating money for the foundation will be exhausted within two weeks. Moody stresses the way in which polio strikes suddenly with no choice of man or woman, rich or poor, at home or abroad.

The Laughing Boy was incorrectly identified as **Charles Ruggles**.

Episode #738, Broadcast of September 17, 1949
Stunts: Movie Premiere, Bull Fiddle, and Pie Face Lyrics
The Laughing Boy conversation concerns a recipe for Swivel Meat Leaf. **Mr. and Mrs. J. Halett** of Alburg, Vermont, are telephoned by The Laughing Boy and they fail to identify the mystery voice. (Their guess was **George Rector**.)

Two-way set-up between the New York studio where the program originates, and the entrance to the El Patio Theater on Hollywood Boulevard, where celebrity guest is **Erskine Johnson**, Hollywood columnist, who interviews five contestants who were sent to the theater from the quiz program. Earlier in the day, bleachers were set up across the street from the theater and an announcement was posted of the premiere of "Stung at 8:30." People immediately crowded around and sat in the bleachers waiting to see the movie stars arrive for the "premiere." Erskine Johnson interviews the contestants just as if they were movie stars – complete with red plush carpet as if it was an authentic premiere. The people who gathered to see the celebrities were invited into the El Patio to see the picture showing there.

"I introduced a plumber, a printer, two housewives and a character in the glare of searchlights and amidst cheers from crowded grandstands at a Hollywood Boulevard premiere, broadcast coast-to-coast. It was Ralph Edwards' idea. So who cared if everyone got stung at 8:30? It was fun," wrote Johnson in his column. "'Stung at 8:30' was the name of the movie that Ralph, on his *Truth or Consequences* show, announced was being premiered at a Hollywood Boulevard theater. There were lights, bleachers, a red carpet, police guards, limousines and even a big poster reading: 'Big Premiere Tonight. Stars, lights, celebrities!' Ralph didn't miss anything except the stars. The 'stars' were his contestants – printer **Harry Schuster**, plumber **Albert Israel**, housewives **Theresa Vecchia** and **Ingrid Mott**. The wonderful character was **Mabel Hall**, who talked faster than Ralph can get ideas. The 'stars' arrived in limousines. The mob in the grandstands cheered and gawked in a confused sort of way. I introduced the 'celebrities.' Then Ralph came in, confessed the hoax and invited everyone in to see a revival of *The Bachelor and the Bobby Soxer*."

Episode #739, Broadcast of September 24, 1949

Stunts: Silly Punishment, Ten Men to Dinner, English Channel Swim B.U., and Grand Rapids Tease

The Laughing Boy phone call was to a resident of Chico, California, who mistakenly thought the mystery voice is **George Mardikian**, the famed restauranteur. The Laughing Boy says he is a plumber who wants to repair the leaking sink.

Contestant **Burt Kennedy** of Hollywood is selected as the trainer for "Otto the Great," better known as "Pierre Cilion," to swim the English Channel. We do not see "Otto the Great" but contestant is sent backstage to consult with Otto, through an interpreter, then returns to report that he and Otto will make a go at it. Edwards says Otto will make trial swims in the U.S. during the next few weeks and then will leave with his trainer, Burt Kennedy, via TWA for Calais, France. The contestant will get $1 per minute for every 60 seconds Otto the Great beats the Channel swimming record-time.

Episode #740, Broadcast of October 1, 1949

Stunts: Skunk Hitchhike, Lights Out Pie, English Channel Swim, and Baby Judging Contest

Broadcast from Grand Rapids Stadium in Grand Rapids, Michigan, celebrating the 25th anniversary of radio station WOOD. The Laughing Boy phone conversation leads the caller to incorrectly identify him as **Robert Lewis**.

A contestant is sent out to hitchhike a ride and bring back his "driver." The contestant has to hitchhike with a pet skunk on a leash.

In another stunt, **Mrs. Howe Taylor** of Grand Rapids is the contestant who judges a baby contest. In the contest are Grand Rapids babies and their mothers, plus Mrs. Taylor's own grown son, **Maurice Taylor**, who is dressed as a baby and wheeled in a baby carriage by his father, disguised as a woman. Also in the contest is Mrs. Taylor's little granddaughter, whom she has never seen until now.

A pick-up from New York City where contestant **Burt Kennedy**, who agreed to act as a trainer for Pierre Cilion, also known as "Otto the Great," for Pierre's attempt to swim the English Channel. Kennedy and Pierre are ready to board a TWA to fly to France where they will start the Channel Swim from Calais. Kennedy tells of practice swims made by Pierre in the Missouri River, and again at Jones Beach, New York. For every minute cut from the existing record of about 11 hours, the record set thus far for Channel swimmers, Kennedy will receive $1 per minute.

Episode #742, Broadcast of October 8, 1949
Stunts: Field Glasses Husband, Choir Shower, Channel Swim, and Call Home Town

Broadcast originates from the Kansas City Municipal Auditorium in Kansas City, Missouri. The feature stunt was to have every inhabitant of the small town of Sibley, Missouri (150 inhabitants transported by Greyhound Bus) on the stage to surprise a contestant from their hometown. The contestant sings "Billy Boy" and is told she will get $250 if she can get anyone in Sibley to answer the telephone and say they heard the contestant sing on the program. The entire town will be treated to a special picnic lunch on their way home after the broadcast.

The Laughing Boy pretends to be a collector of pinecones. The contestant incorrectly identifies the mysterious voice as **Chic Johnson** of the Olsen and Johnson comedy team.

There was an attempt to contact **Burt Kennedy** in Calais, France, but the pick-up from Calais failed to come through. **Allen Adair**, a British sports announcer, was waiting in Calais to report.

Episode #743, Broadcast of October 15, 1949
Stunts: T or C Pie Time, Channel Swim, Dream Stars, and Eskimo Date

The Laughing Boy pretends to be a maker of wigs and a designer of coiffures. The contestant does not answer her telephone although the call is attempted throughout the broadcast. Thus, she forfeits her privilege of trying to identify The Laughing Boy.

Celebrity guests heard first by recordings and then in person are **Robert Young**, **Victor Mature** and **David Niven**, who take part in a "dream sequence" staged for a female contestant who was told to close her eyes and dream while the studio is darkened. She hears the voices of the dream men of the movies and when the lights come on she meets the actors in person.

Burt Kennedy, the contestant who coached the sea lion Pierre Cilion, also known as "Otto the Great," to swim the English Channel, returns to the program. Kennedy received $361, $1 per minute for every minute which the swimmer beat the record Channel swimming time. The fastest time for a human swimmer was made by Czechoslovakian **Vencelas Spacek**, who made the 19-mile Channel crossing in 10 hours and 45 minutes in 1926. Pierre Cilion made the entire swim in five hours and four minutes.

Contestant **Morton Taylor** of Brooklyn, New York, agrees to telephone an unknown girl in an attempt to win $200 if she agrees to go on a date next Saturday evening. He does get the date but his telephone call is to an Americanized Eskimo girl in Nome, Alaska. The contestant will be sent to Alaska to keep his date.

Episode #744, Broadcast of October 22, 1949

Stunts: Own Voice Relative, George Jessel, and Fish Bridge B.U.

Milton Berle is correctly identified as The Laughing Boy by **Mrs. Lincoln Kilbourne** of 3647 14th Street, Milwaukee. Berle's "voluntary services" to solicit funds for the Cancer Drive last year were mentioned as Ralph Edwards thanked the comedian for cooperating in the weekly Laughing Boy telephone calls and recordings.

Broadcast includes a salute to the United Nation's fourth anniversary of the Signing of the U.N. Charter. Celebrity guest is **George Jessel**, who appears on the broadcast with his young daughter, **Jerilyn Jessel**.

Contestants **Frank Kubitschek** and **Pat Moran** agree to fish with a pole and line from the Golden Gate Bridge in San Francisco, and the George Washington Bridge in New York, respectively, until one of them catches a fish. A $500 U.S. Security Bond would be awarded to the one who catches a fish first. A follow-up will be reported next week.

Episode #745, Broadcast of October 29, 1949

Stunts: Fish Bridge No. 1, English Lesson Love, Eskimo Date Payoff, and Model Pilot

Celebrity guests are actor **John Payne** and **Capt. L.M. Williams** of Trans-World Airlines, a senior pilot for the TWA Constellations. Capt. Williams takes part in a consequence with a 13-year-old boy whose hobby is making model planes. The boy will get a Christmas flight from Hollywood to Chicago, riding as copilot, with Capt. Williams on a Constellation. The boy's mother will accompany him on the special trip. This program arranged for special entertainment and all-expenses-paid for the young traveler and his mother.

Brooklyn boy **Morton Taylor**, who spent last week in Nome, Alaska, returns to the program with the Eskimo girl with whom he had a date. The two sing, "Baby, It's Cold Outside."

An announcement was made just before broadcast ended that **Frank Kubitschek**, from the Golden Gate Bridge, caught a fish and would get the $500 U.S. Security Bond. The New York fisherman, **Pat Moran**, is told to fish "from the bank" next week and to keep fishing until he makes a catch when he, too, will get a $500 U.S. Security Bond. The "Bank" from which he will fish is the Bowery Savings Bank at 34th Street and Seventh Avenue in New York City.

Episode #746, Broadcast of November 5, 1949
Stunts: Fish Bridge No. 2, Pretend Mother-in-Law, and Bus Welcome

Broadcast originates from Hollywood, with pick-up from the Bowery Savings Bank, 34th Street and Seventh Avenue, in New York City, where fisherman **Pat Moran** is fishing from the roof of the savings bank with his line leading down four stories below into a tub full of guppies. Moran reports that he simply cannot get a fish and is instructed to fly to Hollywood where he will spend the next week "fly-fishing" – fishing with a troll line while being flown at low altitude across the Pacific Ocean.

From the corner of Hollywood and Vine, Los Angeles, a female contestant acts as Chairman of the Welcoming Committee to greet the first woman who gets off the Pacific Electric Sunset Bus at the bus stop. **Charles Lyon**, actor and announcer, describes the "welcome." **Bernice Oldstein** is the first woman to get off the bus.

The Glass Goblet stunt begins on this broadcast, in which contestants get a chance to try to break a specially-made Corning Glass Goblet that is designed to break when a certain unknown tune is sung. The prize starts at $500 and increases an additional $500 each additional week the goblet remains unbroken. Contestant **Ted Gurr** is the first to attempt to break the glass. The Glass Goblet stunt is tied in with plugs for the movie, *Everybody Does It*, in which **Paul Douglas** shatters a mirror by the notes he hits while singing in the shower.

Episode #747, Broadcast of November 12, 1949
Stunts: Waitress Customer Pie, Bull Whip, Stars Mothers, and Fish Bridge No. 3
Broadcast originates from Hollywood with a pick-up from Coffee Dan's food-

and-coffee bar on Vine Street, just across the street from NBC. A contestant goes there and gets a pie in the face from a waitress.

Celebrity guests include **Dave Kashner**, bullwhip cracker of the movies and stage; and members of the Movie Stars Mothers Club. Two ladies are presented with equipment for their club room. Among the women present are the mothers of **Joan Crawford, Tom Brown, Lou Costello, Robert Page, Helen Mack, Donald O'Connor, Peggy Singleton, Dorothy Lamour, Marguerite Church, Cesar Romero, Pat O'Brien, Edmund MacDonald, Gary Cooper** and **Fred MacMurray**.

A report from **Pat Moran**, the contestant who is trying to "fly fish" from a chartered airplane flying above the Pacific, we find out that he has still not caught a fish. Edwards reports that Moran will be on the studio stage next week and fish from a tank on stage.

Episode #748, Broadcast of November 19, 1949

Stunts: Fish Bridge Payoff, Groucho Marx Celebrity, and Re-enact Thanksgiving Scene

Celebrity guests are **Ronald Reagan** and actor **Ernest Van Diest** is on the program doing an impersonation of **Groucho Marx**.

Special Thanksgiving stunt involves Grandma and Grandpa Hubbard – their 10 children and 19 grandchildren are brought "home for Thanksgiving" to surprise the grandparents.

Pat Moran finally gets a fish while doing "deep-sea diving" in a huge water tank on stage. He receives a $500 U.S. Security Bond.

Episode #749, Broadcast of November 26, 1949

Stunts: Relay Pie, Find Soldier Son, Tight Rope Husband, and Swipe Shoes B.U.

Broadcast from the Cleveland Public Hall in Cleveland, Ohio. The Public Hall was considered the largest in the country, with 16,000 seats. **Barbara Edwards** attended the broadcast, the first time in years that she joined her husband on a business trip. With responsibilities of small children, she was unable to tour with him. Her parents, **Mr. and Mrs. C.N. Sheldon**, lived in Hudson, Ohio, a short distance away from Cleveland.

Special guests are "The Great Vino," a high-wire walking expert, and members of the track team from Baldwin Wallis College in Cleveland, Ohio. The coach is **Eddie Finnegan**. The track team takes part in a relay race both in and out of the studio.

Two male contestants agree to spend the coming week together in a Rhode Island hotel with the purpose of trying to steal the others' shoes while one sleeps. The contestants are from Cleveland: **Ralph Kinsey** and a man named Gus. The contestants get a plane trip to and from Providence, Rhode Island, with all expenses paid while in the state.

Organist Buddy Cole was heard speaking on the broadcast of November 19, 1949.

Episode #750, Broadcast of December 3, 1949

Stunts: Return Contestants, Dog Circus, Swipe Shoes Payoff, Deductions Pie, and Stork

Broadcast from the Rhode Island Auditorium in Providence, Rhode Island, with recorded commercials presented from New York City. Celebrity guest was **Tommy Bartlett**, emcee of the radio program, *Welcome, Travelers*. The animal stunt concerned Herbert, a stork from the zoo, who was also a "guest" on the program, and the "Caninas Choir," composed of 20 dogs that "sang" while the contestant led the "choir."

Contestants taking part in the stunts were **W. Ward Harvey**, a Rhode Island State Representative; **Peter King**, owner of the Boston Shoe Store in Providence, and **Edward Texera**, a landlord of contestant **Charlotte Atkins**, a newcomer to Providence. Mrs. Atkins' father-in-law, unknown to her, is also on stage.

In the "Steal the Shoes" contest started last week, Gus was the winner of $300 for taking off the shoes of his friend, **Ralph Kinsey**, while Kinsey slept.

Episode #751, Broadcast of December 10, 1949
Stunts: Claim Wallet, Sweet Adeliners Hot Seat, and Ventriloquist-Dummy
Broadcast from the Hollywood studio with three pick-ups from Sunset Boulevard, where contestant **Mrs. Opal Voll** was trying to give someone a wallet. In the studio, contestants were **Harry Royal**, a ventriloquist, with his dummy Nibby; and four members of "The Sweet Adeliners," a woman's barbershop quartette singing organization.

Episode #752, Broadcast of December 17, 1949
Stunts: Wife Gift Advisor, Speech Song Joke, Christmas Tree Hat, and Say Hello to Mother
Broadcast from the Hollywood studio with a pick-up from the Gift Counselor's Booth in the Broadway Department Store in Hollywood, where contestant **Bob Barts** was sent to ask the counselor for help in selecting a gift for his wife. The program presented him $50 to spend on the gift. The counselor was really his wife in disguise.

Fred L. Sale, Assistant Advertising Manager of the Coca-Cola Bottling Company in Los Angeles, was seated among the audience, having obtained four tickets for the December 17 broadcast.

Episode #753, Broadcast of December 24, 1949
In order to give complete program content to the Christmas celebration, The Glass Goblet stunt was not included on this broadcast. By transcription, recorded December 15, the program featured three guests, all one-time choir singers.

Don Sweiger, an ex-Pfc., now 26 years old, was once an active member of the Methodist Church Choir in Colome, South Dakota. He heard the choir sing again as transcribed at the Methodist Church in Colome, South Dakota. He also heard messages spoken by his brother, his uncle, members of the choir, etc.

Frank Szinski, age 20, was in the Hollywood studio to tell about the time he spent singing with the Boys Town Choir. He was a student at St. Benedicts and did some singing around Hollywood. By transcription, the Boys Town Choir from Boys Town, Nebraska, sang Christmas carols and various special friends of Frank's wish him "Merry Christmas." **Nicholas H. Wegner**, director of Boys Town, spoke with a Christmas message to Frank and all of the other boys who graduated from Boys Town and hopes they have gone forth to make a name for themselves in the world.

Melvin Vickland was also in the Hollywood studio, formally a baritone in the Plymouth Congregational Choir of Minneapolis. Melvin came to Hollywood and was successful in developing his singing career until, three years ago, he was stricken with polio. Since that time, he worked as a radio producer and announcer, performing his duties from a wheelchair and was now on crutches. His wife, **Jerry Vickland**, and their three children (all girls), appeared on the program with him. Melvin was presented with an Oldsmobile especially constructed so that he could drive it with ease, despite his crippled condition. The program sent a $500 check in his name to the hometown choir back in Minneapolis. The Plymouth Congregational Choir in Minneapolis performed Christmas carols via a transcription made at the Church.

Another special guest was **Mary A. Lyons** of 2520 W. Seventh Street, Los Angeles, now nicknamed the "Christmas Box Lady," her third Christmas visit to the program. In 1947, she was presented with a box labeled, "Do not open until Christmas, 1948." During the 1948 holiday broadcast, she opened the package and found inside another box labeled, "Do not open until Christmas, 1949." Inside this box she finds a 1948 calendar in which certain dates were circled in red. Ralph Edwards tells her the circled dates are part of a code, which she must decode in time to give her answer when she returned on the Christmas program of 1950.

Episode #754, Broadcast of December 31, 1949

Stunts: One More Seat, Rose Bowl Relative, Turkey Jury, and U.C. Football Team
Broadcast from the March Field Army Air Base near Riverside, California. Special guests include **Lynn (Pappy) Waldorf**, Coach of the University of California Rose Bowl Team, and the entire Rose Bowl Team. Various members of the

team talk about the coming game. Feature stunt concerned contestant **Wesley Swearinger** (student at the Ohio State University who was in California for the Rose Bowl game) who does not know that members of the Golden Bears and their coach are on the program.

Episode #755, Broadcast of January 7, 1950

Stunts: Phony Contestant, Star Car Husband, and Sleep Station B.U.

Celebrity guest is actor **Cesar Romero**. Pick-up from the Los Angeles home of contestant **Gustav Bloomquist**, who impersonates a radio quizmaster who is delivering the prize won by the housewife.

Contestants **Bill Corday** and **Virginia Newton**, volunteer to take part in a sleep experiment that will carry over into next week's broadcast. Corday will try to get $5,000 by being asleep in Union Station in Chicago. Newton (brought in by the Super Chief) will try the following week if he fails. They are not allowed to use sleeping pills, etc. The trip to Chicago and entertainment while there will be at the expense of the quiz program.

An announcement that The Glass Goblet contest (sometimes referred to as The Magic Goblet) will be open to listeners via telephone calls; the first call to be made on the broadcast of January 21, if the studio contestants have not broken the goblet by that time. A clue is provided in the form of a riddle: One for the Money, Two for the Sough, Skidoo Two, The Answer is No. Listeners are asked to tune in next week to find out how they may participate.

Episode #756, Broadcast of January 14, 1950

Stunts: Movie Set Reunion, Sleep Station Payoff, Song Lecture, and March of Dimes Parade Gargantua

From Union Station in Chicago, announcer Norman Barry is on the scene, along with a physician from the University of Chicago Medical School, and contestant **Bill Corday**, who is trying to fall asleep at Union Station. The physician uses special instruments to determine if Corday is truly asleep and says that the contestant is not sleeping. Corday then tells of having stayed awake for the better part of seven days and seven nights to try to be sleepy enough during the broadcast. Back in Hollywood, Edwards tells Corday that he will get a consolation prize of $500.

A pick-up from Pictorial Production Studios, contestant **Sally Johns**, a school teacher, thinks she has been flown to her home by jet plane and finds herself in a specially constructed movie set, which is arranged exactly like her family home. Her parents' furniture has been brought to the studio and her parents, family and friends are there to greet her.

Back in the studio, **Barbara Edwards**, a handwriting expert of Honolulu, is a consultant in cases of forgery, to determine handwriting traits. She examines the note attached to The Glass Goblet. There is an announcement that the contest will be opened to listeners next week. Listeners were asked to send in their name, address and telephone number on a card (not a letter). Three listeners will be called each week until someone breaks the goblet. A guest singer will sing the note the listener names. Contestants telephoned will receive a 49-piece set of Sterling Silver. The card can be sent to Truth or Consequences, Box 300, Hollywood 28, California.

Episode #757, Broadcast of January 21, 1950

Stunts: T or C Guessing Game, Husband-Mermaid Water-Tank, and Sleep Station No. 2

From Union Station in Chicago, contestant **Virginia Newton** tries to fall asleep while the physician who was on the program last week, and announcer **Norman Barry**, test the experiment. She was unable to fall asleep. She receives a $500 consolation prize instead of the $5,000 she would have received, had she been asleep. She tells how she tried to exhaust herself in preparation for the evenings' experiment.

Back in the Hollywood studios, actor **Mark Stevens** "christens" The Magic Goblet in preparation for the first telephone call to listeners. He christens the goblet "Willie" and promises that Edwards will be able to tell listeners why he chose the name. Edwards says he must wait until next week for the explanation. Goblet stunt tonight is worth $5,000 and $500. But nobody breaks the goblet so the price will increase an extra $500 for next week. The first listener called lived in Kentucky but did not answer the phone. In the studio, singer **Ernie Newton** sings the notes named by listeners called. Mark Stevens, who christened the goblet, also selected the three cards of writers tonight. Ernie Newton does such a good job as a singer that he remains for the duration of the contest.

Episode #758, Broadcast of January 28, 1950

Stunts: Three Mud, Unveil Horse, and Round the World Pogo Stick B.U.

The first contestant, Mr. Hull of St. Louis, Missouri, answers the "catch question," which is usually planned so that Ralph Edwards can say, "You did not tell the truth, so you must pay the consequence." On this particular broadcast, the contestant turned the tables and answered immediately, "Woodrow Wilson," when asked whose picture appeared on a $100,000 bill. The contestant received $1,000 in cash and did not have to perform any consequence.

A new carryover stunt began: a race between two contestants to get to City Hall in Los Angeles. **Larry Hayes**, a singer, must go around the world via TWA Constellation; **Carol Fieldhouse** goes by pogo stick on a course of 24 miles mapped out by the program. The race will begin in three weeks. The first person to reach City Hall will receive $1,000.

Pick-up from the Hollywood Knickerbocker Hotel, from a session of the Western Harness Racing Association Convention, where announcer **Gerry Lawrence** handled a consequence in which he thought he was unveiling the statue of a horse, "Old Battle Ax," unaware that the statue was his mother-in-law, in the flesh.

The Magic Goblet contest was now worth $6,000. None of the contestants phoned gave the correct answer. Movie star **Dan Dailey** was on hand to assist with the telephone numbers that were called.

Episode #759, Broadcast of February 4, 1950

Stunts: Ralph Recording, Round the World Pogo Stick No. 2, and Three Grandfathers

Ralph Edwards leaves the studio to take part in a contest outside as he drives a car. His recorded voice conducts the show in studio during this time – all to confuse the two contestants, **Larry Haynes** and **Carol Fieldhouse**, who will start a race to Los Angeles City Hall. The contestants tell of their "training" for the race.

Episode #760, Broadcast of February 11, 1950

Stunts: Alarm Clock, Round the World No. 3, Heckle Remote Speaker, and Find Brother B.U.

A female contestant "jumps the gun" on Edwards and beats him to the answer in his opening question so she does not have to take the consequence but receives $15 for her quick wit. The answer concerns the origin of the custom of wearing a wedding and engagement ring on the third finger of the left-hand.

The Magic Goblet is finally broken by the note corresponding with the number nine, selected by **Mrs. Cliff Riebe**, a listener who was telephoned at her home in Waukesha, Wisconsin. In working out the riddle to get the number, she arrived at the number nine and then verified this by the last line of the riddle: "The answer is No." In German, no is "nein" – hence, nine. Mrs. Riebe received $7,000. Ralph Edwards explained why the goblet was christened the name of "Willie" – in honor of **Dan Dailey's** new motion picture, *When Willie Comes Marching Home*.

Contestants **Larry Haynes** and **Carol Fieldhouse** are back on the program still preparing for the race to the Los Angeles City Hall. Eleanor, a kangaroo, appears with Fieldhouse, for publicity photos.

A new feature began on this broadcast. During the week, the producers of the quiz show ran advertisements for people who have special stories concerning missing relatives. From the 150 people who answered the ads, one was chosen: **Lola Phillips Chapin**, formally of Mountain Grove, Missouri, told the story of her missing brother whom she has not seen since the mother left home taking the one-year-old boy with her, leaving the father, Lola and her sister. Today, none of their relatives ever heard of either the mother or the child again. The child was named **Walter Raymond Phillips**. The mother's maiden name was Points and she may have given the child her maiden name as a surname. Anyone having information concerning Walter Points or Walter Phillips was asked to get in touch with *Truth or Consequences*, NBC, Hollywood.

Episode #761, Broadcast of February 18, 1950

Stunts: Foreign Commercials, Find Brother No. 2, Rip Own Hat, Heartbeat, Round-the-World No. 4, and Grab Bag

Ralph Edwards goes through the studio audience and asks various people at random to reach into a grab bag. One person pulls out a dime taped to a card advising them that they will receive a dime a day through the mail for a year. Another person pulls out a small part of a wristwatch and a note to the effect that during the year, various other parts of the watch will be mailed to them.

The Mr. Heartbeat contest began with actual heartbeat of a famous American heard several times during the broadcast. Listeners are told that they could identify "Mr. Heartbeat" by listening to a number clues in the form of a riddle:

> "Sigh, Sigh, Pie,
> Half Prince and Pauper I.
> I'm drab they say,
> But remember Fair Play,
> Ring, Ring High."

Mr. Heartbeat was also heard laughing on the program. From week to week, added clues were given. If the radio listeners thought they knew the identity of Mr. Heartbeat, they were to send a card (letter was not acceptable) with their name, address and telephone number to: Truth or Consequences, Box 300, Hollywood 28, California. The purpose of the contest was to call attention to the great work being done by the American Heart Association to keep the "heart beats of America" going.

Letters and telephone calls from people who think they might have leads in the case of **Lola Chapin's** long-lost brother were received in great numbers and the program was tracking down every available resource.

Carol Fieldhouse and **Larry Haynes** appear on the program to announce that in one hour and 15 minutes following the broadcast, they will start from the Los Angeles Airport on their famous race to Los Angeles City Hall.

Episode #762, Broadcast of February 25, 1950

Stunts: Honest Elephant, Find Brother No. 3, Fake Mystery Voice, and TWA-Pogo Stick B.U.

Three phone calls were made to numbers from the cards that were mailed in, selected at random by the beautiful **Valli**, currently starring in *The Third Man*. The contestants telephoned received a 48-piece set of Sterling Silver. The person who identified Mr. Heartbeat would receive $10,000. All three contestants guessed incorrectly. A public plea was made to send contributions to the local American Heart Association, but that all contributions would have no relation to their participation in the contest.

The race to Los Angeles City Hall ended with the winner being **Carol Fieldhouse**, who made the race on a pogo stick. He received $1,000. An announcement was made that **Larry Haynes**, the contestant making the race via TWA around the world, was still flying due to a 48-hour delay in London, England.

Two-way set up from the home of **George Daviau**, 3945 Orange Drive, Los Angeles, for a special stunt. Daviau was in the Hollywood studio while his wife was at home. Her reaction was broadcast over the air when she was told she won a giant jackpot.

Episode #763, Broadcast of March 4, 1950
Stunts: Talk Marathon, TWA-Pogo Stick Payoff, Find Brother No. 4, and Own Party Line

Three phone calls were made to numbers from the cards that were mailed in, again selected at random by the beautiful **Valli**. A new clue for the identity of Mr. Heartbeat was a recording of sounds such as people applauding or saluting an actor, singer, public speaker or athlete. Ralph Edwards emphasizes that "one out of every three" people in America has heart disease – "Remember the Third Man!"

A follow-up regarding the race to Los Angeles City Hall – both participants in the race were in the studio. **Larry Haynes**, the loser, and **Carol Fieldhouse**, the winner. Haynes confessed that he once was considered as understudy for **Ezio Pinza** and as a consolation prize, for coming in second, was given a chance to sing on the broadcast. He was invited by Fieldhouse to sing at his wedding in the near future. Haynes received a $500 consolation prize for his participation.

A follow-up regarding **Lola Chapin's** long-lost brother: the producers of the quiz program were now looking for information about a man named Harry Cobert. This may be the "missing link."

Outside the studio, contestants **Ken Mayer** and **Faith Moore** positioned themselves outside Melody Lane café and they agreed to conduct a "talking marathon" to see if men or women talk more. They will be relieved during the week by two contestants selected in the studio audience. The contestants must talk in shifts of 24 hours per day for the entire week. The winners would be announced on next weeks' show. The winners would receive $1,000.

Pogo Stick Story

The fabled race between the tortoise and the hare was reprised when Larry Haynes, an unemployed singer, who resided at 1314 Gordon Street in Hollywood, attempted to streak across the globe on a Trans World Airline plane. His opponent was Carol Fieldhouse, of 115½ S. Normandie Ave., who bounced about the streets of Los Angeles on a pogo stick. He tried his best to reach the Los Angeles City Hall before Haynes, knowing the winner would receive $1,000.

Like most consequences on the quiz show, the stunt was dreamed up several weeks in advance. During the broadcast, Haynes and Fieldhouse were asked if they were willing to accept the consequence. When dangling a $1,000 financial carrot in front of someone who was unemployed, the answer was a sure thing. Vancouver-born Carol Fieldhouse, a former Kitsilano High School student who lived in Los Angeles, was a one-time saxophone player. Fieldhouse served in the American Armed Forces during the war, and had since worked as a truck driver, a Beverly Hills police officer, and in a Columbia records plant. While Fieldhouse wore out whole sets of nerves practicing on his pogo stick, Haynes took his shots and clearances for a round-the-world flight. The race commenced on the evening of February 18, from Burbank Airport. When the starting signal was given, Haynes streaked away to New York, London, Brussels, Damascus, Basra, Karachi, Delhi, Calcutta, Bangkok, Hong Kong, Okinawa, Tokyo, Midway, and Honolulu.

Fieldhouse, meanwhile, bounced his way down Sepulveda Boulevard. The itinerary read Sepulveda to Santa Monica Blvd, Santa Monica to Wilshire Blvd., Wilshire to Highland Avenue, Highland to Hollywood Blvd., Hollywood to Sunset Blvd., down Sunset to Main Street, and then to City Hall. For overnight use, there was a trailer always following Fieldhouse on his 23 or 24 mile pogo pilgrimage. A regular caravan followed him on the five-day trip. Ralph Edwards sent along a station wagon and a trailer, equipped with beds, food and a stove. Policemen E.R. Evans and Chet Wolfrum kept confused drivers from mowing him down. "Evans let me go through stop lights. But Chet made me stop for 'em – and kept me hopping up and down all the time."

Fieldhouse reached City Hall first, with three days to spare. He won the $1,000 prize, losing eight pounds in the process. Haynes got fogged in for 48 hours in London, grounded somewhere in Brussels, Belgium, and was somewhere over the Pacific when he received word that his competition succeeded. "It's worth a thousand bucks just to do this," Fieldhouse told reporters upon completion at noon on Thursday, February 23. "I'm the shy type. It takes more guts than a government mule to pogo through. Los Angeles traffic with everybody gawking at you like you were crazy or something. Old ladies followed me like puppy dogs. Kids asked for my autograph. And one lady cussed me out for blocking traffic." Fieldhouse was 23 and single at the time, but planned to use the money to pay off his bills. He told reporters he contemplated getting married on what was left. He wore out six pogo sticks and averaged three miles a day. "I'd hop for two-tenths of a mile real fast and then rest," he explained. "That way I covered a mile for every 50 minutes of hopping."

On the broadcast of March 4, both men appeared before the microphone to talk about their adventures. Fieldhouse explained how he wore out a pair of Army boots, but a clothing storeowner along the route took care of that. "This guy hollers out: 'Come on in and get some new boots.' So I did. He wanted me to wear a cap advertising his store. I took it off, though, as soon as I turned a corner."

Episode #764, Broadcast of March 11, 1950
Stunts: Wild Goose, Indian Drama, Find Brother, and Talk Marathon

Lola Chapin was back on the program. There is still no definite solution to her brother's disappearance but researchers for the program have reason to believe they were successful. The clues might be in Leavenworth, Kansas, where the Old Soldiers Home is.

Contestant **Betty Miller** does an American Indian stunt and finds that her father, sister and grandfather, whom she has not seen for a long time, are the other Indians in costume. Betty Miller was living in Van Nuys, California. Her family was flown from Springfield, Missouri. **Mr. and Mrs. Gilbert Gann** of Rt. 3, Box 45, Springfield, **Olive Ferguson**, and Mr. Gann's father. With the aid of a friend, they arranged to have **Betty Miller** attend the radio broadcast so she could be called out of the audience to participate in the sketch.

There was a two-way set-up for several cut-ins from the corners of Hollywood and Vine, where the "Talkathon" was in progress, a carry-over from last week. The ladies, **Faith Moore** and **Madeline Bolton**, are both on their corner carrying on without any trouble, apparently. The men on the other corner, were not so lucky. **Ken Mayer** had been carrying on alone since 10:30 a.m. when his partner, **Leo Orn**, lost his voice. The "Talkathon" continued until one side conceded.

Episode #765, Broadcast of March 18, 1950
Stunts: Hubby Disguise Bath, Talk Marathon Payoff, Dick Haymes, and Deer for a Day

The winners of the "Talkathon" was a guest on the show: **Madeline Boulton** who, with her partner, **Faith Moore**, won the contest. The race ended during the past week. **Ken Mayer**, the man who had to talk so well after his partner developed laryngitis, was also on the program. He received a $500 consolation prize.

Pick-up from a home in Los Angeles for a stunt in which the wife thought there was a strange man in her bathroom. The "stranger" was actually her husband, a contestant on the quiz show.

Billy Lasker, a handicapped boy and member of the Crippled Children's Society of Los Angeles County, rang the bell for Easter Seals. Billy played the ukulele and received a chance to accompany singing star **Dick Haymes** to perform a special number. Billy's appearance on the show tied in with an appeal on behalf of the Easter Seals. For his participation, the CCS of Los Angeles would receive a Westinghouse television set in Billy's name. Also, a record player with a complete set of albums of Dick Haymes records for Billy.

Screen cowboys aside, Ralph Edwards attempted to incorporate rising trends on the quiz program such as little green men from Mars and flying saucers, which were appearing in newspaper columns and on the cover of national magazines. On this broadcast, Edwards offered $1,000 to the first person to produce a little man from Mars. This was primarily a put-up or shut-up policy as it applied to those who claimed to have seen flying saucers flown by 23-inch high men. "Why didn't he offer $1,000,000, or is he afraid one might show up?" a newspaper columnist remarked. Another newspaper columnist remarked, "Attention, Orson Welles!"

Episode #766, Broadcast of March 25, 1950
Stunts: Joe Palooka, T or C Contestant, Guitar Wager, and T or C New Mexico

Celebrating the quiz program's tenth anniversary, special guest was the first contestant to ever appear on *Truth or Consequences*, back on March 23, 1940, from New York City: **Alvin Raymond Robinson.** (He was a sailor when he appeared on the first broadcast.) Robinson was back to help Ralph Edwards describe the first program, the growth of popularity, naming all of the various announcers to have assisted on the program, and briefly highlighting some of the outstanding contests conducted on the show in the past. Taking part during the broadcast was professional guitarist **Wes Montgomery**.

Ralph Edwards reads a letter from **J.G. Mims,** Mayor of Hot Springs, New Mexico, explaining that Hot Springs is officially changing the name of the town to Truth or Consequences. In recognition, the program next week will be broadcast from Truth or Consequences, New Mexico.

Contestant **Margaret Maher**, manager of the Blair Convalescent Home, was among the lucky callers on this broadcast. For $10,000 cash, she was asked by Ralph Edwards if she could identify "Mr. Heartbeat." She incorrectly guessed Arthur Godfrey. She received the consolation prize worth several hundred dollars – a 48-piece set of Fine Arts Sterling Silver. After the broadcast, the phone in her home was kept busy for several hours as family relatives called to comment on her luck, and to give her "inside tips" on who "Mr. Heartbeat" was. When a local newspaper reporter in Kansas City, Missouri, asked her about the contest, she remarked: "Nobody can tell me from now on that the selection of people being called on those radio quiz shows is a put-up deal."

Episode #767, Broadcast of April 1, 1950
Stunts: Congressman, T or C Museum, T or C Jester, Elephant Butte, County Seat, Calls Letters, and New Editors
Broadcast from the stage of the high school auditorium in Truth or Consequences, New Mexico, formerly Hot Springs, New Mexico. Special guests included **J.G. Mims**, Mayor of Truth or Consequences, New Mexico; **Burton Roach**, New Mexico State Senator; and **John E. Miles**, U.S. Representative of New Mexico. Various citizens of the town were appointed to special positions in the renamed city to serve for a period of one year in this capacity. Among the outstanding appointments were **Mrs. Walter Knox**, member of the Truth or Consequences Woman's Club, appointed custodian of the new Truth or Consequences Museum where various trophies of the program would be on display. Proceeds from visits to the museum would go to the Carrie Tingley Crippled Children's Hospital. **Roy Stovall**, appointed Public Relations Director for the city, is assigned to create signs reading "# of miles to Truth or Consequences, N.M." for placement in various parts of the world including Cairo, Egypt and Grand Central Station in New York City.

Episode #768, Broadcast of April 8, 1950
Stunts: Pink Lemonade Running Gag, Find Wife Clown, Trampoline, T or C New Mexico, Spin Kiss Elephants, Find Wife Mention, and Train Domestic Animals
Broadcast from the Clyde Beatty Circus Grounds in Los Angeles, with celebrity guests **Clyde Beatty**, famous wild animal trainer and owner of the circus; his wife, **Harriett Beatty**, famous woman tiger trainer; the Clyde Beatty Circus

Clowns **Mel Rennick, Abe Goldstein, Lou Walters** and **Charles Hilderra**; **Marc Antony**, the producer clown; and the Manzello Troupe, an acrobatic group who performs on the trampoline.

Contestants take part within the circus personnel in various stunts such as selling pink lemonade, etc. One contestant thinks he will get to kiss the Clyde Beatty Aerialist girls but instead he is blindfolded and the girls are replaced by the famous Circus Elephants! **Billie and Elmer Schroeder** won a television set after Billie was dressed up (with makeup) as a clown for a stunt. (After the broadcast, Elmer informed Edwards that television had not become aware of the advantages of the High Sierra country, where reception was practically zero, so they were promised a list of gifts from which to choose from.)

By transcribed recording there is a two-way conversation between Ralph Edwards and the citizens of Truth or Consequences, New Mexico. These include **State Senator Burton Roach** of New Mexico, speaking from City Hall, **Joe Tafoya**, postmaster of Truth or Consequences, New Mexico, and **Roy Stovall**, Public Relations Director of Truth or Consequences, New Mexico. These citizens tell of the barrage of mail arriving in Truth or Consequences as a result of the publicity of re-naming the city.

Episode #769, Broadcast of April 15, 1950

Stunts: $100 Pie Running Gag, Maternity Reunion, Jo Stafford, Foreign Sentence Payoff, and Golf Mention No. 1

Celebrity guest **Jo Stafford**, singer, was involved in a "foreign sentence" stunt. She was a "plant" in the audience who came up onstage to sing "Dearie" with **Howard Evans,** a 17-year-old Hollywood high school boy. After the unrehearsed (and good) duet, Evans took the courage and planted a kiss in the middle of Stafford's surprised face. She blushed – and after the radio program, took him to dinner at the Brown Derby.

The foreign language sentence which Ralph Edwards has been using near the opening of his broadcasts from time to time is finally translated with "actions that speak louder than words." **Michael Bruce**, who was in the studio audience, runs to the stage when Edwards quotes the sentence and picks up a pie from a table on stage and tosses it into Edwards' face. The foreign-language sentence was Hindustani for, "I will give you $500 if you will come and throw into my face a 'sweetbread' or pie!" (The actual translation of the specified sum was 2,500 rupees, the equivalent of $500 for the person who followed instructions in the sentence.) After the broadcast, Bruce confessed how his brother just returned from India and had taken down the sentence on a wire recorder, translated it and then waited an anxious month for broadcast tickets so he could collect the prize. Bruce received the $500.

Contestant **Al Baker** agrees to play golf on an 823-mile course, from Hollywood, California, to Truth or Consequences, New Mexico. Par was 25,000 strikes. If Baker breaks par, he will receive $500 and the new Nash and Trailer which is accompanying him on the trip. All golfing equipment was furnished by Wilson Golfing.

Episode #770, Broadcast of April 22, 1950

Stunts: Fake Fire Plug, Golf Mention No. 2, Squirt Hugh, Mrs. Chapin Find Brother, and Identify Own Screams

Back on the program was **Lola Chapin**, who made several appearances on the program in connection with the search for her missing brother. The search is still on but she thanks all of the listeners who tried to help her track down her elusive kin.

Pick-up from the front of Coffee Dan's Restaurant on Vine Street, where a contestant was sent out to impersonate a cop and to put a "wrong parking" sticker on a car parked outside the restaurant. The gag was a tie-in with plugs for the local Los Angeles Police Show.

Episode #771, Broadcast of April 29, 1950

Stunts: 1910 Easter Hat, Disown Shoe Shine, Sweetheart Pie, Golf Mention No. 3, and New York Flying Saucers

Ralph Edwards announces that a sign indicating the exact miles to Truth or Consequences, New Mexico, has been set up in Barcelona, Venezuela. An announcement was also made that the souvenir copy of the Truth or Consequences *Herald* was available for .25 cents to cover the cost of handling and mailing to "Truth or Consequences Herald, Truth or Consequences, New Mexico" or to **Paul Tooley**, publisher of *The Herald*.

This broadcast marked the start of the Flying Saucer stunt. On Monday, May 1, five "flying saucers" would be released over New York City – one over each of the five boroughs. Every flying saucer had a message engraved on it. If anyone finds one of the saucers, and decodes the message, following the instructions for turning in the saucers, $50 would be rewarded. If all five saucers were found and returned to the proper place before next week's broadcast, all five would share a $1,000 cash prize. Every week until all five were turned in, the flying saucers would be released over a different city.

Jack Shafer, columnist for the Newark *Star-Ledger* interviewed Edwards regarding this stunt, learning how an airplane above the city launched five facsimiles of small flying saucers. "At the time, I told Ralph it reminded me more of a nickel-back-on-the-bottle stunt than a flying saucer sensation," Shafer wrote.

Episode #772, Broadcast of May 6, 1950

Stunts: Newsboy Water Tank, Golf Mention No. 4, Life Contestant, and Flying Saucers New York

Broadcast from Hollywood with announcer Jerry Lawrence interviewing a newsboy, **Rocky Ruiz**, of San Fernando, California, 39-years-old, and contestant **Charles Metzger**, bus driver for the Santa Monica Sight-Seeing Tours. The object of the interviews was to determine if Hollywood or New York newsboys were the "more intelligent" as reflected in their being able to answer questions correctly regarding the day's newspapers in their city. Every time a newsboy answered correctly, the contestant received $25; every time a newsboy gave an incorrect answer, the contestant was dunked in a tank of water. From New York, at 42st Street and Sixth Avenue, announcer **Ed Herlihy** was interviewing **John David**, a 61-year-old newsboy, and contestant **John Julio**, head waiter at the Radio City Restaurant. David answers three out of three questions correctly; the Hollywood newsboy answered only one of three correctly.

From a studio in New York City, announcer **Ted Bell** reports that none of the five flying saucers (made of paper) were released. Next week, the saucers would be released over Philadelphia and citizens there had the same opportunity that the residents of New York City had.

The story of the housewife "serial" begins. Contestant **Laura Chester**, housewife, agreed to appear on the program each week, ala soap opera, until she has told the story of her life as an American housewife. She dramatizes only a few lines at a time.

The Police Show

The 16th annual Los Angeles Police Show, a 14-day event held at the Shrine Auditorium, opened on May 4. As was customary, Bob Hope opened the event put on by the Los Angeles Police Relief Association. Celebrities included Red Skelton (May 6), Danny Thomas (May 7), Jack Benny (May 8), Dan Dailey (May 9 and 10), Ralph Edwards (May 11 and 12), Donald O'Connor (May 13), Gordon MacRae (May 14 and 15), and Eleanor Powell (May 16 and 17). Actress Janet Waldo became the honorary first lady of the Los Angeles Police Department.

Episode #773, Broadcast of May 13, 1950
Stunts: Mother Cook, Life Story No. 2, Giovanni, Golf No. 5, and Flying Saucers Philadelphia
Broadcast from the Hollywood studios, where guest **Dr. Giovanni**, professional entertainer and "pickpocket," demonstrates how he can remove articles of clothing, wallets, etc., from people without their knowledge.
Pick-up from Nickodell's Restaurant in Hollywood where contestant **John Deeman**, Marine Sergeant, ordered a meal "like his Mother used to cook" and was surprised by finding that his Mother is in the back of the kitchen at Nickodell's. She was reunited with her son for Mother's Day. Mrs. Deeman was flown to Hollywood from Louisville, Kentucky.
Back in the studio, housewife contestant **Laura Chester** tells the next installment in her life story – "The Life of a Housewife."
Follow-up to the flying saucer stunt: Ralph Edwards receives news by telephone from **Norman Brenner** of Philadelphia, that all five flying saucers were found during the week and were decoded and properly returned to Horn & Hardart, located at 12th and Market, as instructed on the saucers. The five finders shared the $1,000 cash prize. Finders were **William Kiss, Harry Cohen, Bernard Fabin, Roscoe Wells** and **Katherine Snyder**.
Ralph Edwards announced that "Elephant Butte Bill," a frog from Elephant Butte Lake in Truth or Consequences, New Mexico, has been entered in the famous annual "Jumping Frog of Calaveras County" being held next week.

Episode #774, Broadcast of May 20, 1950
Stunts: Seal Bed Street, Life Story No. 3, Golf No. 6, and Saw Wood Symphony
Ralph Edwards reports on the progress of **Al Baker**, who was golfing his way from Los Angeles, California, to Truth or Consequences, New Mexico. This

week, Al Baker made 2,004 strokes on his way from Tucson to the next larger city in Arizona. His caddy, **Carl Jochen**, a contestant on last week's broadcast, failed to guess the correct number of strokes Baker would take the week before, so he spent the week with Baker caddying at the rate of ten cents a stroke and collecting $200.40. Baker had 148 miles to go to reach Truth or Consequences, New Mexico.

From Sunset Boulevard, outside the NBC Studios, announcer **Jerry Lawrence** interviewed a contestant who was lying in a bed with a seal named Oscar. The contestant's wife, his boss, and his minister (**Rev. Gahagan**) were all at the scene.

Mr. Heartbeat was finally identified by a contestant, **Dorothea Ziegler** of San Francisco, California, as **Edgar A. Guest**. Transcribed from Detroit, Michigan, Edgar A. Guest congratulated the winner of the $10,000 cash prize. While no contributions for the American Heart Association were solicited during this contest and while there was no direct tie-in with the organization for the contest, the on-going stunt provided public conscious of the work of the American Heart Association and of the way that "every third man, woman or child in America" was a victim of some form of heart disease. Ziegler, age 80, a former Western Union telegrapher, lived in a rented room with her adopted daughter. When asked if she was a regular listener to the quiz program, Ziegler confessed that she was not, but that she sometimes "cut in" on Saturday nights. "They make too much noise to suit me and I get tired of it sometimes. But they sure have a good time and I guess I'm going to myself now."

Episode #775, Broadcast of May 27, 1950

Stunts: Problem Contest, Bridegroom Chase, Golf New Mexico Payoff, and Life Story No. 4

Contestant **Margaret Stude** of Fort Worth, Texas, made continuous telephone calls during the broadcast, numbers submitted by listeners in the Mr. Heartbeat contest. Every five minutes, she sent a report on the success of her phone calls. Working backstage with an NBC telephone operator, **Billy Clavenger**, she attempted to assist the recipients. If there was a winner during the first five minutes of phone calls, the winner would receive a television set. If there was a winner during the second five minutes, the winner would receive an electric fridge. During the third five minutes, the winner would receive a 72-piece set of Sterling Silver. This was the Mr. Heartbeat Dividend Contest. The only winner was the person phoned during the last five minutes, **Mrs. E.L. Majors** of Fresno, California, receiving the cumulative prize of a television set, refrigerator, and Sterling Silver.

Peggy Nelsen, a Los Angeles model, participates in the life story of a housewife, the ongoing soap opera performed by **Laura Chester**.

Pick-up from Truth or Consequences, New Mexico, where **Al Baker** traveled from California to New Mexico, and was interviewed by **Dick Gottlieb** and congratulated by **Burton Roach**, New Mexico State Senator, and **T.B. Williams**, newly-elected Mayor of Truth or Consequences, New Mexico.

Episode #776, Broadcast of June 3, 1950

Stunts: Barrel Race Eggs, Music-Music-Music, Life Story No. 5, and Retired Teacher Vacation

Broadcast included a salute to the National Retail Grocers' Association currently holding an annual convention in Chicago. The first contestant called to the microphone was a retail grocery clerk. Celebrity guests were **William Early**, a singer, formerly of Boston, now on his way to fill an engagement at KNBH; and **Frank G. Swain**, Judge of the Superior Court of Los Angeles, on the program to take part in a consequence with his former schoolteacher who he had not seen in 15 years. Edwards asked the judge, "Aren't you the judge who just granted a divorce to a woman because her husband refused to let her sit on his lap?" asked Edwards. "Yes," giggled Judge Swain, "wasn't that silly?"

Clara A. Bookshy, an 87-year-old school teacher from Canoga Park, was surprised by four of her former students from the class of 1907. They had been flown in from all parts of the country for the occasion.

Episode #777, Broadcast of June 10, 1950

Stunts: Freddie Martin, Commencement Parents, Life Story No. 6, and Telephone Husband Model

Broadcast from Hollywood with a two-way pick-up from Music City Store, at Sunset and Vine. A contestant was giving autographs and pretending that he was **Freddy Martin**, saxophone player, bandleader and popular recording artist. Among those who asked for his autograph was Freddy Martin himself!

In the studio, celebrity guests included **Claire Dennis**, a model, and **Mr. and Mrs. Roy Stovall** of Truth or Consequences, New Mexico. Stovall was the public-relations man for the town and reported on various distant places where highway signs were placed since the city of Hot Springs, New Mexico, changed its name to Truth or Consequences.

Episode #778, Broadcast of June 17, 1950
Taped on May 31, 1950
Stunts: Platoon Census, Man's Gifts, Song Marching Contest, Radar Pie, and Life Story No. 7
Special guests were the 817th Engineers' Platoon Band from the March Air Force Base in California, under the leadership of **Lt. Owen Olden** and **Sergeant George Kirsten**; **Harold Martin**, British actor who was seeking a career in Hollywood; and **Laura Chester**, the carryover contestant who presented another episode in the life of her soap opera, a take-off on the radio daytime serial.
Patricia Draper, the young wife who thought her husband was on army duty in Okinawa, was reunited with her husband whom she had not seen for 14 months. **Bob Draper**, the husband, was flown in from Okinawa through cooperation of the quiz program and arrangements were made for him to spend a 30-day furlough with his wife and baby daughter, **Wendy Jean**, whom he set eyes on for the very first time during this broadcast.

Episode #779, Broadcast of June 24, 1950
Taped on June 7, 1950
Stunts: Vacation Mr. X, Four Songwriters, Life Story No. 8, and Dog Telephone
A woman contestant was told to pretend to be a songwriter, claiming to have written some of the outstanding song hits of the past. Special guests were real songwriters who masqueraded as foreigners visiting this country. The songwriter guests were **Wolfie Gilbert**, writer of "Ramona" and disguised as a German; **Ben Oakland**, writer of "I'll Dance at Your Wedding" and disguised as an Italian; **Ned Washington**, writer of "My Foolish Heart" and disguised as a Swede; and **Johnny Lang**, writer of "Mule Train" and disguised as a Frenchman.
Laura Chester, housewife, agrees to come back to the program next fall to continue her soap opera.

Pick-up from the front of the Biltmore Hotel in Los Angeles, where contestant **Willard Alexander,** a fruit and vegetable vendor, was given a free vacation for himself and his family. Contestant was sent to find the man whose baggage he had been given in the studios. While he was searching for the man, his wife and child drove up in a taxi and told him to join them in a rush to the railroad station. He was the man who was getting the vacation and the baggage. His own clothes, plus a new wardrobe, was packed in the luggage he was guarding!

Episode #780, Broadcast of September 5, 1950
Taped on September 4, 1950
Stunts: Philip Morris Seltzer, Newsboy Miracle, Life Story No. 9, and Star's Image

Episode #781, Broadcast of September 12, 1950
Taped on September 8, 1950
Stunts: Pressure Cooker, T or C Dixieland Band, Life Story No. 10, Disguise Wife Secretary, and Top Sergeant Mud
Broadcast originated from the El Toro Marine Base in Santa Ana, California.

Episode #782, Broadcast of September 19, 1950
Stunts: Alarm Clock Running Gag, Spin Models Pig, Pay Off Soldier Debts, Wrong-Right Relative, and Life Story No. 11

Episode #783, Broadcast of September 26, 1950
Taped on September 22, 1950
Stunts: Water Phone R.G., Apple Over Soldier, Identify Ten Things, Life Story No. 12, and Mom Pop Recording
Broadcast originated from Lompoc, California.

Episode #784, Broadcast of October 3, 1950
Taped on September 28, 1950
Stunts: Remote Sound Effects, McManus Frame, Sing Talk Mill Stream, Life Story No. 13, Kibitz Telephone, and T or C Welcome
Celebrity guest is **George McManus,** cartoonist famous for the syndicated comic strip, *Bringing Up Father*, makes an appearance on this broadcast.

Episode #785, Broadcast of October 10, 1950
Taped on October 7, 1950
Stunts: Egg on Head, Roll Up Sidewalk, Paint Church, Guess Friends, and School Teachers
Broadcast originated from Merino, California, where Ralph Edwards grew up.

Episode #786, Broadcast of October 17, 1950
Taped on October 13, 1950
Stunts: Salute Seltzer, Wife Model Hut, Recreate Home, and Hampton Drum
Broadcast originated from the Port Hueneme Naval Station, California. Celebrity guest was **Lionel Hampton**. Trick question was asked of a contestant: "Who do you know that goes to sleep with his shoes on?" (Answer: a horse.)

Episode #787, Broadcast of October 24, 1950
Taped on October 19, 1950
Stunts: Cut String Mud R.G., Audience Star, Mental Telepathy No. 1, U.N. Mimic, and Stag Party
Celebrity guest, actor **Bruce Cabot**, participates in a stunt. Radio announcer Paul Harvey participates in a stunt titled "Stag Party." **Arline Butler** of Burlingame, California, was a TWA stewardess who helped in the Stag Party. Her stockings were torn by accident, through her efforts, so the producers of the program arranged for Gotham stockings, size 9, to be shipped to her with their compliments.
Ralph Edwards and his fascination with the potential for mental telepathy, starts a new contest that stretches a few episodes, in the hopes that result prove the existence of mental telepathy.

Episode #788, Broadcast of October 31, 1950
Taped on October 26, 1950
Stunts: Find Way Home, Story in Songs, Mental Telepathy No. 2, Alaska Gold Ring and Berlin Telephone Payoff
Radio announcer **Paul Harvey** returns to the program for the Alaska Gold Ring stunt.

Episode #789, Broadcast of November 7, 1950
Taped on November 3, 1950

Stunts: Election Water Tank, Africa Diamond Ring Mention, and Mental Telepathy Payoff

The length of time for this broadcast was cut short due to election returns.

Episode #790, Broadcast of November 14, 1950
Taped on November 10, 1950

Stunts: Millstream Shower R.G., $50 Kiss, Africa Diamond Ring No. 2, Advise Colonel, Live Like a Millionaire, and Mental Telepathy No. 4

Broadcast originated from the Barstow Marine Supply Depot in Southern California.

Episode #791, Broadcast of November 21, 1950
Taped on November 15, 1950

Stunts: Coach Chorus R.G., African Diamond Ring No. 3, Italian Brother Interpreter, Mental Telepathy No. 5, and Thanksgiving Turkey

Episode #792, Broadcast of November 28, 1950
Taped on November 23, 1950

Stunts: T or C Taxi, Bendix McDonald, Give Away Birthday, African Diamond Ring Payoff, and Mental Telepathy No. 6

Celebrity guests include singer/actress **Marie McDonald** and actor **Richard Carlson** participate in stunts on this broadcast.

Episode #793, Broadcast of December 5, 1950
Taped on November 29, 1950

Stunts: Harry the Hipster, Ask for Own Gifts, Taxi-Cab Mention, Mental Telepathy No. 7 and German Song Double Talk

Episode #794, Broadcast of December 12, 1950

Stunts: Three Stories, Kibitz Boss Telephone, Christmas Cartoon, Mention Hot Seat, Gramophone, and Mental Telepathy Mention

Episode #795, Broadcast of December 19, 1950
Taped on December 6 and 18, 1950

Stunts: Crash Own Party, The Thing, Sister Christmas Letter, and Mental Telepathy Winner

Episode #796, Broadcast of December 26, 1950

Stunts: Cat's Meow, Sailor Sister Star, Don't Open 'Til Christmas B.U., and Blind Boy Guitar

Country singer **Jimmy Wakely** makes an appearance on this broadcast, assisting a blind boy who loves to play the guitar.

Episode #797, Broadcast of January 2, 1951
Taped on December 27, 1950

Stunts: Elephant Delivery, Jack Smith Imitation, Don't Open 'Til Christmas Payoff, Postman Appreciation, and Take Out Charlie McCarthy

Celebrity ventriloquist **Edgar Bergen**, and his wooden dummy **Charlie McCarthy**, are on this program to assist with one of the stunts.

Episode #798, Broadcast of January 9, 1951
Taped on December 20, 1950

Stunts: Buy Out Stock, Four War Songs, and Ad Lib Shakespeare

Soldiers who participated in World War II, World War I, the Spanish-American War and the Civil War, were heard on this program, in an act involving veterans of four wars singing the most popular songs of each conflict. The Civil War veteran was 99-year-old, **General James Moore** of Selma, Alabama, and Commander of the Confederate Veterans, who sang "Dixie." Screen stars **Alan Mowbray** and **Rhys Williams** plays a bit of Shakespeare with an unsuspecting contestant.

Episode #799, Broadcast of January 16, 1951
Taped on January 3, 1951

Stunts: Miami Store Vacation B.U., Star Observation Test, and Swami Frame

Bob Davies, a Los Angeles salesman, revealed his wife to emcee Ralph Edwards in order to spend a week at Miami Beach. Within minutes Davies was conducted to Bond's Clothing Store on Hollywood Boulevard, where a replica of Miami Beach awaited him in the store window – complete with beach sand, miniature cabana, and large sun lamp to provide atmosphere. By the time Davies reported back to the radio show a week later, Edwards had a complete and real Miami Beach vacation planned for him. Newspapers in both Miami and California printed a photo of Davies, along with beauty models **Donna Davis** and **Joyce Brainard**, feeding a fake seal while seated comfortable on Miami Beach.

Celebrity guest was **Piper Laurie**, actress, who participated in a "Star Observation Test."

Episode #800, Broadcast of January 23, 1951
Taped on January 10, 1951
Stunts: Grocery Delivery B.U., Postman Appreciation, Amateur Song Writer, and Miami Store Vacation Payoff

Episode #801, Broadcast of January 30, 1951
Taped on January 16, 1951
Stunts: Impossible Scavenger Hunt, Mixed-Up Wives, and Grocery Delivery Payoff

Broadcast originated from Camp Stoneman in Oakland, California. This was to entertain an estimated 5,000 soldiers who were bound for Korea. An act built around a grocer from Charlotte, North Carolina, highlighted the program's tribute to the grocers of America. Several Camp Stoneman soldiers were brought onstage as contestants. Celebrity guest **Joyce MacKenzie**, actress who appeared in the recent movie, *Destination Murder*, makes an appearance in this broadcast to remind the soldiers what they were fighting for.

Episode #802, Broadcast of February 6, 1951
Taped on January 27, 1951
Stunts: Help Old Lady, Scoutmaster vs. Tenderfoot, and Ralph Kiner Scoutmaster

Broadcast originated from Las Vegas, Nevada. Edwards and the gang were helping celebrate the annual Boulder Dam area council banquet of the Boy Scouts of America. For the stunts, Edwards had a group of Boy Scouts, their Scoutmasters and their wives set up as contestants. **Paul H. Henry**, after failing to correctly answer his question, was dressed in a summer Boy Scout uniform and taken to the corner of Second and Freemont streets to assist elderly ladies across the street. After being brushed off by several, he espied an elderly laden with packages and it was not until he had addressed her that he realized it was his mother, **Mrs. Edgar Henry**, who was flown from her home in Lancaster, Ohio.

Episode #803, Broadcast of February 13, 1951
Taped on February 8, 1951

Stunts: Firario, Husbands Likes-Dislikes, Bring 'Em Back Reverse, and Observant Hat Tank

Broadcast originated from the Fresno Memorial Auditorium in Fresno, California. Both the radio and television program originated on stage at the Fresno Fig Festival Show. "If the country at large does not know that all dried figs in the United States are grown in California, the situation will be remedied by the show," said **A.E. Thorpe** of Fresno, the managing director of the California Fig Institute. Television personality **Linda Williams** stood behind a giant fig leaf, with little clothing on, giving the impression that the leaf was the only thing shielding her assets. An estimated 4,000 people were in the audience at the time of the broadcast.

Episode #804, Broadcast of February 20, 1951
Taped on January 17, 1951

Stunts: Commander Rain Barrel R.G., King Sisters, and Buddies Dictate Letter

Broadcast originated from Treasure Island in San Francisco. A student of Northwestern State College, in Phoenix, **Patte Crider**, along with her mother, went on a tour of Los Angeles and San Francisco. The highlight of the trip was a four-day visit with **Jimmie Lee Leathers**, Patte's fiancé, who was in the Navy and stationed at Treasure Island. Jimmie was a contestant and she was the consequence payoff. Patte went home with a 72-piece set of Sterling Silver and Jimmie received a 25-jewel wristwatch plus $50 in cash.

Episode #805, Broadcast of February 27, 1951
Taped on January 31, 1951

Stunts: Roof Blonde, Numbers Kids Gift, Take Out Charlie McCarthy, and Three Nationalities Joke

Ventriloquist **Edgar Bergen** and his wooden pal **Charlie McCarthy** return to the program to restage the stunt they participated in weeks prior, a contestant going out on a date with Charlie.

Episode #806, Broadcast of March 6, 1951
Taped on March 1, 1951

Stunts: Cabby, Joe Howard, and Grandma Hush Contest

Episode #807, Broadcast of March 13, 1951
Taped on March 8, 1951
Stunts: Jam Session, $1,000 Suit, and Imitate Star

Dwight Braden, a real Southerner from Knoxville, Tennessee, was unable to answer a question on the program. After being told that the suit he was wearing had to be cleaned, Braden was ordered to change into the "only other thing available," which happened to be a Confederate uniform. Edwards then declared Braden's suit was being sent to the Anchorage Laundry and Cleaners, located in Alaska. When Braden balked at going to Anchorage to reclaim his suit, Edwards idly remarked that there was a $1,000 bill sewed into the lining of the coat. After the broadcast, Braden, wearing the uniform of the Confederacy, sped to Alaska by Northwest Airlines. There, however, he learned that someone else had picked up the suit and it was headed back to California. So Braden left Anchorage, still in pursuit of his perambulating wardrobe. He left a trail of amazed and mystified people in wake all the way from California. Passengers on board the airplane were cracking jokes. Braden returned home, was made a Colonel in the Confederate Air Force, and won his $1,000.

Episode #808, Broadcast of March 20, 1951
Stunts: Telephone Parcheesi, Guess Where, T or C New Mexico Announcement, and $1,000 Suit No. 2

Broadcast originated from Palm Springs, California. Beginning with this episode, the series was broadcast live from Hollywood and not taped in advance.

Episode #809, Broadcast of March 27, 1951
Stunts: Janis Paige Remote, T or C New Mexico Announcement, and $1,000 Suit No. 3

Episode #810, Broadcast of April 3, 1951
Stunts: Missed Good Gesture, Memory Test Frame, and $1,000 Suit No. 4.

Episode #811, Broadcast of April 10, 1951
Stunts: Indian Girl Train, and $1,000 Suit No. 5

The entire broadcast was live except for the Indian Girl Train stunt, which was taped in advance. **Katchina Mana**, age 14, a Hopi Indian, was accompanied by her aunt, **Lena Charley**, during her appearance as a contestant on this broadcast. She failed to answer a telephone question and as a consequence, was told to leave the reservation and flag down the Santa Fe Super Chief at some isolated point along the line and persuade the crew to give her a ride to New York City. She had never travelled more than 100 miles from her birthplace at Oraibi, and never been on a train, so this was something of a major consequence for her. On the program, she told of the results when she flagged the train down at Suwanee, New Mexico, 40 miles east of Albuquerque, and her stay in New York City.

Episode #812, Broadcast of April 17, 1951
Stunts: $50 Shoe, Elephant Hunt Winner, Casey Ruggles, $1,000 Suit Payoff, and Lipsticks
Warren Tufts, San Jose cartoonist who drew the Western comic strip, *Casey Ruggles*, makes a guest appearance by starting a Los Angeles man to work digging up sections of Main Street opposite the Los Angeles Post Office. Tufts' digger was **G. Dewey Davis** of Glendale, a telephone company employee, a contestant who missed a question and was marched up to the mike with a map for buried gold, a shotgun and miner's tools. Davis was informed that real gold was buried near the Post Office and he could have $500 if he dug the ore up in a week.

Episode #813, Broadcast of April 24, 1951
Stunts: Baseball Game, Casey Ruggles Payoff, and Old Soldier
The "prospector" who camped out in a tent for a week with miner's tools, shotgun and other gadgets amid the stares and smog of Los Angeles, discovered the "ore" under his tent, and as a result won $500. "He could have found it easily if he had followed the map," **Warren Tufts** said during the follow-up on this broadcast. He admitted the map was not easy to follow. A clue was also provided in the daily *Casey Ruggles* comic strip, which is why a local newspaper delivered a complimentary issue every day. In the comic strip, Casey was engaged in trying to halt miners who were destroying Los Angeles with their operations. The clue, Tufts explained on the program, was in contacting the Los Angeles sheriff. In any event, **G. Dewey Davis** relaxed from his ordeal as Tuft's guest at a Los Altos ranch for the balance of the week.

Episode #814, Broadcast of May 1, 1951

Stunts: Grandma Jazz Band, Common Grandchild, and Matinee Idols

Partially transcribed from Las Vegas. **Ida Sterns** of Promise City, Iowa, was a contestant whose appearance was enjoyed by a number of her friends back in her home town. She played "Dinah" on the clarinet, along with four other grandmothers who played various instruments, in a Grandma Jazz Band. Sterns told Edwards that she had been playing the cornet for 60 years, and friends could back up her statement, as the entire Anderson family were noted for their musical ability. She was awarded a cash prize, a radio-phonograph combo, and a carton of Philip Morris cigarettes for her part in the program.

Episode #815, Broadcast of May 8, 1951

Stunts: Model Pass, Morse Code Words, Treasury Spot, and Wife Duffle Bag.

Broadcast live aboard the United States Naval aircraft carrier, the U.S.S. Los Angeles, based in San Diego, California. The carrier, bought with funds raised through the sale of War Bonds in the Los Angeles area, had its sea-going history narrated by Edwards. Crew members were the contestants, having returned from Korean waters. Seaman apprentice **Donald Traylor**, 20, won a 16mm moving picture camera. Motion-picture actress **Andrea King** sat on his lap during the broadcast and the producers arranged for a 72-hour shore leave from his station aboard the U.S.S. Los Angeles.

Episode #816, Broadcast of May 15, 1951

Stunts: Louse Up Contestant, Ronald Reagan, and Grandma Hush Payoff

Celebrity guest participating in a stunt was actor **Ronald Reagan**.

Episode #817, Broadcast of May 22, 1951

Stunts: Sing Praises, Make Up Phone Number, Living Room Surprise, and Board Students

Andrea Anderson receives a phone call informing her that her husband, Mr. Anderson, is out with a blonde. What she did not know was a microphone hidden at home and the audience could hear every word she said. Mr. Anderson was in Hollywood on stage during the broadcast, taking the consequence until the truth was revealed to his wife. Mrs. Griffith, their neighbor, timed the scenario to ensure Mrs. Anderson would be home at the time. **Bill Meers** of station KOIN in Portland, Oregon, helped with the hookup. The "living room surprise" idea was sent in by a little boy in Portland named **Cue Cox**. Other stunts included singing praises (involving three women), and a "make-up phone number payoff."

Episode #818, Broadcast of May 29, 1951

Stunts: Bugle Call Song, Jet Model Test, Soldier Clerk Phone, and Nellis Air Force Base Vacation

Broadcast from the Nellis Air Force Base in Las Vegas, Nevada. **Art Gilmore** was the announcer on this broadcast, with assistance from **Jay Jackson** as the announcer via remote. Ralph Edwards and his crew perform on stage in front of an audience of jet pilots, ground crews, officers, enlisted men and "a smattering of sergeants," along with their commanding officer, **Colonel Avalon Tacon, Jr.** The Nellis Air Force Base is a jet training base, the home of the F-86 Shooting Stars. **Sergeant Ralph Artz** played the bugle and for every call, a private kept one of the five $20 bills that was handed to him.

Songs were different for both the East and West Coast broadcasts: "Oh, How I Hate to Get Up in the Morning," "Charge," "Crazy Over Horses," "Tea for Two," "Hail, Hail, the Gang's All Here," "Pay Call," "I Got Plenty of Nuthin'," and "Chow Call." The contestant receives a Bell and Howell 8mm Sportster movie camera for their participation and Artz received a Crosley portable radio… and a carton of Philip Morris.

A dancer from Las Vegas, **Betty London**, volunteered her time to provide a test to a jet pilot and if he passed the test, he went out on a date with her. One of the questions was to "explain the bail-out procedure in an F-80 equipped with an ejection seat."

Pfc. Gerald Lowell phoned his wife and convinced her to come to Las Vegas for a vacation. The hitch is that he had to pretend to be a clerk in a general store and during those two minutes he had to wait on customers. What Lowell did not realize until after the game has concluded that the producers flew his wife from Grand Rapids, Michigan, on a luxurious TWA Transworld Airlines Constellation and she was already in Las Vegas for the vacation. **Capt. Bill Quinlan** arranged for a three-day pass for Lowell, at the famous Hollywood Roosevelt Hotel, at the expense of the quiz program. **Sergeant Leo Pavelosky**, however, plays a similar game and wins a one-week vacation, expenses paid, to the Nellis Air Force Base!

Lt. Barney Rawlings helped assist with the radio broadcast. With hundreds of military personnel longing to appear on stage to perform consequences, the radio cast and crew performed an additional number of games, even though they were not broadcast live over the air. Following the stage performances, and to celebrate the final broadcast of the season, there was a staff party at the Flamingo Hotel late that evening.

Episode #819, Broadcast of June 17, 1952
Taped on June 6, 1952.
Stunts: Imitate Movie Star, Senior Prom, and Pet Milk Delivery No. 1

Celebrity guests include actors **Lizabeth Scott** and **Aldo Ray**. Contestant **Lillian Beardsley** is told to call a grocery store in Buffalo, New York, and ask the grocer to deliver one can of Pet Milk (the sponsor's product) to her Hollywood address. She places the call during the program and the grocer agrees to make the delivery. **John Tarrantino** of the Boulevard Market at 804 Niagara Blvd., in Buffalo, New York, during his phone conversation, agrees to start at once in his grocery delivery truck to make the cross-country trip to Hollywood. This portion of the broadcast was done in salute to the Grocers of America. NBC engineers at WBEN in Buffalo, New York, were instrumental in broadcasting this stunt.

Diane LeClercq, a senior at the John Burroughs High School in Burbank, California, goes to the senior prom with actor Aldo Ray, courtesy of Columbia Pictures, who pitches Ray's latest picture, *The Marrying Kind*. The contest was arranged courtesy of **Vernon H. Weybright**, principal of the high school. Diane's parents, meanwhile, go to the Brown Derby and have a nice dinner on the expense of the quiz program.

Beginning with this broadcast, a weekly "Surprise Consequence" was featured, ranging from 10 to 12 minutes of the program, with Ralph Edwards taking a roving mike into the audience where he briefly interviewed audience members and surprising them with small gifts, finally descending upon one unsuspecting guest who was lured to the program in some manner, without realizing they would be the person to get a big "Surprise Consequence" prize. The payoff usually invited the recipient to step to the stage and open the "Door of Surprises" – behind this improvised stage door could be the guest's entire family, flown across the continent to join them, gifts in the form of merchandise and clothing articles. With so many people submitting suggestions for *This Is Your Life*, Edwards and crew decided this would satisfy a number of requests without focusing an entire half-hour on the recipient's life.

Letter from Sue Clark, Press Relations for *Truth or Consequences*, to Mr. J.A. Haeffner, program manager of WBEN, Hotel Statler, Buffalo, NY

"Well, looks like we are all jumping with your contestant from Buffalo. I am having the Pet Milk Company send him direct 5,000 very tiny souvenir Pet Milk cans to give out on his way cross country. Would you ask him to be sure and contact the NBC stations in Cleveland, Chicago, Des Moines, Omaha, Denver, Salt Lake City, Reno, San Francisco, and Los Angeles on the way out? Don Cole of the Gardner Agency is sending him direct the names of the agency contacts in the various cities and is writing to alert the cities about the man coming through. On the return, we would like for him to do the same in Phoenix, Truth or Consequences, Albuquerque, Amarillo, Oklahoma City, Tulsa, St. Louis, Indianapolis, Columbus, Pittsburgh and New York. Would you arrange to have made for his truck, both sides and the back a sign reading something like I AM TRUTH OR CONSEQEUNCES CONTESTANT ON MY WAY TO LOS ANGELES TO DELIVER CANS OF PET MILK TO MRS. BEARDSLEY. T OR C, NBC, TUESDAYS. We, of course, will pay for the signs."

Episode #820, Broadcast of June 24, 1952
Stunts: Baseball Roulette, Desk Seat, Love Letter, Ellis Island, and Pet Milk Delivery No. 2
Broadcast live from the Polo Grounds in New York City. Ralph Edwards announces that *Truth or Consequences* is being broadcast from New York just as it was 12 years ago from the very same NBC Studio where the show originated. The first contestant was a New York Giants baseball fan, **Eric Webster**, of East Orange, New Jersey, who was given a chance to win as much as $1,000 if he predicted correctly what the batter would do when the quiz program tuned in to the game between the New York Giants and the Cincinnati Reds. If the batter up at that time gets a home run and contestant predicted the same, Webster receives $1,000… but must run around the diamond touching all four bases tomorrow, before the game, in order to collect.
From the Polo Grounds, **Russ Hodges**, regular announcer for the New York

Giants baseball TV and radio broadcasts, describes the play of the moment. Hodges talks from the WMCA booth overlooking the ball field. The game was in the second inning; Cincinnati leading 3 to 0, **Bob Elliott** of the Giants was up but was retired and the contestant's prediction stunt applies to **Don Mueller**, Giants right fielder. After one strike, which the contestant called earlier, Mueller flies out. Webster receives $100 for his prediction. He also added the prediction that the Giants would win the National League pennant and says his favorite Giant ball player is **Whitey Lockman**, second baseman.

In the Surprise Consequence contest, the surprise visit of the mother of G.I. **Porter Lee Whittington** of Wheeler, Texas, was brought to New York to meet her daughter-in-law to be, **Erica Rus**, who just arrived earlier in the day on the Queen Mary. Erica's fiancé was on his way home from Korea. *Truth or Consequences* gave the girl and the mother paid expenses stay in New York, air trip to Texas, and a number of gifts.

Pick-up from Chicago, **John Tarrantino**, grocer, reports on his progress. He was being entertained everywhere along the route by grocers and station managers of NBC stations. Numerous people were adding gifts to his market delivery truck.

Sierra County Advocate Publisher Arletta Coleman with quiz show contestant delivering a can of Pet Milk from Buffalo, New York.

Episode #821, Broadcast of July 1, 1952
Taped on June 13, 1952.
Pet Milk Delivery Payoff was Taped June 30, 1952.

Stunts: Seal Accompaniment, Citizenship Papers, Star Autograph, Surprise Grandmother, and Pet Milk Delivery Payoff

Surprise Consequence involves **Rock Hudson**, actor and star of *Has Anybody Seen My Gal?*, who appears in person to give an autographed picture to a high school admirer, **Sally Harrison**, of 2565 Woodstock, Hollywood, California.

Leonie Crawford of 1715 Georgia Street, Los Angeles, and her husband, Sergeant Crawford, are guests. She is presented with her Citizenship Papers on this broadcast. She applied and took the necessary tests but getting the papers was a Surprise Consequence for her. She also won a Tappan Gas Range.

Studio feature included **John Tarrantino**, the grocer from Buffalo, New York, who arrived in Hollywood to deliver a small can of Pet Milk ordered by **Lillian Beardsley** of Los Angeles, during the broadcast of June 17. He comes to the microphone to collect the money from her to pay for the milk. For his participation, he receives a new set of tires for his delivery truck, and an all-expenses paid vacation in Hollywood. His wife and two-year-old son have accompanied him on the broadcast. His brother and wife, who were keeping the grocery store running while Tarrantino was away, get a paid vacation at Lake Placid, and she receives a Westinghouse food-mixer. Tarantino received a Tappan Gas Range.

Helen Lee of 693 S. Shatto Place, Los Angeles, was asked "What is worth more after it is broken?" The answer was a horse. Because she did not know the answer, she had to sing with a sea lion (the same who swam the English Channel, featured on *Truth or Consequences* several years ago). This sea lion "sang" a song and Helen Lee received an Evans handbag made of seal skin.

Broadcast of July 8, 1952
Cancelled due to Republican National Convention, sponsored by Philco.

Episode #822, Broadcast of July 15, 1952
Taped on June 20, 1952.

Stunts: Love Count, Old Nightshirt, Old Model "T," Happy Birthday Singing Telegram, and Sealed Room B.U.

Broadcast originated from Chicago, Illinois. Feature spot included **George Libner**, Chicago Marine Corps Veteran, who agreed to enter a closed room in the Conrad Hilton Hotel on Tuesday, June 22, 1952, at 9:30 p.m. Eastern, and attempt to keep track of passage of time so that on the broadcast of July 29, during the first 25 minutes of the broadcast of *Truth or Consequences*, he (Libner) will ring a buzzer connected from his room to the broadcast stage to show that he knows exactly one week has passed. During the time he spends in the Conrad Hilton (Philco air-conditioned) room, he will have no means of telling time. No windows, no radio, no wristwatch, no telephone except an inside phone connecting directly to a desk outside his door where a *Truth or Consequences* representative is on constant guard. Over this phone, he may order and get any kind of service at any hour – food, cleaning and pressing, etc. Two men representing the quiz show staff (**Roland Rude** and **Dick Coyle**) will rotate time spent on guard and will be available to chat with Libner, play cards with him, etc. He will have also a record player and all kinds of books and magazines but no daily papers! He will use his own resources to compute the passage of time. If he guesses the time within the first 25 minutes of the broadcast on June 29, he will receive $1,000.

Surprise Consequence feature included a reunion with contestant **Roy Hess** and his old Model T pushed on stage, and contestant **Grace Ann Harvey** who receives a Happy Birthday singing telegram. She is reunited by her son, **Bill Harvey**, who is flown in on a luxurious TWA Transworld Airlines Constellation from the Naval Amphibious Base at Coronado, California.

A Love Count stunt includes a male contestant and a female judge, actress **Pamela Britton** of *Guys and Dolls*.

Broadcast of July 22, 1952

Program cancelled due to Democratic National Convention, sponsored by Philco.

Episode #823, Broadcast of July 29, 1952
Taped June 27, 1952.

Stunts: English Baseball, Dog Replacement, Maternity Mates, Doctor, Sealed Room Payoff, and Chicago Cubs

Broadcast originated from Chicago, Illinois. **George Libner**, the ex-Marine who agreed to be in a closed room at the Conrad Hilton Hotel in Chicago since July 22, guessed the time lapse of exactly 3 minutes and 45 seconds too early, before airtime, missing the $1,000 prize. As a consolation prize, Libner receives $250 in cash, a home freezer and a week-long vacation at the Flamingo Hotel in Las Vegas, Nevada. Libner spoke on the program from his special room and told how he kept track of time by running a movie on his projector and timing it by an hour glass made of paper through which he poured sugar saved from his meals; by timing phonograph records, timing movies in slow motion, etc.

Contestant **Michael Graham** of London, England, a member of the Piccadilly Bus Tour, watches a movie of the Yankee-Giant World Series Game of 1951 and gives a British broadcast view of the game. Contestant **Evelyn Lundeen**, nurse, attempts to identify two contestants now grown who were babies in the same nursery at the same time she worked in the Premature Babies' Nursery, at Michael Reese Hospital, in Chicago. **Pat O'Donnell**, a youngster in the audience, told the story of how they recently lost their dog, a Collie named Queenie. Edwards surprised the youth with a new Collie, with permission from the parents, of course.

The start of a new contest began on this broadcast. Each week, from a different city in the United States, a famous person disguised as a "Mystery Caller" knocked on the door of a listener who sent their name, address and telephone number to the quiz program, asking that the caller come to their door. The person who correctly identified the Mystery Caller would receive a Spiegel Catalogue gift certificate worth $1,250. For every week that the Mystery Caller remained unidentified, the amount of the gift certificate increased $250.

Episode #824, Broadcast of August 5, 1952
Taped June 17, 1952.
Stunts: Lullaby and $2,000 Sleep, T or C Mystery Caller No. 1, World's Fair 1915 Relic, and Fashion Model
Taped in San Francisco, California, with the Mystery Caller feature via electrical transcription from Atlanta, Georgia. In San Francisco, feature contests included a contestant trying to go to sleep right on the studio stage during the broadcast while all kinds of noises, including recordings of San Francisco cable cars, and a lady contestant singing a lullaby, were in progress. If **Dr. F. Edwyn Garfield's** examination at the end of the half-hour proved that the contestant actually slept, the contestant would receive $2,000.
From Atlanta, Georgia, the Mystery Caller knocked at the door of a Mrs. Whiting,

who incorrectly identified Mr. Mystery, so the amount of the gift certificate increased $250.

Episode #825, Broadcast of August 12, 1952
Stunts: Wife's Likes, Third Grade Composition, Wave Mother, and Mystery Caller No. 2

Broadcast live from Hollywood with the Mystery Caller segment via electrical transcription. The Mystery Caller knocked on the door of **Mrs. Max Wilson** of 518 E. 58th Street, Seattle, Washington. She incorrectly identified the Mystery Caller as **Charlie Andrews**, writer and cast member on **Dave Garroway's** radio program.

In the Hollywood studio, the Surprise Consequence honored a young engaged couple, **Frances Smith**, WAVE, and **Harold Williams**, Medical Dept. Corpsman, both stationed at Moffett Field in California. The bride to be was surprised by having her mother and father, **Mr. and Mrs. Clayton W. Smith** of Cheyenne, Wyoming, appear on the program. They were flown to Hollywood to take part in their daughter's wedding which was to be held next week.

Episode #826, Broadcast of August 19, 1952
Taped in Hollywood on June 30, 1952.
Stunts: England Mind Reader, Library Book Overdue Bill, Minister, Bridal Party, and Mystery Caller No. 3

Mrs. George Stillwell of Sioux Falls, South Dakota, greeted the Mystery Caller but could not identify them. The gift certificate prize was pushed up to $2,000. Stillwell guessed **Ozzie Nelson** and was incorrect but received a Westinghouse Roaster Over for participating.

A Trans-Atlantic phone call between London, England, and Hollywood, California, with Mr. Foster in the Hollywood Studios, talking to another American contestant who answered questions by phone regarding Mrs. Foster. Mr. Foster thought the contestant, a Mrs. Mosely, was a mind reader because she got all the facts about his life correct, unaware that it was his mother, from London, on the other line. He was finally let in on the secret and allowed to talk to his mother, off mike and away from the radio audience.

During the Surprise Consequence segment, **Anna Cherichillo** was asked if she ever read a book titled *The Prince of Foxes* and was informed that the book was overdue at the local library. Her fine was $18.00. Edwards handed her the $18 to pay the fine and gave her a beautiful Bulova Academy Award wristwatch to make sure she got the book back on time. **Charles and Agnes Crawford** were reintroduced to **Rev. W.L. Summers**, who was the minister of the First Methodist Church in Yuma, Arizona, who performed the services for the married couple.

Episode #827, Broadcast of August 26, 1952
Stunts: Groucho Marx Celebrity, Child Letter, Long Lost Relatives, and Mystery Caller No. 4
Mrs. John R. Jenkins of 26 Coffee Drive, Chalmette, Louisiana, a suburb of New Orleans, incorrectly guessed The Mystery Caller as **Meredith Willson**. She received a Westinghouse Roaster Oven as a consolation prize.
In a stunt involving **Groucho Marx, Mr. and Mrs. Sid Spitz** of 6620 Colgate Avenue in Selma, Louisiana, won a Tappan Gas Range and a Shaver and Shavex attachment. Actor **Dale Robertson** was a guest in a stunt involving contestant **Jacqueline Robertson** of 6378 Darby Place in Reseda, California. There was also a plug on the program for his motion-picture, *O. Henry's Full House*.
In the Surprise Consequence spot, a bother and a sister were reunited after 26 years. **Charles Sowers** was located in a Veterans' Hospital in a Western state. His sister, **Kathryn Johnson**, was referred to on the program only by first name. The veteran was also reunited with his daughter, **Colleen Sowers**, who lived on North Vernon Avenue in Louisiana, and his son, **Sergeant Alec K. Bowers**, of Ft. Leonard Wood, Missouri, who now had families of their own.

Episode #828, Broadcast of September 2, 1952
Stunts: Spin-Model-Pig, Lost Elephant, Call Home Town, and Mystery Caller Payoff
The Mystery Caller was correctly identified as aviator **Douglas "Wrong Way" Corrigan** who explained how the clue, "showing a grey suede glove which he wears on this right hand, removes and outs on his left hand" helped the contestant identify him. A right-hand glove would be "wrong way" on the "left hand." Winner was **Mrs. Ann Kappen**, of 400 Wadsworth Ave. in Denver, Colorado, with Corrigan and Mrs. Kappen both heard from Denver. She received the $2,500 gift certificate to Spiegel's Mail Order House.

Program guests include models **Lee Jay**, **Barbara Dodd** and **Sue Mayer**, and a baby pig named Rowena. **Goldie Stanton Cloud**, was presented with a statute of a miniature elephant given to her by **Florence Ziegfeld**, which she lost ten years ago. Special Surprise Consequence saluted small hometowns across the country including the 3,000 residents of Temecula, California, who honored **Frida Knott**, who did much for her community as a teacher and community worker. Her surprise was orchestrated with the assistance of her friend, **Alice Machado**.

Episode #829, Broadcast of September 9, 1952
Stunts: Cross Country Bicycle, T or C Atlas Mention, Thank You Chamber of Commerce, Celebrity Recording, and Mrs. Mystery

A new contest similar to the Mystery Caller, known as Mrs. Mystery, provided a recorded voice: "I have 2 Golden Gloves. You take one. Got it? Okay, let's shake." The first contestant was **Mrs. Richard Wise** of 2829 Anita Drive, Garland, Texas. She correctly identified **Gilda Grey**, famous dancer and actress. Mrs. Wise received a $1,500 gift certificate to Spiegel's Mail Order House.

Pick-up from the Hollywood Paramount Theatre, where actor **Jerry Lawrence** and contestant **Bob Serna** were featured. Serna was wearing a Gay Nineties bathing suit and thought he was at the *Truth or Consequences* studio but was transported via moving van to the lobby at the Paramount.

Celebrity guest was **Champ Butler**, vocalist and Columbia recording artist, singing "Younger than Springtime." Contestant **Allene Kleinman**, a fan of Champ Butler, was tricked into attending the show through her friend, **Shirley Reece**, and Edwards reveals Kleinman's desire to get a copy of Butler's "Younger than Springtime" – so Edwards arranged for a custom recording be made for Kleinman on the program.

There was a three-second fadeout on the applause at 9:58:20 p.m., as a result of an engineer-producer misunderstanding.

Episode #830, Broadcast of September 18, 1952
Stunts: Cow Symphony, Nutcracker, and Stock Company Picture

A new mystery caller contest began, known as "Mr. Mystery Number 3," providing the recorded clues as follows: "I have here a deck of cards. Ralph Edwards says I am a noted man, a colorful character. I don't know about that, but I'm handing you a group of cards that are all of one suit. That's a flush. Someone I loved once handed me a flush, which started my career with a rush. What is my name?" The winner who correctly identifies the mystery voice would receive an Amana Freezer in addition to the $1,500 gift certificate from Spiegel's Mail Order. The first contestant was **Hazel Gaines** of 314 W. Gurley Street, Prescott, Arizona, who incorrectly guesses the Mystery Caller was Papa Dionne. She received a Westinghouse Roaster Oven as a consolation prize.

Mrs. Harry Thornton of Kearney, Nebraska, failed to answer the question: "What is the main function of the liver?" (Answer: It serves as a base for the onions.") As her consequence, she had to participate in a cow symphony, for which she received Amelia Earhart luggage with cowhide trim. (Celebrity guests included **T.B. Williams** and the String Trio, furnishing the music. **Buddy Cole** led the following violinists for this act: **Victor Arno**, **Mischa Russell**, **Armand Kaproff** and **David H. Sterkin**.) The contestant milked a cow in rhythm to the music.

Celebrity guest was actress **Katherine Sheldon**, who began her career in a stock company in 1909 and was still active in radio and motion-pictures. She was reunited with her friend and former trouper, now an author, **Jessica Pan**, who flew to Hollywood from New York. **Dorothy Vaughn**, young radio and movie bit part actress, helped Ralph Edwards arrange the reunion of the two actresses.

Episode #831, Broadcast of September 25, 1952
Taped on September 23, 1952.
Stunts: Bob Richards Obstacle Course, Pie-Cake-Special Dinner, Star Kiss, and Lipstick Kiss

Broadcast originated from the Open-Air Theatre in Camp Pendleton, California, a Marine base for the Second Infantry Training Regiment whose next step was Korea. Contestants were the Marines and their families. Special guest was actress **Susan Cabot**, who kisses **Marine Thomas B. Stanley**, because he once made a statement that he would love to be kissed by "that girl Susan Cabot…"

Celebrity guest was **Rev. Bob Richards**, American athlete, the 1951 Decathlon champion and the 1952 Helsinki Olympics World Polo Vault Champion. He set a new record of 14 feet, 11 1/8 inches. He appeared disguised as an 1890 Bloomer Girl to run a race in competition with two Marines. Edwards claimed that **Mrs. Della Clark** (Richards in disguise) won the Bloomingdale

Broadcloth Bloomer Banner. **Sergeant Donald Booth** from Marble, Minnesota, and **Pfc. Elmer Mogingo** of Plumerville, Arkansas, both receive baked pies as their mother made back in their home town.

Otto H. Hess of 3933 Warwick Blvd., Kansas City, Missouri, received a visit from the Mystery Caller, who knocked on their front door. He incorrectly identifies the Mystery Caller as **Artie Shaw**.

Episode #832, Broadcast of October 2, 1952
Stunts: $50 Kiss, Initialed Hearts, and Tennessee Quartet

The original "Tennessee Quartet," a male quartet popular about 40 years ago, composed of **George Ridley Crump, Arlington Beebe, Kirby Crump** and **Al Langdon**. The reunion of these Quartet members was a surprise for all of them and they sang "I'm Makin' for Macon in Georgia," one of their old-time favorites.

Casey Blunt, a veteran of both World War II and Korea, was surprised when Ralph Edwards revealed his tattoo of **Lola Jean**, Casey's wife, who knew each other in Oakdale High School. The lovebirds' initials on his right arm were a testament of their love... as was the initials and heart on the background scenery of a high school play Casey once participated in, brought to the stage as a gift for the couple to go home with. "You'll be able to show it to your great grandchildren someday," Edwards exclaims.

Celebrity guest was actress **Donna Lee Hickey**, starlet currently seen in 20th Century Fox's *Snows of Kilimanjaro*, who two years later would be known under the stage name of **May Wynn**. The Mystery Caller contest continued with **Ethel O. McLaughlin** of 815 Normal Avenue, Fresno, California, who receives a visit from the Mystery Caller, and she incorrectly guesses **T. Texas Tyler**.

Episode #833, Broadcast of October 9, 1952
Stunts: Buddy Baer, Star Autograph, and Widow's Possessions

Celebrity guests include **Buddy Baer**, ex-boxing champion, and Hollywood actor Dana Andrews. Contestant **Theodore Farrah** of 1829 Mintwood Place in Washington, D.C., a tour guide around the outside of the White House, won a Tappan Gas Range. Contestants **Ann Louise** and **Elinor Smith**, twins, receive autographed photos of **Dana Andrews** and **Bal de Tete** perfume. A plug for Andrews' latest picture, *Assignment Paris*, was mentioned on the air.

- The Flying Tiger Lines (a.k.a. Flying Movers) received a plug on the program as a result of a "Woman's Possessions" stunt. They agreed to fly household goods for a contestant, **Nancy N. Irvine**, from Ohio to California, at no cost to her.
- The Mystery Caller was correctly identified as **Pinky Tomlin**. Among his hit songs were "The Object of My Affection." Contestant **Carolyn V. Kueffer** of 2506 NW Twelfth Street in Oklahoma City, Oklahoma, correctly identified the song writer and won a $2,250 gift certificate from Spiegel's Catalogue Mail Order House in Chicago.
- This broadcast launched the Creamy Peach Pie contest used only for studio contestants. Every contestant who said "Creamy Peach Pie" whenever Ralph Edwards made a clucking noise, received a $10 bill. (Creamy Peach Pie was a Pet Milk recipe.)

Episode #834, Broadcast of October 16, 1952

Stunts: $1,000 Heartbeat, Surprise Phone Call, Mystery Authors, and Creamy Peach Pie B.U.

Contestant **Joseph Leoni**, who was born in Constantinople, Turkey, was sent on a cross-country jaunt via TWA to cities across the nation, leaving under "sealed orders." In some lucky place, when Mr. Leoni says "Cluck, cluck, cluck" in a clucking sound like that used by Edwards on this broadcast, someone who replies, "Hello, Creamy Peach Pie" will receive $1,000. (Just like last week, whenever Edwards made the clucking sound, the studio contestant received $10 for responding appropriately.)

Celebrity guests included **Dave Kashner**, bullwhip artist, who demonstrated his skill with a whip by knocking cigarettes from someone's mouth; and four mystery writers: **James Fox** (his latest mystery was *A Shroud for Mr. Bundy*), **Stuart Palmer** (his latest mystery was *Before It's Too Late*), **Dorothy B. Hughes** (author of *The Davidian Report*) and **Jonathan Latimer** (author of the William Crane mysteries). Bathing suit and cover girl **Spring Mitchell** participated in a $1,000 Heartbeat stunt with contestant **Janice Raffee**, who measured a man's heartbeat when he was kissed by the model.

During the Surprise Consequence segment, from time to time, a listener somewhere in the U.S. was surprised by a telephone call from Ralph Edwards. This listener would get a prize, depending on what the individual needed because the listener telephoned was described by some well-wisher who sent a letter to the program. The phone call during this broadcast went to **Mrs.**

Edwin P. Smith of York, Pennsylvania, whose prize was a free trip for herself and her 2-year-old child to visit her husband who was an ex-G.I. studying at Penn State.

Episode #835, Broadcast of October 23, 1952
Stunts: Elephant-Donkey-Picture B.U., Own Presents, Family Picture, Marine Baby, and Creamy Peach Pie Payoff
The Creamy Peach Pie stunt terminated as contestant **Joe Leone** was a guest in the Hollywood studio to report that he gave away his $1,000 in Memphis, Tennessee, where **Mrs. H.V. Stauber** of 3541 Aurora Circle, Memphis, identified him when he visited her little shop at the jewelry counter.
This broadcast featured a salute to a Pet Milk Baby, two-month-old **Mary Elizabeth Regan**, who was on the program and whose father, **Marine Sergeant William Regan**, was surprised by getting to see her for the first time on this broadcast. One of the special guests was **Captain "Catfish" Williams** of Truth or Consequences, New Mexico, who held the world's championship for the size of the catfish caught, a 71-pound fish in Elephant Butte Lake, Truth or Consequences, New Mexico.
Mrs. Tom Keating was told to guess a number between one and ten. If she guessed correctly, she won an electric food mixer, an electric coffee pot, costume jewelry, a table lamp, a silver candy dish, and a love seat. She was unaware that her husband helped set up the stunt because the prizes were her own possessions. After the ruse was discovered, she received a Wool-o-the-West Gamester, including a beautiful blanket from the Portland Woolen Mills, the new Fryryte deep freezer, a Westinghouse Roaster Oven, a new Westinghouse Odorout Lamp, and a Tappan gas range.
The Democrat-Republican Contest began on this broadcast. **Bill Fletcher**, shoe salesman of Baltimore, was presented with a camera and one week's time in which to bring back pictures of a Republican named Elephant, seated on a Donkey, and a Democrat named Donkey, seated on an Elephant.

Episode #836, Broadcast of October 30, 1952
Stunts: Hospital House, Donkey-Elephant-Picture Payoff, Audience-Dentist Bill, Band Singer, and Campaign Button B.U.
Sixteen-year-old **Sandra Jacaloni**, a young vocalist, was given an opportunity to sing with **Jerry Gray** and his Orchestra. A student at San Fernando High

School in Pacoima, California, she was signed by Gray to sing during the November 15 engagement at the Statler Hotel in Los Angeles.

Program salutes the *Mary Lee Taylor* radio series, also sponsored by Pet Milk, on the occasion of the program's 19th anniversary which would be observed on Saturday. There was also a public service plea on the program for the Multiple Dystrophy Fund, asking listeners to send any contributions to DA, Los Angeles 19, California.

Pick-up from the home of contestant **Wally Williams**, who was blindfolded and put into an ambulance and taken to his own home. He thought he was in a hospital or still at NBC Studios in Hollywood. When he finds he was at home, he said over the air, "By God, I'm at home..." He loses out on the big prize by not knowing where he was, but Edwards heard about the stunt from an executive at NBC the following day because of the contestant's remark.

Contestant **Bill Fletcher** of Baltimore, Maryland, was back on the program with photos of a Republican named Daniel Elephant sitting on a donkey (Elephant comes from Encino, California); and of a Democrat named **Milton Burro** sitting on an elephant (Burro comes from Pacoima, California). The name "burro" was accepted as a synonym for "donkey" and the contestant received an Amana Home Freezer.

Episode #837, Broadcast of November 6, 1952
Stunts: Tiger Tail, Telephone Surprise-Bed Mattress, Peppettes Reunion, and Campaign Button No. 2

Last week a wager was made between a Democrat and a Republican, on the outcome of the Presidential Election. **William J. Fries**, retired businessman of Connecticut, bet on Eisenhower; **Jack Richard Moore** of Zanesville, Ohio, bet on Stevenson. They open their sealed "pay-off" envelopes to find that the loser had to parade up and down Vine Street one week from today wearing the campaign button of the Presidential candidate he supported – plus any other campaign buttons from any other Presidential election, or the most recent one which he could find around the house. Listeners were then asked to mail in all the campaign buttons they could supply and mail them direct to the loser's home address, provided on the air.

Celebrity guests included **Jeanine Shepherd Lonza** who, as **Jean Shepherd**, was star of the "Peppettes" dancing group in Lewiston, Idaho. As a surprise, other members of the former Peppettes appear on stage and Jeannine and the Peppettes perform, "I Got Rhythm." All members of the group received orchid corsages and $20 expense money – tied in with an announcement about National Flower Week. (The Peppettes included **Della Gravelle, Mary Thomas, Maria Harlow** and **Barbara Wipperfurth**.)

Gordon Kibbee, organist, subs for **Buddy Cole** for this episode.

Episode #838, Broadcast of November 13, 1952

Stunts: Campaign Button Payoff, Andy & Della Russell, Apron Picture, Pay Off Soldier Debts, and Mental Telepathy Build-Up

Contestant **Jack Richard Moore** of Ohio, who lost last week's Election bet and voted for **Adlai Stevenson**, is back on the show to pay off his bet as agreed, by parading up and down Vine Street wearing all of the campaign buttons sent to him by listeners. He's completely covered with campaign buttons which reached him during the week – only one State out of the 48 failed to send him a "Stevenson button" – that was Vermont! For his stunt, he received a 12-cubic foot Amana Freezer.

Celebrity guests include singers **Andy and Della Russell**, real-life man and wife. The Surprise Consequence spot involves a pay-all-your-debts stunt in which a Marine and his wife who are in debt to finance companies, **Montgomery Ward**, Industrial Loan & Investment Co., the Telephone Company, etc., get all their debts paid in full! (The total was $209.63.)

An on-going Extra-Sensory Perception Test (ESP) stunt begins with this broadcast. An authentic mind reading test is performed by guest **Dr. Leonard Wendland**, Doctor of Psychology at Pepperdine College, California. He explains his theory of mental telepathy and asks contestant **Marie Henson** of 451 South Ardmore, Los Angeles (it was mentioned Houston, Texas in the program), who volunteers for the experiment, to spend five minutes at 12 noon every day during the week, beginning tomorrow, concentrating on a five-word sentence which Dr. Wendland is trying to "send" her by Mental Telepathy. Next week she will appear on the program to state the sentence she may have "received."

Malcolm Davis, manager of the Sunset & Gower Branch of Bank of America, takes the sealed envelope, with Dr. Wendland's five-word sentence written inside, and put it into a strong box and locks the box – in full view of the studio audience. The strong box will remain in the bank safety vault until next week. This same mental telepathy/ESP test was restaged in the fall of 1966 for the television series.

Episode #839, Broadcast of November 20, 1952
Stunts: Star-Spangled Sailors, Traffic Ticket, Trip to New York, and Mental Telepathy No. 1

Celebrity guest is actress **Audrey Totter**, who participated in the Star-Spangled Sailors stunt in conjunction with Columbia Pictures and a pitch for the movie, *The Happy Time*, starring **Charles Boyer**. Contestant **Gloria Hopkins** of Reseda, California, received the Surprise Consequence. She had her traffic tickets resolved courtesy of Officer Clutterham.

Marie Henson, who tried all week to get **Dr. Leonard Wendland's** mental telepathy message, claims she was told "Do as you are told." This was not the message that was in the sealed envelope produced by **Malcolm Davis**, keeper of the Bank of America strong box. The original message was "Support your Red Feather Drive." This tied in with the Red Feather appeal. Another sealed envelope with a five-word sentence is given by Wendland to Davis, another envelope placed in a Bank of America strongbox. Beginning tonight and for the next three broadcasts, Ralph Edwards will concentrate for 20 seconds on the five-word sentence while there was absolute quiet on the air. Listeners across the nation were encouraged to "concentrate" and mail the "message" they receive to a specific address. Any person who correctly writes the exact message will be the winner on the broadcast of December 18, when the strongbox containing the envelope with the five-word sentence is open in full view of the studio audience. The winner will receive a $2,500 merchandise certificate from Spiegel's Mail Order Catalogue, plus $1,000 in cash. In case of a tie, the prize will be divided.

Episode #840, Broadcast of November 27, 1952
Stunts: Smash Fender, Servicemen Dinner, Thanksgiving Reunion, and Mental Telepathy No. 2

Mrs. Elvira Beale finds herself an unwilling contestant when Ralph Edwards tries to get her to argue with a man who backs into her new car. If, for an entire week, she does not lose her temper, she will receive a large prize. Pick-up from the NBC parking lot to cover the event as it happened. Back in the studio, a special Thanksgiving feature with all of the Army and Navy men and women who were in the studio audience, invited to stand and be recognized. They all receive a free Thanksgiving dinner at famous Hollywood restaurants. The restaurant owners who appear as guests on the program: **Gus Constance** and **Staunton Pillsbury** of the Brown Derby; **Mrs. Fred Glow** of Bit O' Sweden; **Max Lerner** of Mike Lyman's; and **Nick Slovich** of Nickodell's. Some of the servicemen were interviewed on the program: **Roland Reece** of Iowa, **Dale Mitchell** of Massachusetts, **Johnny Calender** of Pennsylvania, **Pfc. Valenti** of New York, **Robert Schaefer** and someone identified merely as "Cornwell." In another Surprise Consequence feature, **Bob Matthews** of Dallas, Texas, who served on the submarine Queen Fish, was surprised by his uncle, **Charles Austin** of Madeira, California, and by a visit from his own family and from his bride's father. Last Sunday, Matthews married **Rosemary Meyer**. (Mrs. Matthews, the bride, is also on the program).

Episode #841, Broadcast of December 4, 1952
Stunts: Happy Birthday Running Gag, Trees, Telephone Orphanage, and Mental Telepathy No. 3

Mrs. Jim Dorsey of 409 Hollywood Blvd., in Birmingham, Alabama, received $35 for the purchase of a U.S. Savings Bond, in a Happy Birthday running gag. Motion-picture star **Virginia Mayo** assisted with a stunt for contestant **Mrs. Don Frank** of Los Angeles. Mayo appeared courtesy of Warner Brothers and on-air mention that her latest picture was *The Iron Mistress*.

Atha Graffort of Olney, Missouri, a 75-year-old foster mother, requested the listening audience to send canned goods to her to help a local orphanage. In response, Pet Milk contributed a year's supply of canned milk. Also donated was a 12-cubic foot Amana freezer, a Tappan gas range and a Westinghouse Refrigerator with 59 pounds of cold storage space.

Episode #842, Broadcast of December 11, 1952
Stunts: Bus Welcome, Return Ring, Song Debut, and Mental Telepathy No. 4

Ralph Edwards delivers a report from **Atha Graffort**, regarding her plea last week to help a Missouri orphanage. The first night the cans of food came in, the kids were unable to eat in the kitchen because food was piled so high with canned goods. Assuming Graffort and the children were listening, Edwards read a wire from **Wayne J. Hackett**, General Manager of KJFJ, an independent radio station in Webster City, Iowa: "KJFJ in Webster City has taken on a canned food raising program for its Christmas project this year to help Miss Graffort in time for Christmas. A large amount has been sent in over the week and more is coming in fast."

Mrs. James Biersach, housewife, wrote a song titled "Every Day is Christmas" and celebrity **Gordon MacRae** sung the song, accompanied by the Buddy Cole Trio. Afterwards, **Mike Gould** of the Ardmore and Beechwood Music Publishing Company appeared on the program and promised publication of the song.

Episode #843, Broadcast of December 18, 1952

Stunts: Guess What, Atha Graffort Mention, Billy Eckstine, Colorado Husband, and Mental Telepathy Payoff

During the Surprise Consequence, **Corporal William Cole** and **Pfc. Darrell Neill** are contestants. Both were known as singers and could do a terrific imitation of **Billy Eckstine**. **Ken Carpenter** informs the radio audience that Neill could not sing. Neill mouthed the words as Billy Eckstine himself, standing next to him behind a screen, did the actual singing. Imagine Cole's surprise! (Eckstine appeared courtesy of MGM records and a plug for his engagement at the Stanley Theatre in Pittsburgh for one week beginning December 24.)

Mary Meredith of Venice, California, is in for a holiday surprise. Her husband is hospitalized in the Army hospital at Camp Carson in Colorado, suffering from tuberculosis. He was not expected to be released for at least 18 months. They were married in Tijuana, Mexico and settled in Milwaukee, Wisconsin. In May 1948, **Dolton Meredith** joined the Army. Because the Army would not recognize a marriage in Mexico, she received none of the allotments or benefits of a serviceman's wife. She was unable to follow her husband abroad. On the program, she received a round-trip ticket on a luxurious TWA Transworld Airlines Constellation to Denver to spend the holiday with her husband, with accommodations at The Hostess House at Camp Carson while she was there. She was also given five $20 bills to cover the cost of the ticket. Dolton sold his wristwatch, among other things, so that he could get the $100 for her. Edwards gave her a brand new Bulova wristwatch to replace her husband's timepiece.

The Mental Telepathy contest concluded with **J.H. Norton** of Winona, Missouri, the winner, accurately predicting the phrase in the Bank of America lock box.

Episode #844, Broadcast of December 25, 1952
Taped December 11 and 18, 1952.
Stunts: Reverse Consequence Gifts, Mary Christmas Hat, Teeth, Surprise Christmas, and Service Men Phone Calls

Jane Barrows agrees to play a game in reverse. Edwards bestowed her with multiple prizes and because she failed to answer the question correctly, had to give the presents away to people in the audience.

Episode #845, Broadcast of January 1, 1953
Stunts: New Year's Calling, Replace Tools, Atha Graffort, and Tall Story No. 1

There was a March of Dimes spot at the opening of the program when Ralph Edwards and contestant **Harry Weinstein**, an insurance man of Los Angeles, talk about the good done through the annual March of Dimes campaign. Listeners were urged to get their dimes ready for the 1953 drive!

An update regarding the canned food campaign for the orphanage in Olney, Missouri, **Atha Graffort** explains the miraculous gift of charity, described by the local papers there as "The Miracle of Olney, Missouri." She thanks all who sent her food, other gifts, and cash to her in response to the publicity she received on the radio program. She reported the receipt of 12,846 packages of food... Enough to last about four years, most of it in cans which would make it safe to keep as long as it lasts; $4,000 in cash; 3,949 letters; fresh fruit by the bushel; a quarter beef and many cards.

The Tall-Story Contest for Service Men began, the start of a six-week contest in which the best "tall-story teller" from some military bases would compete with another tall storyteller from another base to decide on a winner. Each week's winner, who returns to the program the following week to compete with a new contestant, will receive a $50 US Government Bond. The six-week winner will get a $500 U.S. Savings Bond. Eliminations were held at the various camps and the camp determined who would be the contestants. The judges were **Fairley Albert**, President of the San Fernando Sportsman's Club; **Ransom Sherman**, television and radio storyteller; and **Vincent Sherman**, producer and director of Columbia Pictures. The first two servicemen to take part in the new contest were **Tony Cedroni**, Chief, Seabees, hometown Philadelphia, Pennsylvania; and Draftsman Second Class **Granville Judd**, Seabee. Seabee Judd was the winner by unanimous vote of the judges.

Episode #846, Broadcast of January 8, 1953

Stunts: Gisele MacKenzie, Bavarian Plate, Sister Reunion, and Tall Story No. 2

Celebrity guest was singer **Gisele MacKenzie**, who participates in a stunt whereupon a contestant must sing "You'll Never Get Away." She received an on-air plug for her engagement at the Sahara in Las Vegas.

Two sisters were reunited on the program, courtesy of Edwards' "Door of Surprises." Mary discovers her sister, Beatrice, is sitting right next to her the entire time in disguise.

Episode #847, Broadcast of January 15, 1953

Stunts: Tall Story No. 3, Telephone Contest Winner, High School Annual, and Elephant Fable

For a third week in a row, the Tall-Story Contest was performed. This time **Danny Davenport**, Airman Second Class from the March Airforce Base in Riverside, California, told a tall tale against last week's winner, **Sergeant Paul Shaner**, a Marine from the El Toro Marine Base. Davenport was in line for the grand prize of a $500 Savings Bond, but for now wins a $50 Savings Bond and a Westinghouse Clock Radio. Shaner, for coming in second place, won a $25 Savings Bond and an electric shaver with the amazing new Shavex attachment.

Hazel M. Foster wrote to the program informing them of **Miss Ferrol Schiller** of Columbus, Montana, who has been entering contests for years and never won anything. With the arrangement of Foster and friends, Schiller was not listening to the radio while Edwards put in a call to Miss Schiller. "This is the Get-Rich-Quick Program in Hollywood, California," Edwards told the contestant. "If you can answer a certain question you can get rich quick. You have exactly ten seconds to answer the question... Who was the composer of Beethoven's Fifth Symphony?" She answered correctly and won a Westinghouse Roaster Oven, a set of Brockware, a matched set of Amelia Earhart Luggage, a supply of White Rain lotion shampoo, Bal de Tete perfume, and a Bulova Martha Washington watch. And for every room in her home, Varlar Stainproof wall covering from the United Wallpaper Company.

Episode #848, Broadcast of January 22, 1953

Stunts: Tall Story No. 4, Returned Watch, Hope Chest, and German Doubletalk

Celebrity guest was **Vincent Sherman**, film director promoting his latest film,

Affair in Trinidad (starring **Rita Hayworth**) who participated in the tall story segment of the program. **Sergeant Paul Shaner** from last week went up against **Pvt. Peter Markapoulas**, from Camp Roberts.

Mrs. Clarence B. Hoadly was surprised when she became a contestant on the program. Edwards helped her recall how her husband was a graduate of Swarthmore College in Pennsylvania. Her husband once broke the record for the 440-yard dash in 53 seconds. At that time, he received a gold watch, presented by Walter Clothier. The watch bore the following inscription: "To Clarence B. Hoadly. Record 53 seconds. 440 Yard Dash, Swarthmore College, May 23, 1896." She could not remember how she lost the watch but Edwards surprises her with that very watch, which was recently found. It turned up in the possession of a seaman. It later appeared in the establishment of a dealer in old jewelry over 5,000 miles from Hollywood. The watch then made its way to Korea where a boy there sent it to his brother in the United States.

Mary Lou Kay, a senior at UCLA, engaged to marry Airman Second Class **John Pimentel**, stationed at Kelly Field in San Antonio, Texas, received a beautiful hope chest from the Spiegel Catalogue, filled with prizes a bride would need after marriage. Dresses from Deedee Johnson, clothing designer in California, twelve pairs of the Bonnie Kaye Hosiery by Vogue, linens, towels, a certificate for redemption of a Tappan Gas Range, a baby rattle, the new Fryryte deep fryer, and a certificate for a beautiful Westinghouse refrigerator with 59 cubic feet of cold storage space for frozen foods... and her boyfriend who pops out of the hope chest!

Episode #849, Broadcast of January 29, 1953

Stunts: Tall Story No. 5, Magazine Subscriptions, Pawned Object, and Singing Sailor

The Tall-Story Contest continues with **Seaman Bill Allen** of the Naval Ordinance Test Center, a resident of Edinburg, Texas, who went up against **Sergeant Paul Shaner**, who retained his status again as a tall storyteller.

Ralph Edwards spoke briefly about the up-coming Fiesta in Truth or Consequences, New Mexico, encouraging radio listeners to join the fun in the city of health and hospitality. "Rodeo, parades, barbecues, street dancing, Old Fiddler's contest, as well as guessing stunts and a hooded mystery man with big prizes!" Edwards exclaimed.

Young **Barbara "Babs" Rice** was trying to sell subscriptions to *Children's*

Digest Magazine in the hopes of selling subscriptions to be rewarded with enough money to pay for the balance of a bicycle her parents promised to buy. She worked every day after school, door-to-door, but failed to sell many subscriptions. The quiz program gave her a brief minute to explain the importance of the magazine and encourage radio listeners to send in money to buy subscriptions. People in the audience were volunteering to buy subscriptions – enough to ensure she would get the bike... which was brought out on the stage. A beautiful 1953 Monarch Bicycle which included a one-year fire and theft insurance policy.

Celebrity guest as California's Heavyweight champion, **Willie Bean**, telling how he began a boxing career in 1946 and went up the ladder to capture the Pacific Coast crown in 1950. The Inland Boxing Club of Spokane, Washington, awarded him with a championship belt. When things got tough as a result of a sickness in the family, there were doctor bills to pay and he pawned everything he had to make the bills good. The last to go was his championship belt. As a Surprise Consequence, Edwards presented Bean with his belt, which they found.

The Singing Sailor stunt featured celebrity guest **Andy Russell**.

Episode #850, Broadcast of February 5, 1953
Stunts: Tall Story Payoff, Mr. Langdon, Father-Daughter Reunion, and Broderick Crawford

The Tall-Story Contest concludes. In the running for the $500 Savings Bond, **Sergeant Paul Shaner**, the Marine from El Toro Marine Base at Santa Ana, California, went up against **Chief Duane Pople**, an eager opponent who recently won the big elimination contest at the Coast Guard Base on Terminal Beach, Long Beach, California. The latter won the contest while Shaner, who carried the contest for four weeks, won the usual $25 Savings Bond weekly prize, and an additional runner-up prize of a $50 Savings Bond. Judges received a Sterling Silver Zippo lighter, engraved, and a Westinghouse clock radio.

Mr. Joe J. Langdon of Roscobel, Wisconsin, on vacation to California with his wife, was the victim of a Surprise Consequence. By profession a rural mail carrier, he was provided a tour of the Los Angeles Post Office, which included full inspection of the money order department, and to accompany a daily mail carrier on his route... a joke obviously played by his employers for an afternoon of his vacation. Langdon's wife, however, received a Wool-o-the-West Gamester and a beautiful blanket from the Portland Woolen Mills. While the band played "Jolly Good Fellow," a good luck horseshoe of flowers was placed around Mr. Langdon's neck.

Mrs. Florence Mounts of 1714 Wellesley Avenue, West Los Angeles, was married to **Mr. Tracy Mounts** for over 25 years. With two fine boys, **Francis** and **Tracy, Jr.**, she never saw her father in decades. In 1920, her father and mother, two brothers, sister and she were living in Calais, Maine, when her father and mother divorced. Her father went to California alone. He worked many jobs – from lumberjack to cook – and always sent money home to his family. A family reunion was staged on the radio program.

Episode #851, Broadcast of February 12, 1953
Stunts: Empty Hollywood Bowl, Good Luck Dollar, and Margaret Whiting Valentine

Jean Hoffman of 11838 Dorothy Street, Los Angeles, was an Army nurse in the South Pacific during World War II. She performed heroically in her capacity but suffered a serious leg injury which made it impossible for her to drive a car without specially-built controls. Then, not so long ago, someone ran into her car, smashing it up, and injuring her again. Rather than worry about herself, she wrote many letters of cheer and encouragement to others who were in trouble. Among the letters was one to **Mrs. Annie Naulty** of Wickenburg, Arizona, and as Naulty explained, "Some years ago when things looked very dark for us, Jean Hoffman sent us this dollar bill. 'Have faith,' she wrote, 'and may this dollar bill be an omen of good things to come.' It was, and now that Jean herself has had more trouble I would like to have you return it to her with our good wishes, and our hope that it will bring her the luck it brought us." In recognition for her devotion, Hoffman was rewarded with an all-expense paid vacation to the Flamingo Hotel in Las Vegas, Nevada, with a set of Amelia Earhart luggage, and travel provided by a new 1953 Packard, with a chauffeur to take her where she needed.

Pfc. Stephen Sheldon was interviewed by Ralph Edwards, explaining how he kept getting Valentine's cards in the mail from singer **Margaret Whiting**. The most recent card read: "Sometime today, you will hold me in your arms while I sing you a long song – Margaret Whiting." Sheldon was surprised when he discovered the woman sitting next to him the entire time was the singer herself! She let him hold her in his arms while she sang "Take Care My Love," which was recently released through Capitol Records. As a Valentine's present, the Marine received a Bulova wristwatch engraved, "Happy Valentine, 1953, Margaret Whiting." Before leaving, she kisses the Marine.

Episode #852, Broadcast of February 19, 1953
Stunts: Amateur Song Writer, Return Watch, Wheel Chair Phone, Honorary Mayor Mention, and Ride Chief

Bob Hilton, a buyer out at Lincoln-Mercury, wrote a song and his sister secretly sent it in to the producers of *Truth or Consequences*. Chosen as a contestant in advance, Hilton was asked to act as a judge with two other fellows who know something about music – famous orchestra leaders **Dick Stabile** and **Ralph Flanagan**. Announcer **Jack Smith** sang while **Buddy Cole** played the tune.

Billie Clevenger, NBC phone operator, connected Ralph Edwards and his crew to a woman named Mrs. Ball in Colorado, via telephone, who had a daughter who was ill for a long time. They presented her with a surprise in the living room – a brand new wheelchair for her daughter.

Edwards made another pitch for the up-coming Fiesta at Truth or Consequences, New Mexico, asking children to write in to the program telling "Why your dad or mother should be honorary Mayor of Truth or Consequences, New Mexico, during the Fiesta." A committee appointed by officials of Truth or Consequences would judge the entrants and the mother or father chosen would be flown to the Fiesta to participate at the head of the parade, have a box seat at the three-day rodeo, be honored on the radio broadcast that weekend, and take part in all the festivities.

Episode #853, Broadcast of February 26, 1953
Stunts: Rosemary Clooney, Last Fling, Fly Soldier Home, Honorary Mayor Mention, and General George C. Kenny

Celebrity guest was **Rosemary Clooney**, who performed a rendition of "Tenderly," with Buddy Cole supplying the music. **Floyd Croswait**, a soldier, is flown home via TWA to Cincinnati, Ohio. **General George C. Kenny**, President of the National Arthritis & Rheumatism Foundation, spoke for a moment in this episode. Air Force **Lt. Robert B. Siegel** received a $100 Spiegel gift certificate for a stunt involving General Kenny.

Episode #854, Broadcast of March 5, 1953

Stunts: Scotch Kilts Water Tank, Ripe Olive Tuna Ring B.U., return Ring, Lost Father Reunion, and Honorary T or C Mayor

John Bleifer, an actor who appeared in many movies back from the silent days, and was appearing in *The Juggler*, soon to be released, was reunited with a ring once given to him from actor **Rudolph Schildkraut**. Bleifer told the significance of the ring and how he came to lose it.

Eleanor Covington was a surprised contestant when it was revealed that for thirteen years she attempted to locate her father, **Adam Schoveller**. A few months prior she succeeded in her task but they were not able to get together because he could not afford the trip. Because of sickness and finances she has been unable to go to Detroit. He left 26 years ago when her mother and father divorced. Mr. Schoveller has been staying at the Knickerbocker Hotel since he arrived in California at the expense of the quiz show.

Episode #855, Broadcast of March 12, 1953

Stunts: Stars Mothers, Hearing Aid, False Teeth, Repaired Car, Honorary Mayor Mention, and Ripe Olive Tune Ring Payoff

Many prizes were awarded in this broadcast. A Contour chair from the Contour Company was sent to the Motion Picture Mothers' Clubroom. A Zenith Regent hearing aid was awarded to **Ray Hodge** of Hondo, California. His friend Wiley wrote a letter in advance to inform the producers that Hodge needed a new hearing aid and could not afford one. **Mrs. Margaret S. Duester** of 817 W. Santa Barbara, Los Angeles, received a Fryryte deep fryer and two Swift Premium hams. **Tom Zachary** discovered the repair bill for his car, $91.01, has been paid.

Episode #856, Broadcast of March 19, 1953

Stunts: Bathing Suits Package, Pillow Case, Honor Student, and Skunk Hitchhike B.U.

Dolores Lee of La Mirada Street, Hollywood, had two boys serving in Korea. She managed the Children's Department in Sears' Hollywood Store and recently the President of Sears commended her, personally, for her excellent merchandising. In a job such as hers, no little detail must be overlooked – no half-finished displays. But a pillowcase she was embroidering when she was 13 years old was never finished and it was brought to the stage as a gift.

A young high school girl in St. Clairsville, Ohio, an honor student, had a semi-invalid mother. In spite of sickness and extreme financial difficulties, they continued to hold their heads high and look only to the future. Because they had no phone, Principal **John Shannon** arranged for them to be in his office at the St. Clairsville High School to receive a call from Ralph Edwards. She revealed her hardships and the pride she had in her daughter for reaching the honor roll. "It is no disgrace to be poor," she explained to Edwards. "We do the best we can. We live by the good book and the golden rule." Edwards revealed that a special assembly in Lois' honor gathered in the auditorium, where Principal Shannon made a short announcement to this effect: He called a special assembly because Pet Milk wanted to bestow their annual award to an honor student who was deserving. **Lois Bush** was called to the stage and was given a new prom dress and a gown for graduation day, courtesy of Stone and Thomas, West Virginia's largest department store. He mother would also be receiving prizes including a Tappan stove range, and a new Westinghouse refrigerator.

Episode #857, Broadcast of March 26, 1953
Stunts: Taxi Vacation, Stolen Watch, Orphan's Circus, Honorary Mayor Winner, and Skunk Hitchhike No. 1
- **Mr. Bill Bell** of Los Angeles was selected out of the audience to play a "Taxi Vacation" stunt in which his wife was disguised. The couple won a trip to the Flamingo Hotel in Las Vegas, and the use of a 1953 Packard to drive to Las Vegas, along with $75 expense money.
- During the Surprise Consequence segment, **Tom Grant** of Compton, California, has a lost watch returned to him, and he and his wife win a $53 Spiegel gift certificate.
- Clyde Beatty Circus tickets go to the children of the Volunteers of America Children's Home. **Dennis Vivella**, a child from the home, and **Bobby Kay**, a clown from the circus, appeared on the broadcast.
- **Lynne Higinbotham**, age 14, was on the program to help bestow the prize of "Honorary Mayor" in Truth or Consequences, New Mexico, for the upcoming Fiesta, to her father, **Mr. R.L. Higinbotham** of Sunburst, Montana.

Episode #858, Broadcast of April 2, 1953
Taped March 1, 1953

Stunts: Swami-Husband, Boy-Dog Reunion, Beauty Contest, St. Louis Browns, and Skunk Hitchhiker No. 2

This radio episode was kinescope-simulcast from the television series. Audio was re-edited for radio, retaining most of the television contents. Actor **Boris Karloff** makes an appearance on this episode, participating in a "Swami Husband" stunt. **Mr. and Mrs. Frank Lawrence** of Hollywood were the unsuspecting contestants. They received $100 cash for their participation.

Agnes C. Thornton of Palo Alto, California, helped her son **Tommy Thornton** be reunited with his dog, named Spot, and was awarded dog food and a dog house.

Hollywood actress **Marla English** and **Alice Corr**, the Maid of Cotton beauty pageant winner, participate in a beauty contest involving **Mrs. Moreen Ehly**, flown in from England, with her husband **Sergeant Robert L. Ehly**, stationed at Camp Pendleton in Oceanside, California.

Episode #859, Broadcast of April 9, 1953
Taped on April 4, 1953

Stunts: Mystery Man Payoff, Man's Gifts, Governor Mecham, City Hall Sign, Honorary Mayor, Church Essay, Old Fiddler's Contest, and Skunk Hitchhiker Payoff

Broadcast live from Truth or Consequences, New Mexico, as part of the annual Fiesta festivities. The Mystery Man who walked about town in disguise all week was identified by **Bill Perry**, a local resident. During the Surprise Consequence, Ralph Edwards asks **Governor Edwin L. Mecham** of New Mexico, to speak a few words about the great state of Arizona – his competition. **Mayor T.B. Williams** tells the radio audience a few things about Truth or Consequences, New Mexico, including the principal industry and the number of tourists who come to visit the city every year. Edwards and his crew presented the mayor with a neon sign reading, "City Hall, Truth or Consequences, New Mexico." The sign was made by the Luminart Neon Company Electrical Advertising of Los Angeles. Having had all the children of Truth or Consequences write an essay, "What Church means to me," 16-year-old **Mary Faye Leigon** walked up on stage to accept a Bulova wrist-watch and a Schwinn bicycle for writing the winning essay. Actor **James Stewart** read her essay on the air. An old fiddler's contest was performed on the air and the winner received $175 in cash and a new fiddle.

Ralph Edwards at the annual Fiesta in Truth or Consequences, New Mexico.

Episode #860, Broadcast of April 16, 1953

Stunts: Impediment Drama, Telephone-Canary, Letter Award, Sailor's Wallet, and Husband-Mermaid Water Tank

During the Surprise Consequence, the children at the Merced County Hospital Polio Unit receive a 21-inch Westinghouse television set. A female contestant wins a canary and a cage. Winner of the letter award was **Stanley Steinke** of 8567 Eglise Ave., Rivers, California, who received four dozen golf balls from dealers of the Goodyear Tire & Rubber Company. A Husband-Mermaid Water Tank stunt was practically what you think it is, with **Mr. and Mrs. Robert Harding** of Joplin, Missouri, the participating contestants. **Joan Mayberry**, professional model, played the role of the mermaid.

Episode #861, Broadcast of April 23, 1953

Stunts: Opera Star, Gold Football, G.I. Reunion, and Hypnotist Wife

Opera star **Florence McCann** was a celebrity guest on this broadcast, performing a solo with **Buddy Cole** as accompanist. **Jack Petty** of Culver City, California, participated in the contest and won a Tappan Gas Range for his efforts. **Peggy Cox** of Corcoran, California, returned a lost gold football charm during a Surprise Consequence and received a gold Bulova wristwatch as a result. There was a G.I. Reunion, brothers **Lee R. Lee** of Missouri and **Glenn A. Jones** of Nebraska, adopted into separate foster homes. Assisting with the contest was a girl WAVE, Miss McKinnon. A Hypnotist Wife stunt involved **Jim Plummer** of Monterey, California, and his wife – Husband was in town for business and did not recognize his wife in disguise. **Dr. Karl Reinhart** performed the hypnotist act.

Episode #862, Broadcast of April 30, 1953
Stunts: Louse Up Contestant, Airman WAAF Reunion, Bobby Riggio No. 2, and Star

Broadcast from the Flamingo Hotel in Las Vegas, Nevada. A woman was sent to the Hotel Flamingo to perform on stage, billed as a professional singer but in reality, she had no experience. She sung "Stardust," "Enchanted Evening," "Fantasy Impromptu," and "Chasing Rainbows." Among the Surprise Consequences was Airman Second Class **Eunice A. McAmis**, 2243 WAF Squadron, at the Mitchel Airforce Base in New York, and her husband, Airman Second Class **Virgil McAmis** at the Nellis Air base in Nevada, who won a three-day pass and stay at the Flamingo.

The Variety Club School for Handicapped Children receive a 1953 21-inch screen Westinghouse television set, a 12-cubic foot Amana freezer, and a folding wheel chair from Abbey Rents, as a result of Principal **Helen Wilborn** and her arrangement of having **Alan Sanders**, age seven, sing "Over the Rainbow." He received a $500 U.S. Savings Bond, along with $5,000 in donations sent in to the Variety Club, Las Vegas, Nevada, for the benefit of the school.

Celebrity guest was actor **Edmund O'Brien**, courtesy of Columbia Pictures. A pitch for his latest film, *Man in the Dark*, was made during the program. Contestant and movie struck girl **Eunice L. Smith**, a young lady from Las Vegas, won a Bulova wristwatch for her participation in a stunt.

Episode #863, Broadcast of May 7, 1953
Stunts: Plant Wallet, Boy-Dog-Phone, Fraternity Ring, Pet Milk Phone Number, Variety Club Mention, and What's My Name Seltzer

A young boy named **Galen Watson** of Lampasas, Texas, was presented with a new dog in a phone call contest. **Mr. and Mrs. Andrew Streitwieser** of Jamaica, New York, failed to pick up the cash value of a $25 U.S. Savings Bond in the "What's My Name Seltzer" contest, so it was mailed to them instead. They also received a Westinghouse Automatic Electric Blanket.

Episode #864, Broadcast of May 14, 1953
Taped May 11, 1953.
Stunts: Ad-Lib Drama, Phone-Girl-Friend-Band, El Toro Service, and Cross Country Bicycle B.U.
Broadcast originated from the El Toro Marine Base in Santa Ana, California. **Michael McIntyre**, a serviceman, was asked to ad lib in a sketch with actress **Rhonda Fleming**, star of *The Serpent of the Nile*, her up-coming motion-picture. McIntyre played the role of a wealthy bachelor and man-about-town named **Gaylord DuVal**, who meets his mad lover, who begs for him to tell her how much he loves her, asks him to hold her in his arms, recall the name of the little café they enjoyed, and to kiss her... and Edwards directs him to her cheek. For his participation, McIntyre wins a Westinghouse portable radio.
Corporal James Burton from Hamilton, Ohio, confesses he has a girlfriend name Ruth Davis and that it has been almost a year since he saw her. Edwards arranged for the two to connect on the phone while the El Toro Marine band, under the direction of Warrant Officer **Victor Shuel**, played a few bars of music... so loud that he could not hear his sweetheart's voice over the phone. After the gag concluded, Burton was told that Ruth was waiting backstage and he could go meet her and take a Bulova wristwatch as a consolation prize.
Another Marine, **Lawrence Reed** of Danville, Illinois, was a guest on the base and on stage he faced the "Door of Surprise" where various men on the base, **Lt. John Kennedy, Major James Pugh, Capt. Gilbert Meuller**, etc., continue to service his needs by providing his slippers, his fishing rod, a hot water bag, and so on. The catch? His mother was flown to California and would be in town for a few days' visit.

Cross Country Trip

Marine Corporal Donald Mainland, a 21-year-old native of Racine, Wisconsin, had to suffer the consequence of breaking the cross-country bicycle racing record. Corporal Mainland shoved off from Santa Monica on Friday morning, May 15, hoping to pedal the 2,910 miles to New York City in less than 20 days, 7 hours and 29 minutes. "I hope to trim the time by about five days," he told reporters on the takeoff. "With a little luck, I think I can make about 200 miles in a 10-hour day. I'll sleep in motels and eat in restaurants along the highway." The stunt was sponsored by the *Truth or Consequences* radio program, which began the Cross Country Bike stunt on the broadcast of May 14, 1953.

For most of the pedaling, Mainland used an Italian road bike with eight speeds forward, but in the car accompanying him was two American racing bikes, one with a low gear ratio for climbing mountains and another with a high gear ratio for flat lands. To get in shape for his long-distance attempt, Mainland, a communications man in the Third Marine Division, pedaled as much as 100 miles a day over the mountainous roads at Camp Pendleton in California. "I guess I'm one of the few Marines who works harder off duty than on," he joked. Along for the trip was his wife, Ruth, and a Marine buddy, as well as the publicity man representing the radio program.

Along the trip, a transcribed conversation for the radio program reported on their progress, week by week. A few miles west of Albuquerque, New Mexico, Mainland ran into some thorns and needed tire repairs. Weather also played a factor in his attempt to beat the record: rain in California and snow in Arizona.

Meanwhile, back in the triangular traffic island at the intersection of La Brea and Hollywood Boulevard, Sergeant Sam Scherr peddled on a stationary bike. His task was to peddle to a certain goal and see which of the two Marines accomplishes their task first. For the traffic island stunt, Ed Bailey secured the necessary clearances through the Mayor's office, Chief of Police, and the Precinct Captain, as well as the Bureau of Water and Power, and the Board of Public Works in the City of Los Angeles. The entire stunt was in conjunction with the Marine Corps Recruiting.

During the broadcast of May 28, an update was provided on the air, recorded at Indianapolis. During the broadcast of June 11, an announcement was made that the Cross Country bike race was over and a new record was set. Edwards thanked Sunkist Frozen Orange and Lemonade Juice for supplying them with all the Vitamin "C" they needed during the ordeal, Abbey Rents for supplying them with their living equipment on the island and to Schwinn bicycles.

Episode #865, Broadcast of May 21, 1953

Stunts: Rip Own Hat, Fraternity Pins, Liberace-Girl Singer, and Cross Country Bicycle No. 1

Albert Hingston, Professor of Speech and Drama at Pacific University in Oregon, participated in a Surprise Consequence involving two fraternity pins, which he lost many years ago. Edwards reminds the professor of his education, graduation from Washington State College in 1935, choosing a profession as an entertainer at a nightclub, only to lose two fraternity pins, linked together: Pi Kappa Alpha and Phi Mu Alpha. Hingston was surprised to learn that the man sitting next to him is **Ken Kincheloe**, director of the music school at Bradley University, who returns the pins to Hingston and tells how he came across the lost property.

Sherry Dexter, age 16, student attending Alhambra High School, had the ambition of becoming a name singer. Chosen among the Surprise Consequences, she confessed her favorite was **Liberace** and enjoyed his weekly television series. "Wouldn't it be a thrill to sing while Liberace played your accompaniment?" Edwards asked. He told her that one day he might make her wish come true but for now, she was asked to go on stage and sing her favorite song, "For You," for the audience. Liberace comes out on stage and the two perform the song with the performer at the piano. After Sherry Dexter returned to her seat, Liberace provided details about his up-coming tour.

Episode #866, Broadcast of May 28, 1953

Stunts: Filibuster, George Montgomery, Lost Locket, Lost Wedding Book, and Cross Country Bicycle No. 2

Mrs. Gertrude Friedburg of Sussex, England, won an eight-cubic foot Amana Freezer for her participation in a "Filibuster Buildup" stunt. **Mrs. Emma Gilbert** of South Gate, California, won a Westinghouse refrigerator. A lost wedding book was returned to **Corporal Matt Matthews** and his wife, in a Surprise Consequence.

Episode #867, Broadcast of June 4, 1953

Stunts: Cigarette Lighter, Foreign Commercials, Return Wedding Ring, Singing Callicoats, and Cross Country Bicycle Payoff

Mrs. Marsha Lester of 132 South Second Street, Los Angeles, California, became the unsuspecting contestant of a Surprise Consequence when Ralph

Edwards handed her the broken wedding ring, with the diamonds still intact, which she lost a few weeks ago. "The person who sent the ring to us said that you had been visiting them and apparently your ring had been knocked off your dresser and then stepped on, then picked up by the vacuum sweeper," Edwards explained. The Klee-ban Jewelers in Beverly Hills will repair the ring before it is delivered to Mrs. Lester.

Phillip Callicoat and his four sisters and three brothers, along with his parents, are sitting in the audience. The family is known for feeding as many as ten needy people, from adults to children, in his own home. They served this charity up until the last year. The house burned down, Mr. Callicoat was in an accident that kept him from doing heavy work, his daughter **Mary Callicoat** developed rheumatic heart and they had to seek a climate that would help her… so they went to California. The whole family still tried to take in needy people into their new home, and as "The Singing Callicoats," the whole family sang and many of their evenings were spent at the bedside of people who enjoyed hearing them sing. The entire family was invited on stage to sing "The Old Cross Road." As a reward for their devotion, the family received a Pfaff Dial-A-Stitch, a portable sewing machine, a Sealy mattress, and a Kraylor Cushioned sofa and matching chair.

Episode #868, Broadcast of June 11, 1953

Stunts: Memory Test Frame, Bass Violin Return, Texas Mother Son Reunion, and Love Count

Roger Barber of 3216 East Seventh Street in Long Beach, California, worked for the Macco Construction Company and played in an orchestra. Instructed to play the violin, Barber is surprised to discover the instrument being handed to him was his own, which he left at home in Ohio when he came out to California. He was not told the violin was his and the trick was to see if he recognized it. He did not recognize the instrument as that of his own and Edwards mentioned that he could go home with it, and "now you can quit grousing to your wife about not liking the rented one." His wife received a Tappan Gas Range.

Ralph Edwards reminded listeners that **Atha Graffort** of Olney, Missouri, a 76-year-old foster mother who handled the canned goods for an orphanage in the holiday season, would have her story told in the July issue of *Radio-TV Mirror*.

Sergeant Louis Hall, Jr., a 22-year-old Marine from Camp Pendleton, was sent offstage during the warm-up, unaware that his mother was on stage. She had not seen the youth since he was five years old. She and her husband separated and by mutual consent, her husband's parents took the boy in. She had a traveling job and while she was away the grandparents moved and took Louis with them. Until now, she could not locate him. She talked to him on the phone, but he does not know what she looks like. To surprise the Marine, Edwards told him that they had four mothers who had sons in the service and that each had some gifts for him. Then they brought out the mothers one at a time and each of them gave Louis a homey little present. The fourth mother, Louis' mother, gave him a big kiss and the two could make up for the 17 years they had been apart.

The first mother was **Mrs. Carroll Jones**, whose son was a major in the Air Force at a camp in Frankfort, Germany. She donated a pair of socks, which she knitted herself. The second was **Mrs. Bessie Ussery**, whose son was in the Navy in Manilla, Philippines. Her present was an apple pie. The third was **Ida Whitehead**, whose son was a paratrooper in the Army. She gave Louis some homemade candy. The fourth mother was introduced as **Mrs. Nellie Carson**, and the two reunited. Before Louis and his mother left the stage, he was handed a three-day pass while she stayed in town.

Episode #869, Broadcast of June 18, 1953
Stunts: Time Change Running Gag, Hayes and Healy, and Dog Summons

Numerous prizes awarded in this episode. **Mr. and Mrs. Gene Wagner** of San Diego, California, won a 21-inch Westinghouse television set. **Mrs. Ida Strongin** of Hollywood, California, won a Tappan Gas Range. **Mrs. and Mrs. Neighbors** of La Mesa, California, won a Westinghouse electric roaster oven. **Mrs. Katherine Boyce** of Montebello, California, won a $100 Spiegel gift certificate.

Episode #870, Broadcast of June 24, 1953
Taped June 19, 1953.

Stunts: Wife vs. Model, Overseas Duty, Disguise Wife Secretary, and Apple Over Soldier

Broadcast originates from Fort MacArthur in San Pedro, California, where the program is presented for the entertainment of the servicemen stationed at

MacArthur. Celebrity guests were three models: **Neva Gilbert**, **Cheryl Clark** and **Evelyn Lovequist**. Each of them received $50 for their time devoted on the stage. **Corporal Harry Middleton** of Big Spring, Texas, won a three-day pass and a vacation at the Atwater Hotel in Catalina, and a reservation on the S.S. Catalina, plus $25 expense money. **Mrs. Lynn Lusk** was flown in for a stunt to surprise her husband, disguised as a blonde secretary to see if he recognized her. She won a Tappan gas range and a weekend three-day pass to vacation at the Plaza Motel.

Episode #871, Broadcast of July 1, 1953
Taped on June 23, 1953
Stunts: Marble Cake, Telephone Family Race, Goodwill Gifts, and Husband vs. Edwards

Broadcast originated from Thorne Hall at Occidental College in Los Angeles, California, presented in honor of the Goodwill Industries on the 51st anniversary of their organization. Celebrity guest was **Mr. Kavanaugh**, Executive Director of Goodwill Industries in San Francisco. Listeners were invited to send their broken furniture, toys, clothes to be mended, etc., to Goodwill Industries. The company operated across the country and was dedicated to rehabilitating the handicapped, who quickly learned to repair and demand articles, which were then sold to secure other things needed to keep the industries in operation.

Celebrity guest **Don Bragg**, UCLA basketball star, was a contestant using a Pet Milk recipe to make marble cake, with a bag of marbles as an ingredient! Bragg was paid $5 for every marble he removed out of the batter, a potential pot of $100, but he could only use his mouth. Every time he dropped a marble into the empty bowl, he must sing, "If I Knew You Were Coming I'd Bake a Cake!"

Episode #872, Broadcast of July 8, 1953
Taped on June 12, 1953.
Stunts: Mayor's Wife, Coach Chorus, Paper Boy Vacation, and Fire Chief Hotfoot
Broadcast originated from the Municipal Theatre in Oakland, California, in salute to the city of Oakland and its community projects and citizens. Special guest was **Clifford D. Rishell**, Mayor of Oakland. A contestant phones the mayor's wife, carrying on a conversation with her. The gimmick was that the contestant

was complaining to the mayor's wife about things the mayor should be doing for his community! The contestant did not realize that the mayor himself was in the theater, standing right by the side of the contestant while she was talking with his wife over the telephone.

Episode #873, Broadcast of July 15, 1953
Taped on June 12, 1953.
Stunts: French Question, T or C Dixieland Band, Mixed Up Wives, and Advise Colonel

Broadcast originated from Camp Stoneman in Pittsburg, California, near Oakland. Presented with the intent to entertain Army and Air Force Boys at Camp Stoneman. Celebrity guest was actress **Joan Vohs**, currently seen in the motion picture, *Fort Ti*. Vohs tempts four servicemen into kissing her. They received an electric shaver if they kissed her, $25 in cash if they did not. One of the stunts featured **Lt. Colonel Ralph Talbert**, Commanding Officer, replacement Battalion of Camp Stoneman, who pretended to be a sergeant to "pull a gag" on **Pvt. Lester Pearson** who is told to pretend to be the Colonel and to give "orders" to the Sergeant!

Another feature on this program was the performance of a small combination of servicemen musicians: **Bob Melander**, trumpet; **Frank Shrope**, guitar; a G.I. identified merely as "Pete," who played the drums; and another as "Tom" who was a pianist. The men perform their rendition of "Jazz Me Blues."

Episode #874, Broadcast of July 22, 1953
Taped on June 13, 1953.
Stunts: Star Observation Test, Sea Bag, Mind-Reader Telephone, and Identify Ten Objects

Broadcast originated from the U.S. Naval Station on Treasure Island in San Francisco Bay, California, where program was presented to our Navy men and women for their entertainment. Celebrity guest was **Joan Weldon**, movie actress currently seen in *The Stranger Wore a Gun*. She gave two sailors a feast to view for a short time and then stepped behind a screen to give them a chance to answer a question based on what color hair she had, how much she weighed, if she had any rings on her fingers, and what shade of lipstick she was wearing. One of the men samples her lipstick, making his buddy jealous!

Among the Navy personnel on the program for various stunts were **Charlie King** of Denver; **James Burton** of Winston-Salem, North Carolina; **Bob Evans** of Muscatine, Iowa; **Earl Duffy** of Baker, Oregon; **Herald Gish** of Paducah, Kentucky; **Jim Curry** of Columbus, Indiana; and **Pauline Alice**, WAVE of Pennsylvania. **Mary Millie Cozeo**, WAVE of Pennsylvania, received a surprise visit from her mother through this program, with all of her mother's expenses paid.

Episode #875, Broadcast of July 29, 1953
Taped on June 13, 1953.
Stunts: $20 Sox, Whistle Dixie, Sing Grocery List, Plug Store, Prisoner Song, and Italian Cow

Broadcast originated from San Francisco, California, where program was presented as part of the activities of the meeting of the Grocers of the California Area. Program included a special telephone conversation from the San Quentin Prison. Radio listeners heard both sides of the conversation, where **Warden Harley Oliver Teets** presents an inmate identified merely as "Andy," who devoted time to songwriting. Back in San Francisco, on the radio program, celebrity guest was **Pamela Britton**, who sang Andy's song "Café La Rue." Ralph Edwards said that he felt a publisher would be secured for the song. The program sent the San Quentin Prison Library a set of Encyclopedia Americana. Warden Teets said he knew great work and rehabilitation was being done through the application of prisoners like Andy who use their time to their advantage to follow a hobby or to find a vocation.

At the time of broadcast, men incarcerated could not receive the same benefits as John Q. Public. Known as "Andy" on the radio broadcast, his name could not be disclosed on the broadcast for numerous legal reasons. In real life his name was **Virgil Eugene Anderson** (also known as A-17752). Because a recording was furnished to Warden Teets for broadcast over the inmate radio network, he was permitted a copy of the recording, placed with his property at the institution until his release. Director **Ed Bailey** made the arrangements to accommodate.

Episode #876, Broadcast August 5, 1953
Taped on July 31, 1953.
Stunts: Obey Husband Mike, Fred Beaver, and Dressmaker Daughter Reunion

Start of the program was delayed one minute for special news bulletin regarding a prisoner of war released from North Korea.

Celebrity guest was **Fred Beaver**, baritone and artist. Beaver sang a selection, accompanied by Buddy Cole, regular organist and pianist for the series. Beaver, an amateur vocalist, was interviewed regarding his artwork and contact was made for him to sell some Greeting Card sketches to Buzza Cordosa, a greeting card company.

Contestant **David Allen** of Hollywood, California, is in the studio and phones his wife because she believed he was still at work. He tells her to throw a pail of water in his face when he gets home. If she did so without David explaining why, he receives his choice of a 12-cubic foot Amana freezer with a 430-pound capacity, or a Stromberg Carlson 21-inch screen television set with panoramic vision. Towards the end of the broadcast, he attempted to have her open the door, but fails. He discovers his wife was back at the studio and her voice was coming from behind a speaker. For being a wonderful sport on the gag, he won the television set.

Episode #877, Broadcast of August 12, 1953
Taped on July 31, 1953.

Stunts: English Lesson Love, Valentino, Polio Honeymoon, and Millstream Sing-Talk

Broadcast originated from Hollywood, California. Celebrity guest was actor **Rod Cameron**, television star of *City Detective*, who participated in a stunt involving three English teachers wearing raincoats and shower-caps, with their heads through the holes of a large screen on stage. One contestant was a noun, another an adjective, and the third an adverb. Cameron played a romantic scene with a beautiful female and the nouns, adverbs and adjectives were left out of their parts. The men were to call out the blanks and if they miss, they get hit with seltzer water. A pitch for Cameron's next picture, *The Steel Lady*, was made on the program.

A contestant named **Rudolph Florentino** was a stunt man who worked with the silent screen legend, Rudolph Valentino. He tells of how he was a close friend of the romantic screen legend and was the same man who made the jump to the chandelier for *Son of the Sheik*. He once had a prized gift from Valentino, a wristwatch chain, and as a Surprise Consequence, the stuntman was presented with that very watch chain inscribed by Rudolph Valentino, courtesy of **Joan Valentino**, the actor's daughter. This chain, a gift from the great actor to the stuntman, was lost 11 years ago.

Paul and Judy Jackson of Inglewood, California, both polio victims, were soon to be married. They told of their battle against polio and how they wanted everyone to help fight the disease through their local March of Dimes drives and assist the National Foundation for Infantile Paralysis. They were awarded an all-expense paid honeymoon at the Flamingo Hotel in Las Vegas, Nevada. They also received a Westinghouse refrigerator, a Stromberg Carlson 21-inch screen television set, a Tappan gas range, and a $150 merchandise gift certificate from the Spiegel mail order catalog.

Episode #878, Broadcast of August 19, 1953

Stunts: Frozen Pineapple Dessert B.U., Explain Baseball, Orphanage Freezer, and Mothers-In-Law War Bride

Celebrity guest was **Bob Kelly**, sportscaster for the Los Angeles Angels, Pacific Coast League. Kelly did a "typical baseball broadcast" with a female contestant interpreting what he was saying. **Edward L. Pearson**, Baptist Minister, Head of the Children's Baptist Home of Southern California, was a guest on the program and as part of the Surprise Consequence, he received a 25-cubic foot Amana freezer for the home. Contestant **Gladys Dunn** agreed to answer her telephone by saying "Frozen Pineapple Dessert" every time it rang through the week and to return to the program next week to report of her success. This contest was tied in with the Pet Milk recipe for the Frozen Pineapple Dessert. Throughout this entire show, Dunn practiced by answering "Frozen Pineapple Dessert" every time Ralph Edwards addressed her.

Episode #879, Broadcast of August 26, 1953

Stunts: Double Date Telephone, Connie Haines, Major Reunion, and Frozen Pineapple Dessert Payoff

Connie Haines, singing and recording star, performed "You Made Me Love You" after the recording of the selection was used to "fool a contestant," until the real Connie Haines arrived on stage. The young lady with the same name, who was in no relation to the singer, proved she could fool anyone with her talent for lip sync. Haines appeared on the program to promote her new Coral Record, *The World on a String*. **Gladys Dunn**, hold-over contestant from last week, was back to claim her prize of a 12-cubic foot Amana Freezer, for answering her phone all week with "Frozen Pineapple Dessert."

In the Surprise Consequence, **Army Major Ralph E. Martin**, presently stationed at the Beale Air Force Base in California, had not seen his family in almost two years. They lived in Villa Park, Illinois. He was surprised by a visit from his wife and children, flown from Illinois to spend time with Martin. Edwards' provided a reminder of "all the men and officers of all the services who sacrifice so much of their precious family time to help guard us and keep us the free nation we are."

Episode #880, Broadcast of September 2, 1953
Taped August 19, 1953.
Stunts: Mother-in-Law Goat, 200-Year-Old Spoon, and Mothers-in-Law Wedding

Broadcast originated from Hollywood. Program includes a spot recorded at the home of **Ray Field**, on Primrose Avenue in Hollywood, who as a contestant was sent from the program and tried to get his wife to open the front door and allow him to bring a goat inside. In actually, the covered vehicle in which he thought there is a goat contained his mother-in-law, **Ann Marcus** of Beverly Hills, hidden inside.

Episode #881, Broadcast of September 9, 1953
Stunts: Ventriloquist Dummy Husband, Four Prizes, Hotel Worker's Vacation, and Speech Song Joke

Live from Hollywood. Celebrity guests included **Hugh McCormick**, a ventriloquist, and his wooden dummy, Jerry. The dummy was disguised as "The Great Gumbo," a fortune-teller, rigged with a microphone and speaker. While McCormick sat in the back row of the audience, providing the voice of "Gumbo," his wife was on stage to ask the dummy questions. She was surprised when the dummy knew the answers to her questions. She would win $50 if she could stump the dummy, asking questions such as "What is the name of my two cousins?" and "What is my husband's middle name?"

Ida Floe, a chambermaid at the Hollywood Knickerbocker Hotel, was convinced on stage to phone the room clerk and avoid mentioning she worked there. She was to book a reservation for the finest suite in the house, a beautiful dinner, fancy desserts and flowers in the room – and she would arrive in one hour. She succeeded, almost having to bawl him out in order to do so, only to discover that she went as a guest for a full week, at the expense of the radio producers. This include hairdressers, a lovely dress, a new robe and nightgown. Won't room service be surprised when they discover their comrade was a resident of the hotel?

Episode #882, Broadcast of September 16, 1953
Stunts: Jack Smith Imitators, Missed Good Gesture, and Return Editor's Desk
Live from Hollywood. Two men, **Martin G. Sperzel** and **Bernard David Alper**, claiming to be impersonators, discover the punch of the gag after impersonating a celebrity – until they meet the real **Jack Smith**, star of radio, television and motion-pictures.
Surprise Consequences awarded Westinghouse portable radios to **Mrs. Esther Vitro** of Larchmont, New York, and **Mrs. Etha Beck** of Miami, Florida. **Lamount Tupper** of Hollywood, California and **J. Kelly** of New York City, each received a Shaver & Shavex attachment. **Corporal Joel Helm** from the El Toro Marine Base in Santa Ana, won a Bulova watch for his participation in a "Missed Good Gesture" stunt which involved his parents, **Mr. and Mrs. Roe H. Helm** of Chico, California, who went home with a Tappan gas range.

Episode #883, Broadcast of September 24, 1953
Taped September 23, 1953.
Stunts: Squirt High, Help Old Lady, Fryryte Contest Winners, and Brag on Self
Celebrity guest was **Roy Rogers**, who was "in the wings" and tempted to say "hello" when Ralph Edwards greeted him. Special contestants were two ladies who for the first time get the word that they are winners of a recent nationwide Fryryte Contest. **Mrs. Perry E. Thompson** of Litchfield, Michigan, and **Mrs. Susanna C. McKee** of Glencoe, Illinois, were told to try to find out what they have in common. They never met until tonight on the broadcast. After talking amongst themselves for a spell, they discover they both entered the same contest to become members of the studio audience for this broadcast and won. Mrs. Thompson came in first place and won a trip to Paris. Mrs. McKee came in second and received $1,000 in groceries.
Includes a pick-up from outside at Sunset and Vine, for a special Boy Scout feature with one of the Surprise Consequence segments with a Scout Master, **Clarence G. Nellison** of Sherman Oaks, sent out dressed like a Boy Scout, to

"help little old ladies cross the street." One of the ladies turned out to be his mother, **Mrs. Elizabeth Nellison**, who was flown to California from St. Paul, Minnesota, to surprise her son.

Episode #884, Broadcast of October 1, 1953
Stunts: Rain Barrel, Clarence Buildup, Robert Young, and Little Girl Accordion
Celebrity guest was **Robert Young**, star of NBC's *Father Knows Best*. Included on the broadcast was a telephone contest with a female contestant from Memphis, Tennessee, having a chance to name three cities in the United States where she thought it was raining at this very moment. Every time she named a city, she was required to call a police officer in that city to ask him if it was raining. If she was right the first time, she received $500. If she was right the second time, she received $300. If she guessed correctly the third time, she received $100. She decided on Chicago, New Orleans, and her hometown of Memphis, but all three cities provided a "good weather, no rain" report.
Special Surprise Consequence concerned a five-year-old named **Suzanne Carol Bish**, who was partially blind for most of her life. Now, she was overcoming her blindness and she wanted to play an accordion. She receives an accordion as a gift. On the show, she sings "You Belong to Me."

Episode #885, Broadcast of October 8, 1953
Taped on October 6, 1953
Stunts: Word Association Seltzer, Pretend Mother-in-Law, Harvest Gold Peach Pie Man, and Clarence Payoff
Harvest Gold Peach Pie Treasure Truck stunt started with this broadcast. Operated by National Van Lines, the truck would visit 32 cities across the country, stopping at designated points in each city so that citizens could visit the truck, talk with the Harvest Gold Peach Pie Man and choose a key from a gigantic replica of a Pet Milk cylinder. If the key unlocked a secret door to an immense replica of a "Harvest Gold Peach Pie" in the truck, the holder of the key would receive fabulous prizes valued at $5,000, plus a $1,500 gift certificate to be used in ordering merchandise from Spiegel's Mail Order Catalogue in Chicago; a Westinghouse washer and drying machine; a 21-inch Stromberg-Carlson television set, a Tappan Gas Range, a $500 Wright Air Conditioner; and a Bulova wristwatch. Each week on the air, the cities visited during the next week would be announced with a location of the truck.

The truck tomorrow would be in Long Beach, California, and then move east towards New York City.

Contestant **Gilbert Fishman**, known as the Duke of Catalina because he was a lifeguard at Catalina for 18 years, was chosen to be the Harvest Gold Peach Pie Man. When the lucky key opens the secret door later this season, the Harvest Gold Peach Pie Man, who will also serve as the official greeter for the truck, will get $1,000.

Episode #886, Broadcast of October 15, 1953
Taped on October 13, 1953

Stunts: Star Masquerade, Harvest Peach Pie Man No. 2, Marine-Car Repair, and Tank Hamburger

Broadcast originated from Hollywood, with a recorded telephone conversation between Ralph Edwards, and **Gilbert Fishman** at KOB, Albuquerque, New Mexico, with Fishman reporting on his first week with the treasure truck. No one chose the lucky key yet. He told of his reception everywhere along the way, especially reporting on a visit to the Children's Hospital in Truth or Consequences, New Mexico, where a little boy in a wheelchair had the honor of throwing pies at the pie man. (When nobody gets a lucky key, a pie is thrown at the pie man.) All of the patients, nurses and doctors in the Children's Hospital received Harvest Gold Peach Pie for dessert.

Program featured a pick-up from Stan's Drive-In across the street from the NBC Studios in Hollywood, where car hop girls were calling their orders to the cook. Inside the studios, contestant **Paul Horowitz** from New Rochelle, New York, was suspended over a water tank with four ropes. Every time a hamburger was ordered, one of the ropes was cut away. The contestant was dropped into the tank because four hamburger orders were called for in 60 seconds.

Celebrity guest was actor **Robert Cummings** for a masquerade stunt.

Episode #887, Broadcast of October 22, 1953
Taped on October 20, 1953

Stunts: Love Letters, Harvest Gold Peach Pie No. 3, Indian Drama, and Whiffenpoof Lamb

The first winter in the Harvest Gold Peach Pie Treasure Truck was announced. According to a wire sent to Ralph Edwards from station WBLK, in Clarksburg,

West Virginia, **Mrs. Rose Isner**, homemaker, chose the correct key. She was invited to appear as a guest on the program next week. The program included a recording made two days prior to the broadcast, while the treasure truck was in Louisville, Kentucky. (Recorded at station WAVE, Louisville.) **Gilbert Fishman** told of his travels across the country as the Golden Harvest Peach Pie Man. At this time, of course, the Duke did not have a winner.

An announcement followed that a duplicate prize has been set up for the next winner, with the winning key back in the big replica of a Pet Milk cylinder on the truck. The Treasure Truck was now headed for New Jersey and New York. Trenton, New Jersey, on Tuesday, October 27, from 9:30 to 11:00 a.m.; Newark, New Jersey, on Wednesday, October 28, from 9:30 a.m. to 12 noon; and New York City on Wednesday afternoon from 2:30 to 6:30 p.m., in front of the Colonial Theater on Broadway.

Episode #888, Broadcast of October 29, 1953
Taped on October 27, 1953

Stunts: Camp Fire Girls, Harvest Peach Pie Man No. 4, Prospective Bride Shower, and Smith Jones B.U.

Broadcast originated from Hollywood where **Mrs. Rose Isner**, winner of the key contest, received a $1,500 gift certificate from Spiegel's Inc.; $1,000 in cash from "White Rain" lotion shampoo; the Westinghouse "Twins" (Laundromat and Dryer); a 12-cubic foot Amana freezer, a 21-inch television set; a Tappan Gas Range; a $500 Wright air cooler, a man's 21-jewel solid gold Bulova wristwatch and a 21-jewel Lady's Diamond Bulova wristwatch. She did not appear on the program in person.

In the Hollywood studio was the start of a new contest as a Mr. Smith and a Mr. Jones, who have never met before, face each other briefly and are taken by taxi out on different routes to their respective homes. Without knowing their real names, if they find each other in time to return to the studios by next week, each gentlemen would receive a 21-inch television set.

From the NBC Studios in New York City, **Mel Brandt**, NBC staff announcer, interviewed **Gilbert Fishman**, the Harvest Gold Peach Pie Man, who yesterday completed his trip from the West Coast. Fishman said there were no other winners in the Harvest Gold Peach Pie Contest. Mrs. Rose Isner of Clarksburg, West Virginia, was the first and only winter during the trip. He received a $1,000 U.S. Savings Bond for his participation. He discovers his

Savings Bond is locked inside the Harvest Gold Peach Pie and he must go through the 26,000 keys to find the one that opens the secret door.

This broadcast included a salute to Camp Fire Girls with a Camp Fire Girls group from Los Angeles as special guests taking part in a gag in which a woman found her own son dressed as a Camp Fire Girl. For their participation, the Los Angeles Area Council, Camp Fire Girls, received a television set from the show.

Episode #889, Broadcast of November 5, 1953
Taped on November 3, 1953
Stunts: Smith Jones Payoff, Cat's Meow, Three Grandparents, and Song Lecture

Smith and Jones are back on the program. They managed to find each other in time after making contact through a doctor who treated one of the two men. A grandfather stunt involved three grandfathers seeing their grandchildren and a surprise reunion. Also, Ermintrude, a kitten, is featured in a gag with a contestant who is "meeting" her from a station outside the studios at Hollywood and Vine, heard through a loudspeaker.

Episode #890, Broadcast of November 12, 1953
Taped on November 10, 1953
Stunts: Superstition B.U., Mother-in-Law Frame, Horse for a Day, and Children's Prayer

A "Friday the 13th" stunt starts with this broadcast as contestant **Gordon Chandler** agrees to do all the things that are supposed to be bad luck such as walking under ladders, giving everybody he meets cigarette lights (always three-on-a-match), all day tomorrow, Friday the 13th. During this time, he is protected by insurance on a $5,000 Beneficial Hospital Plan in case of accidents occurred during the day. If he returns with the report during the next broadcast that verifies he came through the ordeal without any injury, he would get an Amana freezer.

Harry Blitzsteen, a junk collector, was told that his horse, the one that served faithfully pulling his junk cart was named "Horse for a Day" and crowned Queen. Tomorrow, the horse would get special feed, a new blanket, and the day spent at the movie studios where she met **Roy Rogers'** famous horse, Trigger. Also included was a trip to the race track where she was quartered in a special stable next to a great racehorse, the photograph made in the

Winners' Circle, and special grooming for the entire day. Blitzsteen received $50 cash and a Tappan gas range. This was a spoof of another quiz program, *Queen for a Day*.

Mrs. Albina La Rocca of Encinitas, California, whose husband was in Japan, wrote to the program asking to record her three children's prayers to be sent to her husband. Tonight, right from her home where she was putting the children to bed, a special tape recorder was set up. The radio audience heard the children's bedtime prayers as they were recorded. She later thanked Ralph Edwards through a two-way conversation between her home and the studio. She was presented with the Webster Tape Recorder so she could make recordings of more family events to send her Marine husband.

Episode #891, Broadcast of November 19, 1953
Taped on November 17, 1953
Stunts: Superstition Payoff, Fortune Teller's Son, and Camel's Hair Coat

Contestant **Gordon Chandler** returns from last week's broadcast, having come through his defiance of superstitions and collected his Amana freezer. He also received the Beneficial Hospital Plan which was slated for one day, extended for an entire year for his entire family including his wife and two children.

The reunion of a mother and her son, whom she believed to be overseas, was staged numerous times on the quiz program. This time the son was disguised as a fortuneteller, secretly flown home on furlough. In another stunt, a female contestant was told to deliver a "camel's hair coat" to a certain address. The fur coat was a living and breathing camel and the address was her own home. This stunt was done prior in 1947 and 1949.

Beginning with this broadcast, an International Consequence became a regular feature through December 10. The initial concept was to broadcast a similar rendition of the quiz program from a different country each week, but the set-up was more complicated than the producers wanted so all of the segments originated from London, England. The emcee from London was **Max Bygraves**, comedian, who in the past toured the United States with **Judy Garland**. The three judges for the on-going stunts were an American, an Englishman and a Frenchman. Each of the International Consequence segments lasted about ten minutes.

Episode #892, Broadcast of November 26, 1953
Taped on October 10, 1953

Stunts: Story in Song and Parent's Thanksgiving

International Consequences again has British contestant and **Max Bygraves** as the British emcee. Parent's Thanksgiving feature had parents whose children would not be home for Thanksgiving so invitations were sent out to invite a stray young couple to share their Thanksgiving dinner. Of course, they encounter their own son and daughter-in-law, secretly flown to Hollywood. Taking part on the program was actor **Paul Frees** and musician **Stanley Fletcher**; also a live St. Bernard dog.

Episode #893, Broadcast of December 3, 1953
Taped on November 10, 1953

Stunts: Baby Judging Contest, and Tune-In

Another International Consequences spot featuring **Max Bygraves** as emcee.

Episode #894, Broadcast of December 10, 1953
Taped on November 10, 1953

Stunts: Tuba Frame, and French Drama Seltzer

Contestants **Mr. and Mrs. E. Elgas** thought they were playing the tuba. In actuality, a professional tuba player, Stanley Fletcher, was producing the lovely music. Another stunt included actor **Paul Frees**, introduced as a famous French actor, to take part in a French drama scene with **Mrs. Fred Ryan**, a contestant who understood no French but kept answering "Oui" when the actor asks, "Don't you think your husband should be doused in seltzer water?" (Oui means yes in French.)

International Consequence from London, with **Max Bygraves** as emcee. Contestants were policemen: **Albert Bates**, the London "Bobby"; and **Edward Mitchell**, Los Angeles Police Department.

Episode #895, Broadcast of December 17, 1953
Taped on December 15, 1953

Stunts: Wife Sales Clerk, Christmas Tree, Common Grandchild, Wife Sales Clerk, and Reindeer Search B.U.

Christmas preview show with holiday consequences. The broadcast featured

Christmas Seal plugs tied in with program continuity. Ralph Edwards said, "We're going to have SEALS on the show tonight… Christmas Seals!"

Celebrity guest was **Barbara Louise Schmidt**, the Queen of the Roses for the Tournament of Roses in Pasadena on New Year's Day. Contestant named Mr. Ruggles was given $50 and told to take Queen Barbara out for Christmas shopping at the nearby drugstore. What he did not know until it was too late was that his wife was the salesclerk at the counter where Barbara choose to take him.

A female contestant is told to call Santa's reindeer and "Blitzen," a real live reindeer arrives on stage. **George Neise**, actor, plays the role of Santa and brought every lady in the studio audience a "Christmas gift" or "Raindear" plastic rain boots, compliments of the Raindear Company. There were 300 ladies in the audience. The live reindeer, Blitzen, became part of a new Christmas contest. Blitzen would hide for one week but has to be found by Christmas Eve, next week's broadcast. This was timed so all listeners of any age could guess where Blitzen was hiding and mail a postcard to Truth or Consequences, Hollywood 28, California, with the name of the place, anywhere in the United States, where they thought Blitzen was hiding, plus their name, address and telephone number. The winner would receive a $1,000 U.S. Defense Bond. **Ed Pawlek**, member of the *Truth or Consequences* program staff (usually on the production end of the show) had a "speaking part" as he pitched the giveaway product, announcing that 300 reindeer were pounding their hooves at the door.

Episode #896, Broadcast of December 24, 1953
Taped on December 22, 1953
Stunts: Rose Bowl Relative, Reindeer Search Payoff, and Nativity

The reindeer search contest winner was announced as **Robert E. Barnes**, who wrote the postcard designating the "best hiding place" for Blitzen, the live reindeer who was on the program last week and was "just getting back to the North Pole in time to join Santa and his Christmas Eve deliveries."

The Rose Bowl Relative segment involved contestant **Jim Snook**, told he would get to see the Rose Bowl Game in the company of a "relative" who would later phone him and with car and chauffeur stick right with him during the entire game. The "relative" was a real live pig (relative of the "pigskin" – the football). Live baby pig was on the program, with his former owner, the piglet's chauffeur.

The story of the birth of Christ was the special Christmas feature, taking up a major portion of the broadcast (22 minutes to be exact). The story of the Nativity was performed by Ralph Edwards on the quiz program years prior and by special request of listeners was reprised. Three children, none of them over the age of 6 years, were chosen from the studio audience (including a Negro child) and gathered around Ralph Edwards as he told the story. Afterwards, Edwards told the children about a wonderful belief: that whenever the story of the Nativity was told just before Christmas day, good little boys and girls were visited by Santa Claus wherever they happened to be. Santa Claus came on stage, accompanied by the Angels Chorus singing "Jingle Bells," and chats with the youngsters. The children receive toys and were told that their request for gifts would be fulfilled by Christmas morning. Clothes and toys were included in the gifts, along with a $100 U.S. Defense Bond for each of the children.

Episode #897, Broadcast of December 31, 1953
Taped on December 29, 1953

Stunts: Rose Bowl Tank, New Year's Resolutions, Parents Pie New Years, and Help Boy Scout

Rose Bowl contest with two contestants trying to forecast who would win the Rose Bowl Game, involves the men taking their clothes off and sitting above a huge Rose Bowl tank on stage, filled with water and rose petals. Contestant **Jack Edwards** represented Michigan and contestant **Jack Spargos** represented UCLA. The men dress in old-fashioned bathing suits. The referee was **Mr. D. Fisk**. Contestants had to sing their teams' school songs during the whole show. Edwards of Michigan wins.

New Year's Resolutions Stunt involved a Casper Milquetoast type, **Albert Polisner**, told to make a New Year's resolution that would make his wife appreciate him and realize how wonderful he was – the domineering he-man hero husband. To help him practice, celebrity guest **Bibbs Borman**, French movie star, appeared with the contestant, whose wife was listening.

A New Year's pie-tossing stunt involved a young woman, **Mrs. Viola Wein**, told to telephone her parents to wish them a happy New Year. She could not persuade her father to throw a pie into the face of one of his New Year's guests, so she only received $50. Of course, her father and mother were really back stage and her father tosses the pie at his son-in-law.

Episode #898, Broadcast of January 7, 1954

Stunts: Bride-Groom Chase, Make-Up Phone Number, and Swami Frame

Celebrity guest was **Lorraine Crawford**, magazine-cover model. **Don Smith**, contestant, received a chance to telephone a number which he unwittingly chose by naming a state, a city in that state, giving at random any two letters, likewise two sets of alternate letters at five numbers. If the contestant could get a telephone number and could can get a person named Jack at the place he phoned, he would receive $1,000. **Mr. and Mrs. R. Gentry** took part in a stunt that Mrs. Gentry thought was a real fortune-telling, crystal ball gazing séance with a real swami known as "Adi Sivad" (in actuality, the recorded voice of Mr. Gentry).

Episode #899, Broadcast of January 14, 1954

Stunts: Remote Sound Effects, Surprise Baby, and Choose Hat

Future stunt was the surprise appearance of **Mrs. Edwin Christensen** and her three-week old baby, **Patty**, who were flown to the program from Lake Charles, Louisiana, to surprise her mother and in-laws. The family did not even know the baby was expected in the Christensen household – she had not informed her mother and her husband's parents of the coming event because months ago she had planned to surprise them on this quiz program! Actor **Tom McKee** played the role of a "friend" of Mr. and Mrs. Edwin Christensen.

Episode #900, Broadcast of January 21, 1954

Stunts: Vacation Mr. X, Scoutmaster vs. Tenderfoot, and Observe Model

Episode #901, Broadcast of January 28, 1954

Stunts: Grandma Jazz Band, Italian Brother Interpreter, and Model Pass

Episode #902, Broadcast of February 4, 1954

Stunts: Dreams, Retired Teacher, and Rainmaker B.U.

Episode #903, Broadcast of February 11, 1954

Stunts: Cuckoo Time Running Gag, Studio Names Tour, Band Leader Accompaniment, Rainmaker Payoff, and The Thing Tease

Beginning with the broadcast of February 11, 1954, an object in a box, securely wrapped and thoroughly sealed, was labeled "The Thing." Every week, two to three contestants were phoned with an opportunity to ask one question and then guess what was in the box. In return for plugs for their latest motion picture, *The Command*, starring **Guy Madison**, the staff at Warner Bros. were responsible for selecting two or three listeners to be called by telephone during the course of the weekly broadcasts. The movie studio also paid Ralph Edwards a $1,500 check for the advertising, approved in advance by the weekly radio sponsor, who agreed that the plugs were not originating from a competing sponsor.

Episode #904, Broadcast of February 18, 1954
Stunts: Wife Operator, and The Thing Phone Calls

Episode #905, Broadcast of February 25, 1954
Stunts: Three Stories, The Thing Phone Calls, and Yankee Soldier B.U.

Episode #906, Broadcast of March 4, 1954
Stunts: Laughter, Morse Code Words, T or C Wedding Tease, Telephone Husband Model, The Thing Phone Calls, and Yankee Soldier Payoff

Episode #907, Broadcast of March 11, 1954
Stunts: Tug-O-War Shower, Husband Newspaper Picture, The Thing Phone Calls, and Portland-Seattle Petition B.U.

Episode #908, Broadcast of March 18, 1954
Stunts: Three Nationalities Joke, The Thing Phone Calls, Talk Fast Sailor Count, T or C Wedding Tease, and Portland-Seattle Petition Payoff

Episode #909, Broadcast of March 25, 1954
Stunts: Woman Pie, Kibitz Boss Telephone, The Thing Phone Calls, and Bear Motor Scooter

Episode #910, Broadcast of April 1, 1954
Stunts: Soldier's Sweetheart, The Thing Phone Call, Wife Model Hut, and Mother Bouquet
"The Thing" contest continued with Ralph Edwards making the usual three telephone calls to listeners whose cards were chosen from those mailed in, to

try for a chance to identify The Thing in the *Truth or Consequences* "Mystery Box." Nobody identified The Thing so the prize value was boosted to $10,000 in cash and prizes. The contestants telephoned failed to answer correctly but received a Bulova wristwatch for their participation.

Celebrity guest was **Karolee Kelly**, a professional model.

Episode #911, Broadcast of April 8, 1954
Taped on April 3, 1954

Stunts: Same Name Star, The Thing Payoff, Jack Bailey, Mayor Williams, Fiesta Queen, Wedding Couple, Bear Motor Scooter, and Tin Whistle Symphony

This broadcast was taped in advance at Truth or Consequences, New Mexico, where the cast and crew were performing as part of the festivities at the Fifth Annual Fiesta. Celebrity guests included **Edwin L. Mecham**, Governor of New Mexico, who welcomed the cast and crew to the city; **General George C. Kenny**, president of the Arthritis and Rheumatism Foundation, who told about the way the proceeds from all the activities during the annual Fiesta in Truth or Consequences, New Mexico, were turned over to the Foundation; actor **John Payne**, who took part in a stunt involving a plumber with the same name who found himself trading places with the actor; **Jack Bailey**, well-known as emcee of the *Queen for a Day* radio program, announced as the next emcee for the *Truth or Consequences* series on NBC Television; and **T.B. Williams**, Mayor of Truth or Consequences.

Engaged couples wrote letters to the program stating why they wanted to be married in Truth or Consequences, New Mexico. The winning couple was **Mr. and Mrs. Carl Berg**. Until the ceremony Mrs. Berg was **Miss Polly Jo'anne Simonsen**. The bridegroom was a private in the Anti-Aircraft Artillery Guns at Camp Hartford, New Mexico. In addition to having a beautiful wedding ceremony in the city of their choice, the couple received an all-expenses paid honeymoon and free airline transportation to Truth or Consequences, New Mexico.

"The Thing" contest ended when the first contestant on the phone, **Mrs. Shelley A. Foy** of 3122 Happy Valley Road in Jackson, Michigan, correctly identified The Thing as an automobile jack. Mrs. Foy won over $10,000 in cash and prizes which included a Tappan range, a Sensation MowBlo Model Power Mower, an Insinkerator Food Waste Disposal, a Bulova wristwatch, carpets and carpet cushions, a Pentron High-Fidelity Three Speaker Tape Recorder, a set of American Encyclopedia, and other prizes.

Episode #912, Broadcast of April 15, 1954
Stunts: Dish Pan, Mop the Floor, Wife-Soldier-Telephone, and State Songs Seltzer
Broadcast live from the Municipal Auditorium in Sacramento, California, where the quiz program was part of the activities staged for the benefit of the Junior Museum Fund of California. This was the final broadcast to be recorded solely for the radio program.

THE JACK BAILEY SEASON

Production number and date of filming is indicated next to stunts that were audio from television productions. Any stunts listed with no production numbers and filming dates were taped in advance for the radio program, exclusively. All of the radio broadcasts were numbered among Ralph Edwards's production files. To maintain the "official" count, the numbering system jumps from 912 to 922 as indicated in the files.

Episode #922, Broadcast of March 23, 1955
Stunts: Popcorn B.U. (#42 – March 1, 1955)
Lion's Mouth (#43 – March 8, 1955)
Popcorn No. 2 (#42 – March 1, 1955)
William Tell (#42 – March 1, 1955)
Popcorn No. 3 (#42 – March 1, 1955)
Find Husband (#41 – February 22, 1955)
Jigsaw City (Taped)
Popcorn Payoff (#42 – March 1, 1955)

Episode #923, Broadcast of March 30, 1955
Stunts: Snake Charmer (#41 – February 22, 1955)
Man on Street Reunion (#44 – March 15, 1955)
Reverse Procedure (#44 – March 15, 1955)
Jigsaw City Phone Calls (Taped)

Episode #924, Broadcast of April 6, 1955
Stunts: Pool Romance (#41 – February 22, 1955)
Own Painting (#40 – February 15, 1955)
Jigsaw City Phone Calls (Taped)

Episode #925, Broadcast of April 13, 1955
Stunts: Telescope Husband B.U. (#46 – March 29, 1955)
Wife T.D. (#45 – March 22, 1955)
Telescope Husband Payoff (#46 – March 29, 1955)
Jigsaw City Phone Calls Payoff (Taped)

Episode #926, Broadcast of April 20, 1955
Stunts: Cow Fable (Taped)
City and State Dignitaries (Taped)
Contest Payoffs (Taped)
Jack Smith Act (Taped)

Episode #927, Broadcast of April 27, 1955
Stunts: Girdle Water Tank (#48 – April 12, 1955)
Unicycle (#47 – March 5, 1955)
Actress Frame (#46 – March 30, 1955)
Horse Hitchhike (#47 – April 5, 1955)

Episode #928, Broadcast of May 4, 1955
Stunts: Audience Celebrity (#48 – April 12, 1955)
Hollywood Tour (#48 – April 12, 1955)
Rajah Hoax B.U. (#46 – March 29, 1955)
Snoring Man Contest (Taped)

Episode #929, Broadcast of May 11, 1955
Stunts: Feel Faces (#50 – April 26, 1955)
Rajah Hoax Payoff (#47 – April 5, 1955)
Horse Hitchhike (#49 – April 19, 1955)
Snoring Man Contest (Taped)

Episode #930, Broadcast of May 18, 1955
Stunts: Front Row Kiss (#49 – April 19, 1955)
Cannon Ball (#49 – April 19, 1955)
Snoring Man Contest Phone Calls (Taped)

Episode #931, Broadcast of May 25, 1955
Stunts: Wife Taxi Driver (#50 – April 26, 1955)
Assemble Car B.U. (#50 – April 26, 1955)
Snoring Man Contest Phone Calls (Taped)

Episode #932, Broadcast of June 1, 1955
Stunts: Retired Teacher (#51 – May 3, 1955)
Assemble Car Payoff No. 1 (#51 – May 3, 1955)
Snoring Man Contest Phone Calls (Taped)

Episode #933, Broadcast of June 8, 1955
Stunts: Husband Mermaid (#51 – May 3, 1955)
Hair Dryer Reunion (#53 – May 17, 1955)
Assemble Car Payoff No. 2 (#52 – May 10, 1955)
Snoring Man Contest Phone Calls (Taped)

Episode #934, Broadcast of June 15, 1955
Stunts: Trick Golfer (#52 – May 10, 1955)
Fake Fire Plug (#52 – May 10, 1955)
Snoring Man Contest Payoff (Taped)

The broadcast of June 15 was heard on a limited number of radio stations across the country, due to a special address by Governor Harriman.

Episode #935, Broadcast of June 22, 1955
Stunts: Service Messages (#55 – May 31, 1955)
Uranium Hunt (#54 – May 24, 1955)
What Is It (#55 – May 31, 1955)
Interview with Snoring Man Contest Winner (Taped)

Episode #936, Broadcast of June 29, 1955
Stunts: Helicopter Cage Build-Up (#26 – November 9, 1954)
Bailey Disguise (#57 – June 14, 1955)
Totem Pole (#57 – June 14, 1955)
Helicopter Cage Payoff (#26 – November 9, 1954)

Episode #937, Broadcast of July 6, 1955
Stunts: Bathroom Derrick B.U. (#8 – July 6, 1954)
Choose Bag (#56 – June 7, 1955)
Mixed-Up Wives (#8 – July 6, 1954)
Bathroom Derrick Payoff (#8 – July 6, 1954)

Episode #938, Broadcast of July 13, 1955
Stunts: Elephant Fable (#5 – June 15, 1954)
Ad Lib Drama (#5 – June 15, 1954)
Recreate Home (#5 – June 15, 1954)
Husband Imitator (#56 – June 7, 1955)

Episode #939, Broadcast of July 20, 1955
Stunts: Not Husband (#26 – November 9, 1954)
Soldier Recording (#15 – August 24, 1954)
Retired General (#15 – August 24, 1954)

Episode #940, Broadcast of July 27, 1955
Stunts: Husband Likes-Dislikes (#17 – September 7, 1954)
Love Letter (#17 – September 7, 1954)
Fake Home Town Surprise (#17 – September 7, 1954)
Bermuda Shorts B.U. (#17 – September 7, 1954)

Episode #941, Broadcast of August 3, 1955
Stunts: Sailor Husband (#18 – September 14, 1954)
Grandfather's Clock (#18 – September 14, 1954)
Goat-Cow-Guess (#18 – September 14, 1954)
Bermuda Shorts Payoff (#18 – September 14, 1954)

Episode #942, Broadcast of August 10, 1955
Stunts: Phoney Jackpot Build-Up (#34 – January 4, 1955)
Same Dress Prize (#34 – January 4, 1955)
Tab Hunter – Cab Driver (#35 – January 11, 1955)
Phoney Jackpot Payoff (#34 – January 4, 1955)

Episode #943, Broadcast of August 17, 1955
Stunts: Unknown
The Thing Contest Tease (Taped)

Episode #944, Broadcast of August 24, 1955
Stunts: Moulin Rouge Build-Up (#24 – October 26, 1954)
Japanese Drama (#24 – October 26, 1954)
Manicurist (#37 – January 25, 1955)
Moulin Rouge Payoff (#24 – October 26, 1954)
The Thing Contest Tease (Taped)

Episode #945, Broadcast of August 31, 1955
Stunts: Freeway Hoax (#66 – August 16, 1955)
Boat in Bottle Build-Up (#66 – August 16, 1955)
The Thing Contest Phone Calls (Taped)

Episode #946, Broadcast of September 7, 1955
Stunts: Own Livestock (#67 – August 23, 1955)
Plane in Bottle Build-Up (#67 – August 23, 1955)
Boy Friend Frame (#67 – August 23, 1955)
The Thing Contest Phone Calls (Taped)

Episode #947, Broadcast of September 14, 1955
Stunts: TV Highlights (#68 – August 30, 1955)
Plane in Bottle Payoff (#68 – August 30, 1955)
The Thing Contest Phone Calls (Taped)

Episode #948, Broadcast of September 21, 1955
Stunts: 500 Phones (#69, September 6, 1955)
Identify Sounds (#68 – August 30, 1955)
The Thing Contest Phone Calls (Taped)

Episode #949, Broadcast of September 28, 1955
Stunts: Lie Detector (#70 – September 13, 1955)
Hoop Mind Reader (#69 – September 6, 1955)
The Thing Contest Phone Calls (Taped)

Episode #950, Broadcast of October 5, 1955
Stunts: Police Line Up Build-Up (#69 – September 6, 1955)
Three Bears (#70 – September 13, 1955)
Police Line-Up Payoff (#69 – September 6, 1955)
The Thing Contest Phone Calls (Taped)

Episode #951, Broadcast of October 12, 1955
Stunts: Three Women Sculpture Build-Up (#71 – September 20, 1955)
Gaston Reunion (#71 – September 20, 1955)
Three Women Sculpture Payoff (#71 – September 20, 1955)
The Thing Contest Phone Calls (Taped)

Episode #952, Broadcast of October 19, 1955
Stunts: Stop Son's Wedding B.U (#28 – November 23, 1954)
Mala Powers (#28 – November 23, 1954)
Stop Son's Wedding Payoff (#28 – November 23, 1954)
The Thing Contest Phone Calls (Taped)

Episode #953, Broadcast of October 26, 1955
Stunts: $1,000 Weight (#31 – December 14, 1954)
High Dive Husband (#31 – December 14, 1954)
The Thing Contest Phone Calls (Taped)

Episode #954, Broadcast of November 2, 1955
Stunts: First Phone Call (Taped)
Man on Street Frame (#76 – October 28, 1955)

Ground Observer B.U. (#75 – October 21, 1955)
Road Block (#75 – October 21, 1955)

Episode #955, Broadcast of November 9, 1955
Stunts: Man on Street Frame (#76 – October 28, 1955)
Ground Observer B.U. (#75 – October 21, 1955)
Road Block (#75 – October 21, 1955)

Episode #956, Broadcast of November 16, 1955
Stunts: $100 Switch (#77 – November 4, 1955)
Teletype B.U. (#77 – November 4, 1955)
Ground Observer Payoff (#76 – October 28, 1955)
Teletype Payoff (#77 – November 4, 1955)
Drive-In Remote (#76 – October 28, 1955)

Episode #957, Broadcast of November 23, 1955
Stunts: Masked Marvel (#23 – October 19, 1954)
Father Master of Ceremonies (#22 – October 12, 1954)
Thought Waves (#22 – October 12, 1954)
Tease for "Hush" Contest (Taped)

Episode #958, Broadcast of November 30, 1955
Stunts: Kick Hats (#78 – November 11, 1955)
Man Hunt Remote (#78 – November 11, 1955)
Big Prize Seltzer (#78 – November 11, 1955)
Ice Folly Build-Up (#22 – October 12, 1954)
Tease for Mr. and Mrs. Hush Contest (Taped)

Episode #959, Broadcast of December 7, 1955
Stunts: Ice Folly Payoff (#23 – October 19, 1954)
Gas Station Remote (#79 – November 18, 1955)
Piper Laurie (#79 – November 18, 1955)
Model Home (#79 – November 18, 1955)
Mr. and Mrs. Hush Contest (Taped)

Episode #960, Broadcast of December 14, 1955
Stunts: Marshmallow Chimp Kiss (#80 – November 25, 1955)
Ice Land Reunion (#33 – December 28, 1954)
Model Home Payoff (#80 – November 25, 1955)
Pair 'em Up (#81 – December 2, 1955)
Mr. and Mrs. Hush Contest (Taped)

Episode #961, Broadcast of December 21, 1955
Stunts: TV Store Frame (#81 – December 2, 1955)
Olson & Johnson Build-Up (#80 – November 25, 1955)
Olson & Johnson Payoff (#80 – November 25, 1955)
Mr. and Mrs. Hush Contest Phone Calls (Taped)

Episode #962, Broadcast of December 28, 1955
Stunts: Weatherman Build-Up (#81 – December 2, 1955)
Picture Quiz (#82 – December 9, 1955)
Weatherman Payoff (#81 – December 2, 1955)
Mr. and Mrs. Hush Contest Phone Calls (Taped)

Episode #963, Broadcast of January 4, 1956
Stunts: Service Couple Reunion (#82 – December 9, 1955)
T or C Strikes Again (a.k.a. Skunk-Perfume) (#82 – December 9, 1955)
Mr. and Mrs. Hush Contest Phone Calls (Taped)

Episode #964, Broadcast of January 11, 1956
Stunts: Mention Water Tank (#83 – December 16, 1955)
T OR C Strikes Miami (#83 – December 16, 1955)
Terry Moore (#83 – December 16, 1955)
Mr. and Mrs. Hush Contest Phone Calls (Taped)

Episode #965, Broadcast of January 18, 1956
Stunts: Moulin Rouge Build-Up (#24 – October 26, 1954)
Japanese Drama (#24 – October 26, 1954)
Moulin Rouge Payoff (#24 – October 26, 1954)
Truth or Consequences, New Mexico Tease (Taped)

Episode #966, Broadcast of January 25, 1956
Stunts: That's the Father Build-Up (#86 – January 6, 1956)
That's the Father Payoff (#86 – January 6, 1956)
Wild Bill Hickok (#86 – January 6, 1956)
Husband Recording (#33 – December 28, 1954)
Masked Marvel (#23 – October 19, 1954)
Truth or Consequences, New Mexico Tease (Taped)

Episode #967, Broadcast of February 1, 1956
Stunts: Ass Figures Love (#88 – January 20, 1956)
Split Screen Reunion (#87 – January 13, 1956)
Water Buffalo B.U. (#88 – January 20, 1956)
Superstition B.U. (#87 – January 13, 1956)
Water Buffalo Payoff (#88 – January 20, 1956)
Helen of Troy B.U. (#88 – January 20, 1956)

Episode #968, Broadcast of February 8, 1956
Stunts: Dan Duryea (#89 – January 27, 1956)
Helen of Troy Mention (#89 – January 27, 1956)
Beauty Shop Mention (#89 – January 27, 1956)
Camera Celebrity B.U. (#82 – December 9, 1955)
Town Marshall Contest (Taped)
Truth or Consequences, New Mexico Tease (Taped)

Episode #969, Broadcast of February 15, 1956
Stunts: Telescope Husband B.U. (#46 – March 29, 1955)
Helen of Troy Payoff (#90 – February 3, 1956)
Actress Frame (#46 – March 29, 1955)
Rajah Hoax B.U. (#46 – March 29, 1955)
Telescope Husband Payoff (#46 – March 29, 1955)
Camera Celebrity Payoff (#83 – December 16, 1955)
Town Marshall Contest Tease (Taped)

Episode #970, Broadcast of February 22, 1956
Stunts: Parachute B.U. (#90 – February 3, 1956)
Unicycle (#47 – April 5, 1955)

Old Fiddler's Tease (Taped)
Rajah Hoax Payoff (#47 – April 5, 1955)
Fiesta Tease (Taped)
Parachute Jump Payoff (#90 – February 3, 1956)
Town Marshall Contest (Taped)

Episode #971, Broadcast of February 29, 1956
Stunts: Barber Roulette (#91 – February 10, 1956)
Father Psychiatrist (#91 – February 10, 1956)
Diaper Derby (#92 – February 17, 1956)
Zsa Zsa Gabor (#91 – February 10, 1956)

Episode #972, Broadcast of March 7, 1956
Stunts: Wife T.D. (#45 – March 22, 1955)
Kiss Dog Frame (#92 – February 17, 1956)
Fiesta Tease (Taped)
Be Frank (#93 – February 24, 1956)
Town Marshall Contest (Taped)

Episode #973, Broadcast of March 14, 1956
Stunts: Slide Lecture B.U. (#94 – March 2, 1956)
Pick Soldier (#94 – March 2, 1956)
Town Marshall (Taped)
Star Sister (#94 – March 2, 1956)
Fiesta Queen & Jeep Tease (Taped)
Slide Lecture Payoff (#94 – March 2, 1956)

Episode #974, Broadcast of March 21, 1956
Stunts: Popcorn B.U. (#42 – March 1, 1955)
Father-Daughter Drama (#95 – March 9, 1956)
Fiesta Tease, a.k.a. Willy's Jeep (Taped)
Popcorn Insert No. 1 (#42 – March 1, 1955)
William Tell (#42 – March 1, 1955)
Popcorn Insert No. 2 (#42 – March 1, 1955)
Fiesta Plug (Taped)

Popcorn Payoff (#42 – March 1, 1955)
Town Marshall Contest (Taped)

Episode #975, Broadcast of March 28, 1956
Stunts: Lion's Mouth (#43 – March 8, 1955)
Fiesta Tease (Taped)
Pool Romance B.U. (#41 – February 22, 1955)
Snake Charmer (#41 – February 22, 1955)
Fiesta Tease & Jeep Rally (Taped)
Pool Romance Payoff (#41 – February 22, 1955)
Find Husband (#41 – February 22, 1955)

Episode #976, Broadcast of April 4, 1956
Stunts: Foreign Row Row Row (#97 – March 23, 1956)
Woman Stand-In (#96 – March 16, 1956)
Charade Frustration (#98 – March 30, 1956)
Town Marshall Tease & Payoff (Taped)
Golden Wedding (#98 – March 30, 1956)

Episode #977, Broadcast of April 11, 1956
Taped exclusively for radio on April 7, 1956 in Truth or Consequences, New Mexico
Stunts: Bathing Suit Package B.U.
Governor's Wife
Tab Hunter
Spin Model Pig
Bathing Suit Package Payoff

Episode #978, Broadcast of April 18, 1956
Taped exclusively for radio on April 7, 1956 in Truth or Consequences, New Mexico
Stunts: Whiffenpoof Lamb
Guess Mayor
Ad Lib Song
Prize Winners
Women Sleigh Bells

Episode #979, Broadcast of April 25, 1956
Stunts: Husband Box Hoax (#99 – April 6, 1956)
Miracle in Rain (#99 – April 6, 1956)
Phone Husband Frame (#98 – March 30, 1956)

Episode #980, Broadcast of May 2, 1956
Stunts: Gorilla Switch (#102 – April 27, 1956)
Korean Adoption (#100 – April 13, 1956)
Wash Elephant (#101 – April 20, 1956)
Baby on Doorstep (#101 – April 20, 1956)
Barber Shop Rubdown (#101 – April 20, 1956)

Episode #981, Broadcast of May 9, 1956
Stunts: Pool Wife Boss B.U. (#103 – May 4, 1956)
Chambermaid Surprise (#102 – April 27, 1956)
Identify Husband's Kiss (#102 – April 27, 1956)
Pool Boss Payoff Frame (#103 – May 4, 1956)
Kiss Irish Ladies (#90 – February 3, 1956)

Episode #982, Broadcast of May 16, 1956
Stunts: Graduation Surprise B.U. (#57 – May 14, 1955)
Choose Bag (#56 – June 7, 1955)
Crime Drama (#56 – June 7, 1955)
Miss Hush Tease (Taped)
Graduation Surprise Payoff (#57 – June 14, 1955)

Episode #983, Broadcast of May 23, 1956
Stunts: Reverse Squirt (#58 – June 21, 1955)
Bailey Disguise (#57 – June 14, 1955)
Totem Pole (#57 – June 14, 1955)
Husband Imitator (#56 – June 7, 1955)
Miss Hush Contest Tease (Taped)

Episode #984, Broadcast of May 30, 1956
Stunts: Considerate Husband B.U. (#59 – June 28, 1955)
Considerate Husband Cut-In No. 1 (#59 – June 28, 1955)

Mud Puddle Dress (#59 – June 28, 1955)
Whose Babies (#59 – June 28, 1955)
Considerate Husband Cut-In No. 2 (#59 – June 28, 1955)
Considerate Husband Payoff (#59 – June 28, 1955)
Miss Hush Contest Phone Calls (Taped)

Episode #985, Broadcast of June 6, 1956
Stunts: Return Frustration B.U. (#105 – May 18, 1956)
Recall Faces Reunion (#103 – May 4, 1956)
Return Frustration Payoff (#105 – May 18, 1956)
Miss Hush Contest Phone Calls (Taped)

Episode #986, Broadcast of June 13, 1956
Stunts: $100 Bill Back (#104 – May 11, 1956)
Phone Booth Reunion (#106 – May 25, 1956)
Phoney Chiropodist (#104 – May 11, 1956)
Miss Hush Contest Phone Calls (Taped)

Episode #987, Broadcast of June 20, 1956
Stunts: People Dog Drama (#107, June 1, 1956)
German Mother-In-Law (#107, June 1, 1956)
Fur Coat Hoax (#107, June 1, 1956)
Miss Hush Contest Phone Calls (Taped)

Episode #988, Broadcast of June 27, 1956
Stunts: Pin Tail Reunion (#109 – June 15, 1956)
Zsa Zsa Gabor (#105 – May 18, 1956)
Vacuum Cleaner (#106 – May 25, 1956)
Miss Hush Contest Phone Calls (Taped)

Episode #989, Broadcast of July 4, 1956
Stunts: Water Guillotine (#110 – June 22, 1956)
French Gabor (#108 – June 8, 1956)
Announcer Product Hoax (#108 – June 8, 1956)
Miss Hush Contest Phone Calls (Taped)

Episode #990, Broadcast of July 11, 1956
Stunts: Stop Train B.U. (#111 – June 29, 1956)
Translate Joke (#111 – June 29, 1956)
Stop Train Payoff (#111 – June 29, 1956)
Miss Hush Contest Phone Calls (Taped)

Episode #991, Broadcast of July 18, 1956
Stunts: Relay Record (#112 – July 6, 1956)
Linda Darnell (#112 – July 6, 1956)
Burbank Mayor Remote (#112 – July 6, 1956)
Miss Hush Contest Phone Calls (Taped)

Episode #992, Broadcast of July 25, 1956
Stunts: Husband Masher B.U. (#109 – June 15, 1956)
Husband Masher Payoff (#109 – June 15, 1956)
Mattress Salesman (#109 – June 15, 1956)
Five Grandparents (#110 – June 22, 1956)
Miss Hush Contest Phone Calls (Taped)

Episode #993, Broadcast of August 1, 1956
Stunts: Imitate Singer (#114 – July 20, 1956)
Miss Hush Contest Phone Call Winner (Taped)
Car Hop Remote B.U. (#114 – July 20, 1956)
Star Wager (a.k.a. Arlene Francis Spot, #110 – June 22, 1956)
Car Hop Remote Payoff (#114 – July 20, 1956)

Episode #994, Broadcast of August 8, 1956
Stunts: Musical Punctuation (#115 – July 27, 1956)
High Note Hot Seat (#116 – August 3, 1956)
Maharaja Frame (#116 – August 3, 1956)
Right One Tank (#115 – July 27, 1956)
Magic Reunion (#115 – July 27, 1956)

Episode #995, Broadcast of August 15, 1956
Stunts: Unknown

August 22, 1956 pre-empted

Episode #996, Broadcast of August 29, 1956
Stunts: Own Pool B.U. (#117 – August 10, 1956)
TV Surprise (#117 – August 10, 1956)
Call Husband Frame (#118 – August 17, 1956)
Own Pool Payoff (#117 – August 10, 1956)

Episode #997, Broadcast of September 5, 1956
Stunts: Guess Stork (#118 – August 17, 1956)
Hot Seat Star (#119 – August 24, 1956)
Own Fashion Show (#119 – August 24, 1956)
Bomber Reunion (#120 – August 31, 1956)

Episode #998, Broadcast of September 12, 1956
Stunts: Little League Reunion (#116 – August 3, 1956)
Knife Thrower (#121 – September 7, 1956)
Marilyn Maxwell Act (#121 – September 7, 1956)
Little League Reunion (#116 – August 3, 1956)
Chambermaid Surprise (#102 – April 27, 1956)

Episode #999, Broadcast of September 19, 1956
Stunts: Bailey Janitor (#122 – September 14, 1956)
Husband Box Hoax (#99 – April 6, 1956)
Miracle in Rain (#99 – April 6, 1956)

Episode #1,000, Broadcast of September 26, 1956
Stunts: Pool Boss Frame (#103 – May 4, 1956)
Fake Nose (#122 – September 24, 1956)
Culligan Remote (#122 – September 24, 1956)
Pool Boss Frame Payoff (#103 – May 4, 1956)
Foreign Double Talk (#123 – September 21, 1956)
Blindfold Drill Reunion (#123 – September 21, 1956)

Episode #1,001, Broadcast of October 3, 1956
Stunts: Ash Can Phone (#124 – September 28, 1956)

Fire Bucket Husband (#87 – January 13, 1956)
Split Screen Reunion (#87 – January 13, 1956)
Jimmy Durante (#87 – January 13, 1956)

THE BOB BARKER SEASON

Because the final season of radio's *Truth or Consequences* contained audio tracks of the television counterpart, listeners were unable to watch the proceedings such as a lady contestant who ruins her new hairdo because she has to bob for apples. Physical slapstick was the meat and potatoes for the medium of television so the radio counterpart suffered from this disadvantage. Many payoffs contained dreams-come-true for deserving people: families were reunited, and servicemen after taking part in stunts that rewarded them with a reunion of their wives and children.

As television ultimately dominated the entertainment field, radio programming faded. Even though the final season aired on radio five days a week, NBC had difficulty selling sponsorship on radio. The television program continued on but after 1,091 radio broadcasts (official number count), the final *Truth or Consequences* radio broadcast after a 17-year run concluded on the morning of August 30, 1957.

Index

99 Men and a Girl (radio program) 8
Abbott, Bud 181
Abie's Irish Rose (stage play) 407
Action Comics (comic book) 317
Adair, Allen 283, 547
Adams, Cas 375
Adams, Maude 106
Adelman, Harry 433
Adventures of Rin-Tin-Tin, The (television program) 317
Affair in Trinidad (motion-picture) 601
Against the Storm (radio program) 8, 34
Ai, Lee Ling 365
Albert, Fairley 599
Albin, Jack 464
Albright, Tommy 482
Alexander, Ben 251
Alexander, Joan 68
Alexander, Percy 271, 514
Alexander, Willard 570
Alice, Pauline 617
Allen, Bill 601
Allen, David 618
Allen, Fred 6, 128, 249, 250, 305, 404-407
Allen, Lena 414
Allen, Mel 8, 12, 34, 325, 344, 356, 358, 478, 517
Allison, Joe 308

Allton, Mary 218
Alper, Bernard David 621
Alvin and Betty (radio program) 2
Always Leave Them Laughing (motion-picture) 280
Andereck, Armand 426
Anderson, Albert 474
Anderson, Andrea 579
Anderson, Andy 190
Anderson, Betty 474
Anderson, Eddie "Rochester" 129, 178, 270
Anderson, J. Albin 391
Anderson, Marion 277
Anderson, Roy 279, 448
Anderson, Virgil Eugene 617
Andrews Sisters, The 422
Andrews, Charlie 587
Andrews, Dana 591
Andy, Handy 174
Annabella 18
Annie Laurie (song) 165
Antony, Marc 564
Antwerp, Eugene I. Van 269
Apartment for Peggy (motion-picture) 512
Arkus, Fred 162
Armbruster, Ed 314
Arnaz, Desi 300
Arno, Victor 590
Arnold (famed hairstylist) 403
Arnold, Arch 223
Arnold, Fred W. 541
Arquette, Cliff 441
Arsenic and Old Lace (stage play) 354
Arthur, Bob 513
Arthur, Jean 110
Arthur, Louise 96, 458, 461
Artz, Sgt. Ralph 580
Asher, Johnny 267-270, 509, 511, 512, 514
Ashworth, George 306
Assignment Paris (motion-picture) 591
Atkins, Charlotte 552
Atlanta Journal (newspaper) 443
Austin, Charles 597
Autry, Gene 240
Avallone, G. 410
Avallone, Rose 410
Bach, Louie 466
Bachelor and the Bobby Soxer, The (motion-picture) 545
Backus, Jim 68, 488
Baer, Buddy 591
Bailey, Ed 86, 132, 135, 164, 188, 190, 195, 215, 218, 287-289, 326, 433, 469, 470, 611, 617
Bailey, Jack 305-307, 310, 632, 633
Baker, Al 221-236, 565, 567-569
Baker, Edward J. 165

Baker, Herbert 482
Baker, Kenny 452
Baker, Phil 8, 90, 265, 456
Baldwin, Faith 116
Balinger, Art 22
Ballard, Dave 354, 393
Ballard, John H. 147, 151
Bangor Daily News (newspaper) 175
Bankhead, Tallulah 106
Barber, Helen 379
Barber, Roger 613
Barker, Bob 246, 310-317, 648
Barkley, Alben 285, 506
Barnes, Dr. A.R. 489
Barnes, Robert E. 628
Barnett, Charlie 430, 431
Barnett, Sue 214
Barnick, Buddy 532, 534-539
Barnish, Mary 390
Barron, Bob 445
Barrows, Don 491
Barrows, Jane 599
Barrows, Marilyn 491
Barry, John S. 182
Barry, Norman 555
Bartholomew, Richard 86-88, 435, 436
Bartlett, Tommy 481, 535, 551
Barton, Frank 325
Barton, Otis 543
Barts, Bob 552
Barty, Billy 21, 247
Baruch, Andre 6, 8, 9
Bastow, Raymond 365
Bates, Albert 627
Bats in the Belfry (radio program) 3
Batters, Charles 503
Bauer, Betsy 218
Bauer, Charlie 218
Bauman, Patsy 384
Baxter, Anne 512
Bayuth, Jack 162
Beale, Elvira 596
Bean, Willie 602
Beardsley, Lillian 581, 584
Beat the Band (motion-picture) 57, 281
Beatty, Clyde 563
Beatty, Harriett 563
Beaudry, Mac 231
Beaumont, Grace D. 331
Beaver, Fred 617, 618
Beavers, Dorothy 452
Beck, Etha 621
Beebe, Arlington 591

Before It's Too Late (motion-picture) 592
Bell Jr., Billy 231
Bell, Bill 606
Bell, Charles 73
Bell, George 100, 464
Bell, Rex 100, 104, 464, 471, 473
Bell, Ted 53, 566
Bell, Toni 100, 464
Belt, Dr. Elmer 513
Belton, Eddie 231
Bendix, William 178, 394, 427, 485, 494, 530
Benjamin, Joey 239
Bennett, Constance 403
Benny, Jack 79, 91, 93, 128, 129, 166, 167, 169-171, 174-179, 184, 409, 474, 567
Benson, John 223, 228, 230, 232, 233, 236, 267-269, 509, 511, 512, 514
Benson, Julius 418
Benton, John M. 419
Berg, Gertude 287
Berg, Mrs. Carl 632
Bergen, Edgar 35, 277, 574, 576
Bergerac, Jacques 304
Berle, Milton 280, 548
Berman, Ingrid 222
Bernay, Henry 168
Bernie, Al 369
Bernie, Ben 8, 39
Bertram, Mary Ruth 330
Besser, Joe 310
Betts, Rome 168
Beyer, Mrs. Kenneth 385
Biersach, Mrs. James 597
Billingsley, Sherman 352
Biographies in Sound (radio program) 309
Bish, Suzanne Carol 622
Bishop, Hazel 305
Blair, Janet 418
Blakeley, Rev. Harold 529
Blanchard, Harold 308
Bleifer, John 605
Blitzsteen, Harry 625
Blondell, Joan 388
Blood, Sweat and Tears (book) 65
Bloomquist, Gustav 554
Blore, Eric 396
Blunt, Casey 591
Blurton, Wilma 6
Blyth, Ann 509, 538, 539
Bob Barker Show, The (radio program) 312
Boebel, Bill 386
Boettigr, John 272
Boger, Thom 193
Bolen, Murray 6, 58, 88
Boley, R.V. 330

Bolton, Madeline 561
Bookshy, Clara A. 569
Booth, Adrian 240
Booth, Evangeline 109
Booth, Sgt. Donald 591
Borman, Bibbs 629
Botino, Carl 2
Botkin, Perry 448
Bourne, Jane 485
Bow, Clara 100, 104, 464, 471, 473
Bowers, Sgt. Alex K. 588
Bowman, A.H. 519
Bowman, Lee 418
Bowron, Fletcher 204, 254, 451
Boyce, Katherine 614
Boyer, Charles 308, 369, 447, 477
Bracken, Eddie 520
Braden, Dwight 577
Bradford, Irene 229
Bradley, General Omar 143, 148, 151-153, 495
Bradley, Harry 306
Bragg, Don 615
Brain, Albert G. 507
Brainard, Joyce 575
Brandao, Sampayo 365
Brandt, Mel 624
Brandt, Sgt. Bill 488
Breakfast in Hollywood (radio program) 181
Brennan, Marge 328
Brenneman, Tom 6
Brenner, Jeanette 45
Brian, David 240
Brice, Fanny 363
Bride and Groom (radio program) 180
Bridges, Martin 479
Briggs, Fred 230
Bringing Up Father (comic strip) 571
Britt, Jim 82
Britton, Pamela 585, 617
Brock, Heine 350
Brown, John 541, 542
Brown, Tom 550
Bruce, Michael 564
Bucham, Jerry 400
Buchstane, Lillie 30, 56
Buck, Nolan 509
Buddy Cole Trio 598
Buhler, William I. 216
Bulova, Arde 147, 151
Burch, Bill 327
Burch, William 326
Burgess, Harry 7
Burgmeier, Rev. Father A. 193, 202

Burk, V.C. 208
Burke, Billie 277, 287
Burnett, Leo 1
Burns, Williams 329
Burro, Milton 594
Burton, Cpl. James 610
Burton, James 617
Bush, Ernie 7
Bush, Lois 606
Butler, Arline 572
Butler, Champ 589
Butterfield, C.E. 175
Butterfield, Herb 530
Bygraves, Max 626, 627
Byington, Spring 99, 106
Byrd, Evie 170
Byrnes, Phyllis 542
Cabot, Bruce 572
Cachicame, C. 332
Calder, Mrs. R.G. 331
Calendar, Johnny 597
Callicoat, Mary 613
Callicoat, Phillip 613
Cameron, Bruce 498
Cameron, Rod 279, 501, 529, 618
Campbell, Major General 380
Can You Top This? (radio program) 51
Cannom, Robert C. 524, 525
Cantor, Eddie 79, 165, 272, 409
Card, Bill 269
Carey Jr., Harry 240
Carideo, Eddie 263, 264, 266, 504, 508
Carl, Wilbur 384
Carle, Frankie 281, 414, 488
Carlin, George 318
Carlisle, Kitty 271, 514
Carlson, Richard 573
Carmona, Dr. L.R. 74
Carney, Fred 36, 37, 138, 267, 289, 486
Caroll, Earl 501
Carpenter, Harlow 326
Carpenter, Ken 326, 598
Carrell, Rev. Harvey 202
Carroll, Earl 87, 99
Carroll, Madeleine 392
Carson, Jack 303, 436
Carson, Nellie 614
Carter, Gaylor 325
Carter, Nancy 214
Casey Ruggles (comic strip) 578
Castle, Irene 287
Cedroni, Tony 599
Chadwick, Jim 270, 501

Chalmers, Robert 494
Chambers, Harry 231
Chandler, A.B. 286
Chandler, Gordon 625, 626
Chandler, Jeff 302
Chandler, Norman 272
Chandler, Walter 402
Chaney Jr., Lon 316
Chapin, Lola Phillips 557-559, 561, 565
Charbert, Del 7
Charles, Jesse 420
Charley, Lena 578
Charm (magazine) 308
Chase, Ward 481
Cherichillo, Anna 587
Chester, Laura 566, 567, 569, 570
Chicago Daily Tribune (newspaper) 175
Children of Orphans (radio program) 3
Children's Digest (magazine) 601, 602
Choepheri, The (stage play) 5
Christensen, Edwin 630
Christensen, Patty 630
Christmas, Dorothy 512
Christopher, Kay 541
Church Mouse (stage play) 2
Church, Francis 403
Church, Marguerite 550
Churchill, Winston 165, 176, 474
City Detective (television program) 618
Claire, Eau 116
Clark, Cheryl 615
Clark, Col. Owen 310
Clark, Della 590
Clark, G.H. 538
Clark, Pat 256, 257, 472-474
Clark, Sue 170, 188, 195, 501, 582
Clarke, Thurmond 168
Clavenger, Billy 568
Clayton, Zella 229
Clayworth, June 281
Clevenger, Billie 499, 604
Clinton, Larry 488
Clooney, Rosemary 304, 604
Close, Carl B. 205
Cloud, Goldie Stanton 589
Coalson, Earl 244
Cohan, Agnes 287
Cohen, Alex 147
Cohen, Harry 567
Colbert, Jean 329, 388
Cole, Buddy 84, 91, 94, 325, 434, 448, 551, 590, 595, 604, 609, 618
Cole, Cpl. William 598
Coleman, Arletta 201, 218, 583

Collette, R.C. 106, 481
Collyer, Clayton 326, 396
Colman, Benita 272
Colman, Ronald 272, 477
Colonna, Jerry 58, 251, 265, 486
Command, The (motion-picture) 631
Comstock, Bill 441
Concannon, Charlie 6
Conlon, Pat 420
Connevy, Mrs. C. 330
Connor, Dr. Charles A.R. 168
Conover, Harry 416, 418
Constance, Gus 597
Conway, Ed 231
Cooke, Flora Juliette 110, 111
Coon, Ann 460
Cooper, Gary 550
Cope, Claude 435, 437, 438
Corbley, Vivian 438, 441
Corday, Bill 554
Corr, Alice 607
Corrigan, Douglas 588
Costa, Mickey 390, 391
Costanzo, Jack 304
Costello, Dolores 302
Costello, Lou 181, 304, 550
Cotton, Carolina 240
Coulter, Doug 7
Covington, Eleanor 605
Cowles, Sidney 425, 426
Cox, Cue 580
Cox, Peggy 609
Coyle, Dick 585
Cozeo, Mary Millie 617
Craig, J.L. 205
Crain, Jeanne 448
Crawford, Agnes 588
Crawford, Barbara 493
Crawford, Charles 588
Crawford, Joan 83, 155, 550
Crawford, Leonie 584
Crawford, Lorraine 630
Crew, Virgil L. 182
Crider, Patte 576
Cristoff, E.J. 532
Crosby, Bing 83, 110, 165, 272, 285
Crosby, John 127, 250
Crospell Sr., Ralph 218
Cross My Heart (motion picture) 490
Cross, Dr. George L. 483
Cross, Milton 39, 357, 388, 418
Croswait, Floyd 604
Crump, Boss Ed 164

Crump, George Ridley 591
Crump, Kirby 591
Cudner, Albert 392, 393
Cugat, Zavier 431
Culpsenetter, Earl 512
Cummings, Robert 623
Curry, Jim 617
Curtis, Tony 302
Dahlstead, Dresser 325
Dailey, Dan 513, 556, 557, 567
Daily News (newspaper) 536
Dalberg, Howard 417
Dalton, John 33
Daly, Joe 326
Dander, Edward B. 415
Dane, Marshall 480
Dann, Roger 501
Darland, Jeane 218
Darnell, Donnie 504
Darnell, Linda 304, 310, 646
Darnell, Norris 422
Dating Game, The (television program) 24
Davenport, Danny 600
Davenport, Thomas 193
Daviau, George 558
David, John 566
Davidian Report, The (motion-picture) 592
Davies, Bob 574
Davis, Al 30
Davis, Bill 327
Davis, Donna 575
Davis, G. Dewey 578
Davis, Harvey L. 183
Davis, Malcolm 595, 596
Davis, Phil 30, 531, 536
Davis, Rose 332
Davis, W.A. "Skinny" 198, 199, 218
Dawson, Irmgard 349
Day, Dennis 177, 304
Day, Owen Winston 252
De La Vigne, Louise 414
De Long, Robert 353
De Tete, Bal 591
Dear Ruth (motion-picture) 473
Deeman, John 567
DeFore, Don 541
DeLisle, Grace 508
Dell, Myrna 457
Deltour, Jean 481
Demarest, William 473
Dempsey, Barbara J. 89
Dempsey, Jack 86-89, 114, 161, 162, 314, 353, 435, 485, 524
Dempsey, John 212

Dennis, Clark 569
Dennis, Rev. O.L. 202
Desmond, Mrs. Harry 330
Destination Murder (motion-picture) 575
DeSylva, Buddy 273
Dewey, Gov. Thomas E. 273
Dewey, Harry 141, 476, 477
Dexter, Sherry 612
Diefenbach, Henry V. 205
Dietrich, Marlene 287
Dix, Richard 165
Dixon, Mary 535, 536
Doctor I.Q. (radio program) 318
Dodd, Barbara 589
Dodds, John A. 391
Dodson, Claire 99, 462
Dodson, Sam 529
Doe, Doris 532
Donahue, Jack 419
Donald, Peter 180, 358
Donlevy, Brian 304
Donnelly, Pat 349
Doran, Paul 409
Dorsey, Mrs. Jim 597
Dottson, Maxine 229
Douglas, Kirk 108
Douglas, Paul 6, 549
Doyle, Daniel A. 44, 360
Dragnet (radio program) 309
Draper, Bob 570
Draper, Patricia 570
Drew, Ellen 387
Dubedat, Louis 5
Duchin, Eddie 20
Ducksters, The (cartoon) 318
Duel in the Sun (motion-picture) 457
Duester, Margaret S. 605
Duffy, Earl 617
Dumbo (motion-picture) 351
Dumm, Bob 4
Dumm, Wesley 4
Duncan, Dorothea 544
Dunn, Gladys 619
Dunne, Irene 272
Dunne, Steve 243, 303, 304
Dupont, Larry 118, 484
Durante, Jimmy 303, 304, 310, 648
Duryea, Dan 310, 641
DuVal, Gaylord 610
Dyer, Bob 275, 489
Early, John 477-480
Early, William 569
Eckstine, Billy 598

Edens Jr., W.H. 215
Edwards, Barbara (handwriting expert) 555
Edwards, Barbara (wife) 8-10, 12, 56, 207, 213, 214, 217, 245, 251, 550
Edwards, Chris 312
Edwards, Christine 9
Edwards, Jack 629
Edwards, Joan 279, 425, 448, 514
Edwards, Lauren 9, 312
Edwards, Minnie 478
Edwards, Paul 327
Edwards, Ralph 1-13, 15, 17-24, 29-40, 43-45, 47-59, 63-65, 67-69, 71-73, 78-83, 85-91, 93-100, 102, 104-105, 107, 108, 110, 112, 114, 115, 117-121, 125, 127-129, 131, 132, 134-137, 143, 145, 147, 150-157, 159-162, 164-166, 168-171, 173-184, 187-198, 200, 204-207, 209, 210, 213-215, 217-219, 221-223, 231-234, 239-241, 243, 245-247, 249-253, 255-258, 261-263, 265-403, 405-412, 414-416, 418, 419, 422-427, 429, 430, 432-438, 440-455, 457-465, 467-470, 472-481, 483-493, 496, 498-504, 507, 508, 512-515, 517, 520, 522, 525, 528-530, 532-540, 543-546, 548, 550, 553, 555-557, 559, 560, 562-567, 569, 572, 574, 575, 577, 579-582, 586, 588-592, 594, 596-604, 606-608, 610-615, 617, 619-621, 623, 626, 628, 629, 631, 633
Ehleis, Honey 330
Ehly, Moreen 607
Ehly, Robert L. 607
Eigen, Jack 166
Einstein, Albert 88
Eisenhower, Dwight D. 273
Elbar, Claire 453
Eldridge, Florence 272
Eldridge, Neil 229
Ellen, Arthur 315
Elliott, Bob 583
Emerson, Hope 302, 355, 389, 417, 524
Engineer's Journal (periodical) 37
Engle, Cliff 325, 382, 384
English, Ed 216
English, Marla 607
Erickson, Louise 145
Ericson, Erich 367
Erlich, Isabel 113
Evans, Bob 617
Evans, E.R. 560
Evans, Howard 564
Evans, Maurice, 155, 458
Evans, Steve 255, 452, 453
Eyman, Jack 231
Fabin, Bernard 567
Fairbanks, Jerry 299, 300
Fanning, Michael D. 93, 263, 519
Farber, Dr. Sidney 78, 83
Farmer, Willie 403
Farnell, Jack 10, 37
Farr, Bob 288
Farrah, Theodore 591
Father Knows Best (radio program) 622

Fay, Frank 337, 339
Feeney, Madeline 183
Feller, Bobby 490
Ferguson, Harold G. 512
Ferguson, Olive 561
Fernandez, A.M. 210
Ferrell, Harold 490
Ferrer, Jose 304
Fibber McGee and Molly (radio program) 290, 309
Field, Norman 5
Field, Ray 620
Fieldhouse, Carol 157, 556, 558-560
Fields, W.C. 544
Fifield, Stephen H. 133
Finnegan, Eddie 550
Fisher, Don 71, 418
Fisher, Leon 329
Fishman, Gilbert 623, 624
Fishman, Harvey 420
Fisk, Mr. D. 629
Fitzgerald, Don 452
FitzHugh, Douglass K. 210-212
Flaherty, Ray 454
Flanagan, Ralph 604
Fleenor, Rev. M. Guy 137, 484
Fleming, Rhonda 303, 610
Fletcher, Bill 593, 594
Fletcher, Stanley 626
Floe, Ida 620
Flood, Hal 326
Florentino, Rudolph 618
Floyd, Barbara 214
Ford, Merle 277-279, 527-529
Foreman, Harry 409
Forscht, William 508
Forsythe, John 304
Foster, Frank 524
Foster, Hazel M. 600
Foster, Preston 394
Fowler, Charlie 211, 212
Fox, Harry 45
Fox, James 592
Fox, Jeremy 21
Foy, Shelley 632
Francis, Arlene 310
Frank, Mrs. Don 597
Frazin, Al 347
Freeman, Frank 228
Frees, Paul 308, 477, 627
Friedburg, Gertrude 612
Fries, William J. 594
Froman, Jane 419
Fromme, Harry 488

Front and Center (radio program) 156
Fuhrman, John Ed 53
Funt, Allen 408
Gabbert, Bill 500, 501
Gable, Clark 477
Gabor, Eva 304
Gabor, Zsa Zsa 303, 304, 310, 642, 645
Gahagan, Rev 568
Gaines, Hazel 590
Gallico, Paul 104
Gallop, Frank 6
Gamble, Ted 431
Gammon, Bill 137
Gammon, Kay 362
Gandhi, Mahatma 474, 475
Gann, Gilbert 561
Gans, Anne 327
Garbo, Greta 168
Garday, Hank 209
Garden, Mary 111
Gardey, Henry 200, 201
Gardney, Hank 218
Garfield, Dr. F. Edwyn 586
Garland, Judy 626
Garland, Nancy 513
Garner, James 304
Garroway, Dave 587
Gart, Johnny 325, 396, 410
Garvey, Dan 235
Gary, Bruce 503
Gaston, John E. 308
Gay, Jerry 593
Gehersky, Dale 515
Gentry, Mrs. R.
George Jessel Show, The (radio program) 7
Gerletti, Fred 231
Gesler, Katie 538
Gethers, Clarence 429
Gethers, Sharon 429
Getter, Jane 439
Gibbs, Otto 525
Gibson, Hoot 243, 244
Gilbert, Emma Crooks 298, 612
Gilbert, George 383
Gilbert, Neva 615
Gilbert, Wolfie 570
Gillen, John 395
Gilmore, Art 326, 580
Gilmore, L.D. 386
Gimbel, Sophie 353
Giovanni, Dr. 567
Gish, Herald 617
Glamour Manor (radio program) 441, 452

Glow, Mrs. Fred 597
Godfrey, Arthur 285, 286
Goetz, Billy 176
Goldman, Albert 520
Goldsmith, Peter C. 288
Goldstein, Abe 564
Goldstein, Bob 517
Goodwin, Bill 129
Gordon, Elsie May 347
Gordon, Gale 389
Gospel Singer, The (radio program) 8
Goss, Jim 523
Gott, Guy 445
Gottlieb, Dick 234, 236, 569
Gould, Mike 597
Gould, Robert 288
Graffort, Atha 597, 599, 613
Graham, Martha 104, 115-118, 120-122, 127, 128, 165, 488
Graham, Michael 586
Grant, Elmer 518
Grant, James C. 231
Grant, Tom 606
Grauer, Ben 357, 419, 532
Gravelle, Della 595
Gray, Colleen 513
Great Gildersleeve, The (radio program) 309
Greb, Joe 525-528, 531-534, 536, 538-540
Green, Ivan 153, 445, 449
Green, Virginia 470
Greene, Frances 443
Greenway, Norman 52, 396
Greenwood, Charlotte 107
Greer, Betty Jane 423
Greleck, Harry 117, 483, 494
Grey, Gilda 589
Griffith, Dr. Francis 272
Grimes, Bob 508
Groom, Helen 527
Gross, Ben 115, 127, 492
Gross, Milton 375
Grover, John 325
Gruener, Carl 234
Guadalcanal Diary (motion-picture) 394
Guedel, John 181
Guest, Edgar A. 286, 568
Guillory, Mrs. John 500
Gurr, Ted 549
Gustafson, Einar 81
Guys and Dolls (motion-picture) 585
Haason, Gordon 383
Hackett, Wayne J. 597
Haeffner, J.A. 582
Haffner, Dora Shaw 513

Hafner, Ed 498
Hafner, Louella 498
Hagen, Phyllis 467
Haight, Walter 165
Haines, Connie 303, 619
Halett, J. 545
Halett, Mrs. J. 280
Hall Jr., Sgt. Louis 614
Hall, Jon 304
Hall, Mabel 545
Hallett, Audrey 518
Hallett, Charles 518
Halloran, Col. Mary 107
Hambay, Norma 234
Hammerslag, Victor 404
Hampton, Lionel 572
Haney, Fred 473
Hannah, Joan 89
Hannegan, Robert E. 165
Hansen, Ethel 154
Hansen, Lester 153, 154, 449
Happy Time, The (motion-picture) 596
Harding, Robert 608
Hargrave, Lyn 231
Harlow, Maria 595
Harmon, Mrs. William 100, 112
Harriman, Gov. W. Averell 635
Harris, Phil 69, 79, 177, 530
Harrison, Sally 584
Hart, Moss 271, 514
Hart, Rosa 500
Hartman, Mary 140
Harvey, Bill 585
Harvey, Grace Ann 585
Harvey, Margaret 542
Harvey, Paul 572
Harvey, Richard 417
Harvey, W. Ward 552
Harwood, Zoe 52
Has Anybody Seen My Gal? (motion-picture) 584
Hatchet, C.W. 194
Hatfield, Odell 475
Hawaii Calls (radio program) 6
Hawes, Bill 269, 327
Hayes, Jim 231
Haymes, Dick 530, 562
Haynes, Larry 157, 556-560
Hays, Mrs. James 339
Hayworth, Rita 601
Head, Edith 417
Heatter, Gabriel 503
Hedden, Frances 410
Hedrick Jr., Earl 476

Hedrick, E.R. 476
Heidt, Horace 249, 389, 488
Heifetz, Jascha 174
Heisley, Howard 28
Hellman, Jack 449
Hellzapoppin' (stage play) 23, 343
Helm, Joel 621
Helm, Roe E. 621
Hemingway, Ernest 272
Henderson, Cliff 228
Henry, Edgar 575
Henry, Paul H. 575
Henson, Marie 596
Here Come the Waves (motion-picture) 417
Herlihy, Ed 325, 361, 377, 404, 409, 518, 530, 533, 566
Herman, Woody 379
Hess, Otto H. 591
Hess, Roy 585
Hickey, Donna Lee 591
Higinbotham, Lynne 243, 606
Higinbotham, R.L. 243, 606
Hildegarde 370, 371
Hilderra, Charles 564
Hill, E. Louise 330
Hill, Howard Roy 448
Hill, Sgt. Maj. Barry 512
Hilton, Bob 604
Hingston, Albert 612
Hoadly, Mrs. Clarence B. 601
Hodge, Ray 605
Hoffman, Dr. Samuel 472
Hoffman, Jean 603
Hogan, Ben 506
Hogeman, Wayne 503
Holcomb, Robert M. 216
Holland, Herb 285, 443, 444
Hollywood Star Preview (radio program) 501
Hollywood Theatre of the Air (radio program) 387
Holm, Celeste 262, 493
Holm, Floyd 58
Honolulu Bound (radio program) 8
Hook, Mrs. Joseph S. 168
Hookey, Bobby 351, 357
Hoover, Dorothy 401
Hoover, Herbert 474
Hoover, J. Edgar 164
Hope, Bob 58, 300
Hopkins, Gloria 596
Hopkins, Margaret 183
Hopkins, Mrs. Oliver 287
Hopper, Hedda 287
Horace Heidt Show, The (radio program) 8
Horn and Hardart Children's Hour, The (radio program) 10, 11, 351, 357

Horowitz, Paul 623
Houston, James F. 231
Howard, Bob 467
Howard, Cal 327
Howard, Sidney 5
Howe, Mrs. Glen 145
Hubbard, Florence 166-171, 174, 177, 179, 183, 184, 489
Huber, Mrs. Charles 302
Huckabee, H.B. 196
Hudson, Rock 584
Hughes, Dorothy B. 592
Hull, Josephine 287
Hume, Benita 272
Hunter, Tab 303, 310, 637, 643
Huntington, F.J.F. 67
Hussin, Betty Jane 535
Hussin, Danny 535
Huston, Walter 165
Hutchinson, Harry 355
Hutchinson, Madge 536
Hutton, Betty 490
Hyman, Joseph P. 151
Hynes, John B. 79
I Love Lucy (television program) 300
I Walk Alone (motion-picture) 164, 170, 258
I, Jane Doe (motion-picture) 496
Iden, Chet 232
Information, Please (radio program) 11, 39
Iron Mistress, The (motion-picture) 597
Irvine, Nancy N. 592
Isaac, Omaray 194
Isner, Rose 292, 624
Israel, Albert 545
Jacaloni, Sandra 593
Jacanto, Mario 448
Jack, John J. 66
Jackson, Bill 504
Jackson, Howard 325
Jackson, Jay 326, 580
Jackson, Judy 619
Jackson, Paul 155, 619
James, Harry 368
Jampel, Carl 53
Jarvis, Susan 209, 302
Javna, Jonas 448
Jay, Lee 589
Jean, Gloria 34
Jean, Lola 591
Jean, Wendy 570
Jefferson, Russell 516
Jenkins, Mrs. John R. 588
Jennings, Jo Ellen 197
Jensen, Rose 333

Jessel, George 548
Jessel, Jerilyn 548
Joan of Arc (motion-picture) 222
Jochen, Carl 568
Johns, Sally 554
Johnson, "Box Car" 456
Johnson, A. 208
Johnson, Chic 280, 547, 640
Johnson, Don 425
Johnson, Edward 356
Johnson, Elsa M. 133
Johnson, Erskine 545
Johnson, Gen. Hugh 333
Johnson, Harold 303, 310
Johnson, Joe 371
Johnson, Kathryn 588
Johnson, Lamont 53, 326
Johnson, Thelma 513
Johnson, Van 176, 445
Johnston, Lewis 5
Johnstone, Wayne 542
Jolson, Al 155
Jones, Candy 532
Jones, Carroll 614
Jones, Frank 385
Jones, Glenn A. 609
Jones, Johnny 328
Jones, Joseph 487
Jones, Paul 325
Jones, Spike 307, 519
Jordan, Jim 290
Jordan, Marian 290
Jorgenson, Eiler 494
Joy, Ernest N. 44
Joyce Jordan (radio program) 181
Judd, Granville 599
Judge for Yourself (television program) 305
Juggler, The (motion-picture) 605
Julian, Joseph 417
Julio, John 566
Jungst, Christian 354
Junior Miss (radio program) 39
Jurgens, Dick 488
Juster, Gene 264, 505
Juvenile Jury (radio program) 482
Kaiser, Henry J. 165
Kaiser, R.S. 191
Kaltenborn, H.V. 503
Kapp, John 391
Kappen, Ann 588
Kaproff, Armand 590
Karloff, Boris 172, 274, 310, 453, 516, 607
Kasher, Dave 550

Kay, Bobby 606
Kay, Joe 114, 234, 252, 475
Kay, Mary Lou 601
Kaye, Danny 48
Kaye, Sammy 348
Kayo 385
Keating, Mrs. Tom 593
Keaton, Buster 304
Kee, Charley 537
Keeler, Ruby 302
Keene, Vernon 38, 445, 446
Keith, Allan H. 88
Keith, Claude 273, 521
Keith, Daryl 273
Keith, Gerald 218
Keith, Larry 273
Keith, Linda 273
Keith, Mary 522
Keith, Oscar 273, 520-522
Keith, Phil 481
Keith, Sharon 273
Keith, Viola 240
Kelly, Al 413
Kelly, Bob 619
Kelly, Joe 468
Kelly, Karolee 632
Kennedy, Burt 282, 283, 546, 547
Kennedy, Edgar 467
Kennedy, Lt. John 610
Kenney, Raymond 414-416
Kenny, George C. 604, 632
Kenny, Sister Elizabeth 106, 113
Kenton, Stan 430
Kercher, Pete 454
Kerr, Robert A. 408
Kersey, Dr. Vierling 96
Keuffer, Carolyn V. 592
Keyes, Charles R. 206
Kibbe, Gordon 595
Kilbourne, Mrs. Lincoln 548
Kilgallen, Dorothy 532
Kinard, Mary 451
Kincheloe, Ken 612
King Lear (stage play) 5
King of the Cowboys (motion-picture) 392
King, Andrew 579
King, Carroll Ray 183
King, Charlie 616
King, Gov. Bruce 218
King, Mildred 114
King, Peter 552
Kinneman, Mary 413
Kinser, Don 230

Kinser, Mrs. J.E. 230
Kinsey, Jr. Joe D 212
Kinsey, Ralph 551, 552
Kirsten, Sgt. George 570
Kiss, William 567
Kittel, Clyde 404, 409, 412
Kjellstrom, Nills 190, 195, 210
Klein, Dorothy 329
Kleinman, Allene 589
Klinger, Max 231
Klise, Rod 383
Knott, Frida 589
Knox, Mrs. Walter 198, 199, 563
Koby, James 494
Koe, Steven 536
Kohler, William 218
Koki, Douglas T. 207
Koster, William S. 77, 78, 82
Koukol, Joseph 519
Kovacs, Ernie 304
Kozoll, Julia 459
Kozoll, Mike 459
Kronach, Arthur 487
Krupa, Gene 535, 536
Kruzel, Phil 532
Kubitschek, Frank 548, 549
Kuhne, Charles 218
Kupperman, Joel 420, 468
Kurtsinger, Gene 531
Kushins, Harry 365
L'Hommedieu, Florence 370
La Rocca, Albina 625
Lachelle, Elbert 6
Lackey, Nadine 531
Ladd, Alan 222, 493
Laffin, Bill 542
LaGuardia, Mayor 474
Laher, Bobby 327
Laine, Frankie 304
Lake, Veronica 493
Lamb, Charley 231
Lambert, Lucille 365
Lamont, Bob 531
Lamour, Dorothy 156, 474, 542, 550
Land, Marjorie Ellis 308
Lander, Harry 369
Landis, Carole 419
Lane, George R. 137
Lang, Johnny 570
Langdon, Al 591
Langdon, Joe J. 602
Langford, Frances 57, 58, 421
Lantone, Anthony 386

LaPrade, Janice 400
Lasker, Billy 562
Lasky, Phil 3, 4
Late Springtime (stage play) 5
Latimer, Jonathan 592
Lauder, Sir Harry 474
Laughton, Charles 501
Laurie, Piper 303, 310, 575, 639
Lawrence, Barbara 513
Lawrence, Ernest Orlando 273
Lawrence, Frank 607
Lawrence, Gerry 517, 556
Lawrence, Jerry 537, 543, 568, 589
Lawrence, Larry 326
Layne, Walter 541
Learman, Mrs. R. 514
Leathers, Jimmie Lee 576
Lee, Dixie 272
Lee, Gypsy Rose 388
Lee, Helen 584
Lee, Lee R. 609
Lee, Peggy 304
Legg, Douglas 535
Leigon, Mary Faye 607
Lennstrom, J. Leroy 410
Lennstrom, Mrs. Walter 410
Leone, Joe 593
Leoni, Joseph 592Kashner, Dave 592
Lerner, Max 597
Leslie, Bob 269
Lester, Marsha 612, 613
Lett, Herbert 201, 218
Levitan, Sam 446
Lewis, Elliott 530
Lewis, John L. 474
Lewis, Martin 344
Lewis, Ralsten 6, 8
Lewis, Robert 280, 546
Lewis, Sinclair 437
Lewis, Tommy 397
Lewis, Warren 151
Liberace 612
Libner, George 585
Liebermann, Mildred R. 271
Life (magazine) 99
Life Begins at Forty (book) 357
Life Can Be Beautiful (radio program) 8, 34, 181
Life of Riley, The (radio program) 427, 485, 494, 530
Lind, Willard 458
Lindley, Earnest Kidder 272
Lindsay, Howard 272
Linkletter, Art 180
Little, Wesley 241, 242

Livingstone, Bob 524, 525
Livingstone, Hilliard 176
Livingstone, Mary 171, 174-176
Lloyd, Duncan 492
Lloyd, Harold 272
Lloyd, Olivia 492
Lockman, Whitey 583
Lombardo, Guy 368, 413, 427, 488
London, Betty 580
London, Howard J. 93
Lonza, Jeanine Shepherd 594
Look (magazine) 504, 530
Loomis, Agnes 331
Lopshire, Richard 231
Lorre, Peter 174
Loughrin, Richard 493
Louis, Joe 165
Louise, Ann 591
Love, James 502
Love, Loreen Cox 504
Lovequist, Evelyn 615
Lowell, Pfc. Gerald 580
Luce, Clare Boothe 272
Luce, Henry 272
Lucky Strike Program, The (radio program) 177
Lukas, Paul 108
Lundeen, Evelyn 586
Lupino, Ida 485
Lusk, Lynn 615
Lutcher, Nellie 502
Luyster, Martha 410
Lyman, Abe 222, 343
Lynn, Betty 513
Lyon, Charles 326, 477, 485, 491, 542, 549
Lyons, Mary A. 141, 523, 553
Macbeth (stage play) 5
MacDonald, Edmund 550
MacDonald, Jeanette 277, 527
MacFarland, Dora 483
MacGowan, Lauren 517
Machado, Alice 589
MacHugh, Edward 8
Mack, Helen 550
MacKenzie, Gisele 600
MacKenzie, Joyce 575
MacMurray, Fred 550
MacRae, Gordon 567, 598
Madison, Guy 457, 631
Madsen, Chris 6
Madsen, Junior 145
Magazine Digest (magazine) 461
Magic Town (motion-picture) 477
Maher, Margaret 285, 563

Mahoney, Jock 304
Mahoney, Ralph 116
Mail Call (radio program) 60
Mainland, Cpl. Donald 293-295
Mainland, Donald 611
Mainland, Ruth 293, 611
Major Bowes' Original Amateur Hour (radio program) 8, 12
Majors, E.L. 569
Mallory, Lincoln 429
Malneck, Matty 430, 431
Maloney, Jerrie C. 331
Man in the Dark (motion-picture) 609
Mana, Katchina 577
Manche, Tom 179
Manners, Ginger 327
Mansfield, Jayne 242
Maraia, Kathleen 520
March of Events (radio program) 3
March, Fredric 272
Marcus, Ann 620
Mardikian, George 280, 546
Marino, Buddy 417
Markapoulas, Pvt. Peter 601
Marmaduke, Virginia 170
Marrying Kind, The (motion-picture) 581
Marsh, George 508
Marshall, Herbert 164, 165
Marshall, Jay 378
Martell, Henry 64, 415
Martin, Dude 3
Martin, Freddy 569
Martin, Harold 570
Martin, Harris 415
Martin, James 88
Martin, Ralph E. 620
Martin, Ronnie 477
Martin, Tony 303
Martini, Cleland 520
Marx, Groucho 550, 588
Mary Lee Taylor (radio program) 594
Masi, Phil 81
Mason, George W. 538
Matthews, Bob 597
Matthews, Cpl. Matt 612
Mature, Victor 390, 391, 547
Maverick (television program) 304
Maw, Herbert B. 153
Maxwell, Elsa 106, 481
Maxwell, Marilyn 303, 310, 647
Maxwell, Scotty 225
Mayberry, Joan 608
Mayer, Ken 559, 561
Mayer, Louis B. 164

Mayer, Sue 589
Mayo, Michael 329
Mayo, Virginia 478, 597
McAmis, Eunice A. 609
McAmis, Virgil 609
McCall, L.M. 175
McCann, Florence 608
McCarthy, Charlie 574, 576
McCarthy, Glen 209
McCarthy, Nora 372
McClean, Sergeant 400
McCollen, Lyle 397
McCormick, Hugh 620
McCormick, Mrs. William 100, 102, 103, 111, 463, 464
McCullough, John 308
McDaniel, E.W. 240
McDonald, Marie 419, 573
McElravy, Col. C.A. 54
McElwane, George 498
McEnroe, John 170
McGinn, Margaret 260, 261, 497, 498
McGinn, Tom 260, 261, 496, 497
McIntyre, Michael 610
McKay, Diane 399
McKay, Doreen 399
McKee, Susanna C. 621
McKee, Tom 630
McKenzie, Maude 471
McKinley, Barry 402
McKinney, Jean 328
McLaughlin, Ethel O. 591
McManus, George 571
McMillan, Gordon 331
McMillin, George 492, 495, 499
McMillin, John 9, 11
Mechem, Governor 240
Mecham, Edwin L. 607, 632
Meeder, Bill 9, 325, 338, 366, 375
Meehan, Arthur R. 206
Meers, Bill 579
Melander, Bob 616
Melchior, Lauritz 303
Melvin, Jack 264, 505
Meredith, Dolton 598
Meredith, Mary 598
Merrill, Anna 538
Merry Macs, The 34
Metzger, Charles 566
Meuller, Cpt. Gilbert 610
Meyer, Rosemary 597
Mezies, William Cameron 542
Michaelson, Ruth 329
Middleton, Cpl. Harry 615

Middleton, R.H. 213
Midsummer Night's Dream, A (stage play) 5
Mihld, Mrs. John 537
Miles, John 196
Miles, John E. 210, 563
Milland, Ray 531, 532
Miller, Betty 561
Miller, Madeline 170
Miller, Mrs. Albert 431
Mills, Pelham 500
Mims, Mayor Glen J. 190, 191, 195, 206, 562, 563
Minay, Gloria 462
Mitchell, Dale 597
Mitchell, Dorothy 394
Mitchell, Edward 627
Mitchell, Spring 592
Mito, Mike 444
Mitropoulos, Dimitri 27
Mogingo, Pfc. Elmer 591
Molle Mystery Theatre (radio program) 181
Monroe, Vaughn 368, 408
Montgomery, Wes 562
Montoya, Eddie 218
Moody, Sidney 544
Moon in the Yellow River, The (stage play) 5
Moore, Clement 120
Moore, Colleen 2
Moore, Faith 559, 561
Moore, Gen. James 574
Moore, Jack Richard 594
Moore, Preston J. 483
Moore, Terry 303, 310, 640
Moorehead, Agnes 340
Moorman, Dick 462
Moran, Pat 548-550
Morgan, Henry 532
Morgan, Jack 211, 212
Morgan, Ray 519
Morgan, Tom 3
Mormon, Robert 498
Morrell, Lila 137, 484
Morris, Pat 315
Morrison, George 342
Morteson, Varion 145
Morton, Jerry 314
Mosby, Aline 114, 174, 253
Moses, Grandma 287
Moss, Herb 53, 58, 326
Mott, Dorothy 197
Mott, Ingrid 545
Mounts Jr., Tracy 603
Mounts, Florence 603
Mounts, Francis 603

Mounts, Tracy 603
Mowbray, Alan 574
Moyles, Jack 153, 449
Mr. Peabody and the Mermaid (motion-picture) 509
Mueller, Don 583
Mueller, Helen 344
Mullane, Harold 47, 376
Mullane, Mrs. Dennis J. 47, 376
Mullin, Elizabeth 121
Mulvahill, Joe 503
Murder, My Sweet (motion-picture) 422
Murdock, James 531
Murray, Arthur 26, 349, 418
Murray, Mae 287
Musser, Charlotte 214
My Gal Sal (motion-picture) 44
Nagler, Barney 375
Nail, Mathilda 503
Nastgner, Roy 96
Nathanson, Wynn 162
National Radio Fan Club (radio program) 309
Naulty, Annie 603
Nazarro, Cliff 439
NBC Radio Theatre (radio program) 309
Neas, Hal 137
Nehauser, Edward 470, 471
Neill, Pfc. Darrell 598
Neise, George 628
Nelligan, Ada 155
Nellison, Clarence G. 621
Nellison, Elizabeth 622
Nelson, Ozzie 587
Nelson, Peggy 569
New York City News (newspaper) 479
Newman, Irvine 491
Newman, Mrs. Irvin 491
Newsweek (magazine) 99, 372
Newton, Ernie 555
Newton, Virginia 554, 555
Niemann, Joe 231
Night Before Christmas, The (poem) 120
Niven, David 547
Noah, Donald 397
Noah, Ronald Lester 397
Nocturne (motion-picture) 457
Nolan, Lloyd 394
North, Evelyn 397
Norton, J.H. 598
Novak, Marty 218
Novak, Thomas 218
Nuneville, Emrys D. 66
Nye, George 439
O. Henry's Full House (motion-picture) 588

O'Brien, Edmund 609
O'Brien, Pat 550
O'Connell, Jesslyn 330
O'Connor, Donald 222, 550, 567
O'Connor, J.F.T. 96
O'Daniel, W. Lee 478
O'Donnell, Lillian 349
O'Donnell, Pat 586
O'Dowd, Jack 231
O'Flaherty, Terrence 31, 32
O'Keafe, George Michael 44
O'Keefe, Dennis 527
O'Neils, The (radio program) 8
Oakland, Ben 570
Ocepa, Lorraine 478, 479
Ogden, Dorothy 329
Olander, Fred 201
Olden, Lt. Owen 570
Oldstein, Bernice 549
Oleson, Myrtle 512
Oliver, Dorothy 128
Olsen, Irving 145
Olsen, John 303, 310, 640
On Borrowed Time (stage play) 453
One Man's Family (radio program) 309
Oregon Journal (newspaper) 175
Orn, Leo 561
Ortiz, Peter 155
Osborne, Louise 408
Osborne, Will 430
Our Town (stage play) 360
Outten, Billy 309
Owen, Ethel 348
Owens, Claude 219
Paar, Jack 114
Page, Robert 550
Paige, Janis 577
Palance, Jack 303
Palmer, Stuart 592
Pan, Jessica 590
Pankey, Joe 217
Pankey, Ruben 217
Parker, Lorene 465-471
Parker, Orlan 145
Parks, Bert 6, 318
Parks, Robert 137
Parrot, Harold 375
Parsons, Louella 277
Paschall, Al 17, 53, 65, 93, 94, 97, 102, 103, 106, 114, 117, 124, 143, 144, 151, 170, 171, 260, 288, 289, 314, 300, 326, 485, 497
Passmore, Dorothy 197, 198
Passmore, Ralph Edwards 197, 198
Passmore, Thomas 197, 198

Pastor, Tony 423
Paul, Jeffrey 495
Pavelosky, Sgt. Leo 580
Pawlek, Ed 326, 628
Pawlek, Johnny 36, 37, 108, 326, 470
Payne, Jerry 19
Payne, John 548, 632
Pearce, Madeline 374
Pearson, Drew 181
Pearson, Edward L. 619
Pearson, Ford 325
Pearson, Lester 616
Peck, Gregory 279, 529
Penn, Alfred 2
Penn, Gertrude 485
People Are Funny (radio program) 180, 181, 309, 508
Pepan, Bea J. 249
Pepper Young's Family (radio program) 8, 181
Pepper, Bob 435, 437, 438
Pepper, Sen, Claude 474
Perini, Lou 78
Perrin, Sam 176
Perry, Bill 243, 607
Perry, Vernon 425
Peterson, Louis 520
Peterson, Marie 492
Petrillo, James 165
Petty, Jack 609
Phelps, Alfred 425
Phelps, Bob 425
Phelps, Frances 425
Phil Arden Orchestra, The (radio program) 7
Philips, Sid 508
Phillips, Janice 214
Phillips, Walter Raymond 557
Photoplay (magazine) 517
Pick and Pat (radio program) 8
Pickett, Orville 202
Pickford, Mary 273
Pillsbury, Staunton 597
Pimentel, John 601
Pinza, Ezio 559
Platt, Leonard 457
Plummer, Jim 609
Plunderers, The (motion-picture) 499
Polisner, Albert 629
Pollock, Grant 6
Pople, Duane 602
Porter, Erwin 306
Porter, William 467
Post, Emily 8, 287
Pot o' Gold (radio program) 249
Pouch Sr., Jesse M. 133

Powell, Dick 422, 536, 541, 542
Powell, Eleanor 567
Power, Tyrone 18
Powers, Mala 303, 310, 638
Powers, Ralph 325
Prager, Sammy 325, 415
Pratt, Dr. Dallas 275, 522
Presby, Arch 306, 316, 326
Price, Vincent 303
Prima, Louis 488
Prince of Foxes, The (motion-pictures) 587
Provost, Jon 304
Pugh, Maj. James 610
Purcell, Charles 328
Purcell, George 349
Pyle, Lorayne 67
Queen for a Day (radio program) 499
Queen for a Day (television program) 626, 632
Quinlan, Capt. Bill 580
Quiz Kids, The (radio program) 22, 420, 468
Radio Life (magazine) 170
Radio Mirror (magazine) 168, 396, 490
Radio Stars on Parade (motion-picture) 57, 421
Radio-Movie Guide (magazine) 344
Radio-TV Mirror (magazine) 613
Raffee, Janice 592
Ragsdale, Charles 216
Ralph Edwards Show, The (radio program) 138, 290
Ralston, Gilbert 11
Ralston, Vera 281, 496
Ramsey, William 10
Rand, Sally 34
Randall, Renee 473
Range, Charlie 267-269, 509-512, 514
Raphael, Rick 211
Rarick, Ricki 231
Rateenbury, J. 329
Rathbone, Basil 270
Rau, Sgt. Dick 362
Raulston, Dr. Burrell 513
Ravazza, Carl 418
Rawlings, Lt. Barney 581
Rawlings, Thomas 487
Ray, Aldo 581
Ray, George 494
Raymond, Gene 277
Raywood, John Lloyd 328
Reader's Digest (magazine) 381, 444, 445
Reagan, Ronald 550, 579
Reaver, Lois 216
Rector, George 280, 545
Rector, Roy 257, 264, 472, 505
Reece, Roland 597

Reece, Shirley 589
Reed, Bill 327
Reed, Jo Bradley 107
Reed, Lawrence 610
Regan, Mary Elizabeth 593
Regan, William, Sgt. 593
Reilly, Harold 330, 342
Reilly, Mike 430
Reinhart, Karl 609
Rennick, Mel 564
Reveenman, Ethyle 332
Revelle, Nellie 111
Rey, Alvino 430, 431
Reynolds, R.M. 519
Rhodes, "Dusty" 252-256, 450-455, 459
Ribble, Steve 231
Rice, Barbara 601
Richards, Rev. Bob 590
Riebe, Mrs. Cliff 557
Riggio, Bobby 71, 418
Riggs, Tommy 436
Right to Happiness, The (radio program) 8
Riley, Verne 530
Ring, Jeanne 175
Rio Rita (musical) 391
Ripley, Ida 137, 484
Ripley, Robert L. 491, 492, 495, 499
Rishell, Clifford D. 615
Riskin, Robert 477
Rlgas, Mrs. E. 627
Roach, Burton 188-190, 193, 195, 198, 199, 207, 211, 212, 218, 236, 563, 564, 569
Roach, Hal 544
Roach, Leonard J. 444
Road of Life, The (radio program) 8, 181
Robberson, G.C. 139
Robbins, Maury 509
Roberts, John 331
Roberts, Ken 6, 9, 12, 325, 343
Robertson, Dale 588
Robertson, Jacqueline 588
Robie, Richard 78
Robinson, Alvin Raymond 192, 562
Robinson, Jack 534
Rochelle, Ann 371
Rockford, Mickey 176
Rocking Horse Rhythms (radio program) 351
Rodelle, Mrs. Fred 498
Rodges, Russ 582
Rogers, Buddy 273
Rogers, Ginger 277
Rogers, Roy 23, 73, 74, 262, 304, 392, 413, 490, 621, 625
Roland, Jean 425
Romano, Tony 58

Romanoff, Prince Michael 310
Romero, Cesar 304, 513, 550, 554
Roos, Charlie 442
Roos, Leonard 72-76, 442
Roos, Pearl 73
Roosevelt, Anna 272
Root, Jack 517, 519
Rose, Joe 387
Rosenbloom, Maxie 310
Rosenthal, Herb 11
Ross, Barney 155
Ross, David 6, 39, 357
Ross, Jack 531, 533
Rossi, Angelo 387
Rougier, Mike 501
Rowe, J.J. 413
Roy, Joe 415
Roy, Joseph E. 64
Royal, Harry 552
Ruben, Yale 327
Rude, Roland 585
Ruggles, Charles 280, 545
Ruiz, Rocky 566
Rus, Erica 583
Russell, Andy 595, 602
Russell, Della 595
Russell, Henry 389
Russell, Mischa 590
Russell, Todd 180, 325
Ruth, Babe 73, 74, 79
Rutherford, Jerry 468
Ryan, Mrs. Fred 627
Sabot, Susan 590
Sachs, Mildred 328
Saigon (motion-picture) 493
Sain, Johnny 80, 81
Sale, Fred L. 539, 552
Saluto, Frankie 73
Sanders, Alan 609
Saunders, Felix 541
Saxon Charme, The (radio program) 508
Scafuto, Danny 533
Schaden, Chuck 136
Schaefer, Robert 597
Schaffer, Patsy 397
Schaffer, Richard 397
Schapper, Beatrice 381
Scherr, Herbert 28
Scherr, Sgt. Sam 293, 611
Schildkraut, Rudolph 605
Schiller, Miss Ferrol 600
Schilling, Charlotte 330
Schmidt, Barbara Louise 628

Schoeppel, Andrew 382, 387
Schoveller, Adam 605
Schroeder, Billie 564
Schroeder, Elmer 564
Schuline, Arthur 383
Schuster, Harry 545
Schwab, Benjamin T. 139
Scoggins, J.E. 212
Scott, Carleton 487
Scott, J.W. 190, 210, 212
Scott, Lizabeth 258-260, 485, 581
Scott, Martha 361
SCTV (television program) 318
Seddon, Rev. F.J. 202
Seegers, Mrs. 402
Seltzer, Walter 170
Sergeant, Freeman 6
Serna, Bob 589
Serpent of the Nile, The (motion-picture) 610
Seven Days Leave (motion-picture) 57, 362, 391
Seymour, John 332
Shafer, Jack 566
Shakespeare, William 5
Shalit, Sid 179
Shanahan, Dick 535
Shaner, Sgt. Paul 600-602
Shannon, John 606
Sharrett, Norma 537
Shaw, Artie 591
Shaw, George Bernard 5, 474
Shay, Dorothy 518
Sheath, William 464
Sheldon, C.N. 550
Sheldon, Frances 307, 308
Sheldon, Katherine 590
Sheldon, Stephen 603
Shelton, Chuck 226
Shepherd, Dr. Warren 145
Sheridan, Edith 408
Sherman, Ransom 599
Sherman, Vincent 599, 600
Sherr, Herbert 517
Shirk, Beulah 201, 218
Shore, Dinah 409
Shrope, Frank 616
Shroud for Mr. Bundy, A (motion-picture) 592
Shuel, Victor 610
Shumer, Gerald 542
Shunk, Tom 509
Shute, Hiram 489
Sieder, Otto 470
Siegal, Hyman 518
Siegel, Lt. Robert B. 604

Siegel, Mrs. Hyman 519
Siering, Mrs. 372, 373
Sikes, Beverly 214
Silver Theatre, The (radio program) 8
Simon, Al 64, 187, 188, 301
Simonsen, Polly Jo'anne 632
Sinatra, Frank 73, 266, 300, 401, 486, 504, 515
Sing It Again (radio program) 277
Singer, Sidney 67
Singleton, Peggy 550
Skelton, Red 363, 542, 567
Slade, Ted 35, 326
Slater, Earline 457
Slovich, Nick 597
Smart, Robert 416
Smith, Bert 317
Smith, C. Roy 93
Smith, Clayton W. 587
Smith, Don 630
Smith, Elinor 591
Smith, Eunice L. 609
Smith, Frances 587
Smith, Herman 487
Smith, Hubert Clark 135-140, 156, 161
Smith, Jack 604, 621
Smith, Joan 397
Smith, Kate 277
Smith, Mrs. Edwin P. 593
Smith, Norma 214
Smith, Robert B. 236
Smith, Rubert 484
Snodgrass, Susie 243
Snook, Jim 628
Snows of Kilimanjaro, The (motion-picture) 591
Snyder, Katherine 567
Snyder, William 264, 266, 506, 507
Somerville, Slim 386
Son of the Sheik (motion-picture) 618
Southworth, Billy 499
Southworth, Billy 80, 81
Sowash, Oswald 493
Sowers, Charles 588
Sowers, Colleen 588
Spacek, Vencelas 283, 548
Spahn, Warren 80, 82
Spargos, Jack 629
Sparks, Edith 542
Sparks, Ned 477
Speakman, Betty 400
Spencer, Jasper 267-269, 509, 511, 512, 514
Sperzel, Martin 621
Spitz, Sid 588
Spivak, Charlie 410

Spizza, Sol 359
Sprague, Charles 425
St. John, Adela 287
Stabel, Dell 541
Stabile, Dick 604
Stafford, Hanley 69
Stafford, Jo 564
Stage Door Canteen (radio program) 13
Stanley, Thomas B. 590
Stanwyck, Barbara 155
Starr, Jimmy 116
Stauber, Mrs. H.V. 593
Steel Lady, The (motion-picture) 618
Steinglass, Charles 125
Steinke, Stanley 608
Stephens, Bertie 309
Sterkin, David H. 590
Sterns, Ida 579
Stevens, Mark 555
Stevenson, Dr. George 275, 522
Stewart, Bob 536
Stewart, Dallas 411
Stewart, James 607
Stewart, Jay 326
Stickney, Dorothy 272
Stielmacker, Paul 383
Stillwell, Mrs. George 587
Stone, Lewis 272
Stone, Lloyd 448
Stop Me If You heard This One (radio program) 181
Stop the Music (radio program) 181, 249, 250, 277, 509
Stovall, Roy 194, 197, 201, 206, 563, 564, 569
Strange Lady in Town (motion-picture) 306
Stranger Wore a Gun, The (motion-picture) 616
Strasser, Edwin F. 139
Streitwieser, Andrew 610
Strike It Rich (radio program) 180
Strobo, William E. 207
Strongin, Ida 614
Stude, Margaret 568
Sturgess, Sarah Huntsman 5
Subbie, Ruth Annette 103, 117-127, 174, 482-484
Suchanek, Sgt. Richard 281, 496, 499-501
Suesse, Claudia 411
Sullivan, Dan 78
Sullivan, Ed 175
Sullivan, Margaret 417
Summers, Rev. W.L. 588
Swain, Frank G. 569
Swanson, Gloria 287
Swartz, George 78-80
Swearinger, Wesley 554
Sweeney, Budd 109

Sweiger, Don 552
Szinski, Frank 553
Tacon Jr., Col. Avalon 580
Tafoya, Joseph D. 191, 218, 212, 213, 564
Take It or Leave It (radio program) 265, 456
Talbert, Ralph 616
Tarrantino, John 581, 583, 584
Taylor, Maurice 546
Taylor, Morton 548
Taylor, Mrs. Howe 546
Taylor, Sam 6
Teale, Al 132-134, 432
Teets, Harley Oliver 617
Temple, Shirley 39, 40
Tetrald, T. 328
Texera, Edward 552
Thatcher, Pat 425
Thayer, Mrs. Percy 491
Theodore, Casimir 118, 125
This is Your Life (radio program) 7, 143, 153-156, 204, 289, 290, 298, 582
This is Your Life (television program) 299, 301, 303
Thomas, Col. Lawrence M. 231
Thomas, Danny 567
Thomas, Dave 318
Thomas, John Charles 68
Thomas, Mary 595
Thompson, C.B. 395
Thompson, Marshall 240
Thompson, Mrs. Perry E. 621
Thompson, Tom 466
Thornton, Agnes C. 607
Thornton, Mrs. Harry 590
Thornton, Tommy 607
Thorpe, A.E. 576
Thrush, Nellie 509
Thurston, Carol 411
Till the End of Time (motion-picture) 457
Time (magazine) 99, 114, 173
Tingley, Gov. Clyde 188
Titterton, Lewis 114, 181
To the Shores of Tripoli (motion-picture) 355
Toepfert, Henry J. 67
Tolley, A.F. 538
Tomlin, Pinky 592
Tooley, Mike 215
Tooley, Paul 190, 192, 201, 218, 565
Torrance, Bob 225
Torres, Alerico 197
Toth, Ona 352
Totter, Audrey 596
Towery, H.A. 537
Tracy, Mrs. Thomas 498
Tracy, Spencer 83

Tracy, Thomas 498
Tranter, Dorothy 152, 494
Tranter, Frank 146
Tranter, Lawrence 145-153, 155, 156, 443, 494
Tranter, Leonard 145
Tranter, Lorene 146
Tranter, Mildred 145
Travis, Albert 391
Traylor, Donald 579
Trevor, Claire 422
Troutman, George 452
Truman, Harry 164, 474, 475, 506
Truman, Margaret 113
Tucker, Harold 244, 481
Tufts, Sonny 490
Tufts, Warren 578
Tupper, Lamount 621
Tyana, Madame Babette 361
Tyler, Mrs. O.G. 111
Tyler, T. Texas 591
Uncle Jim's Question Bee (radio program) 297
Underhill, Dave 227
Uninvited Guest, The (motion-picture) 286
Ussery, Bessie 614
Vague, Vera 58
Valdespino, Tom 231
Valenti, Pfc. 597
Valentino, Joan 619
Valentino, Rudolph 618
Vallee, Rudy 270, 358, 421
Valli 558, 559
Van Antwerp, Eugene 514
Van Bolt, Lucille 411
Van Coute, Fred 429
Van Diest, Ernest 550
Van Every, Ed 375
Van Norstrand, Jack 6
Van Sant, E.M. 213
Varipappa, Andy 165-196
Vaughn, Dorothy 590
Vecchia, Theresa 545
Veloz, Frank 273, 274, 520, 521
Ventriglia, Tony 412
Vic and Sade (radio program) 8
Vickland, Jerry 553
Vickland, Mel 128, 156
Vickland, Melvin 553
Victory Parade (radio program) 363
Vinson, Fred 431
Vitis, Efrim 365, 366
Vitro, Esther 621
Vivella, Dennis 606
Vohs, Joan 616

Voll, Mrs. Opal 552
Von Neumayer, Prof. Charles 5
Von Roth, Roger F. 427
Von Zell, Harry 6, 55, 56, 154, 409, 410, 507
Votaw, Mrs. Harold 459
Vrooman, Jack 471, 473 **Voorman?**
Wade, Mary Ruth 499, 500
Wagner, Gene 614
Wahl, Jim 426
Wahlert, William 417
Wain, Bea 10
Wainwright, Gen. Jonathan 273
Waite, Maggie 501
Wakely, Jimmy 574
Waldo, Janet 567
Waldorf, Lynn (Pappy) 553
Walker, Benny 399
Walker, Dick 526
Walker, Moyles 399
Wallington, Jimmy 459
Wallis, Hal 170, 258
Walsh, Leo 397
Walters, Joe 3, 4, 7
Walters, Lou 564
Ward, Allan 7
Ward, Montgomery 595
Warren, Bailey 541
Warren, Earl 272
Warren, Forrest 540
Warren, Frank J. 382
Washburn, Bryant 302
Washington, Ned 570
Waterman, Willard 491, 498
Watras, Rose 330
Watson, Galen 610
Waver, Nina 303
Wayne, John 537
Weatherwax, Jack 502
Weaver, Ned 166
Weaver, Pat 5, 6
Webb, Charles F. 139
Webster, Eric 582
Weddington, Leonard D. 489
Wegner, Nicholas H. 553
Wein, Viola 629
Weingarten, Harry 139
Weinstein, Harry 599
Weiss, Sol 458
Weissmuller, Johnny 303
Welch, Pat 369
Welcome, Travelers (radio program) 481, 535, 551
Weldon, Joan 616
Welk, Lawrence 51

Welles, Orson 129, 562
Wells, Mary 537
Wells, Roscoe 567
Wendland, Dr. Leonard 595, 596
Werner, William G. 489
Wesly, Janice 436
West, Dr. Howard F. 168
West, Harley 508
West, James E. 164
Westmore, Bud 509
Weston, G.W. 531
Weybright, Vernon H. 581
What's Up (musical) 395
Wheeler, Willard 493
When Willie Comes Marching Home (motion-picture) 557
White, Alice 277
White, G.E. 332
White, Jack 204, 368
Whitehead, Ida 614
Whiteman, Paul 180
Whiting, Margaret 603, 604
Whittington, Porter Lee 583
Wickel, Rudolph J. 63-67, 124, 132, 414
Wickel, Rudy 67
Widmark, Richard 513
Wilborn, Helen 609
Wilcox, Harlow 32, 218, 326, 448, 459, 467, 468
Williams, Austin 204, 205
Williams, Barbara 429
Williams, Bob 427
Williams, Capt. Catfish 593
Williams, Carrie 113
Williams, Chili 421
Williams, Esther 315
Williams, Fred 225
Williams, Griffith 429, 430
Williams, Harold 587
Williams, L.M. 548
Williams, Linda 576
Williams, Mayor T.B. 207, 209, 210, 212, 234, 569, 590, 607, 632
Williams, Rhys 574
Williams, Richard 420
Williams, Ted 83
Williams, Wally 594
Williamson, Leo C. 205
Willson, Meredith 588
Wilson, Don 69, 459
Wilson, Earl 418
Wilson, Earlene 491
Wilson, Mrs. Max 587
Wilson, Ward 389
Wilson, Woodrow 287
Winchell, Walter 116, 503

Winn, Marcia 114
Winston, Frank 209
Winters, Shelley 302, 542
Wipperfurth, Barbara 595
Wise, Mrs. Richard 589
Wolfrum, Chet 560
Wolski, Mitchell 289
Wolters, Larry 174, 175
Wons, Tony 8
Wood, J.R. 420
Woodmansee, Jack 512
Woods, Larry 218
Woodward, Don 215
World on a String, The (album) 619
Wormser, Jack 269, 511
Worth, Petie 325, 384
Wortman, Fred 218
Wortman, Grita 218
Wright, Frank 3, 4
Wright, Gerald E. 224
Wyckoff, Harold 329
Wynn, Cliff 225
Wynn, Ed 58
Wynn, Keenan 253, 450
Wynn, May 591
Yellen, Starr 503
Yellow Jack (stage play) 5
Yokum, Carl 231, 232
Yolanda, Casazza 273, 274, 520, 521
Yonker, Fern 531
York, Alvin C. 165
Young, Alan 525
Young, Robert 547, 622
Young, Roger 443
Youngdahl, Luther W. 530, 532, 533
Yount, Jeanne 175
Your Hit Parade (radio program) 8, 266, 486, 504, 506, 515
Zachary, Tom 605
Ziegfeld, Florence 589
Ziegler, Dorothea 286, 568
Zimmerman, Bob 188
Zuckert, Bill 388

About the Author

Martin Grams, Jr. is the author and co-author of more than 30 books about old-time radio and retro television, including *The Twilight Zone: Unlocking the Door to a Television Classic*, *Science Fiction Theatre: A History of the Television Program, 1955-57* and *The Time Tunnel: A History of the Television Program*. Recipient of numerous "Best Book of the Year" awards, editor of the bi-monthly *Radio Recall* and frequent contributor of numerous magazines, Martin continues to research and write about radio and television programs. You can find a complete list of all his books at www.martingrams.com.

Martin is the events co-ordinator of the annual Mid-Atlantic Nostalgia Convention, a three-day non-profit event that benefits children with treatable cancer. Martin loves to garden, read 1950s science-fiction, listen to old-time radio and master the art of perfecting "the God shot" (which is his way of describing how he brews a good cup of coffee).

Martin is completing a new book project, along with co-author Terry Salomonson, together combining over three decades of research documenting the earliest history of the masked man and his faithful Indian companion, titled *The Lone Ranger: The Early Years, 1933–1937*.

OTHER BOOKS BY MARTIN GRAMS

THE SHADOW
The Shadow -- for the consideration of those who never heard a radio broadcast or read a pulp magazine -- was a supernatural sleuth with a sepulchral chuckle. A detective whose success in tracking down criminals became a popular long-running radio program from 1937 to 1954, after beginning a number of years before as a ghost-like voice introducing a bone-chilling murder play that concluded with a sinister laugh. This 850-page book documents the entire history of the radio program.

THE GREEN HORNET
Since The Green Hornet first appeared on radio in 1936, he has made the transition to motion pictures, comics and television. Very little has been written about the masked marvel and what has been recorded in magazine articles and encyclopedias prior to this publication has never explored the character as deeply... or accurately. For the first time, the complete story of this crime fighter is unmasked, as prolific TV and radio historians Martin Grams and Terry Salomonson usher you into the Black Beauty. This 800-page book is the essential one-stop source for everything regarding the masked vigilante.

THE BIG SHOW
The Big Show was an NBC house-built package and an innovation in show business deriving its name from the fact that the talent roster each week included "the biggest names in show business." Bob Hope, Groucho Marx, Phil Harris, the Andrews Sisters, Milton Berle, Judy Holliday, Jimmy Durante, Eddie Cantor and many others were heard on the program -- along with hostess Tallulah Bankhead. It was not until the rehearsal of the premiere broadcast that Bankhead discovered the program was cleverly scheduled in an effort to kill the radio career of Jack Benny, who jumped networks for a shareholder deal. This 370-page book documents the entire history of the radio program.

WAY OUT
In the spring of 1961, CBS premiered a short-lived television program hosted by author Roald Dahl, titled WAY OUT. The creepy late-night horror program aired right before THE TWILIGHT ZONE, but spun a gruesome tale of horror for horror's sake. With no parables or social commentary, devout fanatics with more than a few qualms about the horror material considered the program a bottom feeder's form of entertainment. The TV horror program lasted a mere 14 telecasts and this book documents the history of the program, complete with program guide and scans of archival documents from the production files.

THE TIME TUNNEL
The Time Tunnel was by no means a superb product of Friday night entertainment. If the plot holes were not as large as the tunnel itself, viewers noticed the same props from Allen's other television programs popping up on the show. Fan boys to this day still debate whether the futuristic episodes involving space aliens were better than the historic adventures, but few would deny that Lee Meriwether made a lab coat look sexy. This 546-page book documents the entire history of the program, the origin and conception of the series, why it never ran a second season, almost 200 never-before-published behind-the-scenes photographs, and a detailed episode guide including dates of production, music cues, episode budgets, salary costs, deleted scenes that were filmed, memories from cast and crew, bloopers, trivia and much more!

THE TWILIGHT ZONE

Very few television shows withstand the test of time, and Rod Serling's THE TWILIGHT ZONE is one of the notable exceptions. Proven to be an important part of American culture since its debut on CBS in October 1959, many Hollywood producers, screenwriters and directors have been inspired and influenced by this series. Comic books, magazine articles, numerous television revivals, a major motion picture and even modern audio productions have been produced, showcasing the continuing popularity of this television classic. This definitive history presents a portrait of the beloved Rod Serling and his television program, recounting the major changes the show underwent in format and story selection, including censorship battles, production details, and exclusive memories from cast and crew. The complete episode guide recalls all 156 episodes of the series in detail that has never before been accomplished in any publication. This "Best Book of the Year" winner will make you want to look back at the episodes once again, whether you are a casual fan or serious enthusiast of the series.

SCIENCE FICTION THEATRE

From 1955 to 1957, Science Fiction Theatre, a semi-documentary series, explored the "what ifs" of modern science. Placing an emphasis on science before fiction, television viewers were treated to a variety of complex challenges from mental telepathy, robots, man-eating ants, killer trees, man's first flight into outer space and the possibility of visitation from outer space. Hosted by Truman Bradley, a former radio news commentator, Science Fiction Theatre became an influential program for the time, courtesy of Ivan Tors, a man with a healthy regard for science and nature. Hollywood actors Gene Barry, Ruth Hussey, Gene Lockhart, Basil Rathbone, Howard Duff, William Lundigan and Vincent Price are but a few who lent their talents. For the first time ever, this 530-page book documents the entire history of the television program with biographies about Fred Ziv, Ivan Tors and Truman Bradley; behind-the-scenes production details; over 150 exclusive never-before-published photographs; and an episode guide for all 78 episodes including dates of production, fake science props, cast list, salary fees, location shooting, and much more!

www.ingramcontent.com/pod-product-compliance
Lightning Source LLC
Chambersburg PA
CBHW071148230426
43668CB00009B/871